Argument and Change in World Politics

Arguments have consequences in world politics that are as real as the military forces of states or the balance of power among them. Neta Crawford proposes a theory of argument that focuses on the role of ethical arguments in fostering changes in long-standing practices. Analyzing colonialism and slavery, the author shows how ethical arguments helped bring about the abolition of slavery and forced labor, and decolonization. Suggesting that decolonization is perhaps the most significant change in world politics over the past 500 years, the author examines ethical arguments from the sixteenth century justifying the conquest of the Americas, through the twentieth-century debates over decolonization and humanitarian intervention. The author explicitly considers alternative explanations for decolonization and abolition, and shows that economics cannot fully account for either change. She also offers a prescriptive analysis of the role of ethical argument in humanitarian intervention.

NETA C. CRAWFORD is an Associate Professor (research) at the Thomas J. Watson Jr. Institute for International Studies at Brown University. She is co-editor (with Audie Klotz) of *How Sanctions Work: Lessons from South Africa* (1999) and author of *Soviet Military Aircraft* (1987).

CAMBRIDGE STUDIES IN INTERNATIONAL RELATIONS

Series list continues after index

Argument and Change in World Politics

Ethics, Decolonization, and Humanitarian Intervention

Neta C. Crawford

CAMBRIDGE
UNIVERSITY PRESS

PUBLISHED BY THE PRESS SYNDICATE OF THE UNIVERSITY OF CAMBRIDGE
The Pitt Building, Trumpington Street, Cambridge, United Kingdom

CAMBRIDGE UNIVERSITY PRESS
The Edinburgh Building, Cambridge CB2 2RU, UK
40 West 20th Street, New York, NY 10011-4211, USA
477 Williamstown Road, Port Melbourne, VIC 3207, Australia
Ruiz de Alarcón 13, 28014 Madrid, Spain
Dock House, The Waterfront, Cape Town 8001, South Africa

http://www.cambridge.org

First published 2002

Printed in the United Kingdom at the University Press, Cambridge

Typeface Palatino 10/12.5 pt.   *System* LATEX 2$_\varepsilon$ [TB]

A catalogue record for this book is available from the British Library

Library of Congress cataloguing in publication data

Crawford, Neta C., 1961–
Argument and change in world politics : ethics, decolonization, and
humanitarian intervention / Neta C. Crawford.
    p.   cm.
Includes bibliographical references and index.
ISBN 0 521 80244 X – ISBN 0 521 00279 6 (pb. : alk. paper)
1. International relations – Moral and ethical aspects.   I. Title.

JZ1306 .C73   2001
172′.4 – dc21   2001043120

ISBN 0 521 80244 X hardback
ISBN 0 521 00279 6 paperback

For Rose, Greta and Robert

Contents

Illustrations

Tables

Acknowledgments

I started writing this book in 1992 as a short article on decolonization for a project on norms of humanitarian intervention sponsored by the American Academy of Arts and Sciences. I am grateful to Laura Reed and Carl Kaysen for thinking that I was up to the task. Since then, this book has made its ever-evolving appearance in many places, and I have been inspired, educated, and influenced by the work of scholars and friends, some of whom will no doubt disagree with nearly everything I say. If I leave anyone out, it is because the process was long and frequently interrupted for months at a time.

I am grateful to Hayward Alker. His eclectic mind, scholarship, and intellectual enthusiasm, or more accurately, exuberance and genuine interest in all sorts of approaches to the questions of international relations and philosophies of social science inspires. I have written this book with Hayward in mind: holding an attitude of respect for all modes of inquiry, looking everywhere I could think of for insight, regardless of discipline, and taking everything seriously, at least for the moment, so that I can see what others have to offer.

E. P. Thompson and Joan Scott were vital exemplars of courageous intellectual and political engagement and the best of arguers. It was an education to work with them on something we all cared about in the 1980s. Randy Forsberg's unflagging commitment to making peace and her belief in reasoned discourse has also inspired over the past two decades. Jackie Cock has been a generous and critical reader and the model of intellectual and political engagement. Lynn Eden's work on organizational frames was an inspiration for its economy, vivid writing, and blending of the empirical and theoretical; I know I have not met the standards set by Lynn's example but the effort to do so has made this a better book. And Lynn introduced me to Kathy Goldgeier, without whose help this would be an even longer book. James Der Derian and Barbara Cruikshank, wonderful colleagues at the University of Massachusetts, forced me to read Foucault and other "posties."

Tom Biersteker, Elise Boulding, John Brigham, Carol Cohn, Cynthia Enloe, Matt Evangelista, Sheldon Goldman, Joshua Goldstein, Laura Jensen, Willard Johnson, Robert Keohane, Robert Latham, John Odell, Amir Pasic, Bruce Russett, Steve Smith, Ann Tickner, and Tom Weiss all helped me intellectually, by example, and in the concrete ways that make a career work. Though I rarely ask for advice (preferring to make my own mistakes) all of these colleagues directly or indirectly gave me the benefit of their perspectives. Katherine Sikkink, Bud Duvall, Jim Bennett, Alexander George, Robert Jervis, Deborah Welch Larson, Lily Ling, Jack Levy, John Mercer, Nicholas Onuf, Freidrich Kratochwil, Martha Finnemore, Karen Jacobsen, Jim Rosenau, Beth Kier, and Jutta Weldes are also among those whose work I have found stimulating and provocative.

Support by the National Science Foundation, the Social Science Research Council–MacArthur Foundation program on peace and international security, and a post-doctoral fellowship from the University of Southern California's Center for International Studies were essential early in my career. The Thomas J. Watson Jr. Institute for International Studies at Brown University provided the space and the resources for me to reconceptualize the book. Tom Biersteker and Tom Weiss, in particular, along with all of the support staff, worked to make the Watson Institute a stimulating environment. They succeeded. Students at the University of Massachusetts, and Brown University made teaching enjoyable.

I presented an early version of the arguments at the International Studies Association in early 1994, at Yale University in December 1994, and at Harvard's seminar on Ethics and International Affairs in November 1995. At Yale, Bruce Russett and Alexander Wendt asked me why I wasn't focusing my book entirely on ethical arguments about colonialism and decolonization since there was surely enough material there. They were right, and I thank them for the gentle nudging. I also presented portions of the argument at the International Studies Association in 1994 and at a roundtable for the American Political Science Association meeting in Washington, DC in August 1997. Drafts of the first two chapters were presented at University of California, Riverside and Duke University in March and May 1998. At these talks I benefited from the comments of Juliann Allison, Tom Beirsteker, Seyom Brown,

Peter Feaver, Chris Gelpi, Andrew Kydd, Cecelia Lynch, Amir Pasic, Bruce Russett, Alex Wendt and others. I also thank Beth Kier for arranging a small critical seminar for me at Harvard's Center for Science and International Affairs in December 1998 and for asking me to clarify the table on which arguments occur. The last chapter was first presented at a conference on international ethics organized by Amir Pasic at Brown University in the spring of 1997. Substantially revised it appeared in the 1998 edition of the journal *Ethics & International Affairs*. An invitation by Wayne Sandholtz to talk about the problem of humanitarian intervention at the University of California, Irvine in March 2000 pushed me to further develop the ideas presented in the last chapter. A précis of the whole book was presented at Stanford University in March 2000 and I thank the participants of that seminar, especially Lynn Eden and Judith Goldstein, who went after my arguments relentlessly. Hayward Alker, Jill Breitbarth, Lynn Eden, Martha Finnemore, Peter Katzenstein, Meg McLagan, Barry O'Neill, and Jack Snyder gave me detailed comments on all or parts of the manuscript.

I finished the first draft of the book while I was the Peace Fellow at the Bunting Institute of Radcliffe College. What a privilege. Anthropologist Meg McLagan and economic historian Gail Triner read portions of the manuscript and argued generously with me, while historians Kate Baldwin and Ann Blair gave me many citations. The blessing and problem of conversations with historians and anthropologists is the vastness of their knowledge. I am appropriately humbled. Rachel Manley's gift for passionate expression also humbled. I also benefited from stimulating conversations with Tracy Isaacs, Deborah Valenze, Meridel Rubenstein, Aaronette White, Wu Man, Maggie Keane, Evelyn Barbee, Tamar Diesendruck, Sheila Kennedy, Loretta Mickley, Marsha Moses, Ellen Winner, Christina Shea, Marlene Goldman, Jill Reynolds, Sheila Pepe, Carol Mason, Tytti Soila, Deborah Woodcock, Jeanne Nightingale and Lynnette Bosch. Their work will affect me for years to come in ways I haven't yet figured out.

While colleagues provided example, critical comments, real inspiration, and imaginary audience over the years, my greatest debts are to those who encouraged me to continue to have fun, put work in context, and to aim for clarity. I am sure this book took longer to write because of my propensity for play (and for writing other things when I should have been writing directly about argument), but I wouldn't have had it any other way. Elizabeth Cohen, Lisa Mascaro, Ann Ferguson and Carol Shea were wonderful and too rarely hiking and Indian food eating companions. Taylor, Meredith, and Zoe Adams lent their humor. My brother Robert was endlessly amusing, my sister Greta, full of argument. My parents, Robert and Jeanne Crawford, encouraged in a sort of back door way by continually asking when I would be finished. Lisbeth Gronlund, David Wright and Kirsten were the best of Arlington buddies. Karen Kurlander and Jade McGleughlin gave generous assistance when the going got rough, as did Ellen Grossman and Gail Phillips. Barry O'Neill gave his humor and an occasional song. Bob and Laurel Breitbarth, Jackie Cock, David Fig, Carl Nightingale, Lisa Mascaro, Leslie Vinjamuri, and Oliver Wright opened their homes to me on three continents; though they may not have realized it, I wrote portions of the book in their houses. My dog Shana certainly wished her human would play stick and ball more often; many typos in the manuscript were the result of her long nose nudging my arm and I am grateful to Cambridge University Press for catching those, as well as for all the other work they did on the book. Jill Breitbarth, the *sine qua non*, was a source of both calm and distraction and a wonderful partner through numerous adventures. Finally, my late grandmother, Odell, who reminded me (repeatedly) that she was the grandaughter of Jordan and Amy Ware, American slaves, is never far from my thoughts and I hope this book is something that would have stood up to her supportive criticism.

Introduction

This book follows three lines of inquiry, each equally important. First, it proposes a new theory of argument and change in world politics, focusing in particular on the role of ethical argument and normative change. Second, it intervenes in an older academic dispute, the problem of why colonialism ended.[1] Third, in the prescriptive voice of international political theory and ethics, it suggests how, building on the practices of ethical argument that are already in place, certain practices of international relations might be used to make world politics more just and peaceful.

Why focus on argument and change? International relations theorists have two generic social conditions to explain: order and change. Scholars have done well at explaining more stable aspects of world orders, such as bi-polar and multi-polar systems, but much less well at explaining, or more ambitiously, predicting significant changes in world political and economic relations. Of course accounting for stability, equilibrium, and change is no easy task and probably no single variable can do all or even most of the explanatory work. But that has not stopped international relations theorists from proposing master variable accounts of world politics – for example, stressing the drive for power or the operation of markets.

International relations theory has difficulty accounting for change in part because it has thus far not developed a clear understanding of process. The world is ordered or it changes; stasis or rupture. This view is a consequence of our meta-theoretical building blocks. International

---

[1] These explanatory aims are both constitutive and causal in the sense that Alexander Wendt describes in "On Constitution and Causation in International Relations," *Review of International Studies* 24 (December 1998), 101–117.

relations theorists usually focus on the actors (or agents) of world politics and the big structures of states and alliances within an anarchic environment. Actors or agents have characteristics (rationality) and interests (power), while structures such as anarchy or hierarchy (colonialism) constrain and dispose the relations among states. There is little room for argumentation in this understanding because argument is a process. Once we begin to see world politics as constituted by agents, structures, and processes, it is possible to grasp the role of processes like argument and persuasion and to see how change may occur. I do not intend with my focus on argument to sweep all other accounts to the side or to banish complexity or contingency. Rather, I show that once we pay attention to political argument, we will see the role the making and persuasiveness of arguments plays in maintaining orders, changing relations, and overturning practices. A focus on argument may also allow us to see room for human agency within the operations of seemingly inexorable political and economic forces.

The major arguments are these. First, the usual understanding of agents and structures as constituting the major forces of world politics is incomplete without an understanding of the *processes* of world politics. Second, political argument, persuasion, and practical reason are fundamental processes within and among states. Third, beliefs and culture are respectively the content and the context of political argument; without them actors could not understand the arguments that others make, nor could actors successfully argue with others. Fourth, ethical argument analysis is a way to understand and explain normative change in world politics. Fifth, once the central importance of the processes of argument and reason in world politics is recognized, it is possible to think prescriptively about using ethical argumentative processes to re-make world politics.

I did not begin this work with a clear theory of argument and persuasion. Rather, I began by wanting to understand a puzzle: why did one of the most enduring practices of world politics come to an end so close to the peak of its practice? While some small colonial territories remain, the end of formal colonialism as a legitimate practice is perhaps the biggest change in the structure and practice of international relations in the last 500 years. Many colonies became independent in the 1960s and in 1997, with much ceremony, Great Britain returned Hong Kong to China after more than a century of colonial rule. At least in the popular imagination, the peaceful withdrawal from the island by the empire meant that the sun had finally set not only on the British empire but also on colonialism itself.[2] Why did old-fashioned colonialism end? Why did colonialism end when it did? Why didn't colonialism end much earlier?

Colonialism ended when it was arguably still profitable and colonizers could, if they wanted to, still enforce their will on the colonized. There was nothing inevitable about decolonization in the realm of ideas or normative beliefs. There are probably no "economic laws" that inhibit the profitability of colonialism, even in the age of industrialization and free markets, nor any reasons why militarily powerful states cannot impose themselves on weaker states should they choose to do so. The powerful could still cut off the hands or heads of those who resist imperial rule, they could still deny the weak the franchise, and tell them how they must order their political, economic, and religious affairs. Yet, as Julius Nyerere, Tanzania's first independence political leader said, "Military occupation of another country against the wishes of the people of that country is internationally condemned. This means that colonialism in the traditional and political sense is now almost a thing of the past."[3]

Explaining the end of colonialism is obviously important. Particular colonial systems have risen and fallen over the past several thousand years, but there is something distinctive about the decolonization of the late twentieth century. No new colonies were formed in the last twenty-five years. And colonizers did not just stop acquiring colonies at mid century, they began to give up the colonies they already held. In the few instances during the late twentieth century when states tried to annex land, such as Indonesia's 1975 invasion of East Timor, those actions were contested not only by the subjects of colonization, but by outsiders. In one case, Iraq's attempted annexation of Kuwait in 1990, states used military force under the authority of the United Nations to remove Iraq and nullify its conquest. Colonizers, once proud, now express remorse. In 1993, the president of the United States apologized for the US annexation of the Hawaiian Islands one hundred years earlier. Colonialism made the world map look much as it does, and decolonization began at what was perhaps the peak of that ancient practice.

[2] China's occupation of Tibet is among the exceptions. While Tibet's legal status is hotly debated, the occupation denies the political self-determination and religious freedom of the people of Tibet. Several other territories, many small in terms of population, and others much larger, remain in conditions rather like that of colonies, albeit with crucial differences. See Robert Aldrich and John Connell, *The Last Colonies* (Cambridge: Cambridge University Press, 1998).
[3] Julius Nyerere, "Forward," in Chakravarthi Raghavan, *Recolonization: GATT, The Uraguay Round & the Third World* (London: Zed Books, 1990), pp. 19–25: 19.

Colonialism did not just fade away; it became illegitimate. Why and how did this change occur? To rephrase the question in more abstract terms, how do dominant behavioral norms change? Do normative beliefs have anything to do with those changes? If so, how?

There are competing explanations but no consensus about why colonialism is no longer legitimate. Most observers think that colonialism ended because it began to cost more than it profited the colonizers. Colonizers, being rational, thus let the practice go out of use and found less costly, more profitable, ways of getting what they wanted from former colonies. Or perhaps decolonization occurred not because any one colony was too costly to maintain, but because the imperial powers had overstretched their reach, and could no longer beat down the constant and rising resistance to empire in the periphery. Thus, the most commonly given explanations for the end of colonialism stress both the material world of extraction where conquest does or doesn't pay, and the cognitive world of rational calculators who are either wise or insensible.

I give an account of the end of colonialism that stresses factors other than profit, capabilities, and the rational calculation of costs and benefits. It is certain that those factors were important. Or rather, I should say that the beliefs actors held about profit, military and economic capabilities, and the costs and benefits of colonies mattered causally in terms of motivating colonialism and decolonization. But what mattered more in the long run was the making of persuasive ethical arguments containing normative beliefs about what was good and right to do to others. While the colonized had always resisted colonialism, sometimes with great success, what changed in the twentieth century was the content and balance of normative beliefs and the burden of proof. Whereas colonialism had been the dominant practice, or norm, for thousands of years, supported by strong ethical arguments, colonialism was denormalized and delegitimized in the twentieth century because anti-colonial reformers made persuasive ethical arguments.

Colonialism could still be considered legitimate and acceptable if the powerful still believed in human inequality and thought it was acceptable to take and hold territory by arms and dictate the life of others with brute force. Colonialism ended, ostensibly for good, in the mid twentieth century, because most Westerners no longer think it is acceptable to control others in precisely that same way. The engine for this change was ethical argument, not force, or changing modes of production, or declining profitability. Ethical arguments, once used to support colonialism, were used to undermine and ultimately to eliminate the

4

practice. While it is possible to account for the practices of colonialism, the abolition of slavery, and decolonization with primarily economic or material explanations, such accounts are deficient to the extent that they fail to appreciate the process and content of argument, especially ethical arguments deployed by domestic and transnational advocates. In focusing on the content of the arguments deployed by advocates of reform, I give relatively little attention to the tactics and mobilization strategy of reformers. This is not because social movement strategy is unimportant in understanding how arguments become heard and were, or were not, persuasive. On the contrary, the politics of social movements and reform is vital. However, since the techniques of social movement mobilization are much better understood and well known than the account I give here of ethical argument, the emphasis here is less on who argues and how they organize, and more on the content and process of argument and how arguments may prompt changes in political power.[4]

The first chapter, "Argument, Belief, and Culture," lays the conceptual ground for an understanding of the process of ethical argument. It begins by developing the concept and role of argument as a practice of reason and persuasion.[5] Though argument is only one process in world politics, its role is obviously important, and strangely underemphasized and undertheorized by international relations theorists. World politics is characterized by several kinds of argument. Instrumental or practical arguments are about how to do things most effectively in the social world. Identity arguments suggest that people of a certain kind, such as "we the civilized," ought to act in a particular way. Scientific arguments use the laws of science, technology, or nature to define situations

---

[4] On social movements and transnational activism see: Jeffrey W. Knopf, *Domestic Society and International Cooperation: The Impact of Protest on US Arms Control Policy* (Cambridge: Cambridge University Press, 1998) and Margaret E. Keck and Kathryn Sikkink, *Activists Beyond Borders: Advocacy Networks in International Politics* (Ithaca: Cornell University Press, 1998). Whereas these scholars mention persuasion and influence at several points in their books, they are primarily concerned with demonstrating the existence and effectiveness of domestic and transnational advocacy networks. An excellent book giving more attention to persuasion is Matthew Evangelista, *Unarmed Forces: The Transnational Movement to End the Cold War* (Ithaca: Cornell University Press, 1999).
[5] The chapter focuses on two (ideal-type) forms of reasoning that arguments generally take: top-down (syllogism) and sideways (comparative or associative). Top-down reasoning in the case of a practical argument looks rather like a syllogism where conclusions follow logically from premises. Arguments in the form of side-ways associations, or symbolic arguments, compare cases. They use metaphor, metonym, and analogies to help others draw inferences from one situation that imply actions about other complex situations.

and show how they ought to be addressed. Ethical arguments are about what it is right to do in particular contexts.

Argumentation and persuasion depend on content or beliefs. The content of beliefs held by foreign policy decisionmakers shapes their perceptions, priorities, and preferences, especially as beliefs become institutionalized in practices – organizational routines and knowledge making processes. Yet as Dan Reiter suggests, "There is no space in realist theory to permit states to have different beliefs about how international politics work."[6] Beliefs, which address all areas of social life, are translated into political action through reason – what Aristotle called practical inference – which involves reflection and political, that is, public, argument. I describe philosophical/ontological, normative, instrumental, and identity beliefs. I also review belief system theory, and specify how the theory developed here builds on and is different from that earlier work. In addition, I discuss theories of the foundation of belief and belief change or learning.

Next, I suggest four ways that culture is relevant to an understanding of argumentative processes in world politics. First, shared cultural background allows meaningful conversations and arguments to occur. Without this background meaning, all speech, including argument, would be unintelligible. Second, culture often provides the content for specific beliefs; it is the source of philosophical, normative, identity, and instrumental beliefs. Third, culture provides the background meaning by which particular beliefs and arguments are consciously judged, and cultures contain the metaphors and historical events which actors consciously use to frame problems. That is, culture is a resource that argument makers draw upon when attempting to be persuasive. Fourth, while culture is one source of the rootedness of beliefs, it can be a source of new beliefs.

Practical, scientific, and identity arguments are ubiquitous in world politics and it might be (relatively) easy to convince you that, for example, practical arguments are at work in decisions over whether or not to intervene militarily, or that scientific arguments used within and outside epistemic communities, such as those of atmospheric scientists, can change world politics. But ethical arguments are the hard case. Do ethical arguments make a difference? Are they causal, or are they "epiphenomenal?"

---

[6] Dan Reiter, *Crucible of Beliefs: Learning, Alliances, and World Wars* (Ithaca: Cornell University Press, 1996), p. 5.

Chapter 2, on "Ethical Argument and Argument Analysis," gives a theoretical account of how normative beliefs and ethical arguments work in world politics. I chose to highlight the role of ethical argument because skeptics of the role of argument will probably be most skeptical about the causal significance of ethical arguments. I review several, conflicting, theories of "norms" in world politics, specify the differences between behavioral norms and normative beliefs, and show how ethical arguments may link the two. I discuss the conditions under which ethical arguments can be persuasive and describe the process of persuasive ethical argument. Specifically, ethical arguments are generally used to do one of three things: uphold existing beliefs and practices, extend normative beliefs to new areas of practice, and change dominant practices.

How can ethical arguments be used to change dominant practices? The process occurs in three phases. First, persuasive ethical arguments deconstruct: they denormalize and delegitimize dominant beliefs and practices. Second, persuasive ethical arguments offer a reconstruction, the articulation of an alternative that meets normative criteria. In this phase, alternative conceptions of possibility and interest are discussed and adopted by some actors. And, in the third phase, actors begin to change their social world. If arguments are persuasive among enough individuals and groups (and "enough" depends on the context), then the balance of capabilities between those who favor the dominant normative belief and the new normative belief will begin to change. Further, normative beliefs that change as a consequence of ethical argument may become institutionalized, altering the structures of the world and the starting point for new ethical arguments. In the first two phases, the action is primarily discursive or rhetorical; in the last phase, the action is more obvious in the political and institutional world as capabilities shift and standard practices are modified. This is a dynamic understanding of how ethical argument can be used to change dominant beliefs and practices. To see whether this understanding makes sense, I then propose a method of "informal argument analysis" by which it is possible to analyze ethical argument and the process of persuasion. Finally, some of the methodological objections to the argument analysis approach are raised and answered in the last part of chapter 2.

Chapters 3 through 7 show how ethical arguments shaped colonialism and were also used by reformers who sought to abolish slavery and to end colonialism. Chapter 3, "Colonial Arguments," outlines the content of arguments that characterized early debates on colonialism and describes the famous debate between Bartolomé de Las Casas and Juan Ginés de Sepulveda in 1550 over the humanity of New World Indians. Chapter 4, "Decolonizing Bodies," focuses on the movements to end slavery and forced labor, arguing that these were crucial steps on the path to weakening colonialism. Chapter 5, "Faces of Humanitarianism," describes the height of colonialism in Africa and the ways that humanitarian arguments were used by both colonizers and colonial reformists. Chapter 6, "Sacred Trust," focuses on the role of the League of Nations Mandate system in institutionalizing new normative beliefs about colonial practice. Chapter 7, "Self-Determination," discusses the post-1945 period when decolonization occurred at a rapid pace and became the international norm.[7] Chapters 5 through 7 also include more discussion of colonialism and decolonization in South West Africa/Namibia to illustrate the development of both successful and unsuccessful arguments in greater detail over a 100 year period. Chapter 8, "Alternative Explanations, Counterfactuals, and Causation," summarizes the ethical argument explanation for the end of colonialism, raises competing economic and power political explanations for decolonization, and considers counterfactual possibilities. It also concludes the discussion of South West Africa by comparing economic and strategic factors to the role of ethical argument.

This book could not have been written without utilizing the work of many historians of colonialism, slavery, and decolonization. Too many of the primary sources I consulted – especially the translations of Las Casas' sixteenth-century arguments at Valladolid on behalf of Indians, the anti-slavery briefs of abolitionists, and the British government's Blue Book on German South West Africa – were vivid descriptions of what Joseph Conrad's fictional character Kurtz from *Heart of Darkness* would call "the horror, the horror!" Because relatively little secondary work and analysis has been done on the Mandate system, chapter 6 builds on the work of historians but has been supplemented by deeper investigation into primary material, especially League of Nations documents and the records of the Permanent Mandates Commission.

---

[7] The term decolonization is, of course, problematic because it implies the exit of colonizers and the return of social, economic, and political life in colonies to a pre-conquest status. In every instance, however, the colonized are deeply and forever changed by the colonial experience, specifically by the introduction of wage labor, the concept of the sovereign state, and ties to European and American economies, while pre-existing institutions and social relations are altered or erased. In this sense no former colony has been able to fully decolonize.

If this were a comprehensive history of the rise and fall of colonialism, I would have been compelled to use more primary sources and to discuss, in much greater depth, colonialism and decolonization in areas of the world that I hardly mention. As it is, some may think the historical analysis and case material is too long, too descriptive, too wide-ranging, and contains too many citations and events. On the contrary, this work is surely too short as history and does not even mention many events, actors, and arguments some might consider crucial. My explanation for this brevity is the simple fact that I do not intend a comprehensive account but only to persuade you of the importance of argument, especially ethical argument, in the practice and end of colonialism. My admiration for the skill of narrative historians has only grown through the process of writing this book and I have not attempted to duplicate their work. Rather, I hope to have provided a template for the analysis of argument and historical change from which other, more comprehensive, histories can be read and re-interpreted.[8]

Chapter 9, "Poiesis and Praxis: Toward Ethical World Politics," develops an approach for making the practices of world politics more ethical and legitimate. In a world of clashing cultures and conflicting beliefs about what is right, how *ought* we decide what to do about the pressing questions of world politics? Specifically, how can we decide the important ethical and policy questions of when and how to conduct humanitarian interventions? "Poiesis and Praxis" – unlike previous chapters which are historical and analytical – is forward-looking and prescriptive. Using and elaborating on the approach to argument known as "discourse ethics," it discusses the process of ethical argument by which world politics might be remade with regard to the problem of humanitarian intervention.

International politics and foreign policy decisionmaking involve deliberation and choice, though decisions are made in highly constrained choice situations. The answer to the why question – why this thing and not another – is found in the content of the arguments and the process of reason. The process and content of argument are fundamental forces in world politics – they are constitutive of the world. The beliefs that actors hold about the world and the outcome of political arguments, whether

---

[8] Careful readers will note that in a few cases in the book my spelling of place names and organizations change. The inconsistency is not mine, but the fact that over decades, the names themselves sometimes changed or were written differently by sources. Similarly, to avoid anachronism, I use names for groups of people, in their historical context, e.g. "Hottentot," which are now or might be considered derogatory. No offense is intended.

they are considered persuasive, make world politics and foreign policy what it is, as much or more than the distribution of power among
states. The content of world politics is found in particular beliefs, and the
process of politics is shaped by the arguments and beliefs of everyday
discourse, public political rhetoric, legislation, court proceedings, and
private memos. In turn, the process of argument and the content of
beliefs are institutionalized in practices – organizational routines and
knowledge-making processes – that are part of the cultural environments of domestic and world politics. This argument about arguments
offers an alternative theory of choice in international relations that is not
based on rational actor theory, but on the role of practical reason and
the importance of beliefs rooted in culture. The major evolutionary or
revolutionary changes of world politics are thus a consequence of reasoned choice – as much as change is due to accident or material forces
and structures.

1 Argument, belief, and culture

Soldiers and their generals fight for many causes, worthy and unworthy, and when it comes to the battlefield the considerations are pretty much the same, whatever the cause. The generals study each other's tactics across the battle lines, often with admiration. They are the technicians of warfare. The soldiers of the contending armies display courage (and sometimes cowardice), and the people they fight for make heroic sacrifices (or exploit the war for gain) on both or all sides, although perhaps to different degrees and in different ways. To learn what the fighting and the courage and sacrifices meant one must look elsewhere, behind the physical contest to loyalties and emotions, thoughts and ideas, moral convictions and arguments. One must ask what moral and mental content shaped the decisions that brought these people to the battlefield.[1]

To be of greatest interest to us, the act of demolishing another must be enshrined in justifications. The muscle movements must occur in a context of verbal legitimacy.[2]

Why do people, either alone or in groups, choose one action and not another? How do they even come to know that they must make a decision? Why choose blockade over invasion, or confrontation over appeasement? Indeed, how do people decide what is worth fighting for at all? Surely actors are often circumscribed by resources, or their options seem limited by the structure of choice (such as time pressure), but generally decisionmakers still have options even within constraint. Individuals and groups make decisions through a process of practical

---

[1] William Lee Miller, *Arguing About Slavery: The Great Battle in the United States Congress* (New York: Alfred A. Knopf, 1996), p. 4.
[2] Harold Lasswell, *World Politics and Personal Insecurity* (New York: The Free Press (1935) 1965), pp. 23–24.

reason or argument, while the beliefs contained in those arguments help actors, both in groups and by themselves, decide what to do. Reason is the process individuals go through in deciding how the world works and how they will act in it.[3] Political argument is public reason.

The necessity of making good arguments, ones that convince others, preoccupies domestic governments, social movements, and associations. Why? Because justification is necessary. What is not clear to scholars of world politics is how argument could have any importance outside the domestic realm. Focusing on argument thus runs against the grain of international relations theory.[4] However, analysis of the process and content of arguments is crucial for understanding constancy and change in world politics. Argument is not "merely" rhetoric.[5] Even those who use brute force make arguments about why it was "necessary" or "wise" to do so.

The tendency to downplay argument, belief, culture, and political discourse has deep roots. Political philosopher Thomas Hobbes proclaimed "covenants, without the sword, are but words, and of no strength to secure a man at all."[6] Hans Morgenthau, in *Politics Among Nations*, urges scholars of international politics to assume rationality and a drive for

---

[3] Rational actor theories describe one kind of reasoning but certainly do not encompass all forms of reasoning.
[4] Exceptions include: Thomas Risse, "'Let's Argue!' Communicative Action in World Politics," *International Organization* 54 (Winter 2000), 1–39; Thomas Risse, Stephen C. Ropp, and Kathryn Sikkink, eds., *The Power of Human Rights: International Norms and Domestic Change* (Cambridge: Cambridge University Press, 1999); Hayward R. Alker, *Rediscoveries and Reformulations: Humanistic Methodologies for International Studies* (Cambridge: Cambridge University Press, 1996); Friedrich V. Kratochwil, *Rules, Norms and Decisions: On the Conditions of Practical and Legal Reasoning in International Relations and Domestic Affairs* (Cambridge: Cambridge University Press, 1989); Thomas F. Homer-Dixon and Roger S. Karapin, "Graphical Argument Analysis: A New Approach to Understanding Arguments Applied to a Debate about the Window of Vulnerability," *International Studies Quarterly* 33 (September 1989), 389–410; Anatol Rapoport, *Fights, Games, and Debates* (Ann Arbor: University of Michigan, 1960); Gavan Duffy, Brian K. Federking, and Seth A. Tucker, "Language Games: Dialogical Analysis of INF Negotiations," *International Studies Quarterly* 42 (June 1998), 271–294; Michael Walzer, *Just and Unjust Wars: A Moral Argument With Historical Illustrations* (New York: Basic Books, 1992); and Martti Koskenniemi, *From Apology to Utopia: The Structure of International Legal Argument* (Helsinki: Finnish Lawyers' Publishing Company, 1989); Andrew Linklater, *The Transformation of Political Community: Ethical Foundations of the Post-Westphalian Era* (Cambridge: Polity Press, 1998). Outside international relations see: Brian M. Barry, *Political Argument: A Reissue with a New Introduction* (London: Routledge, 1990); Deirdre N. McCloskey, *The Rhetoric of Economics, 2nd edn* (Madison, WI: University of Wisconsin Press, 1998) and Michael Billig, *Arguing and Thinking: A Rhetorical Approach to Social Psychology* (Cambridge: Cambridge University Press, 1996).
[5] And like casuistry, rhetoric is not bad, though in recent years both terms have the connotation of empty speech that is separate from and/or conceals real interest.
[6] Thomas Hobbes, *Leviathan* (New York: Penguin (1651) 1986), p. 223.

power.[7] Given an assumption of rationality, defined as the pursuit of one's interests, it matters little what actors think or how they use arguments to persuade others to act. Structural theories of international politics, which emphasize the anarchical character of the international system and suggest that most outcomes can be explained by reference to the distribution of capabilities (most importantly, power) among states, similarly assume and emphasize a narrowly defined rationality. Kenneth Waltz argues that systemic forces of international politics (the balance of power) push actors to be "'sensitive to costs' . . . which for convenience can be called an assumption of rationality."[8] Further, even constructivists – who argue that rules regulate behavior and constitute actors' identities – appear to hold the view that there is a rational core to behavior in international politics.[9] Post-structural and critical theory approaches to world politics, which emphasize discourse, come closest to articulating a role for argument.[10]

The *process* of foreign policy decisionmaking and international relations is characterized by political arguments that occur among elites, within organizations, between elites and masses, in the public sphere, within authoritarian states, and in the anarchical international system. There is a tight relationship between belief and argument: beliefs are translated into political action through reasoned argument. Even when beliefs appear, by themselves, to lead to actions such as the use of force by states, actors reason and give reasons to others about why force must be used. Reasoning involves both individual reflection and political, or public, argument. Arguments and beliefs gain their content and are

[7] The tendency of Hobbes and Morgenthau to downplay the role of ideas and argument is ironic given the centrality of political argument in Thucydides.
[8] Kenneth N. Waltz, "Reflections on Theory of International Politics: A Response to My Critics," in Robert O. Keohane, ed., *Neorealism and its Critics* (New York: Columbia University Press, 1986), pp. 322–345: 331.
[9] Constructivist primers include Peter Katzenstein, ed., *The Culture of National Security: Norms and Identity in World Politics* (New York: Columbia University Press, 1996); Alexander Wendt, *Social Theory of International Politics* (Cambridge: Cambridge University Press, 1999); Emanuel Adler, "Seizing the Middle Ground: Constructivism in World Politics," *European Journal of International Relations* 3 (September 1997), 319–364; Audie Klotz, *Norms in International Relations: The Struggle Against Apartheid* (Ithaca: Cornell University Press, 1995); Nicholas Greenwood Onuf, *World of Our Making: Rules and Rule in Social Theory and International Relations* (Columbia: University of South Carolina Press, 1989).
[10] See David Campbell, *Writing Security: United States Foreign Policy and the Politics of Identity* (Minneapolis: University of Minnesota Press, 1992); Karen Litfin, *Ozone Discourses: Science and Politics in Global Environmental Cooperation* (New York: Columbia University Press, 1994); Roxanne Lynn Doty, *Imperial Encounters: The Politics of Representation in North–South Relations* (Minneapolis: University of Minnesota Press, 1996).

intelligible through and within cultures. In other words, arguments depend on and refer to beliefs and those beliefs are embedded in a context of other beliefs which may or may not be explicit or structured. Argument in foreign policy decisionmaking and international politics is only one species of the processes of international politics.[11]

Argument

The dominant view of how issues are decided was well articulated in 1862 by German Chancellor Otto von Bismarck: "The great questions of the age are not settled by speeches and majority votes . . . but by iron and blood."[12] Yet, as foreign policy decisionmakers come to believe it is time to act, and there is no obvious course of action dictated by preexisting beliefs and policies, they begin to argue over the correct action. Arguments are an effort to persuade others to see the world in a particular way and to act in accordance with the conclusion that follows from the argument. Practical arguments are about how to act in the social world; scientific arguments are about the natural world; ethical arguments are about what it is right to do in particular situations; and identity arguments are about how different understandings or actions in the world are implied on the basis of identity.

Argument as reasoning and persuasion

Political argument is a form of persuasion and intersubjective reasoning. While decisionmaking is characterized by reflection and often keen intelligence, it is not rational, at least not in the sense scholars usually think of as rational (dispassionate utility maximizing). Rather, foreign policy decisions are the product of preexisting beliefs and the process

[11] Processes are the regular practices that the agents of world politics engage in as they create, maintain, and transform themselves and the structure of world politics. Other processes are: constitutive, reproductive, communicative, discursive and oppositional. Arguments communicate beliefs and information about how others understand the world. Argumentation is also a discursive practice; arguments only make sense within discursive or knowledge structures and within the larger cultural/historical context within which they take place. Arguments can bolster, modify, or destroy knowledge structures. Arguments are also constitutive in that they define, make, and maintain corporate/collective agents and some aspects of social structure. Reproductive and oppositional processes are also dependent on arguments. We could oppose each other or reproduce ourselves in any number of ways. How groups choose to do so, or to change from one mode of production or opposition to another, is by a process of persuasive arguments and reasoning.
[12] Quoted in Hagan Schulze, *Germany: A New History* (Cambridge, MA: Harvard University Press, 1998), p. 140.

of argument within and among groups – they are reasoned. Such political reasoning takes the form of an argument that contains beliefs and a logic or logics of inference.[13] The goal of political arguments may be to convince or persuade another (or some third party), or discourse ethical argument can be used by interlocutors to reason or to find "truth" together. In the former instance, the focus of most of this book, those who argue are convinced of their position and are trying to persuade the other or an important audience that they are right.[14] In the latter case, actors are more open to challenges to their position and to changing their beliefs and conclusions.

Practical reasoning or inference is an internal act of deliberation that individuals can use to work through problems; it is "a route to *discovery*, not just to retrospective explanation or justification, or to self-encouragement."[15] Public or political arguments attempt to influence private reasoning and affect a group's choice: political arguments provide reasons that actors think and hope others will find persuasive. Of course, coercion is possible and frequently used, but it is very expensive to coerce others over prolonged periods. To get other states to go along with yours, whether in a coalition, alliance, or large international organization (or at least not to oppose your state) those others must be convinced to act, or at least not to block your action. Thus, politics is thick with places where arguments can and must be persuasive. When practical reason is a public process of argument, advocates in effect take their audience through the steps of practical inference and/or associative reasoning.[16] Thus, a strict division between internal and external reasoning breaks down in practice since individuals acquire and understand history and historical analogies as part of a social process.

Reason and persuasive argument have been discussed for millennia by philosophers and rhetoricians. Aristotle distinguished practical from theoretical reasoning (or wisdom) in the *Nichomachean Ethics*, where he says that "practical wisdom is concerned with action."[17] Theoretical reasoning or wisdom concerns answering the question of what is or is not

[13] I say more about logics of inference later.
[14] Risse, "Let's Argue," calls this rhetorical action.
[15] Robert Audi, *Practical Reasoning* (New York: Routledge, 1989), p. 184.
[16] Aristotle links practical reasoning and politics in book 6 of *The Nichomachean Ethics*, translated with an Introduction by David Ross (Oxford: Oxford University Press, 1980).
[17] Aristotle, *Nichomachean Ethics*, p. 146 (book 6, ch. 7). Also see Aristotle, *The Art of Rhetoric*, translated with an Introduction by Hugh Lawson-Tancred (New York: Penguin, 1991). Habermas relates Aristotelian practical reason to discourse ethics in Jürgen Habermas, *Between Facts and Norms: Contributions to a Discourse Theory of Law and Democracy* (Cambridge, MA: MIT Press, 1996).

true, while practical reasoning is concerned with answering the question of how to act in response to practical problems.[18] Practical reasoning "concludes with an answer to a practical question, such as, paradigmatically, 'What am I to do?', asked in the context of a felt problem."[19] Further, as Aristotle notes, deliberation over practical problems may consist of chains of practical reasoning, as people reason about how to achieve something they have defined as a good.

> We deliberate not about ends but about means . . . Having set the end, they consider how and by what means it is to be attained; and if it seems to be produced by several means they consider by which it is most easily and best produced, while if it is achieved by one only they consider how it will be achieved by this and by what means *this* will be achieved, till they come to the first cause, which in the order of discovery is the last . . . and what is last in the order of analysis seems to be first in the order of becoming.[20]

Forms of argument: top-down, rule-based and sideways, associative

There are different ways to deconstruct and represent practical reason and arguments.[21] Political debates and arguments may often be described as Aristotelian practical reason where actors, who are goal – or norm – driven make arguments that move from general premises to specific conclusions. For example, "si vis pacem para bellum/ if you want peace prepare for war." Though we seldom make arguments in a form where the architecture is so transparent, practical reasoning may be illustrated in the form of a syllogism or practical inference: the first,

---

[18] Aristotle distinguished episteme or theoretical knowledge from phronesis, or practical wisdom, used for resolving particular problems. Theoretical statements or arguments are idealized, atemporal, and "necessary" in the sense that they depend on the initial axioms being correct and on the consistency of subsequent deductions. Practical statements or arguments are concrete (resting on experience), temporal, and "presumptive" in the sense of being revisable. Albert R. Jonsen and Stephen Toulmin, *The Abuse of Casuistry: A History of Moral Reasoning* (Berkeley: University of California Press, 1988), pp. 26–28.
[19] Audi, *Practical Reasoning*, pp. 18–19.
[20] Aristotle, *Nichomachean Ethics*, pp. 56–57. Toulmin calls larger arguments "macro-arguments," and the arguments embedded in larger arguments "micro-arguments." Stephen Toulmin, *The Uses of Argument* (Cambridge: Cambridge University Press, 1958), p. 94.
[21] I am for the most part omitting explicit discussion of formal theories of argument and discourse because I have chosen to emphasize the process of argument in world politics – specifically in understanding colonialism, decolonization, and humanitarian intervention – rather than theories of argument. Further, I am not developing a formal method for analyzing arguments but rather, in chapter 2, proposing an informal method.

16

or major, premise expresses a goal, the second, or minor, premise articulates a cause-effect belief, and the conclusion regards a practical necessity, the statement of an action to bring about the desired goal realizing,
of course, that there may be more than one way to achieve the goal.[22]

Form of practical syllogism/Inference

Premise: desired goal or norm/good
Premise: cause–effect argument or representation of the situation
Conclusion: description of action implied by the argument

Practical inferences are the "single step from a set of premises to a
conclusion" and practical reasoning is "a sequence of practical inferences linked by more than one step of inference."[23] Practical reasoning
may then be represented as a syllogism with prior syllogisms, linked in
inferential or purposive chains, and such arguments may be analyzed
in terms of their deductive logic. Good arguments of this sort ought to
have conclusions that follow logically from their premises, and whether
something follows "logically" depends on the content of beliefs embedded in the argument and the wider background of culture.

All practical arguments are vulnerable to being questioned. First, an-
tagonists may debate the *desirability* of the proposed goal and whether
the goal is worth the actions required to achieve it (meta-argument).
Second, they may focus on the second premise, specifically on whether
the particular *means–end relationship* given as part of the argument is
correct – whether the beliefs given about how the world actually works
in the ways presumed by the argument are correct. Third, interlocutors may question the *validity* of a practical inference; in other words,
whether the correct conclusion was drawn from the argument. Fourth,
actors may agree on the goal, the ends–means premise, and the inferences drawn from the argument, but argue over whether the actions
required to reach the goal are *feasible*. Or finally, using a powerful rhetorical move, opponents to a dominant argument may raise a competing
syllogism or suggest different relevant comparisons.

In contrast to top-down reasoning, when actors perceive similarities
between situations they may reason horizontally, by association, that it
is wise to act in ways that worked in the first instance, assuming that
what applies in one situation ought to apply in a similar case. Arguments

---

[22] Douglas N. Walton, *Practical Reasoning: Goal-Driven, Knowledge-Based, Action-Guiding
Argumentation* (Savage, MD: Rowman and Littlefield, 1990), pp. 16-21 discusses alternative
formulations of premises and conclusions of a practical inference.
[23] Ibid., p. 129.

which take this form "depend for their power on how closely the *present* circumstances resemble those of the earlier *precedent* cases for which this particular type of argument was originally devised . . . the truths and certitudes established in the precedent cases *pass sideways*, so as to provide 'resolutions' of later problems."[24] Inferences in horizontal/associative reasoning are based on simplifying, or in some cases caricaturing complex situations through the use of metaphor, metonym (recalling a part or aspect of something to refer to characteristics of the whole), or analogy, and comparing them with other situations.

Metaphor, metonym, and analogy are thus a crucial part of the internal reasoning of individuals – how they come to understand, learn, and decide by themselves – and public argument. Intended analogies may often be conveyed in one word or phrase that is synonomous with "lessons" learned: "Munich" recalls appeasement and ultimately the failure to prevent aggression; "Pearl Harbor" recalls a surprise attack with devastating consequences. Yuen Foong Khong argues that as a form of reasoning, "analogies are cognitive devices that 'help' policymakers perform six diagnostic tasks central to political decision-making. Analogies (1) help define the nature of the situation confronting the policymaker (2) help assess the stakes, and (3) provide prescriptions. They help evaluate options by (4) predicting their chances of success, (5) evaluating their moral rightness, and (6) warning about dangers associated with the options."[25] In sum, actors are asserting that the present situation is like the one recalled, attempting to frame a situation and simultaneously implying that one ought to act according to the "lessons" of the analogy. "Metaphor is one, if not the major, cognitive means that communicating minds have for simplifying and 'making sense' of highly complex phenomena."[26]

In sum, reasoning can be used by an individual actor as a "route to discovery" to help them determine the right course of action to solve a particular problem and also as a form of public reason or political argument.[27] In making arguments, individuals give reasons, and evidence to support those reasons, to persuade others of the rightness of a course of action or opinion that they advocate. Although psychologists

---

[24] Jonsen and Toulmin, *The Abuse of Casuistry*, p. 35.
[25] Yuen Foong Khong, *Analogies at War: Korea, Munich, Dien Bien Phu, and the Vietnam Decisions of 1965* (Princeton: Princeton University Press, 1992), p. 10.
[26] Paul Chilton, *Security Metaphors: Cold War Discourse from Containment to Common House* (New York: Peter Lang, 1996), p. 28.
[27] Audi, *Practical Reasoning*, p. 184.

may debate whether human reasoning is top-down, rule-following, or associative, research on foreign policy decisionmaking suggests that arguments and inferences are made both ways.[28] Major political arguments, especially those involving ways of life and fundamental social concerns, usually occur over long periods of time and sometimes feature discrete debates over supporting issues and points of evidence. Meta-arguments are also part of the process.

Meta-arguments: the real, the good, the frame

Coherent arguments are unlikely to take place unless and until actors, on at least some level, agree on what they are arguing about. The at least temporary resolution of meta-arguments – regarding the nature of the good (the content of prescriptive norms); what is out there, the way we know the world, how we decide between competing beliefs (ontology and epistemology); and the nature of the situation at hand (the proper frame or representation) – must occur before specific arguments that could lead to decision and action may take place.

Meta-arguments over epistemology and ontology, relatively rare, occur in instances where there is a fundamental clash between belief systems and not simply a debate within a belief system. Such arguments over the nature of the world and how we come to know it are particularly rare in politics though they are more frequent in religion and science. Meta-arguments over the "good" are contests over what it is good and right to do, and even how we know the good and the right. They are about the nature of the good, specifically, defining the qualities of "good" so that we know good when we see it and do it. Ethical arguments are about how to do good in a particular situation.

More common are meta-arguments over representations or frames – about how we ought to understand a particular situation. Sometimes actors agree on how they see a situation. More often there are different possible interpretations. Thomas Homer-Dixon and Roger Karapin suggest, "Argument and debate occur when people try to gain acceptance for their interpretation of the world."[29] For example, "is the war defensive or aggressive?" Defining and controlling representations and images, or the frame, affects whether one thinks there is an issue at

---

[28] On the debate in psychology, see Steven A. Sloman, "The Empirical Case for Two Systems of Reasoning,"*Psychological Bulletin* 19 (January 1996), 1–22; Gerd Gigerenzer and Terry Regier, "How Do We Tell an Association from a Rule? Comment on Sloman," *Psychological Bulletin* 19 (January 1996), 23–26.

[29] Homer-Dixon and Karapin, "Graphical Argument Analysis," p. 390.

stake and whether a particular argument applies to the case. An actor fighting a defensive war is within international law; an aggressor may legitimately be subject to sanctions.

Framing and reframing involve mimesis or putting forward representations of what is going on. In mimetic meta-arguments, actors who are struggling to characterize or frame the situation accomplish their ends by drawing vivid pictures of the "reality" through exaggeration, analogy, or differentiation. Representations of a situation do not re-produce accurately so much as they creatively re-present situations in a way that makes sense. "Mimesis is a metaphoric or 'iconic augmentation of the real,' imitating not the effectivity of events, but their logical structure and meaning."[30] Certain features are emphasized and others de-emphasized or completely ignored as the situation is recharacterized or reframed. Representation thus becomes a "constraint on reasoning in that it limits understanding to a specific organization of conceptual knowledge."[31] The dominant representation delimits which arguments will be considered legitimate, framing how actors see possibilities. As Roxanne Doty argues, "the possibility of practices presupposes the ability of an agent to imagine certain courses of action. Certain background meanings, kinds of social actors and relationships, must already be in place."[32]

If, as Donald Sylvan and Stuart Thorson argue, "Politics involves the selective privileging of representations," it may not matter whether one representation or another is true or not.[33] Emphasizing whether frames articulate accurate or inaccurate perceptions misses the rhetorical import of representation – how frames affect what is seen, or not seen, and subsequent choices.[34] Meta-arguments over representation are thus

[30] Alker, *Rediscoveries and Reformulations*, p. 298.
[31] Donald A. Sylvan and Deborah M. Haddad, "Reasoning and Problem Representation in Foreign Policy: Groups, Individuals and Stories," in Donald A. Sylvan and James F. Voss, eds., *Problem Representation in Foreign Policy Decision Making* (Cambridge: Cambridge University Press, 1998), pp. 187–212: 189.
[32] Roxanne Lynn Doty, "Foreign Policy as Social Construction: A Post-Positivist Analysis of U.S. Counterinsurgency Policy in the Philippines," *International Studies Quarterly* 37 (September 1993), 297–320: 298.
[33] Donald A. Sylvan and Stuart J. Thorson, "Ontologies, Problem Representation, and the Cuban Missile Crisis," *Journal of Conflict Resolution* 36 (December 1992), 709–732: 731.
[34] Erving Goffman, *Frame Analysis* (New York: Harper, 1974); Paul Slovic, Baruch Fischhoff, and Sara Lichtenstein, "Response Mode, Framing, and Information-Processing Effects in Risk Assessment," in David E. Bell, Howard Raiffa, and Amos Tversky, eds., *Decision Making: Descriptive, Normative, and Prescriptive Interactions* (Cambridge: Cambridge University Press, 1988), pp. 152–166; Amos Tversky and Daniel Kahneman, "Rational Choice and the Framing of Decisions," in Bell, Raiffa, and Tversky, eds., *Decision Making*, pp. 167–192.

crucial elements of political argument because an actor's arguments about what to do will be more persuasive if their characterization or framing of the situation holds sway. But, as Rodger Payne suggests, "No frame is an omnipotent persuasive tool that can be decisively wielded by norm entrepreneurs without serious political wrangling."[35] Hence framing is a meta-argument.

Associative reasoning, especially analogies, are particularly useful in meta-arguments about the frame. Thus, Dwain Mefford argues, "the process of reasoning by analogy probably exerts greatest impact in the initial steps of the overall process. It helps shape the decision makers' initial orientation and posture. It is here that candidate interpretations are first marshaled, later to be scrutinized and reworked or rejected."[36] Historical analogy is *both* a frame and a mechanism for internal discovery and reason. "The ambiguous and incomplete information that a new situation typically presents is often pieced together and completed on the basis of parallels drawn to past incidents. The parallels, once recognized, guide actors' expectations as to what may ensue from the present situations if the parallel holds."[37] In some cases, analogies that in retrospect seem misplaced or poorly remembered helped policymakers settle on what are regarded as mistaken policies.[38]

Some scholars are wary of analogy because it seems to do too many things in argument. For example, Jack Levy distinguishes between analogies that help us reason and those that are "rhetorical." "Some fail to differentiate between genuine learning and the rhetorical or strategic use of historical lessons to advance current preferences or fail to construct research designs that expedite the empirical distinction between these causal processes."[39] Levy discounts the rhetorical. "Instead of genuinely learning from historical experience, individuals might use

[35] Rodger Payne, "Persuasion, Frames, and Norm Construction," unpublished manuscript (University of Louisville, 2000).
[36] Dwain Mefford, "Analogical Reasoning and the Definition of the Situation: Back to Snyder for Concepts and Forward to Artificial Intelligence for Method," in Charles F. Hermann, Charles W. Kegley, Jr., and James N. Rosenau, eds., *New Directions in the Study of Foreign Policy* (London: HarperCollins Academic, 1987), pp. 221–244: 222.
[37] Ibid., p. 223.
[38] See Robert Jervis, *Perception and Misperception in International Politics* (Princeton: Princeton University Press, 1976), pp. 275–279; Yaacov Y. I. Vertzberger, *The World in Their Minds: Information Processing, Cognition, and Perception in Foreign Policy* (Stanford: Stanford University Press, 1990), pp. 296–341. Also see Khong, *Analogies at War*; Ernest May, *"Lessons" of the Past* (New York: Oxford, 1973); Richard Neustadt and Ernest May, *Thinking in Time: The Uses of History for Decision-Makers* (New York: Hill and Wang, 1989).
[39] Jack S. Levy, "Learning and Foreign Policy: Sweeping a Conceptual Minefield," *International Organization* 48 (Spring 1994), 279–312: 282.

Argument and change in world politics

history instrumentally. They often select from historical experience those cases that provide the greatest support for their preexisting policy preferences, or they reinterpret a given case in a way that reinforces their views, so as to rally support for their preferred policies, whether they be driven by views of the national interest or partisan political interests."[40] Discounting instrumental uses of analogy misses the purpose and effects of historical/analogical statements as meta-arguments. The intention is precisely to persuade and the framing effect is often quite powerful.[41] As Khong says, "that policymakers use the same analogies to *justify* their choices does not vitiate the diagnostic role of the analogies in helping policymakers *arrive* at those choices."[42]

Why do actors find one framing analogy or metaphor more persuasive than another? The answer probably lies in the personal histories and cultural contexts of decisionmakers. Further, as Vertzberger argues, the "logic of analogical reasoning dictates that the greater the perceived correspondence between the past and the present or future, the greater the credibility of the analogy and the appropriateness of analogical reasoning are perceived to be."[43] This "perceived correspondence" is crucial. "Consequently the weight given to inferences and definitions of the situation based on lessons from history is higher than the weight given to competing inferences and definitions of the situation based on other knowledge structures, such as deductive logic. In the same vein, the greater the perceived correspondence, the more likely is high credibility and trust in the validity of the analogy. . . ."[44] But "correspondence" is not merely recognized or "perceived." Rather, policymakers often *argue* that the case corresponds with their preferred analogy, *making* the situation correspond with the past that they want to emphasize. Further, framing is shaped and constrained by dominant cultures.

To understand which arguments are persuasive, and how one argument is chosen over another, it is important to know which representation or characterization of the situation was believed and why one representation was chosen over competing frames. Winners of the framing contest, or more importantly, the content of the representation they employ, have powerfully set the terms of subsequent argument. The content of the accepted representation focuses debates simply because

[40] Ibid., 306.
[41] For a psychological approach, see Keith Holyoak and Paul Thagard, *Mental Leaps: Analogy in Creative Thought* (Cambridge, MA: MIT Press, 1995).
[42] Khong, *Analogies at War*, p. 16.
[43] Vertzberger, *The World in Their Minds*, p. 319.   [44] Ibid.

22

when the same issues are framed one way versus another, some arguments will seem more persuasive than others. Further, the at least temporary settling of meta-arguments over the good, ontology, epistemology, and representations, is the *topoi* or starting point of other arguments.[45] Among like-minded individuals, and in cases where the issue was less what the starting point was than what to do about a particular question, decisionmaking will likely feature much less meta-argument than debate on the content of arguments on the table, a search for consensus, and a focus on the best means of implementing decisions. The settling of arguments can lead to a new round of meta-argument, however, as the practices implied and entailed by the conclusion of arguments change the way the world works and is understood.

Content of argument

Political arguments can be classified into four ideal-type categories that vary in terms of their content: practical/instrumental, ethical, scientific, and identity. In complex situations that demand complex arguments, more than one, in some cases all these types of arguments may be deployed. Although the bulk of the empirical part of this book concerns the role of ethical argument the other types are also common in world politics.

Practical or *instrumental* arguments involve beliefs about cause and effect relations among individuals; they are about how to do things in the social world. For example, prior to World War I, strategists in the French, German, and Russian militaries argued that offensive military doctrines were the best defense, and convinced the civilian leaders of those states to adopt offensive strategies.[46] Practical arguments work by giving good accounts of the social world, and thus they rely on hearers being convinced by the practical beliefs that support those arguments. Practical arguments may also show that a previous or alternative process for accomplishing a certain task in the social world was inadequate or ineffective. Words like "counter-productive," "futile," or "ineffective" will convey this sense. Those employing practical arguments may also then make the claim that an alternative process is better (e.g. more efficient, more effective, or less costly) than the dominant practice. Such a claim may or may not rest on the belief that advocates of the new practical alternative have a better understanding of how the social world works.

---

[45] Kratochwil, *Rules, Norms and Decisions*, pp. 38–39, 41, 218–219.
[46] See Jack Snyder, *The Ideology of the Offensive: Military Decision Making and the Disasters of 1914* (Ithaca: Cornell University Press, 1984).

Scientific arguments are about the constraints and possibilities of the physical and natural world, using the "laws" of science, technology, or nature, as they are understood at the time. Scientific arguments are often made by members of scientific epistemic communities and by others who invoke "natural" laws.[47] For example, the interlocutors in international policy debates about global warming rely on scientific (and economic) arguments. Old-fashioned realist theories and a good deal of contemporary foreign policy rely on what are thought to be scientific views of human nature as at root concerned with the acquisition of power. Scientific arguments work, or are persuasive, to the extent that they make powerful ontological claims about the natural world that are coupled with epistemological, procedural, claims about how to make new knowledge. These procedures for producing new knowledge become the only valid grounds for judging whether or not information and arguments should be heard and how they should be judged. Scientific arguments work by defeating other claims to understanding the natural world and by posing plausible accounts of the processes of the natural world that cohere with other scientific accounts.

Ethical arguments concern how to act in a particular situation so as to be doing good, assuming that the good has been defined through cultural consensus or meta-argument. Ethical arguments may assert that an existing normative belief or moral conviction ought to be applied in a particular situation, and they are used to promote new normative beliefs. To simplify in a way that parallels the model of practical inference, ethical arguments may take the form of positing the existence of an ethical or prescriptive normative belief (premise 1), then specifying that the particular context is an instance covered by the prescriptive norm (premise 2), which implies (conclusion) that to do good, one ought to act in ways consistent with the prescription. Ethical arguments may also be characterized by sideways reasoning, where similarities and differences between cases suggest what is right to do in a new situation.[48] Chapter 2 describes in detail how ethical arguments work.

Identity arguments posit that people of a certain kind act or don't act in certain ways and the audience of the argument either positively or negatively identifies with the people in question. Identity arguments

[47] See Peter Haas, "Introduction: Epistemic Communities and International Policy Coordination," *International Organization* 46 (Winter 1992), 1–36.
[48] See Jonson and Toulmin, *The Abuse of Casuistry*.

may apply to groups or to individuals, but they are specifically about the characteristics of those individuals and what those characteristics imply in terms of actions or reactions. A simple example is the following: "civilized nations do not permit genocide" (premise 1); "we are civilized" (premise 2); "those who permit or conduct genocides are barbarians and we, the civilized should not allow this practice" (conclusion).

Identity arguments work by producing or calling upon previously existing identities and differences among groups and claiming that specific behaviors are associated with certain identities. Identity arguments therefore depend heavily on the depth and taken-for-grantedness of identities or identity beliefs. To be most persuasive, identity and difference must be seen as deeply embedded and natural. Identity arguments work to the extent that hearers are not immediately conscious of the ways that identity and difference are produced and naturalized by the individual performance of actions, the discourses of insiders and outsiders which articulate the characteristics and reproduce the histories of groups, and the institutions that produce identities such as schools, religious societies, or states. Further, identity arguments are often linked with practical or scientific arguments, as for example in this statement by a member of the French parliament in 1930:

> France has not yet become sufficiently conscious of the extent to which its colonies offer possibilities of prestige, elements of power and prosperity for its material recovery and opportunities to diffuse and display the splendor of its spirit. None of our national preoccupations is as important as that one. They all, whether they concern our security, our financial recovery, problems of population or of the reinforcement of our influence in the universal concord of people, they all have their full significance and precise implications only if viewed from this aspect. In fact on reflection one may rightly say: France will be a great colonizing power, or it will cease to be France.[49]

Identity and ethical arguments are often tightly linked. To be a good person, or in the above case, a great and splendorous nation, implies or perhaps even requires, certain "good" behaviors. "France will be a great colonizing power, or it will cease to be France." Identity arguments, perhaps more obviously than other arguments, also make use of and are bolstered by emotions or feelings of belonging and love, or alternatively

---

[49] Léon Archimbaud quoted in Rudolf von Albertini, *Decolonization: The Administration and Future of the Colonies, 1919–1960* (Garden City, NY: Doubleday & Company Inc., 1971), p. 265.

of hatred and contempt. Nationalist discourses, for example, depend on ethnocentric and national identity, which entails love and we-feeling for the ingroup and imply a political program of state-building. Thus, arguments do not depend solely on "cold" cognitive processes for their persuasiveness, but also on emotions.[50]

Emotion and argument

Arguments are more or less well received depending on the emotional status of the hearer and the emotional content of the argument. When individuals are angry or hostile toward an interlocutor, they are less open to persuasion than if they are neutral or feeling empathetic. More subtly, some arguments may trigger feelings as well as thoughts. Historical analogies are cognitively persuasive in arguments if they convince us that there are similarities between one situation and another; the lesson learned in the previous situation, therefore, ought to be applied to the new situation. If the events "match" (are similar in respects deemed significant) it is more likely that individuals who belong to generations with direct experience of an event used in the analogy, or who have had some direct contact with those who experienced the event, will likely have a greater emotional reaction.

Analogies may also be emotionally persuasive. Emotions are often purposefully evoked by political actors to increase our receptivity to their arguments. Nationalist leaders may promote fear of outsiders and love of country. International and non-governmental organizations use guilt and empathy to prompt disaster relief and foreign aid. Emotional appeals may be particularly effective when conflicts are represented in ethnic or racial terms, and when there is a reservoir of pre-existing negative beliefs and feelings toward outgroups, or where those beliefs and feelings can be easily stimulated and stoked. Both ethical and identity arguments are emotional and derive much of their persuasiveness from how well they elicit appropriate emotions, such as love or shame.

Both cognition and emotion influence persuasiveness, but the effects are not straightforward or easily disentangled. Persuasiveness that depends on careful cognition may be impaired by positive moods. Conversely, attempts to evoke emotions such as fear may backfire since "the kind of arguments used in fear appeals appear to disrupt careful

---

[50] See Neta C. Crawford, "The Passion of World Politics: Propositions on Emotion and Emotional Relationships," *International Security* 24 (Spring 2000), 116–156.

evaluation of message content."[51] But arguments that evoke fear may have positive consequences when interlocutors want fearful subjects to pay less attention to logic.

Process and meaning

If the process of political argument is ubiquitous, why do one thing and not another? And why are particular arguments understood to be persuasive enough to change the prevailing practice? In other words, the entire causal story is not captured by the process of argument. To answer questions about the particular constitution of the world at one moment, and how world political practices change, one must turn to content.[52] Meaning-content is found in the individual words used by those who are making arguments, and in the context that is readily apparent to participants because of their cultural background and immediate historical experience.

> Words are a part of human behaviour. They are mental categories which both represent, and are part of, the world and which impose intentionality and coherence on that world. Language is not just an intellectual activity distinct from the material world. Concepts and contexts are inseparable. Language is part of the social and political structure; it reveals the politics of a society. Hence analysis of political discourse will indicate how the political world is perceived, and a diachronic analysis of concepts can be helpful in uncovering long-term structural changes by showing how words acquire new meanings in the contexts of such changes.[53]

Further, as Aristotle noted, arguments are nested: more difficult social and political issues will often be tied to other complex and contested arguments and belief systems, linked to chains of prior argument. Consider the following syllogism about achieving peace. The first premise articulates the goal of actors, the second premise makes a claim about a causal relationship, and the conclusion states a "logical" action that

---

[51] Francine Rosselli, John J. Skelly, and Diane M. Mackie, "Processing Rational and Emotional Messages: The Cognitive and Affective Mediation of Persuasion," *Journal of Experimental Social Psychology* 31 (March 1995), 163–190: 167.
[52] Meaning is the manifest understanding of beliefs and arguments and the related web of associations including the background beliefs held by interlocutors and observers by which they are able to understand the arguments and beliefs. Linguists call this "deep structure." Associative arguments are particularly rich with meanings that may not be obvious to interlocutors and which may vary among interlocutors.
[53] K.H.F. Dyson, *The State Tradition in Western Europe: A Study of an Idea and Institution* (Oxford: Martin Robinson, 1980), pp. 1–2 quoted in Chilton, *Security Metaphors*, p. 25.

follows from the premises. The context is a question about how to use one's military to promote peace.

Example of Practical Inference in Foreign Policy Arguments

Premise: We desire international peace. (goal of actor)
Premise: The best way to achieve peace is through a strong military. (causal argument)
Conclusion: We ought to make a strong military. (An action is required or desired; follows from premises)

There are nearly always competing practical arguments on the table or in the background. An alternative position to the argument presented above is the confidence-building perspective where the goal or major premise is the same – the expression of a desire for peace – but the premise concerned with end-means relations makes an alternative claim based on different beliefs. The causal argument might be phrased, "The best way to achieve peace is through assuring the other side that you have peaceful intentions" where the conclusion might be "communicate" or "disarm."

Both examples illustrate that there are multiple supporting beliefs and arguments that underpin complex arguments.[54] Instrumental beliefs frequently come into play in arguments about practical questions such as how shall the state defend itself. For example, military doctrines include a mix of strategic, operational, and tactical beliefs about the most efficient and effective ways to deter and fight wars. Those beliefs affect decisions about the acquisition of equipment, the structure and content of training, and the conduct of military campaigns. But those beliefs are also used in arguments by those within and outside militaries to legitimize or delegitimize other arguments about which weapons to acquire in what number, how forces ought to be trained, and how wars ought to be fought. Thus, reasoning is contextual, including particular knowledge or larger belief contexts (culture).

Actors, persuasive context, and non-ideal speech

Political argument is institutionalized in world politics, albeit under different rules of procedure and standards of evidence, in several venues. Indeed, diplomacy is not only the mediation of estrangement and alienation, as James Der Derian suggests, it is the formal and institutionalized process of argumentation among states carried on by official or unofficial

---

[54] On using artificial intelligence to model practical reasoning see Alker, *Rediscoveries and Reformulations* and Walton, *Practical Reasoning*.

representatives of governments.[55] Besides bilateral diplomacy, venues for argument in world politics include international courts, commissions, and the resolution-making bodies of international organizations as well as transnational movements. In domestic settings, argumentation is institutionalized in the peer review process of disciplinary journals, in the op-ed and letter pages of newspapers, and in public institutions such as courts, legislatures, and political campaigns. Many kinds of actors in world politics are involved in making arguments, from individuals in governmental bureaucracies to diplomats who wish to make treaties to avoid or end wars, to members of the press and intellectuals who write opinion pieces about foreign policy, to staff members of non-governmental organizations (NGOs) who desire a change in a state's foreign policies or the policies of inter-governmental organizations such as the United Nations or the World Bank.[56]

If argument-making is institutionalized and ubiquitous, it is not unaffected by the purpose, context, and the identities of speakers and hearers. Some scholars of argument, notably Jürgen Habermas, talk about the conditions for "ideal speech" where only the force of the better argument convinces.[57] No institutional power, physical threats, or lies get in the way of the logic of argument and inference. In an ideal speech situation, all actors are competent and able to challenge the premises of their interlocutor, and the interlocutor must be prepared to justify their claims to validity.

Thus, those who presume that argumentation is primarily "a procedure whereby two or more individuals try to arrive at an agreement" or truth potentially miss an important context of argumentation.[58] A search for agreement may characterize some interpersonal arguments, but political arguments are different in significant respects.[59] First, participants

[55] See James Der Derian, *On Diplomacy: A Genealogy of Estrangement* (New York: Basil Blackwell, 1987).

[56] Much of what transnational advocacy networks do involves making meta-arguments and arguments. See Margaret E. Keck and Kathryn Sikkink, *Activists Beyond Borders: Advocacy Networks in International Politics* (Ithaca: Cornell University Press, 1998).

[57] See Jürgen Habermas, *Justification and Application: Remarks on Discourse Ethics* (Cambridge, MA: MIT Press, 1993) and Habermas, *Between Facts and Norms*.

[58] Frans H. van Eemeren, Rob Grootendorst, Sally Jackson, and Scott Jacobs, *Reconstructing Argumentative Discourse* (Tuscaloosa: University of Alabama Press, 1993), p. 12. Also see H.P. Grice, "Logic of Conversation, " in P. Cole and J.L. Morgan, eds., *Syntax and Semantics 3: Speech Acts* (New York: Academic Press, 1979), pp. 41–58; Denis J. Hilton, "The Social Context of Reasoning: Conversational Inference and Rational Judgement, " *Psychological Bulletin* 118 (September 1995), 248–271.

[59] While I share the desire of political theorists who seek to create non-coercive ideal speech communities I am here describing world politics, not at this point trying to remake it. The last chapter is prescriptive.

in political argument, while they may sincerely want to persuade the other and come to agreement, sometimes have no thought of trying to persuade their immediate interlocutor; rather they are playing to a larger audience, hoping to persuade non-participants and thus shift the political balance of power. Moreover, while persuasion of one's counterpart is often the point of making arguments, there are also other reasons to argue. Specifically, advocates of a particular position may be attempting, by stating their case, to rally their own supporters as a way of mobilizing their preexisting political power. Or advocates may be attempting to lay the rhetorical grounds (change the frame) as the background for a future argument. Or someone may give an argument in order to proclaim and establish their identity as a "standard bearer" or person who holds particular beliefs.

Second, in major political arguments that occupy domestic and international societies over long periods of time, larger issues and relations of power – in addition to the ostensible issue being debated – are usually at stake. The occurrence of a major political argument means the dissatisfaction that is characteristic of all political arrangements is occurring in a context of shifting ideas and power relations: there would be no argument if all were settled. Rather, justifications in the form of arguments would perhaps be used to maintain the taken for grantedness of the existing relationship. The occurrence of political argument indicates that there is either a normative belief that the issues at stake *should not* be decided by force alone or a *practical judgment* that a conflict *cannot* be decided by force. This is the case in all domestic societies, regardless of the level of authoritarianism.

Third, the scope for argument varies within and across institutional settings. For example, there is potentially greater scope for argument in democracies if only and simply because the dominant institutions have regular occasions, times, and venues for hearing arguments. A normative belief in public deliberation underlies the institutionalization of argument. In a democracy, when no side has the power to simply impose their view (and they often get that power by having won prior arguments and institutionalizing their victory), a decision often comes about as a result of the process of argument. The scope for argument is decreased in authoritarian settings. Specifically, one cannot neglect the important role of both simple allegiance (unreasoned faith) or unquestioned belief in the normality and legitimacy of certain institutions and practices, and fear, which can be quite effective in holding authoritarian states together. For fear to work, it requires that people believe adverse consequences will come about if they violate the dictates of the leadership. Authoritarian elites demonstrate their power against potential dissenters by making dissidents the subject of, for example, ridicule, job loss, kidnapping, torture, or execution.

But the role of argument is not entirely absent in authoritarian settings. Hegemons often make arguments so that they may maintain their position and because they believe what they argue. Even coercion requires arguments that are persuasive enough to convince those who will operate the mechanisms of coercion that coercion is necessary and that they must participate. Intimidation intended to produce fear cannot go all the way to the top at all times. Indeed, political arguments occur even among elites in authoritarian societies and the felt need and the practice of using arguments to mobilize constituencies testifies to the importance of argument.[60] Counter-arguments may be raised by those who are already in a counter-hegemony, or who seek to form one; they are using these arguments to change not only the beliefs and practices of the society but also the capabilities of the hegemonic social order, perhaps to overturn it. In other words, the people who make arguments come from and constitute elements of civil society that seek either to maintain or to overturn social practices. In the case of those who seek to overturn practices, their arguments may be successful enough to change the arrangement of authority and power within the civil society. In fact, they may have to do so to change dominant social practices.

Fourth, though everyone may argue, not all are persuasive. Politics, even in democratic contexts, is certainly not an ideal speech situation where preexisting power and authority have been removed from the scene or equalized and only the force of the better argument convinces. Political argument occurs on a decidedly *unlevel* playing field of discourse between differently powerful actors. Those whose beliefs are dominant usually hold an advantage in arguments; their position has set the terms of debate, defining what will be considered at all, and within that realm, what will be considered legitimate. In addition, those who hold the dominant position are usually the dominant class, with all the tools of privilege – media access, positions of political and social visibility and authority, recognized expertise, and presumed legitimacy – at their disposal. These elites are, in other words, hegemonic in a

[60] I thank Seyom Brown for suggesting this clear phrasing of my argument.

Gramscian sense.[61] Moreover, authority is not accidental. "To advance the 'new thinking' in the Soviet Union, for example, Gorbachev replaced many 'old thinkers' with 'new thinkers' who could further promote those ideas in their agencies."[62] Further, as the work on decisionmaking under conditions characterized by high degrees of uncertainty and complexity suggests, interlocutors with specialized knowledge may have rhetorical power disproportionately greater than their ostensible rank.[63] For example, in a Western medical context physicians will have greater authority attributed to their arguments over non-physicians in discussions of human health and neurologists will have greater authority than oncologists in discussions on treating multiple sclerosis or Parkinson's disease.

Finally, although in ideal speech situations, everything should be on the table, in most political arguments, much goes unsaid. For example, actors commonly make other assumptions about fellow conversationalists and inferences about content that go beyond the *explicit* contents of arguments. Hearers may assume that speakers' utterances are true. "If the hearer attributes properties such as sincerity, reliability, and knowledgeability to the speaker, then the hearer may well consider the probable truth value of an utterance to be high. If, on the other hand, the hearer considers the speaker to be insincere, unreliable or unknowledgeable, then the hearer may well consider the probable truth of the utterance to be low."[64] And hearers also use contextual knowledge to fill in the blanks of explicit arguments.[65] "Contextual factors generally held exogenous to game models may prove decisive for outcomes. These factors include actors' beliefs about the nature of the interaction, their beliefs about other actors' beliefs, and the means by which actors convey and infer intentions to and from one another."[66]

In sum, while meta-arguments as well as more specific identity, scientific, practical, and ethical arguments are made all the time by many actors, not all arguments have the same chance to be persuasive. Persuasive context – the purpose and intended audience of the argument,

[61] Antonio Gramsci, *Selections from the Prison Notebooks of Antonio Gramsci* (New York: International Publishers, 1971). Also see Stephen Gill, ed., *Gramsci, Historical Materialism and International Relations* (Cambridge: Cambridge University Press, 1993).
[62] Levy, "Learning and Foreign Policy," p. 300.
[63] Haas, ed., "Special Issue: Knowledge, Power, and International Policy Coordination."
[64] Hilton, "The Social Context of Reasoning," p. 250.
[65] Grice called this practice "conversational implicature." See H.P. Grice, "Logic of Conversation"; Duffy, Frederking, and Tucker, "Language Games."
[66] Duffy, Frederking, and Tucker, "Language Games," p. 271.

whether larger issues are on the table, the relative power and identities of the interlocutors, and the relevant cultural contexts – affect the success of persuasive efforts. The existence of argument as a practice is consistent; what varies across social formations and depending on the structure of power within groups, are the resources of authority and publicity (the ability to make arguments heard). Those who wish to form counter-hegemonies must make persuasive arguments to bolster their position and form a social movement.

Argument, belief, and legitimation

Even in cases where one side has imposed their views or practices on another, the process of argument and persuasion is still crucial: hegemons must convince others to carry out their wishes because even the leviathan falls asleep. In other words, although it is especially important to politically insecure elites, legitimation is a preoccupation of all ruling elites because at all times, even in totalitarian systems, governance requires some level of voluntary submission to authority.[67] To minimize resistance leaders of states must convince people that their actions are legitimate (done for a good reason and/or under right authority) on some level, or else they could not govern without the use of expensive surveillance and coercive mechanisms. "To a greater or lesser degree leaders have to legitimate their policies, to themselves, to their legislators, and to their electorates. They do this by the use of language and concepts. Consequently they must draw, proactively or retroactively, on the discourses (beliefs, practices and associated linguistic realizations) of the society of which they are a part."[68]

Elites can use any number of legitimating ideologies to show that "there are good arguments for a political order's claim to be recognized as right and just."[69] Legitimating ideologies used in political orders have included divine right, meritocracy/elitism, democratic/republican representation, and socialism. Legitimating ideologies are more or less

[67] Michel Foucault, "The Subject and Power," in Herbert L. Dreyfus and Paul Rabinow, eds., *Michel Foucault: Beyond Structuralism and Hermeneutics, 2nd edn* (Chicago: University of Chicago Press, 1984) and Thomas Franck, "The Emerging Right to Democratic Governance," *The American Journal of International Law* 86 (January 1992), 46–91. Loyalty and idealism can, to a certain extent, function in place of good reasons. See David Lumsdaine, *Moral Vision in International Politics: The Foreign Aid Regime, 1949-1989* (Princeton: Princeton University Press, 1993), p. 12.
[68] Chilton, *Security Metaphors*, p. 31.
[69] See Jürgen Habermas, "Legitimation Problems in the Modern State," in Jürgen Habermas, *Communication and the Evolution of Society* (Boston: Beacon Press, 1979), pp. 178–205: 178.

acceptable as societies move from one historically distinct situation to another – that is, as their beliefs change. Fascism and divine right are now mostly discredited legitimating ideologies, made unacceptable to Western societies as the belief assumptions behind those ideologies were understood differently and were delegitimized.

Legitimation crises are a sense that the government or governing group does not deserve the allegiance and compliance of the people because their actions are no longer understood as being done for a good reason. A *fundamental* legitimation crisis occurs when a government's legitimating ideology is discredited or successfully challenged, for example, when divine right is no longer seen as a legitimate basis for rule. A *regime* legitimation crisis occurs when a particular clique, for example a social class or ethnic group, is seen as illegitimate. A *policy* legitimation crisis occurs when specific policies of a government are seen as so troubling as to throw into question the policy or programs of the ruling group. A *personal* legitimation crisis occurs when the leadership of a particular individual is seen as illegitimately obtained or they have misused the trust of the people. A personal legitimation crisis is likely when a government's leader and/or their close associates are suspected of or proven to have broken the law or social norms by, for example, accepting bribes or intimidating political opponents. There may also be *cultural* or *societal* legitimation crises, when longstanding practices are no longer taken for granted and seen as legitimate.[70]

States that cannot convince their populations that their actions are legitimate eventually suffer legitimation crises; if those crises are not remedied through persuasion, the state may modify its policy or be forced to undergo a serious restructuring, perhaps a revolution. Individuals may be more receptive to ethical arguments if they live in societies that are in the midst of a legitimation crisis; and vice versa, ethical arguments may become the seeds of a legitimation crisis. Of course a legitimation crisis of one type may spark other sorts of legitimation crises as, for example, when the anti-slavery movement created problems for conservative rule in Britain and when it sparked tensions over states' rights and federalism in the United States.[71]

---

[70] This is a simpler model of legitimation needs and crisis than Jürgen Habermas, *Legitimation Crisis* (Boston: Beacon Press, 1975) where Habermas focuses on the consequences of the decreasing role of the "lifeworld" and the decline of cultural expectations as rationality and expectations about the state's role in providing well being increase.

[71] Habermas suggests stages of legitimation are "connected with social-evolutionary transitions to new learning levels" and that the "legitimations of a superseded stage, no matter

States must provide arguments, which are seen to be legitimate, for their actions. Environments thick with international institutions (such as the United Nations, the world court, regional organizations of states, and non-governmental organizations) and transnational advocacy networks provide venues where states, corporations, and individuals have to justify their international behavior. International institutions and governments must also increasingly justify their actions and inactions to attentive international and domestic publics.[72] As Martha Finnemore argues: "When states justify their interventions, they are drawing on and articulating shared values and expectations held by other decision makers and other publics in other states." Finnemore suggests that this is "literally an attempt to connect one's actions to standards of justice, or perhaps more generically, to standards of appropriate and acceptable behavior. Thus, through an examination of justifications we can begin to piece together what those internationally held standards are and how they may change over time."[73] Within international society, arguments and behaviors are judged on the basis of prevailing international belief systems, including normative beliefs. Thus, successful arguments in world politics must pass *both* domestic and international muster.

Why do arguments succeed?

To say that argument is ubiquitous, and how certain arguments might work, does not yet fully answer the question of whether argument is causally important. Meta-arguments are causally important when their exponents succeed in setting the framework for understanding events. This framing effect is particularly important in crises, when actors may

what their content, are depreciated with the transition to the next higher stage; it is not this or that reason which is no longer convincing but the kind of reason." Habermas, "Legitimation Problems," p. 185. I agree with Habermas that once certain types of justification are understood as illegitimate, a state is not likely to successfully resort to another variety of the same type of legitimating ideology. But whether there are progressive "stages" of legitimation connected to social-evolutionary stages is not clear. Nor is it clear that a society must hold only one type of legitimating ideology at a time. Indeed, it seems possible to use two or more legitimating ideologies simultaneously, with perhaps one reinforcing the weaknesses of the other. In sum, all political institutions face legitimation problems, but those problems do not always become fundamental, regime, policy, or personal legitimation crises.

[72] Thomas Risse-Kappen, "Public Opinion, Domestic Structure, and Foreign Policy in Liberal Democracies," *World Politics* 43 (July 1991), 479–512; Paul Wapner, "Politics Beyond the State: Environmental Activism and World Civic Politics," *World Politics* 47 (April 1995), 311–340.

[73] Martha Finnemore, "Constructing Norms of Humanitarian Intervention," in Katzenstein, ed., *Culture of National Security*, pp. 153–185: 159.

have little time to reconsider a frame once it has been accepted or become dominant. We can infer that scientific, identity, ethical, and practical arguments were causally important if actors change their beliefs and behavior after they have heard arguments and if other explanations fail to account for the change. A more detailed discussion on cause and ethical arguments appears in chapter 2.

If argument is ubiquitous, why are some arguments persuasive and others not? Persuasive arguments often have one or more of the characteristics of being emotionally appealing, accounting for evidence, and addressing the concerns raised by counter-arguments. Persuasive arguments are also often consistent with preexisting beliefs. Further, some arguments are persuasive simply because the frame has been set so well by advocates that no other argument seems plausible. Additionally, there may be a bias toward coherentism, with successful meta-arguments disposing hearers to accept subsequent arguments that cohere with them. Further, especially in the case of practical arguments, the logic of certain arguments may be more compelling than the alternatives. Other arguments are persuasive because they are made by authorities or experts, and the culture defers to those experts. (The literature on epistemic communities is implicitly an example of the effectiveness of scientific arguments.)[74] Persuasive arguments must also often change underlying beliefs. Finally, arguments may, as suggested above, resonate with or evoke an important emotional response. Thus, the content of arguments is important in explaining their persuasiveness, but so too is the cultural context within which arguments are made and heard.

Why do some arguments win out over others? Of course, more "persuasive" arguments may win. But we know that not all compelling arguments succeed in changing minds or behavior, and thus we must take into account the four aspects of the discursive context that affect the success of arguments: access, organizational ability, chance, and coherence with the larger material and ideational context. First, to have a possibility of succeeding, arguments must be heard. Since politics is far from an ideal speech community or level playing field, many arguments will never be heard or achieve the same legitimacy as those made by advocates with the power to squash alternative perspectives or to pay for media access. Second, successful arguments are made by savvy political actors who mobilize support, while those who do not mobilize and change the balance

74 See Haas, "Introduction."

of political power may have good arguments, but poor organizing ability. Third, there is a degree of chance involved in the success of some arguments over others. For example, if the proponents of an argument happen to be unskilled rhetoricians, their arguments may fail decisively while "weaker" arguments may have more skilled proponents.

Finally, arguments are less likely to be persuasive if the social and material context – economics and strategic interests – do not align with the argument. This does not mean that argument actually boils down to material conditions, but rather it acknowledges the complexity of the relationship between arguments and preexisting cultural, strategic, and economic factors. On the other hand, arguments that have already succeeded in reframing actors' understanding of their interests, and assisting social movements or reformers in restructuring important elements of economy and politics, are more likely to be persuasive.

Belief

> Decisions for war will always be affected by the *beliefs* about war which prevail within the society in question and the effect these have on national behaviour. These beliefs have varied greatly from one age to another. In some war has been seen as glorious and honourable, in some as wicked; in some as cheap and in some expensive. A widespread belief that war is a normal and inevitable feature of international life must affect the behaviour of all states (if only because every one must be in a position to counter the expected onslaught of others). In other words, it is not only beliefs that exist within particular states that will affect their propensity to war, but also the beliefs they know to exist elsewhere within their [international] society. All are affected by the expectations and assumptions of the international community as a whole.[75]

There are essentially three views of the role of belief in decisionmaking. Many scholars suggest that we should start analysis of decisions by assuming rationality or else we will be lost in a realm of thick description and mired in the quicksand of idiosyncratic explanations and unpredictability.[76] Different rational actors, given the same situation, should essentially be interchangeable as they weigh costs, risks, and

[75] Evan Luard, *War in International Society* (New Haven: Yale University Press, 1986), p. 21.
[76] See Gary S. Becker, *The Economic Approach to Human Behavior* (Chicago: University of Chicago Press, 1976).

benefits and maximize given utilities. The content of beliefs seems less important, in this view, than the rational *process* of decisionmaking given particular beliefs, preferences, and probabilities.

A second view supposes that the process of decisionmaking is essentially rational, but because individuals are limited in their cognitive capacities and are occasionally, especially in crisis situations, influenced by feelings or other (ir/rational) considerations, beliefs may *bias* an individual's processing of information and their decisions. Herbert Simon, for instance, distinguishes between substantive, ideal type decisionmaking, and procedural or bounded rationality, which recognizes a decisionmaker's cognitive limits.[77] In this view, we can use tools that include an understanding of belief (cognitive belief systems, misperception theory, organization theory, or even psychological analysis of individual decisionmakers) to fill in the gaps of the master rational actor narrative. From this perspective, we expect both affective (emotion driven) and cognitive (information processing) biases inside the "black box."[78] Or, as Max Weber said: "the construction of a purely rational course of action . . . serves the sociologist as a type . . . By comparison with this it is possible to understand the ways in which actual action is influenced by irrational factors of all sorts . . . in that they account for the deviation from the line of conduct which would be expected on the hypothesis that the action was purely rational."[79] Sydney Verba argued that "[o]ne of the major values of the rationality model may be that it facilitates the systematic consideration of deviations from rationality."[80]

Thus, even those who use cognitive and abnormal psychology to explain decisionmaking under stress, or those who look to explain unsuitable military doctrines by the "pathologies" of militarism and nationalism, presume a rational outline for decisionmaking and a rational–irrational dichotomy. Similarly, rationalist scholars have begun to

[77] Herbert Simon, "Human Nature in Politics: The Dialogue of Psychology with Political Science," *The American Political Science Review* 79 (June 1985), 293–304.
[78] See Jervis, *Perception and Misperception*; Richard Ned Lebow, *Between Peace and War: The Nature of International Crises* (Baltimore: The Johns Hopkins University Press, 1981); Robert Jervis, Richard Ned Lebow, and Janice Gross Stein with contributions by Patrick Morgan and Jack Snyder, *Psychology and Deterrence* (Baltimore: The Johns Hopkins University Press, 1985); Deborah Welch Larson, *Origins of Containment: A Psychological Explanation* (Princeton: Princeton University Press, 1985); Janice Gross Stein, "Building Politics into Psychology: The Misperception of Threat," *Political Psychology* 9 (June 1988), 245–271.
[79] Max Weber, trans. A.M. Henderson and Talcott Parsons, *The Theory of Social and Economic Organization* (New York: Oxford University Press, 1947), p. 92.
[80] Sidney Verba, "Assumptions of Rationality and Non-Rationality in Models of the International System," in Klaus Knorr and Sidney Verba, eds., *The International System: Theoretical Essays* (Princeton: Princeton University Press, 1961), pp. 93–117: 116.

acknowledge the role of "ideas" but regard them as "*always* a valuable supplement to interest-based, rational actor models."[81] Barry Weingast regards belief systems, when held by all actors in a system as a "co-ordinating device" that functions like complete information, solving a "large scale coordination problem."[82]

A third view, taken here, argues that beliefs are neither rational nor irrational: beliefs are the propositions that individual people and groups have about themselves, others, and the world around them. They think those ideas are "true" – they believe them. When nearly everyone in a group holds a certain belief, and it is taken for granted, perhaps even confirmed by "experience," then beliefs may have the status of knowledge, truth, or "reality." More often than not, however, although one particular belief may be "dominant" (have the most political and social clout), other beliefs about the same subject may compete with a dominant belief. The meaning statements that members of a society don't believe at all, or don't yet believe, are described by skeptics – with varying degrees of respect – as a notion, idea, knowledge, theory, myth, ideology, faith, or dogma.[83] If others don't share our beliefs, we may try to convince them of their truth. But regardless of the truth of a belief, as Luard argues, "All are affected by the expectations and assumptions of the international community as a whole."[84]

Philosophical, instrumental, normative, and identity beliefs

Philosophical beliefs are ontological and epistemological. They are about the kind of "reality" humans inhabit, the general qualities of human beings or human nature and the natural world, and about how to know more about the world. Philosophical beliefs include views about how to decide between competing beliefs and when to add new beliefs or modify or even eliminate already held beliefs. For example, we could believe that we will know more about the world if a god reveals truth to us, or we might believe in the scientific method, or we might trust that history

[81] John Kurt Jacobsen, "Much Ado About Ideas: The Cognitive Factor in Economic Policy," *World Politics* 47 (January 1995), 283–310: 285.
[82] Barry R. Weingast, "A Rational Choice Perspective on the Role of Ideas: Shared Belief Systems and State Sovereignty in International Relations," *Politics and Society* 23 (December 1995), 449–464: *passim* 460–461. Similarly, Katzenstein says, "Collective expectations can have strong causal effects." Peter J. Katzenstein, "Introduction: Alternative Perspectives on National Security," in Katzenstein, ed., *Culture of National Security*, pp. 1–32: 7.
[83] My emphasis on belief and the process of argument does not mean that other aspects of agents, such as their dispositions (e.g., to be skeptical or accepting), desires, habits, and feelings, are unimportant.
[84] Luard, *War in International Society*, p. 21.

repeats itself and our guide to the present and the future lies in an under-standing of the past. "Realist" foreign policy decisionmakers generally believe that humans are by nature aggressive or at least interested in acquiring power. Realists also tend to hold "positivist" epistemologies in the sense of believing that observation of the empirical world – the world "revealed" by our senses – is trustworthy.[85] Philosophical beliefs are often the content of meta-arguments.

Normative beliefs are ideas individuals and groups hold about how they ought to act (or not act) to do what is "right" or expected. They are prescriptions with justifications attached to them. Prescriptive norma-tive statements follow from normative beliefs, e.g. thou shall not kill. Normative beliefs are the content of ethical arguments.

Although "multiple, conflicting meanings attributed to the term norm" may not be "the greatest shortcoming in the work on international norms," there is conceptual confusion about the idea of norms.[86] Many use norm to mean the most common practice, while others talk about norms as "oughts" or ethical prescriptions. Unfortunately, international relations theorists frequently use "norms" to denote both senses.[87] Fur-ther, it is also not uncommon to imply norms are synonymous with shared ideas, a form of common knowledge. For example, Kratochwil says that norms are "standards of behavior defined in terms of rights and obligations."[88] But Kratochwil also says that norms reduce uncer-tainty, allow the pursuit of goals and shared meaning, define situations and rules of the game, and provide the template for solutions. In these senses, for Kratochwil, norms are not prescriptive, but like other forms of common knowledge or shared belief.[89]

A distinction between norms and normative beliefs should minimize confusion. Norms *describe* the *dominant practice* or *behavior.* The behav-ioral norm is the behavior that typifies the "mode" in a distribution of be-haviors, while those that fall outside of the range of dominant practices are often considered "abnormal." Behavioral norms (or conventions), may, like common knowledge, create expectations about how actors

---

[85] See Alker, *Rediscoveries and Reformulations,* pp. 6–12 on ontological, epistemological, and methodological orientations in international relations theory.

[86] Gregory A. Raymond, "Problems and Prospects in the Study of International Norms," *Mershon International Studies Review* 41 (November 1997), 205–245.

[87] See Janice E. Thompson, "Norms in International Relations: A Conceptual Analysis," *International Journal of Group Tensions* 23 (1993), 67–83. Thompson argues that we should reserve the term "norms" to describe "normal practices."

[88] Kratochwil, *Rules, Norms and Decisions,* p. 59.

[89] Ibid., *passim,* e.g., pp. 9, 10, 48, and 50.

will behave in certain situations. When discussing "norms" as dominant practices or expectations about such practices, I use the phrases convention, dominant practice, norm or behavioral norm. If the behavioral norm is respect for sovereignty, defined as non-interference in the domestic affairs of governments, then actors expect non-interference. What if a practice is not universally adhered to? It may still be considered a behavioral norm if the behavior is commonly expected, and if, when actors do not follow the expected behavior, sanctions are considered and/or applied against those who violate the norm. In sum, statements about social conventions or behavioral norms describe the dominant practice and the shared expectation that actors will follow the norm in the appropriate context.

Principles, rules, and laws are prescriptive normative statements that rest on *normative beliefs*. Behavioral norms are identified by wide compliance and are usually justified with normative beliefs that are themselves justified by other normative or practical beliefs.[90] Behavioral norms and prescriptive norms/normative beliefs are clearly related but should not be equated. A "norm" describes the dominant practice or behavior, and normative beliefs often justify the "normal" practice.[91] Legal or social sanctions for violating norms signal the existence of prescriptive norms and normative beliefs. Beliefs that are prescriptive statements about what dominant practices ought to be, are termed prescriptive norms or normative beliefs depending on whether I am describing an injunction to behave a certain way, or the beliefs about why it is good to behave this way. Ethical arguments are characterized by the use of prescriptive statements that rest on normative beliefs.

Instrumental beliefs are the practical ideas we have about cause and effect in the natural and social worlds and about how to get what we want accomplished. They are both general and specific guides to action, with the level of specificity usually related to the specificity of the task. They suggest what to do once we have perceived and evaluated the nature of a situation and identified our goals. Instrumental beliefs may be codified

[90] Conventions or behavioral norms are similar to Jon Elster's "social" norms and prescriptive norms are similar to his "moral" norms. See Jon Elster, "Norms of Revenge," *Ethics* 100 (July 1990), 862–885, especially 863–866.
[91] Douglas Foyle argues that in the realm of public opinion foreign policy decisionmakers hold "normative beliefs" about the "*desirability* of input from public opinion affecting foreign policy choices." Douglas C. Foyle, "Public Opinion and Foreign Policy: Elite Beliefs as a Mediating Variable," *International Studies Quarterly* 41 (March 1997), 141–169: 145.

in organizational routines (institutionalized) and used, in combination with philosophical (ontological and epistemological) beliefs, to produce new knowledge. Instrumental beliefs are often the content of scientific and practical arguments. For example, one can think of foreign policies, which are composed of many different elements, as instrumental beliefs. One element of a state's foreign policy is military doctrine, instrumental beliefs that help determine how a state organizes its military forces and intends to use those forces in war. Military doctrines rest on ever-more specific instrumental beliefs, such as the utility of certain weapons (based on experience and scientific-technical knowledge/beliefs) under various conditions or the ratio of offensive to defensive forces needed to successfully engage in a "breakthrough" assault.

Identity beliefs include related and probably co-dependent beliefs about self and other. Self-identity beliefs are the beliefs we hold about our individual selves and about our group, including who belongs in the group. Self-identity beliefs are often, perhaps always, paired with beliefs about other individuals or groups. They include stereotypes, whether positive or negative, and notions of essential self and essential other, including the idea that self and other do not change and that groups are homogeneous – there is little variation among individuals who belong in certain categories of us and other/them. Yet according to the pragmatic and historically contingent view of the foundation of beliefs, there is not much about identities that is natural or fixed (except by our understanding of our history); identities, like norms, are socially constructed and simultaneously constitutive of the social world. Identities seem to be both mutually constitutive and historically/sociologically determined.

Often "identities" include conceptions of roles – arguably different from and overlapping with identities – for both self and others. Roles are a combination of situation-specific behaviors (driven by normative beliefs) and identity: individuals know which roles to assume in part because of their identity, and they know who they are, their identity, in part by the roles they perform. Roles – expectations and customs about behavior – only make sense in certain contexts.[92] There is often a reflective and reasoned interaction of identity, role expectations (context- and norm-influenced) and prescriptive social norms.[93] For example, US Senator Richard Russell's identity argument for a surprise attack

[92] See Martin Hollis and Steve Smith, *Explaining and Understanding International Relations* (Oxford: Clarendon Press, 1991), pp. 155–159, 164–170.
[93] On national role conceptions see, for instance, Stephen G. Walker, ed., *Role Theory and Foreign Policy Analysis* (Durham: Duke University Press, 1987). Similarly, "constitutive

42

during the Cuban missile crisis included a role belief: "It seems to me that we are at a crossroads. We're either a first class power or we're not."[94]

Foundations of belief

Foundations are the grounds for holding a particular belief or set of beliefs. To focus on foundations, ask: "on what is the belief based" and "how can it be justified" or shown to be true.[95] There are at least four views about the foundations of belief.

Foundationalists, or materialists, argue that well-founded beliefs about the world reflect a material reality (ontology) that we come to know through our sense experiences or observations (epistemology). Individuals base their beliefs on observation just as empiricists base their science on observables or sense impressions. Perceptions can be more or less accurate; accurate perceptions correspond to reality and directly justify basic beliefs. Beliefs based on observation may in turn indirectly, or inferentially, justify other beliefs. Rational individuals only hold those beliefs which they can justify rationally either directly or indirectly from empirical observation. Others' beliefs will be intelligible to us, if the other is rational, because their beliefs rest on the same foundations. A justified belief is grounded on some observation, or it is grounded on or entailed in some other belief that is itself grounded on observation. In other words, one can give a reason, rooted in the world of material observation, for the particular belief being held. Good arguments rest on empirically justified beliefs.

The anti-foundationalist position holds that beliefs are accidental, historically contingent, and essentially arbitrary. "We must accept the introduction of chance as a category in the production of events."[96]

---

norms" are those which "create new actors, interests or categories of action." They are beliefs about the properties or characteristics of a role. Martha Finnemore and Kathryn Sikkink, "International Norm Dynamics and Political Change," *International Organization* 52 (Autumn 1998), 887–917: 891.

[94] Ernest R. May and Philip D. Zelikow, eds., *The Kennedy Tapes: Inside the White House During the Cuban Missile Crisis* (Cambridge, MA: Harvard University Press, 1997), p. 258.

[95] This is similar to but not the same as asking how a person came to hold a particular belief. Someone may acquire a belief second-hand, e.g. through education or hearsay, rather than by coming to hold the belief in some first-hand (experiential or reflective) way. For an introduction to philosophical approaches to belief, see Robert Audi, *Belief, Justification and Knowledge* (Belmont, CA: Wadsworth, 1988). An introduction to psychological approaches is Susan T. Fiske and Shelley E. Taylor, *Social Cognition* (Reading, MA: Addison-Wesley Publishing Co.: 1984).

[96] Michel Foucault, *The Archaeology of Knowledge and the Discourse on Language* (New York: Pantheon, 1972), p. 231.

In this case we would expect a wide variety of beliefs. According to anti-foundationalists, beliefs should also be highly sensitive to cultural context and the arrangement of discursive power within social groups. "[W]hat ties Dewey, Foucault, James and Nietzsche, together – the sense that there is nothing deep down inside us except what we have put there ourselves, no criterion that we have not created in the course of creating a practice, no standard of rationality that is not an appeal to such a criterion, no rigorous argumentation that is not obedience to our own conventions."[97]

In the coherentist perspective, one's beliefs, no matter how they are derived, are mutually supporting, forming a coherent network: one accepts as justified those beliefs which "fit" with other beliefs. "A basic criterion for a coherent epistemic state is that it should be *logically consistent*."[98] The beliefs in a coherent belief system entail each other, they are tied to other beliefs in a system where beliefs are justified if they are part of that system.

In the pragmatic view, beliefs do not necessarily accurately reflect a material reality, nor are they necessarily consistent with other beliefs, but they come about and remain because they work to help an individual get along psychologically or they coordinate social and practical activity. Correspondence to "reality" is not necessarily the foundation of belief.[99] The "foundation" of a belief is its utility. A justified belief in the pragmatic view is one that works or is useful in a particular context. According to pragmatists, beliefs that do not work will or ought to be rejected or revised.

There is good evidence for all of these perspectives on the foundation of belief. That is, some kinds of belief seem to be founded on observation, others on nothing in particular but habit or social convention, while some beliefs are held because they cohere with some other belief, or because they work to help actors understand or act with efficacy. It is not necessary to decide that particular beliefs are well justified to see that beliefs are used and useful in arguments. However, beliefs and arguments that rest on foundations that

---

[97] Richard Rorty, *Consequences of Pragmatism* (Minneapolis: University of Minnesota Press, 1982), p. xlii.

[98] Peter Gardenfors, "The Dynamics of Belief Systems: Foundations Versus Coherence Theories," in Cristina Bicchieri and Maria Luisa Dalla Chiara, eds., *Knowledge, Belief and Strategic Interaction* (Cambridge: Cambridge University Press, 1992), pp. 377–398: 380.

[99] See Richard Rorty, *Philosophy and the Mirror of Nature* (Princeton: Princeton University Press, 1979).

are perceived as shaky will obviously be more vulnerable to counter-arguments.

Belief system theories

The theory of belief systems presented here grows out of, but diverges in significant ways from, earlier theories of belief systems and operational codes. Yet, as Steve Smith notes, "a bewildering variety of terms is used in international relations to describe the essential features of the concept of belief system: terms such as 'the image', 'operational code', 'cognitive map' ... All of these focus on basically the same factor: the nature of the filtering device of existing beliefs about empirical and normative issues."[100] Most scholars of belief systems in world politics hold foundationalist or coherentist views of beliefs. They also tend to presume that belief systems affect decisionmaking by influencing information processing tasks – specifically that beliefs *bias* perceptions (assuming that objective observers, not influenced by preexisting beliefs, would have "accurate" perceptions and make rational decisions unbiased by their prejudices).

For example, Ole Holsti characterizes belief systems as composed of a group of images of the past, present, and future: they are a "set of lenses through which information concerning the physical and social environment are received" that establish goals and order preferences.[101] Holsti argues: "[O]ur behavior is in large part shaped by the manner in which we perceive, diagnose, and evaluate our physical and social environment. Our perceptions, in turn, are filtered through clusters of beliefs about what has been, what is, what will be, and what ought to be." He says "beliefs provide us with a more or less coherent code by which we organize and make sense out of what would otherwise be a confusing array of signals picked up from the environment by our senses."[102] Similarly, Stephen Walker argues that belief systems influence, but do not determine, diagnostic and choice propensities. "The dominant inference pattern is the principle of cognitive consistency, from which are derived two general propositions: (a) beliefs tend to reinforce one

---

[100] Steve Smith, "Belief Systems and the Study of International Relations," in Richard Little and Steve Smith, eds., *Belief Systems and International Relations* (Oxford: Basil Blackwell, 1988), pp. 11–36: 11.

[101] Ole Holsti, "The Belief System and National Images: A Case Study," *Journal of Conflict Resolution* 16 (September 1963), 244–252; 245.

[102] Ole R. Holsti, "Foreign Policy Decision Makers Viewed Psychologically: 'Cognitive Process' Approaches," in James Rosenau, ed., *In Search of Global Patterns* (New York: The Free Press, 1976), pp. 120–144: 122.

another to form a coherent belief system; (b) under specified conditions beliefs constrain the range of alternative choices and thereby influence the final decision."[103]

Robert Jervis argues that preexisting beliefs are "rational" in the sense that they help actors make sense of the world. Beliefs can help decision-makers increase the signal-to-noise ratio of environmental cues, but they can also be misleading if they are inappropriate or held without critical reflection.[104] As Jervis suggests, "There is no way to draw a neat, sharp line between that degree of holding to existing beliefs and disparaging discrepant information that is necessary for the intelligent comprehension of the environment and that degree that leads to the maintenance of beliefs that should be rejected by all fair minded men."[105] Individuals may ignore discrepant information because it simply does not make sense from within their paradigm – and perhaps they do not see what they can't understand. Or individuals may misperceive the information, assuming that the presently held paradigm accounts for the incoming data. Those lacking firm preexisting beliefs may be more prone to being swayed by the latest argument or alternative presented, while those who hold firm beliefs may be prone to premature cognitive closure, cutting off analysis of information or policy alternatives because they are already convinced of the correct path.[106] Individual and group belief systems may change over time, for instance due to changes in personnel, or dramatic historical events which cause people to learn something new because their previous beliefs were inadequate. Jervis argues quite persuasively, however, that individuals are often quite resistant to change and they may employ any number of strategies to avoid changing their beliefs.[107]

Alexander George, building on the work of Nathan Leites, proposed identifying an actor's operational code belief system through a systematic content analysis of an actor's philosophical and instrumental beliefs.[108] George argued that the way to determine the effect of

---

[103] Stephen G. Walker, "The Evolution of Operational Code Analysis," *Political Psychology* 11 (June 1990), 403-418: 409. Also see Stephen G. Walker, "Operational Codes and Content Analysis: The Case of Henry Kissinger," in Imtrad Gailhofer, William E. Saris, Marrianne Melman, eds., *Different Text Analysis Procedures for the Study of Decision Making* (Amsterdam: Sociometric Research Foundation, 1986), pp. 13–27; and "Coding Instructions for the OC Procedure," in ibid., pp. 111–120.

[104] Jervis, *Perception and Misperception*, pp. 143ff., 156–161.   [105] Ibid., p. 177.

[106] Ibid., pp. 175, 187. Also see Larson, *Origins of Containment*, p. 65.

[107] See Jervis, *Perception and Misperception*, especially pp. 291–296, on the methods individuals employ to preserve their beliefs.

[108] Alexander George, "The 'Operational Code': A Neglected Approach to the Study of

operational code beliefs on decisions is either by demonstrating congruence between beliefs and decisions or by tracing the process of decisionmaking. In process tracing one "seeks to establish the ways in which the
actor's beliefs influenced the receptivity to and assessment of incoming
information, his definition of the situation, his identification and evaluation of options, as well as, finally, his choice of a course of action."[109]
The congruence method requires much less information about the actual
decision process. The researcher identifies the nature of the subject's beliefs and policy preferences and then determines whether the decisions
follow from those beliefs. The causal significance of operational codes
is not necessarily proven by this procedure, its plausibility is merely
established.[110]

In sum, work on belief systems has been primarily cognitive
and focused on perceptions, assuming that preexisting beliefs bias
perceptions.[111] Beliefs are understood to be privately held by individuals and those beliefs affect perceptions and sometimes help them
organize their responses to situations. For example, Dan Reiter suggests
that "states act as if they have beliefs, or ideas about international
politics."[112] Alexander George argues: "Neither . . . diagnosis of situations nor . . . choice for action is rigidly prescribed and determined by
these beliefs."[113] Despite this last caveat, there is little discussion of the
exact role of beliefs in the decisionmaking processes of individuals or
groups. These cognitively influenced theories of belief presume that
beliefs are first of all (biasing) lenses, and secondly lead reflexively or
somewhat unreflectively (though not "rigidly") to policy choices. Actors
behave in ways that are essentially *unreflectively* consistent with their
beliefs.

Political Leaders and Decision-Making," *International Studies Quarterly* 13 (June 1969),
190–222. Nathan Leites first suggested the phrase "operational code" in *The Operational
Code of the Politburo* (New York: McGraw-Hill, 1951).
[109] George, "The Causal Nexus," p. 113.
[110] Ibid. pp. 106–113.
[111] Others have examined the role of beliefs and related concepts in social life – e.g.
cognitive psychology, the sociology of knowledge, the history of ideas, and philosophy
of science: schemas, wertrationality, discourse, episteme, ideas, ideology, and paradigms.
Some of these concepts from outside political science, namely Max Weber's ideas about
wertrationality, Michel Foucault's ideas about discourse, episteme, and knowledge, and
Thomas Kuhn's arguments about scientific paradigms, and feminist theorists of gender,
are similar to mine.
[112] Dan Reiter, *Crucible of Beliefs: Learning, Alliances, and World Wars* (Ithaca: Cornell University Press, 1996), p. 12.
[113] George, *Presidential Decisionmaking in Foreign Policy*, p. 45.

The emphasis on perception is partly explained by the close relationship belief system scholars have had with cognitive psychology, drawing particular inspiration from "schema" theory. Schemas help decisionmakers deal with complexity by providing a framework of concepts and connections; they are "higher order knowledge structures . . . that embody expectations guiding lower order processing of the stimulus concept."[114] Schemas are, in a sense, like grammar, providing the framework for understanding incoming information and quickly articulating a response.[115] So schemas are abstract concepts and notions about expected relationships, theories that influence perception by organizing incoming information and influence behavior by providing a guide to successful responses in similar instances. In certain stylized situations, one type of schema, known as a "script", may describe the way that individuals approach frequently encountered situations that offer little variance.

> In sum, a script is a hypothesized cognitive structure that when activated organizes comprehension of event-based situations. In its weak sense, it is a bundle of inferences about the potential occurrence of a set of events and may be structurally similar to other schemata that do not deal with events. In its strong sense, it involves expectations about the order as well as the occurrence of events. In the strongest sense of a totally ritualized event sequence (e.g., a Japanese tea ceremony), script predictions become infallible – but this case is relatively rare.[116]

Vertzberger argues: "information that fits into existing schemata – that is cognitive structures of organized prior knowledge abstracted from specific experiences – is noticed earlier, considered more valid, and processed much faster than information that contradicts or does not fit into any particular schema."[117]

While schema and belief system theory point to the ways individuals respond to what they see as routine situations, it is deterministic. This kind of theorizing too often neglects both the reflective characteristics of humans, how we deal with multiple, sometimes contradictory, ideas at once, and ignores the *political* context of decisionmaking in foreign policy where individuals must make arguments to justify their perceptions

---

[114] Robert Abelson, "Psychological Status of the Script Concept," *American Psychologist* 36 (1981), 715–729: 715.
[115] See George, "The Causal Nexus," p. 97, and Larson, *Origins of Containment*, pp. 50–57; Deborah Welch Larson, "The Role of Belief Systems and Schemas in Foreign Policy Decision-Making," *Political Psychology* 15 (March 1994), 17–33. Also see chapter 6 in Fiske and Taylor, *Social Cognition*.
[116] Abelson, "Psychological Status of the Script Concept," p. 717.
[117] Vertzberger, *The World in Their Minds*, p. 60.

and actions. The process of political argument and the fact that individuals are reflective – sometimes changing beliefs – suggests that observers ought not to expect a determinative relationship between beliefs, decisions, and behavior. Rather, beliefs are part of the process of political argument that characterizes foreign policy decisionmaking. Nor should we necessarily be concerned with whether beliefs "accurately reflect" the real world or "bias" perceptions. What is of concern is the *content* of beliefs, whether or not they are true, and the ways beliefs, which can change, are used in inference and argument.

Beliefs and belief system theory revised

Beliefs are arguments that we have become convinced of, whose conclusions we take for granted. Beliefs help us not only to perceive the world and organize our "perceptions," they also help us constitute the social world, make the world according to our beliefs. As John MacLean argues, beliefs are not separate or apart from the social world: "what the beliefs, practices and institutions of a society actually are depends on what they mean to its members and, in this sense, meaning is not merely descriptive of 'things' in society; it is necessarily constitutive of them too."[118] That is, when we believe our beliefs, and others believe them, we often act as if they were real. Belief has meaning and gives meaning. We act according to those meanings. Further, we use beliefs to reason, to figure out new meanings.

And while beliefs are privately held, their content is a product of the individual's social interactions. Put another way, beliefs are not simply private but *both* individual and social. The fact that beliefs are intersubjectively shared, or at least publicly contested, is important for understanding their role beyond structuring individual cognition. Beliefs are held by individuals and groups – they are intersubjective.

It is common to draw a distinction between interests and belief – "Choices of specific ideas may simply reflect the interests of actors"[119] – as if interests were self-evident, and beliefs followed unproblematically from interests. But as Mark Laffey and Jutta Weldes argue, "by maintaining this distinction, the investigation of the social *construction* of interests is in practice disavowed because it is assumed . . . that interests are given and can be determined in isolation from 'ideas.' " Further, they argue this distinction "creates a tendency to understand 'ideas'

[118] MacLean, "Belief Systems and Ideology," p. 76.
[119] Goldstein and Keohane, "Ideas and Foreign Policy," p. 11.

merely as tools which are used by policy-makers to manipulate various audiences, such as international elites, domestic publics or bureaucracies." As a consequence, when "decision-makers' interests are defined as analytically distinct from ideas, then 'ideas' are easily dismissed as 'mere justification', as post-hoc rationalizations of policies made on the grounds of already given material interests."[120] Thus, a distinction between interests and beliefs should not be drawn too sharply if only because beliefs and arguments help people decide what they think of as interests.

A cluster of beliefs is a belief system when it is characterized by a focus on a *particular subject or problem* (although the exact nature of the subject and its relation to other subjects may at times be under dispute) and there are multiple and overlapping belief systems within societies. For example, within the issue area of domestic policy there may be health care or welfare belief systems that are themselves related to different beliefs about the role of the state. Foreign policy belief systems are focused on the problem of a state's relation to other states and the content of the beliefs articulates how to understand and deal with other states. Within a general foreign policy belief system, particular sets of beliefs are focused on political, economic, cultural, and military components of the subject. And, as suggested earlier, there may be contentious disagreements within groups about whether certain beliefs are properly part of the larger subject area. For example, beliefs about human rights may or may not be considered part of the realm of foreign policy.

A focus on a particular problem is not enough to make a collection of beliefs a belief system. The adherents to a particular set of beliefs will usually argue that the beliefs themselves come out of or were revealed from within an historical *tradition*. In addition, those who hold the particular belief system, and perhaps even the critics of the belief system, argue that the ideas are *related* to each other somehow (besides their historical relationship). They argue that there is an internal "logic" to the system that is sometimes claimed to be religious, or natural, or at other times scientific. Belief systems consist of related beliefs at various levels of generalization – core, contingent, and role-specific. Assuming that the beliefs in a belief system are characterized by both coherence and a historical relationship, one will often be able to predict elements of a belief system from knowledge of a few core elements and the history of

[120] Mark Laffey and Jutta Weldes, "Beyond Belief: Ideas and Symbolic Technologies in the Study of International Relations," *European Journal of International Relations* 3 (1997), 193–237: 200–201.

the belief system. But beliefs and belief systems are not always coherent. And within societies different, even conflicting, belief systems may be held within and among social groups.

Previous work on foreign policy decisionmaking notes variation in the relative importance, taken-for-grantedness, and flexibility of beliefs within a belief system, suggesting that there are hierarchies of belief.[121] For example, Douglas Blum argues that there are core, intermediate, and peripheral beliefs. "The core level of the belief system consists of 'philosophical beliefs,' or basic assumptions and values from which everything else in the belief system is ultimately derived. Because international politics is by definition an interactive realm, we may postulate that core beliefs provide the most basic concepts relevant to interaction." Intermediate beliefs are abstract but presuppose and are logically subordinate to core beliefs: they "function to provide normative direction as well as additional analytic concepts." Peripheral beliefs "include detailed, tactically relevant information about the political world."[122] Others propose that beliefs are hierarchically structured and that these structures compare across states; individuals hold general foreign policy postures which rest on underlying core values which structure more specific policy beliefs.[123]

While one can agree or disagree with these particular schemes, some beliefs in belief systems are clearly more central, and possibly more difficult to modify, than others. *Core* beliefs, whether philosophical, normative, instrumental, or about the identities of self and others, are general and fundamental and they seem to be held with little variation, regardless of context. Like the foundations of a building, core beliefs provide

---

[121] Ideologies are belief systems that are consciously articulated, developed, promoted, and defended. They often have explicit agendas or action orientations that adherents promote. Thus, the difference between belief systems and ideologies is the consciousness with which beliefs are held and the explicitness of the action agenda.

[122] Douglas W. Blum, "The Soviet Foreign Policy Belief System: Beliefs, Politics, and Foreign Policy Outcomes," *International Studies Quarterly* 37 (December 1993), 373–394: 375–376. Also see George, "The 'Operational Code.'"

[123] Jon Hurwitz, Mark Peffley, and Mitchell A. Seligson, "Foreign Policy Belief Systems in Comparative Perspective: The United States and Costa Rica," *International Studies Quarterly* 37 (September 1993), 245–270; Hurwitz and Peffley take a cognitive approach: "because humans have severe cognitive limitations, they often behave as cognitive misers, coping with their shortcomings by taking short cuts whenever possible." Jon Hurwitz and Mark Peffley, "How are Foreign Policy Attitudes Structured? A Hierarchical Model," *American Political Science Review* 81 (December 1987), 1099–1120: 1099. Philip Tetlock's hierarchy is fundamental, strategic and tactical beliefs. Philip E. Tetlock, "Learning in U.S. and Soviet Foreign Policy: In Search of an Elusive Concept," in George W. Breslauer and Philip E. Tetlock, eds., *Learning in U.S. and Soviet Foreign Policy* (Boulder: Westview, 1991), pp. 20–61: 27–31.

the support and basic architecture around which other beliefs are held. *Contingent* beliefs and their relation to behavior are more contextually specific. They are like rules of thumb that are evoked, referred to, and used to guide action, depending on a particular circumstance. And like rules of thumb, contingent beliefs may be ignored or overruled if they are seen to conflict with core beliefs. *Role-specific* beliefs are the ideas that people have about how they or others ought to behave when they are performing a particular role or job. As noted, role-specific beliefs and normative beliefs are connected. For example, an identity – one is a citizen of the United States – may be further specified by the context of an individual and the situation: the individual is a male over the age of 18 who must, they believe, register for the military draft. Thus, it is that individual's duty in their "role" as a good citizen to register for the draft. Here, identity and behavioral norms are both constituted and reinforced by laws about who is a citizen and the rights and obligations of those citizens. Whether or not individuals behave in accordance with the law and social expectations will further depend on the particular social pressures they confront, their personal religious and philosophical beliefs, and their personal reflection/reasoning. Of course this example shows that roles are not always completely voluntarily assumed or enacted and such an understanding is implicit in such terms as "reluctant imperialists" and the involuntary roles of "international pariah" and "rogue states."

Belief systems are held intersubjectively and produced by groups of individuals at various levels of aggregation. Belief systems may be held by small decisionmaking groups, such as military planners, or there may be a dominant institutional belief system, shared by members of particular bureaucracies such as the US State Department. Further, within larger and smaller groups there will often be dominant belief systems as well as rival belief systems that challenge core, contingent, and perhaps even the role-specific elements of the dominant belief system.

The idea of coherence and interdependence of beliefs in a belief system does not necessarily mean that there is a *naturally logical* relationship between beliefs; the beliefs may simply be related by historical circumstances. In this sense, the "system-ness" of the belief system may only make sense internally and historically, while individual beliefs that are part of a larger belief system, may contradict each other. Moreover, belief systems consist of "a set of beliefs that are organized and relatively constant over time – that is, the beliefs do not fluctuate abruptly from day to day."[124] Still, beliefs and belief systems do change.

Belief change and "learning"

Belief systems held by individuals and groups may be elastic (malleable) or inelastic (fixed). Individual belief systems are probably formed (or adopted) early in one's life and the flexibility of an individual's beliefs probably decreases over time. States' leaders and propagandists recognize this property of belief systems, which is why the control of institutions that shape the ideas of youth have been so important to states and political movements. Dan Reiter argues that formative events, specifically world wars, structure the beliefs of states.[125] However, individual beliefs and belief systems tend to persist, even in the face of disconfirming evidence as individuals ignore information that disconfirms the schema or, in some cases, struggle to make the evidence fit the existing schema.[126] Yet we know that individual beliefs do change and such change is a crucial aspect of the persuasiveness of arguments. How is it that people change their beliefs and under what circumstances will they do so?

Theories of belief change generally follow from the foundational, pragmatic, coherentist, and accidental perspectives on the foundations of belief. Foundationalists expect belief change to occur either if the material world changes, or if the rational justifications for holding a particular belief change or can no longer be supported. According to theories in cognitive psychology, schemas may change if the incoming evidence is undeniably, unambiguously, not in keeping with the existing schema. Belief systems are sometimes gradually modified, but, at other times, individuals may experience a dramatic conversion where, if core beliefs are revised, large portions of preexisting belief are jettisoned in favor of new beliefs.

According to the pragmatic view, beliefs are revised or jettisoned when they no longer "work" in a particular context. This "working" may or may not be dependent on material "realities." For example, the perceived failure of Soviet-style communism to produce material prosperity led many to abandon their belief in it.

---

[124] Jerel A. Rosati, *The Carter Administration's Quest for Global Community: Beliefs and Their Impact on Behavior* (Columbia: University of South Carolina Press, 1987), p. 16.
[125] Reiter, *Crucible of Beliefs*.
[126] See Jervis, *Perception and Misperception*, pp. 217–287.

Coherentists, while not providing a unique argument about the causes of belief revision, argue that belief change will be minimal. Peter Gardenfors describes this as a "conservative" process of belief revision. "When we change our beliefs, we want to retain as much as possible of our old beliefs; information is in general not gratuitous, and unnecessary losses of information are therefore to be avoided. We thus have a criterion of *informational economy* motivating the coherentist approach."[127] Foucault argued that the field of the history of ideas was itself characterized by a coherentist bias.

> The history of ideas usually credits the discourse that it analyzes with coherence. If it happens to notice an irregularity in the use of words, several incompatible propositions, a set of meanings that do not adjust to one another, concepts that cannot be systematized together, then it regards it as its duty to find, at a deeper level, a principle of cohesion that organizes the discourse and restores it to its hidden unity. This law of coherence is a heuristic rule, a procedural obligation, almost a moral constraint of research . . . But this same coherence is also the result of research . . . It appears as an optimum: the greatest possible number of contradictions resolved by the simplest means.[128]

Finally, if beliefs are historically contingent, we would expect them to change either willy-nilly like fashion in clothing; or according to changes in the discursive, cultural, and institutional context. As the relations of power change, so might the content of beliefs.

While these questions are discussed at greater length below, I remain agnostic on the question of the source of beliefs and on the way that beliefs change. All four views of the grounding and change of belief – foundational, pragmatic, coherent, and anti-foundational – may be "correct" depending on the beliefs in question. In any case, arguments play a role in all these methods of belief change.

How are beliefs spread? Individuals are, for the most part not passive receptacles of beliefs. Reflective individuals consider new beliefs and arguments and make decisions about whether to adopt those beliefs on the basis of the form of reasoning they are using, the "fit" of those beliefs with other beliefs they hold, their "need" for the belief to explain something, and whether others whom they respect take the belief seriously. Thus, beliefs do not spread like contagious disease, by simply being "in the air" or through mere "contact." Individuals and groups

---

[127] Gardenfors, "The dynamics of belief systems," p. 381.
[128] Foucault, *The Archaeology of Knowledge*, p. 149.

must be receptive to new beliefs, and people usually reflect on beliefs before adopting them or modifying longstanding beliefs. And as Jack Levy argues, individuals "learn how to learn. They learn new decision rules, judgmental heuristics, procedures, and skills that facilitate their ability to learn from subsequent experience."[129]

Of course there are exceptions to the rule of reflectivity: some individuals are relatively passive and malleable and this probably varies over time and cultures. For example, in places and eras where charismatic authority, in the sense described by Max Weber of personnal charisma, is dominant, one would expect many individuals to simply adhere to the beliefs espoused by the charismatic authority. Others may require some other form of conviction.

> In traditionally stereotyped periods, charisma is the greatest revolutionary force. The equally revolutionary force of 'reason' works from without by altering the situations of action, and hence its problems, finally in this way changing men's attitudes towards them ... Charisma, on the other hand, may involve a subjective or internal reorientation born out of suffering, conflicts or enthusiasm. It may then result in a radical alteration of the central system of attitudes and direction of action with a completely new orientation of all attitudes toward the different problems and structures of the "world."[130]

Mass and elite beliefs

The public is generally considered less interested, less well informed, and less powerful in determining the foreign policies of states than are elites.[131] Yet non-elite input into the making of world politics occurs more frequently, and is more fundamental to the process of foreign policy, than is generally assumed.

---

[129] Levy, "Learning and Foreign Policy," p. 286.

[130] Max Weber, "The Principal Characteristics of Charismatic Authority and its Relation to Forms of Communal Organization," in J.E.T. Eldridge, ed. *Max Weber: The Interpretation of Social Reality* (New York: Schocken Books, 1971), pp. 229–234: 234.

[131] For instance, authoritarian personality literature examines this question. Also see Paul Sniderman and Philip Tetlock, "Interrelationship of Political Ideology and Public Opinion," in Margaret Hermann, ed., *Political Psychology: Contemporary Problems and Issues* (San Francisco: Jossey-Bass Publishers, 1986), pp. 62–96; Ofira Sliktar, "Identifying a Society's Belief Systems," in Herman, ed., *Political Psychology*, pp. 320–354; Philip Converse, "The Nature of Belief Systems in Mass Publics," in David Apter, ed., *Ideology and Discontent* (London: The Free Press of Glencoe, 1964), pp. 206–261; William A. Gamson and Andre Modigliani, "Knowledge and Foreign Policy Opinions: Some Models for Consideration," *The Public Opinion Quarterly* 30 (Summer 1966), 187–199.

Is there a divergence between mass and elite beliefs? There are significant differences.[132] The notion of the "masses" needs disaggregation into, for example, classes, races, genders, social formations, and political parties. Mass beliefs appear to be less tightly structured, and more flexible than elite beliefs, perhaps only because the masses that constitute public opinion are of many different types with more or less coherent and clearly structured beliefs about world politics. Elites tend to be more homogeneous.

Does public opinion influence policy and elite beliefs? There is some evidence for consistency between public opinion and foreign policy.[133] Douglas Foyle argues that mass beliefs or public opinion, influence foreign policy when decisionmakers believe that such influence is desirable and that public support is necessary for a foreign policy to succeed: decisionmakers' "beliefs and attitudes" about public opinion "can profoundly influence their reaction to public opinion."[134] Mass beliefs constrain decisionmaking behavior at the extremes and in the general conduct of world politics. More precisely, mass beliefs have little effect if the beliefs are not strong in one direction or another. But when mass beliefs are strongly held in one direction, foreign policy decisions and behavior will be constrained because elites need to mobilize public support (in both democracies and non-democracies) for the implementation of labor and/or capital intensive decisions. That is, mass beliefs are especially important because the masses provide much of the capital (in the form of taxes) and labor (for armed forces, extraction of natural resources, and industrial production) necessary for modern warfare.[135] Elites may successfully appeal to mass beliefs to increase the acceptability of a preferred policy option (to the masses and other elites) while they may, conversely, feel unable to select options they feel the masses will find unacceptable. Thus, mass beliefs influence elite decisionmaking behavior by setting acceptability constraints. Decisionmakers who hope to

---

[132] For example, see Benjamin I. Page and Jason Barabas, "Foreign Policy Gaps between Citizens and Leaders," *International Studies Quarterly* 44 (September 2000), 339–364.

[133] See Bruce Russett, *Controlling the Sword: The Democratic Governance of National Security* (Cambridge, MA: Harvard University Press, 1990); Foyle, "Public Opinion and Foreign Policy."

[134] Foyle, "Public Opinion and Foreign Policy" p. 164.

[135] This point is not new, yet we tend to forget it. See, for instance, Vasquez: "War cannot be initiated, as Bueno De Mesquita would have us believe just by a simple decision of the leader. The public must be mobilized not only to accept the decision, but to fight and sacrifice enthusiastically in order to give the state the highest chances of success. For this reason, even if the decision maker wants to go to war, he (or she) may not initiate it because of domestic constraints." John A. Vasquez, "Foreign Policy, Learning and War," in Hermann, Kegley, and Rosenau, eds., *New Directions*, pp. 366–383: 367.

retain power over the long haul believe that they must make decisions that are acceptable to the masses and other (non-decisionmaking) elites, and they are constrained by this belief.[136]

In addition, the size and level of sophistication of the politically active masses determines their effect on elites. Of course, if the decision requires little in the way of mass mobilization, or if the effects of mobilization can somehow be minimized or deferred, then the content of mass beliefs and public opinion will be less important as a constraining force unless elite opinions or behavior precipitate a legitimation crisis. While the content of elite beliefs, especially those of foreign policy decisionmakers, will most often be at the forefront here, the content of beliefs held by other members of society is still important. This is because elites come from the wider social milieu, are dependent upon it for political support – even in authoritarian states – and must make their decisions in ways that can be justified to these more attentive and organized "masses." This is the role of "public opinion."

Perhaps more immediately important in shaping elite behavior than "mass belief" is the role of *organized* publics. When "masses" are organized into coherent social movements and "transnational advocacy networks" of activists driven "by values rather than by material concerns or professional norms" they may be both "norm entrepreneurs," deploying arguments based on principled beliefs, and shape the political context or conditions of acceptability within which states and other social actors try to act.[137] Through direct action, these movements may also make large-scale behavioral change, without the direct involvement of governments, desirable, possible, and a fact on the ground. In sum, the content of beliefs held by both unorganized and organized publics affects the making and receptivity of arguments.

Culture

No man ever looks at the world with pristine eyes. He sees it edited by a definite set of customs and institutions and ways of thinking. Even

---

[136] See Philip Tetlock, "Accountability: The Neglected Social Context of Judgement and Choice," in *Research in Organizational Behavior*, vol. VII (London: JAI Press, 1985), pp. 297–332; Barbara Farnham, "Political Cognition and Decision-Making," *Political Psychology* 11 (March 1990), 83–111; and Jennifer S. Lerner and Philip E. Tetlock, "Accounting for the Effects of Accountability," *Psychological Bulletin* 125 (March 1999), 255–275. Note that acceptability, accountability, and responsibility are not necessarily rational concepts.
[137] Keck and Sikkink, *Activists Beyond Borders*, p. 2.

> in his philosophical probings he cannot go behind those stereotypes; his very concepts of the true and the false will still have reference to his particular traditional customs.[138]

> Most history, when it has been digested by a people becomes myth. Myth is an arrangement of the past, whether real or imagined, in patterns that resonate with culture's deepest values and aspirations. Myths create and reinforce archetypes so taken for granted, so seemingly axiomatic, that they go unchallenged. Myths are so fraught with meaning that we live or die by them. They are the maps by which cultures navigate through time.[139]

> A culture makes some things possible, some things desirable, and some things unimaginable.[140]

If there were one global culture and humans lived without a sense of history we might not be conscious of culture as a concept, nor think it was interesting. Yet historical experience and contact with others who believe differently and have different practices makes us conscious of culture. For example, in the 1490s, a Catholic Pope, not war, decided the New World boundaries between Spanish and Portuguese explorers, and the Pope's decision was ratified by the Treaty of Tordesillas in 1494. The foreign policy practices of European states in the late 1400s were embedded within both Christian religious and secular beliefs and practices, while *international* authority was vested in the Catholic Church. The foreign policy practices of the early twenty first century, at least in most Western states, are more strongly embedded in the rational belief system, and authority is vested in separate states whose leaders and peoples are for the most part loathe to give power to international religious authorities. Chronological distance makes the practices of fifteenth-century international actors seem strange.

In the late 1950s Margaret Mead summarized anthropology's concept of culture as the "systematic body of learned behavior which is transmitted from parents to children."[141] Ruth Benedict, Mead's teacher, described culture as the "ideas and standards" that people have in common and that hold them together; culture includes the "motives and emotions and values that are institutionalized . . . habits of thought."[142]

---

[138] Ruth Benedict, *Patterns of Culture* (Boston: Houghton Mifflin, 1959), p. 2.
[139] Ronald Wright, *Stolen Continents: The New World Through Indian Eyes* (New York: Houghton Mifflin, 1992), p. 5.
[140] Elizabeth Kier, *Imagining War: French and British Military Doctrine Between the Wars* (Princeton: Princeton University Press, 1997), p. 165.
[141] Margaret Mead, "A New Preface" in Benedict, *Patterns of Culture*, p. vii.
[142] Benedict, *Patterns of Culture*, pp. 16 and 49.

Further, Benedict argued, "The significance of cultural behavior is not exhausted when we have clearly understood that it is local and man-made and hugely variable. It also tends to be integrated. A culture, like an individual, is a more or less consistent pattern of thought and action."[143]

Culture, a property of social groups, is the organization and practice of interconnected belief systems in particular places and times. When societies organize meaning and make their social reality through practices that conform with widely held beliefs, they are maintaining their culture. Just as beliefs are arguments whose conclusions we have become convinced of, cultures are the beliefs, symbols, and practices that social groups are convinced of or in great measure take for granted. While keeping in mind that simple cultural explanations may seem satisfying when they are made about another culture, and simplistic if applied to one's own culture, the challenge is to understand how culture (understood as a system of background beliefs and practices which make life meaningful in particular settings) may influence, but not necessarily determine, argument-making and the reception of arguments.[144]

Culture is important for understanding the process of argument in world politics for several reasons. First, culture is the background of shared interpretations (unconsciously held intersubjective beliefs) and practices, the starting point or topos that allows meaningful conversations and arguments to occur among individuals and groups; culture is the "lifeworld" that serves as the stable foundation upon which action and arguments are understood. Second, because cultures contain and organize belief systems, they provide the content for specific identity, normative, practical, and scientific beliefs. Third, culture provides the background meanings – the metaphors and historical events – by which specific beliefs and arguments are consciously judged and which actors intentionally use to frame problems. Fourth, culture can be a source of new beliefs and arguments and can thus be a source of innovation.

Culture in international relations theory

Rational actor theories tend to treat culture as irrational and exogenous, and for many realist scholars of world politics, culture is irrelevant. This view is, however, relatively recent. In the 1930s, students of world politics argued that culture was relevant and in fact that certain institutions

---

[143] Ibid., p. 46.
[144] Belief systems focus on specific issue areas while cultures contain webs of belief systems and practices.

of international relations were deeply influenced by culture. Margaret
Mead argued that war is a social invention, and Freud contended that
civilization and culture could tame human instincts and reduce the
drives toward war.[145] After Mead and Freud, however, culture was not a
term that saw much use among international relations theorists and Rob
Walker could justifiably argue that there is a "relative neglect of culture"
among mainstream scholars of international relations.[146] "To an extent,"
Vertzberger notes, "this neglect is understandable, since ultimately sub-
societal units are the bodies actually carrying out decisionmaking tasks,
whereas societal factors are less apparent to the observer."[147] When
culture is noted and theorized by mainstream international relations
scholars, it is usually assumed that cultures exist within states and civilizations while conflict reigns between cultures, as is the argument in
Samuel Huntington's ideas about the "clash of civilizations."[148] Yet, as
Walker argues:

> If questions about culture turn out to be little more than questions
> about sovereignty and national identity, then there are only two inter-
> esting avenues worth exploring. One is the way in which "culture,"
> understood as anthropological difference, constitutes the central prob-
> lem to overcome, a corroboration of the deeply fractured character of
> human communities. The other is the way such divisions have in fact
> been overcome by the fragile accommodations of statesmanship.[149]

Scholars of comparative politics have paid more attention to culture.
For example, Lucien Pye, Sydney Verba, and others described what they
thought were distinctive national political cultures.[150] This work was

---

[145] Margaret Mead, "Warfare is Only an Invention – Not a Biological Necessity," in Leon
Bramson and George W. Goethals, eds., *War: Studies from Psychology, Sociology and Anthropology* (New York: Basic Books, 1964), pp. 269–274; and Sigmund Freud, "Why War?" in
Bramson and Goethals, *War*, pp. 71–80.
[146] R.B.J. Walker, "The Concept of Culture in the Theory of International Relations," in
Jongshuk Chay, ed., *Culture and International Relations* (New York: Praeger, 1990), pp. 3–
17: 9.
[147] Vertzberger, *The World in Their Minds*, p. 260.
[148] Samuel Huntington, "The Clash of Civilizations?" *Foreign Affairs* 72 (Summer 1993),
22–49.
[149] Walker, "The Concept of Culture in the Theory of International Relations, p. 11.
[150] Gabriel Almond and Sydney Verba, *The Civic Culture* (Princeton: Princeton University
Press, 1963); Lucian W. Pye and Sidney Verba, eds., *Political Culture and Political Development* (Princeton: Princeton University Press, 1965); Robert D. Putnam, *Making Democracy
Work: Civic Traditions in Modern Italy* (Princeton: Princeton University Press, 1993); John S.
Duffield, "Political Culture and State Behavior: Why Germany Confounds Neorealism,"
International Organization 53 (Autumn 1999), 765–803.

criticized for reifying and stereotyping cultures, and interest in culture waned, until recently. Writing in what has become a new wave of attention to political culture, Lucien Pye argues, "Since political power rests largely upon expectations, communications, and shared sentiments and values, politics is essentially a cultural phenomenon. Indeed, politics would be impossible without culture, and cultures, of course, differ according to time and place."[151] For the anthropologists Sonia Alvarez, Evelina Dagnino, and Arturo Escobar, political culture is the "particular social construction in every society of what counts as 'political.' In this way, political culture is the domain of practices and institutions, carved out of the totality of social reality, that historically comes to be considered as properly political (in the same way that other domains are seen as properly 'economic,' 'cultural,' and 'social')."[152] So, there are two concepts of culture – a wider one, and a narrower, political culture.

Contrary to the idea of "relative neglect," international relations scholarship on culture does exist, though culture is often confused with belief in this literature. In the late 1970s, Ken Booth argued that ethnocentrism was both an important feature of politics among nations and deeply embedded in international relations theory and the practice of threat assessment.[153] Stephen Rosen suggests that culture, specifically social structure, may influence military effectiveness.[154] Elizabeth Kier, who defines a military's organizational culture as "collectively held beliefs within a particular military organization," suggests that culture, especially beliefs about the role of armed force, affects the formation of military doctrine.[155] Military organizations' cultures shape their members' understandings and choices: "military organizations develop strong collective understandings about the nature of their work and the conduct of their missions, and these organizational cultures influence their choices between offensive and defensive military doctrines."[156] Further,

---

[151] Lucien W. Pye, "Introduction: The Elusive Concept of Culture and the Vivid Reality of Personality," *Political Psychology* 18 (June 1997), 241–254: 247.
[152] Sonia E. Alvarez, Evelina Dagnino, and Arturo Escobar, "Introduction: The Cultural and Political in Latin American Social Movements," in Sonia E. Alvarez, Evelina Dagnino, and Arturo Escobar, eds., *Cultures of Politics, Politics of Cultures: Re-visioning Latin American Social Movements* (Boulder: Westview Press, 1998), pp. 1–29: 8.
[153] Ken Booth, *Strategy and Ethnocentrism* (New York: Holmes and Meyer, 1979).
[154] Stephen Peter Rosen, "Military Effectiveness: Why Society Matters," *International Security* 19 (Spring 1995), 5–31.
[155] Elizabeth Kier, "Culture and French Military Doctrine Before World War II," in Katzenstein, ed., *The Culture of National Security*, pp. 186–215: 203.
[156] Kier, *Imagining War*, p. 4.

she argues, "civilians' cultural understanding of the role of military force in the domestic arena governs their participation in developing doctrine."[157] Similarly, Alastair Johnston argues that strategic cultures affect military strategy, defining "strategic culture" as an "integrated system of symbols (i.e. causal axioms, languages, analogies, metaphors, etc.) that acts to establish pervasive and long-lasting strategic preferences by formulating concepts of the role and efficacy of military force in interstate political affairs, and by clothing these conceptions with such an aura of factuality that the strategic preferences seem uniquely realistic and efficacious."[158]

Culture has also been hypothesized as a factor in promoting peace and war. Echoing Mead and Luard, John Vasquez argues that, "Not all historical periods and not all actors (or dyads) experience the same amount of war. This suggests that war is not as culturally acceptable in some times and places as in others."[159] Johan Galtung warned against "cultural violence" or cultural elements "used to justify or legitimatize direct or structural violence."[160] Bruce Russett has suggested, among other possible explanations, that the peace observed among democracies may be due to common culture.[161] Marc Howard Ross argues that "psychocultural dispositions shape how groups and individuals process events and the emotions, perceptions, and cognitions the events provoke." These dispositions "link particular events to culturally shared threats to self-esteem and identity" and the "culture of conflict" is "specific norms, practices, and institutions associated with conflict."[162] Elise Boulding argues that to promote peace one should promote a peace culture.[163] Samuel Huntington believes that in the post-cold war world the "great divisions among humankind and the dominating source of conflict will be cultural."[164] Huntington regards civilizations as the "highest cultural

---

[157] Ibid. p. 21.

[158] Alastair Iain Johnston, "Cultural Realism and Strategy in Maoist China," in Katzenstein, ed, *The Culture of National Security*, pp. 216–278.

[159] John A. Vasquez, "Foreign Policy, Learning and War," in Hermann, Kegley, and Rosenau, eds., *New Directions*, pp. 366–383: 372.

[160] Johan Galtung, "Cultural Violence," *Journal of Peace Research* 27 (August 1990), 291–305: 291.

[161] Bruce Russett, *Grasping the Democratic Peace: Principles for a Post-Cold War World* (Princeton: Princeton University Press, 1993), p. 35.

[162] Marc Howard Ross, *The Culture of Conflict: Interpretations and Interests in Comparative Perspective* (New Haven: Yale University Press, 1993), pp. 10 and 21.

[163] Elise Boulding, *Cultures of Peace: The Hidden Side of History* (Syracuse: Syracuse University Press, 2000).

[164] Huntington, "The Clash of Civilizations?" p. 22.

grouping of people and the broadest level of cultural identity people have."[165]

Others emphasize the cultural foundations of regional and global international society. Luard argued that, "It is not possible to consider the behaviour of states without regard to the social context, the international environment, within which they exist; nor to consider a society of states without regard to the motivations and behaviour which characterize the individual states which are its members."[166] As Bull argued, "a common feature of . . . historical international societies is that they were all founded on a common culture or civilization."[167] Further, Bull distinguished between diplomatic culture and "international political culture" or the "intellectual and moral culture that determines the attitudes towards the states system of the societies that compose it."[168] Bull believed that "the future of international society is likely to be determined, among other things, by the preservation and extension of a cosmopolitan culture, embracing both common ideas and common values, and rooted in societies in general as well as in their elites, that can provide the world international society of today with the kind of underpinning enjoyed by the geographically smaller and culturally more homogenous international societies of the past."[169] Bull and Adam Watson argued that international society grew out of and follows a Western European pattern and that, "it is not our perspective but the historical record itself that can be called Eurocentric."[170] Ronald Jepperson, Alexander Wendt, and Peter Katzenstein argue that an "international cultural environment" is the context of national security policymaking where culture refers to "both a set of evaluative standards, such as norms or values, and to cognitive standards, such as rules or models defining what entities and actors exist in a system and how they operate and interrelate."[171] Specifically, they suggest, this international cultural environment includes a "layer of formal institutions or security regimes," a layer of "world

[165] Ibid., p. 24.   [166] Luard, *War in International Society*, p. 13.
[167] Hedley Bull, *The Anarchical Society: A Study of Order in World Politics* (New York: Columbia University Press, 1977), p. 16.
[168] Ibid., p. 316.   [169] Ibid., p. 317.
[170] Hedley Bull and Adam Watson, "Introduction", in Hedley Bull and Adam Watson, eds., *The Expansion of International Society* (Oxford: Clarendon Press, 1984), pp. 1–9: 2. Also see Adam Watson, "European International Society and its Expansion," in Bull and Watson, eds., *Expansion of International Society*, pp. 13–32.
[171] Ronald L. Jepperson, Alexander Wendt, and Peter J. Katzenstein, "Norms, Identity, and Culture in National Security," in Katzenstein, ed., *Culture of National Security*, pp. 33–75: 34 and 56.

political culture" which includes "elements like rules of sovereignty and international law, norms . . . and standardized social and political technologies," and finally, a layer of "international patterns of amity and enmity."[172]

Thus, while it would be an exaggeration to say that culture figures prominently in international relations theory, many scholars give culture an important role in shaping beliefs, practices, and identities in organizations, nations, and international societies.

Character and location of culture

Culture is often conceptualized as having the same properties as belief. For instance, Vertzberger describes culture in such a way that it is synonymous with a cognitive understanding of belief. "Culture represents a unified set of ideas that are shared by the members of a society and that establish a set of shared premises, values, expectations, and action predispositions among members of a nation that as a whole constitute a national style."[173] Vertzberger hypothesizes several cultural affects on foreign policy decisionmaking (that are not distinct from the affects others attribute to beliefs), arguing that "Individuals', organizations', and groups' information processing and definitions of the situation are affected and sometimes actually dictated by their being part of a distinct societal-national environment, culture, and experience."[174] He also argues that, "At the core of culture, in most cases, are broad and general beliefs and attitudes about one's own nation, about other nations, and about the relationships that actually obtain or that should obtain between the self and other actors in the international arena."[175] Culture thus biases attention to danger, assessment of risk, modes of cognitive operation such as associative versus abstract thinking, and perceptions about the most acceptable means of conflict resolution, and interferes with correctly understanding what actors from another culture say.[176]

Yet culture is more than belief. As a set of practices culture contains behavioral norms, symbols (meanings attached to objects, social events, and action), and ways to reproduce philosophical, instrumental, normative, and identity beliefs. Within cultures, the belief systems of individuals and groups are embedded in, and sit side by side with,

---

[172] Ibid., p. 34.   [173] Vertzberger, *The World in Their Minds*, p. 267.
[174] Ibid., p. 260.   [175] Ibid., p. 268.
[176] Others attribute these effects to individual beliefs.

other belief systems (such as religious, ethical, and scientific traditions). Together these webs of beliefs and practices constitute a society's culture or rather its multiple cultures. Thus, culture is the larger background of beliefs and practices (sometimes routinized and standardized within institutions) within which the particular belief systems and sub-cultures of groups sit. Culture is conveyed in a group's language or more precisely in the *meaning* of discourse. "A discourse, i.e., a system of statements in which each individual statement makes sense, produces interpretive possibilities by making it virtually impossible to think outside of it. A discourse provides *discursive spaces*, i.e. concepts, categories, metaphors, models and analogies by which meanings are created."[177] As Kier argues, when actors are totally inside their culture, it "consists of many assumptions that are rarely debated and seem so basic that it appears impossible to imagine things could be different."[178] Further, cultures exist in time and place, they are situated within groups.

While actors are more or less unself-conscious about aspects of their culture, they may be quite self-conscious about other elements of it. Further, actors must constantly work to reproduce their cultures as new members are born and old members die. And because groups are rarely completely homogenous and/or devoid of contact with other groups, challenges to a dominant culture are constant. Part of the socialization of new members into a community with a particular culture includes teaching members their group's history. This history is inculcated alongside the practices, rules, and philosophical, instrumental, normative, and identity beliefs held by most group members. For example, to be part of a monetary culture, one must learn the norm of paying for things with money rather than taking them or trading for them. Of course, analyzing another's culture is also rather like holding up a mirror to one's own culture.[179] Thus, another part of the work of making a culture, and maintaining it, can include comparing a culture with itself at a previous time or comparing one culture with other cultures.

So far, I have described culture as if it were located somewhere in an exclusive community. But it is possible to locate complex webs of meaning and regular practices among groups of individuals, and within larger cultures among groups who are characterized by race, class, religion, occupation, and sex as well as by political affiliations. I consider

---

[177] Doty, "Foreign Policy as Social Construction," p. 302.
[178] Kier, *Imagining War*, p. 26.
[179] See Edward W. Said, *Orientalism* (New York: Vintage Books, 1979).

cultures in five locations: epistemic communities, formal organizations, bounded political communities (nations and states), civilizations, and global cultures. Obviously, any one person may participate in several cultures.

Epistemic communities and formal organizations have belief systems and culture in the sense of regular and accepted practices. Peter Haas defines an epistemic community as "a network of professionals with recognized expertise and competence in a particular domain and authoritative claim to policy relevant knowledge within that domain or issue area." Epistemic communities have "(1) a shared set of normative and principled beliefs ... (2) shared causal beliefs ... (3) shared notions of validity ... (4) a common policy enterprise."[180] Epistemic communities share a culture in the sense that these beliefs entail larger world views that they subscribe to and which make their practices and discussions meaningful.

Culture also exists within organizations, shaping the way organizations do their job. Elizabeth Kier defines organizational culture as, "the set of basic assumptions, values, norms, beliefs, and formal knowledge that shape collective understandings."[181] Lynn Eden shows how the particular knowledge-making practices of nuclear weapons organizations frame their understandings of nuclear weapons effects.[182] Organizations have methods for socializing their members into the beliefs characteristic of members of the organization. They have ways of ridding blatant non-believers from the group, and they have practices, or "standard operating procedures," which they recognize as normal and which guide their actions in particular contexts.

Cultures also exist in bounded political communities. Martin Sampson suggests that a "set of norms, standards, rules or collective mental programming refers to a national culture that has certain properties."[183] Sampson says "these socially created and learned factors exist across a variety of institutions within a single nation-state; one may detect them in many different functional settings – families, associations, businesses, and governmental organizations – and one may also detect them over a large range of time periods ... " and he argues that these factors affect

[180] Haas, "Introduction," p. 3.
[181] Kier, *Imagining War*, p. 28.
[182] Lynn Eden, *Whole World on Fire: The Making of Organizational Knowledge about U.S. Nuclear Weapons Effects* (Ithaca: Cornell University Press, forthcoming).
[183] Martin W. Sampson, "Cultural Influences on Foreign Policy," in Hermann, Kegley, and Rosenau, eds., *New Directions*, pp. 384–405: 385.

the processes of foreign policy decisionmaking.[184] Similarly, Vertzberger argues that national political cultures are the source of biases in information processing. While these national political cultures are much less homogenous than they are generally described, there are such cultures.

In addition, groups of states and groups of organizations that transcend states may share more general historical, religious, ethical, and scientific traditions. Shared beliefs, common institutions, and regular interaction of states and non-state actors (such as multinational corporations and social movements) constitute international societies.[185] Hedley Bull argues that, "if contemporary international society does have any cultural basis, this is not a genuinely global culture, but is rather the culture of so-called 'modernity.' And if we ask what is modernity in culture, it is not clear how we answer this except by saying that it is the culture of the dominant Western powers."[186]

It is possible now more than at any other point in world history to speak of emergent world cultures. Globalization, the catch-phrase for the emergence of these world cultures, the spread of international markets, and the growing interdependence of productive processes, suggests the technological capacities and the economic, social, and political interactions that have created the emergent world culture. Further, some twentieth-century events – the cold war, ozone depletion, global environmental change, and the AIDS pandemic, as well as the development of a universal human rights discourse – were experienced and interpreted as global phenomena. As Scott Turner argues, "civil society is increasingly global not only because groups are establishing linkages across national borders, but also because of the nature of the issues around which NGOs and social movements converge."[187]

There are at least three overlapping spheres of an emerging global culture: political structures and processes, economic structures and processes, and issue-specific belief systems. The global culture is characterized by: dominant belief systems that sometimes conflict with each other (namely, individual human rights, commercialism, capitalism, militarism, increased respect for the rule of law or liberalism); a set of common international institutions (such as the United Nations, the

---

[184] *Ibid.*, pp. 385–386.
[185] See Christian Reus-Smit, "The Constitutional Structure of International Society and the Nature of Fundamental Institutions," *International Organization* 51 (Autumn 1997), 555–589.
[186] Bull, *Anarchical Society*, p. 39.
[187] Scott Turner, "Global Civil Society, Anarchy and Governance: Assessing an Emerging Paradigm," *Journal of Peace Research* 35 (January 1998), 25–42: 31.

World Court, and the World Trade Organization); and transnational epistemic communities of scientists, social scientists, financial experts, critical social movements, and cultural intellectuals. In the political sphere, as Dorothy Jones has noted, there is an emerging "Code of Peace" resting on international law alongside the older international cultures of military force and realpolitik.[188] Critical transnational social movements challenge the militarism, profit-orientation, and authoritarianism of dominant social institutions and "cultural representations play a pivotal role in the formation and maintenance of social protest."[189] To highlight the emergence of a global culture is not to say that local, national, and regional cultures are dying, though they might be, or to say that the now dominant cultures will always be dominant. Rather, the shape of global cultures is emerging out of sometimes contradictory cultures. Finally, to some extent, the dominant emerging world culture is marked by a certain respect for pluralism, which probably means that despite the form of globalization that is synonymous with homogenization, other cultures will remain for centuries.

But simply noting that groups hold some shared beliefs, and participate in common practices that may or may not be institutionalized, does not tell us how culture affects the process of argument. I go further than those who suggest that culture (like belief) is the source of misperceptions and cognitive biases. Culture is the stable foundation that makes and allows intelligible argument; cultures are the source of specific beliefs; culture is consciously used to frame and judge arguments; and culture can foster belief innovation.

Culture as "lifeworld" or stable foundation

Culture is the background of shared interpretations and practices, the unstated topos or starting point that allows meaningful conversations and arguments to occur. Beyond language, taken for granted beliefs that members of a society share, and the practices associated with these beliefs, allow and enable actors within a community to understand each other without having to make everything explicit. Culture provides the

---

[188] Dorothy V. Jones, *Code of Peace: Ethics and Security in the World of Warlord States* (Chicago: The University of Chicago Press, 1989).

[189] Richard G. Fox and Orin Starn, "Introduction," in Richard G. Fox and Orin Starn, eds., *Between Resistance and Revolution: Cultural Politics and Social Protest* (New Brunswick: Rutgers University Press, 1997), pp. 1–16: 6. Also see R.B. J. Walker, *One World, Many Worlds: Struggle for a Just World Peace* (Boulder: Lynn Reinner, 1988), pp. 61–62; Keck and Sikkink, *Activists Beyond Borders*.

floor or background of meaning on which actors can construct other meanings and interpret each other.

Habermas' development of Edmund Husserl's idea of *Lebenswelt*, or lifeworld, best captures this aspect of culture "formed from more or less diffuse, always unproblematic, background convictions."[190] The lifeworld seems real or "objective" to those who share it even as it "stores the interpretive work of preceding generations."[191] This fundamental background which enables hearers to understand speakers is

> an *implicit* knowledge that cannot be represented in a finite number of propositions; it is a *holistically structured* knowledge, the basic elements of which intrinsically define one another; and it is a knowledge that *does not stand at our disposition*, inasmuch as we cannot make it conscious and place it in doubt as we please. When philosophers nevertheless seek to do so, then that knowledge comes to light in the form of commonsense certainties. . . .[192]

Actors who hold different ideologies (understood as explicitly developed belief systems) may share a lifeworld and this allows arguments between ideologies to be intelligible, at least to a certain extent, to participants. Conversely, as Habermas suggests, lifeworlds constrain what will be seen as a valid argument since the taken-for-granted aspect of cultures is the first level, or order, of interpretation of arguments, although the act of interpretation at this point is generally unconscious. "The linguistic worldview is reified as the world order and cannot be seen as an interpretive system open to criticism."[193]

Antonio Cassese's understanding of the role of "prevailing ideologies" of international law illustrates the relationship between belief systems and the lifeworld. "International legal rules are, however, a simple

---

[190] Jürgen Habermas, *Theory of Communicative Action, Volume One: Reason and the Rationalization of Society* trans. Thomas McCarthy (Boston: Beacon Press, 1984), p. 70. Fred Dallmayr argues: "In the weak conception, the life-world is basically viewed as a preamble to reason or rational reflection, as a non- or pre-rational antechamber to cognition – but the antechamber that pliantly submits to thought (as the result of an inherent affinity between prereason and reason). In the strong version, by contrast, the life-world functions no longer as a mere precursor of reason or as its relatively immature or embryonic modality, but rather emerges as an integral dimension of thought, a dimension impinging powerfully on the status of rational or cognitive claims (not by nullifying them but by changing their sense)." Fred R. Dallmayr, "Life-World: Variations on a Theme," in Stephen K. White, ed., *Life-World and Politics: Between Modernity and Postmodernity* (Notre Dame: University of Notre Dame, 1989), pp. 25–65: 26.
[191] Habermas, *Theory of Communicative Action*, p. 70.
[192] Ibid., p. 336.   [193] Ibid., p. 71.

reflection of the constellation of power in the world community, as well as the prevailing ideologies and political concerns." For Cassese, both power and the content of the prevailing international culture provide the content and limits of international law. "The scholar, however dissatisfied he may be with this state of affairs, cannot but take note of the present legal regime with all its flaws and lacunae, and pinpoint the emerging strands of the international system."[194] Cassese's legal regime is a belief system, embedded within a lifeworld where legal systems or "prevailing ideology" make sense, and is essentially taken for granted. Legal practices, including argument and proof, are institutionalized and legitimate.

The importance of this background stock of meaning has not gone unnoticed by scholars of domestic and foreign policy. For example, Charles Elder and Roger Cobb argue that "a political culture acts to limit the range of problems and problem solving alternatives that are likely to be considered, or for that matter, even entertained or recognized."[195] Vertzberger argues that "accumulated historical experience, political culture, as well as geopolitics, provide enduring perspectives, attitudes and beliefs, within which defense and security policy predispositions emerge."[196] Michael Shapiro argues that "it is important to recognize that policy thinking is not unsituated . . . representational practices arise out of a society's more general practices . . ."[197] Shapiro further suggests that "Representations of public policy, then, have an ideological depth to the extent that they engage in a stock of signs with which people make their everyday lives intelligible."[198] Similarly, Roxanne Doty argues: "The reception as meaningful of statements revolving around policy situations depends on how well they fit into the general system of representation in a given society."[199]

The taken-for-granted aspect of culture provides stability. And, like other forms of common knowledge, culture can make communication, cooperation, and coordination easier among those who share beliefs and expectations because they can anticipate how others within the culture

[194] Antonio Cassese, *Self-determination of Peoples: A Legal Reappraisal* (Cambridge: Cambridge University Press, 1995), p. 162.
[195] Charles D. Elder and Roger W. Cobb, *The Political Uses of Symbols* (New York: Longman, 1983) p. 85.
[196] Vertzberger, *The World in Their Minds*, p. 272.
[197] Michael J. Shapiro, "Representing World Politics: The Sports/War Intertext," in James Der Derian and Michael J. Shapiro, eds., *International/Intertextual Relations: Postmodern Readings of World Politics* (Lexington: Lexington Books, 1989), pp. 69–96: 71.
[198] Shapiro, "Representing World Politics," p. 73.
[199] Doty, "Foreign Policy as Social Construction," p. 303.

will think and act in particular contexts. These aspects of culture – as communicative background, stable arena, the common knowledge that facilitates cooperation and coordination, and boundary for argument – are generally in the background of social interactions, where members of a group are unaware or unconscious of their situatedness within that culture. This property also makes understanding other cultures in and on their own terms difficult.

Finally, as the deep background of social interaction and discourse, culture and the particulars of a decisionmaking situation influence a group's openness to argument as a process. In a culture that places a high value on agreement and conformity, arguments will be rare and relatively minor. Culture may also delimit the scope of arguments, that is, how deeply one can raise objections to beliefs and practices. In some contexts, it may not be possible to challenge core beliefs, especially if this suits elites who wish to maintain their hold on the reins of cultural power. "Dominant hegemonic practices attempt to achieve some sort of closure of the social, that is, to produce a relatively unified and normalized set of categories to understand reality . . . "[200]

Culture as a source of specific beliefs

Perhaps most obviously, culture often provides the content for specific philosophical, instrumental, normative, and identity beliefs at the core, contingent, and role levels. Further, epistemic communities, small groups, and organizations may develop beliefs that are particular to their culture.

One can see how cultures are the source of particular foreign policy beliefs by examining the beliefs that are dominant in a state's foreign policy. Vertzberger, for example, argues that concepts of national "belonging" in the sense of which group of nations the state sees itself as belonging to, as well as international role and status, are culturally determined.[201] Nationalists posit continuity of past and present culture, history, and genetic material. But while we can argue that there are certain common characteristics of nationalism, the specific character of nationalist beliefs varies. For instance, one of the first uses of the term nationalism was in an essay published in 1774 by the German pacifist Johann Gottfried Herder.[202] Herder's conception of nationalism was

---

[200] Arturo Escobar, "Culture, Practice and Politics: Anthropology and the Study of Social Movements," *Critique of Anthropology* 12 (December 1992), 395–432: 406.
[201] Vertzberger, *The World in Their Minds*, p. 282.
[202] Anthony Smith, *Theories of Nationalism*, 2nd edn (New York: Holmes & Meier Publishers, 1983), p. 167.

both spiritual and linguistic in the sense that he believed in an evolved organic *volkgeist* (folk-spirit), and that only through expression in one's native tongue could humans reach their fullest potential.[203] A generation later, Prussian nationalist Johann Fichte espoused the idea that Germans were specially suited for leadership because their language, unlike other European languages, was original and unpolluted.[204]

The ingredients of a particular dominant foreign policy belief system within a state are based on the particular history of the state (or dominant political group) as mythologized by national historians, dramatic personal and group experiences such as war or occupation, and individual socialization (parents/family, schools, peer groups). As Dan Reiter argues, foreign policy beliefs are "often lessons drawn from past events."[205] The most vivid events will have the greatest impact. And, as Robert Jervis argued two decades earlier, individual learning and belief change may occur when foreign policy decisionmakers are confronted with dramatic stimuli.[206] Certain events are seen and coded as paradigmatic for members of a culture. For example, members of post-World War II European and North American policy elites came to see "Munich" as a paradigm of appeasement, with the lesson that appeasement only encourages aggressors. Thus, to understand the source and substance of the foreign policy belief system of states, one has to understand the particular history of the state as it has been mythologized by national historians, and also the social and political history of the individuals dominant in foreign policy decisionmaking. Foreign policy belief systems are embedded in larger belief systems (religious, ethical, and scientific traditions) and common historical experience; in other words, they are grounded in the historically situated culture(s) of the community in question. As in the case of common historical analogies, the transmission of culture involves the socialization of its members in the dominant discourse, that is the symbols and interpretations of historical events.

Cultural framing

Some symbols are so widely understood within a culture, so taken for granted, and so powerful, that they merely have to be invoked for

---

[203] Hans Kohn, *Nationalism: Its Meaning and History* (Princeton: D. Van Nostrand, 1955), pp. 30–32.
[204] Ibid., p. 36.
[205] Reiter, *Crucible of Beliefs*, p. 12.
[206] Jervis, *Perception and Misperception*.

participants in a conversation to make the standard emotional and cognitive associations. Yet, as Vertzberger argues, "the images of particular past events or situations are often based to some degree on a mélange of fact and fiction not always clearly distinguished from each other. There are historical facts, mass media reports, national mythologies, artistic impressions in writing, painting, or artifacts – all reinforced by the person's own imagination and selective memory."[207] Further, multiple and conflicting cultural frames are available as actors view events from epistemic, organizational, national, or international cultural perspectives. As Kier argues, "there are not definitive meanings attached to an objective empirical reality. As important as material factors may be, they can be interpreted in numerous ways."[208] Actions are thus intelligible first through an unconscious cultural lens, the lifeworld.

But the effect of culture is not only deep and unconscious. Advocates consciously and unconsciously use culturally dominant interpretations in their meta-arguments to represent situations to others. They use historical experience, cultural signs (including metaphors, myths and common analogies), and beliefs to *reason* and to make arguments to others.

> Contemplating the sins of the system, painting banners, making speeches, marching – these bold actions are wound around an armature of cultural meanings before they power up social protest. As dissent grows and protest erupts, there may be improvisation, there must be inclusion (and exclusion), there can be persistence and success and, very often, there will be failure. Every step in the process involves the creation and diffusion of cultural meanings. At every step, too, historical events create new social conditions within which these meanings deploy. [209]

Cultural framing may be used as part of a justification for positions already taken, or as part of publicly communicated evaluations of the validity of positions others have taken. The fact that actors consciously employ culture, perhaps even cynically or disingenuously, as a part of their rhetorical menu does not mean that we should discount cultural framing. Rather, this use underscores the importance of culture's role in argumentation and the grounding of particular beliefs.

---

[207] Vertzberger, *The World in Their Minds*, p. 297.
[208] Kier, *Imagining War*, p. 3.
[209] Fox and Starn, "Introduction," p. 8.

Culture as obstacle to and source of innovation

Though there is sometimes a tendency to think of culture as monolithic, resilient and unchanging, culture is not static, nor does "culture" simply constrain and dispose. Cultures can enable innovation in at least three ways.

First, and most obviously, when people from a relatively homogenous culture come into contact with a different set of cultural beliefs, new beliefs and practices may be introduced into both cultures. After some reflection, some of these beliefs may be adopted wholesale or melded in a syncretic way. Sub-cultures within a dominant culture may also expose new beliefs to the larger culture. But it is important to emphasize that the transmission of beliefs does not guarantee their adoption. Members of cultures often resist new beliefs, and why any new belief is adopted must be explained since some beliefs and practices are adopted while others are not. The cultural aspects of resistance to, and adoption of, new beliefs is perhaps best seen in debates within traditions, such as those documented by scholars of the philosophy and history of science who have written about debates within scientific belief systems when scientists proposed radical new ideas.[210]

Highly cohesive groups or cultures that are isolated from outside influences and who hold rigid, self-reinforcing, standards of proof for the adoption of new beliefs may be most resistant to change. They may also be prone to groupthink where group "members' strivings for unanimity override their motivation to realistically appraise alternative courses of action."[211] Irving Janis suggests that "in circumstances of extreme crisis, group contagion occasionally gives rise to collective panic, violent acts of scapegoating, and other forms of what could be called group madness." But, Janis argues, "much more frequent ... are instances of mindless conformity and collective misjudgement of serious risks, which are collectively laughed off in a clubby atmosphere of relaxed conviviality."[212] Thus, according to Janis, a policymaking group which displays the symptoms of groupthink will not survey all

---

[210] Thomas Kuhn, *The Structure of Scientific Revolutions* (Chicago: University of Chicago Press,1955); Paul Thagard, *Conceptual Revolutions* (Princeton: Princeton University Press, 1992).

[211] Irving Janis, *Groupthink: Psychological Studies of Policy Decisions and Fiascoes* (Boston: Houghton Mifflin, 1982), p. 9; Irving Janis, *Victims of Groupthink* (Boston: Houghton Mifflin, 1972). Also see Irving L. Janis, *Crucial Decisions: Leadership in Policymaking and Crisis Management* (New York: The Free Press, 1989).

[212] Janis, *Groupthink*, p. 3.

the objectives and policy alternatives, nor candidly assess the risks and costs of alternatives.[213] Moreover, individual decisionmakers in group-think settings tend to think in less cognitively complex ways.[214] Janis is correct in pointing to the contributing role of homogeneity in the group-think process: the primary cause of groupthink is the desire to maintain consensus in a group of like-minded individuals. Crisis situations may be more likely to generate groupthink because decisionmaking groups tend to decrease in size at those times and there may be great pressures felt to come to consensus quickly. [215]

Groupthink and censorship are, of course, not the same. Censorship is a more direct and conscious process where individuals with information or opinions that directly contradict the dominant view are silenced or their views systematically screened out of the discourse and the decisionmaking process. In totalitarian settings, individuals with such views may frequently silence themselves (self-censorship), to preserve their lives or their position within the hierarchy. Thus, censorship and self-censorship may contribute to groupthink and both may be more likely in extremely homogenous cultures that stress cohesion and consensus.

Second, when individuals and groups face new social and material challenges, such as overpopulation or climate change, innovation is possible. But innovation is not guaranteed. Groups may hold on to their old beliefs and ways of acting even if others might consider change imperative. The content of webs of preexisting belief, and a group's knowledge-making practices will affect whether changes in social and material conditions will be understood as challenges to old beliefs, and whether the pre-existing beliefs are changed.[216] In either case, those who

---

[213] Ibid., pp. 174–175.

[214] Philip Tetlock, "Identifying Victims of Groupthink From Public Statements of Decision Makers," *Journal of Personality and Social Psychology* 37 (August 1979), 1314–1324.

[215] Ole R. Holsti, "Crisis Decision Making," in Philip E. Tetlock, Jo L. Husbands, Robert Jervis, Paul C. Stern, and Charles Tilly, eds., *Behavior, Society and Nuclear War, Volume One* (Oxford: Oxford University Press, 1989), pp. 8–84: 20–21. Of course, even in crisis situations small groups do not always fall prey to groupthink. For critiques of groupthink and discussion of small group decisionmaking, see Ramon J. Aldag and Sally Riggs Fuller, "Beyond Fiasco: A Reappraisal of the Groupthink Phenomenon and a New Model of Group Decision Processes," *Psychological Bulletin* 113 (May 1993), 533–552; Paul t'Hart, Eric K. Stern, and Bengt Sundelius, eds., *Beyond Groupthink: Political Group Dynamics and Foreign Policy-Making* (Ann Arbor: University of Michigan Press, 1997); and Robert Abelson and Ariel Levi, "Decision Making and Decision Theory," in Gardner Lindzey and Elliot Aronson, eds., *The Handbook of Social Psychology*, 3rd edn (New York: Random House, 1985), pp. 231–309: 292–293.

[216] On change and resistance to it, see Elder and Cobb, *The Political Uses of Symbols*, pp. 106–109.

advocate belief change will have to make arguments to others to show why they should adopt new beliefs.

Even if the group is not confronted by substantially novel circumstances, new beliefs and arguments may be developed by those who for some reason (their economic, social, or cultural position or the "logical" development of their beliefs) have come to see the world differently from the social formations or classes of the dominant culture. These individuals may attempt to develop a cohort of likeminded people, promoting a social movement, who work to develop an analysis that re-frames the dominant understanding of the world and outlines a program for reform or revolution. For example, human activity had long affected the environment. The environmentalism of the 1960s and 1970s grew out of the experiences and understanding of individuals who felt the prevailing actions of humans harmed the environment and ultimately the quality of human life. Activists work to persuade others to see the world as they see it, and set about trying to change aspects of the dominant culture. As Fox and Starn suggest, "protest builds and sometimes transforms the cultural meanings shared by communities and groups."[217] Powerful new beliefs and arguments have the capacity to fracture the prevailing belief consensus and consequently fracture the political consensus among the dominant elites themselves.

Third, cultures may contain within them the attitudinal seeds for belief revision and innovation. Specifically, conservative cultures may go to great lengths to preserve and transmit unchanged beliefs and practices. On the other hand, cultures that contain belief systems that are extremely self-reflective, putting their own beliefs and modes of reasoning on trial, or that contain elements which consciously foster innovation in the arts and sciences, may be more prone to belief revision and change. It is possible that these cultures are characterized by a form of reasoning that de-emphasizes formal logic as the sole mode of reasoning and prizes diversity and experimentation.

The source of culture

Not surprisingly, there are intense debates among anthropologists about the source of culture. Specifically, is culture autonomous, is it an effect of biological forces, or does it reflect the material base and the organization of production? The latter is a naturalist functional utility account

---

[217] Fox and Starn, "Introduction," p. 7.

of culture where culture is an effect of material forces.[218] As Marshall
Sahlins argues: "At first glance the confrontation of the cultural and
material logics does seem unequal. The material process is factual and
'independent of man's will'; the symbolic, invented and therefore flexible. The one is fixed by nature, the other is arbitrary by definition.
Thought can only kneel before the absolute sovereignty of the physical world."[219] If culture is an ideational effect of material forces, then
those who argue that material forces are the cause of social behavior have not been defeated by an account that stresses the importance
of culture. Politics still boils down to material causes and biological
drives.

Yet there is good reason to doubt materialist/functionalist accounts
of the origins of culture. As Sahlins argues, "nothing in the way of their
capacity to satisfy a material (biological) requirement can explain why
pants are produced for men and skirts for women, or why dogs are
inedible but the hindquarters of the steer are supremely satisfying of
the need to eat. Nor are the relations of production – the division of
labor by culturally defined categories and capacities – deducible from
materially determined categories and capacities of the population."[220]
In other words, while it is true that cultural practices include activities that are motivated by material factors and biological needs (e.g.
building houses to stay warm or dry; eating meat to satisfy hunger),
one ought not to fall into the functionalist trap of assuming that there
is only one way to satisfy a "need." Humans could and do satisfy
their material needs for shelter and food in other ways. "The material forces taken by themselves are lifeless."[221] As Sahlins suggests,
nature "rules only on the question of existence, not on specific form."[222]
He argues:

> So far as the definite properties of a cultural order are conceived,
> the laws of nature are indeterminate... Culture is not merely nature
> expressed in another form. Rather, the reverse: the action of nature un-
> folds in the terms of culture; that is, in a form no longer its own but
> embodied as meaning. Nor is this a mere translation. The natural fact
> assumes a new mode of existence as a symbolized fact, its cultural de-
> ployment and consequence now governed by the relation between its

[218] This dichotomy is familiar as the free will versus determinism and the agent versus
structure debates.
[219] Marshall Sahlins, *Culture and Practical Reason* (Chicago: University of Chicago,
1976), p. 207.
[220] *Ibid.*   [221] *Ibid.*   [222] *Ibid.*, p. 209.

> meaningful dimension and other such meanings, rather than the rela-
> tion between its natural dimensions and other such facts. All of this of
> course within the material limits ... From the moment of cultural syn-
> thesis, the action of nature is mediated by a conceptual scheme ... Such
> being the feature of nature culturalized, nature as it exists in itself is
> only the raw material provided by the hand of God, waiting to be
> given meaningful shape and content by the hand of man. It is as the
> block of marble to the finished statue; and of course the genius of the
> sculptor – in the same way as the technical development of culture –
> consists in exploiting the lines of diffraction within the material to his
> own ends.[223]

But if materialist-functionalist accounts of culture seem inadequate, especially in the face of contemporary and historical cultural diversity, then what accounts for culture? Sahlins puts a premium on human re-flection, how we actively make meaning out of the natural world, order it and our relations to each other. Which leaves social scientists in the awkward position of being interpreters of interpretation. Despite the importance of the question, an account of origins is not necessary at this juncture if what one wants to understand is the consequences of culture.

Summary and caveats

Political arguments and debates are forms of reasoning in a political context where the aim can be both private discovery or deliberation as well as public motivation, justification, and mobilization. Ethical, sci-entific, practical, and identity arguments are frequent in world politics, as are meta-arguments over framing, the nature of the world, how we know it, or what is good. Arguments may occur in a simple form, such as single practical or identity arguments, or they may be more complex concatenations of arguments. Further, the contexts of arguments (the who, when, why and where) affects their persuasiveness. Arguments may be subject to dissection as one moves back and forth along infer-ential and belief chains of reasoning to support or attack elements of a particular argument or supporting arguments.

Good arguments are ones that give hearers good reasons to believe their conclusions. Persuasive arguments also use emotional appeals and draw on our feelings as much as they use vertical logic or horizontal associative reasoning. Arguments are not necessarily *rational* in a simple utility maximizing sense, but they will be reasoned: they will aim to answer some questions and consist of beliefs and supporting beliefs,

[223] *Ibid.*, pp. 209–210.

giving reasons for conclusions. Similarly, symbolic arguments which use sideways or associative forms of reasoning, such as analogies, may or may not be appropriate. Nevertheless, inappropriate analogies may be persuasive.

The reason one argument wins over another is first of all that its advocates have been heard, while many arguments are never heard. Second, successful arguments are made by savvy political actors who mobilize political support. Third, accidents of history, such as the skill and access of those making the case, may affect the success of arguments. Fourth, arguments are less likely to be persuasive if the social and material context does not cohere with the argument. Again, this does not mean that argument actually boils down to material conditions. Rather the relationship between arguments and preexisting cultural, strategic, and economic factors is complex since previous argument shaped the world in which present arguments occur.

Beliefs are neither "rational" nor "irrational" features of a decision-making process. Beliefs – philosophical, instrumental, identity, and normative – are historically and socially contingent. The persuasiveness of arguments and judgments about the validity (legitimacy) or logic of political arguments are also contingent. There is no rational (or irrational) foundation for social beliefs. We can only understand beliefs historically, by examining their unfolding within particular historical contexts or as the result of reason. Moreover, there are few "real" material interests that cannot be viewed in more than one way. That does not mean certain actions should not be considered counter-productive, but the criteria for judging foreign policy decisions should be the framework of *reason*, not ideal-type rationality. Rational actor theory itself consists of a set of beliefs organized in a belief system that stresses natural foundations for belief and accurate assessments of costs, risks, and benefits.

The argument rests on several key premises and assumptions. First, though we often speak of individuals alone as making decisions, foreign policy decisionmaking and policy implementation is both an individual and a group activity. Many are involved in its various steps, from information gathering to option formulation, decision, and implementation. Even in dictatorships, it matters what participants think about the reasons given for a particular decision, and action. In other words, the non-coercive aspects of politics are ultimately about legitimacy and thus we must understand the processes by which certain activities become legitimate and normal and by which individuals are persuaded to act or believe.

Second, in the process of making arguments, decisionmakers must constantly remind each other of their identities, goals, reasons, and justifications. Thus, shared belief systems are crucially important for the simple reason that shared beliefs help individuals see the same things, share a vision of the group, and come to an agreement about goals and policies. Belief systems do what rational actor theorists and game theorists would describe as facilitate coordination. But philosophical, instrumental, normative, and identity beliefs also shape understanding and interests: the content of these coordinating ideas is crucially important.

Third, what is "self-evident," and taken for granted in an individual's belief system is not necessarily based on real, objective, and obvious material interests. Much of the scholarly literature and popular discussion of foreign policy assumes that the material interests of states are obvious and essentially unproblematic and can be "taken for granted." Indeed, the terms self-interest and national are rarely defined and their meaning has usually been unproblematized, as were the ways foreign policy decisionmakers argued for their particular view of national interest.[224] But, I argue, both individual and intersubjectively shared beliefs are the foundation for most of these taken-for-granted assumptions. Little is self-evident about "national interests."

Fourth, there is nothing firm, everlasting, or immutable about these beliefs whether they are philosophical, instrumental, normative, or about identities. Foreign policy beliefs are constructed, maintained, and modified through social practices. Beliefs are as constructed and open to reinterpretation as the arguments that decisionmakers use to convince themselves and others of the "correct" foreign policy decision. Major foreign policy shifts are as likely to be the result of changes in belief systems as they are to be the result of changes in the "structure" of international politics or in the composition of the ruling elite of an individual nation.

Fifth, beliefs do not recognize borders inside states or outside them. As Luard argues, international politics is a milieu of social interaction and there are dominant beliefs in this environment which structure actions: "it is the ideology of international society – the set of assumptions and expectations which are established there – which determine the thinking of individual decisionmakers, and so the way they will respond when faced with a particular threat, dignity, or affront."[225] Luard argues that it

---

[224] Exceptions include Katzenstein, ed., *Culture of National Security* and Martha Finnemore, *National Interests and International Society* (Ithaca: Cornell University Press, 1996).
[225] Luard, *War in International Society*, p. 3.

is "not possible to consider the behavior of states without regard to the social context, the international environment, within which they exist; nor to consider a society of states without the motivations and behavior which characterize the individual states which are its members."[226] Interdependence includes belief in his view. "No state is an island (whatever its geographical situation). All states at all times have had regular contact with some other states."[227] Thus, individuals and groups do not come up with beliefs, evaluate them, or make persuasive arguments in a social vacuum. Foreign policy belief systems are embedded within and reflect larger social and historical complexes of meaning.

While we can see cultures in various social and political groups including epistemic communities, organizations, states, civilizations, and international or global settings, scholars must take care not to reify cultures in particular locations. Rather, it is possible to recognize that in certain times and places, people share beliefs and practices and ways of understanding their history, at least enough to superficially understand the arguments of those within their culture. The practice of colonialism varied over time as cultures changed and those who tried to alter aspects of colonialism constantly ran into culture. It would be extremely difficult to understand how colonialism changed from the dominant practice to one that is considered illegitimate without examining the larger cultural context which shaped, and was used to shape, its constitutive arguments and practices.

This theory of the causal and constitutive role of arguments offers a specification of how beliefs (or what most call ideas) work in world politics. A theory of argument offers a way to understand the links between domestic political processes, nongovernmental organizations, and international institutions to international structures and processes – not simply as multilevel games but also as multilocal and multivocal arguments where the goal is to persuade others and change practices. By focusing on the *content* of beliefs and the role of argument and reason, this theory moves away from the implicit rational/irrational dualism that dominates international relations theory. My argument focuses instead on how the meaning-content of beliefs and arguments is both historically and logically related to, and dependent upon, the meaning of other beliefs and arguments that are themselves *not necessarily* related to material interests or perceptions/misperceptions of the social world.

---

[226] Ibid., p. 13.   [227] Ibid., p. 15.

2   Ethical argument and argument analysis

> I want to account for the ways in which men and women who are not lawyers but simply citizens (and sometimes soldiers) argue about war, and to expound the terms we commonly use. I am concerned precisely with the present structure of the moral world. My starting point is the fact that we do argue, often to different purposes, to be sure, but in a mutually comprehensible fashion: else there would be no point in *arguing*. We justify our conduct; we judge the conduct of others. Though these justifications cannot be studied like the records of a criminal court, they are nevertheless, a legitimate subject of study.[1]

Ethical argument is ostensibly the hard case for demonstrating the importance of argument in world politics. To make an ethical argument, as opposed to any other kind of argument is to propose three things simultaneously: that a behavior or course of action is good and right; that others ought to do this good thing; and that despite the strength of my conviction, I will not force you to do what I believe is the good, but rather I seek to persuade you to believe as I do and act according to that belief. Further, ethical arguments clearly rest on normative beliefs, but they are also usually closely related to identity and constitutive beliefs. To do the right thing is to be a good human either as an individual or a member of a group (identity) or as part of one's role (constitutive belief). And ethical arguments, because of their relation to beliefs about how it is that we are good, how it is that we relate to others, are emotional and this is part of their distinctive appeal and power. Those who make ethical arguments at least want to be seen as good and at most believe that they are suggesting what is good.

[1] Michael Walzer, *Just and Unjust Wars: A Moral Argument With Historical Illustrations* (New York: Basic Books, 1992), p. xxvii.

The dominant account of the role of ethics in international relations is that it is a "stand in" for material interests and is the product of power. Such is the view of E.H. Carr:

> Theories of social morality are always the product of a dominant group which identifies itself with the community as a whole, and which possesses facilities denied to subordinate groups or individuals for imposing its view of life on the community. Theories of international morality are, for the same reason and in virtue of the same process, the product of dominant nations or groups of nations ... morality is the product of power.[2]

These and similar claims are found in the writings of Thucydides and Hobbes.

Arguments about the irrelevance of ethics or morality are powerful. Translated into their assumptions, those who say that "morality is the product of power" are actually making several claims. First, they suppose that when individuals make ethical claims, those statements mask some "real" interests that are not "moral." Rather, the interests are "selfish." Further, these selfish interests or "self-interested" behavior and arguments are motivated at root by material causes such as the desire for power or survival. Moreover, to act self-interestedly is to be rational, in the sense of utility maximizing, while action motivated by ethical concerns is irrational. Since states are rational, and since in the world of international politics militarily/materially powerful states dominate (the strong do as they will, the weak as they must), international ethics is an oxymoron. Representatives of states who say they act for moral reasons are covering up some other, self-interested motive. In this view, theories of world politics that give ethical accounts of behavior are at best mistaken and at worst misleading.

Another strong argument, as articulated by Joshua Cohen, grants some causal weight to morality but suggests that morality has been internalized and is part of the interests of individuals. He argues that "some ethical explanations ... have force. That force derives from the general claim that the injustice of a social arrangement limits its viability." Cohen continues: "Social arrangements better able to elicit voluntary cooperation have both moral and practical advantages over

---

[2] Edward Hallett Carr, *The Twenty Years' Crisis, 1919–1939: An Introduction to the Study of International Relations* (New York: Harper & Row, 1964), pp. 79 and 81.

their more coercive counterparts."[3] Cohen makes this argument with specific reference to the demise of slavery, suggesting that slavery conflicted with slave interests in "material well-being, autonomy, and dignity." Slavery is "unjust" because it could not be the result of a free, reasonable, and informed agreement.

> Suppose, then, that one comes to understand certain facts, all of which can be recognized independent from the procedures of moral reasoning: that slaves share the natural properties that are sufficient for being subjects of legitimate interests, that they have the fundamental interests, and that slavery sharply conflicts with those interests. Moral reasoning about slavery, proceeding in light of these facts, and giving due consideration to the interests of slaves, is bound to recognize the interests as legitimate and to condemn slavery as unjust. To say, then, that the wrongness of slavery explains the moral belief is to note the following: that moral reasoning mandates the conclusion that slavery is unjust; and that the moral belief is produced in part by that kind of reasoning. And once the injustice is recognized, it is reasonable to expect that recognition plays some role in motivation, that it contributes to the antagonism of slaves to slavery, that it adds nonslave opponents to slave opponents, and that, once slavery is abolished, it helps to explain why there are not strong movements to bring it back.[4]

Cohen's arguments are actually a version of rational actor theory, where it is rational to act in accordance with normative beliefs. "The moral weight also figures implicitly in the conflicting interests view . . . The conflict of slavery with legitimate slave interests, and the fact that masters' interests in preserving slavery are not legitimate, plausibly helps to 'tip the balance' in favor of stable departures from slavery."[5]

The basic assumptions of rational actor theory are familiar yet bear repeating. First, people are means to ends rational: they devise strategies and engage in behaviors that move them efficiently toward achieving their goals. Second, people are utility maximizers: they will choose the course of action with the greatest perceived benefits. Third, people calculate costs, risks, and benefits in an unbiased manner. Fourth, preferences are given and stable. Rational actor theory does not pretend to tell us about the source of preferences or interests, nor how preferences change. In sum, human behavior can be explained in terms of rational

---

[3] Joshua Cohen, "The Arc of the Moral Universe," *Philosophy & Public Affairs* 26 (Spring 1997), 91–134: 93.
[4] Ibid., p. 131.   [5] Ibid.

decision processes. Individuals weigh costs, risks, and benefits of alternative actions, and they choose the course of action with the least costs and risks, and the greatest benefit. In the case of Cohen's argument about the demise of slavery, an ethical explanation makes sense because slavery conflicts with the *rational* slave's interest, and because it conflicts with slave interests the institution of slavery is *costly*, in fact more costly than beneficial in most circumstances. Morality and self-interest are thus still distinct from each other in this view, although as Gregory Raymond argues, "self-interests and norms frequently coexist."[6]

However, normative beliefs can have force, and the power of those beliefs in argument is related specifically to their content. People use arguments (instrumentally) because they want to persuade the other and they find that ethical arguments are often persuasive. In the case of ethical arguments they want to persuade the other that behaving in a certain way is normatively good and therefore they ought to behave that way. Convincing ethical arguments provide good normative reasons to do one thing versus another. The reasons given in a persuasive ethical argument seem good, first because people believe in the values put forward in the argument, and second, because they believe that the proposed course of action will help to realize those values. In other words, when they are successful, ethical arguments work primarily because of their persuasive power and the source of this persuasive power is their content. Ethical arguments may also have political power if the balance of belief shifts to the position articulated by the ethical argument, which means that those who deploy successful ethical arguments must be as politically savvy as those who deploy practical, identity, or scientific arguments. Ethical arguments that occur within political groups and among them are as important and ubiquitous as practical, scientific, and identity arguments in world politics.

The key question is whether there is a causal relationship between normative beliefs and behaviors that become dominant. I argue that there is, and that the causal power of normative beliefs lies in ethical argument. The aims in this chapter are to articulate the workings and role of ethical argument; to explicate the relationship between ethical arguments, normative beliefs, and behavioral change; and to suggest a way to study ethical arguments in world politics. I make my case for the importance of ethical argument in several steps. First, I develop

---

[6] Gregory A. Raymond, "Problems and Prospects in the Study of International Norms," *Mershon International Studies Review* 41 (November 1997), 205–245: 232.

the concepts of behavioral norms and normative beliefs, distinguishing between them and discussing their potential relationships. Second, I briefly discuss alternative theories of behavioral norm and normative belief change. Third, I develop the theory of ethical argument that shows how ethical arguments can be persuasive. Fourth, I explore some of the reasons behavioral norms and normative beliefs are difficult to change, but how, nevertheless, ethical arguments might seem persuasive. Finally, I discuss methodological questions and propose a method of ethical argument analysis.

Behavioral norms and normative beliefs

International relations scholars frequently talk about "norms" but do so in ways that frustrate analysis by blurring the distinction between behavioral norms and normative beliefs. They also emphasize common knowledge properties of "norms" that are not unique to "norms." Further, it is not uncommon for the "norms" literature to proceed as if the dominant practice were the same as the normative belief.

Behavioral norms are simply "typical, or modal, behavior" or the dominant practice in certain contexts.[7] Normative beliefs are beliefs about what it is *right* to do. What is distinctive about prescriptive normative statements and normative beliefs is their emphasis on what is *right* and *good*. This prescriptive *normative* quality is precisely what theorists are asserting or denying has causal import, so it is vital not to confound normative beliefs and behavioral norms or else one risks circular and imprecise arguments (in the form of "norms" cause "norms").[8]

It is not unusual, even among the most careful scholars, to procede as if common knowledge and normative beliefs are one and the same. For instance, Friedrich Kratochwil suggests that norms are used to ascribe praise or blame, but he highlights the function of "norms" in decisionmaking and problem solving – ordering and coordination effects – arguing that norms decrease uncertainty, allow the pursuit of shared

[7] Robert O. Keohane uses the phrase "typical, or modal, behavior" in "The Demand for International Regimes," in Stephen D. Krasner, ed., *International Regimes* (Ithaca: Cornell University Press, 1983), pp. 141–171: 145.
[8] See Raymond, "Problems and Prospects in the Study of International Norms," and Janice E. Thompson, "Norms in International Relations: A Conceptual Analysis," *International Journal of Group Tensions* 23 (1993), 67–83.

meanings, and help actors coordinate by defining situations and the rules of the game.[9] For Audie Klotz, norms are beliefs, or "shared (thus social) understandings of standards for behavior."[10] Klotz says that "Discrimination based on raciálly defined categories, evident in racist language, personal actions, or social policies, is bad, and individual equality (lack of racial discrimination) is good."[11] Failing to distinguish dominant behaviors from the beliefs that might cause them, Klotz says: "Nor are all norms moral, since these standards can have functional and nonethical origins and purposes."[12] Christopher Gelpi also confounds common knowledge with normative, that is, prescriptive force, when he "emphasizes the role of norms as focal points for interpreting behavior" and as "reputational constraints."[13] Gregory Raymond argues that "contrary to the Hobbesian assertion that 'the independence of states implies that there are no rules', acknowledged normative standards exist in the absence of a common power to keep everyone in awe."[14] But when Raymond argues that "Norms are ubiquitous . . . The web of expectations created by norms guide behavior; even in the absence of centralized mechanisms to enforce compliance," he does not distinguish normative beliefs from other kinds of beliefs or common knowledge.[15] And while focusing on the "prescriptive" aspect of norms "as a standard of appropriate behavior," Finnemore and Sikkink nevertheless say, "Norms channel and regularize behavior; they often limit the range of choice and constrain actions."[16]

As shared expectations about behavior, both behavioral norms and normative beliefs may have common knowledge effects, decreasing uncertainty about what actors are likely to do in certain circumstances, and facilitating coordination because "norms," that is, both behavioral norms and normative beliefs, are "functional" in ways that are similar

---

[9] Friedrich Kratochwil, *Rules Norms and Decisions: On the Conditions of Practical and Legal Reasoning in International Relations and Domestic Affairs* (Cambridge: Cambridge University Press, 1989), *passim*, esp. pages 9–11; 48; 50; 58–59; 69–70 and 100.

[10] Audie Klotz, *Norms in International Relations: The Struggle Against Apartheid* (Ithaca: Cornell University Press, 1995), p. 14.

[11] Ibid.   [12] Ibid.

[13] Christopher Gelpi, "Crime and Punishment: The Role of Norms in Crisis Bargaining," *American Political Science Review* 91 (June 1997), 339–360: 339.

[14] Raymond, "Problems and Prospects in the Study of International Norms," p. 207.

[15] Ibid., p. 208.

[16] Martha Finnemore and Kathryn Sikkink, "International Norm Dynamics and Political Change," *International Organization* 52 (Autumn 1998), 887–917: 891 and 894.

to the role of other ideas (conventions) or knowledge and institutions.[17] In this sense, "norms" are not unique. Non-normative beliefs (e.g. scientific propositions), habits, and rules – indeed any form of common knowledge and agreed upon procedures – may help actors coordinate or limit the range of choice. Because there is nothing unique about this aspect of normative beliefs, scholars ought to take care not to confuse the *possible* coordinating effects of normative beliefs (that are similar to the effects of any form of common knowledge and focal-point agreements) with the unique prescriptive characteristic of *normative* beliefs.

Both behavioral norms and normative beliefs usually have a traceable history; actors will often be able to say when and sometimes why they or their ancestors began a practice and why they thought a normative belief was right. But behavioral norms may also be arbitrary. In other words, there may be no good ethical or practical reasons for a behavioral norm, yet, for some accidental reason, the practice is accepted and ex-pected. In this situation, no one seems to have what might be recognized as an ethical or logical argument to justify the practice, though *post-hoc* rationalizations for the practice might spring to mind if practitioners are pressed. Finally, in the sense that dominant practices and expectations do these things (normalize, decrease uncertainty, shape interests and the scope of consideration, and legitimize behaviors), they are "struc-tural" features of international and domestic politics. In other words, behavioral norms and normative beliefs are both constitutive (meaning making) and regulative (constraining).

An illustration may help clarify the distinctions and overlaps between behavioral norms and normative beliefs. It is possible to view complex international practices, such as warmaking, colonialism, diplomacy, and trade in certain contexts, as behavioral norms. These complex prac-tices are composed of other behavioral norms (regular behaviors) and normative beliefs. For instance, war is composed of several behavioral norms regarding violence that leads to injury, mutilation, and death. And within the conceptual domain of these particular practices, there are normative beliefs – prescriptions about how injury, mutilation, and death ought to (or ought not to) come about, that rest on other normative beliefs about what it is good and right to do. Since the widespread adop-tion of the convention on chemical weapons in the twentieth century, as

---

[17] Institutionalists stress the role that institutions and ideas can play in reducing trans-action costs, providing focal points, and decreasing uncertainty among rational actors. Also see Gary Geortz, *Contexts of International Politics* (Cambridge: Cambridge University Press, 1994), p. 98.

Richard Price and Nina Tannenwald argue, the use of chemical weapons in war has been seen as something that ought not to be done, according to international law, while other methods of injury, mutilation, and death, such as machine guns, remain more or less acceptable and expected or normal.[18] But even the acceptability of methods in war is constrained by the pre-existing web of normative beliefs in a culture – such as the belief that it is not right to kill prisoners of war or non-combatants.[19]

Types and variations of behavioral norms and normative beliefs

As Raymond notes, "Over time all norms vary with regard to communal meaning, perlocutionary effect, degree of internalization, extent of conformity, patterns of deviance, and so on."[20] It is worthwhile saying more about the variations in behavioral norms, normative beliefs, and the possible relationships between behavioral norms and normative beliefs. Normative beliefs, as propositions about what it is good and right to do, vary along several dimensions: basic type; scope of obligation; specificity; and links to other normative beliefs. Behavioral norms vary in terms of prevalence, degree of institutionalization, links to normative beliefs or normativity, and the costs of non-compliance.

It is possible to distinguish four basic types of normative belief: substantive (more commonly called regulative norms), procedural, constitutive, and meta-normative.[21] Substantive normative beliefs define and prescribe what qualities and behaviors are good, for example the belief that truth is good. Procedural normative beliefs prescribe how to decide what is good and right, for example that democratic or republican procedures ought to be used. Constitutive normative beliefs are about the characteristics of a good social entity or what makes individuals or social groups count as something.[22] For example, those who follow the particular prescriptions entailed by the normative belief in question are ("good") soldiers, states, allies, and so on. Those

---

[18] See Richard Price and Nina Tannenwald, "Norms and Deterrence: The Nuclear and Chemical Weapons Taboos," in Peter J. Katzenstein, ed., *The Culture of National Security: Norms and Identity in World Politics* (New York: Columbia University Press, 1996), pp. 114–152.
[19] On the constraining effects of culture see Tracy Isaacs, "Cultural Context and Moral Responsibility," *Ethics* 107 (July 1997), 760–684.
[20] Raymond, "Problems and Prospects in the Study of International Norms," p. 235.
[21] It is more common to distinguish regulative and constitutive norms.
[22] These are sometimes related to identity beliefs.

who do not follow the particular normative prescriptions may cease to be considered soldiers, states, and allies. Meta-normative beliefs prescribe that normative prescriptions ought to be followed. The distinction between substantive normative beliefs and meta-normative beliefs is that "Moral codes and various moral taboos have a connection with custom . . . But rules such as that promises ought to be kept, or that it is immoral to tell a lie seem to be rather different . . . Their existence cannot truly be said to depend on historical contingencies . . . the rule such that promises ought to be kept presupposes the existence of the *institution* of promising . . . [that] need not be universal."[23] Some normative beliefs – such as those promoting truth-telling, promise-keeping, treating like cases alike, and following legitimate rules – are *meta-normative* since they are prescriptions that are intended to guide norm following in general and help create an intersubjective expectation that normative prescriptions will be followed because it is good to do so.

Despite the existence of meta-normative beliefs, prescriptions are not always followed. There are context specific beliefs about the scope of obligations arising from a particular normative belief about when to behave in the ways prescribed by the normative belief. Universal normative beliefs define the scope of obligation such that *everyone* must *all the time* without exception, follow the prescription (in international law, the principle of *jus cogens* where absolutely no derogation is permissible). Role normative beliefs limit the scope of obligation to those whose formal or informal role it is to comply with the prescribed or proscribed behavior. For example, neutral states are expected to behave one way and not another, while allies can be expected to follow different prescriptions. Normative beliefs are also often conditional; the scope of obligation depends on the conditions of the specific situation. Under conditional normative beliefs, for example, actors ought to follow the prescription if there is time, if they are able, if doing so does not conflict with another specified normative belief, such as not causing greater harm, and so on. For example, food-rich states ought to contribute to famine relief while food-poor states are not expected to do so.

Normative beliefs also vary by the explicitness of their specification. The normative belief may be vague in terms of the scope of the

---

[23] Georg Henrik von Wright, "Norms, Truth and Logic," in Georg Henrik von Wright, *Practical Reason* (Ithaca: Cornell University Press 1983), pp. 130–209: 138.

obligation, or the belief may be well specified, with the conditions for its scope of obligation well elaborated. Further, the articulated justification (persuasive reasons to hold the belief) for the normative belief may be vague or explicit.

Finally, normative beliefs also vary by the density of their relation to other normative beliefs. Normative beliefs are articulated in laws, myths, and religious doctrines and they rarely stand alone. Behavioral norms and prescriptive normative statements are linked to, and embedded in, wider webs of normative beliefs and behavioral norms which are in turn embedded in wider social institutions and networks of beliefs or culture.

Like normative beliefs, behavioral norms vary in their prevalence, degree of institutionalization, normativity, and the cost of non-compliance. By definition, behavioral norms are a dominant practice. Publicity about behavioral norms becomes common knowledge and may have the property of easing coordination. But several behaviors may be possible in different situations, and the prevalence of a behavior may vary from always, to frequently or infrequently practiced. For example, in the last several centuries most, though not all, states have established organized armed forces. In cases where a practice is infrequent, it ought not to be considered a behavioral norm.

The degree of institutionalization of behavioral norms is the extent to which routines and procedures that facilitate or constitute the performance of the behavioral norm are built into standard operating procedures and regulations of organizations that function in the relevant issue area. Institutionalization is how normative beliefs are both internalized within organizations – as they are incorporated into practices, policies, and rules – and externalized, as rules are adopted by other bodies. Highly institutionalized norms will be associated with rules about when to engage in practices that facilitate the conduct of the behavioral norm and actors will consciously practice the behavioral norm and devise routines for its execution. Moreover, institutionalization can contribute to changing actors understandings of their interests; as Kathryn Sikkink has argued about human rights norms in US policy, "ideas embodied in institutions created bureaucratic interests based on the perpetuation of those policies."[24]

---

[24] Kathryn Sikkink, "The Power of Principled Ideas: Human Rights Policies in the United States and Western Europe," in Judith Goldstein and Robert Keohane, eds., *Ideas and Foreign Policy: Beliefs, Institutions, and Political Change* (Ithaca: Cornell University Press, 1993), pp. 139–170: 167. Sikkink also stresses the importance of NGOs.

Table 2.1 *Variations in normative beliefs and behavioral norms*

Normative Beliefs	Behavioral Norms
Type	*Prevalence*
substantive	infrequent
procedural	frequent
constitutive	invariable
meta-normative	
Scope of Obligation	*Degree of Institutionalization*
universal	none
role	some
conditional	highly
Specificity	*Normativity*
vague or explicit scope	none: habit
vague or explicit justification	weak/implicit
	strong/explicit w/ sanctions if violated
Links to Other Normative Beliefs	*Costs of Non-compliance*
few	low
many	high

Behavioral norms may also vary in terms of "normativity," the articulation of justificatory links between behavioral norms and normative beliefs. Sovereignty, for example, has high normativity. Habits are the behavioral norms that are not at all explicitly and consciously linked to normative beliefs. Those behavioral norms that are linked may be tied strongly and explicitly, or weakly and implicitly, to normative beliefs. Violations of behavioral norms that are strongly linked to normative beliefs are probably more likely to be sanctioned than those with weak or non-existent links to normative beliefs. It may still be costly to violate norms which are not strongly linked to normative beliefs, but the costs will be due more to the loss of efficiency and ease of coordination.

Alternative theories of norms and normative belief

There are several ways to think about the possible causal relationships between normative beliefs and behavioral norms: normative beliefs as irrelevant; normative beliefs and behavioral norms as rational; and normative beliefs as part of reason or elements of ethical argument.

Some realist theories of international relations argue, as noted above, that normative beliefs are causally irrelevant. As Hans Morgenthau claimed, "A realist theory of international politics will also avoid the other popular fallacy of equating the foreign policies of a states- man with his philosophic or political sympathies, deducing the for- mer from the latter."[25] Thus, Morgenthau argued, the role of nor- mative beliefs may be simply embodied in the tendency of foreign policy decisionmakers to think that their own views are right. Mor- genthau implored scholars of foreign policy to avoid making that mistake. "To know that nations are subject to the moral law is one thing, while to pretend to know with certainty what is good and evil in relations between nations is quite another...On the other hand, it is exactly the concept of interest defined as power that saves us both from that moral excess and that political folly."[26] If normative content does matter, realists see the role of ethical argu- ments as only "instrumental," as "moral justification for the power quest."[27] Realists answer the question of the origins of behavioral norms with the argument that behavioral norms are contingent, accidental historical phenomena that are maintained by habit and ex- tended by custom or further accident. Or, as E.H. Carr argued, morality reflects the interests of the dominant power.

The second view, that "norms" are rational and functional, is ar- ticulated by both realist and liberal international relations theorists. In this view, the causal force of normative beliefs, and actors' re- ceptivity to particular ethical arguments, derives from the extent to which "norms" are seen as customary. Several scholars take this approach. As Keohane argues, international regimes "perform the function of reducing uncertainty and risk by linking discrete is- sues to one another and by improving the quantity and quality of information available to participants."[28] As Robert Axelrod argues, norms may reduce uncertainty and facilitate coordination by pro- viding a focal point.[29] Similarly, Christopher Gelpi suggests that

[25] Hans J. Morgenthau, *Politics Among Nations: The Struggle for Power and Peace* sixth edition, revised by Kenneth W. Thompson (New York: Knopf, 1985), p. 6.
[26] Ibid., p. 13.
[27] Nicholas Spykman, quoted in Jack Donnelly, "Twentieth Century Realism," in Terry Nardin and David R. Mapel, eds., *Traditions of International Ethics* (Cambridge: Cambridge University Press, 1992), pp. 85–111: 94.
[28] Keohane, "The Demand for International Regimes," p. 162.
[29] Robert Axelrod, "An Evolutionary Approach to Norms," *American Political Science Review* 80 (December 1986), 1095–1111.

"Norms are enabling when they serve as focal points, which I label normative referents, to help states coordinate their behavior. In this case, norms alter state behavior by helping them interpret the behavior of other states in an uncertain international environment."[30] Conceptual confusion – confounding prescriptive norms with common knowledge effects and dominant behaviors – is evident in these statements. This has the effect that, rather like the first "normative beliefs are irrelevant" view, the rational and functional explanation for the causal force of "norms" boils down to the position that specific qualities of perceived goodness are irrelevant. This is because the causal force of norms, under this hypothesis, derives from their ability to decrease uncertainty and coordination costs by, for example, providing focal points.

Another version of the rational norms perspective is an evolutionary/ practical account of behavioral norms, such as proposed by Robert Axelrod, where "what works well for a player is more likely to be used again while what turns out poorly is more likely to be discarded."[31] There is some randomness, but the emphasis is on functionality and trial and error processes. More efficient "norms" triumph; states do what works and "the analysis of what is chosen at any specific time is based upon an operationalization of the idea that effective strategies are more likely to be retained than ineffective strategies."[32] Ann Florini, who argues that norms are like genes, suggests that the "reproductive success" of "norms" depends on natural selection processes. First, "whether a norm becomes prominent enough in the norm pool to gain a foothold"; second, "how well it interacts with other prevailing norms with which it is not in competition, that is the 'normative environment'"; and finally, the "external environmental conditions" such as the distribution of power and the availability of human or natural resources.[33]

Rational norms theorists also sometimes argue, consistent with the norms are irrelevant school, that behavioral norms and normative beliefs (to the extent that there are normative beliefs) are imposed and maintained by hegemons to suit their material interests.[34] The reason the hegemon prefers one norm over another is not a normative belief in the goodness or rightness of the behavior. Under this hypothesis, the causal

---

[30] Gelpi, "Crime and Punishment," p. 340.
[31] Axelrod, "An Evolutionary Approach to Norms," p. 1097.   [32] Ibid.
[33] Ann Florini, "The Evolution of International Norms," *International Studies Quarterly* 40 (September 1996), 363–389: 374.
[34] For instance suggested by Axelrod in "An Evolutionary Approach to Norms" p. 1108 and Carr, *The Thirty Years Crisis*.

force behind behavioral norms is rational material interests and the fact that the behavior has become a norm is only a testament to the power of the hegemon to impose the desired behavior and impose costs on transgressors. The norm simply suits the "interests" of a hegemon and the "preferences of more powerful actors will be accorded greater weight."[35]

In sum, according to these rational/functional accounts of behavioral norms, the adoption of norms is a rational activity which facilitates coordination and reduces uncertainty for many, or at least for one powerful actor. Normative content is basically irrelevant – normative beliefs are epiphenomenal; any ethical meaning is essentially a gloss on material interests. Particular behavioral norms are preferred because they provide stability rather than the instability of having no expectations; they are "devices to overcome the barriers to more efficient coordination" in an anarchic environment.[36] Actors keep their normative commitments because of the "costs that international audiences (i.e. other governments) may impose on state leaders if they do not keep their commitments."[37] But, as the discussion above should have made clear, any common knowledge and agreement on a convention could be "rational." The specifically *normative* content would seem to be irrelevant in the rational actor account of "norms." Thus, for the most part, the rational interest account boils down to the position that normative beliefs are irrelevant/epiphenomenal.

A third view is that the prescriptive content of normative beliefs matters in how one behavioral norm is chosen over another.[38] For example, Robert Jackson argues that normative ideas "that originated in the West were a crucial factor in the abolition of colonialism and the institution of self-determination in the greater part of the non-Western world . . ."[39] Ethan Nadelmann argues that "norms emerge and are promoted because they reflect not only the economic and security interests of dominant members of international society but also

[35] Keohane, "The Demand for International Regimes," p. 146.
[36] Ibid., p. 151.   [37] Gelpi, "Crime and Punishment," p. 341.
[38] Klotz, *Norms in International Relations*; Gary Geortz and Paul F. Diehl, "Toward a Theory of International Norms: Some Conceptual and Measurement Issues," *Journal of Conflict Resolution* 36 (December 1992), 634–666; David Welch, *Justice and the Genesis of War* (Cambridge: Cambridge University Press, 1993); Martha Finnemore, "Norms, Culture, and World Politics: Insights from Sociology's Institutionalism," *International Organization* 50, (Spring 1996), 325–347. An analysis of how normative beliefs affect politics is of course different from making the claim that world politics ought to be concerned with ethics.
[39] Robert H. Jackson, "The Weight of Ideas in Decolonization: Normative Change in International Relations," in Goldstein and Keohane, eds., *Ideas and Foreign Policy*, pp. 111–138: 112.

their moral interests and emotional dispositions."[40] This suggests that for new behavioral norms to become dominant, the most powerful actors must find that their economic and security interests must coincide with the proposed new norm, or at least not be counter to it, and that they may also believe the prescription is good on substantive normative grounds.[41]

My arguments are closest to this school. Yet these accounts of behavioral norm change are often vague about the precise relationship they suggest between behavioral norms and normative belief. For instance, John Mueller suggests that norms are "sold" by norm entrepreneurs, that is, people who peddle norms. Mueller argues that "people sort through this huge market of ideas and prove receptive to some while remaining immune to others."[42] But in Mueller's account one has to explain receptivity, that is, the conditions under which people and states "buy" a particular norm and internalize certain normative beliefs and not others. Nadelmann suggests an answer. "This is not to argue, I should stress, that 'states' or governments hold moral views; rather, the capacity of particular moral arguments to influence government policies, particularly foreign policies, stems from the political influence of domestic and transnational moral entrepreneurs as well as that of powerful individual advocates within the government."[43] Again, after a certain point, the particular normative content of "norms" doesn't seem to matter so

[40] Ethan A. Nadelmann, "Global Prohibition Regimes: The Evolution of Norms in International Society," *International Organization* 44 (Autumn 1990), 479–526: 524.
[41] *Both* argument and imposition are necessary unless actors share a common normative framework. This applies to both "good" and "bad" norms. In other words, "bad" normative beliefs like unequal treatment of women or persons of a different race must be imposed by force because those who are treated unequally will not submit without resistance. Similarly, those who hold "good" normative beliefs may not be able to persuade the holders of "bad" norms to change their practices without compulsion.
[42] For example, John Mueller, "Changing Attitudes Towards War: The Impact of the First World War," *British Journal of Political Science* 21 (January 1991), 1–28: 25–27. Mueller may have been the first to use the phrase "norm entrepreneurs." Mueller does not specify how norm entrepreneurs succeed, only that their work is difficult. Robert Keohane uses the phrase "political entrepreneur" to describe those who promote regimes, "usually ... a government." Keohane, "The Demand for International Regimes," p. 155. Laffey and Weldes argue that describing "entrepreneurs" and the "marketing" of ideas suggests a metaphor of ideas as commodities. They propose instead to use the metaphor of ideas as capital. Mark Laffey and Jutta Weldes, "Beyond Belief: Ideas and Symbolic Technologies in the Study of International Relations," *European Journal of International Relations* 3 (1997), 193–237.
[43] Nadelmann, "Global Prohibition Regimes," p. 483. Similarly, Wapner credits transnational interest groups with promoting "ecological sensibility." Paul Wapner, "Politics Beyond the State: Environmental Activism and World Civic Politics," *World Politics* 47 (April 1995), 311–340.

much for either Mueller or Nadelmann. "Morality" among states boils down to power and "political" influence inside them; it is difficult in these accounts to say why one normative belief and a practice entailed by it, was preferred over another, only that one side had more political power than another.[44]

Martha Finnemore and Kathryn Sikkink propose an account of the "life-cycle" of "norms" (although they seem to be eliding the distinction and possible causal connection between prescriptive normative beliefs and behavioral norms). The first stage in their life-cycle, when norm entrepreneurs "persuade" others to embrace their norm, is "norm emergence." The second stage in the life-cycle, "norm acceptance," is a "cascade" characterized by a "dynamic of imitation as norm leaders attempt to socialize other states to become norm followers." In this stage, norm cascades are facilitated by "a combination of pressure for conformity, desire to enhance international legitimation, and the desire of state leaders to enhance their self-esteem." The third stage, "internalization" of the norm, is when "norms acquire a taken-for-granted quality and are no longer a matter of broad public debate." They further suggest that though there is no guarantee that a norm will inevitably go through the process they describe, in those cases where norms cascade and are internalized, they "may eventually become the prevailing standard of appropriateness against which new norms emerge and compete for support."[45] Finnemore and Sikkink may be on the right track, but normative content has faded from view with the emphasis on stages.

What is interesting and important about these accounts is their assertion that the *prescriptive* normative content of "norms" is, more or less, causally important in changing dominant practices. In general terms, I agree with these scholars but fear that an account which insufficiently explains the process of persuasion, and fails to show how the prescriptive content of normative beliefs is causally important, will not itself be persuasive.

Thus, I give an explicitly normative account of behavioral norm change. Certainly the adoption of behavioral norms could be accidental or rational, but it is also often a consequence of people being convinced

---

[44] For example, see Chaim D. Kaufmann and Robert A. Pape, "Explaining Costly International Moral Action: Britain's Sixty-year Campaign Against the Atlantic Slave Trade," *International Organization* 53 (Autumn 1999), 631–668.

[45] Finnemore and Sikkink, "International Norm Dynamics and Political Change," p. 895. The life-cycle metaphor also suggests scholars of "norms" ought to try to account for the decline, metamorphosis, and death of both behavioral norms and normative beliefs, as well as the emergence, acceptance, and internalization of norms.

by persuasive ethical arguments. Specifically, some behavioral norms, namely those with a normative content, are developed and adopted because they reflect or are implied by normative beliefs; these behavioral norms are adopted over other possible practices because the advocates of the norm made persuasive ethical arguments that appealed to normative beliefs. It is not to say that the normative beliefs are in "reality" good or true or will always be seen as so; only that actors, when they make ethical arguments, are trying to convince others that the beliefs they champion are good and the practices that necessarily follow from subscribing to those beliefs are good. What makes an ethical argument persuasive? How is it seen to be good? In this ethical argument explanation of the adoption of normative beliefs and behavioral norms, interpretation and meaning are a central element of a theory of behavioral norm and normative belief change.

Ethical arguments, like other kinds of argument, are ubiquitous in world politics. Advocates for new behavioral norms certainly engage in horse-trading, propaganda, and coercion, but they also engage in debate and argument. This is so even in the case of inter-state war. As Michael Walzer argues: "whether or not its specific terminology is adopted, just war theory has always played a part in official arguments about war. No political leader can send soldiers into battle, asking them to risk their lives and to kill other people, without assuring them that their cause is just – and that of their enemies unjust."[46] Successful ethical arguments set the terms of debate, even to the point where people who are moved by other reasons, for instance by emotions or practical considerations, feel compelled to make ethical arguments. Walzer recognizes this. "And if the [just war] theory is used, it is also misused. Sometimes it serves only to determine what lies our leaders tell, the complex structure of their hypocrisy, the tribute that vice pays to virtue."[47] The question, then, is understanding the ethical arguments that people make and the force those arguments have to persuade.

Ethical arguments
Maintaining beliefs and practices

Normative beliefs are the ethical arguments we already hold as true. When people make ethical arguments they are first using normative

[46] Walzer, "Preface to the Second Edition," *Just and Unjust Wars*, pp. xi–xii.
[47] Ibid., p. xii.

beliefs in an attempt to get others to believe as they believe, and then often trying to get them to act in ways that are implied by or entailed in holding such a belief. Ethical arguments are used in three contexts: to uphold existing practices, to extend normative prescriptions to new areas of practice, or to change dominant practices and normative beliefs.

When advocates use them to uphold practices, ethical arguments normalize, legitimize, and also support and reproduce the existing cognitive, political, and institutional order. Specifically, normative beliefs can be enunciated in prescriptive statements that indicate what is normal. In other words, normative beliefs can "normalize" – make certain actions and actors appear to be "normal" (and often unquestioned) and others "abnormal."[48] Even practices that are not done by the majority of a population may be considered "normal" if they fit into the dominant framework or web of normative beliefs. If actions can be related to a normative belief, they can be seen as legitimate more than actions which are not prescribed by a normative belief. Ethical arguments also legitimize behaviors by giving good reasons for a practice. Ethical arguments that we already believe thus support and reproduce a larger cognitive world order (because people believe the normative prescriptions and ethical arguments), and help maintain relations of power as people act in accordance with the prescriptions implied by the dominant normative beliefs.[49] Ethical arguments that are used to uphold dominant practices are institutionalized: the routines or standard operating procedures of an institutional practice performed for normative reasons being justified by ethical arguments. Much of the work done by ethical arguments occurs in the context of upholding existing or dominant practices and remains part of the background, taken for granted.

Advocates may also use ethical arguments to apply or extend existing normative beliefs (rules, laws, standards of conduct) to new situations or problems. To apply existing normative beliefs in new contexts, one must win the contest of representations and successfully frame a situation as an instance covered by the existing normative belief. The argument may be extended by an analogy that takes this form: We do X in certain situations because it is good; this other case, or new situation, is very much like or the same as the situations where we do X: therefore we must

[48] See for example Geortz, *Contexts of International Politics*, p. 27.
[49] Ethical arguments are a discursive strategy in a Foucauldian sense although Foucault did not emphasize the process of argument in the way I do here. Michel Foucault, *The Archaeology of Knowledge and the Discourse on Language* (New York: Pantheon, 1972).

extend the practice of X to this new situation if we want to do good.[50] This use of ethical arguments to extend practices is perhaps the most common form of such arguments where we are conscious that ethical arguments are being made. One should not assume, however, that the attempt to apply and extend ethical arguments to a situation is always genuine. One of the best ways to make something "bad" look "good" is to say that it is so. "Hypocrisy is rife in wartime discourse, because it is especially important at such a time to appear to be in the right. It is not only that the moral stakes are high; the hypocrite may not understand that; more crucially, his actions will be judged by other people who are not hypocrites, and whose judgments will affect their policies toward him."[51]

Ethical arguments and normative change

Actors use ethical arguments when they try to change dominant normative beliefs and behaviors. Advocates use prescriptive normative beliefs in arguments to "normalize" and proclaim the abnormal, to legitimize or delegitimize their actions and the actions of others, and to influence the construction of interests and the sense of possibility in decisionmaking. Challenging old normative beliefs and creating new normative-ethical standards is more difficult, however, than maintaining old practices or applying dominant normative beliefs to new situations.[52] Advocates of a new normative belief or new behavioral norm, even one within the bounds of the dominant belief system, must persuade others that their position is superior on ethical grounds, or that ethical grounds are outweighed by or, conversely, trump other considerations.[53]

In the role of resisting dominant (behavioral) norms or establishing new norms, ethical arguments can be used to denormalize (that is

---

[50] For example, after World War II, it became increasingly clear to the majority of white males in the U.S. that the "norm" that all "men" were created equal clashed with the unequal treatment and political rights of minorities and women. Those who advocated change deployed arguments that rested on already accepted arguments of equality and claimed that therefore political rights must be extended.

[51] Walzer, *Just and Unjust Wars*, p. 20.

[52] There are parallels here to Thomas Kuhn's understanding of scientific revolutions. Thomas Kuhn, *The Structure of Scientific Revolutions* (Chicago: University of Chicago Press, 1962).

[53] If someone argues only on practical grounds, they argue within the dominant discourse though practical arguments may also be deployed by those who wish to win on ethical grounds. Thus, ethical arguments may be given as purely ethical arguments, but they are often linked to practical, identity, philosophical, and scientific arguments.

defamiliarize or make strange) the dominant norm. Ethical arguments may also delegitimize a dominant norm, showing how it is wrong and ought to be questioned. If successful, denormalization and delegitimation deconstruct the existing discourse. Next, ethical arguments offer a reconstruction. Those making an ethical argument may pose alternative prescriptions and suggest that an alternative order is conceivable, desirable, and possible, and this may have the effect of changing actors' conceptions of their interest. And persuasive ethical arguments may help overturn the status quo as the powerful who uphold the dominant norm can no longer convince others to abide by or impose the old norm. Even hegemons must convince their henchmen that they must uphold an existing order or impose a new one. If they can't do that, their political support may wane. Finally, new normative beliefs, and the practices implied by holding such beliefs, may be institutionalized. In sum, world politics is always already based on ethical argument. Note however that arguments do not necessarily proceed in the orderly way I have laid out: reconstruction may precede and indeed cause deconstruction and not all may be convinced at once, with significant portions of the population coming to change their beliefs only after the social world has been reorganized.[54]

Deconstruction of dominant beliefs and practices

Denormalization. Widespread and traditional practices are familiar and seem normal to the majority, and there is little reason to question those beliefs and behavioral norms as long as they are considered normal and good. For such practices to be changed, they must be questioned. Why were actors engaged in these particular practices? Why believe one thing or engage in one particular behavior and not another? Unquestioned practices are normal, while "normal" practices are unquestioned. Simply asking "why?" may cause participants in a system to question dominant beliefs and behaviors, while posing an alternative may also defamiliarize or denormalize the dominant practice, making it seem strange. Symbolic arguments, especially analogies, are also often successful strategies for denormalizing practices. Beliefs and practices that are successfully denormalized will be seen as one of many possible options or may even seem abnormal. Denormalization is thus actually a meta-argument, where what is at stake is the framing of a practice as

---

[54] As utopians know, simply asserting an alternative may denormalize and delegitimize the dominant practice.

normal or abnormal. The move to denormalize is successful to the extent that previously taken-for-granted practices are no longer seen as givens. If denormalization succeeds, the framing of a dominant practice shifts from unquestionable and unproblematic to questionable and problematic. Without denormalization, it is unlikely that delegitimation will be successful.

Delegitimation. Legitimate actions are done for a good reason (as opposed to being performed out of habit or fear of punishment). Legitimate commands are developed using the right process, given under the direction of the appropriate authority, and made for a good reason. Ethical arguments may upset or alter the perceptions of legitimacy associated with a dominant practice by showing a disjuncture or hypocrisy between present behavior and an already existing normative belief. In this case, what once seemed acceptable is no longer acceptable on the basis of arguments that mobilize logic, empathy, or analogy to question the legitimacy of a practice. "The exposure of hypocrisy is certainly the most ordinary, it may also be the most important form of moral criticism."[55] Delegitimized practices can no longer pass the test of being done for good reason because we no longer think the reason is good, or at least, good enough. Criticism of the action or behavior may shade over into an implicit or explicit critique of the institution conducting the behavior, prompting the sorts of legitimation crises described above. Linkages of non-dominant prescriptive norms to already established dominant beliefs and norms may help boost the legitimacy of new practices. As Finnemore and Sikkink suggest, the "construction of cognitive frames is an essential component of norm entrepreneurs' political strategies, since, when they are successful, the new frames resonate with broader public understandings and are adopted as new ways of talking about and understanding issues."[56]

Denormalization and delegitimation are crucial meta-arguments: without this initial step of deconstruction, subsequent steps in the ethical argument, especially the posing of alternatives, are unlikely to be understood or successful. Denormalization and delegitimation, together serve to deconstruct the dominant beliefs, and throw into question previously unquestioned behaviors. Dominant normative beliefs and the practices associated with them are unlikely to be abandoned unless and

[55] Walzer, *Just and Unjust Wars*, p. xxix.
[56] Finnemore and Sikkink, "Norm Dynamics and Political Change," p. 897.

until actors also see new possibilities for action and understand their moral interests in new ways. Deconstruction is crucial in this regard because it creates a moral space, an opening, through which new beliefs and arguments may be heard.

Reconstruction

Changing conceptions of possibility and interests. By positing a new normative belief and advocating new behaviors, ethical arguments may change actors' conceptions of what is possible or what is desirable. As some new good is seen as possible or more urgent, ethical arguments can even result in actors reframing their "interests," or the order of their preferences. This is the power of utopian or visionary narratives: utopians not only critique the normality and legitimacy of the present order by contrasting it with a "better place," they are obviously articulating the particulars of the better place and, they hope, making that better place seem both desirable and achievable. New normative beliefs are also more likely to win acceptance if advocates succeed in changing actors' conceptions of their interests (what they want or believe they need). An interest is formulated when agents believe in the value or goodness of something.[57] For example, in the early 1990s, promoting democratization was seen as a good, and (re-)defined as a U.S. interest that would structure foreign policy. The order of preferences would be changed by adopting this normative belief if promoting democracy became more important than promoting free trade and profits.

Political and institutional change

Changing capabilities. Change can certainly occur in the absence of normative consensus; not everyone has to be persuaded by ethical arguments for the influence of ethical arguments to be felt.[58] Ethical arguments that have persuaded enough people that a dominant practice is strange, illegitimate, and undesirable can mobilize groups to take strategic action to change the dominant practice. Normatively based and motivated resistance, when focused in the political arena in the form of organized

---

[57] As Finnemore and Sikkink argue, "many norm entrepreneurs do not so much act against their interests as they act in accordance with a redefined understanding of their interests." Ibid., p. 898.

[58] Scholars of social movements have already observed this. See for instance, Jeffrey Knopf, *Domestic Society and International Cooperation: The Impact of Protest on U.S. Arms Control Policy* (Cambridge: Cambridge University Press, 1998).

boycotts, sanctions, op-eds, electoral campaigns, legislation, court challenges, and lobbying, may alter the capacity of the actors who held the dominant normative belief to carry out the practices associated with that belief as they change the balance of belief within a population. Those who take strategic action based on normative commitments may be particularly committed, dedicated to long-term, seemingly losing, struggles with dominant institutions.[59] And as Keck and Sikkink argue, some issues may be easier than others to mobilize around: "Issues that involve ideas about right and wrong are amenable to advocacy networking because they arouse strong feelings . . . and infuse meaning into these volunteer activities."[60] Indeed, ethical arguments that resonate with the emotions and pre-existing normative commitments of activists are probably more likely to mobilize activists to take the sort of sustained strategic action that can change the balance of capabilities within states and across borders.

Those who hold the dominant normative belief may be disabled by a strategically powerful minority who hold a different belief, or the balance of those holding new normative beliefs may shift so that those who were once in the majority become a minority. Ethical argument explanations do not, therefore, completely replace accounts of change based on the rational political action of politicians who, for instance, want to remain in office by pleasing the voters; rather, an ethical argument explanation can show why one behavior, and not another, pleased the voters. Pragmatic reformers, discussed at greater length below, may thus initiate reforms sought by those motivated by normative concerns, just so that they can maintain their position.

Further, piecemeal reforms may alter the system, and the capabilities of actors within it, in ways that either normatively or pragmatically motivated reformers do not anticipate and perhaps never intended. As Robert Jervis powerfully argues, this is because of interconnections within social systems which mean that "many effects are indirect, mediated and delayed."[61] Thus, relatively small changes may avalanche into large, unanticipated, openings for reform, further argument, and

---

[59] Finnemore and Sikkink rightly focus on the affective and principled components of those who deploy ethical arguments: "it is very difficult to explain the motivations of norm entrepreneurs without reference to empathy, altruism, and ideational commitment." Ibid., p. 898.

[60] Margaret E. Keck and Kathryn Sikkink, *Activists Beyond Borders: Advocacy Networks in Transnational Politics* (Ithaca: Cornell University Press, 1998), p. 26.

[61] Robert Jervis, *System Effects: Complexity in Social and Political Life* (Princeton: Princeton University Press, 1997), p. 29.

institutionalization. For example, ending slavery decreased the profitability of colonialism and the power of colonial actors to press for their interests in the metropole. Weakened colonizers could not resist the efforts of colonial reformers, who, for example, pushed for improvements in political representation and working conditions within colonies, which in turn enabled the colonized to more effectively resist the colonizer and push for greater reform.

Institutionalization. Once new prescriptive normative beliefs have been accepted, they may become institutionalized in a two-step process. First, practices designed to enact and ultimately realize the normative belief are articulated and measures of successful compliance are devised. The beliefs are instantiated in rules, laws, regulations, standard operating procedures, or other kinds of expected practices within institutions; they become practical and measurable. Second, compliance is monitored by administrators or bureaucrats, and even outsiders, to ensure that the normative prescriptions implied by the normative beliefs are followed. Actors become accountable. Institutionalization may create new structures of political opportunity for actors who would seek to expand the scope of application for newly accepted normative beliefs.[62] For example, normative beliefs about the treatment of slave and then forced labor in colonies was gradually institutionalized in domestic law and international organizations in the nineteenth and twentieth centuries, eventually leading to the outlawing of both practices.[63]

Institutionalization of normative beliefs both requires some base level of consensus and, in turn, usually entails even more ethical and practical (perhaps even scientific and identity) arguments as actors choose among options for realizing the prescriptive normative beliefs they have adopted. Failures at institutionalization or implementation may prompt a reevaluation of underlying normative beliefs and ethical arguments.

[62] Doug McAdam, John D. McCarthy, Mayer N. Zald, eds., *Comparative Perspectives on Social Movements: Political Opportunity, Mobilizing Structures, and Cultural Framings* (Cambridge: Cambridge University Press, 1996).

[63] Several scholars have rightly stressed the importance of institutionalization. See for example, Edward Weisband, "Discursive Multilateralism: Global Benchmarks, Shame, and Learning in the ILO Labour Standards Monitoring Regime," *International Studies Quarterly* 44 (December 2000), 643–666; Sikkink, "The Power of Principled Ideas"; Ronald Jepperson, Alexander Wendt, and Peter J. Katzenstein, "Norms, Identity, and Culture in National Security," in Katzenstein, ed., *The Culture of National Security*, pp. 33–75; and Finnemore and Sikkink, "Norm Dynamics and Political Change."

Once institutionalized, or made practical by diplomats, lawyers, bureaucrats, and administrators, normative beliefs are implemented as part of the taken for granted of international politics, further changing the structure of world politics. The articulation of expectations in the form of benchmarks and timetables, and the establishment of new routines and standard operating procedures allows other ethical arguments to be bootstrapped into the system, accelerating the dynamic of ethical argument and normative change. United Nations treaty making on self-determination is one example of the process and consequences of institutionalization by the making of international agreements:

> Treaty-making has contributed to the emergence and consolidation of general rules in two ways. Firstly, when the treaty rules were elaborated, Member States of the UN had an opportunity to take a stand, to voice their views and concerns as well as to react to the statements of other governments. All these pronouncements had an impact that went beyond their final result – the treaty provisions – because they stimulated debate and prompted States to adopt positions that were conducive to their gradual acceptance of general standards on the matter. Treaty-making is also relevant in another respect. Once adopted, treaty rules had a significant spin-off effect, in that – together with the monitoring mechanisms overseeing their implementation – they led to contracting States being increasingly amenable to the adoption of the course of action dictated by the rules. As membership in the UN came practically to coincide with membership of the world community and the number of contracting Parties to the Covenants increased at a rapid pace, a growing number of States became bound by international legal standards on self-determination and consequently behaved as required by those standards.[64]

Institutionalization has two important consequences. First, future actions that can be represented as relevant in terms of the new normative standard are judged differently once the new standards, and in particular, the criteria for approval and disapproval – including rewards and sanctions – have been articulated. Once normative beliefs are institutionalized, they are measurable, enabling compliance and non-compliance with the prescriptive standards to be identified

---

[64] Antonio Cassese, *Self-determination of Peoples: A Legal Reappraisal* (Cambridge: Cambridge University Press, 1995), p. 67.

and named.[65] Second, with institutionalization, the table on which all subsequent arguments occurs has changed, with newly institutionalized normative standards becoming the starting point, topoi, for future ethical arguments. Normative belief change that becomes institutionalized may create a path dependent dynamic for subsequent cognitions, emotional reactions, political arguments, and behaviors as "initial choices preclude future options" and make other options available.[66]

In sum, complex prevailing international practices (behavioral norms) may change as a result of a process of ethical argumentation.[67] Ethical arguments that are intended to change dominant beliefs and behavioral norms work by denormalizing/defamiliarizing dominant practices, delegitimizing them, changing actors' conceptions of their interests, and sometimes by changing the capabilities of dominant actors to carry out the practices associated with those norms.[68] Institutionalization articulates and embeds prescriptive normative standards in the

[65] As Finnemore and Sikkink argue, institutionalization "contributes strongly to the possibility of a norm cascade both by clarifying what, exactly, the norm is and what constitutes a violation (often a matter of some disagreement among actors) and by spelling out specific procedures by which norm leaders coordinate disapproval and sanctions for norm breaking." Finnemore and Sikkink, "Norm Dynamics and Political Change," p. 900. Finnemore and Sikkink talk about tipping and threshold points, arguing that tipping occurs after about one-third of states in the system adopt the norm or if crucial or "critical" states adopt the norm. Some states may be crucial, for instance, Britain was crucial in the case of ending the slave trade in the nineteenth century, but as Finnemore and Sikkink acknowledge, tipping does not have a theoretical underpinning. Ibid., p. 901.
[66] Walter Powell, "Expanding the Scope of Institutional Analysis," in Walter Powell and Paul DiMaggio, eds., *The New Institutionalism in Organizational Analysis* (Chicago: University of Chicago, Press, 1991), pp. 183–202: 192.
[67] Finnemore and Sikkink stress socialization arguing that states change their behavior because of emulation, praise, and ridicule. Finnemore and Sikkink, "Norm Dynamics and Political Change," pp. 902–903.
[68] I agree with much of Freidrich Kratochwil's excellent book *Rules, Norms and Decisions*. Like him, I argue that normative beliefs are part of the discourse of actors in international and domestic politics. Kratochwil emphasizes the process of practical and legal reasoning as an antidote to the conception of international politics as anarchic and points out the importance of what might be called meta-norms of argument: fairness, predictability, and reliability. I emphasize the prescriptive, normative *content* of ethical arguments and thus their ability to legitimate, normalize, and so on. I also focus more directly on the source of normative beliefs and ethical arguments by suggesting that normative beliefs and receptivity to ethical arguments are based on the dominant belief systems and identities of actors. Some scholars hypothesize the source of norms, but many who study norms often have little to say about the sources of particular practices and normative beliefs. Exceptions include Martha Finnemore, "Constructing Norms of Humanitarian Intervention," in Katzenstein, ed., *The Culture of National Security*, pp. 153–185; David Halloran Lumsdaine, *Moral Vision in International Politics: The Foreign Aid Regime, 1949–1989* (Princeton: Princeton University Press, 1993); Paul A. Kowert, "The Cognitive Origins of International Norms: Identity Norms and the 1956 Suez Crisis," paper prepared for delivery at the 1994 Annual Meeting of the International Studies Association.

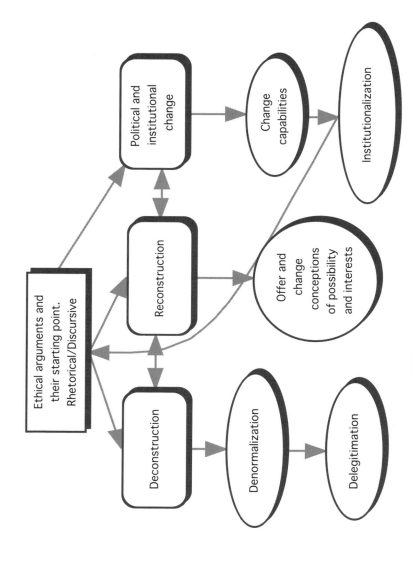

1. Ethical argument and new starting points

routine practices of states, international organizations, and even corporations, which in turn changes the starting point for future perceptions, evaluation, and behavior with reference to the issue area covered by the now dominant normative belief. Institutionalization changes the starting point (topoi) of future arguments. Institutionalization of normative beliefs, adopted because ethical arguments have been successful, changes the course of politics as it opens some paths and closes off others. Figure 1 includes an arrow representing the pathway from institutional change to a new rhetorical starting point.

This argument about ethical argument will be supported if the content and process of arguments follows certain patterns. Dominant behaviors will be challenged with ethical arguments that question the normality, legitimacy, and the conception of interests inherent in the dominant practice. Second, an alternative prescription will be put forward. Third, those who make ethical arguments may seek to mobilize the masses or particularly influential elites (e.g. depending on the issues, members of the media or religious groups) in order to force the dominant practice to change; in so doing, they will alter the capabilities of those who carry out the dominant practice.

Resilience of behavioral norms and normative beliefs

While ethical arguments may be effective in changing normative beliefs and behavioral norms, it is not easy to bring such changes about.[69] Both behavioral norms and normative beliefs are quite resilient for several reasons, some having to do with the normativity of the belief or practice, and others having to do with the difficulty of changing any belief or long-standing practice.

There are several *non*-normative reasons that belief and behavior change are difficult. First, change can be costly, because, to the extent that a convention or prescriptive norm coordinates behavior, actors will comply with a behavioral norm if they expect others to conform.[70] Further, actors may comply with dominant practices or beliefs simply out of unreflective habit and/or the difficulty of bucking deeply institutionalized normative beliefs.

---

[69] Keck and Sikkink put this even more strongly, "Normative change is inherently disruptive or difficult because it requires actors to question this routinized practice and contemplate new practices." Keck and Sikkink, *Activists Beyond Borders*, p. 35.
[70] Cristina Bicchieri, "Norms of Cooperation," *Ethics* 100 (July 1990), 838–861: 842.

Further, individuals and groups may be reluctant to alter normative beliefs, as well as behavioral norms which are strongly normative, if doing so requires rethinking an entire complex of related normative, scientific, practical, and identity beliefs which an individual has become convinced are good and sees no other reason to challenge. Resistance to taking on new normative beliefs if they require massive belief revision may also be due perhaps to desire for economy, or a wish for coherence, or because putting many beliefs up to re-evaluation is cognitively difficult or even emotionally painful.

Perceptive and articulate individuals may acknowledge their reluctance to change normative beliefs specifically because it requires them to change many other beliefs and behaviors. This was the case in 1917 when Charles Buxton, a member of the Anti-Slavery and Aborigines' Protection Society, argued against a post-World War I peace arrangement that included consulting with African natives. "*Are* we prepared to say that what we would apply to the natives of Africa should apply also to the natives of India? If not, then we lay ourselves open to this charge of hypocrisy."[71] Thus, once established and institutionalized, it is particularly difficult for behavioral norms to change. In these instances, when people adhere to established practices because it may be inefficient or costly to alter behavior, or they do not think to try something else, or because deeply institutionalized behaviors are difficult to alter because they are tightly linked to other beliefs and behaviors, the goodness or normativity of the practice is not the primary reason for resilience.

In addition, individuals may conform if doing so brings approval and/or there is a clear material benefit to conformity, while non-conformity leads to disapproval or sanction. If individuals or groups want to do what is required by law or social pressure because they fear disapproval, they may comply with prevailing normative beliefs and practices. But again, the normativity of the behavior (its link to prescriptive normative beliefs) may not be what motivates individual compliance, although normativity may motivate the imposition of sanctions for non-compliance.

Groups and cultures also vary in their openness to argument, and this may account for the resilience of some beliefs and practices. Though people may hold divergent views, they may go along to get along if they and others place a high value on conformity and group cohesion. "Every group of any kind whatsoever demands that each of its members

---

[71] See chapter 6, note 17 this vol.

shall help defend group interests. Every group stigmatizes any one who fails in zeal, labor and sacrifices for group interests . . . The group force is also employed to enforce the obligations of devotion to group interests. It follows that judgments are precluded and criticism is silenced."[72] Moreover, homogenous groups may be less likely to entertain changes in practice, simply because it never occurs to them.

I have emphasized several non-normative reasons why it is difficult for arguments to change beliefs. Is there something distinctly normative about the resilience of normative beliefs? In other words, do actors adhere to them because they are thought to be good? Actors could be moved (or not) by other kinds of non-ethical arguments, for instance practical arguments. If, to change a practice, it is unnecessary for actors to deconstruct (denormalize and delegitimize) normative beliefs, then one could argue that it was not normative belief, but other kinds of belief that underpinned a dominant practice and resilience was due to the non-normative reasons, for example, the costliness of any change, or the failure to consider other alternatives.

Yet there are reasons for normative belief resilience and adherence to established behavioral norms that appear to be uniquely normative. The simplest reason to resist change implied by new ethical arguments would be because an individual agrees with the dominant normative belief and thinks its content is good in itself. Or someone could believe that in following the prescription they are likely to bring affirmation of their own "goodness" as a person in a specific role – they are good because they follow the existing prescription. In this case, they have internalized the role, they believe it, and also believe in the content of the normative beliefs. An ethical argument that is unpersuasive in this instance fails to convince the actor that they ought to change their evaluation of an already held normative belief, and fails to convince the person that they ought to think differently about their role.

In sum, there are powerful reasons – both normative and non-normative – why individuals adhere to pre-existing practices. Ethical arguments that succeed in changing beliefs and practices must be extremely persuasive in order to overcome the inertia of habit, the obstacles of institutionalization, the possible confusion and loss of efficiency associated with change, the personal identification and stakes individuals may have in the practice, and the belief that the old practice is good.

---

[72] William Graham Sumner, *Folkways: A Study of the Sociological Importance of Usages, Manners, Customs, Mores and Morals* (Boston: Athenaeum Press, 1906), p. 15.

Increasing receptivity and persuasiveness

Ethical arguments are unlikely to be persuasive if actors are unreceptive. Receptivity depends on a number of factors that are both intrinsic and extrinsic to the content of the ethical arguments, and those seeking to identify factors that, *ex ante*, indicate which arguments will succeed over others, should pay careful attention to extrinsic and intrinsic conditions. The extrinsic characteristics of persuasive ethical arguments described in chapter 1, in the discussion of persuasive context, are briefly recalled here.

Arguments must first be heard. Since most domestic and international political arguments do not occur on a level playing field, whether or not an argument is heard depends on the discursive space within which the argument takes place. In other words, if those who challenge dominant normative beliefs cannot get a broad hearing of their arguments, those arguments are unlikely to have a chance or opportunity to be persuasive. Democracies and egalitarian groups may be more open to ethical arguments that compete with the dominant belief system because those groups already hold substantive normative beliefs about freedom of expression, they may have forums where new ideas can be articulated, and in the case of relatively egalitarian settings, the economic barriers to broadcasting speech may be relatively lower than in non-democracies or highly stratified societies.

A second extrinsic constraint is the credibility of those who are making the ethical argument. If those who make the ethical argument can claim some relevant expertise or have been granted authority by an institution, the audience is usually more likely to give their arguments a hearing. The relevant expertise and institutions from which individuals can gain authority of course varies with the culture, although religious authorities and moral philosophers are often given great credence in making and judging ethical arguments. Yet even here, extrinsic and intrinsic constraints overlap because who will be considered a legitimate interlocutor depends on the institutionalization of beliefs, since as Jepperson, Wendt, and Katzenstein note, "institutionalization of ideas – in research institutions, schools of thought, laws, government bureaucracies" determines not only policy, as they say, but who is able to critically comment on policy.[73]

---

[73] Jepperson, Wendt, and Katzenstein, "Norms, Identity and Culture in International Security," p. 50.

Once heard, how might an ethical argument defeat the formidable intrinsic barriers to changing normative beliefs? First, the pre-existing system must be deconstructed – but not entirely. Those who hear ethical arguments usually compare those arguments with the beliefs they already hold. This view of receptivity is related to a school of ontology known as "coherentism," which supposes that beliefs are justified by their connection and similarity to other already held beliefs. Ethical arguments that hearers find persuasive usually make sense within the framework of an individual's already existing beliefs about the particular issue area, their identity, and fit the existing social structure. Thus, the meaning of the web of beliefs that normative arguments are made within and against helps to determine the receptivity of individuals to a particular ethical argument.

But even if ethical arguments do not "naturally fit" within dominant webs of belief, advocates of new beliefs and practices can try to make them fit by reinterpreting the pre-existing webs of belief, or by fabricating plausible connections with analogical arguments. As Mark Laffey and Jutta Weldes argue, "'fit' does not just happen; rather, it is *made*. That is, the 'fit' between new and existing ideas is actively *constructed* rather than simply 'there' in the ideas themselves."[74] Just as successful meta-arguments reframe existing practices so that they are denormalized and delegitimized, new normative beliefs are often framed as consistent with some pre-existing normative beliefs. Those wishing to block adoption of normative beliefs, and the practices associated with them, could argue that those beliefs do not fit with the culture and therefore ought not be adopted.

What does it mean exactly for normative beliefs to cohere with pre-existing beliefs and for receptivity to ethical arguments to depend on the congruence between the content of ethical arguments and the dominant belief systems of actors? Normative beliefs gain their legitimacy by their substantive content (meaning) relationship to other beliefs.[75] Ethical arguments that match or complement the content of religious, social, or scientific belief systems that are part of the dominant culture are more likely to be successful than arguments that clash with existing webs of belief. The pre-existing "logic" of accepted behavioral norms

---

[74] Laffey and Weldes, "Beyond Belief," p. 203. Similarly, Finnemore and Sikkink argue that "Activists work hard to frame their issues in ways that make persuasive connections between existing norms and emergent norms." Finnemore and Sikkink, "Norm Dynamics and Political Change," p. 908.
[75] See Audi, *Belief, Justification and Knowledge*.

and normative prescriptions will influence receptivity to new normative beliefs and practice. Symbolic arguments, in particular those using analogies, may be particularly useful in showing or constructing a
coherent fit.

Further, receptivity to ethical arguments also depends on the "fit"
between the self-conceptualization of actors' identity and the proposed
normative belief. There are at least three components to political identity:
(1) a sense of the political self, and what is distinctive about self in
relation to others[76]; (2) a historical narrative about self – often partly
mythical and religious, involving certain "lies" or constructions about
the homogeneity of the self and how good and honorable the self is; and
(3) an ideology or political program. Advocates of a new practice often
say that their proposed norm better fits with the kind of people that they
are or would like to see themselves as. The identities of actors will be
used as part of the argument usually by appealing to the consistency
of the argument with the identity being evoked. For example, if we
are good, virtuous, just, and superior to others – as most ethnocentrists
believe – then we are justified in imperial conquest. If we are good,
virtuous, just, and equal to others, then imperialism cannot be justified.
Similarly, arguments for humanitarian intervention may rest on identity
and conceptions of roles in a particular situation. "America was founded
on a moral purpose, and its people retain a strong commitment to a moral
foreign policy. They are also extremely generous. Given able and forceful
leadership, it should be possible to generate a spirit of disinterested
altruism that will support humanitarian intervention."[77]

Foreign policy decisionmakers and members of the public hold multiple identities that include their nation, race, gender, class, family,
religion, age, occupation, and education.[78] States are collections of
individuals and groups, with both distinct and overlapping identities, and transnational identities are not uncommon. These multiple
identities, and their malleability, are important in the context of ethical arguments to the extent that argument makers call upon, create,
and manipulate identities. These identities or roles may offer conflicting normative guidelines even as they are potential openings for

[76] This is similar to what Wendt calls "social identity." Alexander Wendt, "Collective
Identity Formation and the International State," *American Political Science Review* 88 (June
1994), 384–396: 385.
[77] Guenter Lewy, "The Case for Humanitarian Intervention," *Orbis* 37 (Fall 1993), 621–632:
624.
[78] See Katzenstein, ed., *The Culture of National Security.*

normative appeals. Conversely, ethical appeals may at the same time include the techniques of constructing new identities or not recognizing or disavowing other identities. If an existing conception of identity cannot be changed actors may try to change the composition of the decisionmaking group so it will be more receptive to the particular ethical arguments they want to see adopted.

And because ethical arguments are about how to act toward others so as to be a good person, ethical arguments are inherently emotional. Specifically, most humans want to be good, do good, and feel well regarded by others. Thus, one can increase receptivity to ethical arguments that seek to change practices that affect others by showing that the "other" deserves our empathy and good treatment even while existing practices mean that we are not doing good by them. Greater empathy may enable actors to get past the first threshold, that of being heard, thus increasing the hearers' receptivity.

Receptivity of actors to new ethical arguments also depends on the prescriptions' fit with existing social structures (which are themselves dependent on beliefs). It is common sense that if the majority of a society is, for example, dependent on unequal relationships of extraction and exploitation, it will be more difficult for people to reconceptualize their interests, see hypocrisy, or to mobilize resistance to the dominant behavior.[79] Radically new prescriptive norms that clash with many social practices are likely to take hold only gradually, or piecemeal. In a context where advocates of new normative beliefs and practices face a complex institution with multiple sources of support, a great deal has to be changed to achieve the desired state. When many of the supporting constitutive practices and prescriptive normative beliefs have to be changed the advocates of new normative beliefs will be regarded as utopians. Advocates of new normative beliefs and practices may then attempt to gradually change the aspects of the world that are obstacles to normative change so that individuals will be more receptive to their larger ethical argument.

Emphasizing the dependence of receptivity on existing social practices and structure is not to fall back on interest. Rather, social practices and structures are in great measure a consequence of the belief systems that rationalize and order societies as, for instance, modes of production or class relations. Capability is also obviously important but it is also

---

[79] Aside from providing greater political opportunities for discourse, democracies may also be more vulnerable to ethical arguments than non-democracies because democracies are relatively more vulnerable to the charge of hypocrisy.

clear that societies make resources available for those activities, however costly, that they consider important, e.g. national military forces and the arts. Outside of the rare extreme cases where there is absolutely no way to do something, material capabilities and constraints matter little unless and until they are perceived.

In sum, successful ethical arguments are able to reframe issues and set the terms of debate, even to the point where people who are moved by other reasons, such as practical considerations, feel compelled to make ethical arguments. Ethical appeals work well when their content is linked to the dominant belief systems, social institutions, and identities of actors. Those who make arguments often intuitively recognize the importance of increasing receptivity by explicitly or implicitly making links to larger ethical belief systems, identities, and existing social structures.[80] The plausibility and extent of those links are then judged by interlocutors.

When the proposed ethical argument does not fit or even strongly conflicts with dominant beliefs, identities, and institutions, advocates of new normative beliefs and practices must try to win the meta-argument of representation and completely reframe the situation, or at least seriously destabilize the dominant frame. The persuasiveness of ethical arguments that clash with the dominant beliefs and institutions of a society may increase if the argument offers an entirely new conception of a situation or problem that individuals find persuasive.[81] In this way, the fit of the new beliefs with the dominant beliefs, identity, and social structure will not matter so much and ethical arguments can escape the conservatism of being judged by existing ethical world views. Those making ethical arguments that attempt to alter the dominant frame will try to denormalize and delegitimize not only the particular beliefs and practices they seek to alter but will denormalize, delegitimize, and offer alternatives for the larger web of beliefs and institutions that support the dominant behavioral and prescriptive norms. If interlocutors succeed in entirely reframing the situation, the ethical argument is then judged by other criteria, standards of its own making, and this may increase receptivity to the ethical argument.

Ethical arguments are made in different venues or forums; or to borrow from parliamentary discourse, arguments are put on a table. Some

---

[80] On social movements and framing, see Sidney Tarrow, *Power in Movement: Social Movements and Contentious Politics*, 2nd edn. (Cambridge: Cambridge University Press, 1998), pp. 106–122.
[81] These are conceptual revolutions or paradigm shifts.

venues may lower the extrinsic constraints to ethical argument by being relatively egalitarian and having rules of procedure that provide opportunities for ethical argument. Other forums will be relatively closed procedurally or substantively in terms of the kinds of arguments that can be brought up. The intrinsic constraints of the table have to do with the lifeworld aspect of cultures (whether the relevant cultural venue is an epistemic, organizational, political community, civilizational or global context), where the background of shared interpretations is the unconscious basis for understanding arguments. The importance of the table and venue become clear when the table changes over time or across social settings.

There is no way to know for certain which arguments will be persuasive and over what period of time. But we can predict that arguments which fail to overcome extrinsic constraints (cannot be heard and do not come from authority) will be less likely to succeed than arguments that can be heard. Further, advocates who are unable to win the meta-argument and reframe prevailing practices so that they are vulnerable to ethical critique are unlikely to succeed. Argument is a dynamic process conducted by reflective individuals – advocates can alter their rhetorical tactics in an attempt to increase their persuasiveness, and opponents of change may try to counteract potentially successful challengers.

Reason versus rationality

Some scholars of "norms" are concerned that their arguments not be taken as a repudiation of rational actor theories where actors are supposed to make choices and behave accordingly in ways that will bring them the greatest rewards at the least cost. This view of rationality stresses cold cognitive processes. But ethical arguments are neither rational nor irrational. They are convincing to the extent that they give persuasive reasons for believing and doing. Neither receptivity to ethical arguments, nor the intrinsic appeal of arguments, is necessarily rational in the former sense. In other words, scholars of world politics are better off thinking in terms of the process of reason rather than in terms of rationality.

Those who make arguments are giving reasons for a belief or course of action and their appeals may be emotional as well as cognitive. Emotional appeals work because individuals want to feel good about themselves by knowing they are doing good, and others see them as doing good.[82] Or emotions may help individuals feel empathy toward others. Cognitive appeals, for instance arguing that holding one normative belief is consistent with or entails holding another belief, are also not necessarily entirely un-emotional. Strong emotions that are associated with some normative beliefs may affect, either positively or negatively, the receptivity to ethical arguments on the basis of coherence. As the following chapters on slavery, forced labor, and colonialism show, emotional and cognitive appeals were important aspects of ethical arguments whether those arguments were made by people who wanted to keep or overturn these institutions. The process was internal reasoning or public argumentation that involved giving reasons. Some of the reasons took the form of rational calculation, especially on the issue of whether colonial institutions were profitable, but that was only one form of reasoning at work. In other words, argumentation is not simply and only a rational process, if what one means by rationality is the unemotional and narrow pursuit of real "interests" using cost–benefit analysis. Persuasive ethical arguments are emotional, rooted in social contexts, and related to webs of other arguments.

Is a theory of ethical argument merely a reiteration of rational actor theory? Ethical argument explanations are different from rational actor accounts in at least two senses. First, rational actor theories generally regard normative beliefs, when they are considered at all, as secondary to interests, whereas a theory of ethical arguments regards normative beliefs on equal ground with other beliefs, and suggests that normative beliefs sometimes constitute "interests." Second, to the extent that at the point of final decision, decisionmakers follow what might be considered a "rational" process of weighing options and choosing among alternatives, every part of reasoning before then was based on the content of pre-existing beliefs and the outcome of prior arguments. The implementation of the final decision will also essentially be determined by how those same or evolving beliefs are used in arguments. In other words, the work of decisionmakers is reason and persuasion, not so much rational calculation. The work of scholars is to interpret their reasoning and the effects of actors' persuasive efforts.

---

[82] See Vaughn P. Shannon, "Norms are What States Make of Them: The Political Psychology of Norm Violation," *International Studies Quarterly*, 44 (June 2000), 293–316; Weisband, "Discursive Multilateralism."

Ethical explanations

Ethical arguments made by participants in a practical situation are different from ethical explanations which are given by people who are observing a behavior and trying to say what caused it. When normative beliefs are used in arguments about what it is good to do, people are making ethical arguments. When someone says that they or someone else acted ethically, or that an individual or group behaved in a certain way because of ethical reasons, they are giving an ethical explanation of social behavior. That ethical arguments occur everywhere, all the time, does not mean that they are necessarily significant causally. Arguments could be "merely" rationalization or *post-hoc* justification.

A method of informal argument analysis

While it may be that one method of argument analysis suits all types of political arguments, it is more likely that the method would vary with the scope and types of arguments to be understood. Most scholars of political argument use formal and semi-formal approaches. Formal argument analysis, or artificial intelligence modeling of logic, focuses on validity and the structure of inferences, tracing the logical structure and identifying the substantive support (warrants) for arguments.[83] Formal argument analysis is better suited to tracing debates that are relatively short term, where moves and counter-moves are immediate and explicit, and focused on relatively small areas of contention in instances where we can assume that actors were trying to come to an agreement with their interlocutors and their arguments are relatively clearly laid out in a logical form. Similarly, semi-formal argument analysis is also focused on specific exchanges.[84] An example of one approach, taken from Gavan Duffy, Brian Federking, and Seth Tucker is summarized below.[85]

Obviously not all political arguments are about relatively narrow or technical issues; in some instances, political arguments address major social and political institutions and therefore require comprehensive

[83] For an example of formal approaches used in international relations theory, see Hayward R. Alker, "The Dialectical Logic of Thucydides Melian Dialogue," *American Political Science Review* 82 (September 1988), 805–820; Hayward R. Alker, *Rediscoveries and Reformulations* (Cambridge: Cambridge University Press, 1996), pp. 23–63; Gavan Duffy, Brian K. Federking, and Seth A. Tucker, "Language Games: Dialogical Analysis of INF Negotiations," *International Studies Quarterly* 42 (June 1998), 271–294.

[84] See Thomas F. Homer-Dixon and Roger S. Karapin, "Graphical Argument Analysis: A New Approach to Understanding Arguments Applied to a Debate about the Window of Vulnerability," *International Studies Quarterly* 33 (September 1989), 389–410.

[85] See Duffy, Federking, and Tucker, "Language Games," p. 272.

Table 2.2 *A method of formal argument analysis*

---

1. List explicit moves, including non-verbal actions that convey meaning.
2. Specify an inventory of propositions (non-controversial facts or beliefs of the relevant parties) that express the background knowledge necessary to understand the dialogue.
3. Pragmatic analysis of the dialogue, constructing inventories of propositions conveyed implicitly, noting those aspects of meaning that are context dependent.
4. Formal argument analysis of moves conveyed implicitly and explicitly. Test: certain action theorems follow logically from the contents of the inventories.

Source: From Duffy, Federking, and Tucker, "Language Games," p. 272.

arguments. Nor do political arguments only occur in a focused way in one forum where advocates are intent on coming to an agreement with fellow interlocutors. In many cases, it may not be the intention of participants to directly influence their immediate counterparts; rather, the point is to sway a wider audience and influence the balance of belief and power. These larger political arguments may occur over several years, some for decades or centuries and are often characterized by an informal style. To focus on the formal structure of the smaller debates that comprise long, comprehensive, and informal arguments would certainly be illuminating, but one runs the risk of missing the larger landscape. I use a method of informal argument analysis that may be better suited to understanding and tracing the effects of the looser, and more long-term arguments that characterize these long informal discourses.

The method of informal argument analysis developed here occurs in five steps.[86] First, having identified a problem or issue area, analysts seek to identify the purpose of particular arguments that are being used in efforts to maintain or challenge a practice. Analysts must then specify the argument's role. Whether arguments are intended to facilitate deliberation, reframe the issues, persuade others, or do all of these things, may be inferred from what the speaker says and by the

---

[86] I could just as well have called my approach rhetorical analysis since I am concerned with what Aristotle called rhetoric. Both rhetoric and casuistry have negative associations in our present context, so I use the more neutral, or relatively less laden term 'argument.' See Aristotle, *The Art of Rhetoric*, translated with an introduction by H.C. Lawson-Tancred (New York: Penguin Books, 1991); Thomas B. Farrell, *Norms of Rhetorical Culture* (New Haven: Yale University Press, 1993).

location (forum) where the arguments are made.[87] Argument analysis is easier in some instances than in others. In the transition from established behavioral norms to new norms, there are likely to be periods of confusion and uncertainty. With two or more conflicting (and perhaps nearly equally legitimate) prescriptive normative beliefs on the table, expectations will be uncertain, coordination will be more difficult, and the sense of approval or disapproval associated with certain practices may be in flux. It is at these points that ethical arguments may be the most prolific and explicit, as interlocutors strive to be clear and persuasive in their attempts to maintain an existing practice or establish a new mode of behavior. South African arguments to maintain their rule over South West Africa/Namibia after many powers had given up their colonies are an example. Similarly, crisis may make ethical arguments more pointed, as President Kennedy's Secretary of State Dean Rusk suggests in a discussion of the Cuban missile crisis: "at the end of the day, moral and ethical considerations play a very important part, even though people don't wear these things on their shirtsleeves or put these things in official memoranda . . . People act in reference to their basic moral commitments [which] are likely to come to the fore when situations become critical."[88]

Second, one must identify the specific beliefs (core, contingent, and role) that are held by dominant actors and that are at work in a particular political context. As Jonson and Toulmin note, "Each discipline has its special field of debate, within which people of experience share *konoi topoi* ('commonplaces') – that is, bodies of experience that underlie the forms of argument that guide deliberation and discussion in the particular field."[89] The goal is to find the topoi (starting point) of the arguments actors used to uphold or change practices and the background of preexisting beliefs that interlocutors presupposed in making their arguments. "By intending, implicating, presupposing, and entailing, speakers convey far more than they say. Efforts to analyze the contents of political talk that restrict themselves to surface utterances are thus likely to miss much of the politically relevant content."[90]

---

[87] On forums, see Stephen Toulmin, Richard Rieke, and Allan Janik, *An Introduction to Reasoning* (New York: Macmillan, 1979), pp. 14–16. Also see, Farrell, *Norms of Rhetorical Culture*, pp. 280–288.

[88] Quoted in James G. Blight, *The Shattered Crystal Ball: Fear and Learning in the Cuban Missile Crisis* (Savage, MD: Rowman & Littlefield: 1990), p. 93.

[89] Albert R. Jonson and Stephen Toulmin, *The Abuse of Casuistry: A History of Moral Reasoning* (Berkeley: University of California Press, 1988), p. 74.

[90] Duffy, Frederking and Tucker, "Language Games," p. 276.

Third, informal argument analysis expands the time horizon and asks where immediate and background beliefs came from and why and how they changed. As Nardin suggests, "arguments about international affairs, like ethical and political arguments more generally, have a history. Accordingly, the study of international ethics must be, at least in part, historical."[91] Analysis of political arguments must thus be context sensitive, looking for the deeper beliefs that are the starting points and background assumptions without which the arguments would be unintelligible. This entails examining the process and content of decisionmaking over long periods of time within particular historical and cultural contexts.

> The idea of a tradition encourages us to ask what kinds of arguments were characteristic of particular communities at particular moments. It also suggests the importance of looking at the concepts or "languages" employed by particular kinds of argumentation. And because these conceptual languages change through time, in some cases becoming transformed into new languages, the study of tradition leads naturally to the study of conceptual change.[92]

Fourth, informal argument analysis attempts to show how and why some beliefs and arguments won out over others and ultimately why certain policies were chosen. In practice this means tracing whether and how the ethical arguments put forward succeeded in changing the terms of debate (winning meta-arguments and reframing the issues), and whether an ethical argument meant to overturn a practice was able to denormalize, delegitimize, change actors' conceptions of possibility and their interests, alter the balance of political power, and have its normative beliefs institutionalized. This also entails looking at the grounds for change in the support for conformity and receptivity to new arguments.

Informal argument analysis thus emphasizes the content and process of arguments – the words used (and not used), appeals actors make to dominant (unquestioned) beliefs and other normative beliefs, claims about legitimacy, and the use of evidence. This method focuses on how the arguments develop over long periods of time, in particular social settings, including definition and redefinition of the problem (meta-arguments), and the evolution of the features in the argument that are taken for granted or contested.

---

[91] Terry Nardin, "Ethical Traditions in International Affairs," in Nardin and Mapel, eds., *Traditions of International Ethics*, pp. 1–22: 19.
[92] Ibid.

What is central is the discourse(s) which construct a particular "reality" ... This approach suggests that what foreign policy *is* need not be limited to the actual making of specific decisions nor the analysis of temporally and spatially bounded "events."

Similarly, 'foreign policy makers' need not be limited to prominent decision makers, but could also include those rather anonymous members of the various bureaucracies who write the numerous memorandums, intelligence reports, and research papers that circulate within policy circles. The discourse(s) instantiated in these various documents produce meanings and in so doing actively construct the "reality" upon which foreign policy is based.[93]

Fifth, the results of informal argument analysis ought to be compared with other plausible explanations for behaviors to see whether the arguments are important causally. There are several "tests" for the causal significance of ethical argument. (1) temporal ordering – normative beliefs and ethical arguments should be given as a justification for the behavior before or simultaneous to a behavior change, not after; (2) after an ethical argument succeeds, one would expect a (not necessarily universal) congruence between the normative beliefs that underpinned the ethical arguments and the behavior; (3) the relevant normative beliefs should be used in arguments about correct behavior and those who use those arguments are not ignored or mocked; (4) when the prescriptions for behavior implied by the ethical argument are not adhered to, those who do not adhere to the standards of normative belief attempt to justify their (non-normal) behavior on ethical or practical grounds; (5) the normative belief is linked with other normative beliefs, becoming part of the arguments used to advance these other norms. For example, anti-slavery, human rights, and self-determination beliefs should be discussed with each norm's reasoning being used to legitimize the other norms.[94]

Two stronger tests of the role of normative belief and ethical argument are: (6) the presence and use of international sanctions by the majority

[93] Roxanne Lynn Doty, "Foreign Policy as Social Construction: A Post-Positivist Analysis of U.S. Counterinsurgency Policy in the Philippines," *International Studies Quarterly* 37 (September 1993), 297–320: 303.
[94] Even if normative beliefs and ethical arguments pass all of these "tests," we still cannot *prove* causality. However, passing all or several of these tests make it more *likely* that normative belief and ethical argument had a causal role. If, after analysis of the type that I propose, there is little reason to think that normative beliefs and ethical argument had much influence on behavior, then advocates of new behavioral norms should focus their attentions on changing the interests and capabilities of actors – not on winning arguments and changing beliefs.

of the international community to change the behavior of those who violate the normative prescriptions or those who support such norm violators. Finally, (7) ethical arguments may be viewed as causally important whether and to the extent that actors with incentives to violate normative prescriptions act counter to their "interests" and follow the new normative prescriptions, or to the extent that actors re-frame their interests in light of coming to hold new normative beliefs. For the last test to be valid three conditions should hold: states (or rather the influential elites that shape government policies) and other actors should "know" their interests (or at least believe they do); actors should not have been compelled by other (non-normative) circumstances, such as a change in their ability to pursue their interests; and some more efficient solution for achieving the same ends, while not technically violating the normative prescriptions that followed from ethical arguments, was not found. This "interest" test should not be seen as creating a dichotomy between the normative and the self-interested behavior or actors. Ethical arguments may be used to change actors' conceptions of their interests, and successful ethical arguments may alter the political situation to the point where it changes the material capabilities of actors. Rather, this test focuses our attention on the crucial relation between the ideational and material. Table 2.3 summarizes the steps of informal argument analysis.

Examining the role and causal significance of ethical argument thus entails operating at three levels. First, scholars using this method must show that argumentation or practical reasoning was a part of the process. Second, an informal argument analysis must determine if the ethical arguments were used to deconstruct and reconstruct normative beliefs and to change the political and institutional facts on the ground. Third, scholars have to determine the relevance or explanatory weight of ethical arguments. Persuasive ethical arguments may be one of several reasons or the sole reason for a change. If analysis suggests that there were other reasons that beliefs and behavior changed, and ethical arguments were not explicit or implicit, then an ethical explanation for change does not hold.

Objections

Claims about the role of beliefs and argument must answer important objections. First, how can any scholar talk about beliefs and claim a relationship between beliefs and behavior? How can we be sure that the beliefs and justifications for action that are articulated by foreign policy decisionmakers are the actual reasons for their behavior, rather

Table 2.3 *Informal argument analysis of ethical arguments*

1. Identify the main arguments on the table over the course of the debate.
2. Identify the immediate beliefs contained in the arguments that are the topoi/starting point.
3. Identify the background (historical and cultural) beliefs.
4. Trace form and fate of the ethical arguments. Do ethical arguments that seek to overturn a dominant practice
   – denormalize the dominant beliefs and practices?
   – delegitimize the dominant beliefs and practices?
   – change conceptions of possibility and interests?
   – change the political capabilities of actors as the balance of belief changes?
   – become institutionalized?
5. Compare the plausibility of an ethical argument explanation with a material interest explanation. Do ethical arguments pass the tests of
   – temporal ordering
   – congruence between normative beliefs and behavior
   – the relevant normative beliefs are taken seriously
   – those who do not adhere to the standards of normative belief attempt to justify their (non-normal) behavior on ethical or practical grounds
   – the normative belief is linked with other normative beliefs, becoming part of the arguments used to advance these other norms
   – international sanctions are used by the majority of the international community to change the behavior of those who violate the normative prescriptions or those who support norm violators
   – actors with incentives to violate normative prescriptions act counter to their "interests" and follow new normative prescriptions, or re-frame their interests in light of new normative beliefs.

than public justifications, private rationalizations, or perhaps the ranting and ravings of the mad? No scholar can know for certain what someone else believes. We can only show what someone claims to be thinking, what they claim to believe, by examining their public utterances. Some utterances are obviously more credible as a reflection of beliefs than other statements. For example, it is likely that statements made to insiders are more closely related to shared beliefs than are public statements. Rational actor theorists face the same problem of knowing what someone thinks and what counted when they made decisions.

Does it matter whether people mean what they say and say what they mean? Clearly people sometimes believe the ethical arguments they make, and sometimes they do not believe them. Establishing whether normative beliefs and ethical arguments are actually causes, versus rationalizations or justifications, must be dealt with by any argument about beliefs. Jack Snyder has warned against taking justifications too seriously: "many explanations are flawed because they take the justifications of statesmen and strategists at face value. . . ."[95] Rather, Snyder argues, some arguments are just "*not* to be believed" because the "oblique justifications . . . were largely debating points masking a variety of economic, bureaucratic, and political interests."[96]

It is clear that sometimes people lie and do things for reasons other than the ones they claim to be the true motives for their actions. In individual instances, it is difficult to tell the "real" beliefs and reasoning that underlie a particular action. And, as Snyder suggests, arguments and beliefs can constrain or "blowback": "Even if the elite avoids internalizing its own myths, it may nonetheless become equally entrapped in its own rhetoric."[97] Fortunately, decisionmaking in world politics is a process of repeated decision and actions. If decisionmakers are inconsistent in areas and among cases where we would expect consistency, then we may suspect their beliefs are being articulated as justifications. In addition, there are layers of reasons for any foreign policy decision and action: if the publicly articulated beliefs do not seem to match the motives for action, that does not necessarily mean that normative beliefs had no influence on the decision. The fact of the argument being sincere or insincere may be irrelevant if the argument is what convinces others to act in accordance with the conclusion of the ethical argument. And even if the first use of an ethical argument was disingenuous, it may have force in future situations because it may be seen as having set a precedent.

Second, it may be possible to establish that decisionmakers made ethical arguments for action, but those arguments could be beside the point. Unless actors honestly disclose their full reasoning, observers cannot discount non-ethical reasons for their behavior. In other words, ethical arguments may have some force, but a solely ethical explanation may be insufficient. For example, a US policymaker could argue that the United States ought not use nuclear weapons because such use is immoral. In

---

[95] Jack Snyder, *Myths of Empire: Domestic Politics and International Ambition* (Ithaca: Cornell University Press, 1991), p. 10.
[96] *Ibid.*, p. 10. Actually, in this book, Snyder talks about the role of argument, e.g. the "blurring of sincere belief and tactical argument has been common" (pp. 41–42) but he does not offer a systematic treatment of argument.
[97] *Ibid.*, p. 42.

fact, ethical arguments against nuclear use may have come up in every instance when policymakers considered using nuclear weapons in war. Nuclear weapons may not have been used because such use was considered wrong. But an ethical explanation for non-use may be insufficient. Non-use could also be explained by practical considerations, such as the inability of nuclear weapons to be used for military effect, or the fear of nuclear retaliation and escalation. Still, to argue that nuclear weapons were not used for political reasons, namely that their use would be unpopular, is to fall back on an ethical explanation if the unpopularity of their use is founded on normative beliefs such as the view that nuclear weapons violate principles of non-combatant immunity.[98]

But there is an even more subtle problem of establishing whether ethical explanations are appropriate. Specifically, people may arrange their social institutions because they believe that they are right in the sense of being normatively good. But this can lead to two different outcomes. On the one hand, an individual may seek to arrange their world so as to do good; these individuals are motivated by a belief in fairness and justice – that others deserve the same "rights" as they do. On the other hand, a system that some might consider unjust, for instance slavery or colonialism, might be deemed acceptable to its practitioners. In this instance, oppression and discrimination are considered warranted because the practitioners of the unjust system do not believe in the equality of the other; they may never have considered the "rights" of the other; or they may have found the other undeserving of the same treatment as themselves. In fact, they believe that the "injustice" is appropriate and good. Here an ethical explanation applies. In both these instances we can plausibly give ethical explanations.

But what about those instances where people do what we might consider the good and right thing, but they are motivated not by a concern for justice but rather driven by a desire to contain reform? They see that if some concessions are not made, the unjust system may fall altogether as the oppressed revolt. And according to Joshua Cohen, revolt is inevitable since unjust systems are not in the interest of the oppressed. These individuals who make concessions to prevent revolt, let's call them pragmatic reformers, act out of a concern that their unjust world not fall apart under the pressure of those who want to create an ethically just system. Although pragmatic reformers do not hold the same

---

[98] See Nina Tannenwald, "The Nuclear Taboo: The United States and the Normative Basis of Nuclear Non-Use," *International Organization* 53 (Summer 1999), 433–468.

normative beliefs as those who are motivated by a concern for justice, they are willing to reform the unjust system along lines that the person motivated by a concern with justice would approve of, in order to save it. Pragmatic reformers may even give ethical arguments for reform alongside their practical arguments. Does an ethical explanation fit here, or are we in the realm of the practical or pragmatic justice? On the face of it, it seems that an ethical explanation cannot be applied to those who make reforms in order to save the unjust system.

Yet even if arguments given by pragmatic reformers are "merely" justifications, the fact that these actors feel they must make a justification in the form of an ethical argument indicates the importance of these arguments. The content of the justification is not incidental. The elaborateness and vehemence of justifications tells us as much about the character of the culture as do the genuine utterances. "The clearest evidence for the stability of our values over time is the unchanging character of the lies soldiers and statesmen tell. They lie in order to justify themselves, and so they describe for us the lineaments of justice. Wherever we find hypocrisy, we also find moral knowledge"[99] So it is important to trace the content of justifications, even if we know they are not the "real" or only reasons for action. If genuine or disingenuous arguments are made, we know that argument is an important process in world politics. The content of the lies we tell ourselves is part of the architecture of ethical world politics; lies indicate the bounds of the acceptable. Those who are motivated by a belief in justice create the conditions where pragmatic reforms or pragmatic justice is required. (And the unintended consequence of pragmatic reforms may be to catalyze greater reform.)

I use an interpretive method of informal argument analysis, yet, there are strong objections to interpretivism, especially the choice of interpretation. "But how does one know that this interpretation is correct? Presumably because it makes sense of the original text: what is strange, mystifying, puzzling, contradictory, is no longer so, is accounted for."[100] Interpretations can make "sense" and still be wrong. That is, there can be *mis*-understandings, that may not articulate what the actors intended or believed either privately or intersubjectively. I don't think that there is a way around this potential problem for positivist, rationalist, or

---

[99] Walzer, *Just and Unjust Wars*, p. 19.
[100] Charles Taylor, "Interpretation and the Sciences of Man," in Paul Rabinow and William Sullivan, eds., *Interpretive Social Science: A Reader* (Berkeley: University of California Press, 1979), pp. 25–71: 27.

interpretivist approaches. One can only try to get closer to the "data" through thinking thoroughly historically and simultaneously by granting the role that one's own beliefs and context/culture are playing in the interpretive process.[101]

This argument raises the problem of "falsifiability." This theory of foreign policy beliefs and arguments is so comprehensive, because it first of all supposes that argument is a ubiquitous and causally important process – how can we tell when and if it is wrong? At the most fundamental level, I am not sure that any social science theory, especially rational actor theory, much less a theory of argument, belief, and culture, is falsifiable.[102] Rather, theories can be more or less useful for understanding. This theory of arguments would not be useful if outcomes were regularly explained by non-normative factors.

Establishing the causality of arguments and beliefs is not the only aim. The other aim is to understand the content of world politics, which may tell a great deal about how and why actors do what they do. On the other hand, one should suspect a theory if it doesn't "fit" the evidence– that is, if the theory's implicit and explicit predictions don't match the record of the process and the content of foreign policy. A theory is also uninteresting if it fails to tell us anything that we did not already know using other theories. For example, neither rational actor theories, nor the theories of bounded rationality most often used to correct rational actor accounts, tell us about the sources of foreign policy goals, or how those goals change. The theory of political argument will be interesting and worthwhile if it can tell us something about the source of foreign policy goals, illuminate the processes that decisionmakers engage in to make their decisions, and help us see better than before the content of world political action.

Can ethical explanations still have causal force if actors fail to make explicit ethical arguments? Ethical arguments may not be made explicitly and still have causal force in a situation where everyone agrees with the good. "Consensual cultures do not need to justify or defend their

---

[101] Discussion of interpretation and social science is vast and grounded in both anthropological and philosophical literatures. For more on these issues with particular reference to international relations theory see: Mark Neufeld, "Interpretation and the 'science' of International Relations," *Review of International Studies* 19 (January 1993), 39–61; Richard Price, "Interpretation and Disciplinary Orthodoxy in International Relations," *Review of International Studies* 20 (April 1994), 201–204.

[102] Lakatos argues that at their hard core theories cannot be falsified. Imre Lakatos, *The Methodology of Scientific Research Programmes* (Cambridge: Cambridge University Press, 1978). I thank Jack Snyder for helping me to clarify my argument here.

beliefs against a competing set of beliefs."[103] In other words, in cases where there are no arguments specifically about the practice in question, one can assume that everyone agrees (silence means consent) and takes the particular practice for granted to the extent that they don't feel the need to justify it. Silence in the context of coercion however should signal just the opposite.

---

[103] Elizabeth Kier, *Imagining War: French and British Military Doctrine Between the Wars* (Princeton: Princeton University Press, 1997), p. 141.

3   Colonial arguments

What we have to do is analyze specific rationalities rather than always invoking the progress of rationalization in general.[1]

The sense of humanity was narrowly limited by race and religion. People of different blood and different faith were hardly considered human beings at all, and the highest moral requirements were satisfied by tendering them the blessings of Christianity and civilization.[2]

Humanist values could be invoked and at the same time violated through the hierarchical classification of human beings that implied different standards of treatment for different kinds of subjects ... the ethical prescriptions implied by Enlightenment values applied to some kinds of subjects but not to others.[3]

For thousands of years, from ancient Persia, to Greece, Rome, China, and Aztec and Inca America, to the enormous colonial empires of Britain, Spain, and France in the nineteenth and twentieth centuries, colonialism was claimed by leaders of the metropole to be good for both the imperial power and the colonial holding. Colonialism – the political control, physical occupation, and domination by one group of people over another people and their land for purposes of extraction and settlement to benefit the occupiers – was considered a "normal" practice until the early twentieth century. In most cases, occupied land was distant from the center, or metropole, of

---

[1] Michel Foucault, "The Subject and Power," in Herbert L. Dreyfus and Paul Rabinow, eds., *Michel Foucault: Beyond Structuralism and Hermeneutics*, 2nd edn (Chicago: University of Chicago Press, 1984), pp. 208–226: 210.

[2] Quincy Wright, *Mandates Under the League of Nations* (Chicago: University of Chicago Press, 1930), pp. 7–8.

[3] Roxanne Lynn Doty, *Imperial Encounters: The Politics of Representation in North–South Relations* (Minneapolis: University of Minnesota Press, 1997), p. 42.

the people from the occupying state and control was against the express wishes of the occupied people. Until the mid-nineteenth century, when the institution began to change in significant ways with the end of slavery, colonialism also entailed the control of people's bodies and minds, as well as their social and political organization.[4] Normative beliefs and ethical (as well as practical, identity, and scientific) arguments were used by proponents of colonialism to uphold the practice.

Yet, by the mid-twentieth century the behavioral norm and prescriptive normative beliefs were just the opposite – decolonization of former colonies. Sovereignty, self-determination, and non-intervention became dominant international normative beliefs applicable not only to Europeans and North Americans, but to all. Why, after thousands of years has colonial empire, as an accepted system of political organization, ended? Or, why wasn't colonialism as a system overturned much earlier? It is common to argue that decolonization is explained by the changing material interests and capabilities of colonizers and interveners, that "Empire ceased to be a paying proposition with the rise of capitalism."[5] Marxists argue that imperialism was largely replaced by neo-colonial relations of extraction and domination. The alternative explanation is that ethical convictions or "norms" were at work and "virtually wiped out colonialism."[6] In other words, the colonizers changed their minds about the rightness of colonialism.[7] Why and how did they change their minds?[8]

[4] Empire is the political control of the core country, the metropole, and these distant colonies by leaders of the metropole.
[5] Michael Mandelbaum, "The Reluctance to Intervene," *Foreign Policy* 95 (Summer 1994), 3–18: 14.
[6] Robert Axelrod, "An Evolutionary Approach to Norms," *American Political Science Review* 80 (December 1986), 1095–1111: 1096.
[7] Robert H. Jackson, "The Weight of Ideas in Decolonization: Normative Change in International Relations," in Judith Goldstein and Robert Keohane, eds., *Ideas and Foreign Policy: Beliefs, Institutions, and Political Change* (Ithaca: Cornell University Press, 1993), pp. 111–138; Ethan Nadelmann, "Global Prohibition Regimes: The Evolution of Norms in International Society," *International Organization* 44 (Autumn 1990), 479–526; James Lee Ray, "The Abolition of Slavery and the End of International War," *International Organization* 43 (Summer 1989), 405–439; Gary Geortz and Paul F. Diehl, "Toward a Theory of International Norms: Some Conceptual and Measurement Issues," *Journal of Conflict Resolution* 36 (December 1992), 634–666.
[8] There are other explanations for the end of colonialism. One is that the colonizers overstretched, their reach exceeded their grasp, and they had to retreat. Another is that the colonized overthrew the colonizer; guerrilla wars succeeded where wars of resistance failed. See chapter 8.

Those who sought to change the dominant regime of colonialism used ethical arguments to denormalize and delegitimize colonialism and self-interested military interventions. They also used practical, identity, and scientific arguments to bolster their ethical arguments against colonial practices. Thus, over the course of several hundred years, the characteristic beliefs and constitutive practices of colonialism were challenged, modified, and gradually abandoned in line with a growing belief in the equality of others and increased respect for the "rights" of colonized human bodies and politics. The process of these challenges was ethical argument; the content of the argument was more or less persuasive given the preexisting beliefs and cultures of the societies in which the arguments took place. In some cases, the preexisting beliefs that underpinned colonialism were challenged. The agents who made these arguments were a new set of "humanitarians," distinct from the old-fashioned humanitarians who thought colonialism was good for the colonized because it brought them civilization and Christianity. Further, ethical arguments changed the cultural and material context of colonialism.

Colonialism did not end all at once. Rather, it was gradually dismantled, in part by actors who had little or no idea that their advocacy and partial reforms would lead to the questioning and ultimately the elimination of an entire political order. Colonialism was revised and modified because of the influence of ethical arguments about the very practices that made colonialism what it was – slavery, forced labor, torture, expropriation of land and resources, denial of the protections of the rule of law, and denial of political representation. Colonialism was first significantly modified when the slave trade and then slavery were abolished (and abolition itself was a consequence of ethical arguments) in the early and mid-nineteenth century. Colonialism was further modified with the introduction of the League of Nations Mandate system and later the United Nations Trusteeship system where, by international law, certain colonies were to be administered in more humane ways and the goal gradually (and to some degree unintentionally) became to increase the prospect of self-determination for the inhabitants of these territories.

Ethical arguments against colonial practices were only successful because the beliefs about colonial subjects held by colonizers were widely reassessed. Those who argued against colonialism, whether the colonized or reformers based in the metropole, linked their preferred normative beliefs to established belief systems (legal, religious, ethical, and political) that stressed human equality and the rule of law. The cluster of principles and normative beliefs – of equality, self-determination, nationalism, democracy, human rights, non-intervention, and anti-racism – which all in various ways assert and argue for the equality of former colonial subjects, gained broader persuasive power as they were first applied in the heart of the colonial powers, the "mother" countries, and as these arguments were generalized to cover all human beings.

This chapter begins unraveling the causes for the end of colonialism by describing the beliefs and practices of the institution of colonialism, that is, by sketching the outlines and some of the content of the European colonial culture. I rehearse the arguments that supported and opposed colonialism, and include thick descriptions of colonial practices for several reasons. First, it is not possible to fully comprehend the significance of the end of colonialism without understanding exactly what colonialism (an extremely complex political, social, and economic system) was and how it was justified, and recalling the specific taken-for-granted beliefs that supported colonial practices. Those who argue that there is no difference between colonialism and neo-colonialism have perhaps forgotten what colonialism entailed. If we re-focus our eyes on colonialism as it was practiced when it was largely taken for granted, we will better see the disjunctures (and continuities) in arguments, beliefs, and practices between colonialism, decolonization, and humanitarian intervention. For instance, the slavery, mutilation, massacre, and outright theft of land that were common colonial practices are not characteristic of the decolonized world, while the arrogance of the colonizer and former colonizer may be similar.

Second, I review colonial beliefs and arguments to emphasize how ethical arguments not only are used by advocates of social change in attempts to overturn practices, but are deployed by those in dominant positions to support and normalize dominant practices. European colonialism was a cultural production; religious, scientific, economic, and political beliefs and practices all worked to make colonialism what it became in the Americas, Africa, and Asia and the colonizers made ethical arguments to justify and support colonial practices. Though it seemed natural, colonialism depended on practical, scientific, identity, and ethical arguments. The ethical arguments of the colonizers rested on two key sets of beliefs, neither of which was new: the identity belief in European superiority and the firm belief in expanding the scope, with force if necessary, of the Christian religion.

Third, I begin with early colonial arguments regarding the conquest of the Americas and the treatment of Indians in order to emphasize the obvious but frequently overlooked historical fact that there were ethical arguments about elements of colonial practice and belief – if not fundamental challenges to colonialism as an institution – for hundreds of years before colonialism was ultimately delegitimized. Even at the two zeniths of modern European colonialism – conquests of the "New World" in the sixteenth century and of Africa in the nineteenth century – there were ethical debates about its justness. Ethical arguments for reform frequently failed to spark significant change in the short term. This chapter recalls some of the early arguments about colonialism, most notably the sixteenth-century debate between Bartolomé de Las Casas and Juan Ginés de Sepúlveda over the treatment of the Indians in the Spanish conquest of the new world.

Colonialism and decolonization defined

Though colonialism varied over time and place, its characteristic practices were political control, economic expropriation (including slavery, forced labor, extraction of land and natural resources for little or no compensation, the payment of tribute to the colonizer), and cultural control, such as forced religious conversion and education in the language of the metropole. A schematic outline of the colonial plot after 1492 would look like this: a new land populated by barbarians and savages is "discovered"; missionaries and explorers chart the area, imparting the colonizer's values and marking out what is worth taking. Next, private and public companies backed by the might of governments stake claims ("concessions"), and begin settlements in order to do business. Metropolitan governments move military forces into the region to protect the missionaries, explorers, and settlers and also the investments of these private corporations. The language, religion, political, and economic systems of the first inhabitants of the area are recognized only long enough to subdue the local people and cement alliances with local "collaborators" that help smooth the way. Roads, ports, and railways are constructed by the colonizer, usually with the heavy input of colonized labor, to facilitate settlement and resource extraction. A colonial government is developed to coordinate these activities and signal to other potential colonizers that the area is already taken. That government enforces language instruction, religious conversion, and the economic system of the metropole, displacing or crushing the preexisting "backward" language, religion, and economy. Colonial economies are controlled for the colonizer's benefit: manufacturing is restricted so that often only those goods the colonizer deemed appropriate are manufactured in colonies while imports into colonies usually come from or through the ports of the colonial power. Colonial practices were linked to political, religious, economic, and scientific belief systems in the metropole, and colonialism would likely have looked quite different if they had not been so linked. Colonialism is the most intrusive, comprehensive, and institutionalized form of intervention, or coercive interference, in the affairs of others.[9] And, until recently, colonialism conferred prestige on the colonizer.

What causes colonizers to make colonial systems? The theories are well known. Most liberal and Marxist scholars favor economic explanations, arguing that when the economies of metropolitan countries need new markets, raw materials, less expensive labor, or a new place to invest, economic interests push their states to expand.[10] Another explanation stresses colonialism for strategic, balance-of-power, reasons: great powers seek colonies to balance against rivals, or to protect the geopolitical assets they already hold, such as trade routes.[11] A third set of explanations stresses domestic sources: colonies are established because of the interests of some dominant coalition which benefits politically or economically from colonies or the wars needed to get them; or colonies are established to deal with a domestic political crisis, such as overpopulation; or because of atavistic, militarist tendencies.[12]

Decolonization is commonly understood as the end of formal political, economic, and military control of a colonized territory by another power. With decolonization, formal independence is granted to the colony and sovereignty (legal autonomy) is declared by the inhabitants of the former colony. The new state is then recognized by other states and admitted to international society and international organizations as a member of equal standing.

Yet the end of formal political domination by colonizers did not entail an immediate and complete break in relations of control. Economic and sometimes political interference by former colonizers and multinational

---

[9] On defining intervention, see R.J. Vincent, *Nonintervention and International Order* (Princeton: Princeton University Press, 1974), pp. 3–13.

[10] For example, J.A. Hobson, *Imperialism* (New York: James Pott and Co., 1902); V.I. Lenin, *Imperialism: The Highest Stage of Capitalism* (New York: International, 1939); Anthony Brewer, *Marxist Theories of Imperialism: A Critical Survey*, 2nd edn (New York: Routledge, 1990).

[11] Ronald Robinson and John Gallagher with Alice Denny, *Africa and the Victorians: The Official Mind of Imperialism* (London: Macmillan, 1961).

[12] Joseph Schumpeter, *Imperialism and Social Classes* (New York: A. M. Kelly, 1951).

corporations in "developing" countries' governance, finance, and trade is not infrequent, and some would thus argue that decolonization is a fiction or at least an unfinished program. Indeed, there is a strong case to be made that colonizers replaced colonialism with neocolonialism, a more subtle relationship of dependency and control – informal political influence, unequal economic relations, and even occasional military intervention. As Adebayo Adedeji argues: "*negative decolonization* is like emancipation from slavery – freedom from being owned by others. But real *positive decolonization* will only arrive when Africans are effective participants in the world economy and have commensurate share in global power."[13]

Nonetheless, there are significant differences between colonialism and neocolonialism. Under colonialism, the "native" inhabitants of colonies had few if any political rights *vis-à-vis* the colonizer. Land and resources were often taken and occupied by settlers, corporations, and colonial governments with little or no compensation by military force and no end was in sight. Native people were forced to work, under pain of corporal punishment or imprisonment, for the companies and governments of the colonizer for little or no wages. Brutality was common and accountability for it was absent or quite distant. While there is still inequality, with decolonization political freedom has been greater, and financial compensation for resources and labor has generally improved. With the greater political freedom following decolonization, there has also been increased scope, although not complete freedom, for economic self-determination. To suggest that little if anything has changed, that neocolonialism is just as bad as colonialism, is to make an ethical argument by analogy, one that relies on the arguments that helped bring about the end of colonialism.[14] I have chosen to focus on decolonization, stressing the political and military aspects of the relations between colonizers and colonized. How and why decolonization did not include significantly rearranging the world economy so that it is more equitable, and that the inhabitants of former colonies had more economic control, should become evident after an examination of the arguments, beliefs, and culture that produced decolonization.

[13] Adebayo Adedeji, "Comparative Strategies of Economic Decolonization in Africa," in Ali A. Mazrui, ed., *UNESCO General History of Africa VIII: Africa Since 1935* (Oxford: James Curry, 1999), pp. 393–431: 431. Decolonization, as a blanket term, also ignores the different political forms and arrangements that characterized the granting of formal independence to states in the twentieth century.
[14] The fact that neo-colonialism has a pejorative connotation may presage more persuasive and effective future arguments about international political economy.

Decolonization is a context-specific regime (which grew in opposition to the colonial regime) that included normative beliefs, administrative practices in colonies, international law, and other procedures to eliminate colonialism and prevent its reimposition. Following Ethan Nadelmann, decolonization might be called a "global prohibition regime" where "those who refuse or fail to conform are labeled as deviants and condemned not just by states but by most communities and individuals as well."[15] In discussing decolonization as a cluster of beliefs (including the ideas of political self-determination, human rights, non-intervention, and sovereignty) and practices, I am emphasizing the normative element of the regime. The focus here is on how colonialism became delegitimized and was replaced with new normative beliefs – namely, that states should not keep colonies because it is wrong to deny nations and individuals political self-determination. Colonialism was formally delegitimized as an acceptable international practice, and the behavioral norm decisively shifted to decolonization in 1970, when the United Nations called colonialism a "crime" and instituted sanctions against remaining colonial powers, such as Portugal and South Africa. The timing of the change depended on the ability of actors to change the balance of political power within and among states. And that change depended on the success of ethical arguments in changing the beliefs and constitutive practices of colonialism.

Early Colonial arguments and beliefs

The first step in understanding the role of arguments in maintaining and later dismantling colonialism is to identify the main arguments on the table, though the table itself can change, as it did in the case of European colonialism. In the fifteenth and sixteenth centuries, the table where colonial arguments were made was inhabited by important members of the dominant religious culture. After the Reformation, secular and legal actors joined the debate, though religious arguments remained important because of the eighteenth and nineteenth-century religious revival. In the twentieth century colonial arguments took place among, and were judged increasingly by, bureaucrats at international organizations and the general public.

But before the colonial arguments of the sixteenth century, colonialism had been debated for thousands of years. Even at the height

---

[15] Nadelmann, "Global Prohibition Regimes," p. 479.

of the ancient Athenian empire, colonizers found it necessary to justify colonialism. The Athenian leader Pericles reasoned that empire
was natural and beneficial to the glory and economic strength of
the imperial state and argued that all states would desire empire if
they had the military might to acquire it. The Athenians told the
Spartans:

> We have done nothing extraordinary, nothing contrary to human na-
> ture in accepting an empire when it was offered to us and then refusing
> to give it up. Three very powerful motives prevent us from doing so –
> security, honour, and self-interest. And we are not the first to act in this
> way. Far from it. It has always been the rule that the weak should be
> subject to the strong; and besides, we consider that we are worthy of
> our power.[16]

Further, the Athenians argued, "Our opinion of the gods and our
knowledge of men lead us to conclude that it is a general and necessary
law of nature to rule whatever one can."[17] Even while making ethical
arguments, advocates of colonial empire obviously felt that it was important to belittle their causal force; as Pericles asserted in the Melian
dialogue, to argue against imperialism on the basis of justice in interstate
relations was irrelevant, unless there was equal power to compel each
side in a dispute.[18] That the Athenians felt they had to make arguments
for their actions is a testament to the need for justification of the "natural," whether on grounds of normative, philosophical, instrumental, or
identity beliefs.

Colonial arguments are first of all meta-arguments that try to fix the
representation of the other. The other is weak, inferior, and deserves
domination by the strong, the superior. Colonial policies follow from
the meta-argument: genocidal violence is acceptable. Yet the colonizers'
beliefs about themselves clashed with colonial practices. How could the
benevolent and superior colonizer be so cruel? This question caused an
internal critique of colonial practice which emerged powerfully in the
early and mid-sixteenth century.

This emphasis on the narrative, arguments, and actions of the colonizer is not to suggest that there was a complete lack of resistance
to colonialism. Just as colonialism was a behavioral norm, so was

---

[16] Thucydides, *History of the Peloponnesian War*, trans. Rex Warner (New York: Penguin
Books, 1986), p. 80.
[17] Ibid., p. 404.   [18] Ibid., p. 402.

resistance to it.[19] Further, colonialism as a system of practices that embodied prescriptive normative beliefs (as well as philosophical, instrumental, and identity beliefs) was increasingly challenged within the metropole itself by those who held other beliefs. Especially after 1492, the legal and religious debates in Europe over colonialism were articulated with great and intensifying clarity. There were essentially three positions.[20]

In the positive law tradition, colonialism was justified and good because the inhabitants of the colonized lands were less-than-human savages who lacked the attributes Europeans believed were marks of civilization, including government. Further, these savages were not using the land "properly" (in accordance with Western agricultural and scientific practices). And since the international law that Europeans practiced was developed among Christian European states, it did not apply to uncivilized and non-Christian peoples. Moreover, such laws as there were between states derived (echoes of Pericles) from superior force. Since the non-Europeans lacked sufficient force to consistently repel European colonizers, and were also non-Christian and uncivilized in European ways, their land was fair game – *terra nullius*. But even after missionaries converted indigenous peoples, often with the use of force or bribes, conquest obviously continued.

From the beginning, as Robert Jackson argues, the European "colonial enterprise was deeply normative."[21] And it was also as deeply religious as the Christian Crusades against Moslems and Jews that preceded the conquest of the Americas. Since political authority in the late middle ages was based on religious authority, authorization for colonialism by the Church was a necessary part of its legitimation. Columbus' conquests were legitimized by his charter from the Spanish monarchs Ferdinand and Isabella, while their right to conquest was legitimized by Pope Alexander VI in the 1493 papal bull *Inter Caetera*, which gave the monarchs all the land they had already found and "to be discovered."

---

[19] For example, see: William B. Taylor and Franklin Pease, eds., *Violence, Resistance, and Survival in the Americas: Native Americans and the Legacy of Conquest* (Washington, DC: Smithsonian, 1994).

[20] Concise summaries of these arguments are found in Lynn Berat, *Walvis Bay: Decolonization and International Law* (New Haven: Yale University Press, 1990); Christos Theodoropoulos, *Colonialism and General International Law: The Contemporary Theory of National Sovereignty and Self-Determination* (New York: New Horizon Publishing House, 1988) and Michael Donelan, "Spain and the Indies," in Hedley Bull and Adam Watson, eds., *The Expansion of International Society* (Oxford: Oxford University Press, 1984), pp. 75–85.

[21] Jackson, "The Weight of Ideas in Decolonization," p. 119.

Papal authorization for conquest in the fifteenth and sixteenth centuries was conditional on converting infidels to Christianity. "Among other works well-pleasing to the Divine Majesty and other things desirable to our heart, certainly the most outstanding is that the Catholic Faith and the Christian Religion especially in our times is being exalted and spread and extended everywhere and the salvation of souls procured and barbarian nations subdued and brought under that faith."[22] The Treaty of Torsedillas in 1494 – the foundation of which was papal authority – demarcated zones of conquest in the New World between Spain and Portugal. The mark of discovery and possession in both the Americas and Africa, upon whose southern shores the European explorers had also begun to land, was typically the erection of a stone cross.

Sixteenth-century Spanish monarchs, though perhaps particularly zealous, were not alone in articulating a religious rationale for exploration and conquest. In 1541, the French king's commission to explorer Jean de la Rocque said he should "inhabit the aforesaid lands and countries and build there towns and fortresses, temples and churches, in order to impart our Holy Catholic Faith and Catholic Doctrine, to constitute and to establish law and peace, by officers of justice so that they [the Native Americans] may live by reason and civility."[23] Sir Humphrey Gilbert, who took possession of New Foundland for Britain, was given authority to "discover . . . such remote, barbarous, and heathen lands, countries, and territories not possessed by any Christian prince or people nor inhabited by Christian people and the same to have, holde, occupy and enjoy."[24] Table 3.1 articulates some of the core beliefs that grounded the arguments in favor of European colonialism in the Americas. These are the familiar topoi (starting point) for arguments that were also used to justify later colonialism in Africa and Asia.

---

[22] Pope Alexander VI, *Inter Caetera* quoted in Donelan, "Spain and the Indies," p. 79. This was not the first time a Pope had sanctioned war and slavery. In 1455, following Ottoman seizure of Constantinople, Pope Nicholas V authorized Spanish and Portuguese conquests against "all enemies of Christ wheresoever placed," which was viewed as license for expeditions not only against the Turks, but Africa as well. Nicholas V, *Romanus Pontifex*, quoted in Francis Jennings, *The Invasion of America: Indians, Colonialism, and the Cant of Conquest* (New York: W.W. Norton, 1975), p. 4.

[23] Quoted in Anthony Pagden, *Lords of All the World: Ideologies of Empire in Spain, Britain and France, c. 1500–1800* (New Haven: Yale University Press, 1995), p. 33.

[24] Quoted in Patricia Seed, "Taking Possession and Reading Texts: Establishing the Authority of Overseas Empires," in Jerry M. Williams and Robert E. Lewis, *Early Images of the Americas: Transfer and Invention* (Tucson: The University of Arizona Press, 1993), pp. 111–147: 112–113.

Table 3.1 *Topoi for early arguments in favor of colonialism*

Philosophical	Colonialism and empire are natural.
Instrumental	The colonizer will make better, more productive, use of the land than natives because European agricultural techniques are more advanced than those of the natives.
Normative	It is good to spread the Christian faith, to convert pagans, and to bring civilization to barbarians. There are, in an Aristotelian sense, natural slaves, incapable of reason, and masters must reason for them.
Identity	The colonized (e.g. Aztecs and Incas) think that the *conquistadors* are gods (e.g. Quetzacoatl and Viracocha respectively). The colonizers are "racially superior" to the colonized by virtue of and as evidenced by all their accomplishments.

The core belief underpinning the arguments in favor of European colonial practices – from slavery to the expropriation of land and the forced religious conversion of the inhabitants of colonies – was the conviction that European colonizers were superior in every way to the colonized. Aristotle, in a passage widely quoted and debated by New World colonizers, argued that "From the hour of their birth, some are marked out for subjection, others for rule."[25] Although in their early encounters with Africans, Americans, and Asians, the Europeans tended to stress religious differences between themselves and others, European material, military, navigational, and technical competence were also taken as evidence of European superiority.[26] The indigenous inhabitants of newly conquered lands were viewed by the majority of the colonizers as less civilized, less intelligent, and even less human than Christian Europeans. The clearest evidence of the inferiority of the colonized was the fact that even though indigenous populations resisted colonialism,

[25] This is perhaps the most famous statement of Aristotle on slavery, quoted in David Brion Davis, *The Problem of Slavery in Western Culture* (Ithaca: Cornell University Press, 1966), p. 70. In *Politics*, Aristotle's remarks on slavery are embedded in a wider discussion of natural order. There can be little question that Aristotle believed in slavery as a natural institution. "For he is by nature a slave who is capable of belonging to another (and that is why he does so belong), and who participates in reason so far as to apprehend it but not to possess it; for the animals other than man are subservient not to reason, but to feelings." Aristotle, *Politics*, trans. H. Rackham (Cambridge, MA: Harvard University Press, 1990), p. 23.
[26] Michael Adas, *Machines as the Measure of Men: Science, Technology, and Ideologies of Western Dominance* (Ithaca: Cornell University Press, 1989).

142

the imperialists generally won. Anthropology and evolutionary bio-
logy of the nineteenth century later gave scientific "proof" of European
superiority. In this view, colonialism, with all of its constitutive practices – slavery, forced labor, the theft of land for cultivation and raw
materials for industries in Europe – was just because the natives were
considered less deserving than Europeans. Thus, colonialism was not
only the international behavioral norm, it was a regime (rules, norms,
and procedures) that codified and reflected the colonizers' belief in the
inferior status of the conquered.

The dominant positive law position was challenged most forcefully
by those who adhered to a natural law tradition, who argued that colonialism was illegitimate because it violated the "natural" rights of the
inhabitants of colonized regions. In this view, "savages" had sovereignty
and political institutions of their own and all humans, not just Christians, were subjects of international law. Advocates of the natural law
position argued, along the lines of Thomas Aquinas, that divine law
did not vitiate human law, and therefore the religious status of non-
Christians did not mean that they were necessarily without rights.
Though not always entirely consistent in their views, "these publicists
thus held that any land inhabited by people who were linked by some
political organization, no matter how primitive or crude, was not terra
nullius."[27]

A third position was that colonialism could be legitimate in some
circumstances but not in others. Specifically, colonial acquisitions were
just if the land was "empty" or if the natives made little productive use of
the land. For instance, in 1539 Francisco de Vitoria argued that native
populations had rights but that all humans had the right to commerce.
"If the Spaniards were to use this right inoffensively and the Indians
were to prevent this maliciously, a situation might arise in which the
Spaniards might justifiably go to war against them . . . " and take their
labor and their land.[28] Since "the object in question was not without an
owner," Vitoria argued, Spain had no right to take the land, and Spain's
claim to title "gives no support to a seizure of the aborigines any more
than if it had been they who had discovered us."[29] Eighteenth-century
legal theorist Vattel argued, "When the nations of Europe, which are too
confined at home, come upon lands which the savages have no special

[27] Berat, *Walvis Bay*, p. 107.
[28] Quoted in Donelan, "Spain and the Indies," p. 84.
[29] Quoted in Stephen Greenblatt, *Marvelous Possessions: The Wonder of the New World* (Chicago: University of Chicago Press, 1991), p. 61.

need of and are making no present and continuous use of they may lawfully take possession of them and establish colonies in them."[30]

There were heated debates about colonial practices. The first of these was over the nature of those who the conquistadors and religious evangelists met in the New World. A second great debate, described in chapter 4, was over slavery and forced labor. Few, if any, participants in these debates challenged the legitimacy of colonialism *per se*. Rather, even as reformers tried to make colonialism conform to certain normative beliefs while preserving the institution as a whole, the pillars of colonial domination were made strange, undermined, destabilized, and delegitimized.

The first of the great debates: "Are these Indians not men?"

The conquistadors and later Spanish settlers took possession of the land and people in the Americas as quickly as they could. Those conquistadors and settlers who served the Spanish king well were given grants of land and *encomienda*, a system that entitled them to the use of Indian labor for two or three years, during which time the *encomenderos* were also supposed to instruct the natives in Christian doctrine. The Indians made captive as slaves or personal servants worked in gold and silver mines, built roads, dams, and residences for *encomenderos*, transported goods as porters (*tamemes*), labored on the farms established by *encomenderos*, and were even soldiers for the conquering army. In addition to direct labor, Indians were forced to pay a tax tribute to the Spanish.

Immediately after their first encounters with the Indians, Europeans began to argue about how to treat those they met, debating whether the Indians were capable of understanding Christianity and becoming Christians, whether intermarriage was allowable, and whether the Indians were beasts and natural slaves. The answers were not immediately apparent. Christopher Columbus' writing about the New World shows both awe and abhorrence for those he met.[31] Cortez, who conquered the Aztecs just a few decades later, similarly articulated both contempt and respect for the culture he found: "these people live almost like those in Spain, and in as much harmony and order as there,

---

[30] E. Vattel, from the *Law of Nations*, quoted in Berat, *Walvis Bay*, p. 107.
[31] Lewis Hanke, *All Mankind is One: A Study of the Disputation Between Bartolomé de Las Casas and Juan Ginés de Sepulveda in 1550 on the Intellectual and Religious Capacity of the American Indians* (DeKalb, IL: Northern Illinois University Press, 1974), p. 4.

and considering that they are barbarous and so far from the knowledge of God and cut off from all civilized nations, it is truly remarkable to see what they have achieved in all things."[32]

The most intense debates were perhaps among members of the Catholic Church and so one of the first challenges to Spanish colonialism in the New World came from members of the Dominican religious order who charged that the Spanish had failed to convert the natives, the crucial condition of Pope Alexander's 1493 right to conquest.[33] There was widespread attention when, in 1511, Antonio de Montesinos, a member of the Dominican order living on Hispaniola, preached a sermon urging that Indians be Christianized, but questioned the violent methods of the conquistadors. "With what right and with what justice do you keep these poor Indians in such cruel and horrible servitude? By what authority have you made such detestable wars against these people who lived peacefully and gently on their own lands?"[34] And, going to the core of the issue, Montesinos asked, "Are these Indians not men? Do they not have rational souls? Are you not bound to love them as yourselves?"[35] Another Dominican, Matias de Paz, argued around the same time, that, "It is not licit for Christian princes to make war on the infidels for a whim of domination or for the desire to gain riches, but only inspired by the zeal of faith . . . so that the name of our Redeemer be exalted and praised throughout the entire world."[36] The Dominicans' criticisms reached Spain and sparked a wider debate and an ambiguous period of conquest where the Spanish were alternately solicitous and brutal, as if no one wanted to be as cruel as the Dominicans had charged.

Spanish laws of conquest exemplified and institutionalized the features of the argument. The Laws of Burgos in 1512 were the first regulations on Spanish conquistadors' use of Indians as servants, and the conditions in which Indians could be kept (such as providing hammocks so that Indians did not have to sleep on the ground). Under these laws, Indians would work nine months per year for the Spanish and three months for themselves. After their fourth month of pregnancy, women

[32] Quoted in ibid., p. 12.
[33] Seed, "Taking Possession and Reading Texts," pp. 124–125.
[34] Quoted in Anthony Pagden, *European Encounters with the New World: From Renaissance to Romanticism* (New Haven: Yale, 1993), pp. 70–71.
[35] Quoted in Hanke, *All Mankind is One*, p. 4. Also see Hayward R. Alker, *Rediscoveries and Reformulations: Humanistic Methodologies for International Studies* (Cambridge: Cambridge University Press, 1996), p. 168.
[36] Quoted in Luis N. Rivera, *A Violent Evangelism: The Political and Religious Conquest of the Americas* (Louisville, KY: Westminster/John Knox Press, 1992), p. 39.

were not to work in mines or fields, and the exemption continued until their children were three. Law number 24 said, "no one may beat or whip or call an Indian dog (*perro*) or any other name unless it is his proper name."[37] The Laws also ordered Spanish conquerors to educate Indians in the Christian faith and baptize their children.

After further debate, the royal lawyer for Ferdinand and Isabella drew up another document, the *Requerimiento* ("Requirement"), in 1513, which the Spanish were supposed to read to the natives when they came upon them. The Requirement obliged the natives to acknowledge their submission to both the Church and the Spanish monarchy. Natives usually did not understand the Spanish or Latin reading, or perhaps did not hear the words at all because the Spaniards often did not bother to read it to them within hearing distance. Even under these conditions, failure to immediately submit was the authority for conquest and the Requirement warns of severe punishment for the crime of not submitting:[38]

> We shall take you and your wives and your children, and shall make slaves of them, and as such shall sell and dispose of them as their Highnesses may command; and we shall take away your goods, and shall do all the harm and damage that we can, as to vassals who do not obey, and refuse to receive their lord, and resist and contradict him; and we protest that the deaths and losses which shall accrue from this are your fault, and not that of their Highnesses, or ours, nor of these gentlemen who come with us. And that we have said this to you and made this Requirement, we request the notary here present to give us his testimony in writing, and we ask the rest who are present that they should be witnesses of this Requirement.[39]

The royal historian, Gonzalo Fernández de Oviedo y Valdéz, not known for his sympathy for Indians, described one reading of the Requirement this way.

---

[37] Laws of Burgos quoted in Hanke, *All Mankind is One*, pp. 8–9.

[38] That potential subjects of New Spain might understand and still reject proselytizing, as Montezuma did, was also ostensibly irrelevant. Montezuma's response to Cortez's explanation of his Christianizing mission, according to Bernal Díaz, was "I have understood your words and arguments very well before now, from what you have said to my servants at the sand dunes, this is about three Gods and the Cross, and all those things that you have preached in the towns through which you have come. We have not made any answer to it because here throughout all time we have worshipped our own gods, and thought they were good, as no doubt yours are, so do not trouble to speak to us any more about them at present." Quoted in Greenblatt, *Marvelous Possessions*, p. 139.

[39] Quoted in Hanke, *All Mankind is One*, p. 36.

It appears that they had been suddenly pounced upon and bound before they had learnt or understood anything about Pope or Church, or any one of the many things said in the Requirement; and that after they had been put in chains someone read the Requirement without knowing their language and without any interpreters, and without either the reader or the Indians understanding their language, they had no chance to reply, being immediately carried away prisoners, the Spaniards not failing to use the stick on those who did not go fast enough.[40]

If this was how such occasions typically went, why bother writing the Requirement and reading it to the natives? In whose eyes must conquest be legitimate? Obviously the only relevant audiences were God and other Europeans.

The Spanish conquerors were faithful to elements of the Requirement. Indians were routinely enslaved. Technically, two categories of slaves were allowed: those acquired in war, *esclavos de guerra*, and those who were already slaves among the Indians, *esclavos de rescate*. In practice, such distinctions were not widely observed. Slaves were branded on their face, arms, and legs, to indicate their status, and if freed were branded again on the face. As historian William Sherman recounts, contemporary observers documented frequent slaving expeditions in Central America with some Spaniards, such as Diego López de Salcedo, widely known for their cruelty. One observer, named Pedraza, "charged that when the Indians were taken on the road in chains by López de Salcedo and his men some of the carriers faltered under the strain and could not continue. In order to avoid the delay caused by opening the chains to release the stragglers, their heads were cut off and the victims were left on the road, 'the head on one side and the body on the other; and they went on their way.'"[41] Brutality was the main feature of conquest.

> On their way from Honduras to Nicaragua, the Spaniards burned towns and caused great destruction. Recently-delivered babies were taken from their mothers' breasts and tossed aside. Caciques [chiefs] and *principales* were put in collars and chains in groups of ten. More than four hundred Indians were taken from the valley of Guamira loaded down with the merchandise of the governor and his companions. If an Indian fell his head was cut off.

[40] Ibid., pp. 36–37.
[41] William L. Sherman, *Forced Native Labor in Sixteenth-Century Central America* (Lincoln: University of Nebraska Press, 1979), p. 45.

> In Aguatega 200 Indians were punished: one-third of them were put in
> a large hut and burned to death; another one-third were torn to pieces
> by dogs; eyes were plucked out, arms were cut off, and other cruelties
> were practiced on the remaining one-third of the Indians.[42]

Debates about the treatment of Indians took place in both secular and
religious settings. In 1524, King Charles V established the Council of
the Indies which governed Spain's colonies in the Americas until 1834.
Meeting in Madrid, the six to ten members of the council appointed by
the king were charged with issuing all legislation, and approving expenditures and official acts by colonial officials. In 1526 King Charles
proclaimed "Ordinances about the Good Treatment of the Indians" requiring that "at least two religious men or ordained clerics" accompany
all expeditions.[43] The Church hierarchy generally supported conquest
and *encomienda*. Still, some members of the Franciscan and Dominican
orders hotly debated the humanity of Indians and Charles V seems to
have been swayed by arguments on both sides.

For several decades, arguments about how to treat the Indians focused on the question of their humanity and suitability for indoc-
trination in Christian beliefs, with many arguing that Indians were
beasts. The Bishop of Ávila, Francisco Ruiz, said, "Indians are malicious
people . . . but they are not capable of natural judgment or of receiving
the faith . . . and they need, just as a horse or a beast does, to be directed
and governed by Christians who treat them well and not cruelly."[44]
About two years later, in 1519, in an audience before King Charles V,
the Franciscan Bishop Juan de Quevedo said Indians were "*siervos a
natura*."[45] Quevedo said, "If any people ever deserved to be treated
harshly, it is the Indians, who resemble ferocious beasts more than
rational creatures."[46] The Dominican friar Tomás Ortiz said in 1525 that
Indians were "incapable of learning . . . God has never created a race
more full of vice . . . the Indians are more stupid than asses and refuse to
improve in anything."[47] Ortiz charged that Indians "do not have
any human artistry or skills . . . they turn into brute animals."[48] The
Royal historian Oviedo said that Indian heads were different than
European heads: "They were not, in fact, heads at all, but rather hard and
thick helmets, so that the most important piece of advice the Christians

---

[42] Ibid., p. 46.   [43] Rivera, *A Violent Evangelism*, p. 43.
[44] Quoted in Hanke, *All Mankind is One*, p. 11.   [45] Quoted in ibid.
[46] Quoted in Sherman, *Forced Native Labor*, p. 154.
[47] Quoted in Hanke, *All Mankind is One*, pp. 11–12.
[48] Quoted in Rivera, *A Violent Evangelism*, p. 137.

gave when fighting in hand to hand combat with them was not to strike them on the head, because that broke the swords. And just as their heads were hard, so their understanding was bestial and evilly inclined."[49] In about 1532 or 1533, Domingo de Betanzos charged that the Indians were incapable of religious instruction, and later he argued that they were beasts, destined for extinction.[50] Betanzos' views, whose precise wording has in many cases been lost, were widely discussed and provoked a strong reaction among those who thought Indians were not beasts but humans.

What was at stake in the question of whether Indians were human was the legality of the conquest. As Francisco de Vitoria wrote in 1535 about the wars in Peru:

> I do not understand the justice of this war . . . . In truth, if the Indians are not men but monkeys, *non sunt capaces iniuriae*. But if they are men and our fellow creatures, as well as vassals of the Emperor, I see no way to excuse these conquistadores, nor do I know how they serve your majesty in such an important way by destroying your vassals.[51]

Pope Paul III, upon hearing arguments that Indians were beasts and incapable of learning to be Catholics, and the counter-claim that those who were making such arguments were doing the work of the devil, issued the Bull, *Sublimis Deus*, in June 1537. In it he said, "the Indians truly are men and that they are not only capable of understanding the Catholic faith but, according to our information, they desire exceedingly to receive it . . . they may and should, freely and legitimately, enjoy their liberty and the possession of their property; nor should they be in any way enslaved; should the contrary happen it should be null and of no effect."[52] Charles V reacted to both Pope Paul's statements, and those of Vitoria, whose 1539 lectures on *De Indis* questioned unfettered conquest, by trying to squash debate unless he had authorized it.[53] The king was unsuccessful at muzzling the pope and other members of the Church.

At the same time the monarchy also tried to curb the colonizers' worst abuses. In 1542, Charles V proclaimed, "New Laws of the Indies for the Good Treatment and Preservation of the Indians," restricting the *encomenderos'* practices. The New Laws specifically prohibited enslaving any more Indians and forbade using Indians as *tamemes* (porters) except in extraordinary cases (which colonists were quick to proclaim), and

[49] Quoted in Pagden, *European Encounters*, p. 57.
[50] Hanke, *All Mankind is One*, pp. 13, 19, 27.   [51] Quoted in ibid., p. 16.
[52] Quoted in ibid., p. 21.   [53] Rivera, *A Violent Evangelism*, pp. 84–85.

certainly not without paying them.[54] Existing slaves were to be set free unless *encomenderos* could prove just title to them. Further, the law forbade the establishment of new *encomiendas*, and upon the death of the owners of existing *encomiendas* their title was to revert to the king.

Spanish settlers protested against the New Laws, many officials of New Spain delayed their implementation as much as possible and, in Peru, settlers revolted. Resistance to reform was nothing new. *Encomenderos* had long evaded the laws protecting the Indians, and it was difficult for the crown to enforce its regulations, so rules were frequently redrafted. In 1545, the Council of the Indies modified the New Laws, allowing continuation of the *encomienda* land and forced labor system. Slavery was still prohibited, but only with the appointment of a vigorous judge in Central America, Alonso López de Cerrato, who served from 1548 to 1555, were laws protecting Indians more vigorously enforced and large numbers of Indian slaves freed.

The debate in Spain and the Americas over treatment of the Indians thus reached a peak at mid-century. In 1549 Betanzos made a deathbed retraction of his views about the "bestial" nature of Indians.[55] Meanwhile, Judge Cerrato's enforcement of the New Laws was opposed by many Spanish colonizers although supported by some members of the church based in the colonies. Some Spanish settlers traveled to Spain from the New World in order to push for making their *encomienda* grants perpetual – the Indians could be held forever (in perpetuity) as laborers and this status would be inherited by their children. *Encomenderos* and conquistadors argued that *encomienda* should be perpetual since this was the best way to reward them, as agents of the king, and to promote the

---

[54] Spanish conquistadors and *encomenderos* used *tamemes* to carry their personal effects, food, and the goods that flowed to and from Spain, on their backs. *Tamemes* often traveled hundreds of miles carrying loads of 75 to 100 pounds in all sorts of weather through lowlands and mountains. They were given little to eat and though they were supposed to be paid, were often enslaved. "In one of the most catastrophic examples, one expedition saw 4,000 *tamemes* loaded for a journey from which no more than 6 survived to return to their homes." Sherman, *Forced Native Labor*, p. 114. The Spanish government gradually regulated the use of *tamemes*, for instance, saying in 1530, that they should not carry loads from coasts to highlands or the other way around, because such extremes in climate were devastating. In 1533, Spain ordered that no one could carry more than 50 pounds, and that distances ought to be limited. The New Laws said *tamemes* must be paid and some Spanish governors (notably Contreras of Nicaragua, after 1535) prohibited the use of *tamemes* and encouraged instead cart-building and road construction. Crown money was allocated for the purpose of road construction from the 1540s onward. Still, the laws were selectively implemented and enforced, and *tamemes* were widely used until roads and draft animals were more widely available. Ibid., pp. 222–224.
[55] Hanke, *All Mankind is One*, p. 30.

religious conversion of Indians. Further, they argued, "the very natives will benefit because if they are held in perpetuity they will be treated well . . . "[56]

In the same period, Juan Ginés de Sepúlveda was trying to get his long treatise on the inferiority of Indians and the justice of conquest in the Americas, then circulating in manuscript form, published in Spain and Rome.[57] Sepúlveda had earlier, in the 1520s and 1530s, made arguments for the justice of Spain's campaigns against heresy and its war against the Turks.[58] Sepúlveda's argument against Indians' rights was based on Aristotle's distinction between rulers and natural slaves, and bolstered by evidence from Oviedo who regarded the Indians as incapable of becoming Christians and wrote, in any case, that "God is going to destroy them soon."[59] Further, Sepúlveda argued that Pope Alexander's 1493 Bulls were "a right to conquer in order to civilize."[60]

One of the most vocal supporters of Indians, and of the judge Cerrato, was Bartolomé de Las Casas, who had for decades argued for Indian rights. Before becoming a harsh critic of European treatment of the Indians, Las Casas participated in and benefited from the cruelest aspects of the conquest, including holding *encomienda* until 1514 and participating in the conquest of Cuba with Diego Velazques.[61] Although he apparently heard Montesinos' 1511 sermon, Las Casas said his revised understanding of the situation of the Indians resulted from a personal religious experience.[62] Acting on his new beliefs while Bishop of Chiapa, Las Casas denied absolution to those Spaniards who practiced slavery and urged others to do so.

Las Casas wrote an indictment of Spanish conquest, *Brevísima relación de la destruccíon de las Indios* (*Most Brief Relation of the Destruction of the Indies*), published in 1542, that turned the religious mission on its head. He argued that Spanish brutality was so awful that "the more

[56] Quoted in Rivera, *A Violent Evangelism*, p. 129.
[57] Juan Ginés de Sepúlveda, *Democrates Segundo o de las Justas Causas del la Guerra Contra los Indios*, ed., Angel Losada (Madrid: Consejo Superior de Investigaciones Cientificas, Instituto Francisco de Vitoria, 1951). The Council of the Indies refused to publish the manuscript. The Royal Council of Castile, the University of Salamanca, the University of Alcala, and the Council of Trent all either refused to consider the manuscript or refused to publish it. Sepúlveda could not get the manuscript published in Spain or Rome, and a summary of it, published in Rome in 1550, was banned in Spain, with Charles V ordering confiscation of any copies that made it to Spain. See Hanke, *All Mankind is One*, pp. 62–63.
[58] Hanke, *All Mankind is One*, pp. 61–62; Pagden, *Lords of All the World*, p. 100.
[59] Oviedo quoted in Hanke, *All Mankind is One*, p. 45.
[60] Pagden, *Lords of All the World*, p. 100.   [61] Hanke, *All Mankind is One*, pp. 6–7.
[62] Pagden, *European Encounters*, pp. 71–73.

they proceeded to discover, and destroy, and lose people and lands, the more remarkable were the cruelties and iniquities against God and his children that they perpetrated."[63] Las Casas argued that kindness was more certain than cruelty to bring converts to Christianity and he urged that all conversion should be through peaceful persuasion. Las Casas criticized *encomienda* because it showed the contempt Spaniards had for the "unfortunate Indians, whom the Spaniards did not love and adore as people but rather as use, work, and sweat, as one does with wheat, bread or wine."[64] Las Casas was apparently "one of the prime movers behind the legislation" of the New Laws in 1542.[65] In 1546, Franciscans, Dominicans, and Augustinians, including Las Casas, convened a conference in Mexico to discuss slavery.[66] Las Casas railed against the "vehement, blind and disorderly greed from which all harm and evil come" and after his return to Spain furiously lobbied the Council of the Indies and the king in 1549 against *encomienda* and forced conversions.[67]

Las Casas *versus* Sepúlveda

Critics of Spain's colonial practices in the Americas were able to force a formal debate. In July 1549, the Council of the Indies proposed to King Charles V that all conquest be suspended until they decided "how conquests may be conducted justly and with security of conscience."[68] In April 1550 the king briefly halted all conquests until a method for conducting them could be found, and a "disputation" between Sepúlveda and Las Casas began in August at Valladolid in front of the "Council of Fourteen" to debate the question: "Is it lawful for the King of Spain to wage war on the Indians, before preaching a faith to them, in order to subject them to his rule, so that afterward they may be more easily instructed in the faith?"[69] The king sent "outstanding theologians" and members of the Council of the Indies to judge the arguments of Sepúlveda and Las Casas.[70] Las Casas and Sepúlveda agreed that

[63] Quoted in Stephanie Merrim, "The Counter-Discourse of Las Casas," in Williams and Lewis, eds., *Early Images of the Americas*, pp. 149–162: 152.

[64] Quoted in Santa Arias, "Empowerment Through the Writing of History: Bartolemé de Las Casas's Representation of the Other(s)," in Williams and Lewis, eds., *Early Images of the Americas*, pp. 163–179: 171.

[65] Sherman, *Forced Native Labor*, p. 273.

[66] David Traboulay, *Columbus and Las Casas: The Conquest and Christianization of America, 1492–1566* (New York: University Press of America, 1994), p. 177.

[67] Las Casas quoted in Rivera, *A Violent Evangelism*, p. 139.

[68] Council of the Indies quoted in Hanke, *All Mankind is One*, p. 66.

[69] Ibid., p. 67.   [70] Ibid., p. 67.

conversion of Indians to Christianity was the goal; they differed about the Indian's capacity for such conversion and the methods which could be used legitimately to impose Spanish rule. Both men used a mix of ethical, identity, practical, and philosophical arguments.

Sepúlveda, who spoke for three hours on the first day, summarized his unpublished *Democrates Segundo* to the Council, making essentially four points in his argument that war against Indians was just. First, he said that Indians were barbarians and thus ought to be subjects of the Spanish; second, Indians committed crimes against natural law, including human sacrifice and idolatry; third, Indians oppressed and killed innocent people; fourth, war may be waged against infidels in order to prepare them for learning the Christian faith.

Sepúlveda's arguments clearly rested on the assertion of Indian inferiority. Sepúlveda relied on Oviedo's claims that Indians had actually heard and accepted the gospel before but had forgotten it and later fallen into idolatry, and furthermore, that Indians were unteachable, and anyway, the land belonged to Spain and conquest was only recovery.[71] Sepúlveda argued that Indians were "little men (*homunculos*) in whom you will scarcely find traces of humanity . . . "[72] Further, Sepúlveda believed: "In prudence, talent, virtue and humanity they are as inferior to the Spaniards as children to adults, women to men, as the wild and cruel to the most meek, as the prodigiously intemperate to the continent and temperate, that I have almost said, as monkeys to men."[73] He said:

> But if you deal with the virtues, if you look for temperance or meekness, what can you expect from men who were involved in every kind of intemperance and wicked lust and who used to eat human flesh? And don't think that before the arrival of the Christians they were living in quiet and the Saturnian peace of the poets. On the contrary they were making war continuously and ferociously against each other with such rage that they considered their victory worthless if they did not satisfy their monstrous hunger with the flesh of their enemies, an inhumanity which in them is so much more monstrous since they are so distant from the unconquered and wild Scythians, who also fed on human flesh, for these Indians are so cowardly and timid, that they scarcely withstand the appearance of our soldiers and often many thousands of them have given ground, fleeing like women before a very few Spaniards, who did not even number a hundred.[74]

---

[71] Ibid., pp. 40–41. Oviedo argued that North Americans were the descendants of a Visigothic diaspora.
[72] Quoted in ibid., p. 85.   [73] Quoted in ibid., p. 84.   [74] Quoted in ibid., p. 85.

In rebuttal, Las Casas reportedly read his entire manuscript *In Defense of the Indians Against the Persecutors and Slanders of the Peoples of the New World Discovered Across the Seas* to the Council over the course of five days.[75] The *Defense* is scathing: "I think Sepúlveda wrote that little book hastily and without sufficiently weighing the materials and circumstances."[76] Las Casas responded to Sepúlveda on the basis of both "law" and "fact" and argued that Sepúlveda and Oviedo were wrong about the incapacity of the Indians and that it was the Spaniards who "in the absolutely inhuman things they have done to those nations they have surpassed all other barbarians."[77] Domingo de Soto, a member of the Council of Fourteen recalled Las Casas' arguments for his fellow Council members this way:

> The bishop [Las Casas] described at length the history of the Indians, showing that though some of their customs were not particularly civil, they were not however barbarians on this account but rather a settled people with great cities, laws, arts, and government who punished unnatural and other crimes with the death penalty. They definitely had sufficient civilization that they should not be warred against as barbarians.[78]

Las Casas supported his *Defense* with earlier works and another document, what he called the "second part."[79] The first part, 63 chapters, summarized Sepúlveda's arguments, critically reviewed Sepúlveda's and Oviedo's histories, and finally asserted that "Indians are our brothers, and Christ has given his life for them," and therefore war against them ought to end, since "they are docile and clever, and in their diligence and gifts of nature, they excel most peoples of the known world."[80] Las Casas also charged that the methods of conquest were counterproductive and against "natural" law which requires humans to treat others as they would like themselves to be treated:

> What good can come from these military campaigns that would, in the eyes of God, who evaluates all things with unutterable love,

---

[75] Bartolomé de las Casas, *In Defense of the Indians Against the Persecutors and Slanders of the Peoples of the New World Discovered Across the Seas*, trans. and ed. Stafford Poole (DeKalb, IL: Northern Illinois University Press, 1974).
[76] Ibid., p. 297. [77] Ibid., p. 29. [78] Quoted in Hanke, *All Mankind is One*, p. 80.
[79] Las Casas, *In Defense of the Indians*, p. 362. For example, Las Casas wrote a plea for peaceful evangelism, rather than forced conversion, in the late 1530s, *De Unico Vocationis Modo* [The Only Way of Attracting all Peoples to the True Faith] and his *Entre Los Remedios* proposed alternative methods of governing the Indies.
[80] Las Casas, *In Defense of the Indians*, p. 362.

154

compensate for so many evils, so many injuries, and so many unaccustomed misfortunes? Furthermore, how will that nation love us, how will they become our friends (which is necessary if they are to accept our religion), when children see themselves deprived of parents, wives, husbands, and fathers of children and friends? When they see those they love wounded, imprisoned, plundered, and reduced from an immense number to a few?[81]

After Las Casas had finished reading his manuscript, the Council adjourned the proceedings to consider the arguments. The Council reconvened for a second round of debate at Valladolid in May 1551. According to Sepúlveda, this round focused on the meaning of Pope Alexander's Bulls of donation. Since the records of the Council have been lost, one may assume that Las Casas repeated many of his earlier arguments.[82] The Council did not make any formal decision about the merits of either man's position. But, politically, in the short run, Las Casas lost, and perpetuity was granted in Peru by King Philip in 1556, who argued that Indian labor was needed to run the colonies.[83]

However, in the long run, Las Casas' views did have some effect. First, the king continued to support the reformer Cerrato in Central America who persisted in his vigorous implementation of the New Laws. Second, though Las Casas later publicly regretted his advocacy of African slavery as a substitute for Indian bondage, the practice became widespread in the Americas, replacing Indian slavery by the end of the seventeenth century.[84] Third, religious conversion was made more voluntary and treatment of the remaining Indians, by then the area had been largely depopulated, was made less harsh. The Requirement was replaced in 1573 with the "Instrument of Obedience and Vassalage," which was also to be read to the Indians.[85] With this document, and the "Ordinances Regarding New Discoveries and Towns," the word conquest was banned and "pacification" was substituted, signifying that future conversion should be peaceful. Most important, Indian slavery was ended and debt bondage or *naboria* was curbed. Tribute was also reduced. Further, the *encomienda* system, where Indians were required to do labor without pay for the Spanish, instead of or in addition to paying tribute, was eventually replaced by the *repartimiento* system. Under

---

[81] Ibid., p. 29.   [82] Hanke, *All Mankind is One*, pp. 68–69.
[83] Rivera, *A Violent Evangelism*, p. 130.
[84] Spain exported enslaved Africans to the Americas before Las Casas made his arguments about African slavery replacing Indian slavery. See Arthur F. Corwin, *Spain and the Abolition of Slavery in Cuba, 1817–1886* (Austin: University of Texas Press, 1967), p. 4.
[85] Hanke, *All Mankind is One*, pp. 120–121.

repartimiento Indian villages were required to send a certain number of workers per week to a Spanish town for compulsory wage labor, either for private or public works. Less brutal than its predecessor, *repartimiento* also existed side by side with various combinations of wage and forced labor, such as Indian contract and free labor, and African slavery.[86]

Summary

The behavioral norm and dominant normative belief in the late fifteenth century was colonization and religious crusade. Yet, even in this background, those who paid for and conducted colonization in the New World felt they had to justify their actions. The way they did so was to try to extend their previous ethical arguments about conquest and slavery from the European context to the New World by arguing that Indians were inferior, and that conquest was a religious act of reclamation. Identity, practical, and philosophical arguments were also deployed.

Las Casas' and Vitoria's comments on the treatment of Indians were not intended to be, nor were they, deep criticisms of colonialism *per se*. Rather, both Dominicans wanted Christianization to occur, and Vitoria thought brute force was acceptable if the Indians continually refused to take up Christianity. Even the judge Cerrato – who enforced laws against Indian slavery in Central America and argued against colonists who said Indian slavery was necessary (telling Spaniards to do the labor themselves) – saw himself as a faithful servant of imperial interests.[87]

In line with these modest goals, early victories against the worst abuses of colonialism in the New World were modest yet significant. Even when Indian slavery ended, the *encomienda* and later *repartimiento* systems of forced labor for Indians continued. Las Casas wrote in 1562: "For days upon days, years upon years we have overlooked the two kinds of tyranny by which we have destroyed countless republics; one called conquest when we first entered . . . The other was and is tyrannical government . . . to which they gave the name repartimiento or encomienda."[88] And even after the mid-sixteenth-century reforms, "Any sign of rebelliousness became the pretext for slave raids. For

---

[86] Elinor G. K. Melville, "Land–Labour Relations in Sixteenth-Century Mexico: The Formation of Grazing Haciendas," in Paul E. Lovejoy and Nicholas Rogers, eds., *Unfree Labour in the Development of the Atlantic World* (Portland, OR: Frank Cass, 1994), pp. 26–35.
[87] See Sherman, *Forced Native Labor*.
[88] Quoted in Trabouley, *Columbus and Las Casas*, p. 183.

example, in 1620 governor Alonso de Guzman of Costa Rica invented a rebellion among the Aoyaque Indians in order to attack and enslave them."[89]

Brutality toward Indians continued in the Spanish controlled parts of the New World, although it was less horrific and less commonly lethal. As historian William Sherman notes: "While in the second half of the sixteenth century one does find examples of clearly abusive, and sometimes cruel, treatment, the extreme cases are appreciably less common."[90] Sherman argues that in part this was because the next generation of Spanish elites were born and raised in New Spain; they were Creoles who socialized intimately from birth with mestizo and Indian people. "Certainly they mistreated Indians, but they were less likely to kill them."[91] The difference is significant and symbolizes, as Sherman suggests, that there was greater empathy and that the first debate, over the humanity of the Indians, was decided in favor of the Indians. Las Casas' position was ultimately successful because he was able to change the identity beliefs of the conquistadors and their emotional relationship to the Indians.

Nonetheless, Las Casas and other reformers did not intend to overthrow the system, only to curb its excesses on behalf of Indians. Thus, it is true that some of the burden of abuse was shifted from Indians to Africans.[92] Africans had already been brought to the Americas by the English, Spanish, and Portuguese for slavery. Holding Africans in lower regard than Indians, Las Casas for at least three decades had proposed African slavery as a substitute for Indian enslavement.[93] While the debates and reforms of the sixteenth century were part of the process of reforming colonialism to make it less brutal, declining populations of Indians, due to epidemic disease and harsh treatment, ironically boosted the rationale for African slavery.

Finally, while the immediate effect of the debates was ambiguous – modest reforms in the treatment of Indians and greater reliance on

[89] O. Nigel Bolland, "Colonization and Slavery in Central America," in Lovejoy and Rogers, eds., *Unfree Labour*, pp. 11–25.
[90] Sherman, *Forced Native Labor*, p. 331.   [91] Ibid., p. 332.
[92] In North America, Indians were also enslaved, though usually in smaller numbers than Africans. Indians, too, often allied with or harbored escaped African slaves, and it was more common to attempt to keep the two populations separate. The French governor in Mississippi called for an end to Indian slavery in 1728. Indians were still enslaved by English colonists and Americans well into the nineteenth century, though the policy that prevailed was more characteristically war, extermination, and/or treaties and forced resettlement.
[93] Rivera, *A Violent Evangelism*, pp. 180, 183.

African slaves – the arguments of the critics of colonialism gained international attention. For example, Las Casas' *The Destruction of the Indies* was translated into Dutch (1578), English (1583), Latin (1598), and German (1599).[94] Las Casas won the meta-argument, reframing the role of slavery in conquest and, with Vitoria, he inadvertently planted the seed of colonialism's denormalization. Many of the arguments used in the sixteenth century to limit the ill treatment of Indians were to reappear 200 years later in debates about modifying and ending African slavery. Thus, the starting point for future arguments about colonialism, in particular the treatment of slaves and colonial subjects, was changed by the sixteenth-century debates over the treatment of Indians.

[94] Trabouley, *Columbus and Las Casas*, p. 187.

4 Decolonizing bodies: ending slavery and denormalizing forced labor

> Too much time has been lost in declamation and argument – in petitions and remonstrances against *British* slavery. The cause of emancipation calls for something more decisive, more efficient than words.[1]

Slavery and forced labor, two of humanity's oldest institutions, were among the defining characteristics of colonial practice and understanding their demise is vital for understanding decolonization.[2] Between 1500 and the mid-nineteenth century, "What moved in the Atlantic in these centuries was predominantly slaves, the output of slaves, the inputs to slave societies, and the goods and services purchased with the earnings on slave products."[3] Forced labor was also important in the economic development of African colonies. Africans, forcefully recruited, were often the mainstay of the troops of colonial conquest, and forced laborers built the roads, bridges, and railways that took out the commodities produced by forced labor. Since colonizers were too few or unwilling to do the work required to maintain and expand colonial holdings, and the colonized often wanted little or nothing to do with the colonizer, none of these colonies would have endured without unfree

---

[1] Elizabeth Heyrick, *Immediate, Not Gradual Abolition; Or, an Inquiry into the Shortest, Safest, and Most Effectual Means of Getting Rid of West Indian Slavery* (London pamphlet 1824), quoted in Claire Midgley, "Slave Sugar Boycotts, Female Activism and the Domestic Base of British Anti-Slavery Culture," *Slavery and Abolition* 13 (December 1996), 137–162: 153 emphasis in the original.

[2] In addition to the well-known slave trading and slavery institutions of France, Britain, Spain, and the United States that endured into the nineteenth century, Ancient Egyptians, Greeks, Romans, Sub-Saharan Africans, Asians, Aztecs, and some nations of Native North America practiced slavery (often getting slaves from conquest in war). But, as with colonialism, slavery was not the same in practice at all places at all times.

[3] Barbara L. Solow, "Introduction," in Barbara L. Solow, ed., *Slavery and the Rise of the Atlantic System* (Cambridge: Cambridge University Press, 1991), pp. 1–20: 1.

labor. That it was legitimate for the main part of the required labor to be performed by slaves or forced laborers was the dominant belief and assumption for most of the era of colonialism.

The abolition of slavery and amelioration of forced labor are relevant for understanding the end of colonialism in several respects. First, disagreements about the causes of abolition are both parallel to and a precursor of debates about the end of colonialism.[4] Second, colonialism consisted of more than one set of beliefs and practices, including, most importantly, the belief that those who were colonized deserved and even benefited from their subjugation. Once these core beliefs and practices of colonialism came under widespread criticism – they were denormalized and delegitimized – colonialism itself was vulnerable to denormalization and delegitimation. Third, the demise of slavery and forced labor significantly altered the institution of colonialism in ways that were generally unanticipated, even by the advocates of change. Though colonialism remained in many instances profitable for colonizers, profitability diminished with the end of slavery and forced labor, and some of the economic incentive for having colonies was undermined. Further, the political fortunes of colonial interests declined as their economic clout waned. And, as long as colonialism included slavery and forced labor, large police forces were required to make those systems work in the face of slaves' and forced laborers' resistance and rebellion. With the end of slavery and decline of forced labor, the institutions which required the most police power, reasons for political domination and physical occupation, were diminished. Thus, if the roots of decolonization are in the demise of the practices of slavery and forced labor, and the cause of abolition was changing normative beliefs through ethical argument, then ethical arguments are a powerful underlying cause of decolonization.

After being practiced in the West for thousands of years, legal abolition of the slave trade and slavery was relatively quick, though abolition did not come all at once and there were even setbacks. For example, Britain's policy on slavery took decades to resolve, even as Britain led other European and American states in abolishing slavery. British Chief Justice Lord Mansfield ruled in 1772 that slaves brought to England

---

[4] See, Eric Williams, *Capitalism and Slavery* (Chapel Hill, NC: University of North Carolina, 1944); Thomas Bender, ed., *The Anti-Slavery Debate: Capitalism and Abolitionism as a Problem in Historical Interpretation* (Berkeley: University of California Press, 1992); David Brion Davis, *Slavery and Human Progress* (Oxford: Oxford University Press, 1984); Orlando Patterson, *Slavery and Social Death: A Comparative Study* (Cambridge, MA: Harvard University Press, 1982); Suzanne Miers and Richard Roberts, eds., *The End of Slavery in Africa* (Madison: University of Wisconsin Press, 1988).

could not be forcibly deported by their masters to a slave colony. This ran counter to a 1729 ruling by Judge Philip Yorke and Judge Charles Talbot that a slave could be forcibly returned from England to the colonies. Britain regulated the slave trade to make it more humane in 1788 with Dolben's Act, reducing the number of slaves per ship to decrease mortality during voyages.[5] Both the US and Britain made the trade in slaves illegal in 1807. After British slave traders got out of the business, Spanish, Portuguese and other slavers took up most of the slack of the trade in the nineteenth century. It was only in 1833, with the Emancipation Act, that Britain formally abolished slavery in its colonies in the West Indies, Mauritius, Cape of Good Hope, and Canada – though it introduced an "apprentice" system in its place – and emancipation followed four years later. But emancipation of British-held slaves in India and Ceylon did not occur for another decade. And, though Spain outlawed Indian slavery in the sixteenth century, it maintained African slavery well into the nineteenth century. The French allowed Indian and African slavery in their colonies in the Americas and when the Spanish took control of French Louisiana in 1769, Spain allowed Indian slaves to be kept in that territory. In 1792, Denmark, not then a significant participant, decided to gradually outlaw the slave trade, to be accomplished over the course of ten years. Emancipation for Danish Caribbean slaves was granted in 1848. French policy was perhaps most vacillating. While the law did not initially allow African slaves in France, in 1716 the law was amended so that slaves could be brought to France. Revolutionary France, after proclaiming the Rights of Man, abolished slavery in 1794, reinstated slavery in 1802, abolished it again for a short time under Napoleon, and restored it in 1814. France outlawed the slave trade in 1821 and finally abolished slavery in 1848.

The late history of slavery was characterized by both the rise of industrial capitalism and the increased articulation of the rights of slaves and of the obligations of masters to treat slaves better. I begin with a brief discussion of the economics of abolitionism and the economic arguments on the table during the anti-slavery movement and argue against a simple economic explanation for abolition. Economics generally favored keeping the slave trade and slavery in place. Slaves and forced laborers incrementally gained legal recognition and protections

---

[5] Also in 1788, the House of Commons began an impeachment proceeding against the British proconsul of India, Warren Hastings, for violating his "trust" by committing injustices against the people of India.

that were gradually enforced before the abolition of both practices, and well before industrialization took hold in the colonies.

Rather than economic forces, it was the movements to end the slave trade and abolish slavery that worked to change beliefs, interests, and even the capabilities of the pro-slave forces. The normative and constitutive beliefs which supported slavery and forced labor were gradually undermined and new, more egalitarian, beliefs supplanted previous beliefs. Identity and role beliefs also changed. Where once good social entities kept slaves or used forced labor for the purpose of uplifting the undeveloped, beliefs reversed: only bad social entities used slavery and forced labor. The process that led to belief change was ethical argument, which mobilized individuals to form and join social movements to change the domestic political and international conditions that supported slavery. After abolition, the anti-slavery movement turned its attention to forced labor. Like slavery, forced labor was gradually regulated in the nineteenth century, with abolition of forced labor following in the early and mid-twentieth century. The abolition of slavery and forced labor were gradual processes that began with denormalization and delegitimation, then regulation, and ultimately the abolition of unfree labor.

Slavery

Economics of abolition

Were the slave trade and slavery profitable? Did the institutions end because they became less profitable? These questions are still hotly debated among economic historians and, to answer them, it is important to understand the complex role of slavery in colonial economies.

Three modes of production were common in colonies and slave societies after 1500: simple extraction of raw materials such as animal pelts, timber, and mineral wealth; plantation farming; and manufacturing. All three required labor that was in extremely short supply if natives avoided Europeans or were killed by disease and war, and if workers from the metropole were reluctant to move to the colonies. Slavery and forced labor do not work well for hunting and timber harvesting when it is easy for workers to escape into forests where they can subsist. Compulsory labor does work for mining, farming, manufacturing, and for public works such as road building.

Land was abundant in the New World while labor for expansion and development was scarce. At the same time that Native American

populations were diminished by Spanish conquest and literally deci-
mated by disease (including measles, plague, typhus, and small-pox),
the settlers' demand for labor grew with their appetite for gold, silver,
wood, road-building and portage. There was little incentive for free
people to work for others if they could work for themselves, and
until the nineteenth century, Europeans did not flock in droves to the
Americas. Only in the 1840s did the net migration of free persons to
the New World finally exceed the forced migration of slaves.[6] The
Spanish, and then other colonizers, enslaved tens of thousands of Native
Americans, a practice that began almost as soon as the first explorers
arrived. As natives died in epidemics, more were captured from areas
where they still lived in large numbers and moved to meet the demand
for unfree labor. But as Native Americans died at too great a rate, or ran
off, the initially more expensive African slave labor became more attractive to colonizers and importation of African slaves began even before
Native American slavery was outlawed. Later, East Indian, Chinese, and
Irish indentured laborers were imported, gradually at first, to supplement African slave and forced labor in the Americas. In many places in
the Americas, especially in the Caribbean, African and Native American
slaves often exceeded 50 percent of the population, and in some
colonies, slaves were more than 90 percent of colonial populations.[7]
However, since the African slave population in the Americas
was usually not self-sustaining – more male slaves were brought to the
Americas from Africa (men were worth more on the block), infant mortality was high among slaves, and suicide by slaves was not uncommon –
slave economies depended on continuing to extract slaves from
Africa.

In 1713, provisions in the Treaty of Utrecht between England and
Spain granted England a monopoly on the African slave trade for thirty
years, with monarchs of both countries receiving a quarter of the profits
of the trade, and the British expected to pay a duty to Spain for each
imported slave. The monopoly ended in 1750, and the Royal African
Company, charged with carrying out the trade, went bankrupt.[8] There-
after, the British slave trade was privatized, though still subsidized by
the Crown. A new holding company, granted an annual sum of 10,000,

---

[6] David Eltis, *Economic Growth and the Ending of the Transatlantic Slave Trade* (Oxford: Oxford University Press, 1987), p. 24. Also see Solow, "Introduction".
[7] See Patterson, *Slavery and Social Death*, Appendix C, pp. 353–364.
[8] See W.E. Burghardt Du Bois, *The Suppression of the African Slave Trade to the United States of America, 1638–1870* (New York: Longmans, Green, and Co., 1896), p. 3.

maintained the forts necessary for African slavery. Any trader, as long as they paid a small fee (2) to the government for the use of African ports could legally engage in the trade.[9] By the mid-eighteenth century, Britain dominated the slave trade.

Estimates vary, but from the 1500s to 1870, between 9 million and 10 million people were transported to North and South America by the major British, Portuguese, French, US, Dutch, and Danish slave carriers. Not all are counted in this figure. No one knows for sure how many died after capture, *en route* to slave ships, and in crossing from Africa to the Americas in the middle passage. Records for mortality rates on the ships that succeeded in crossing (and not all did, whole ships went down) generally range from 4 percent to 55 percent, though much higher mortality rates were not unusual. In 1773, one Dutch slave ship, the *Nooitgedacht*, lost 89 percent of the 157 slaves aboard to a scurvy epidemic, though the mortality rates for Dutch slave traders were an average of 17 percent.[10] French mortality rates in the eighteenth century averaged about 14 percent.[11] One English slaver, "Captain Collingwood of the *Zong* threw his cargo of 132 diseased slaves overboard in order to claim the insurance which would not have been payable if they had died a natural death."[12] In the last century of the trade, however, mortality aboard ship was declining for slaves (although not for the crews) and in 1848 the British Foreign Office estimated mortality rates for slaves aboard ship of about 25 percent.[13] One assumes that, despite these risks, the slave trade must have been alluring to those Europeans and Americans who profited from it.

> The fortunes of Bristol and Liverpool were thus built upon the bodies of tens of thousands of negroes. . . . The profits of the Round Trip, as it came to be called, made it the most paying of all regular trade routes.

[9] Hugh Thomas, *The Slave Trade: The Story of the Atlantic Slave Trade, 1440–1870* (New York: Simon and Schuster, 1997), p. 265.

[10] Johannes Postma, "Mortality in the Dutch Slave Trade," in Henry A. Gemery and Jan S. Hogendorn, eds., *The Uncommon Market: Essays in the Economic History of the Atlantic Slave Trade* (New York: Academic Press, 1979), pp. 239–260: 252–253.

[11] Herbert S. Klein and Stanley L. Engerman, "A Note on Mortality in the French Slave Trade in the Eighteenth Century," in Gemery and Hogendorn, eds., *Uncommon Market*, pp. 261–272.

[12] Christopher Lloyd, *The Navy and The Slave Trade: The Suppression of the African Slave Trade in the Nineteenth Century* (London: Frank Cass, (1949) 1968), p. 8.

[13] Mortality rates for the white crews were generally higher than for slaves both before and after reforms on the condition of slave transport. See Philip D. Curtin, *The Atlantic Slave Trade: A Census* (Madison: University of Wisconsin Press, 1969), especially pp. 268, 276 and Postma, "Mortality in the Dutch Slave Trade."

It was commonly divided into three 'passages.' On the outward passage [from Britain] the cargo consisted of textiles, hardware, alcohol and antiquated firearms. These were traded on the [African] coast for slaves, who were shipped to America and the West Indies in the notorious Middle Passage. The principal cargoes taken on there for the homeward passage were sugar, tobacco and rum.[14]

Though profitability of the slave trade varied – with demand, transportation, and insurance costs, mortality of slaves on ships, and the costs of repressing slave resistance and rebellions on ships – it was, overall, extremely profitable. While the figure of 30 percent profit is often cited, Roger Anstey conservatively calculates that British slave traders averaged closer to 10 percent profits for the period 1760 to 1810, when the trade was at its peak.[15] Christopher Lloyd suggests that it was possible for British slavers to net as much as 60,000 in a single voyage.[16] Profitability and demand for the slave trade may have been higher in markets where slave populations were not self-sustaining and had to be bolstered by continuing imports from Africa. By the eighteenth century, female slaves were reproducing at rates in the US that could sustain and enlarge the slave population, thereby decreasing US demand for imported slaves. But demand for imported slaves remained high in the Caribbean and South America, where female slaves generally were far fewer in proportion to male slaves (e.g. in Cuba one-third of slaves were female), and slave populations were generally not self-sustaining.[17]

British colonies in the West Indies depended heavily on slave labor for production of exports in the eighteenth century. Eric Williams argues that slavery and the other legs of the "triangular" trade of humans and

[14] Lloyd, *The Navy and The Slave Trade*, p. 5.
[15] Roger Anstey, *The Atlantic Slave Trade and British Abolition 1760–1810* (London: Macmillan, 1975) pp. 46–47. E. Phillip LeVeen, *The British Slave Trade Suppression Policies, 1821–1865* (New York: Arno Press, 1977), p. 22 calculates that slave trade profits were 8.8 percent in the Caribbean in 1800. But profit was never the sole justification given by advocates. British admirals claimed that the slave trade was a valuable way of training seamen who would be available at times of war. On the other hand, "Wilberforce showed that the Slave Trade was not so much a nursery as the graveyard of seamen, since the mortality aboard slave ships was well beyond all comparison greater than that on board vessels engaged on other trades, and the hardbitten seamen pressed from that type of ship were more of a hindrance than a help on board a man-of-war." Lloyd, *The Navy and The Slave Trade*, p. 10.
[16] Lloyd, *The Navy and The Slave Trade*, p. 6.
[17] Arthur F. Corwin, *Spain and the Abolition of Slavery in Cuba, 1817–1886* (Austin: University of Texas Press, 1967), p. 15.

goods among Africa, the West Indies, and Britain, "made an enormous contribution to Britain's industrial development. The profits from this trade fertilized the entire productive system of the country."[18] Thus, British anti-slave policy in the nineteenth century does not seem to make sense economically because, as David Eltis argues,

> In 1800, if one were to argue in terms of economic self-interest, the British should have been actively encouraging the slave trade and slave settlements throughout the world. Such a policy would have been highly effective in achieving national goals as laid down by the amalgam of London merchants and landed gentry who dominated British government at this time. It would have best served the aims of manufacturers and wage earners alike.[19]

Furthermore, when its policy toward the slave trade changed, British efforts to suppress the international slave trade were enormously costly. Not only were slave economies doing better than non-slave economies, the British government paid for suppression of the trade. Three squadrons of naval patrols on the east and west coasts of Africa and in Latin America were involved in slave trade suppression. Naval patrols alone by the British Africa Squadron (based off the west coast of Africa) cost hundreds of thousands of pounds annually, and although the number of ships on station varied with Britain's other uses for naval power (for instance, the Crimean War) by the 1840s, when the Africa Squadron was at its peak, Britain often devoted over 10 percent of its naval manpower and "between a sixth and a quarter of its warships to suppressing slave traffic."[20] From 1811 to 1870, the Africa Squadron alone cost 6.8 million in direct expenses and some 5,000 seamen and officers died, mostly of malaria, in suppression duty.[21] "The cost of maintaining the Africa Squadron far exceeded the value of Britain's annual trade with Africa."[22] Britain's total direct costs from 1810 to 1870 for slave trade suppression, including bounties for naval crews, the special court at Sierra Leone, compensation for wrongful arrests, and the money

---

[18] Williams, *Capitalism and Slavery*, p. 105.   [19] Eltis, *Economic Growth*, p. 6.

[20] Ethan Nadelmann, "Global Prohibition Regimes: The Evolution of Norms in International Society," *International Organization* 44 (Autumn 1990), 479–526: 492. Also see Eltis, *Economic Growth*, pp. 92–93.

[21] LeVeen, *British Slave Trade Suppression Policies*, p. 78 and Lloyd, *The Navy and The Slave Trade*, p. xi.

[22] Howard Temperley, *British Antislavery, 1833–1870* (London: Longman, 1972), p. 45; Williams, *Capitalism and Slavery*, p. 171.

paid to other governments to obtain treaties to end the trade, were at least 13.9 million.[23]

Although the increased cost to slave traders of doing business cannot be estimated with great confidence, British suppression certainly made the slave trade more difficult and costly. Eltis estimates that the costs of acquiring slaves rose between 8 and 11 percent after the British set about curbing the slave traffic to the Americas.[24] In fact, because slaves could command such a high price, profitability grew even under suppression, until the Brazilian and Cuban slave imports halted at mid-century. If a slaver could make it to Cuba in the period between 1856 and 1865, profits averaged over 90 percent, though profits of around 20 and 30 percent were more common for slaves sold in Cuba or southern Brazil between the 1820s and 1850.[25] Such high rates of profit are no surprise to students of sanctions and trade embargoes: those who are caught can lose all while those who succeed in busting embargoes can command premium prices.

In sum, slave trading was, until very late, a lucrative venture for slave traders. The slave trade even remained profitable after Britain began to suppress the trade, because though risks of capture increased, over time, the price of slaves grew. The slave trade did not end because it was no longer profitable. Indeed, the price to Britain, which led the effort to abolish the trade, was extremely high. Rather, the slave trade ended because it was suppressed for normative reasons and because after abolition demand for slaves ended.

But what about slave labor itself? Did slavery become less profitable? Arguments stressing economic causes for the end of slavery claim that slavery became too costly or was gradually outmoded with improvements in agricultural production and early industrialization. Economic arguments also suggest the ways that slave resistance, including slave revolts, and the costs of supervision and work slow-downs by slaves, increased the costs of slavery so that wage labor became relatively more attractive.

[23] LeVeen, *British Slave Trade Suppression Policies*, pp. 78–80. Eltis, who does a more comprehensive accounting than LeVeen, argues that direct costs of suppression to the British government were much higher. Eltis, *Economic Growth*, pp. 91–94. Also see Suzanne Miers, *Britain and the Ending of the Slave Trade* (New York: Longman Group, 1975). Other country's navies patrolled the coast for slave ships, though they were not as effective as the British.
[24] Eltis, *Economic Growth*, p. 140. Indeed, after 1807, because of the profits involved, British merchants participated in the trade in other ways, for instance in outfitting the ships for slavers. Parliamentary laws after this point gradually constrained and criminalized this activity.
[25] Ibid., p. 161 and LeVeen, *British Slave Trade Suppression Policies*, p. 22.

As with the economic gains of the slave trade, the profitability of slave labor is disputed. Slavery could be more or less profitable depending on a number of factors, including the cost of acquiring slaves and the productivity of slave labor versus the costs of feeding, housing, and training slaves. The costs of fending off slave rebellions and revolts also varied. Need for repression was constant, although the aggregate costs of repression probably declined as slave revolts decreased. The successful slave revolt in Haiti in 1791, which resulted in French decolonization, was certainly frightening to slave holders throughout the New World, but it was the exception. Large-scale slave revolts in English colonies, such as the maroon rebellion in Jamaica in 1739, seemed to be declining in the Americas prior to the establishment of abolition movements, and only increased during the decades (1790–1832) when abolitionists were already most active.[26]

Again, the crucial case is probably Britain, which was at the forefront of the industrial revolution and whose huge West Indian empire depended on slave labor. Did Britain abolish slavery because it was no longer profitable as a means of production? If free labor were less expensive than slave labor in the British colonies, it should have been so all along, and slave systems should never have taken hold on such a large scale in the first place. (And the price of obtaining slave labor for other colonial powers did not grow until after Britain moved to abolish its part in the trade.) Still, early on, British abolitionists stressed the economic benefits of free labor, and the *laissez-faire* policies championed by Adam Smith and others stressed morality and used the rhetoric of freedom current in Europe after the French Revolution and the war against Napoleon.[27] Lord Palmerston, in 1842, argued that anti-slavery activity brought *both* economic and moral reward:

> Let no man imagine that those treaties for the suppression of the slave trade are valuable only as being calculated to promote the great

[26] Seymour Drescher, *Capitalism and Antislavery: British Mobilization in Comparative Perspective* (Oxford: Oxford University Press, 1987), pp. 100–103. Some of the largest revolts were fueled by news of abolitionist activity: revolts in Barbados in 1816 involved some 20,000 slaves, Demerara in 1823 involved 30,000 slaves, and Jamaica 1831–32 involved 60,000 slaves. These revolts were ruthlessly squashed by colonists who killed 400, 250, and 540 slaves respectively during or after these revolts. Michael Craton, "Emancipation from Below? The Role of British West Indies Slaves in the Emancipation Movement, 1816–34," in Jack Hayward, ed., *Out of Slavery: Abolition and After* (London: Frank Cass, 1985), pp. 110–131.

[27] See James Walvin, "Freedom and Slavery and the Shaping of Victorian Britain," in Paul E. Lovejoy and Nicholas Rogers, eds., *Unfree Labour in the Development of the Atlantic World* (Portland, OR: Frank Cass, 1994), pp. 246–259.

interests of humanity, and as tending to rid mankind of a foul and detestable crime. Such was indeed their great object and their chief merit. But in this case as in many others, virtue carries its own reward; and if the nations of the world could extirpate this abominable traffic, and if the vast population of Africa could by that means be left free to betake themselves to peace and innocent trade, the greatest commercial benefit would accrue, not to England only, but to every civilized nation which engages in maritime commerce. The slave trade treaties therefore are indirectly treaties for the encouragement of commerce.[28]

But most people didn't think abolition would bring growth. They feared just the opposite, and those concerns proved correct. For Britain, the toughest anti-slavery crusading state, slavery was quite profitable even at the time it was abolished by Parliament. The most lucrative and fastest-growing segments of the colonial economy – sugar, coffee, and tobacco – depended on slave labor. Dependence on slave labor for British colonial production of cotton, which fed Britain's textile mills, and sugar, in fact grew over the course of the abolition movement. For instance, slaves provided labor for 70 percent of Britain's cotton industry in 1787; by abolition in 1838, slaves/apprentices provided 90 percent of the labor.[29] As Seymour Drescher notes, the "world economy as a whole seems to have been as optimal for expanding the Atlantic slave system at the end of British slavery in the 1830s as it was at the beginning of popular abolitionism in the 1780s."[30]

And abolition was economically costly. Productivity in British West Indian economies immediately declined following abolition, while Cuba and Brazil, which still practiced slavery, had robust economies and their demand for slaves grew. Only high duties on Cuban and Brazilian sugar somewhat protected British West Indian planters, and those were reduced after 1846. Declining competitiveness after abolition explains why British West Indian planters eventually joined international abolitionist efforts.[31] For Drescher, British abolition is thus paradoxical. "The real economic paradox of abolition is that in one major region after another – the British colonies, the American South, Cuba, and Brazil – *political* power had to intervene to constrict or to abolish major slave systems whose economic advantages remained intact well after the transformation of British abolitionism into a world human rights

[28] Quoted in ibid., pp. 252–253.
[29] Drescher, *Capitalism and Antislavery*, p. 7.   [30] Ibid., p. 4.
[31] LeVeen, *British Slave Trade Suppression Policies*, p. 69; Corwin, *Spain and Abolition of Slavery in Cuba*, pp. 53 and 60.

movement."[32] Similarly, David Eltis argues, since land was still abundant and labor in the New World remained scarce at the time of abolition, "there was a profound incompatibility between economic self-interest and anti-slavery policy."[33]

The paradox of abolition for Britain is further heightened once one factors in the costs of compensation to slave holders for abolition. The British government paid colonial slave owners 16.7 million in 1836 and 4.1 million in 1837 in compensation for emancipation. Spending on compensation in 1836, at 25.6 percent of total government expenditures, exceeded total spending for the army, ordnance, and the navy combined. And though spending on compensation for slave owners in 1837 was much less, 7.6 percent of total government expenditures, it was close to total British spending on its navy for that year.[34]

Many in France who were contemporary observers of British abolition thought British policy in freeing almost 800,000 slaves was folly, and the pro-slavery French emphasized the decline in British revenue and productivity that followed emancipation in the West Indies. One French pro-slavery advocate argued in 1844 that "production in the English West Indies had fallen by more than a third."[35] The president of the Council of Ministers, Adolphe Thiers, told the Chamber of Deputies in 1840 that British "emancipation has considerably diminished work and production."[36] Although French abolitionists said these claims were exaggerated, as Lawrence Jennings argues, pro-slavery forces in France nevertheless used the British economic difficulties following emancipation to bolster their cause, hoping perhaps that practical arguments would trump ethical ones.[37]

Changes in modes of production could explain the demise of slavery in such a relatively short period (if colonial economies had, in fact, been subject to dramatic changes in production), but such changes do not account for moral or religious arguments about the evil of slavery. If slavery were no longer profitable, there would have been little reason to outlaw it. And, if slavery were uneconomical there would have been little opposition to abolition; rational actors would simply have acted to

[32] Drescher, *Capitalism and Antislavery*, p. 5. Emphasis in the original.
[33] Eltis, *Economic Growth and the Ending of the Transatlantic Slave Trade*, p. 15.
[34] Spending in 1836 on the army, ordnance, and navy totaled 11.7 million; spending on the navy for 1837 was 4.2 million. Calculations based on figures in B.R. Mitchell, *British Historical Statistics* (Cambridge: Cambridge University Press, 1988), pp. 587, 595.
[35] Joseph Napoléon Ney, quoted in Lawrence C. Jennings, *French Reaction to British Slave Emancipation* (Baton Rouge: Louisiana State University Press, 1988), p. 76.
[36] Quoted in ibid., pp. 78–89.   [37] Ibid., p. 206.

use the more efficient forms of free labor. As Martin Klein argues: "Most slave systems were functioning well when slavery came under attack."[38] Indeed, during the period in which Spain used slave labor and Britain did not, Spanish colonial resistance in Cuba to British abolitionism grew, with Cubans insisting that abolition would bring economic ruin.[39]

As Martin Klein suggests, though slavery was used and abandoned, and used again through history, something different occurred in the eighteenth century.

> There were times in many parts of the world when slavery declined, often replaced or absorbed by other forms of exploitation. During the late medieval period, slavery disappeared in northern Europe, and in seventeenth-century Russia it was absorbed within a rather harsh form of serfdom. The use of slaves was declining in South-East Asia during the nineteenth century, most strikingly in Thailand. There is no evidence, however that slavery was seriously attacked in any part of the world before the eighteenth century.[40]

Thus, declining profits cannot explain the end of slavery. Something else was going on. Growing belief in the greater profitability and moral virtues of free labor, and the belief that slavery was wrong, explain the outlawing of slavery. Abolitionists made persuasive ethical arguments.

Constructing and deconstructing slavery

The argument for slavery in Western culture was grounded in the ancient Aristotelian belief that some humans were natural slaves. Voltaire said of black people, whom he called "animals," that it was "a serious question whether they are descended from monkeys or whether the monkeys come from them."[41] French dictionaries in the eighteenth century frequently defined negroes as "slaves which are extracted from the African coast."[42] In 1858, an American scholar of slave law, T. R. R. Cobb, wrote:

> this inquiry into the physical, mental, and moral development of the negro race seems to point them clearly, as peculiarly fitted for a laborious class. The physical frame is capable of great and long-continued

[38] Martin A. Klein, "Slavery, the International Labour Market and the Emancipation of Slaves in the Nineteenth Century," in Lovejoy and Rogers, eds., *Unfree Labour*, pp. 197–229: 212.
[39] See Corwin, *Spain and Abolition of Slavery in Cuba*.
[40] Klein, "Slavery," p. 201.
[41] Quoted in William B. Cohen, *The French Encounter with Africans: White Response to Blacks, 1530–1880* (Bloomington: Indiana University Press, 1980), p. 88.
[42] Quoted in ibid., p. 145.

exertion. Their mental capacity renders them incapable of successful self-development, and yet adapts them for the direction of the wiser race. Their moral character renders them happy, peaceful, contented and cheerful in a status that would break the spirit and destroy the energies of the Caucasian or the native American.[43]

Advocates of slavery and the trade also argued that the practices benefited the enslaved and the society from which slaves were taken. An eighteenth-century pamphlet said, "In certain vast regions of the Africa [*sic*] Continent, where the Arts are almost as little known of rural as of civil cultivation, inhabitants grow faster than the means of sustaining them; and Humanity itself is obliged to transmit the supernumeraries, as objects of traffic, to more enlightened, or less populous countries; which, standing in constant need of their labour, receive them into property, protection and employment."[44] Later, the Englishman Boswell said: "To abolish [slavery] . . . would be extreme cruelty to the African savage, a portion of whom it saves from massacre or intolerable bondage in their own country, and introduced into a much happier life, especially now when their passage to the West Indies, and their treatment there, is humanely regulated."[45]

Not all agreed with these views, even in the eighteenth century. The American Quaker anti-slavery activist Anthony Benezet argued that the slave trade hurt Africans and he disputed the arguments that slavery was natural in Africa. "The . . . natives were an inoffensive people, who, when civilly used, traded amicably with the Europeans . . . And . . . there is no reason to think otherwise, but that they generally lived in peace amongst themselves."[46]

Some philosophers and political commentators portrayed slavery as a corrupt and corrupting institution. In 1748 Montesquieu wrote, "The state of slavery is in its own nature bad. It is neither useful to the master nor to the slave; not to the slave because he can do nothing through a motive of virtue; nor to the master, because by having an unlimited

---

[43] T.R.R. Cobb, *An Inquiry into the Law of Negro Slavery in the United States of America: To Which is Prefixed, An Historical Sketch of Slavery*, 1858 quoted in Thomas D. Morris, *Southern Slavery and the Law, 1619–1860* (Chapel Hill: University of North Carolina Press, 1996), p. 18.

[44] Stephen Fuller, *Remarks on the Resolutions of the West India Planters and Merchants* (1789) quoted in Anstey, *Atlantic Slave Trade and British Abolition*, p. 293.

[45] Quoted in Lloyd, *The Navy and The Slave Trade*, pp. 6–7.

[46] Anthony Benezet, *Some Historical Account of Guinea, its Situation, Produce, and General Disposition of its Inhabitants with an Inquiry into the Rise and Progress of the Slave Trade, its Nature, and Lamentable Effects* (London: (1771) 1788), pp. 50–51, quoted in Anstey, *Atlantic Slave Trade and British Abolition*, p. 216.

authority over his slaves he insensibly accustoms himself to the want of all moral virtues, and thence becomes fierce, hasty, severe, choleric, voluptuous, and cruel."[47] Rousseau also argued vociferously against slavery, turning Aristotle on his head in *The Social Contract*, by saying that "no matter how we look at it, the right of enslavement is invalid, not only because it is illegitimate, but also because it is absurd and meaningless. The words 'enslavement' and 'right' are mutually contradictory; they exclude each other."[48] And Tom Paine in 1775 noted that Americans "complain so loudly of attempts to enslave them while they hold so many hundreds of thousands in slavery."[49]

Adam Smith's *Wealth of Nations*, published in 1776, made a strong economic argument against slavery and in favor of free labor. "The experience of all ages and nations, I believe, demonstrates that the work done by slaves, though it appears to cost only their maintenance, is in the end the dearest of any. A person who can acquire no property, can have no other interest but to eat as much, and to labour as little as possible." And while Smith argued that free labor was generally superior to slave labor, he nonetheless implied slavery was based on a natural human impulse. "The pride of man makes him love to domineer, and nothing mortifies him so much as to be obliged to condescend to persuade his inferiors. Wherever the law allows it, and the nature of the work can afford it, therefore, he will generally prefer the service of slaves to that of freemen."[50] Though Smith is generally understood to say that slavery was never profitable, he did argue that in some cases slavery could be extremely profitable. "In our [British] sugar colonies . . . the whole work is done by slaves, and in our tobacco colonies, a very great part of it." In this instance: "The profits of a sugar-plantation in any of our West Indian colonies are generally much greater than those of any other cultivation that is known either in Europe or America: And the profits of a tobacco plantation, though inferior to sugar, are superior to those of corn . . . Both can afford the expense of slave cultivation, but sugar can afford it still better than tobacco."[51]

[47] Quoted in Anstey, *Atlantic Slave Trade and British Abolition*, p. 103.
[48] Jean Jacques Rousseau, *The Social Contract or the Principles of Political Right* in Rousseau, *The Essential Rousseau*, trans. Lowell Bair (New York: Times Mirror, 1974), book 1, ch. IV, p. 15.
[49] Paine quoted in Ira Berlin, *Many Thousands Gone: The First Two Centuries of Slavery in North America* (Cambridge, MA: Harvard University Press, 1998), p. 220.
[50] Adam Smith, *An Inquiry into the Nature and Causes of the Wealth of Nations* (New York: Modern Library, 1994), book II, ch. II, p. 418.
[51] Ibid., pp. 418–419.

Economic arguments became increasingly important, but given the culture of Europe in this era, Christianity was the primary table on which to represent slavery and judge arguments about it. Building on the arguments of those who advocated better treatment for slaves, abolitionists tried to persuade the majority that slavery was not "natural" after all, and that it ought to be abandoned because it was immoral, against the plan of God's Providence. The Quaker Benezet suggested that slavery was inconsistent with Christian principles, arguing that slaves were "undoubtedly" the "children of the same Father . . . for whom Christ died."[52] British and American Quakers and evangelical abolitionists of the eighteenth and nineteenth centuries, such as Granville Sharp, attempted to "sufficiently prove that *slavery* was ever detestable in the sight of God."[53] Sharp used the history of the Israelites as evidence against slavery, saying that they

> were reminded of their *Bondage in Egypt*: for so the almighty *Deliverer* from *Slavery* warned his people to limit and moderate their *bondage*, which the Law permitted, by the remembrance of *their own former bondage* in a foreign land, and by a remembrance also of his great mercy in *delivering them* from that *bondage*: and he expressly referred them to *their own feelings*, as they themselves had experienced the intolerable yoke of Egyptian Tyranny! 'Thou shalt not oppress a Stranger; for ye know the heart of a *stranger*, seeing ye were strangers in the land of Egypt' (Exodus 23:9). And again: 'Thou shalt remember that thou wast a *Bond-man* in the land of Egypt, and the Lord thy God redeemed thee' (Deuteronomy 15:15).[54]

Evangelical British abolitionists warned that failure to abolish the slave trade was against God's order and could lead to divine retribution on *both* a personal and national level.[55] Abolitionists argued that the American Revolution and the later war against France were divine

---

[52] Benezet, *Some Historical Account of Guinea*, p. 79, quoted in Anstey, *Atlantic Slave Trade and British Abolition*, p. 214.

[53] Granville Sharp, *The Law of Retribution* (London: 1776), pp. 2–3 quoted in Anstey, *Atlantic Slave Trade and British Abolition*, p. 185.

[54] Granville Sharp, *The Just Limitation of Slavery in the Laws of God* (London: 1776), pp. 6–7, quoted in Anstey, *Atlantic Slave Trade and British Abolition*, p. 188.

[55] In line with their views, evangelical abolitionists often favored other benevolent social policies. For example, the prominent English abolitionist William Wilberforce, a member of parliament, was also against hanging, in favor of penal reform, and argued for a more generous welfare provision for the poor. In England, "Antislavery was part of a religious, philanthropic and reform complex which embraced missionary activity, temperance, peace, free trade and limited political reform." David Turley, *The Culture of English Antislavery, 1780–1860* (London: Routledge, 1991), p. 6.

174

punishment against Britain.[56] In 1807, James Stephen, a leading abolitionist, argued that the ravages of Napoleonic wars were divine wrath
for England's failure to give up the slave trade despite their knowledge
that it was wrong.

> Who are the people that have provoked God thus heinously, but the
> same who are among all the nations of the earth, the most eminently
> indebted to his bounty? He has given to us an unexamined portion of
> civil liberty; and we in return drag his rational creatures into a most se-
> vere and perpetual bondage. Social happiness has been showered upon
> us with singular profusion; and we tear from oppressed millions every
> social, nay almost every other comfort. In short, we cruelly reverse in
> our treatment of these unhappy brethren, all the gracious dealings of
> God towards ourselves. For our plenty we give them want; for our ease,
> intolerable toil; for our wealth, privation of the right of property; for
> our equal laws, unbridled violence and wrong. Science shines upon us,
> with her meridian beams; yet we keep these degraded fellow-creatures
> in the deepest shades of ignorance and barbarity. Morals and manners
> have happily distinguished us from the other nations of Europe; yet we
> create and cherish in two other quarters of the globe, an unexampled
> depravity of both. A contrast still more opprobrious remains. God has
> blessed us with the purest effulgence of the Gospel; and yet we dishon-
> our by our slave trade the christian name; and perpetuate the darkness
> of paganism among millions of our fellow creatures.[57]

These arguments, which denormalized, delegitimized, and proclaimed the trade and slavery against Britain's national interests and
identity were powerful precisely because of their religious grounding. Not surprisingly, much of the argument occurred among theologians. Granville Sharp, for instance, met with twenty-two of twenty-six
bishops in 1779 in order to press his anti-slavery arguments and he was
apparently well received.[58]

In response, pro-slavery forces mounted powerful arguments. For
example, some religious figures cited support for slavery in the Bible.
One such attempt, by the Reverend Raymond Harris in 1788 was titled:
*Scriptural Researches on the Licitness of the Slave Trade. Shewing its Confor-
mity with the Principles of Natural and Revealed Religion. Delineated in the
Sacred Writing of the Word of God.*[59] British advocates of slavery at the

[56] See Anstey, *Atlantic Slave Trade and British Abolition*, p. 193; Turley, *Culture of English
Antislavery*, pp. 28–29; 205.
[57] James Stephen, *The Dangers of the Country* (London: 1807), pp. 195, 212 quoted in
Anstey, *Atlantic Slave Trade and British Abolition*, pp. 195–196.
[58] Anstey, *Atlantic Slave Trade and British Abolition*, p. 246.
[59] Turley, *Culture of English Antislavery*, p. 23.

turn of the nineteenth century also argued that abolition would give trade and military advantages to Britain's enemies, especially France.[60]

Abolitionist movement strategy

Some abolitionists responded to the concern about British interests by suggesting that emancipation itself could follow slowly after abolition of the trade.[61] But the strategy and tactics of the movement were not self-evident, and British abolitionists debated whether to go for total abolition and risk losing all (immediatists), or to start with more modest goals, namely first curbing the trade and then seeking abolition (gradualists). The official name of one London group illustrates their tactical and strategic vision: "The London Society for the Mitigation and Gradual Abolition of Slavery throughout the British Dominions." Their tactics for rousing public ire and pressuring the government included letters to prominent officials, petitions, direct appeals, pamphleteering, and mass meetings.

A gradual approach to slave questions is evident even among those who became the most ardent advocates of abolition. Quakers, while at first loathe to bring up an issue that might divide the community of Friends, since some Quakers favored and practiced slavery, took progressively strong positions against the trade and slavery. For example, at the Philadelphia Yearly Meeting in 1758, members decided to exclude from the business of the church any Friends who bought or sold slaves and urged members to free any slaves they had. In 1776, the Philadelphia Yearly Meeting disowned anyone who still had slaves. Other Yearly Meetings had also taken up the question of slavery, and the American Quakers turned to lobbying their colonial governments and, after Independence, the United States government, to end the slave trade and slavery.[62] Further, in an early example of transnational activity by a non-governmental organization, Anthony Benezet and other American Quakers, notably John Woolman, attempted to influence English Quakers against slavery, for instance in pamphlets such as Benezet's 1766 *A Caution to Great Britain and her Colonies in a Short Representation of the Calamitous State of the Enslaved Negroes in the British Dominions*, which was published in London.[63] The Pennsylvania Abolition Society and other American Quakers corresponded with English

---

[60] Ibid., p. 26.   [61] Ibid., p. 28.
[62] Anstey, *Atlantic Slave Trade and British Abolition*, pp. 211–212.   [63] Ibid., p. 214.

abolitionists, feeding them news of their tactics in both state legislatures and the US Congress.[64] Benezet and Woolman made frequent business trips to England in the 1760s and 1770s. English Quakers, following the American lead, established an anti-slave trade committee in London in 1783, writing articles for newspapers, distributing anti-slave trade tracts, such as *the Case of Our Fellow Creatures, The Oppressed Africans* (1783), and lobbied against slavery, presenting their first anti-slave trade public petition to Parliament in 1783. In May 1787, the Committee for the Abolition of the Slave Trade (or the London Committee) was formed, with Quakers comprising nine of its twelve founders.[65] The movement also included members of the legislature, notably William Wilberforce, who put the question of abolishing the trade to Parliament for many years before it finally succeeded in 1807.

Both American and British anti-slavery movements, dominated by upper-class men, believed persuasion would succeed, as the minutes of a meeting in July 1787 of the London Committee show. "Our immediate aim is, by diffusing knowledge of the subject, and particular modes of procuring and treating slaves, to interest men of every description in the Abolition of the Traffic; but especially those from whom any alteration must proceed – the Members of our Legislature."[66] The London Committee published and distributed thousands of copies of such titles as Thomas Clarkson's *Summary View of The Slave Trade* and John Newton's *Thoughts upon the African Slave Trade* (both 1788). In addition, the London Committee printed and distributed copies of a slave ship plan and sections (a dramatic image of slaves packed horizontally, side by side and head to toe) to members of parliament and copies of relevant parliamentary debates to the public.[67] In addition, parliamentary petition campaigns were coordinated by the London Committee and abolitionists in Manchester. In early 1788, 102 petitions with about 60,000 signatures were sent to Parliament by abolitionists. In 1792, 519 petitions with about 400,000 signatures were presented to the House of Commons from all over England, more petitions than had been sent on

[64] J. R. Oldfield, *Popular Politics and British Anti-Slavery: The Mobilization of Public Opinion Against the Slave Trade, 1787–1807* (Manchester: Manchester University Press, 1995), pp. 51–53.
[65] James Walvin, *An African's Life: The Life and Times of Olaudah Equiano, 1745–1797* (London: Cassell, 1998), p. 155; Oldfield, *Popular Politics*, p. 42.
[66] Quoted in Anstey, *Atlantic Slave Trade and British Abolition*, p. 255.
[67] The Committee financed printing of 8,000 ship plans in 1788–1789 alone. Oldfield, *Popular Politics*, p. 166.

any subject in a single session.[68] The petitions, rooted in Christian belief, focused on the humanity of the slaves and the inhumanity of the trade, often called Britain's participation in the trade a "national disgrace."[69]

In 1788 British abolitionists sought to reassure the public that the movement's aim was only to end the trade, not slavery itself: "however acceptable a temperate and gradual abolition of slavery might be to the wishes of Individuals it never formed any part of the Plan of this Society."[70] Yet advocates of immediate abolition, such as Elizabeth Heyrick quoted at the opening of this chapter, argued that petitioning, "declamation and argument" were insufficient and other tactics – hopefully "more efficient than words" – notably boycott, must be used. British and American Quakers first practiced personal abstention from slave produced products in the 1760s. Later, abstention grew into a movement tactic that not only well-educated upper-class males could participate in, but that encompassed women and members of other classes. In 1791–1792, and again from 1825 to 1829 British abolitionists organized boycotts of sugar grown with slave labor.[71] Slave-grown produce was an important part of the English economy and, by 1800, tropical groceries, including sugar, comprised about 35 percent of the total value of imports to Britain and sugar was Britain's largest import by value in the eighteenth century.[72] When British abolitionists set out to halt West Indian grown sugar consumption in 1791, within six months "an estimated 100,000 people had stopped using sugar."[73] Later, Thomas Clarkson estimated that 300,000 people had stopped in 1791–1792. As Claire Midgley notes, "[t]his compares with the estimated 390,000 (adult male) signatories to anti-slavery petitions in 1792."[74] In both the slave-grown sugar boycotts of 1791–1792 and 1825–1829, abolitionists promoted the sugar grown in the East Indies by free labor, arguing that it wasn't tainted. If West Indian farmers were weakened at all economically by the boycotts, their influence in Parliament may have suffered, though in 1823, the Anti-Slavery Society counted five Lords and fourteen members of the House of Commons, while at least fifty-six members had a personal interest in slavery.[75]

[68] See Drescher, *Capitalism and Antislavery*, p. 76 and Oldfield, *Popular Politics*, pp. 49 and 61.
[69] See Oldfield, *Popular Politics*, pp. 115–119.
[70] Quoted in Temperley, *British Anti-Slavery*, p. 7.
[71] Drescher, *Capitalism and Antislavery*, p. 79.   [72] Midgley, "Slave Sugar Boycotts."
[73] Ibid., p. 146.   [74] Ibid., p. 146.
[75] William A. Green, *British Slave Emancipation: The Sugar Colonies and the Great Experiment, 1830–1865* (Oxford: Clarendon Press, 1976), p. 100.

The transnational abolition movement also included slaves and "free blacks," who in the seventeenth and eighteenth centuries described the conditions of slavery and articulated the reasons for abolition. By 1750 there were about 20,000 black people in England, and by the late eighteenth century, some were quite visible in the abolitionist movement. Eighteenth and nineteenth-century anti-slavery movements used published slave narratives, organized public forums for the live testimony of "freedmen" and escaped slaves, and circulated reports by journalists and abolitionists of the conditions of slaves as evidence that slavery was evil and that slaves deserved better treatment. In written and live testimonies, both former slaves and white abolitionists portrayed the brutality of slavery in vivid language and with clear physical evidence. In the late eighteenth century, about twenty black abolitionists were active in England and the best known of this group included Ottobah Cugoano and Olaudah Equiano. Equiano, for example, authored a 520 page book, *The Interesting Narrative of the Life of Olaudah Equiano, or Gustava Vassa, the African* (1789), toured Britain widely, and wrote for English papers.[76] In March 1788, Equiano petitioned Queen Charlotte, the wife of George III, "on behalf of my African brethren" for an end to the slave trade and for giving slaves the "rights and situation of men."[77] Among the most famous former slave activists in the US during the nineteenth century were Nat Turner, Soujourner Truth, and Frederick Douglass, though narratives by many others were widely read and the live testimony of former slaves was often part of anti-slavery meetings.[78] Never before had slaves found a voice that slave holders and non-slave holders heard in relatively large numbers. The fact that slaves were participants in the discourse was doubly important because it facilitated the development of empathy between slave and non-slave and helped to break down the core belief held by many Europeans of the African as savage. Freed slaves and their descendents also began to criticize the larger institution of colonialism.[79]

Eighteenth and early nineteenth-century advocates of abolition, whether gradualists or immediatists, were really arguing two cases. First,

[76] See Oldfield, *Popular Politics*, pp. 125 and 126.
[77] Quoted in Walvin, *An African's Life*, p. 156.
[78] A selection of slave narratives is found in William L. Andrews and Henry Louis Gates, eds., *Slave Narratives* (New York: Library of America, 2000).
[79] For example, the booklet by the Reverend James Theodore Holley, *A Vindication of the Capacity of the Negro Race for Self-Government and Civilized Progress, as Demonstrated by the Historical Events of the Haytian Revolution and the Subsequent Acts of that People Since their National Independence* (New Haven, CN: 1856).

they argued for ending the slave trade on ethical grounds: it corrupted Africa and Africans and was evil, a sin, "a wicked, cruel, and unnatural trade."[80] This was their most powerful argument – a meta-argument on the nature of the good, about the virtues of slavery in the eyes of God – and they succeeded in reframing the practice as being against God's providence to the point that in 1806 Wilberforce was able to argue in Parliament that he found it unnecessary to refute the religious arguments given in favor of the slave trade since he could take it for granted that the scriptural basis for slavery had been disproved. "Indeed, among the various final proofs of the purity and excellence of the religion we possess, it is not the least remarkable that not only is the *practice* of the Slave Trade forbidden, and the *principle* on which it proceeds held out for our abhorrence; but it is specifically denounced as the worst of robbery, those concerned in it being branded as the 'stealers of men.'"[81] The abolitionists' second argument, in response to pro-slave trade interests, was that it was practical to end the slave trade.

Having essentially lost the meta-argument about the religious sanction for slavery in the scriptures, advocates of the slave trade began to emphasize practical arguments. For example, in the 1806 Parliamentary debate, General Tarleton argued against outlawing the slave trade on several practical grounds. First, he claimed that the "prosperity of Liverpool is intimately connected with the African Slave Trade" and the amount that taxes from Liverpool alone "contributes to the public purse, is near 3 millions annually."[82] If Liverpool suffered, he argued, all shipping would be impaired, leading to serious negative consequences for the entire colonial empire. Tarleton also claimed that if the slave trade were ended the war with France would be hurt because government revenue would fall.

> Nor is this all: those who suffer will come to Parliament for compensation for their losses. There will be no pretense for refusing such compensation, because, whatever may be said about the injustice or the inhumanity of this trade, it is not to be denied that it is a trade which has been carried on under the auspices of this House, and agreeably

[80] Quoted in Du Bois, *The Suppression of the African Slave Trade*, p. 43.
[81] Wilberforce quoted in *Substance of the Debates on a Resolution for Abolishing the Slave Trade which was moved in the House of Commons 10th June 1806 and in the House of Lords 24th June 1806* (London: Dawsons of Pall Mall, 1968), pp. 29–30. (Spelling has been made consistent with modern English).
[82] Quoted in ibid., p. 11.

to law; and if it is now to be abolished, all those who have carried it on must have their losses made up . . . and this compensation, I can assure his Majesty's Ministers, will be very considerable in its amount.[83]

Similarly, Lord Castlereagh, while granting the desirability of abolishing the trade on moral grounds, questioned whether it was possible to do so. Indeed, he argued that the whole movement was counterproductive because without Britain the slave traffic "will be conducted by others [France, Spain, and Portugal] under their flags, so that the trade will be carried on in a more inhuman manner hereafter than it is at present."[84] Castlereagh argued instead for using a gradually rising system of duties to discourage the slave trade.

In response, abolitionists also deployed practical arguments about the timing and economic risks of abolishing the slave trade. Wilberforce, for example, argued that Castlereagh's proposed duty on slave imports would not work. He asked, "does not my noble friend recollect, that although during the time we have been discussing this subject, the price of slaves has increased 100 percent, that is to say from thirty to seventy pounds a head, a much larger increase than any duty which he would think imposing, yet that the number of slaves imported into the Colonies has not diminished?"[85]

Many advocates of abolishing the trade, as part of their long-term strategy for abolition, were willing to put up with slavery for a time, thereby hoping to diffuse the arguments of those who said abolition would ruin the colonial economy. Abolishing the British slave trade, they claimed, would still be a significant feat given the fact that at the peak of their involvement in the fifty years prior to ending the slave trade, British slavers controlled 50 percent of the slave trade. As Anstey writes, advocates of the gradual approach also claimed that any economic damage caused by abolishing the trade could be minimized: "With proper encouragement a slave population could reproduce itself, there would be no need for slave imports, and there was no threat to the plantation owner and to the West Indian plantation economy."[86]

Abolitionists turned to the project of ending slavery after Parliament voted to end British participation in the slave trade.[87] In the years of the abolition movement, petitions organized by anti-slavery societies to

---

[83] Quoted in ibid., p. 12.   [84] Quoted in ibid., p. 17.   [85] Quoted in ibid., pp. 31–32.
[86] Anstey, *Atlantic Slave Trade and British Abolition*, pp. 312–313.
[87] On the links and continuity between British and American anti-slavery organizing see Betty Fladeland, *Men and Brothers: Anglo-American Anti-Slavery Cooperation* (Urbana: University of Illinois Press, 1972).

the British parliament often outnumbered petitions for all other causes until slavery was abolished.[88] In 1823 the London Anti-Slavery Society pressed Parliament into urging West Indian colonial governments to reform slave practices, but planters resisted the efforts.[89] In 1825 the anti-slavery societies began publishing the *Anti-Slavery Monthly Reporter* (London) which included such articles as "On the Demoralizing Influence of Slavery" ("men accustomed to govern slaves are unfit to manage free labourers").[90] Another article was "The Question Calmly Considered – What will be the probable consequences, as affecting the public peace of the Colonies and the well-being of the Slaves themselves, of the early and entire extinction of Colonial Slavery, by an act of the British Parliament?"[91] In the latter, abolitionists responded directly to pro-slavery arguments that emancipation would bring chaos.

> The evils which the colonists affect to dread, from such an emancipation of their slaves, are of two kinds – first civil insubordination, tumult, and disorder issuing in pillage, conflagration, and massacre; and secondly, the deterioration of the slave's condition, and his return to all the miseries and privations of the savage state. In argument, it has been hitherto assumed by the colonists as indisputable, that such would necessarily be the consequence of an immediate or even very early emancipation of the slaves; and we must admit that not a few of those who are decided enemies of colonial slavery, both in its principle and practice, have far too readily yielded their assent to this unwarranted assumption. We call it *unwarranted*, because we are not aware of any attempt ever having been made to prove its truth . . . We are acquainted with no such evidence. We know even of no single case in which emancipation of slaves proceeding from the legal authorities of the state, and unresisted by violence on the part of the masters has led either to public disorder, or to the unhappiness and discomfort of the slave, or to the deterioration of his moral, intellectual, and political condition. If there be such a case, let it be stated and proved.[92]

In the 1830s alone, several new organizations formed in Britain to work for abolition and emancipation and over 5,000 anti-slavery petitions were sent to Parliament in early 1833.[93] When Parliament passed the Emancipation Act in 1833, freeing 800,000 slaves in Mauritius, the

[88] Drescher, *Capitalism and Antislavery*, pp. 59 and 91–92.
[89] Temperley, *British Antislavery*, p. 12.
[90] Appearing in *Anti-Slavery Monthly Reporter* 2 (January 1828), 161–174: 164.
[91] "The Question Calmly Considered," *Anti-Slavery Monthly Reporter* 3 (10 November 1830), 453–475.
[92] "The Question Calmly Considered," pp. 454–455, emphasis in the original.
[93] Roger Anstey, "Religion and British Slave Emancipation," in David Eltis and James

West Indies, Canada, and the Cape of Good Hope, abolitionists were disappointed in its provisions for an apprenticeship system of four and six years and for compensation to slave owners, so they kept organizing, ultimately securing an early end to the apprenticeship system in 1838. The British and Foreign Society for Universal Abolition of Negro Slavery and the Slave Trade was founded in 1834; the Central Negro Emancipation Committee founded in 1837 became the British and Foreign Anti-Slavery Society in 1839. Also founded in 1839 were the Aborigines Protection Society and the Society for the Extinction of the Slave Trade and the Civilization of Africa. There were about 100 local chapters of national anti-slavery organizations in Britain between 1839 and 1869.[94]

Anti-slavery activists formed the British and Foreign Anti-Slavery Society in London in 1839 for the "universal extinction of slavery and the slave trade." A descendent of previous anti-slavery organizations, the group's constitution stated that "the extinction of Slavery and the Slave-trade will be attained most effectively by employment of those means which are of a *moral, religious,* and *pacific character.*" The "means to be employed" were to be ethical and practical argument *and* economic leverage:

> 1. To circulate, both at home and abroad, accurate information on the enormities of the Slave-trade and Slavery; to furnish evidence to the inhabitants of Slave-holding countries, not only of the practicability, but of the pecuniary advantage of free labour; to diffuse authentic intelligence respecting the results of emancipation in Hayti [*sic*], the British Colonies and elsewhere; to open a correspondence with Abolitionists in America, France, and other countries; and to encourage them in the prosecution of these objects by all methods consistent with the principles of this Society.
>
> 2. To recommend the use of free-grown produce (as far as practicable) in preference to Slave-grown; and to promote the adoption of fiscal regulations in favour of free labour.

Walvin, eds., *The Abolition of the Atlantic Slave Trade: Origins and Effects in Europe, Africa, and the Americas* (Madison: University of Wisconsin Press, 1981), pp. 37–61: 48. Although most abolitionist activity focused on slavery, some abolitionists advocated the establishment of colonies of former slaves. British abolitionist Granville Sharpe, in 1787, helped freed slaves establish a colony in Sierra Leone. The American Colonization Society formed in December 1816 to support former slave colonies in West Africa took what would become Liberia at gunpoint and established a colony for freed slaves. Though many in the US and Britain had enthusiastically supported colonization of West Africa by former slaves, public opinion was more divided by the 1830s. Fladeland, *Men and Brothers*, pp. 80–105.
[94] Christine Bolt, *The Anti-Slavery Movement and Reconstruction: A Study in Anglo-American Co-operation, 1833–77* (London: Oxford University Press, 1969), p. 4.

3. To obtain the unequivocal recognition of the principle that the Slave, of whatever clime or colour, entering any portion of the British Dominions, shall be free . . .

4. To recommend that every suitable opportunity be embraced for evincing in our intercourse with Slave-holders and their apologists, our abhorrence of the system which they uphold, and our sense of its utter incompatibility with the spirit of the Christian religion.[95]

Institutionalization: suppressing the slave trade

When the British Parliament abolished the slave trade in March 1807 it set stiff penalties for violators: slave trade vessels would be forfeited and a fine of 100 would be imposed for each slave found on board. In 1811, slave trading was made a felony and in 1824 a capital offense. Making the trade illegal and eventually punishable as a felony was a great step in institutionalizing the now dominant normative belief in Britain that the trade in slaves was wrong. The next step, a decades-long effort by Britain to suppress the entire international slave trade, was itself the occasion of another long domestic and international argument.

The scope of the British effort to suppress the slave trade, initially small, grew to be enormous. The British Royal Navy stationed ships off the coast of, first, West Africa, and later, East Africa and American waters to intercept slave ships.[96] The British Africa Squadron between 1816 and 1865 ranged from three to a peak of thirty-six ships (in 1845) patrolling the coasts at any one time to interdict slave ships, while other cruisers were also empowered to search suspicious ships.[97] The British government also established a Slave Trade Department in 1819 to monitor the traffic.[98]

The slave trade was regularly on Britain's nineteenth-century diplomatic agenda. Abolitionists sent 800 petitions to Parliament in 1814, with about 1 million signatures, urging the government to push the French to end the trade.[99] In 1815, the Congress of Vienna passed a resolution on suppressing the slave trade as "repugnant to the principles of humanity

---

[95] *Constitution of the British and Foreign Anti-Slavery Society*, confirmed at a public meeting at Exeter Hall, 17 April 1839 (emphasis in original).

[96] The US intermittently made a commitment to patrols between 1820 and 1864, as did France from 1811 to 1870.

[97] Curtin, *Atlantic Slave Trade*, pp. 249–250.

[98] See D. Eltis, "The Direction and Fluctuation of the Transatlantic Slave Trade, 1821–1943: A Revision of the 1845 Parliamentary Paper," in Gemery and Hogendorn, eds., *Uncommon Market*, pp. 273–301: 276.

[99] Temperley, *British Antislavery*, p. 8.

and universal morality."[100] The slave trade was also raised at the Aix-la-Chapelle meeting in 1818, and at the Congress of Verona in 1822 it was called a "pest which has too long desolated Africa, degraded Europe, and afflicted humanity."[101] By 1839, Britain had treaties "with all major maritime powers except the United States providing for the right to search each other's merchant vessels."[102] According to historian Arthur Corwin, "standard British procedure was to withhold diplomatic recognition or ratification of a treaty of commerce, amity and peace or to refuse to facilitate a loan in the London money market until the lesser power agreed to cooperate with British cruisers in closing the traffic."[103] The treaties were expensive; in 1817 Britain paid Spain 700,000 for the right to search ships under the Spanish flag and for agreements to prohibit slave traffic north, and then 3 years later, south of the equator.[104] Since Spain did not found an Abolitionist Society until 1864, external pressure for abolition was practically all there was apart from the efforts of a few, isolated, individuals.[105] Britain also paid Portugal 300,000 to end its part in the slave trade north of the equator after 1820.[106] Thus, suppression was associated with high moral purpose: many British righteously condemned other states who participated in the slave trade. In 1864 Prime Minister Palmerston wrote: "The Portuguese are . . . the lowest in the moral scale and the Brazilians are degenerate Portuguese, demoralized by slavery and slave trade, and all the degrading and corrupting influences connected with both."[107]

The British signed several bilateral treaties and coordinated their naval patrol efforts off the coast of Africa with a number of countries after 1816. Britain even established international courts, joint courts of

---

[100] Text of Declaration of the Eight Powers, relative to the Universal Abolition of the Slave Trade, quoted in Suzanne Miers, *Britain and the Ending of the Slave Trade* (New York: Longman Group, 1975), p. 11. James Walvin, "The Public Campaign in England Against Slavery, 1787–1843," in Eltis and Walvin, *The Abolition of the Atlantic Slave Trade*, pp. 63–79: 67–68.

[101] Text of the resolution quoted by Sir Edward Mallet at the Berlin Conference in R. J. Gavin and J. A. Betley, *The Scramble for Africa: Documents on the Berlin West Africa Conference and Related Subjects 1884/1885* (Ibadan, Nigeria: Ibadan University Press, 1973), p. 187. Notably, the members of the Congress could not agree on Britain's recommendation to "denounce the trade as piracy" and a "refusal to admit to their domains the produce of the colonies of States allowing the trade." Du Bois, *Suppression of the African Slave Trade*, p. 138.

[102] Klein, "Slavery," p. 202.

[103] Corwin, *Spain and Abolition of Slavery in Cuba*, pp. 31–32.

[104] Miers, *Britain and the Ending of the Slave Trade*, p. 14.

[105] Corwin, *Spain and Abolition of Slavery in Cuba*, pp. 20 and 22–25.

[106] Ibid., p. 30.   [107] Quoted in Eltis, *Economic Growth*, p. 85.

"mixed commission," through bilateral treaties with Spain, Portugal, the Netherlands, Sweden, Norway, and later Brazil. The courts sat in several locations, including Sierra Leone, Cape Town, Havana, Rio de Janeiro, and New York to try slave traders. International cooperation of this sort was unprecedented, though not without controversy. For instance, Britain claimed that the captured slaves freed by the mixed court in Havana were nevertheless being sold in Cuba.[108]

Yet international diplomatic arguments and insults were mild compared to Britain's domestic debate over the suppression policy. Both Houses of Parliament issued separate reports on British efforts to end the trade after hearings in 1848 and 1849 in the House of Commons, and hearings in 1849 and 1850 in the House of Lords. Members heard evidence and arguments at the hearings that came to opposite conclusions. Opponents of suppression suggested the effort was a huge expense for little result. And the financial costs of suppression were staggering. On the other hand, supporters of suppression argued that Britain had already succeeded in greatly diminishing the slave trade and said that without interdiction, the trade would grow in Africa and in the colonies in Central and South America.[109] Some abolitionists estimated that slave traffic actually grew in the 1830s and 1840s but that suppression should continue nevertheless.[110]

Was suppression a success? More than 1,635 ships were captured between 1808 and 1867 and over 160,000 Africans were freed, mostly by the British (over 85 percent).[111] But the overall success of the British interdiction effort is difficult to know given the efforts slave traders went to to conceal the traffic. Christopher Lloyd argues that the success of interdiction efforts "fluctuated violently," and it is "doubtful if the preventive cruises ever captured more than 10 percent of the shipping involved until they were given more latitude in the treatment of foreign vessels and the demand for slaves was stopped by the importing countries themselves."[112] Philip Curtin estimated that despite Britain's effort

---

[108] See ibid., p. 86; Corwin, *Spain and Abolition of Slavery in Cuba*, pp. 39–42.

[109] *Extracts from the Evidence Taken Before Committees of the Two Houses of Parliament Relative to the Slave Trade, with Illustrations from Collateral Sources of Information* (London: Davidson, 1851); reprinted (New York: Negro Universities Press, 1969).

[110] Thomas Fowell Buxton, a prominent English abolitionist, claimed in the late 1830s that the trade might have doubled. Lloyd, *The Navy and the Slave Trade*, p. 105.

[111] Eltis, *Economic Growth*, p. 97–98. Lloyd estimates that 149,843 slaves in the Atlantic slave trade were liberated by the Royal Navy between 1810 and 1864. Lloyd, *The Navy and the Slave Trade*, pp. 275–276.

[112] Lloyd, *The Navy and the Slave Trade*, p. xii.

at interdiction, except for periods of war, "trade nevertheless continued, at a level about a third less than its eighteenth century peak."[113] Since the revolutionary leaders San Martín, Bolívar, and Hidalgo of the Spanish colonies abolished slavery in Argentina (1816) Gran Columbia and Chile (1821), Peru, Guatemala, and Uruguay (1828) and Mexico (1829), the major traffic in slaves from Africa to the New World went to Cuba and Brazil. LeVeen credits the British with rates for interdicting slave traffic to Cuba and Brazil as 15.3 percent from 1821 to 1830, 46.5 percent from 1831 to 1840, 35.6 percent from 1851 to 1860.[114]

The evolution of slavery as practiced in the United States

All thirteen American colonies had slaves. The changing status of slavery – from accepted institution to increasingly suspect practice – is illustrated by the ambiguous and contradictory slave law of the colonial and pre-civil war United States. Slave law varied by state because the United States was much more a collection of states in the late eighteenth and early nineteenth centuries, under the philosophy of states' rights, rather than one uniform nation.[115] After the Declaration of Independence, Northern states under pressure from abolitionists moved to abolish slavery. Vermont was first to make slavery illegal in 1777, and Massachusetts did the same in 1781. The slave trade resumed after the war and slavery, of course, remained legal in the South, with slave states dominating the government through much of the pre-civil war era: the Electoral College and the House of Representatives, because of the constitutional provision that counted a slave as three-fifths a person for purposes of apportioning seats, was overrepresented by slave states.

As slavery was denormalized and delegitimized in the colonies and later the United States, new practices to protect the slave were institutionalized in slave law, even in the southern United States. In the seventeenth century, for instance, the homicide of a slave was allowed in South Carolina if it was done as a "correction" but not if it was done maliciously. By the 1740s, there were fines for killing a slave in South Carolina. In 1791, North Carolina said the killing of a slave who was not resisting his/her master, was murder. In 1798, Georgia's new constitution said, "Any person who shall maliciously dismember or

[113] Curtin, *Atlantic Slave Trade*, p. 269.
[114] LeVeen, *British Slave Trade Suppression Policies*, p. 30.
[115] See Du Bois, *The Suppression of the African Slave Trade*.

deprive a slave of life shall suffer such punishment as would be inflicted in case the like offence had been committed on a free white person, and on the like proof, except in case of insurrection by such slave, and unless such death should happen by accident in giving such slave moderate correction."[116] Later, Alabama, Missouri, and Texas adopted similar laws.

Even before the American abolitionist movement led by Quakers, former slaves, and other human rights advocates gathered political force in the nineteenth century, cruelty toward slaves was also gradually regulated.[117] In colonial South Carolina, while whipping was legal, a 1740 law imposed a fine of up to 100 for cutting out the tongue, eye, or testicles of a slave. A slave would become free according to an 1860 Maryland law if their master was convicted of abuse three times.[118] There were also laws requiring that masters provide food and clothing for slaves, and in 1852, a law in Alabama requiring a master to "treat his slave with humanity."[119]

The US Congress debated slavery many times from its first session in 1789 to abolition.[120] And, as in England, Congress was subjected to popular petitions on the slave trade and slavery from abolition societies in Connecticut, Massachusetts, Maryland, New York, Pennsylvania, and Virginia. Congress acted in 1794 to prohibit US citizens from supplying slaves to foreigners. The later "Act to Prohibit the Importation of Slaves" into the US after 1 January 1808, was passed by Congress and signed by President Jefferson in March 1807. Though the slave trade was prohibited by law, it continued to be conducted clandestinely, and the several Congressional acts to suppress the trade were not consistently or vigorously enforced.

In 1818 the US passed the Antislaving Act and, in 1820, the US declared the slave trade piracy and sent a few ships to the West African coast to conduct interdiction. Between 1818 and 1821 US naval ships stationed off the African coast caught eleven slave ships with 573 Africans on board. But after this initial burst of activity, US interdiction efforts essentially halted. The idea of letting ships with US flags be searched by the British

[116] Quoted in Morris, *Southern Slavery and the Law*, p. 172.
[117] There are dozens of excellent books on anti-slavery activism in the US. Because it is well known, and parallels British anti-slavery movements, I will not recapitulate that history here.
[118] Morris, *Southern Slavery and the Law*, p. 183.　　[119] Quoted in ibid., p. 184.
[120] See William Lee Miller, *Arguing About Slavery: The Great Battle in the United States Congress* (New York: Alfred A. Knopf, 1996), and Du Bois, *The Suppression of the African Slave Trade*.

had been raised several times in the US Congress in the 1820s, and also by the British, but never approved by the US administration. Many slavers took to flying under American flags, making them immune to British searches. With the 1842 Webster–Ashburton Treaty, the US and Britain promised to maintain more substantial anti-slavery patrols on the coast of West Africa. Despite the Webster–Ashburton Treaty, the small US squadron sent to patrol the African coast for slave traffic was ineffective and unable to interdict many slavers. Only in 1862 when the US and Great Britain signed the Treaty of Washington, granting the mutual right of search at sea and establishing "mixed" courts in New York, Cape Town, and Sierra Leone to try slave traders, was suppression of slavers flying the US flag successful.[121]

In sum, much as Indian slavery had been regulated in South America by Spain before it was abolished in the colonies, and well before the Civil War, slavery in the United States was gradually regulated by legislation and the courts, protecting slaves from the worst behavior of their masters. Were reforms primarily motivated by pragmatism (in the belief that better treated slaves would perhaps produce more offspring and be less likely to revolt or attempt escape), or was there a genuine change in how slaves were regarded? Some reforms were undoubtedly motivated and supported for pragmatic reasons. Adam Smith argued that, "The protection of the magistrate renders the slave less contemptible in the eyes of his master, who is thereby induced to consider him with more regard, and to treat him with more gentleness. Gentle usage renders the slave not only more faithful, but more intelligent and, therefore, upon a double account, more useful."[122]

But there are reasons to believe that pragmatism was not at the main root of the reforms.[123] First, though convictions for offenses against slaves were not frequent, by the early nineteenth century, as Thomas Morris notes, "There was truth in the remark of William Gaston of the North Carolina Supreme Court: 'A cruel Master is a term of opprobrium which would be as bitterly resented and is as carefully avoided as that of a dishonest tradesman or of a drunken mechanic.'"[124] The occasions when masters were brought to court to be held to account for

---

[121] Lloyd, *The Navy and the Slave Trade*, pp. 55–59; 175–181; Thomas, *The Slave Trade*, pp. 616–620: 775.

[122] Smith, *Wealth of Nations*, book IV, chapter VII, p. 634.

[123] And though morally motivated reformers probably would have balked at the notion, pragmatic reformers inadvertently made the process of moral reform easier.

[124] Morris, *Southern Slavery and the Law*, p. 185.

their actions were instances where the justice of slavery itself was argued. Second, the regulation of slavery was generally opposed by slave masters and the governments in slave states on the grounds that slaves had to fear their masters or the institution would fall apart. As North Carolina's Judge Ruffin said in 1829, in overturning the conviction of a master in the murder of his slave, "The power of the master must be absolute to render the submission of the slave perfect."[125] Thus, while most masters were probably little moved by anti-slavery arguments, anti-slavery arguments changed the beliefs of the rest of US culture, gradually changing the balance of political forces in the US so that reform was gradually institutionalized.

Forced labor

Several humanitarian ironies were occasioned by the end of the slave trade and slavery. First, as it had in Latin America when Indian slavery ended, abolition gave impetus to forced labor practices (which allowed corporal punishment) that continued well after slavery's demise in both Latin America and Africa. Second, ending slavery became an argument in the mid and late 1800s for the imposition of colonies in parts of Africa that were not yet subject to European rule.[126] As Joseph Chamberlain, then British colonial secretary, said in 1900 about Nigeria: "sooner or later we shall have to fight some of the slave dealing tribes and we cannot have a better *casus belli* . . . public opinion here requires that we shall justify imperial control of these savage countries by some serious effort to put down slave dealing."[127] Humanitarians would later take up arguments against both those practices. And third, processes of international cooperation developed to halt the traffic in slaves facilitated smoother colonization.

---

[125] Ruffin's opinion in *State* v. *Mann*, quoted in Mark V. Tushnet, *The American Law of Slavery, 1810–1860: Considerations of Humanity and Interest* (Princeton: Princeton University Press, 1981) p. 60. Also see Alan Watson, *Slave Law in the Americas* (Athens, GA: University of Georgia Press, 1989).

[126] Lloyd, *The Navy and the Slave Trade*, p. 105.

[127] Quoted in Miers, *Britain and the Ending of the Slave Trade*, p. 294. Miers writes, when the Imperial East Africa Company said in 1892 that it had to leave Uganda for financial reasons, "The Liberal government of the day was prepared to let the territory go but the issue was carried to the electorate in a widespread press and propaganda campaign which resulted in a spate of petitions urging its retention largely on the grounds that the slavery and slave trade would be abolished. Other reasons such as economic advantages and the need to save the Christian missions were also cited but the biggest single consideration was the suppression of slave traffic." Ibid., p. 294.

Forced labor in many forms, for example, indentured servitude, *encomienda* (until 1550) and *repartimiento* for private or public work (after 1550), had long coexisted with slavery and free labor. Similarly, by a French law of 1686 the number of *engagés* or indentured servants was to be equal to the number of slaves in Saint Domingue. In some cases, slave emancipation led directly to forced labor, as when Great Britain ended slavery by law in 1833 (not covering colonies controlled by the East India Company, including India), but allowed six years of "apprenticeship" (labor without pay for 45 hours a week) in the West Indies and Africa. As soon as Britain halted apprenticeship in 1838, plantation farmers faced a labor shortage, since, if they could, apprentices left plantations. In response, colonial assemblies enacted laws, such as the Contract Act in Antigua, to force workers back to the farm while others were compelled to work for fear of arrest under the vagrancy laws passed in many colonies.[128] Further, as in Jamaica, farm wages were purposefully kept lower than rents so many former slaves went into debt and were forced to work for former masters. Where former slaves were not enough, East Indians and Chinese laborers were imported. Indentured workers often had no idea of the terrible conditions they would face in Asia, the Americas, or Africa.[129] Some 28 million Indians left India between 1846 and 1932, mostly to work in some form of forced labor.[130] Seymour Drescher notes that of the "total intercontinental flow of indentured labourers to ex-slave colonies after 1838, two-thirds, went to British frontier colonies deprived of African labour during the previous 30 years. For a generation after apprenticeship more than 95 percent of indentured labourers from Africa and India went to ex-slave colonies as a whole."[131]

Forced labor by Africans for Europeans was also widespread in Africa. Even as Europeans crusaded to end slavery, Africans were not only required to "volunteer" their labor, but the punishment for not volunteering, and for other "crimes" such as vagrancy and failure to pay hut and head taxes, was forced labor.[132] It was the "colonial custom"

---

[128] Vagrancy laws had been similarly used in the 1500s by Spain in Central and South America against both Spanish and Indians. See William L. Sherman, *Forced Native Labor in Sixteenth-Century Central America* (Lincoln: University of Nebraska Press, 1979), pp. 194–196.

[129] W. Kloosterboer, *Involuntary Labour Since the Abolition of Slavery: A Survey of Compulsory Labour Throughout the World* (Leiden: E.J. Brill, 1960).

[130] Klein, "Slavery," p. 207.   [131] Drescher, *Capitalism and Antislavery*, p. 10.

[132] Elizabeth Elbourne, "Freedom at Issue: Vagrancy Legislation and the Meaning of Freedom in Britain and the Cape Colony, 1799–1842," in Lovejoy and Rogers, eds., *Unfree*

to indenture the African "free children born on white farms" in Dutch South Africa "until the age of eighteen or twenty-five."[133] While the Portuguese ended slavery in their African colonies in 1878, according to Gann and Duignan, until the system of *indigenato* was ended in 1961, "Portuguese Africans were under obligation to work in a manner approved of by the administration for at least six months of the year, or else be contracted by the government."[134] British and French colonies also used forced labor in their colonies, especially during the world wars, to build and maintain roads, work on farms, and serve in the military.[135] Forced labor in French West Africa grew after slavery was abolished there in 1905.

Forced labor arguments

Some of the most ardent advocates of forced labor were evangelical Christians, who claimed forced labor would bring moral uplift. Advocates believed forced labor was good since it transformed people living in a "pre-civilized" condition, where they were supposedly idle and lazy, and put them to useful work. Elizabeth Elbourne argues that this system reflects the evangelical and philosophical world view dominant in England at the time which saw nomadic cultures as backward and empty and in need of assistance in rising out of a state of nature.[136] One colonial officer, Colonel Collins, in a report on the Khoikhoi and San of Southern Africa to the British governor of the Cape in 1808, said native South Africans were "multitudes of savages, of the fiercest disposition, dispersed throughout such a vast extent of country, in no part of which they have a settled residence, and from which they plunder their neighbours in every direction; – without the idea of any law, divine or human; connexion among themselves, except such as arises from the ties of parental, or conjugal affection; and even without the least knowledge of the manner of cultivating corn or rearing cattle."[137] French advocates of forced labor made similar arguments in the early 1900s.[138]

Labour, pp. 114–150; Commission on International Justice and Goodwill, *The System of Forced Labor in Africa* (New York: Federal Council of the Churches of Christ in America, 1926).
[133] Elbourne, "Freedom at Issue," p. 117.
[134] L.H. Gann and Peter Duignan, *Burden of Empire: An Appraisal of Western Colonialism in Africa South of the Sahara* (New York: Praeger, 1967), p. 379.
[135] Ibid., p. 256. [136] Elbourne, "Freedom at Issue," pp. 118–120.
[137] Quoted in ibid., p. 118.
[138] Alice Conklin, *A Mission to Civilize: The Republican Idea of Empire in France and West Africa, 1895–1930* (Stanford: Stanford University Press, 1997).

Colonial law articulated and reflected these beliefs. The Caledon Proclamation, or Code, as it was also known, issued by the British governor of the Cape Colony in 1809 made it possible to impress any "Hottentot" (non-European) considered "vagrant" who could not provide evidence of work and a fixed residence. Since "Hottentots" were not allowed to own land, fixed residence implied living in a colonial institution. According to the Code, this was supposed to be good for all parties. "[I]t is necessary that not only the inhabitants of the Hottentot nation, in the same manner as the other inhabitants, should be subject to proper regularity in regard to their place of abode and occupations, but also that they should find an encouragement for preferring entering the service of inhabitants to leading an indolent life, by which they are rendered useless both for themselves and the community at large."[139] These ideas were persistent. As the famous British explorer Sir Richard Burton wrote in 1864: "I see no objection to render liberated labour forcible until the African race is educated for wages, and such habits are not learned in a day."[140]

Reforming forced labor

As with slavery, many religious communities eventually switched positions on the desirability of forced labor, leading campaigns to end various forms of coercion. For example, coinciding with the abolitionist movement, British humanitarians and Christians in the London Missionary Society campaigned to end forced labor in Southern Africa in the early nineteenth century. The "Hottentots" or rather Khoi, themselves also argued for free labor, mobility, and the return of their land.[141] Reformers eventually succeeded in ameliorating labor conditions in Southern Africa. Forced labor by Hottentots was halted in 1828 in Ordinance 50, which ended the Caledon Code, although forced labor for up to a year by black Africans found without passes was still allowed in Ordinance 49.[142] British protection of "Hottentots" became one of the main reasons Boers moved from the coast to the interior in their "Great Trek" to escape British interference.

The campaign to completely end forced labor used ethical arguments that denormalized the practice. In 1835, some anti-slavery activists formed the British and Foreign Aborigines Protection Society, which

[139] Proclamation quoted in Elbourne, "Freedom at Issue," p. 122.
[140] Burton quoted in Eltis, *Economic Growth*, p. 28.
[141] Elbourne, "Freedom at Issue," pp. 139–142.   [142] Ibid., pp. 128–129.

publicized forced labor and other conditions that were against the interests of the people the British were now calling aborigines and natives.[143] Forced labor was documented in journals such as the *Anti-Slavery Reporter and Aborigines' Friend* (London) and by journalists in mainstream papers. Reformers stressed the humanity of the laborers, and the inhumanity of the practice, arguing that forced labor was corrupting, not elevating. Christian groups distributed pamphlets containing testimony such as: "I could not get my mind away from the comparison between the life which these people led in the old days, and that which they are living now. That was called heathenism; the present is hell. That was primitive liberty and comfort; this is the backwash of civilization – grinding servitude and moral degradation."[144] This was implicitly an argument stressing the hypocrisy of Western practices.

But, as with the anti-slavery campaigns, reformers did not only deploy a moral discourse. Reformers' identity arguments attempted to demonstrate the humanity of the African laborer.

> I found them to be a moral people. Not with the morality of civilization, with its niceties and hypocrisies, but they had a morality of their own which they scrupulously observed ...
>
> They were an honest people. In my five years of dealing with them I lost nothing by theft, when there was unlimited opportunity for them to steal. They kept their bargains when their word was passed to one whom they respected and trusted ...
>
> They were a hospitable people. No stranger, especially a white man, who came to their kraals was refused a place to sleep and food to eat, such as they had to give. They did not charge a price for their hospitality, they regarded it good manners on the part of the guest to be as generous as they had been.
>
> They were a courteous people. There was a strict system of etiquette among themselves and towards strangers ...[145]

The identity argument aimed specifically to humanize and in some cases esteem African culture as compared with the culture of the colonizers.

---

[143] For a discussion of their activity see Alpheus Henry Snow, *The Question of Aborigines in the Law and Practice of Nations* (New York: G.P. Putnam's Sons, 1921), pp. 8–11.
[144] Commission on International Justice and Goodwill, *System of Forced Labor*, p. 8.
[145] Ibid., p. 8.

Their clothing was sometimes nearly as brief as that which can be seen nowadays at Coney Island; their house-keeping was about as crude as may be found in more civilized communities; their superstitions were much the same as other peoples who have passed through in their racial infancy; but my experience among them led me to believe that they were about as decent, and much more kindly, than any person who would call them heathen. I would have trusted myself or my family to their tender mercies more readily than to those of some persons who would call them savages.[146]

Practical arguments – that forced labor had terrible consequences for the social order of African society – echo Benezet's late eighteenth-century arguments about the corrupting influence of the slave trade. "But now this [morality, honesty, hospitality, and courtesy] has largely changed. The customs and laws which governed them in the past under their chiefs have been almost entirely displaced by the regulations of a commercial company, administered very largely by hostile black policemen. They have in the change lost not only their liberties, but their decencies as well."[147] Forced labor, it was argued, fostered disruption of families, drunkenness, and prostitution. Further, to elicit empathy, the advocates of reform quoted "data" from reports of Western scholars documenting abuse. They also noted the practical costs of policing forced labor.

A Chief told Professor Ross the following: "A man who was the best carpenter in the district furnished his own tools and food and got nothing, not even a tax receipt. Informed that his wife was sick he obtained a day's leave to go home. Finding her in child-birth and with no one but a little girl to help her he outstayed his leave one day. A *ciapaio* came, tied him up, and brought him to the Post where the Administrator had him given a severe beating with the *palmatorio* [a hammer like instrument for beating the palms of the hand of a prisoner] and thrown into prison. Next morning early the Chief saw them bring this man out of prison with his hands too swollen to close, give him a hoe and set him to work on the road. An armed *ciapaio* stood over him and kept him steady at work. He was weak from lack of food and could not hold the hoe handle between thumb and palm."[148]

The turn against forced labor was linked to both humanization of the laborer and changing religious beliefs, as Christian theology became thoroughly imbued with free market ideology. "Free labour was a means

[146] Ibid., pp. 8–9. [147] Ibid., p. 9. [148] Ibid., p. 20.

by which the individual expiated guilt and constructed his own salvation: slavery and bonded labour were morally damaging to the slave-owner as well as preventing the slave or labourer from having an equal opportunity to rise in civilization through economic advancement."[149] Perhaps not coincidentally, while the freedom of "free" labor varied in Europe, increasingly greater protection was given to free labor as master–servant relations and wage labor were first criticized and then better regulated to protect workers in Europe and North America from the mid-1500s onward.[150]

But as with slavery, pragmatic reformers inadvertently bolstered the cause of normatively motivated reformers. For example, forced labor in French West Africa was gradually reformed in the 1920s even as its use was approved by the colonial government as a form of both civilizing Africans and, obviously, as a way to get the fruits of their labor. This contradiction was possible because the main impetus for reform was pragmatic. African labor was scarce and better treatment, including the provision of basic health care, could, reformers argued, both increase the population and increase its productivity.[151]

Thus, the existence of forced labor and efforts to reform and end the practice are important in two senses. First, it shows how colonizers saw free versus unfree labor. As Martin Klein argues, the "continued importance of labour coercion suggests that capital could not get the labour it wanted in other ways, at least in some areas."[152] Many still saw an economic reason for coercion. Second, the debate over ending forced labor illustrates how anti-slavery principles were generalized, using analogies, by those who fought against forced labor. Evangelical Christians, already having decided that slavery was evil, eventually reframed the practice of forced labor as slavery, and recycled their critiques of slavery to undermine the institutions of forced labor. A Council of Churches pamphlet argues that forced labor was slavery or "worse than slavery."[153] The League of Nations appointed a Temporary Slavery Commission in 1924 which discussed both forced labor and slavery. One British official argued, for example, that "concubinage in this sense

---

[149] Elbourne, "Freedom at Issue," p. 131.
[150] Paul Craven and Douglas Hay, "The Criminalization of 'Free' Labour: Master and Servant in Comparative Perspective," in Lovejoy and Rogers, eds., *Unfree Labour*, pp. 71–101; Nicholas Rogers, "Vagrancy, Impressment and the Regulation of Labour in Eighteenth-Century Britain," in Lovejoy and Rogers, eds., *Unfree Labour*, pp. 102–113.
[151] See Conklin, *Mission to Civilize*, pp. 213–245.   [152] Klein, "Slavery," p. 207.
[153] Commission on International Justice and Goodwill, *System of Forced Labor*, p. 19.

means 'slavery' (slave status)..."[154] Long after most colonial powers had limited or halted forced labor, Portugal continued the practice. A senior administrator in Portuguese Angola argued, "Under slavery, after all, the native is bought as an animal: his owner prefers him to remain as fit as a horse or ox. Yet here [in Angola] the native is not bought – he is hired from the State, although called a free man. And his employer cares little if he sickens or dies, once he is working, because when he sickens or dies his employer will simply ask for another."[155] This was associative reasoning: since most agreed that slavery is bad, if forced labor is the "same" as slavery or "worse," then surely it too must be abolished.[156]

An ethical argument explanation for decolonizing bodies

To show that ethical arguments explain the end of slavery and forced labor, I must first demonstrate that ethical arguments were made in favor of ending these practices and that other forces, namely declining profitability, were not the underlying cause of their demise.[157] The slave trade, slavery, and forced labor remained profitable during most of this period. Or, at least, they were widely thought to be profitable by those who used those institutions and fought against their abolition. Slavery was still profitable in the colonies when it was ended, while ending slavery hurt economically. But the actual profitability of slavery and forced labor rose and fell depending on the context. In any case, either free labor or slavery could have worked well to promote economic growth, and indeed, both did. Both free labor and slavery proved profitable and the institutions existed side by side for centuries. What matters in

[154] Quoted in Paul E. Lovejoy and Jan S. Hogendorn, *Slow Death for Slavery: The Course of Abolition in Northern Nigeria, 1897–1936* (Cambridge: Cambridge University Press, 1993), p. 241.

[155] H. Galvão quoted in Davidson, *Let Freedom Come*, p. 109.

[156] Forced labor was only abandoned in African colonies by France in 1946 and it was used by Portugal into the 1970s. The "dop" system in South Africa, where winery workers were paid in wine rather than cash, only ended in the mid 1990s. More will be said below about how forced labor was regulated in colonies during the inter-war period by the International Labor Organization and the Mandate system.

[157] James Lee Ray and Ethan Nadelmann also suggest that slavery was ended because of changed ethical convictions and the persuasive efforts of those in the secular and religious communities that advocated emancipation. James Lee Ray, "The Abolition of Slavery and the End of International War," *International Organization* 43 (Summer 1989), 405–439; Nadelmann, "Global Prohibition Regimes."

terms of explaining the end of slavery and forced labor is what people thought about profitability. Or rather whether they thought profitability (or morality) was the right frame from which to understand and represent the questions of slavery and forced labor.

And clearly, though economic arguments were made both for and against slavery and forced labor, what seems to have mattered more were religious and philosophical arguments. This is no surprise, since during the eighteenth, nineteenth and early twentieth centuries, the life-world of Europeans, the basis on which they held and judged arguments, was dominated by religion. When the dominant religious-political community viewed slavery as just and good, and as contributing to the uplift of the enslaved, slavery was allowed and even admired. When the religious community thought that idleness was evil, and forced labor good, then forced labor was likewise admired. When some Christian theologians no longer held such views, they attempted to persuade others with their ethical-religious (and practical) arguments against slavery and forced labor, which eventually denormalized and delegitimized these practices. Opponents of slavery argued that the Bible did not encourage slavery, and that slavery was wrong. Religious arguments were persuasive because the dominant culture was Christian.

But secular arguments also became important and help explain why, after failing for thousands of years, anti-slavery arguments were increasingly persuasive. When by the 1780s the secular culture began to stress the rights of man, free labor, and a belief in progress, anti-slave arguments could gain a foothold. As the Earl of Abingdon said in parliament in 1793: "the idea of abolishing the slave trade is connected with the levelling system and the rights of man . . . what does the abolition of the slave trade mean more or less, than liberty and equality? What more or less than the rights of man?"[158] In other words, without greater empathy for slaves, which was actively fostered by the abolitionists, and without a way to frame anti-slavery arguments as consistent with the background of dominant religious/cultural beliefs and the rising "rights of man" discourse, anti-slave trade and emancipation arguments would likely have been as unsuccessful as they had been in the past. Similarly, with the slave trade and slavery abolished, the starting point for other ethical arguments had moved. Ethical arguments that questioned and opposed forced labor, equating forced labor with slavery, delegitimized forced labor by analogy and thus depended on the success of anti-slavery

---

[158] Quoted in Walvin, *An African's Life*, p. 183.

arguments for their persuasive force. Further, with the rise of free labor beliefs, an alternative practice was not only imagined, but said to be better for economic and spiritual reasons. As Martin Klein argues:

> In the context of European history, it is impossible to argue that society became more humane, but people certainly began to regard certain kinds of exploitation as immoral. Slavery eventually became redundant, an inefficient way of getting labour, but emancipation took place long before that happened. Abolition was often forced on the periphery by a centre committed to a free labour ideology and convinced that free labour was essential to dramatic growth and transformation of the capitalist world. This ideology was given its loftiest expression by the abolition movement spawned by and consistently supported by Christian Churches. It was also powerful enough that those non-Western elites who sought to understand Europe's ascendancy invariably saw free labour as a crucial part of that ascendancy. It is only these ideological agendas that can explain why Europe turned against slavery when it was still profitable . . . Dependent on democratically elected European parliaments for their budgets, colonial administrations were vulnerable to the pressures of abolitionist groups and increasingly had difficulty controlling the flow of information about their policies.[159]

At a deep level, the cultural background within which arguments about slavery and forced labor occurred, changed, allowing arguments against slavery which had been available for centuries to be heard anew by a wider audience. Yet to emphasize the role of ethical arguments, articulated primarily in religious terms during the period of contestation over slavery and forced labor, does not mean that practical arguments about the economics of slavery and forced labor, or scientific, and identity arguments were not at work. All sorts of arguments were used by both the advocates of slavery and forced labor and by those who fought for abolition. Ethical-religious arguments were especially salient when the table was dominated by those with strongly held religious beliefs. Economic (practical) arguments became more salient with growing secularization and the rise of capitalist economic beliefs. Slavery and forced labor ended because those who made ethical arguments against those practices were able to convince enough people to support abolition. They did so by first denormalizing and delegitimizing slavery and then by humanizing the slave. If domestic politics was crucial

---

[159] Klein, "Slavery," p. 213.

in ending British or American slavery, the domestic balance of forces changed because of ethical argument.

Regulating and ending slavery and forced labor had important and often unanticipated consequences for the institution of colonialism. With the end of slavery and the increasing freedom of colonial labor, some of the profitability of empire decreased. More importantly, however, by the time the United States, in 1865, and Brazil in 1888, finally ended slavery, several generations had debated the issue and thousands had died over the question.[160] Core beliefs had been challenged and altered, while core practices of colonialism were no longer considered normal and legitimate. Not only was involuntary labor at issue: European and American abolitionists directly challenged the notion of the less-than-human and inferior status of the dark races.[161] Not only was the material world different, the starting point, or topoi, of colonial arguments altered once slavery had been abolished and forced labor was challenged. Which arguments were successful depended on changed identity beliefs about others and greater empathy. Abolitionist and free labor arguments helped humanize the inhabitants of the colonies in the minds of the colonizers. In both cases, reformers institutionalized new normative beliefs which had ripple effects throughout the entire colonial system. For example, forced labor was only abolished in French colonies in 1946 while forced labor continued in Portuguese colonies much longer. The end of widespread belief in natural slaves, the Aristotelian ideal, was the end of slavery, while the abolition of colonialism began with the "decolonization" of slave and forced laborers' bodies.

---

[160] Of course, unfree labor continued well into the twentieth century. Stalin and Hitler used slave labor during World War II, and only in 1963 did Saudi Arabia formally abolish slavery. What is significant beyond the continued existence of unfree labor is that those who practice slavery and forced labor seek to conceal it, whereas in previous eras, concealment was not considered necessary. See Roger Sawyer, *Slavery in the Twentieth Century* (Routledge & Kegan Paul: London, 1986).

[161] Gann and Duignan, *Burden of Empire*, p. 10, argue that slavery was the first of the "great social issues" of the colonies.

5   Faces of humanitarianism, rivers of blood

> I made war against them. One example was enough: a hundred heads cut off, there have been plenty of supplies at the station ever since. My goal is ultimately humanitarian. I killed a hundred people . . . but that allowed five hundred others to live.[1]

> I cannot forget that the natives are not represented among us, and that the discussions of the Conference will, nevertheless, have an extreme importance for them.[2]

> The fundamental principle of our colonial policy must be scrupulous respect for the beliefs, habits and traditions of the conquered or protected peoples.[3]

Colonialism wore two humanitarian faces in the late nineteenth and early twentieth centuries, aggressive and reformist. Aggressive humanitarianism – a modified, "benevolent," colonialism – was the famous "white man's burden" which European powers took up in Africa, and the US shouldered in the Philippines. With the gradual turn to aggressive humanitarianism, Western colonialism in Africa thus began an uneven transformation from brute force to what Foucault called disciplinary power or the panopticon. In the former, power is exercised through

[1] Leon Fiévez, a Belgian Congo official, in 1894, quoted in Adam Hochschild, *King Leopold's Ghost: A Story of Greed, Terror and Heroism in Colonial Africa* (Boston: Houghton Mifflin Company, 1998), p. 166.
[2] Sir Edward Malet at the Berlin West Africa Conference quoted in R. J. Gavin and J. A. Betley, *The Scramble for Africa: Documents on the Berlin West Africa Conference and Related Subjects 1884/1885* (Ibadan, Nigeria: Ibadan University Press, 1973), p. 131. Spelling as it was in the original.
[3] French Minister of Colonies, Georges Léygués, in 1906, quoted in R.F. Betts, "Methods and Institutions of European Domination," in A. Adu Boahen, ed., *Africa Under Colonial Domination, UNESCO General History of Africa, VII* (Paris: UNESCO, 1985), pp. 313–331: 315.

terror and destruction; in the latter, while naked force is still used, power is increasingly exercised through discipline, socialization (eliciting compliance by instilling in the other a coincidence of interests and beliefs), and surveillance.[4]

Aggressive humanitarianism became dominant as colonial powers used anti-slavery arguments to justify greater intervention and colonial settlement in Africa. In 1883, Lord Granville, Britain's minister of foreign affairs, would insist to the Portuguese that ending slavery justified colonial conquest: "Her Majesty's Government . . . stated their chief objects to be the abolition of slavery and the civilization of Africa by the extension of legitimate commerce."[5] Further, the habits and techniques of international cooperation that grew out of the Concert of Europe and the anti-slavery patrols fostered more orderly colonization of Africa, at least among colonial rivals, than had been the case in the Americas. The aggressive face of humanitarianism and international cooperation in colonization were exemplified in arguments and beliefs expressed at the Berlin West Africa Conference in 1884 and in the reality of colonialism in Africa.

Humanitarianism's second face was modestly reformist, though reformers ultimately and unwittingly articulated increasingly powerful anti-colonial arguments and sparked reforms they had little idea would ultimately mortally weaken colonialism itself. Emerging from the anti-slavery movement, and fueled by vivid journalistic accounts of colonial excess, primarily in Africa, organizations like the Aborigines Protection Society, the African Association, and the Congo Reform Associations, called for reform, gradually denormalizing and delegitimizing both naked colonialism and the practices of the aggressive humanitarians. Even as armed resistance to European expansion and revolts in already colonized areas led by traditional leaders continued, Africans educated in European schools also took up the call for reform. Just as the anti-slavery movement succeeded in shifting the grounds of argument from assuming that the brutal exploitation of slavery was an acceptable means and outcome of European interaction with "natives," the colonial reform movement (inadvertently) denormalized colonialism itself by placing reform on the agenda of colonial governments and into the practical administration of colonies.

---

[4] Michel Foucault, *Discipline and Punish: The Birth of the Prison* (New York: Vintage Books, 1979).
[5] Letter from Granville to D'Antas, 15 March 1883, in Gavin and Betley, *The Scramble for Africa*, pp. 2–5: 2.

The turn of the century was a period of complexity and contradiction for colonizers. Slavery was no longer a legitimate practice, and therefore it was to be fought against, yet for the Victorians, as Ronald Robinson and John Gallagher argue, "Expansion in all its modes seemed not only natural and necessary but inevitable; it was preordained and ir-reproachably right."[6] So it was entirely consistent with the dominant beliefs of the 1880s for British Prime Minister Gladstone to argue for principled expansion: "Remember the rights of the savage, as we call him. Remember the happiness of his humble home, remember that the sanctity of life in the hill villages of Afghanistan, among the winter snows, is as inviolable in the eye of almighty God as can be your own."[7] Gladstone's contradictory arguments did not seem contradictory at the time.

The transition from naked aggression to aggressive humanitarian-ism is perhaps not so difficult to understand. Aggressive humanitarian views (we dominate you for your own good, and to show you how well you are being treated, we will feed you better and give you reli-gion) were usually articulated by aggressors and it made sense from a practical standpoint – if only to leave some labor to utilize – to become less brutal. The more difficult question is: why and how did aggressive humanitarianism yield to reformism? That colonial expansion would ul-timately be seen as conflicting with "remembering" the "rights" of the "savage" resulted from several factors: changing normative and iden-tity beliefs; a reframing of colonial practices; and greater opportunity for reformists, including the colonized themselves, to influence colonial practices.

First, as discussed at length above, the victory of the anti-slavery movement challenged or changed core normative beliefs about colo-nialism and the colonizers' relationship to the colonized. The "savage" had economic and political rights and deserved progress in both those realms. Further, while indigenous diplomatic and military resistance to the colonial effort was fierce, it was joined in Europe and the Americas when the descendants of North American and Caribbean slaves artic-ulated a Pan-African challenge to colonial oppression and argued for self-determination. The fact that Western-educated Africans, Indians, and former slaves in the Americas were able to articulate their criticisms of colonialism helped decrease, and in some cases bridge, the cultural

---

[6] Ronald Robinson and John Gallagher with Alice Denny, *Africa and the Victorians: The Official Mind of Imperialism* (London: Macmillan, 1961), p. 3.
[7] Quoted in Michael W. Doyle, *Empires* (Ithaca: Cornell University Press, 1986), p. 289.

distance between colonizer and colonized, and evoked empathy for the colonized. While a colonial discourse of expansion and conquest was still hegemonic in European capitals, it was increasingly challenged by humanitarian reformers and by the internal logic of normative beliefs held among the colonizers. White Europeans who were increasingly supportive of and allied with Pan-Africans slowly realized that their arguments were compelling in ways they had not anticipated; arguments for self-determination could not, logically, be limited.[8]

Second, the colonial project was reframed when Europeans, who held these new beliefs about the rights of the natives, learned more about conditions in colonies, especially those in Congo and Southern Africa. Prior generations had, of course, learned about and participated in colonial massacres and other atrocities, but they did not do so while holding new background beliefs about the rights of natives. Earlier generations had, as a consequence, generally not seen these practices as massacre and atrocity; their new belief in the humanity of the "savages" helped them to understand colonialism in a different way. In other words, there was greater press coverage of the realities of colonial conquest and administration, in part occasioned by the new beliefs mentioned above, but knowledge of atrocities alone would not have led to critique and oversight. New normative beliefs reframed the practices recharacterizing colonialism from benevolent and legitimate, to at least suspect.

Third, nineteenth-century Europeans and Americans were more politically active and democratic than ever before. Liberal democratic and socialist ideas were in full bloom, trade unionism was on the rise, and suffrage and literacy were expanding. Political organizations dedicated toward educating the public and persuading them to take action about conditions in the colonies used the media and democratic institutions to pressure their governments to reform. Though they used roughly the same techniques as the abolitionists, greater democracy at home meant their efforts saw fruition much more quickly in the realm of colonial policy, because as social movement theory suggests, they had greater political opportunity. This was a crucial part of changing the balance of capabilities and power that supported colonial practice.

---

[8] Neta C. Crawford, "Decolonization as an International Norm: The Evolution of Practices, Arguments, and Beliefs," in Laura Reed and Carl Kaysen, eds., *Emerging Norms of Justified Intervention* (Cambridge: American Academy of Arts and Sciences, 1983), pp. 37–61: 53.

The peak of colonial expansion was initially characterized by great confidence in colonialism, but became increasingly marked by criticism of colonial practice. At the outset of this period, inaugurated by the Berlin West Africa Conference of 1884–1885, colonialism was still understood as normal by the majority of the colonizers, and enthusiasts of colonialism formed pro-colonial lobbies. With the exception of the abolition of slavery, European colonial practices in Africa were about as brutal as colonialism had been in the Americas. This is most obvious in the case of the German conquest of South West Africa and Belgian conduct in the Congo, so that it is possible to say that in many ways colonialism reached its peak in Africa, especially in terms of intensity. But late nineteenth-century European colonialism in Africa was also the historical moment and location of some of colonialism's greatest tensions. Over the next thirty years, colonialism was denormalized by the humanitarians so that even these horrible practices did not pass unnoticed.

Africa

Making rules of legitimate conquest

Europeans began their voyages to Sub-Saharan Africa in the late 1400s. For example, Portuguese explorers Jacob Canus and Bartholemew Diaz landed on the coasts of South West Africa and South Africa, respectively, in the 1480s, setting up crosses to mark their landfall. Missionaries and small commercial companies followed over the next centuries but Europeans did not enter Africa's interior or remain on the coast in large numbers, in part because they feared unknown, and as yet untreatable, disease and saw little loot, besides humans, to acquire. With some help from philanthropists and churches, freed slaves set up colonies in Liberia and Sierra Leone in the late eighteenth and early nineteenth centuries, and like their white European counterparts, they largely believed in the virtues of imperialism and the civilizing mission. In the mid-1800s, Africans were still represented as savages and Africa was generally considered dangerous and without economic significance. The greatest European–African interaction had focused on the slave trade – first enlarging it and then curbing it. Except for the Dutch trading settlement in South Africa pushed further into the interior by the British, Europeans were ostensibly content to stay close to the coasts, in trading posts and small settlements. As late as 1880, some 90 percent of the continent was stilled ruled by Africans.

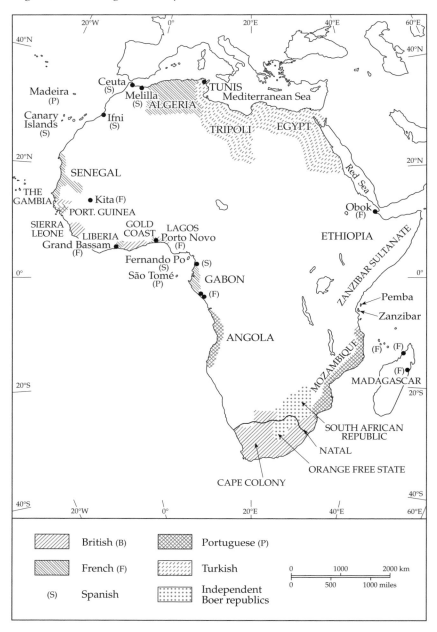

2. Europeans in Africa in 1880

But European interest in Africa grew, generated by an ambitious Belgian king, white explorers, commercial interests, and missionaries. At mid-century, King Leopold of Belgium had great ambitions to set up a colony somewhere in the world and in 1862 he went to Seville, Spain, to study records of Spanish colonialism: "I am very busy here going through the Indies archives and calculating the profit which Spain made then and makes now out of her colonies."[9] In 1876, Leopold, who was by then set on acquiring a colony in Africa, convened a Geographical Conference in Brussels of experts on Africa and famous humanitarians. He used the meeting to set up an International African Association, ostensibly for humanitarian purposes, of which he was president. Through various guises, such as the Committee for Studies of the Upper Congo and the International Association of the Congo, Leopold established his interest in the Congo region. Leopold also financed "exploration" by Henry Morton Stanley, who made treaties of free trade for Leopold along the Congo river. In April 1884, a representative for Leopold got the US Congress to recognize his claims to the International Association of the Congo and the International African Association.

Also during the mid and late 1800s, German missionaries and merchants began to buy land in South-West Africa. Bismarck early on had been opposed to colonial expansion but there was mounting public and political pressure for colonization. Germany was drawn into Africa after the missionaries and merchants appealed for protection from natives and other European interests, and, in April 1884, Germany declared the commercial venture of Adolf Lüderitz in South-West Africa a protectorate. In November 1884, Bismarck called an international conference to deal with the international rivalry over the area known as the Congo.[10]

Although widely thought to be the place where the map of Africa was redrawn, few borders were actually decided at the Berlin West Africa Conference of 1884–1885, though Leopold's new Congo state was recognized by the conference attendees.[11] Diplomatic recognition of the Congo would have enormous significance for people who lived under Leopold's rule, but the most important issues discussed in Berlin, and in the diplomatic exchanges that preceded and followed it, were the basic rules for the partition of Africa by European states. Because the conference set the terms for conquest by defining the condition of legitimate

[9] Leopold quoted in Hochschild, *King Leopold's Ghost*, p. 37.
[10] An overview is S.E. Crowe, *The Berlin West Africa Conference, 1884–1885* (London: Longmans, Green and Co., 1942).
[11] Leopold was not at the meeting.

colonial territory as "effective occupation," and developed provisions for notifying other powers of the acquisition of new territory, the Berlin meeting ensured that European governments' partition and occupation of Africa would proceed without undue risk of war between the great European powers.

European interest in Africa was propelled by humanitarian, economic, and power political reasons. Like the famous African explorer David Livingston – whose African travels, along with those of Stanley and the French explorer de Brazza had fascinated the European and American world – the Europeans present at the Berlin meeting believed commerce, Christianity, and civilization were inextricably intertwined. Colonizers desired the "glory" of empire, an end to slavery, the resources and trade of Africa, and they wanted to hold territory that would help them protect their other colonial interests in the Middle East and across the Indian Ocean. There was a general acceptance, indeed a positive glorification, of colonialism among the Great Powers.

Yet tensions that would become contradictions over the next thirty years were already evident at Berlin. In the face of serious anti-colonial critiques, diplomats felt compelled to make complex arguments, grounded in liberal beliefs, to support colonial expansion. Berlin Conference participants frequently mentioned the political rights of native occupants and discussed efforts to curb the internal African slave trade, all of which would be ensured through the benefits of conquest and free trade.[12] At the opening of the conference, for instance, Otto von Bismarck noted that the purposes of meeting were to end the slave trade and promote free trade, saying that the meeting should "facilitate the access of all commercial nations to the interior of Africa."[13] Britain's representative, Sir Edward Malet, speaking just after Bismarck, agreed that the point of the meeting was to ensure "freedom of commerce" but he then immediately stated, "I must not, however, lose sight of the fact that, in the opinion of Her Majesty's Government, commercial interests should not be looked upon as the exclusive subject of the deliberations of the Conference." Malet said, "While the opening of the Congo markets is to be desired, the welfare of the natives should not be neglected; to them it would be no benefit, but the reverse, if freedom of commerce,

[12] This is in marked contrast to previous legal treatment of natives: for example, neither the treaty between Britain and France ending their war in North America in 1763, nor the treaty between the US and Britain, ending the Revolutionary War, mentioned the natives whose land was occupied, although natives had fought for both sides in each case.
[13] Gavin and Betley, *The Scramble for Africa*, p. 129.

unchecked by reasonable control, should degenerate into licence." The link between humanitarian ideas and commerce are evident.

> I venture to hope that this will be borne in mind, and that such precautions will be adopted for the regulation of legitimate commerce as may tend to insure, as far as possible, that its introduction will confer the advantages of civilization on the natives, and extinguish such evils as the internal Slave Trade, by which their progress is at present retarded.
>
> I cannot forget that the natives are not represented among us, and that the discussions of the Conference will, nevertheless, have an extreme importance for them. The principle which will command the sympathy and support of Her Majesty's Government will be that of the advancement of legitimate commerce, with security for the equality of treatment of all nations, and for the well being of the native races.[14]

There were other prominent discussions of native rights at the Berlin conference. For example, the US delegate, Mr. Kasson, attempted to insert into the final act, without success, the idea that "Modern international law steadily follows the road which leads to the recognition of the right of native races to dispose freely of themselves and of their hereditary soil. In conformity with this principle, my Government would gladly adhere to a more extended rule to be based on a principle which should aim at the voluntary consent of the natives whose country is taken possession of in all cases where they may not have provoked the aggression."[15] Declaring that the US had a special interest in slavery given its recent civil war, Kasson proposed that anyone engaged in slave trafficking ought to be refused the right of residence and that slave traders should be "treated as an enemy of the whole world, just like a pirate."[16]

Humanitarianism and commerce were thus deeply entwined in the resulting General Act, with the consequence that its second paragraph stated twin purposes for colonial powers coming to agreement: managing the process of conquest and rule, and promoting civilization.

> Wishing, in the spirit of good and mutual accord, to regulate the conditions most favourable to the development of trade and civilization in certain regions of Africa, and to assure to all nations the advantages of free navigation on the two chief rivers of Africa flowing into

[14] Ibid., p. 131.
[15] Quoted in Quincy Wright, *Mandates Under the League of Nations* (Chicago: University of Chicago Press, 1930), p. 15. A slightly different version is quoted in Malcolm Shaw, *Title to Territory in Africa: International Legal Issues* (Oxford: Clarendon Press, 1986), p. 42.
[16] Gavin and Betley, *The Scramble for Africa*, p. 228.

the Atlantic Ocean; being desirous, on the other hand, to obviate the misunderstanding and disputes which might in future arise from new acts of occupation ("prises de possession") on the coast of Africa; and concerned, at the same time, as to the means of furthering the moral and material well-being of the native populations . . .[17]

Chapter I spelled out the guarantees for free trade, and Chapter II articulated opposition to slavery, declaring an agreement to "employ all the means at its disposal for putting an end to this trade and for punishing those who engage in it."[18] That this was a transition moment is clear in Chapter I, Article 6, which states in part:

All the Powers exercising sovereign rights or influence in the aforesaid territories bind themselves to watch over the preservation of the native tribes, and to care for the improvement of the conditions of their moral and material well-being, and to help in suppressing slavery, and especially the Slave Trade. They shall, without distinction of creed or nation, protect and favour all religious, scientific or charitable institutions, and undertakings created and organized for the above ends, or which aim at instructing the natives and bringing home to them the blessings of civilization.[19]

The terms for effective occupation were articulated in the General Act and by the Institute of International Law at its session in Lausanne in 1888 and published in volume 10 of the Institute's *Annuaire* (1888–1889). Occupation was deemed "effective" when the act of taking possession was done in the name of a government, other European governments were notified diplomatically, and order was maintained by a local government. Any disagreements among Europeans about the status of a territory would be worked out diplomatically, and if this was unsuccessful, the parties "will appeal to the good offices, the mediation, or the arbitration of one or several third powers." With these rules in place, it was less likely that the Europeans' scramble for Africa would lead to the kinds of wars that characterized the British and French race for territory in North America. And although there were no power political or economic reasons for this to be part of an international understanding of European cooperation for conquest, Europeans were obliged to treat the natives, or aboriginals, with respect.

Art. IV. All wars of extermination of aboriginal tribes, all useless severities, and all tortures are forbidden, even by way of reprisals.

---

[17] Ibid., p. 288.   [18] Ibid., p. 292.   [19] Ibid., p. 291.

Art. V. ... local authority will respect or will cause to be respected all rights, especially of private property, as well of the aborigines as of foreigners, including individual and collective rights.

Art. VI. The local authority has the duty of watching over the conservation of the aboriginal populations, their education, and the amelioration of their moral and material condition.[20]

Cooperation among European governments and aggressive humanitarianism became increasingly institutionalized in 1889–1890 when the Conference of Brussels, attended by more than a dozen states, agreed to suppress the Arab slave trade and slavery in Africa, as well as limit the trade in liquor to Africa.[21] Article I of the Brussels General Act enunciated how the slave trade would be combated through the "progressive organization of the administrative, judicial, religious, and military services under the sovereignty or protectorate of civilized nations," the establishment of "strongly occupied stations" in the interior, the "construction of roads" and railways connecting the coast to the interior, and other means, including the "restriction of the importation of firearms, at least those of a modern pattern, and of ammunition" in the areas where slave trading was being conducted which, according to the treaty, was most of Sub-Saharan Africa.[22] The colonizers were also to "diminish intestine [*sic*] wars between tribes by means of arbitration; to initiate them in agricultural labor and the industrial arts so as to increase their welfare; to raise them to civilization and bring about the extinction of barbarous customs ... "[23] Further, the Brussels Act proposed creating institutional mechanisms to promote abolition, namely international offices in Brussels and Zanzibar and the regular exchange of information between governments about the slave trade. Although the Brussels office apparently never opened, other aspects of the act were adhered to; specifically, from the perspective of conquest, the attendees agreed to restrict the flow of weapons to Africa and they did so with increasing effectiveness.

---

[20] Lausanne Institute of International Law quoted in Alpheus Henry Snow, *The Question of Aborigines in the Law and Practice of Nations* (New York: G.P. Putnam's Sons, 1921), pp. 289–291: 290.

[21] The participants included representatives from: Austria-Hungary, Belgium, Britain, Congo, Denmark, France, Germany, Holland, Italy, Norway, Persia, Portugal, Russia, Spain, Sweden, Turkey, the United States, and Zanzibar. See Suzanne Miers, *Britain and the Ending of the Slave Trade* (New York: Longman Group, 1975), pp. 236–291.

[22] Snow, *Aborigines in the Law and Practice of Nations*, pp. 294–306, General Act quotes from p. 296.

[23] Quoted in ibid., p. 297.

In sum, at Berlin, Lausanne, and Brussels the aggressive humanitarian tone was deeply intertwined with the concerns of free trade and effective occupation. Diplomats at Berlin felt convinced that both missions – commerce and civilizing – were necessarily accomplished with occupation, and that civilizing would come about through commercial activity. At Lausanne and Brussels they spelled out how colonial expansion would be conducted so as to be both safe for Europeans and legitimate. Thus, while Europeans and North Americans were self-conscious about the potential illegitimacy of colonialism, late nineteenth-century colonialism was still imbued with high moral fervor, bolstered by theories of Social Darwinism and white racial superiority.

The civilizing mission and colonial lobbies

By the late nineteenth century, the idea in Europe of a civilizing mission was already several centuries old. Indeed, for all his concern about Indians, even Bartolomé de Las Casas wanted to bring religion to the natives of Central and South America. The Final Act of the Berlin West Africa Conference provided for the protection of missionaries and others who would bring Christianity and other benefits of civilization to Africa. Indeed, Christian missionaries often preceded commercial ventures and settlers in Africa.

The wider cultural support and content for the ideas of a European civilizing mission were deep in Western European beliefs in the superiority of their culture and were articulated in new beliefs about European biological/racial superiority. While earlier in the nineteenth century strong arguments for monogenism (a single origin for human beings) were made by the British physician James Pritchard and others, polygenism had found wider support in anthropology and the biological sciences by the middle of the century. "Polygenists argued that the different races of man were so different from each other in their physical, mental and moral attributes as to form not mere varieties of one single species, but instead several different biological species of their own."[24] Physical anthropologists continued to measure humans and to classify them

---

[24] Nancy Stepan, *The Idea of Race in Science: Great Britain 1800–1860* (London: Macmillan, 1982), p. 29. Also see Michael Banton, *Racial Theories*, 2nd edn (Cambridge: Cambridge University Press, 1998); Pat Shipman, *The Evolution of Racism: Human Differences and the Use and Abuse of Science* (New York: Simon and Schuster, 1994); Robert Bannister, *Social Darwinism: Science and Myth in Anglo-American Social Thought* (Philadelphia: Temple University Press, 1979); Greta Jones, *Social Darwinism and English Thought: The Interaction Between Biological and Social Theory* (Atlantic Highlands, NJ: Humanities Press, 1980).

according to their physical differences while phrenologists argued that differences in the human skull corresponded to differences in the human brain and mental capacities. Charles Darwin's *Descent of Man* (1871) and his *The Origin of the Species* (1859), took for granted a hierarchy of lower and higher races and were also widely understood to support ideas of racial hierarchy.

It is well known that these beliefs spread beyond the scientific community into popular culture and political discourse. In simple terms, if social life was like the natural order, imperial expansion was natural. Or as Theodore Roosevelt said at the turn of the century, "In this world the nation that has trained itself to a career of unwarlike and isolated ease is bound, in the end, to go down before other nations which have not lost the manly and adventurous qualities."[25] Conquest proved the manliness and superiority of the conqueror, while to be conquered demonstrated inferiority, childlikeness, and femininity. Many Europeans were convinced, as well, of their scientific and technical superiority.[26]

Popular European and American enthusiasm for colonialism probably peaked between 1880 and 1900, and it was during this period that the pro-colonial lobbies, who found their support in the widespread belief in the civilizing mission, had perhaps their greatest visibility and success at influencing colonial policy. German public interest and pressure for colonialism at the time of the Berlin West Africa Conference was high. In Germany, the Central Society for Colonial Geography, was founded in 1878 and the German Colonial Union, founded in 1882, had some 121 branches and 12,500 members by 1886. The Society for German Colonization, founded in March 1884, merged with the German Colonial Union in 1887, forming the Deutsche Kolonial Gesellschaft with about 16,000 members.[27] Some members of these societies personally participated in German colonization in East and South West Africa and the societies pushed for government support of the colonies.

---

[25] Quoted in Richard Hofstadter, *Social Darwinism in American Thought*, Revd edn (New York: George Braziller, Inc.: 1955), p. 170.
[26] See Michael Adas, *Machines as the Measure of Men: Science, Technology and Ideologies of Western Dominance* (Ithaca: Cornell, 1989).
[27] W. O. Henderson, *The German Colonial Empire, 1884–1919* (London: Frank Cass, 1993), pp. 31–32; Wolfe W. Schmokel, *Dream of Empire: German Colonialism, 1919–1945* (New Haven: Yale University Press, 1964); Richard A. Voeltz, *German Colonialism and the South West Africa Company, 1884–1914* (Athens, OH: Ohio University Center for International Studies, 1988).

In France, two congresses convened on colonialism in 1889 and 1889–1890. The latter, the National Colonial Congress, specifically aimed to coordinate the activities of the many smaller pro-colonial organizations and included four dozen members of parliament. The Comité de l'Afrique française, founded in 1890, sponsored exploration of Africa, published a monthly newspaper to persuade the public of the benefits of colonization, and lobbied the French government in favor of expansion in Africa. The Union Coloniale Française founded in 1893 was explicitly concerned with promoting economic development of the colonies for French commercial interests. Both societies included members of parliament as did later organizations, such as the Parti Colonial, formed in 1892, and the Comité du Maroc, formed in 1904, to promote French colonialism in Morocco. The French colonial lobby stressed both nationalist reasons for expansion and the potential economic benefits of empire.[28] As Jules Ferry, an ardent advocate of empire argued: "Colonies are for rich countries one of the most lucrative methods of investing capital . . . I say that France, which is glutted with capital and which has exported considerable quantities, has an interest in looking at this side of the question . . . It is the same as that of outlets for our manufactures."[29]

Ronald Robinson and John Gallagher argue that British advocates of expansion were driven similarly by economic, spiritual, and moral fervor. "Since the Evangelical revival and the rise of secular liberalism, the issues presented by tropical Africa to the British nation had been derived from the ethical constructs of these movements." They suggest that "Concern for Africa flowed from some of the most vivid experiences of Victorian religious and political life. And for this reason the chief African questions for the Victorians were ones of atonement and duty. The chains had to be struck from the African's neck. He must be converted. He would be civilized. He should be traded with. But for all their enthusiasm, the earlier Victorians refused to rule him."[30] However, late Victorians did rush to rule Africa.

---

[28] Stuart Michael Persell, *The French Colonial Lobby, 1889–1938* (Stanford, CA: Hoover Institution Press, 1983).

[29] Quoted in A. Adu Boahen, *African Perspectives on Colonialism* (Baltimore: Johns Hopkins University Press, 1987), p. 31.

[30] Robinson and Gallagher, *Africa and the Victorians*, p. 27. They also argue that aside from those with financial and trading interests, the impetus for actual formal colonial rule in Africa, when it came, was official concern for larger strategic goals – British rivalry with France and protection of routes to their lucrative colonial assets in India. Ibid., pp. 191, 463–464. But this ignores British colonialism in Africa that could not be clearly or indirectly linked to strategic assets.

Conquest, resistance, revolt

The rush to establish effective occupation of Africa's interior after the Berlin West Africa Conference was called the Scramble for Africa and European states did just that, conquering and swindling African nations out of their land and political independence, and establishing European colonies that covered almost the entire continent.[31] Conquest often followed the same script. African leaders were offered treaties of protection and free trade by the representatives of a European government interested in the region. The "protection" was against war by other European or African nations and in some cases quite welcome. The "free" trade was a monopoly granting exclusive trading rights to the European state. An African leader's refusal to accede to treaties generally led to war. Declarations and treaties on free trade and ending slavery were thus not only rules for Europeans' conduct in Africa with other Europeans, but also legal rationalizations for dispossessing African rulers of their land if they refused to conduct commerce on European terms or if they practiced slavery or allowed slave trading. Some "African rulers who refused to succumb to the exigencies of British imperialism were arrested or treacherously trapped and deported from their own countries."[32] For example, King Jaja of Opobo and others, resisted offers of "protection" by the British.

> It was only after painstaking explanations and assurances by Consul Hewett that they consented to sign the treaty less the clauses dealing with freedom of trade. This consul invited him to dinner on board a British boat in 1887 and ordered the boat to sail away after King Jaja and his party had settled down to their dinner. King Jaja was taken to Accra, and tried and convicted on phony charges of trade monopoly. He was then deported to the West Indies where he died in 1891. Other famous African rulers who were deported to the Seychelles included King Prempeh I of Asante, Bai Bureh of Sierra Leone, and Mukama Kabarega of Bunyoro. King Prempeh, who was deported in 1896, was allowed to return to Kumasi in 1924, when the British adjudged him to be an old and broken man.[33]

Because most African leaders thus arrested were exiled for many years, Boniface Obichere argues that banishment by the British was a

---

[31] See Thomas Pakenham, *The Scramble for Africa, 1876–1912* (London: Weidenfeld and Nicolson, 1991).
[32] Boniface I. Obichere, "African Critics of Victorian Imperialism: An Analysis," *Journal of African Studies* 4 (1977), 1–20: 3.
[33] Ibid., p. 3.

"very effective method of implanting their own authority in the political vacuum which they created."[34] African leaders who weren't killed or kidnapped and banished wrote letters, negotiated with British colonial officials on the frontier, and many took up arms to halt colonial expansion.

Of course, because Africans resisted the Europeans, colonizers also used brute force, as these lines from a widely quoted poem by Hilaire Belloc suggest: "Whatever happens, we have got/The Maxim Gun, and they have not."[35] Because Europeans usually had fewer soldiers on the battlefield, they recruited or coerced Africans to join their militaries. But the most important factor weighing against the Africans was that the European militaries deployed superior weapons, and this was ensured after they agreed at the Brussels meeting in 1889–1890 to prohibit export of firearms to Africa. Though some arms merchants evaded the embargo, it was effective at preventing even wealthy African nations from getting the most advanced weapons in sufficient numbers to halt the European advance.

Despite their military disadvantage, African resistance to occupation was often intense and sustained. In many cases, African militaries managed to postpone for years the advance of European forces. For instance, the Ashanti and the Zulu beat the British several times. The Ethiopians, with an army numbering over 100,000, held off the Italians until 1935 by defeating them in 1896. Even with the embargo, some Africans were able to acquire modern arms and mobilize large military forces. Samori Touré of West Africa built a force of well over 30,000 in 1887 armed with modern European guns – a combination of domestic manufactures and imports – paid for partly by trading slaves. Though lacking artillery, Samori forestalled French conquest for years.[36] The Barue of the Zambesi similarly opposed Portuguese colonial expansion for several decades in the late nineteenth century, in part with homemade modern arms.[37] Still, even with these and other exceptions, prolonged African military resistance was generally unsuccessful.

[34] Ibid., p. 4.   [35] Quoted in Hochschild, *King Leopold's Ghost*, p. 90.
[36] See M'Baye Gueye and A. Adu Boahen, "African Initiatives and Resistance in West Africa, 1880–1914," in Boahen, ed., *Africa Under Colonial Domination*, pp. 114–148: 123–127.
[37] See Alan F. Isaacman, *The Tradition of Resistance in Mozambique: Anti-Colonial Activity in the Zambesi Valley, 1850–1921* (London: Heinemann, 1976). For summaries of the armed resistance and revolts, see Boahen, *African Perspectives on Colonialism*, pp. 64–66 and Bruce Vandervort, *Wars of Imperial Conquest in Africa, 1830–1914* (Bloomington, IN: Indiana University Press, 1998).

Once occupied, some Africans collaborated, trying to make the best of colonial rule, while others attempted to modify and resist it by whatever means necessary. As Terrence Ranger argues, "virtually every sort of African society resisted, and there was resistance in virtually every region of European advance."[38] Some used work stoppages and strikes to modify colonial governance, and to obtain better working conditions and wages. Major armed revolts included the Hut Tax Rebellion of 1898 in Sierra Leone, the Asante Rebellion of 1900 in the Gold Coast, the long Ekumeku Rebellion of 1893–1906 in Nigeria, and the Ndebele-Shona Rebellion of 1896–1897 in Southern Africa. The 1905–1906 Maji Maji rebellion in Tanganyika against the Germans was perhaps the largest, engaging over twenty African ethnic groups spread over 10,000 square miles. It was also the most brutally repressed uprising in East Africa, with 75,000 Africans killed, and the German starvation strategy leading to a famine causing 250,000–300,000 more deaths.

Some anti-colonial forces used the pen and formed political institutions to lobby for the maintenance of their own legal institutions and autonomy. African organizations, such as the Fantsi Amanbuhu Fekuw of Gold Coast, often combined political and cultural resistance to the colonizer, and there were a number of Aborigines' Rights Protection Societies and similar organizations in the continent. One early reformer, Reverend Alexander Crummell, born in New York in the early nineteenth century and educated in Cambridge, England, was part of the African-American movement that founded Liberia. Crummell believed in the virtues of commerce and the progressive force of Western civilization in Africa, but he also questioned aspects of the colonial situation. "I am not satisfied that the wealth of this, our Africa, should make *other* men wealthy and not ourselves. It troubles me in the night, and in the day it vexes me, that of all the moneys poured out here, so little stays at our own water-side."[39] The intellectuals John Africanus Horton, Edward Blyden, and James Johnson, were less enamored with Western civilization. The British-educated West African Horton rejected the idea that Africans were inferior to any others and he devoted several of his books to refuting the scientific and anthropological arguments of the mid-nineteenth century that proclaimed African inferiority. Horton was

---

[38] T.O. Ranger, "African Initiatives and Resistance in the Face of Partition and Conquest," in Boahen, ed., *Africa Under Colonial Domination*, pp. 45–62: 47.
[39] Quoted in J. Ayo Langley, *Ideologies of Liberation in Black Africa, 1856–1970: Documents on Modern African Political Thought from Colonial Times to the Present* (London: Rex Collings, 1979), p. 26.

also an early advocate of Pan-Africanism. Blyden, a West Indian who moved to Liberia in 1851, and a professor of Greek and Latin at Liberia College, wrote admiringly in several books of traditional African social, economic, and political systems and was also an early advocate of Pan-African solidarity. Johnson, a Yoruba who argued for Nigerian nationalism, believed in "Africa for the Africans."[40]

Though the European scramble and partition were often effected by force, argument was still important. The fact that Europeans gave African leaders' opposition to "free" trade and "protection" as a rationale for conquest, rather than proclaiming a natural right to conquest, signifies a shift toward the legalist view of conquest espoused by Vitoria and Vattel in opposition to the "anything goes" positive law view dominant in the past.

Indirect rule

Like its incarnation in the Americas, European colonialism in Africa consisted of political control, economic expropriation, forced labor, extraction of land and natural resources for little or no compensation, the payment of tribute to the colonizer, and cultural control, such as forced religious conversion and education in the language of the metropole. Colonization in Africa followed a familiar plot: a new land populated by barbarians and savages was "discovered" or, in the case of Africa, "explored" by missionaries and individual charismatic explorers who charted the area. Next, as in the Americas, private and public companies backed by the might of governments staked claims ("concessions"), and began settlements in order to do business. European governments deployed militaries to protect settlers and investments. Colonizers made treaties of European "protection" with Africans, while preexisting disagreements and differences between native populations were exploited so that a divide and rule strategy would succeed. The language, religion, political, and economic systems of the first inhabitants of the area were recognized only as long as it took to subdue the local people. Colonizers constructed roads, ports, and railways, with colonial labor, to facilitate the extraction of resources and settlement of the land and developed local government in order to coordinate these activities and signal to other potential colonizers that the area was already taken.

[40] Boahen, *African Perspectives on Colonialism*, pp. 20–22 and Langley, *Ideologies of Liberation*, pp. 32–38.

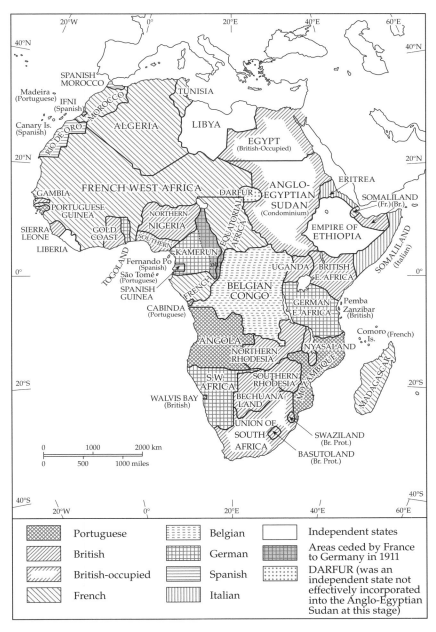

In this way, Africa was completely colonized, with the exceptions of the independent states of South Africa and Ethiopia, by 1914, only a few decades after colonization began. Italy held Somaliland; Germany controlled South West Africa, Kamerun, and a portion of East Africa (Tanzania); Portugal had Guinea, Angola, and Mozambique; Spain had Rio De Oro (now Western Sahara). Most of the rest of the continent was run by either Britain or France.

Of course, one major difference between colonialism in the Americas and Africa was that, after the late nineteenth century, slavery was not legal in most European colonies in Africa, and all the colonizing nations that met at Berlin had pledged to combat it. However, since most Africans were little interested in working on the roads, railroads, mines, and farms of white settlers, and slavery was outlawed, forced labor was widely used. A second important difference was due to demographics. While, in the Americas, native populations declined at an astounding rate, and Europeans found the climate hospitable for colonization and settlement, Africans did not die in great numbers upon contact with colonizers, and Europeans were not immediately comfortable in African climates. Thus, Europeans were well outnumbered by Africans, and in order to govern Africa without the constant use of force, some sort of cooperation had to be devised. This meant that in the era of conquest European armies made use of African troops, usually mercenaries or conscripts drawn from a different region. It also meant that when it came time to rule, European governments relied on local African rulers and collaborators more than they had in the Americas, which meant keeping some aspects of African political systems in place and using them in a system of "indirect" rule.[41] As a French colonial administrator explained, "There is no colonization without native policy; no native policy without a territorial command; and no territorial command without native chiefs who serve as links between the colonial authority and the population."[42]

In terms of concrete everyday practice, indirect rule meant that after Europeans established military authority, they ruled natives through

---

[41] Much is often made of differences among styles of French, British, German, Portuguese, and Belgian administration in Africa. The sharpest contrast is usually described as between French (direct) and British (indirect) rule. The French tended to crush traditional authority systems and insert their own method of governance while the British tended to rule through traditional leaders and leadership structures. While there were important differences, colonial administration generally embodied varying degrees of indirect rule.

[42] Robert Delavignette in 1946, quoted in Betts, "Methods and Institutions of European Domination," p. 317.

settler administrations which in turn governed through African leaders whose authority Europeans both borrowed and enhanced. Local chiefs collected taxes, organized the labor pools necessary to satisfy the demands of the colonizers, and handled disputes among natives. The police forces were primarily staffed by Africans under the directions of Europeans. European administrations governed the European settlers directly through settler administrations.

European governments paid for colonial administration and infrastructure primarily with taxes on "huts" or persons, or on profitable European-run concessions. Taxes also forced Africans out of their subsistence economies and into the wage economy. As Kenya's governor said in 1913, "We consider that taxation is the only possible method of compelling the native to leave his reserve for the purpose of seeking work. Only in this way can the cost of living be increased for the native . . . it is on this that the supply of labour and the price of labour depend. To raise the rate of wages would not increase, but would diminish the supply of labour."[43] Colonial governments typically required free Africans, prisoners, and "vagrants" to provide periods of labor to the government for the construction of roads and other infrastructures. Forced labor for public works and taxes thus subsidized administrative costs.

German South-West Africa

When Germany tried to establish colonies in East and South West Africa, it met with determined African resistance. The Germans crushed this resistance with enormous brutality, and on the face of it, there seems no room in this history for the play of argument, much less ethical argument. As Bismarck said, "The great questions of the age are not settled by speeches and majority votes . . . but by iron and blood."[44] Ultimately, the Germans killed tens of thousands of Africans in South-West Africa, subjected most of the rest to forced labor, and took the land and cattle. After they found diamonds, they took those and made enormous profits. Nevertheless, arguments – identity, practical, scientific, and ethical – *were* an important part of the process, though more often than not native South-West Africans lost their arguments.

[43] Quoted in M.H.Y. Kaniki, "The Colonial Economy: The Former British Zones," in Boahen, ed., *Africa Under Colonial Domination*, pp. 382–419: 397.
[44] Quoted in Hagan Schulze, *Germany: A New History* (Cambridge, MA: Harvard University Press, 1998), p. 140.

As they had elsewhere in Africa, religion and commerce preceded colonial government in South-West Africa. The Portuguese, English and Dutch had all set foot on what was to become South-West Africa starting in the fifteenth century, but only German missionaries made an effort to stake out a settlement. The missionaries were followed decades later, in 1882, by the entrepreneur Adolf Lüderitz, who sought German protection. Assured of at least qualified protection in 1884, Lüderitz successfully acquired a great deal of land, mainly on the coast, and thus German interest in the area grew. As Bismarck's agent Count Münster wrote to Britain's Lord Granville to forestall British interest in the area, "The Imperial Government regards itself bound to afford protection and encouragement to German subjects carrying on trade in districts where sufficient protection is not guaranteed by a recognized Civil organization."[45] Later, when Lüderitz was failing financially, he sold his assets to the Deutsche Colonial Gesellschaft für Südwest Afrika, a private German corporation which expanded its assets by purchasing other land from the natives.

Like other colonial powers, German policy was first to take land from natives by treaty if possible, and to exploit preexisting disagreements and conflict between native leaders, especially the long-standing conflict between the two largest groups in the area, the Herero and the Nama. Those natives who resisted incorporation were to be made to submit. In 1885 Bismarck sent Dr. Heinrich Goering (Hermann Goering's father) to negotiate treaties of protection with the South West African natives, and thus the official German presence was extended. The Germans gave their newly acquired land to other commercial companies, to concessions, and to settlers, taking the rest as crown land. Some African leaders took German protection from Goering or later emissaries as part of their strategy against other groups. For example, in part to help them in their war with the Nama, the Herero submitted to German "protection" in 1890. Questioning the wisdom of the alliance, Hendrik Witboi, a Nama chief, wrote to the head of the Herero after he learned of the treaty:

> But dear captain, you have now accepted another Government; you have surrendered to that Government in order to be protected by another human Government from all dangers, chiefly and foremost to be protected from me in this war ... You are to be protected and helped by the German Government, but dear captain do you appreciate what

[45] Letter quoted in I. Goldblatt, *History of South West Africa from the Beginning of the Nineteenth Century* (Cape Town: Jutta & Company Limited, 1971), p. 86.

you have done? ... but it appears to me that you have not sufficiently considered the matter, having in view your land and people, your descendants who will come after you and your Chieftain's rights. Do you imagine that you will retain all the rights of your independent chieftainship after you shall have destroyed me (if you succeed)? That is your idea, but dear Captain in the end you will have bitter remorse, you will have eternal remorse, for this handing of your land and sovereignty over to the hands of white people ... But this thing which you have done, this giving of yourself into the hands of white people for government, thinking that you have acted wisely, that will become to you a burden as if you were carrying the sun on your back.[46]

The Germans tried to force a treaty with the Nama in 1892 but some, under Witboi, repeatedly declined and instead made a peace treaty with the Herero in November. In 1892 Witboi wrote to the British magistrate in Walvis Bay seeking information:

> Germans are encroaching on my land and now even my life is threatened they come to destroy me by War without my knowing what my guilt is ... I have been told that it is their intention to shoot me and I ask Your Honour. Perhaps you can tell me why? Perhaps you will know because you are parties to a treaty and of you English and Germans the other nation can do nothing without the knowledge of the other; because as I have heard (and I ask Your Honour) that the English Government and the German Government held a big meeting and discussed to whom this land Africa should be assigned – for the purpose of concluding Protection Agreements with the Chiefs of the land; and thereupon you English surrendered the land to the Germans. But you also said at the meeting that no Chief should be compelled by force.[47]

Witboi appealed to Britain to curb the Germans. His appeal framed German behavior as profoundly unjust:

> So also has it come to pass that some Chiefs have accepted German protection. ... The Germans told those Chiefs that they wished to protect them from other strong nations, which intended to come into the land with armies and deprive the Chiefs, by force, of their lands and farms; and that therefore it was their (the Germans) desire to protect the Chiefs from such stupid and unjust people ... but so far as I have seen and heard, it appears to me wholly and entirely the reverse. The German himself is that person of whom he spoke, he is just what he described those other nations as. He is doing those things because he

---

[46] Quoted in Union of South Africa, *Report on the Natives of South-West Africa and their Treatment by Germany* (London: His Majesty's Stationery Office, 1918), p. 20.
[47] Quoted in *ibid.*, p. 25.

rules and is now independent, with his Government's laws; he makes
no requests according to truth and justice and asks no permission of
a chief... He personally punishes our people at Windhuk and has already beaten people to death for debt... It is not just and worthy to
beat people to death for that... He flogs people in a scandalous and
cruel manner. We stupid and unintelligent people, for so he regards
us, we have never yet punished a human being in such a cruel and
improper way. He stretches persons on their backs and flogs them on
the stomach and even between the legs, be they male or female...[48]

Seeking to crush them if they would not sign up for protection, Germans under Commander Curt von François attacked the Nama by surprise in April 1893 at Hornkranz, killing at least eighty people, mostly
women and children. Witboi escaped and decided to go on the offensive. After some fighting during which neither side could gain the upper
hand, the new German officer in charge of South West Africa, Theodore
Leutwein, wrote Witboi a letter, and in May the Nama and Germans
came to a truce that would last until 1 August 1894.[49] During the
truce, Leutwein proposed an unconditional surrender, "submission,"
and charged the Nama with making war against his African neighbors,
which he said was an affront to the German emperor.[50] Witboi refused
to submit and asked instead for a peace that respected both sides.

Witboi and Leutwein's arguments

On 18 August 1894, Witboi wrote to Leutwein in an attempt to keep his
autonomy and avoid battle with the Germans. Witboi's letter was an
argument for the extension of the principle of self-determination to his
territory, and he again used arguments he thought the colonizer would
recognize and must logically extend to apply to the Nama people. "My
dear highly honoured Mr. Leutwein, Major, God has created different
states, and therefore I know and believe that it is no sin or crime that I
should remain Kaptain of my land and my people. If you wish to kill
me on account of my independent rule over my country, and without
any cause on my part, that cannot do me any harm or occasion me any
disgrace, for then I shall die in honour, in defence of my rights."
Witboi's letter demonstrates his recognition of the importance of legal
justification for the Germans "before the world." He says "I bear no

[48] Quoted in ibid. The *Report* notes that Witboi's letter was received and transmitted to
the British government.
[49] Horst Drechsler, *"Let Us Die Fighting:" The Struggle of the Herero and Nama against German
Imperialism (1884–1915)* (London: Zed Press, 1980), pp. 70–71.
[50] Leutwein to Witboi, quoted in *Report on the Natives*, p. 84.

guilt in respect of the things you impute to me as crimes, and which you employ as grounds for condemning me to death. These are things which you have conjured up in order to appear before the world as a man who has honour, right and truth on his side. But dear friend, I tell you that I am truly free and at ease in my mind, because I know myself to be innocent of any guilt." Witboi also acknowledged that the German military was superior to his forces, but, consistent with his strong religious beliefs, he presumed that the Lord would help him. "But you say that might is right, and in accordance with that, you act towards me because you are mighty in that you possess arms and all the other weapons. I agree that you are powerful, and I cannot hold a candle to you. But dear friend, you come to me with an armed force, and you say you are going to shoot at me. Well then, I shall return the fire; but not in my name, or in relying on my strength; rather in the name of the Lord and relying on His strength, and I defend myself with His aid." Finally, Witboi implied that the Germans would lose the ethical argument in the eyes of the world and made a last plea for peace: "You wish to lay on me the blame for the shedding of blood, but that is out of the question. I have offered you peace, and still do so – a genuine peace – and I ask you to leave me in peace."[51]

Witboi's letter was probably written too late, since Major Leutwein had already called for reinforcements and planned to attack again once those forces arrived. In any case, Leutwein replied a few days later: "all further letters in which you do not offer me your submission are useless . . . ."[52] Witboi said nothing and German troops, reinforced, went to war against the Nama. Witboi and the Nama lost when their ammunition and food ran out, and they were forced to sign a treaty with the Germans in mid-September.

Leutwein's treaty was, after all, not premised on a total surrender for the Nama – they were allowed to keep their weapons – and many in Germany, and a number of settlers in South-West Africa, thought the treaty should not be approved by the chancellor. The settlers, and the officer Leutwein had replaced, argued that Leutwein's terms were too lenient. François said: "Compared with the damage Witbooi has caused, I regard the . . . peace as far too mild. The war against Witbooi has cost the German Empire approximately four million Marks. The damage it

---

[51] Witboi letter to Leutwein quoted in Goldblatt, *History of South West Africa*, pp. 122–123. This is similar to statements the Melians made to the Athenians during the Peloponnesian War.
[52] Quoted in *Report on the Natives*, p. 85.

has caused in the colony is at least as great. But he appears to have lost only areas that are at great distance from Gibeon [Witboi's home]; his tribe remains united; he retains his weapons and, it seems, the captured rifles as well; and he receives a salary of 2,000 Marks."[53]

Leutwein was compelled by the criticism to explain his conduct in the war and make a practical argument for the German government's recognition of his treaty with Witboi. In a letter to the German chancellor, Leutwein humbly said he thought his negotiated settlement was the wisest move given the possibility of a prolonged war if total surrender was the object. He wrote:

> All my detractors operate on the premise that I was free to treat Witbooi as I wished and that I acted in the way I did for reasons that are impossible to understand. I must submit, Your Grace, that this was not so. In all colonial wars in which one faces a really formidable enemy, it is a question of either destroying him or coming to an understanding with him. As we have seen on more than one occasion, victory alone is of no avail and severe punishment will only produce a secret enemy intent on casting off his shackles. This is a lesson I have drawn from the study of English colonial history from which we Germans can learn much more than that.[54]

Rather than trying to totally defeat the Nama, a negotiated settlement was the wisest thing for Germany since Witboi was still strong and defeating his forces would have required "3,000 instead of 300 rifles." Leutwein was, of course, making an economic argument as well as a diplomatic one – Germany could ill afford the expense of a long war – and he implored the chancellor to make the case to the emperor. But, he said, "If Your Grace does not subscribe to my view, nothing has been lost either," since he could easily resume war against the Nama: "I should have no difficulty in finding a pretext that would put Kaptein Witbooi in the wrong."[55]

The emperor did agree to Leutwein's treaty, and this inaugurated an almost eleven-year period of coexistence between the Germans and Nama where Witboi's forces even assisted the Germans' divide and conquer strategy, helping to suppress other Africans. Leutwein successfully fed the friction between Nama and Herero. Leutwein said:

> The war with Witboi had, at the very beginning of my colonial activity, opened my eyes to the difficulty of suppressing native risings in

---

[53] Quoted in Drechsler, *"Let Us Die Fighting,"* p. 78.   [54] Quoted in ibid., pp. 78–79.
[55] Quoted in ibid., p. 79.

South-West Africa. Since that time I have used my best endeavor to
make the native tribes serve our cause and play them off one against
the other. Even an adversary of this policy must concede to me that it
was more difficult, but also more serviceable, to influence the natives
to kill each other for us than to expect streams of blood and streams of
money from the Old Fatherland for their suppression. . . .[56]

Despite their great numerical superiority, the Nama, Herero, and
other peoples of South-West Africa were unable to keep German settlers,
of whom there were about 3,700 in 1903, at bay.[57] Only the Ovambo, who
lived farthest from the majority of German settlers and their military,
were left relatively alone. The Africans' weakness was due in part to
the Germans' military superiority, but was also because they were dev-
astated by epidemics. A rinderpest epidemic in 1897 wiped out much
of the cattle on which they depended for subsistence; an epidemic of
typhoid fever the following year further weakened the Africans. The
German expropriation of land continued, and a system of Native Reserves was established in 1898. Thus, the German colonial government
reduced the Africans to "the state of rightlessness." And, "Displaying
a blatantly racist attitude, the Germans described Africans as baboons
and treated them accordingly."[58]

German behavior in South-West Africa was not natural; it had to be
argued before it could be implemented. The colonists' arguments depended on social Darwinist identity and normative beliefs, namely the
belief in German superiority, and the ability to dominate militarily justified such domination. As one high-ranking German colonial official,
Paul Rohrbach, wrote:

> The decision to colonise in South-West Africa could after all mean
> nothing else but this, namely that the native tribes would have to give
> up their lands on which they had previously grazed their stock in order
> that the white man might have the land for grazing his stock.
>
> When this attitude is questioned from the moral law standpoint,
> the answer is that for the nations of the "Kulture-position" of the

[56] Leutwein, quoted in *Report on the Natives*, p. 10.
[57] Drechsler, *"Let Us Die Fighting,"* p. 244.
[58] Ibid., p. 132. As one missionary observed "The real cause of the bitterness among the
Hereros toward the Germans is without question the fact that the average German looks
down upon the natives as being about on the same level as the higher primates (baboon
being their favorite term for the natives) and treats them like animals. The settler holds
that the native has a right to exist only in so far as he is useful to the white man. It follows
that the whites value their horses and even their oxen more than they value the natives."
Quoted in Jon M. Bridgman, *The Revolt of the Hereros* (Berkeley: University of California
Press, 1981), p. 62.

South African natives, the loss of their free national barbarism and their development into the class of labourers in service of land and dependent on the white people is primarily a "law of existence" in the highest degree.

It is applicable to a nation in the same way as to the individual, that the right of existence is justified primarily in the degree that such existence is useful for progress and general development.

By no arguments whatsoever can it be shown that the preservation of any degree of national independence, national property, and political organization by the races of South-West Africa, would be of a greater or even of an equal advantage for the development of mankind in general or of the German people in particular, than the making of such races serviceable in the enjoyment of their former possessions by the white races.[59]

Consistent with these beliefs and arguments, German colonial rule over Africans was harsh. German settlers who took land and cattle from the Africans and coerced them into labor were ignored or assisted by the German police. The few German settlers who were tried for murdering or flogging Africans were often given light sentences or acquitted, while the rule of thumb in cases where Africans killed Germans was a death sentence. As German director of land settlement, Karl Dove, said: "leniency towards the natives is cruelty to the whites."[60] The large-scale theft of thousands of head of cattle under the pretext that the grazing cattle were trespassing on German land, or later through swindling, was particularly enraging to Africans though they could do little about it.[61] One African, Daniel Kariko, described the cattle swindle this way:

Our people were being robbed and deceived right and left by German traders, their cattle were taken by force; they were flogged and ill-treated and got no redress. In fact the German police assisted the traders instead of protecting us. Traders would come along and offer goods. When we said we had no cattle to spare, as the rinderpest had killed so many, they said they would give us credit. Often . . . the trader would simply off-load goods and leave them saying that we could pay when we liked, but in a few weeks he would come back and demand his money or cattle in lieu thereof. He would then go and pick out our very best cows he could find. Very often one man's cattle were taken to pay other people's debts. If we objected and tried to resist the police

[59] Rohrbach, quoted in *Report on the Natives*, p. 19.   [60] Quoted in *ibid.*, p. 49.
[61] Drechsler, *"Let Us Die Fighting,"* pp. 117–119.

228

would be sent for and, what with the floggings and the threats of shooting, it was useless for our poor people to resist.... They fixed their own prices for the goods, but would never let us place our own valuation on the cattle. They said a cow was worth 20 marks only. For a bag of meal they took eight cows . . . Some debts they claimed had never existed . . .[62]

Rebellion and "rivers of blood"

In late 1903 the "Bondelswartz" of the southern region of South-West Africa rebelled after the Germans promulgated regulations compelling them to "regard a white man as a superior being," and proclaimed that the "evidence of a white man can only be outweighed by the statements of seven coloured persons" in court.[63] German authorities had also interfered in an internal dispute, despite treaty provisions granting autonomy to the Bondelswartz in such matters, and in the process they killed a Bondelswartz leader. When German troops moved south to crush the Bondelswartz' uprising, the Herero people, led by Samuel Mahero, began a revolt that shocked the Germans with its intensity and initial success. The Herero only targeted German men and would spare the Boers, British, and other African groups: "We decided that we would wage war in a humane manner and would kill only the German men who were soldiers, or would become soldiers."[64] Even with these limitations, in a few weeks in January 1904, the Herero mounted a serious challenge to the German presence, and despite a shortage of arms and ammunition, they again took the initiative in April and May. Only when Governor Leutwein was reinforced by troops from Germany did German forces take the initiative. By August, the Herero were in retreat. The chief of the Army General Staff, Graff Schlieffen, was put in charge of the operation, which he ran from Germany.

Because he was considered too lenient, inadvertently encouraging the uprising, Leutwein was replaced in July as military commander by General Lothar von Trotha, already well known for his ruthlessness in colonial wars in China and East Africa. Trotha told Leutwein in 1904: "I know enough tribes in Africa. They all have the same mentality insofar as they yield only to force. It was and remains my policy to apply this force by unmitigated terrorism and even cruelty. I shall destroy the rebellious tribes by shedding rivers of blood and money."[65] Von Trotha

[62] Quoted in *Report on the Natives*, pp. 47–48.   [63] Leutwein quoted in *ibid.*, p. 33.
[64] Quoted in ibid., p. 57.
[65] Trotha quoted in Drechsler, *"Let Us Die Fighting"*, p. 154.

gave orders on 2 October 1904 to shoot every Herero: "I believe that the Herero must be destroyed as a nation."[66] Cash bounties for rebellion leaders, dead or alive, were offered by the general. On 29 October, the general asked Herero leaders to come in to arrange a peace treaty and when they arrived, he had them shot.[67]

Von Trotha then issued orders that every Herero "within German boundaries" was to be shot regardless of whether or not they were armed. Although the orders were later revised to be less harsh, von Trotha nevertheless continued the policy with the support of General Schlieffen, who wrote on 23 November: "One may agree with Trotha that the whole nation must be destroyed or driven out of the country. After what has happened the co-existence of whites and blacks will be very difficult, unless the blacks are kept in a state of forced labour, indeed a kind of slavery. Racial war, once it has broken out, can only be ended by the destruction of one of the parties."[68] To escape the German troops, the Herero went east into the desert and the General Staff decided that driving them into the desert would be their policy: "The arid Omaheke was to complete what the German Army had begun: the extermination of the Herero nation."[69] Under Trotha's orders, and with the knowledge of the General Staff, the military then blocked off other routes, and forced the Herero into the desert where many died of thirst.

Many Germans objected to the policy of exterminating the Herero.[70] Those who opposed German policy, and especially von Trotha's extermination order, included the chancellor, Prince von Bülow, who argued to the kaiser that the order was "contradictory to all Christian and humane principles."[71] Notably, Bülow did not oppose "concentration camps where the rest of the Herero people would be placed and kept for the time being."[72] Rather, von Bülow argued pragmatically that extermination was unwise since the native population was "essential both for farming and stock-breeding and for mining" and was "detrimental to Germany's place among the civilized nations and would add

[66] Quoted in Peter Katjavivi, *A History of Resistance in Namibia* (Trenton, NJ: Africa World Press, 1988), p. 10. Also see Goldblatt, *History of South West Africa*, pp. 132–133 and Helmut Bley, *Namibia Under German Rule* (Hamburg: Lit Verlag, 1996), p. 164.
[67] *Report on the Natives*, pp. 59–60.
[68] Quoted in Bley, *Namibia Under German Rule*, p. 165.
[69] General Staff, *Die Kämpfe der deutschen Truppen in Südwestafrica, auf Grund amtichen Materials bearbeitet von der Kriegsgeschichtlichen Abteilung I des Grossen Generalstabes* (Berlin: 1906), vol. I, p. 207, quoted in Drechsler, *"Let Us Die Fighting,"* pp. 155–156.
[70] Henderson, *German Colonial Empire*, p. 86.
[71] Quoted in Bley, *Namibia Under German Rule*, p. 163.
[72] Quoted in Drechsler, *"Let Us Die Fighting,"* p. 165.

fuel to the violent campaign already being waged against Germany."[73] The head of the German Colonial Department, Stübel, argued that the extermination program was damaging to the Germany army.[74] On the other hand, Schlieffen thought von Trotha was correct: "The intention of General von Trotha can therefore be approved. The only problem is that he does not have the power to carry it out."[75] The General Staff felt constrained by public opinion which Schlieffen noted was against extermination, and therefore, he said, Trotha's plan "could not be carried through successfully in the face of present opinion."[76] On 8 December 1904, though much of the damage had already been done, Trotha's extermination order was countermanded. A few thousand Herero were able to cross the desert into other territory, while others were able to slip across German lines and find shelter elsewhere in South-West Africa. The remaining Herero were put in concentration camps.

The Herero, who had asked the Nama to join them at the outset of their rebellion, fought alone and were essentially defeated when the Nama, again led by Hendrik Witboi, finally took up arms against the Germans in October 1904. Since the settlers were calling on the German army to exterminate the Nama as well as the Herero, they feared attack after von Trotha finished with the Herero. About 1,200–1,400 Nama fought a German force in South-West Africa of about 10,000. Even with far superior firepower, due to their limited mobility, the Germans were unable to quickly defeat the Nama.[77] Thus, the war dragged on and General von Trotha was withdrawn from South-West Africa in November 1905 before he was able to defeat the Nama.[78] The Nama were able to fight for several years, but like the Herero, they faced a *de facto* policy of extermination and were slowly crushed, with the last Nama rebels finally being put down in March 1908.

The 1911 census reveals how efficient German strategy and the subsequent camps were: about 50 percent of Nama people (whose population had been estimated at about 20,000 in 1904) and 75 to 80 percent of the Herero population (estimated at about 80,000 in 1904) had been killed by German forces by the end of 1905.[79] On the other hand, a total of 676

[73] Quoted in Bley, *Namibia Under German Rule*, p. 166.
[74] Bley, *Namibia Under German Rule*, pp. 166–167.
[75] Quoted in Bridgman, *Revolt of the Hereros*, p. 130.
[76] Quoted in Bley, *Namibia Under German Rule*, p. 165.
[77] See Bridgman, *Revolt of the Hereros*, pp. 140 and 169.
[78] Still, General von Trotha was given the Order of Merit by the Kaiser in 1905. Pakenham, *The Scramble for Africa*, p. 615.
[79] *Report on the Natives*, p. 35. Bley, *Namibia Under German Rule*, p. 150.

Germans were killed in action, 689 died from illness, 907 were wounded, and 76 were missing; the cost of putting down the rebellion, up to 1906, was estimated at 182 million Marks.[80] By its end in 1908, the war was estimated to have cost Germany nearly 500 million Marks.[81]

Conditions were brutal for Africans following German victory. Herero and Nama survivors were sent to camps where about 45 percent of them died.[82] Hosea Mungunda, described by the British as a Herero headman at Windhuk, testified about conditions for survivors:

> Those who were left after the rebellion were put into compounds and made to work for their food only. They were sent to farms, and also to the railways and elsewhere. Many were sent to Luderitzbucht and Swakopumund. Many died in captivity; and many were hanged and flogged nearly to death and died as a result of ill-treatment. Many were mere skeletons when they came in and surrendered, and they could not stand bad food and ill-treatment.
>
> ... The young girls were selected and taken as concubines for the soldiers; but even the married women were assaulted and interfered with ... When the railways were completed and the harbour works, we were sent out to towns and to farms to work. We were distributed and allocated to farmers whether we liked them or not.[83]

A 1907 law obliged all natives over the age of seven to carry passes. Other ordinances prohibited natives from owning land, riding animals or cattle, and decreed that natives "without visible means of subsistence" would be treated as vagrants.[84] Punishment for vagrancy, desertion, negligence, disobedience and insolence included lashes and/or imprisonment. One European, Johann Noothout, who visited South-West Africa after the rebellion noted, "If a prisoner were found outside the Herero prisoners' camp, he would be brought before the Lieutenant and flogged with a sjambok. Fifty lashes were generally imposed. The manner in which the flogging was carried out was the most cruel imaginable ... pieces of flesh would fly from the victim's body into the air."[85] German farmers were also widely known to abuse the Africans who worked for them.

---

[80] Bridgman, *Revolt of the Herero*, pp. 164; Henderson, *German Colonial Empire*, p. 81.
[81] John H. Wellington, *South West Africa and its Human Issues* (Oxford: Oxford University Press, 1967), p. 212.
[82] Bley, *Namibia Under German Rule*, p. 151.   [83] Quoted in *Report on the Natives* p. 101.
[84] German colonial law quoted in ibid., p. 111.   [85] Noothout quoted in ibid., p. 100.

Role of argument

German colonizers certainly used arguments as well as the whip and rifle. But Witboi's arguments, their futility, and the history of German slaughter of Nama and Herero people in South-West Africa appear to be powerful evidence against my claim that ethical arguments are important in world politics. Indeed, this history illustrates the obvious: not all ethical arguments are successful.

Witboi's arguments failed for at least three reasons. First, and most important, the prevailing beliefs among the Germans did not allow the majority of German settlers to see the humanity of the Nama and other people of South-West Africa. Witboi's arguments simply did not make sense. Second, the most important argument was not between Witboi and Leutwein or between any South-West African and German. What determined German behavior were arguments within Germany and among Germans and other "civilized" countries. Witboi's arguments might have been more effective had the audience that the Germans themselves had to address been less convinced of the rightness of colonial conquest. As it was, Reichstag debates over German South–West Africa policy showed that many members were convinced of the less than fully human status of the South-West Africans, and a policy of extermination was therefore acceptable, at least for a time. As Graf Ludwig zu Reventlow said in 1904 during the Reichstag debate: "Of course we are for humanity with respect to human beings of all kinds; but in contradiction to some of the orators preceding me, I would conclude by abjuring the interested authorities: Do not apply too much humanity to bloodthirsty beasts in the form of humans." German colonial theorist Paul Rohrbach argued that the Herero "lacked the capacity to be educated to moral independence."[86] Yet ethical arguments were also made against German policy. During one debate in the Reichstag, Social Democrat August Bebel called the German actions, "not just barbaric, but bestial."[87] The extermination order was ultimately countermanded by the civilian government, although it was too late for the majority of the Herero and Nama.

[86] Quoted in Helmut Walser Smith, "The Talk of Genocide, the Rhetoric of Miscegenation: Notes on Debates in the German Reichstag Concerning South West Africa, 1904–14," in Sara Friedrichsmeyer, Sara Lennox, and Susanne Zantop, eds., *The Imperialist Imagination: German Colonialism and its Legacy* (Ann Arbor: The University of Michigan Press, 1998), pp. 107–123: 107, 114.
[87] Quoted in ibid., p. 111.

Third, the dominant European culture (the table on which German arguments were made) was consistent with German beliefs and behavior. German behavior was not unusual for conquerors, though the scale of killing in 1904 might have been unusual for colonial policy in the early twentieth century. Indeed, it was only during and after World War I, when Europeans argued that captured German colonies should not be returned to Germany, that Europeans paid much attention to the German slaughter and their subsequent treatment of the natives in South-West Africa.[88] For instance, Britain published the famous Blue Book, the *Report on the Natives of South-West Africa and their Treatment by Germany*, in 1918, with testimony of South-West Africans and other evidence of German atrocities in South-West Africa, including photographs of manacles, hangings, and the shredded backs of natives who had been lashed.[89]

Reform

German policy toward the Africans in South-West Africa changed in several important respects after 1908. The Center and Social Democratic Parties in Germany advocated reforming colonial policy toward Africans. The Reichstag and the Colonial Office, under its new secretary, Bernhard Dernburg, passed laws for reforming the treatment of Africans in South West Africa. The Lüderitz Bay Chamber of Mines and the railway construction concerns made native welfare an explicit preoccupation.[90] Why? First, the extermination program turned stomachs in Germany and South-West Africa and some farmers and missionaries advocated more humane policies.[91] Second, there was an inadequate supply of labor. After the natives lost the right to own cattle and land, most of the remaining African labor worked on white farms or in copper mining. Though there had been an extensive search for diamonds and gold, diamonds were not discovered in South-West Africa until April 1908.

[88] D. Chanaiwa, "African Initiatives and Resistance in Southern Africa," in Boahen, ed., *Africa Under Colonial Domination*, pp. 194–220. Wm. Roger Louis, *Great Britain and Germany's Lost Colonies, 1914–1919* (Oxford: Clarendon Press, 1967), p. 16; Wright, *Mandates Under the League*, p. 28.
[89] The Germans replied in 1919 with a "White Book" that argued that German treatment of natives in the colonies was no worse than what the British did against the Boers and elsewhere and suggested that some officers in South West Africa had refused to follow von Trotha's extermination order. *Die Behandlung der einheimischen Bevölkerung in den Kolonialen Besitzungen Deutschlands und Englands* (Berlin, 1919). Also see Wellington, *South West Africa and its Human Issues*, pp. 236–237.
[90] Henderson, *German Colonial Empire*, p. 114.
[91] Bley, *Namibia Under German Rule*, p. 226.

234

After their discovery, South-West Africa, which had not been a profitable colony, became profitable, at least for the shareholders of the German South-West Africa Company on whose land the diamonds were found.[92] By 1913, whites in South-West Africa, who numbered 14,840 in 1913, depended even more on African labor, of which 12,523 were employed on farms and 9,541 were employed in industry such as railroad construction and mining for copper and diamonds.[93]

While on a visit to South-West Africa in August 1908, Secretary Dernburg framed the reasons for reform in practical terms.

> At the moment, 2 percent of the country has been colonized and yet already there is a notable shortage of labour. We therefore are forced to improve living conditions for the natives, in order to preserve them as a labour force both for present needs and as a healthy new generation in the future. Appropriate measures include medical attention, the provision of the natives' former foodstuffs – particularly milk for the Herero – and permission for the Herero to buy cattle.[94]

In March 1909 Dernburg also gave an ethical argument for aggressive humanitarian reforms:

> It has often been said ... that everywhere in Africa where Europeans can work ... the destruction of the blacks is a law of nature which will be fulfilled in native wars. This is a very questionable assumption. It is out of keeping with our position as a civilizing and protecting power. It makes colonization a process of deliberate exploitation and – as the history of South-West Africa shows – it causes Germany endless sacrifices. It also offends the moral sensitivity of the greater part of our nation, on which our colonial policies are based. In Germany we do not attempt to live according to Darwinist principles: on the contrary, civilization has the task of offering assistance and protection to the weak and helpless, to the morally and economically underprivileged. This must remain our policy towards our fellows in SWA, at least towards those who remain loyal to us.[95]

This statement articulates the rift between the majority of German settlers and the colonial administration and suggests how naked aggression slid toward aggressive humanitarianism and made room for reformist arguments and action. Colonial administrators and civil servants, taking

[92] Drechsler, *"Let Us Die Fighting,"* p. 244. Drechsler argues that, with the exception of Togo, none of the German colonies were profitable, p. 247.
[93] Ibid., p. 244; Bley, *Namibia Under German Rule*, p. 198.
[94] Quoted in Bley, *Namibia Under German Rule*, p. 230.   [95] Quoted in ibid., p. 231.

their lead from the Colonial Office, began to defend Africans against the excesses of colonial settlers for both pragmatic and normative reasons. Local newspapers also talked of colonial excesses committed by so-called "dubious elements" in the settler community, the "black sheep" and "scoundrels," and there was an admission by some of the settlers that, in at least a few cases, a settler disciplining his African workers went too far.[96] Though sentences were light, some whites were prosecuted for ill-treating their African workers and the practice of flogging with sjamboks, although it continued, met with greater scrutiny and was more often prosecuted when it went to what the settler administration thought was extremes.[97] German administration of South-West Africa came to an end in 1915 when the colony was invaded by South African troops in World War I, so it is not possible to say how far the Germans would have gone with these modest reforms.

The United States and the Philippines

In response to an anti-colonial revolt in Cuba, Spain imprisoned Cuban civilians in "reconcentration camps" where terrible conditions killed more than 200,000 people. Citing Spanish abuses, the US government framed their war against Spain in 1898 as an anti-colonial exercise, while others represented the war and other elements of US turn of the century foreign policy as part of a struggle of the fittest. In an 1899 speech, "The Strenuous Life," Theodore Roosevelt said: "We cannot avoid the responsibilities that confront us in Hawaii, Cuba, Porto [*sic*] Rico, and the Philippines. All we can decide is whether we shall meet them in a way that will redound to the national credit, or whether we shall make of our dealings with these new problems a dark and shameful page in our history." It was an identity argument: real men are imperialists:

> The timid man, the lazy man, the man who distrusts his country, the over-civilized man who has lost the great fighting, masterful virtues, the ignorant man, and the man of dull mind, whose soul is incapable of feeling the mighty lift that thrills "stern men with empires in their brains" – all these, of course shrink from seeing the nation undertake its new duties . . .
>
> I preach to you then, my countrymen, that our country calls not for the life of ease but for the life of strenuous endeavor. The twentieth

[96] Ibid., pp. 254–255, 264–265.
[97] Drechsler, *"Let Us Die Fighting,"* p. 235; Bley, *Namibia Under German Rule*, pp. 263–267.

century looms before us big with the fate of many nations. If we stand idly by, if we seek merely swollen, slothful ease and ignoble peace, if we shrink from the hard contests where men must win at hazard of their lives and at the risk of all they hold dear, then the bolder and stronger peoples will pass us by, and will win for themselves the domination of the world.[98]

The US took Cuba, Puerto Rico, Guam, and the Philippines in the war and set up the administrations in these islands despite intense domestic opposition to the policy. The argument for the US occupation of the Philippines was aggressive humanitarianism. The US Philippine Commission, set up to govern the archipelago islands, issued a proclamation on 4 April 1899 stating that the "aim . . . is the well-being, the prosperity, and the happiness of the Philippine people, and their elevation and advancement to a position among the most civilized people in the world." Further, the "commission emphatically asserts that the United States is not only willing, but anxious, to establish in the Philippine Islands an enlightened system of government under which the Philippine people may enjoy the largest measure of home rule and the amplest liberty consonant with the supreme ends of government." The proclamation promised that the US would "enforce" its sovereignty: "those who resist it can accomplish no other end than their own ruin." The proclamation then articulated the rights of the Philippine people and the obligations of the US government to provide "the most ample liberty of self-government . . . which is reconcilable with the maintenance" of US administration as well as roads, railroads, and schools.[99]

On 3 December 1900, President McKinley said to the American people that US possession of the Philippines was an "unsought trust which should be unselfishly discharged."[100] Politicians and academics at the turn of the century described Filipinos as semi-civilized, good "imitators," "imprudent," with characteristics of a "faithful dog" or "monkey."[101] Consequently, Filipinos must be led to civilization, or as President McKinley said, they were "wards" of the US. "Our obligation was not lightly assumed; it must not be otherwise than honestly fulfilled, aiming first of all to benefit those who have come under our

[98] Quoted in Hofstadter, *Social Darwinism in American Thought*, p. 180.
[99] Quoted in Snow, *Aborigines in the Law and Practice of Nations*, pp. 329–331.
[100] Quoted in League of Nations, *The Mandates System: Origin, Principles, Application* (Geneva: League of Nations, 1945), p. 11.
[101] Quoted in Roxanne Lynn Doty, *Imperial Encounters: The Politics of Representation in North-South Relations* (Minneapolis: University of Minnesota Press, 1997), pp. 38–41.

fostering care."[102] Elihu Root, secretary of war from 1899 to 1904, when the US was establishing the administration of the Philippines by force, said of US government:

> We undertook to go a little farther than other countries had gone, and to make the first consideration of our government in the islands the training of the inhabitants in the difficult art of self-government, so that they would as soon as possible become competent to govern themselves instead of being governed by us. Accordingly, one of the first things that we did was to send over teachers by the shipload – thousands of them – and to establish schools all over the islands. And then we provided a form of government under which the Philippines should receive what may be called clinical instruction in administration and in the application of the principles which we consider vital to free self-government and we provided that, step by step, just as rapidly as they became familiar with the institutions of free government and capable of continuing them, the powers of government should be placed in their hands. I am sure that this view of suitable treatment of the Philippines, so long as we are to be in the islands at all, commends itself to the best intelligence and practical idealism of the American people.[103]

While stressing American benevolence in contrast to Spanish corruption and brutality, Root and others underemphasized the consequences of the US government's counter-insurgency war in the Philippines. Some 20,000 guerrilla rebels died, and about ten times that number died of war-related disease and hunger.

The US government generally argued that occupation was temporary, while opponents, including socialists and Democratic Party leader William Jennings Bryan, made ethical, practical, and identity arguments against war and occupation. One black newspaper editorialized: "For the question of self-government or subjection for the Filipinos is the

[102] Quoted in Wright, *Mandates Under the League*, p. 13. Later presidents also framed the US role as guardianship: Theodore Roosevelt said, in December 1904, that he "earnestly hoped that in the end they will be able to stand, if not entirely alone, yet in some such relation to the United States as Cuba now stands." The US was attempting to "develop the natives themselves so that they shall take an ever-increasing share in their own government." Robert Taft said in December 1912, "We are seeking to arouse a national spirit and not, as under the older colonial theory, to suppress such a spirit." Woodrow Wilson called the US a "trustee of Filipino people" in 1915. Wright, *Mandates Under the League*, pp. 13–14.
[103] Quoted in Snow, *Aborigines in the Law and Practice of Nations*, pp. 333–334. Similarly, in 1901 the US Supreme Court implied that US occupation of Cuba was temporary when it held that the island was "territory held in trust for the inhabitants of Cuba to whom it rightfully belongs and to whose exclusive control it will be surrendered when a stable government shall have been established by their voluntary action." US Supreme Court in *Neeley* v. *Henkel* (1901), quoted in Wright, *Mandates Under the League*, p. 13.

old slavery question put in another form."[104] In 1898, US labor leader Samuel Gompers argued against expansion, saying it was against "the great principle of self-government of the people, for the people, by the people." And, he said, "Is it not strange that now, for the first time, we hear that the Cubans are unfit for self-government..." Gompers warned with regard to the Philippines, "Can we hope to close the flood gates of immigration from the hordes of Chinese and the semi-savage races coming from what will then be part of our own country?" Gompers rejected economic arguments for expansion: "it is not necessary that we shall subjugate by the force of arms any other people in order to obtain that expansion of trade."[105] US expansion into the Philippines attracted perhaps the most vehement opposition because the anti-colonial movement there, having nearly defeated the Spanish, did not throw down their arms and welcome the US but kept fighting, requiring thousands of US soldiers to suppress them over several years, while thousands of Filipinos died mounting resistance. The US managed to suppress the rebels, and occupied the islands until the Japanese invaded in World War II.

The second face: reform and anti-colonial organizations

Religious missionaries, educators, and medical personnel went to the colonies with the aim of improving the conditions of Africans under European rule. These men and women worked alongside or directly with private corporations and colonial governments, even as they championed indigenous rights. As historian Frederick Cooper notes: "The reformist critique of imperialism gone wrong emphasized the morality and normalcy of colonial rule."[106] Yet, despite their initial support for colonialism, reformers' arguments gradually became more anti-colonial. How did qualified support and minimal reformism become a major critique of colonialism? First, some missionaries and journalists who went to the colonies became ardent critics of aggressive humanitarianism because they so believed in colonialism but saw that it had

---

[104] Quoted in Philip S. Foner and Richard C. Winchester, eds., *The Anti-Imperialist Reader: A Documentary History of Anti-Imperialism in the United States. Volume I, From the Mexican War to the Election of 1900* (New York: Holmes & Meier, 1984), p. 168.

[105] Quoted in *ibid.*, pp. 202, 205, 207, 210.

[106] Frederick Cooper, *Decolonization and African Society: The Labor Question in French and British Africa* (Cambridge: Cambridge University Press, 1996), p. 27.

failed in its civilizing mission. Second, several anti-colonial organizations grew from abolitionist movement roots and the logic of their arguments pulled them incrementally toward increasingly harsh critiques of colonial practices.

Colonial reformers used the same tactics as their abolitionist forebears: they conducted mass public meetings on colonialism and published journals and pamphlets detailing colonial abuses and their efforts to ameliorate them. The reformers' primary tools were meta-argument and ethical argument: they directly lobbied parliaments and heads of state for more humane conditions in colonies, and in some cases supported African and Asian efforts for independence. For example, in England, the Aborigines Protection Society formed in the late 1830s "to assist in protecting defenceless, and promoting the advancement of, uncivilized tribes."[107] Less critical of colonial policy was the Anti-Slavery Society, though there was considerable overlap in the top membership of both organizations.

And as with the anti-slavery movement, some Aborigines Protection Society members, for example Thomas Fowell Buxton, were also prominent members of the House of Commons. Partly through Buxton's efforts, parliament established a Select Committee on Aborigines. Reporting in 1837, the Select Committee was critical of certain colonial practices: "It is not too much to say that the intercourse of Europeans in general, without any exception in favor of the subjects of Great Britain, has been, unless when attended by missionary excursions, a source of many calamities to uncivilized nations. Too often, their territory has been usurped, their property seized; their numbers diminished, their character debased, the spread of civilization impeded."[108] The remedy for these harms was expressed in the committee's "conviction that there is but one effectual means of staying the evils we have occasioned, and of imparting the blessings of civilization, and that is the propagation of Christianity, together with the preservation, for time to come, of the civil rights of the natives."[109]

Activists sought to increase public awareness of the conditions in the colonies in order to build broad public support for their amelioration. In the late 1800s the Aborigines Protection Society (APS) protested the deportation and exile of African leaders, such as Jaja of Opoba and Chief

---

[107] Quoted in "Amalgamation of the Anti-Slavery Society and the Aborigines Protection Society," *Anti-Slavery Reporter* 28 (March–May 1909), 27–28: 27.
[108] Quoted in Snow, *Aborigines in the Law and Practice of Nations*, p. 10.
[109] Quoted in ibid., p. 11.

Nana of the Isekiri, and the use of chartered companies to colonize and form colonial governments. As Annie Coombes notes: "the Aborigine Protection Society made no bones about what they saw as one of the central contradictions of using chartered companies as governing bodies – namely the contradiction of maintaining a 'just' government while at the same time being necessarily constrained to make all decisions on the basis of achieving the highest dividend. The Society's journal, the *Aborigine's Friend*, frequently carried vigorous criticisms of traders."[110]

The British and Foreign Anti-Slavery Society merged with the APS in 1909 to form the Anti-Slavery and Aborigines Protection Society. The merger was practical and strategic. "Now . . . that slavery is so commonly found under a disguise, and the great evil which has to be fought is the exploitation and coercion of natives in order to secure their labour for the white man, it has appeared to those interested that nothing but good could result from uniting the two similar bodies, and that one strong Society, representing the cause of the native races of mankind, could more effectively serve their interests than two separate organizations working independently, and often hampered by want of adequate resources."[111] The new organization published the *Anti-Slavery Reporter and Aborigines' Friend*, with articles on colonial conditions all over the globe, reports of British parliamentary and colonial office activities, and summaries of the proceedings of the Society. The Anti-Slavery and Aborigines Protection Society's journal thus attempted to create a different kind of public knowledge of colonialism, by printing reports of colonial abuses, that fueled the emotions that became part of the anti-colonial critique and ethical arguments for reform.

Some socialist, labor, and communist movements also supported and publicized anti-colonial activism in the Americas and Europe. In Africa, the reform movement was represented by, for example, the Aborigines' Rights Protection Society in Cape Coast (Gold Coast), founded in 1897, and in Nigeria by the Anti-Slavery and Aborigines' Rights Protection Society. Both lobbied the British government to protect African land ownership. [112] The African Association, founded in London in 1897 and

---

[110] See Annie Coombes, *Reinventing Africa: Museums, Material Culture and Popular Imagination* (New Haven: Yale University Press, 1994), p. 33.
[111] "Amalgamation of the Anti-Slavery Society and the Aborigines Protection Society," p. 28.
[112] Kaniki, "The Colonial Economy: The Former British Zones," p. 390. Also see Boahen, *African Perspectives on Colonialism* and contemporary issues of the *Anti-Slavery Reporter and Aborigines' Friend*.

dissolved in 1901, signaled the development of an international collaboration between Africans in "diaspora" and those on the continent, for improving the lot of those in African colonies. It attracted the support of white liberals in the Aborigines Protection Society and significant attention in the mainstream British press. During its brief existence, the Association lobbied colonial administrators for bettering conditions in Africa and conducted a Pan-African Conference in London, 23–25 July 1900, inaugurating a vital Pan-African movement.[113] Conference attendees, including W.E.B. Du Bois, petitioned Queen Victoria to improve labor conditions and eliminate pass laws in Southern Africa. The official response to the petition by Colonial Minister Joseph Chamberlain was that the queen would keep the "interests and welfare of the native races" in mind.[114]

Revulsion and reform in the Congo and South Africa

Although it is certain that none of the colonized valued colonialism, indeed long reviled it, European and American discomfort with the practice did not take root until the turn of the century. Two cases in particular were widely discussed by the humanitarians and used to frame arguments about colonial excess: the Congo and South Africa.

Belgian King Leopold's brutal conquest of the Congo first came under intense international scrutiny in the 1890s. Recall that Leopold's Congo Free State (his private colony) had achieved international recognition and backing as a humanitarian effort: it was to abolish slavery, bring missionaries and hospitals, and open the Congo to free trade. At the Brussels Anti-Slavery Conference, King Leopold continued to frame his actions in the Congo on humanitarian grounds. But, in 1890 and 1891 the first severe criticisms of Leopold's governance of the Congo by George Washington Williams, who exposed terrible labor practices, received attention in the European and American press. Roads were constructed and rubber was gathered by conscripted Congolese men. Men, whose wives and children might also have been kidnapped, were forced to gather rubber under the lash or at gun-point or else in the fear that they might never see their families again. Women also suffered the same

---

[113] There had been earlier meetings of the same sort, for instance the Chicago Congress on Africa in August 1893 and the Congress on Africa in Georgia in December 1895. P. Olisanwuche Esedebe, *Pan-Africanism: The Idea and Movement, 1776–1963* (Washington, DC: Howard University Press, 1982), pp. 45–47.

[114] See Immanuel Geiss, *The Pan-African Movement: A History of Pan-Africanism in America, Europe and Africa* (New York: Africana Publishing, 1974), pp. 176–198. Quote on p. 190.

fate. Headline coverage in *The New York Herald* of Williams' report on the Congo, published as a pamphlet, read: "The Administration of the African Free State Declared by an American Citizen to be Barbarous– Investigation Demanded."[115] Williams was also one of the first to call for self-rule or international trusteeship in Africa.[116]

Because of Leopold's high humanitarian proclamations, when conditions were disclosed – including the enslavement of Africans and the practice of chopping off of hands and heads – the irony and hypocrisy revealed were startling. Leopold responded with a campaign to vilify and discredit Williams, who died shortly after he made his reports, and the story faded. Thus, little was achieved in ameliorating conditions in the Congo. Leopold continued for another decade to claim humanitarian motives despite evidence of slavery, forced labor, and hostage taking. Leopold had tremendous incentive not to modify the system. Leopold's administration made huge profits from rubber gathering, and claimed half of the private concessionary company profits from rubber (which ran as high as 700 percent due to "cheap" labor and high demand).[117]

Leopold's management of the Congo eventually received more scrutiny from E.D. Morel, another reporter.[118] Morel, who was also a clerk for the company that ran all of the Congo's shipping, Elder Dempster of Liverpool, noted that weapons went into the Congo and ivory and rubber came out. He wrote, "These figures told their own story . . . Forced labour of a terrible and continuous kind could alone explain such unheard of profits . . . forced labour in which the Congo Government was the immediate beneficiary; forced labor directed by the closest associates of the King himself."[119] Whereas Morel had previously criticized the humanitarians and been a supporter of colonialism, at the turn of the century he began to work with anti-colonial critics in the Aborigines Protection Society in England to expose and promote reform of Leopold's practices. Morel left Elder Dempster and began a full-time career as journalist and Congo reform activist, publishing in the space of a few years three books on the Congo. Morel and the other Congo reform activists, most of them also members of the Anti-Slavery

---

[115] Hochschild, *King Leopold's Ghost*, pp. 101–114.   [116] Ibid., p. 111.

[117] Ibid., p. 160. Also see Packenham, *The Scramble for Africa*, pp. 588–589.

[118] Morel's unfinished history of the movement was compiled and published after his death by Wm. Roger Louis and Jean Stengers, eds., *E.D. Morel's History of the Congo Reform Movement* (London: Oxford University Press, 1968).

[119] Quoted in Hochschild, *King Leopold's Ghost*, pp. 180–181. Also see Packenham, *The Scramble for Africa*, pp. 590–592.

and Aborigines Protection societies, publicized many abuses, especially the colonizer's practice of chopping off the hands of Congolese, and got the Congo on the legislative agenda in Britain. The British parliament passed a resolution in May 1903 urging that "natives should be governed with humanity" and Leopold himself proposed some modest reforms to meet his critics.[120] But, Morel and others wanted to show that despite so-called reforms, little had changed in the Congo. He argued against the Congo state on ethical and practical grounds. His ethical argument was that slavery is wrong and the Congo was slavery.

> Such then was the main task: to convince the world that this Congo horror was not only and unquestionably a fact; but that it was not accidental or temporary, or capable of internal cure. To show conclusively that it was deliberate, and that the consequences would be identical in any part of the tropics where similar conceptions might be introduced. To demonstrate that it was at once a survival and a revival of the slave-mind at work, of the slave-trade in being.[121]

Morel's practical argument was that the situation in Congo was the reverse of the free trade principles under which the Congo state had been established.[122] Morel's effort to reframe debate over the Congo received crucial support in 1904 when the British consul to the Congo, Roger Casement, witnessed and exposed atrocities in a report to the Foreign Office and in interviews with the press. Morel and Casement then formed the Congo Reform Association and Morel spent the next decade giving public speeches in Britain, and writing articles that were picked up by British newspapers, including the *Morning Post*, the *Manchester Guardian*, and *The Times*.[123] An American Congo Reform Association also formed. Because of the negative publicity, Leopold was compelled to set up a commission of inquiry to investigate the charges. Unfortunately for the king, his handpicked commission, in 1905, essentially agreed with Casement's observations. So did reports from the US consul-general to the Congo.

The Congo Reform Association in London proposed in 1905 that the Congo be taken from the king as his private property and run instead

[120] Quoted in Hochschild, *King Leopold's Ghost*, p. 194.
[121] Morel, '*History of the Congo Reform Movement*', in Louis and Stengers (eds.), *E.D. Morel's History of the Congo Reform Movement*, p. 63.
[122] Ibid., pp. 64–69.
[123] Wm. Roger Louis, "Morel and the Congo Reform Association 1904–1913," in Louis and Stengers (eds.), *E.D. Morel's History of the Congo Reform Movement*, pp. 171–220: 173, 187, 196–197.

244

by Belgium. This idea was supported by the British Foreign Office, elite opinion in Britain, and increasingly in the Belgian parliament. The Reform Association kept up the pressure for reforms. Finally, in December 1906, international and domestic pressure forced Leopold to turn his private colony over to the Belgian government. Conditions in the Congo improved somewhat because of the international attention and after Belgium formally took over the colony from Leopold in 1908.

The Boer War also affected English beliefs about African colonialism, at least as regards their treatment of white settlers. Britain had taken the Cape Colony from Dutch/Boer settlers in 1814 and over the course of the century, many English settled in the Cape while the Boers moved inland to avoid them, setting up two colonies, Transvaal and Orange Free State. From 1880 to 1881 the Boers fought unsuccessfully to halt British encroachment. Still, the Boers faced a greater influx of English when enormous deposits of diamonds and gold were found in the Transvaal. Just over twenty years later, Boers fought again to keep the English settlers out, while the British wanted ostensibly to ensure the political rights of the English (who the Boers called "uitlanders") against discrimination by the Boers. Although British foreign policy decisionmakers feared that another military action in South Africa would be unpopular at home, the Transvaal and Orange Free State governments were considered to be too independent and also too close to Germany.

After provoking the war in 1899, the British government thought defeating the Boers would be easy.[124] They were wrong: the British effort required 500,000 soldiers and cost both sides a total of almost 55,000 lives. The war claimed the lives of about 15,000 Africans as well. Britain used concentration camps to intern Afrikaners, and between 20,000 and 26,000 men and women, but mostly children, died in the camps, mainly of dysentery and other diseases.

British conduct in the Boer War was so disturbing to both popular British and international opinion that, "Support groups were formed in Germany, Holland, France, and Belgium to collect money and send it to the suffering Boers in South Africa. Foreign brigades were formed, as in the Spanish Civil War, to fight on the Boer side against the forces of English oppression and capitalist imperialism."[125] The war and the almost gratuitous harshness of the subsequent British colonial

[124] Basil Davidson, *Let Freedom Come: Africa in Modern History* (Boston: Little, Brown and Company, 1978), p. 29.
[125] Allister Sparks, *The Mind of South Africa: The Story of the Rise and Fall of Apartheid* (London: Mandarin, 1990), p. 129.

administration, which, for example, forbade instruction in Afrikaans in Boer schools, turned elite and popular opinion in England against British control and galvanized Afrikaner nationalism. As Gann and Duignan argue, the Boer War helped alter popular and elite British views of the glories of colonial war. "The British won a barren victory on the field; the imperial idea sustained a blow from which it never recovered. From the military point of view the conduct of the war brought scant prestige to the British ruling class."[126] So while South Africa remained just as rich in diamonds and gold as before the British victory over the Afrikaners, British opinion turned around so completely that South Africa was given autonomous status by Britain in 1910 as a white-controlled self-governing dominion.

Conclusion

European expansion in Africa was noted for a mix of legalism, international organization, benevolence, and brute force. Though from the reading of the Requirement in the Americas to the conquest of Africa, brutal force was often used to capture and maintain territorial holdings, treaties between native leaders and the colonial powers were generally obtained. Again, although these treaties were usually made through fraud or compulsion, the fact that treaties were obtained at all suggests that the colonists desired at least an aura of legitimacy.[127] Indeed, as Dorothy Jones argues, in North America between 1796 and 1871, "Outright land-grabbing was not nearly so widespread as is commonly believed. There was no need. The treaty system itself was the primary vehicle of transfer."[128] She suggests that, "This can happen because accountability is not built into the diplomatic system. The only check is the assumption of countervailing force. When that is absent, as it invariably is in situations of colonialism, the whole treaty system becomes a weapon in the arsenal of the stronger power."[129]

---

[126] L.H. Gann and Peter Duignan, *Burden of Empire: An Appraisal of Western Colonialism in Africa South of the Sahara* (New York: Praeger, 1967), p. 37. Also see Leonard Thompson, *The Political Mythology of Apartheid* (New Haven: Yale University Press, 1985).

[127] Berat, in *Walvis Bay,* argues that the treaties were primarily a method of notifying other European colonial powers that a nation had begun the process of colonial occupation of the region. The treaties were also sometimes temporary holding actions for both sides as they sought to augment their forces for another battle.

[128] Dorothy V. Jones, *License for Empire: Colonialism by Treaty in Early America* (Chicago: The University of Chicago Press, 1982), p. xi.

[129] Ibid., p. xii.

Yet, accountability was evident: outright land-grabbing was constrained by the normative beliefs of statesmen, diplomats, and domestic opinion. Outright land-grabbing was illegitimate; it had to be justified in terms that would seem right at the time. Thus, although colonialism was as yet a largely unquestioned practice, the issues of legitimacy and the rights of the indigenous populations, were not entirely ignored because the dominant culture, the table on which arguments occurred, was affected by arguments over slavery and the humanity of others. Colonial reformers fought to frame colonialism as against its own principles.

Supporters of colonialism had always argued that it did something good in itself, or was a means to a good end. Nearly all involved in the conquest and colonization said they were motivated by humanitarian concerns. The argument was that "free trade" (although in many cases nothing was traded so much as loot and labor were just taken) would bring civilization. Open doors were required for commerce and the free access of missionary societies. During the height of conquest and consolidation of colonial rule, it was clear that Africans and Asians were to be objects of European control, not the authors of their own aspiration and actions – unless it was to sign a treaty of "protection" under Europeans. Few argued that the colonized could govern themselves. This paternalism made sense in the views current at the turn of the century because it was commonly believed that the "backward" races were like "children," who if they weren't completely overwhelmed by the colonizer would need the care of their elders to get along in the world. But, by the late nineteenth and early twentieth centuries, however, the specific practices of colonialism were under greater scrutiny by the reformers who had moved on from the anti-slavery movement to challenge colonial practices. As Quincy Wright suggests, this humanitarianism had a long lineage:

> Humanitarian considerations for subject races was from the first demanded by moralists and theologians. Queen Isabella in her letter of February 19, 1495, urged generous treatment of the Indians. The Missionary Bartoleme de las Casas and the half-blood Inca, Garcilaso de la Vega, popularized the cause of the Indian in Spain while the learned theologian Francis de Victoria assured his students at Salmanca that the law of nations protected the Indians even though they were infidels. It was not, however, until the later eighteenth century that humanitarianism became organized and effective. Through the efforts of the Quakers John Woolman (1720–73) and Anthony Benezet (1713–84) in America; the Christian philanthropists Thomas Clarkson (1760–1846), William

Wilberforce (1759–1833), and Thomas Fowell Buxton (1786–1845) in England; and the revolutionary humanitarians Condorcet (1743–94), L'Abbe Gregoire (1750–1831), and Mirabeau (1749–91) in France: societies were formed in these countries to abolish the slave trade and protect the aborigines. Their agitation brought legislation against the slave trade early in the nineteenth century, and their scrutiny was a continuous stimulus to colonial offices. Although barbarities against natives were still frequent enough, public sentiment was sometimes successfully mobilized for reform, as in the Congo in the early twentieth century.[130]

Criticisms of colonialism in the heart of the colonial metropole began quite modestly but gradually expanded as anti-colonial reformers realized that their beliefs and arguments about rights could not be arbitrarily limited. Still, many reformers, including those cited by Wright, did not yet question the main premises of colonialism and would perhaps have been surprised by the enormous changes wrought from their modest challenges to colonial practice. As a French critic of forced labor in the colonies, Joseph Folliet, wrote in 1934: "It is precisely because we accept the general and abstract justice of colonization that we desire, in the specific and concrete instance, to purify it of all that soils it."[131] Folliet articulates one face of humanitarianism while German colonial theorist Paul Rohrbach's social Darwinism is its ugliest representation. But on the eve of World War I, practices which were acceptable to the majority in the context of colonization of the Americas, were suspect in the African context precisely because democratic arguments had won the day in Europe and had only to be fully implemented there. The extension and institutionalization of reformist beliefs, and how they changed colonial practices, are addressed in chapter 6.

[130] Wright, *Mandates Under the League*, p. 9.
[131] Quoted in Cooper, *Decolonization and African Society*, p. 27.

6   Sacred trust

But if the extent of the offence be measured by the professions of high moral purpose previously laid claim to, then, iniquitous as has been the conduct of the European Governments toward their own peoples, it pales in comparison with their conduct towards the peoples of Africa, whose territory they parceled out among themselves with the name of God upon their lips, of whose rights they declared themselves to be the jealous guardians, whose helplessness they invoked to justify their own "protective" aegis, and to whom they sent their missionaries that these backward folk might be duly instructed in the gospel of the Prince of Peace. "Civilizing" the African, forsooth! There was a pretty strong element of barbarism in Europe's civilizing methods in Africa before the war.[1]

Whether or not people speak in good faith, they cannot say just anything they please. Moral talk is coercive; one thing leads to another.[2]

The previous chapter showed how the anti-slavery movement's humanitarian arguments rationalized colonial expansion in Africa, yet also denormalized and began to delegitimize some colonial practices. In this chapter I show how reform arguments came to dominate colonial discourse, and how, with the League of Nations Mandate system, new normative beliefs first articulated by the colonial reform movement were institutionalized. The paternalistic and aggressive humanitarianism of the Berlin West Africa Conference, which was coupled with conquest, gradually gave way to the less paternalistic beliefs characteristic of the Aborigines Protection Society and of W.E.B. Du Bois, E.D. Morel, and Woodrow Wilson. The aim became uplift, and better that this uplift would be accomplished non-violently. Because the humanitarians'

[1] E.D. Morel, *Africa and the Peace of Europe* (London: National Labour Press, 1917), p. 67.
[2] Michael Walzer, *Just and Unjust Wars: A Moral Argument with Historical Illustrations*, 2nd ed. (New York: Basic Books, 1992), p. 12.

critique was damning it opened up the space for reconceiving, or re-framing, colonialism. As old-style colonialism was less and less considered normal and legitimate, the political balance of power shifted from naked and unashamed colonialists to those who wanted to at least reform colonialism. Reformist arguments prompted the reconceptualization of colonial practices and development of the League of Nations Mandates system. The Permanent Mandates Commission of the League of Nations changed the context in which arguments about colonialism occurred, providing a venue for new arguments and the institutionalization of new normative beliefs.

World War I and mounting pressures for colonial reform

Humanitarians critiqued colonialism and asserted new normative beliefs during World War I in pamphlets, books, and in their lobbying of colonial governments. The discussions among diplomats about what to do with the colonies the victors had captured in World War I was fundamentally influenced by this wider reformist discourse, and this discourse was in turn embodied in the international innovation known as the League of Nations Mandate system. But it was not obvious that reform of colonialism would be an outcome of the war.

During World War I, European governments used their colonies to produce food, revenue, and manpower for production and military conscription. More than one million Africans fought as conscripts and volunteers for European governments, with the majority being forced to serve; some 150,000 African soldiers and carriers died in the war.[3] France raised nearly 430,000 soldiers and several hundred thousand laborers from its African colonies during the war and pushed its colonies to expand their food production for export. French West African, "Blaise Diagne was promised a package of post-war reforms in French Black Africa if he could recruit the additional men France required for the European front. This he did, but the reforms were never put into effect."[4] Belgium raised up to 260,000 from its Congo colony most of whom

---

[3] M. Crowder, "The First World War and Its Consequences," in A. Adu Boahen, ed., *Africa Under Colonial Domination, UNESCO General History of Africa,* VII (Paris: UNESCO, 1985), pp. 283–311: 283, 295. Also see Myron Echenberg, *Colonial Conscripts: The* Tirailleurs Sénégalais *in French West Africa 1857–1960* (London: James Currey, 1991) and Basil Davidson, *Let Freedom Come: Africa in Modern History* (Boston: Little, Brown and Company, 1978), pp. 114–115.

[4] Crowder, "The First World War and Its Consequences," p. 306.

served as porters. Britain benefited from over 1.5 million "Indian and coloured" colonial subjects serving in the empire's military forces.[5] Further, both white and black South Africans fought against the Germans in East Africa and South West Africa.[6] During the war, revolts against European rule, both as protests against conscription and to take advantage of the return of Europeans to their home countries, surged in number. Though they sometimes required thousands of European troops to put down, the revolts were not successful.

By the end of the war, the Japanese military had captured German islands in the Pacific, while Britain, or the British Dominions, Australia, New Zealand, and South Africa, held German territory in Asia and Africa. The Allies agreed that captured colonies would not go back to their former masters, but no one in allied governments appears to have seriously entertained the possibility of independence for these colonies. Rather, the British Imperial War Cabinet committee on territorial questions was in favor of annexation. As Lord Curzon, a member of the War Cabinet said: "we were meditating the carving up of the world to suit our own interests."[7] The British and Japanese governments secretly agreed in early 1917 to support each others' claims to captured territory, and public opinion was generally in favor of annexation.[8] Self-determination for the territories was ruled out by Britain's Foreign Secretary Balfour who wanted the territory in hand to work out a peace settlement.[9]

---

[5] The majority were Indians and "colored" South Africans, but some 10,000 "colored" West Indians also served. British colonies also provided some 1.4 million white enlistees. "The Military Effort of the British Empire," *The Round Table*, no. 35 (June 1919), 495–508: 498.

[6] Several anti-colonial independence leaders were combatants in World War I for their respective colonial powers. For example, Norman Manley, a leader of the Jamaican independence movement, served in the European theater, where his brother was killed. One of the first post-independence heads of state for Jamaica, Manley was also the father of Michael Manley who served in World War II and later became prime minister of Jamaica and a staunch pan-Africanist.

[7] During March and April 1917, the Imperial War Cabinet in Britain discussed whether some African territory should be returned to Germany after the war. Most argued against the return. The group also discussed various other methods for changing colonial territory, including a South African proposal for trading land with Portugal so that South Africa would have "a natural frontier and round it off as a compact block of subtropical territory." Minutes of the Territorial Desiderata Committee of the War Cabinet meeting quoted in Wm. Roger Louis, *Great Britain and Germany's Lost Colonies, 1914–1919* (Oxford: Clarendon Press, 1967), p. 83. The fact of the Imperial War Cabinet's existence highlights the extent to which the self-governing dominions of Britain were well on their way to total independence. The dominions (Australia, Canada, New Zealand, South Africa) and India became members of the League of Nations.

[8] Ibid., pp. 78–79.   [9] Ibid., p. 106.

Why did the Western allies ultimately agree – despite their privately expressed interest in annexation, that they would not keep captured territory? The concern for applying self-determination to the colonies did not originate with heads of state. The question of what to do with the captured territory, and the idea of mandates or international control, was on the table years before the Paris Peace Conference convened. "The press and the war literature were full of such ideas, as were unpublished private discussions."[10] This was particularly so in Britain, where some of the most far-reaching proposals for reform were widely discussed. Since Britain, or its dominions, occupied and controlled the majority of land formerly held by Germany or Turkey, its position on post-war settlement was crucial. What happened during the latter part of the war was that ethical arguments moved the center of the debate from annexation to some kind of international political control.

The left, and eventually the center, of British intellectual and political elites argued for some kind of international control of captured German colonies. For example, J.A. Hobson published *Towards International Government* in 1915, calling for international colonial control. In 1917, E.D. Morel participated in public debates on the subject and published *Africa and the Peace of Europe*, which proposed internationalization of African commerce, though certainly not decolonization.[11] The British Labour Party, in late December 1917, called for the administration of all colonies in Africa to be transferred to "the proposed Super-National Authority or League of Nations" and proposed that this administration would take account of the "wishes of the people," and also the "protection of the natives against exploitation and oppression and the preservation of various tribal interests."[12]

In 1917, the Anti-Slavery and Aborigines' Protection Society, which still counted members of parliament in its ranks, lobbied British foreign policy officials to include the concerns of native races in the peace talks or in a separate meeting to consider colonial policy, "whatever

[10] H. Duncan Hall, *Mandates, Dependencies and Trusteeship* (Washington: Carnegie Endowment for International Peace, 1948), p. 108. On previous uses of the words mandate and mandatory in connection with colonial policy, see Quincy Wright, *Mandates Under the League of Nations* (Chicago: University of Chicago Press, 1930), pp. 19–20. The idea of countries administering colonies was also not new: Britain had granted South Africa the right to administer Basotoland and Bechuanaland in 1909.

[11] Moreover, colonialism and imperialism were popularly blamed for causing World War I.

[12] Quoted in Louis, *Great Britain and Germany's Lost Colonies*, p. 91.

the final outcome of the European hostilities may be....".[13] The Society used both practical and ethical arguments. "We also point out that such a step appears to be not only morally imperative, but in the truest interests of the Colonizing Powers no less than the native peoples, because the white races have become largely dependent on the coloured races for a large proportion of their food stuffs and raw materials."[14] According to the Society, native "inhabitants should be given a voice in shaping their own destiny"; although it was not a "practical proposal ... this very fact appears to make it more than ever incumbent on the stronger Powers to devise means for adequately safeguarding the rights and welfare of the native inhabitants."[15] The Society's ideas for reform were comprehensive: for example, lynching, forced labor for private profit, and criminal punishment for breaches of civil labor contracts should be halted and land for natives should be reserved.

Yet even the reformers argued among themselves. In July 1917, the Anti-Slavery and Aborigines' Protection Society held a conference on the future of German colonies where some members argued that German colonization was unjust because the Germans rarely made treaties with the local chiefs and they treated the inhabitants badly. Travers Buxton argued that "colonies should not be used like pawns on a chess board, or merely for bargaining purposes."[16] But, Society members disagreed about the proper line to take in lobbying for reforms. Charles Buxton, for example, said the argument for consultation with the natives in former German colonies had no logical limit and this had far-reaching implications; if the Society stated that it is in favor of consultation, "We are laying ourselves open as a Society to the charge of hypocrisy." The entire colonial system was at stake.

> Are we prepared to say that what we would apply to the natives of Africa should apply also to the natives of India? If not, then we lay ourselves open to this charge of hypocrisy ... We have hitherto accepted the principle of parceling out Africa. We have wished that something better could be found, but, as a matter of fact, we have accepted the usual view that tropical Africa has got to be parceled out ... If we are

[13] "Letter to British Foreign Secretary Arthur J. Balfour from the Anti-Slavery and Aborigines Protection Society," 22 January 1917, published in the *Anti-Slavery Reporter and Aborigines' Friend* (April 1917), pp. 3–6:3
[14] Ibid., p. 3.   [15] Ibid., p. 3–4.
[16] Quoted in "Conference upon the Future of German Colonies," *Anti-Slavery Reporter and Aborigines' Friend* (October 1917), pp. 50–59: 52.

going to adopt this new and startling principle, then we ought to adopt it all around. It should be a general policy.[17]

Finally, the Society agreed to a resolution which read: "That in any reconstruction of Africa which may result from this War, the interests of the native inhabitants and also their wishes in as far as those wishes can be clearly ascertained, should be recognized as among the principle factors upon which the decision of their destiny should be based."[18] The resolutions were then forwarded to the British Foreign Office and London-based representatives of the Allied powers. In November 1917 the Society held a conference on international control of colonies. The attendees again disagreed on which measures were practical and politically feasible but they seemed to agree that some form of international supervision was desirable.[19]

In addition to pressure at home from humanitarians, British decision-makers also knew that American President Wilson would probably not agree to annexation.[20] In January 1918, G.L. Beer, who was later chief of the colonial division of the US delegation to the Paris Peace Conference, proposed that the former colonies be dealt with under a Mandate system. Wilson's speeches echo Beer's tone and language. Beer, in written testimony to the US Congress, said:

> Under modern political conditions apparently the only way to determine the problem of politically backward peoples, who require not only outside political control but also foreign capital to reorganize their stagnant economic systems is to entrust the task of government to that state whose interests are most directly involved ... If, however, such backward regions are entrusted by international mandate to one state, there should be embodied in the deed of trust most rigid safeguards to both protect the native population from exploitation and also to ensure that the interests of other foreign states are not injured ... But far more important than any arrangement of this character to secure the interests of the European and American states in such backward countries is the necessity of clearly defined provisions to protect the natives from exploitation.[21]

[17] Quoted in ibid. p. 54, emphasis in the original.   [18] Ibid., p. 59.
[19] "Conference upon International Control," *Anti-Slavery Reporter and Aborigines' Friend* (January 1918), 89–95.
[20] Louis, *Great Britain and Germany's Lost Colonies*, p. 93.
[21] George Louis Beer, *African Questions at the Paris Peace Conference* (New York: Macmillan, 1923), pp. 424–425. In January 1918 the US State Department also commissioned the colonial legal scholar Alpheus Henry Snow, who produced the historical study *The Question*

After the war the Anti-Slavery and Aborigines Protection Society corresponded with both the British Foreign Office and President Wilson in the months before the Peace Conference. To Wilson, on 28 December 1918, the Society wrote, "We beg to urge upon your Excellency that the motive for Colonial expansion should be that implied in the term 'Protectorate.' "

> This term implies that the overseas Powers should be in the position of Trustees for the well being of the inhabitants regardless either of national or colour distinction, a position which involves: – The abolition of every form of compulsory labour for private profit; the preservation of indigenous land rights; the rigid restriction of the sale of ardent spirits within the boundaries of all such Protectorate territories, such restrictions again to be impartially imposed; the recognition of some Protectorate and Native rights over sub-surface values, forest and virgin produce; the prevention of communicable diseases.[22]

Wilson's representative acknowledged the letter but said the president did not have time to meet with the Society on his way to Paris for the Peace Conference. The Society's representative was also prevented by the British government from attending a Pan-African meeting also organized in Paris. The Society then sent another letter to all delegates of the great powers attending the Paris Peace Conference that included a longer, more comprehensive, version of their proposal to President Wilson.

Framing its case as a continuation of the anti-slavery struggle, the Society said: "the time has arrived for the stronger Powers to accept as the soundest economic and ethical relationship that of Trustee for the inhabitants and their territory, and that the old policy of regarding such territories primarily from the point of view of possessions to be developed in the interests of the Metropolitan Government is out of date in practice and indefensible both on political and moral grounds."[23] The strongest Society proposals included an appeal to end forced labor and to create an international tribunal where indigenous people could appeal their treatment. The Society further urged that these reforms be extended beyond the captured territories – that "all Colonizing Powers" adopt the reforms – and suggested that they be applied "first as conditions

---

of Aborigines in the Law and Practice of Nations in December 1918 (New York: G. P. Putnam's Sons, 1921).
[22] Letter to President Wilson quoted in "Peace Terms and Colonial Reconstruction," *Anti-Slavery Reporter and Aborigines' Friend* 9 (April 1919), 2–9: 5.
[23] Letter to Delegates quoted in ibid., p. 7.

attaching to any territory where status is changed as a result of the war and generally as a standard which every Colonizing Power should accept for tropical countries and peoples under its National Control."[24] The Society's position was, just as some in the Society feared, an attack on the whole institution of colonialism, not simply a proposal for how to treat captured territories. Thus colonial reform became a mainstream project.

By late 1918, under public and elite pressure, a consensus was thus forming among allied diplomats and elites around the idea of a Mandate system. Public pressure was in part persuasive because it was consistent with the already officially expressed beliefs in self-determination. Annexation could not be allowed if the victors, especially Woodrow Wilson and Lloyd George, were to be bound to their war-time rhetoric. In January 1917, President Wilson told the US Congress, "I am proposing, as it were, that the nations should with one accord adopt the doctrine of President Monroe as the doctrine of the world: that no nation should seek to extend its policy over any other nation, but that every people should be free to determine its own policy, its own way of development, unhindered, unthreatened, unafraid, the little along with the great and powerful."[25] On 5 January 1918, Prime Minister Lloyd George of England argued for a "general principle of national self-determination," to be applied to the German colonies.[26] In his "Fourteen Points" speech of 8 January 1918, President Wilson argued for, "A free, open-minded and absolutely impartial adjustment of colonial claims, based upon a strict observance of the principle that in determining all such questions of sovereignty the interests of the populations concerned must have equal weight with the equitable claims of the government whose title is to be determined."[27] If Wilsonian self-determination did not necessarily mean complete independence and self-rule, it meant people should have some say in their affairs. On 11 February 1918, President Wilson said,

[24] Ibid., p. 9.
[25] Quoted in Gaddis Smith, "Monroe Doctrine," in Bruce W. Jentleson and Thomas Patterson, eds., *Encyclopedia of U.S. Foreign Relations*, vol. III (New York: Oxford University Press, 1997), pp. 159–167: 162. President James Monroe told Congress in 1823 that "American continents, by the free and independent condition which they have assumed and maintain, are henceforth not to be considered as subjects for the future colonization of European powers." Quoted in ibid., p. 160. The Roosevelt Corollary, announced in December 1904, asserted a US right to intervene to keep Europeans out of Latin America.
[26] Quoted in Wright, *Mandates Under the League*, p. 25.
[27] Woodrow Wilson, "Fourteen Points," 8 January 1918. Quoted in Antonio Cassese, *Self-determination of Peoples: A Legal Reappraisal* (Cambridge: Cambridge University Press, 1996), p. 21.

"Peoples and provinces are not to be bartered about from sovereignty to sovereignty as if they were mere chattels and pawns in a game, even the great game, now forever discredited of the balance of power; but every territorial settlement involved in this war must be made in the interest and for the benefit of the populations concerned, and not as a part of any mere adjustment or compromise of claims amongst rival states."[28] The Bolsheviks also called for peace without annexation and blamed imperialism for the war. During and after the conflict, V.I. Lenin pushed the idea of self-determination and decolonization and made the argument that imperialism caused the war.[29]

In November 1918, a group of US and British elites, known as the Round Table, met in London and discussed the idea of mandates, publishing a summary of their deliberations in their journal *Round Table*. Despite his private efforts to keep captured territories, General Jan Smuts of South Africa, who probably had read the work of the Round Table before writing his draft plan for a League of Nations, also proposed a Mandate system.[30] Smuts' plan, published as a pamphlet in December 1918, said the Mandate system should be confined to Middle East and European territories of the losers of World War I, because he felt that, "The German colonies in the Pacific and Africa are inhabited by barbarians, who not only cannot possibly govern themselves, but to whom it would be impracticable to apply any ideas of political self-determination in the European sense."[31] If Smuts' idea of who was ready for self-determination was narrow, he saw Mandate status as temporary, on the route to independence. President Wilson drew upon Smuts' draft for his own draft of the League of Nations Covenant, but broadened the Mandate system to include former German colonies in Africa.

While the Peace Conference was under way, in February 1919 delegates of the First Pan-African Congress also met in Paris. Opposed by the United States and Britain, which denied passports to some of its citizens

---

[28] Quoted in Wright, *Mandates Under the League*, p. 24.

[29] V.I. Lenin, *Theses on the Socialist Revolution and the Right of Nations to Self-Determination* (March 1916) and *Imperialism: the Highest Stage of Capitalism* (1917). See Robert C. Tucker, ed., *The Lenin Anthology* (New York: Norton, 1975), pp. 204–274. Also see Cassese, *Self-determination of Peoples*, pp. 14–21 and L.H. Gann and Peter Duignan, *Burden of Empire: An Appraisal of Western Colonialism in Africa South of the Sahara* (New York: Praeger, 1967), pp. 55–71.

[30] Campbell L. Upthegrove, *Empire by Mandate: A History of the Relations of Great Britain with the Permanent Mandates Commission of the League of Nations* (New York: Bookman Associates, 1954); Wright, *Mandates Under the League*, pp. 22–23.

[31] Jan Smuts, *The League of Nations: A Practical Suggestion* (London: Hodder & Stoughton, 1918), quoted in Hall, *Mandates, Dependencies and Trusteeship*, p. 13.

who wished to attend (including a representative of the Anti-Slavery and Aborigines Protection Society), the meeting focused on strategies for the liberation for Caribbean and African people.[32] Blaise Diagne, made famous for recruiting over 60,000 West Africans in 1918 for French military service, helped W.E.B. Du Bois organize the meeting and convinced France's leader, Clemenceau, to authorize it over the objections of British and US governments.[33] Despite the travel restrictions, fifty-seven delegates from fifteen countries attended, including sixteen from the US, twelve from Africa, and twenty-one from the West Indies. At least one participant in the Paris Peace Conference, C.D.B. King, a member of the Liberian delegation, also attended the Pan-African Conference.[34]

The Pan-Africanist proposals were comprehensive in a humanitarian reformist sense. Du Bois proposed that all Africa be internationalized, with the former German colonies as the core, adding other territories to this base as time went on.[35] Du Bois said: "This Africa for the Africans could be under the guidance of international organization. The governing international commission should represent not simply governments, but modern culture, science, commerce, social reform, and religious philanthropy. It must represent not simply the white world, but the civilized Negro world."[36] Notably, the 1919 Pan-African Congress did not demand an immediate end to colonialism; rather, its proposals

---

[32] On US and British government efforts to scuttle the 1919 Pan-African Conference, see Paul Gordon Lauren, *Power and Prejudice: The Politics and Diplomacy of Racial Discrimination* (Boulder: Westview Press, 1996), pp. 83–84; George Padmore, *Pan-Africanism or Communism* (Garden City, NY: Anchor Books, 1971), pp. 99–100. Immanuel Geiss, *The Pan-African Movement: A History of Pan-Africanism in America, Europe and Africa* (New York: Africana Publishing, 1974), p. 237. Also see *Anti-Slavery Reporter and Aborigines' Friend* 9 (April 1919), p. 6.

[33] Clemenceau reportedly told Diagne, "Don't advertise it, but go ahead." Quoted in Geiss, *The Pan-African Movement*, p. 237.

[34] Ibid., p. 238.

[35] W.E.B. Du Bois also took a proposal urging self-determination for Africa to Paris for President Wilson. According to the *Chicago Tribune*: "Dr. Du Bois sets forth that while the principle of self-determination cannot be applied to uncivilized peoples, yet the educated blacks should have some voice in the disposition of the German colonies. He maintains that in settling what is to be done with the German colonies the Peace Conference might consider the wishes of the intelligent Negroes in the colonies themselves, the Negroes of the United States, and South Africa, and the West Indies, the Negro governments of Abyssinia, Liberia, Haiti . . . " *Chicago Tribune*, 19 January 1919, quoted in W.E. Burghardt Du Bois, *The World and Africa: An Inquiry into the Part Which Africa Has Played in World History* (New York: International Publishers, 1965), p. 9.

[36] Du Bois quoted in the *Chicago Tribune*, 19 January 1919. Du Bois is also quoted as saying: "We can, if we will, inaugurate on the dark continent a last great crusade for humanity. With Africa redeemed, Asia would be safe and Europe indeed triumphant." Du Bois, *The World and Africa*, p. 9.

were modest in political terms, though radical with respect to economic issues:

> The Negroes of the world demand that hereafter the natives of Africa and the peoples of African descent be governed according to the following principles:
>
> 1. *The land*: the land and its natural resources shall be held in trust for the natives and at all times they shall have effective ownership of as much land as they can profitably develop.
>
> 2. *Capital*: the investment of capital and granting of concessions shall be so regulated as to prevent the exploitation of the natives and the exhaustion of the natural wealth of the country. Concessions shall always be limited in time and subject to state control. The growing social needs of the native must be regarded and the profits taxed for social and material benefit of the natives.
>
> 3. *Labor*: slavery and corporal punishment shall be abolished and forced labor except in punishment for crime; and the general conditions of labor shall be prescribed and regulated by the State.
>
> 4. *Education*: it shall be the right of every native child to learn to read and write in his own language, and the language of the trustee nation, at public expense, and to be given technical instruction in some branch of industry. The State shall also educate as large a number of natives as possible in higher technical and cultural training and maintain a corps of native teachers.
>
> 5. *The State*: the natives of Africa must have the right to participate in the government as fast as their development permits, in conformity with the principle that the government exists for the natives and not the natives for the government. They shall at once be allowed to participate in local and tribal government, according to ancient usage, and this participation shall gradually extend, as education and experience proceed to the higher offices of state; to the end that, in time, Africa is ruled by consent of the Africans . . . .[37]

Du Bois claimed that the Pan-African Congress "influenced the Peace Conference."[38] That was certainly the intent, since the resolutions adopted by the Pan-African Conference were addressed to the Allied and Associated Powers assembled in Paris and called for a "permanent Bureau" in the League of Nations to oversee protection of Africans. Still, none of the standard histories of the Paris Peace

---

[37] Quoted in ibid., pp. 11–12. [38] Ibid., p. 10.

Conference mention the 1919 Pan-African Congress, though it was certainly noticed by the governments involved, given the efforts of some of them to prevent its occurrence.[39] Yet despite Du Bois' claim, it is not clear that the Pan-African Congress' proposals for a system of oversight for African colonies had an influence on the shape of the League of Nations Mandate system: "At best, the resolutions had only a minor impact upon the deliberations of the Paris Peace Conference."[40] The importance of the Pan-African Congress, then, lay not in the uniqueness of the proposals, nor necessarily with any direct influence on many delegates to the Paris Peace Conference, but rather in the fact that colonial subjects demonstrated their ability and willingness to organize politically and attract public attention and campaign for the amelioration of colonialism. If they were slightly more militant, the Pan-Africanists were part of a larger movement which pushed for some degree of self-determination.

The League of Nations Mandate system

The activists' proposals for colonial reform and for managing the former colonies of Germany and Turkey were much more comprehensive than the measures ultimately adopted by the Paris Peace Conference of 1919 and written into the Covenant of the League of Nations drafted there. This was because, "[f]ar from envisaging the eventual independence of colonies such as German East Africa, Allied statesmen at the Peace Conference regarded 1919 as the renewal, not the end, of an imperial era."[41] Equality and self-determination, not just securing peace, were on the agenda for the first time, although there was not a consensus on implementing these beliefs. In an important sense, these ideas were nascent or immanent, not yet believed widely or strongly enough among the representatives of the Great Powers to radically reshape foreign and colonial policy, but held just enough to change policy on the margins. For example, when the Japanese-proposed statement of racial equality won a majority of votes at the Peace Conference, President Wilson, as chair of the meeting, rejected it, saying the issue was too serious to be

[39] For instance, see H. W. V. Temperley, ed., *A History of the Peace Conference of Paris* (London: H. Frowde, and Hodder & Stoughton, 1920–1924), 6 vols.; David Hunter Miller, *The Drafting of the Covenant* (New York: G.P. Putnam's Sons, 1928), two vols.
[40] Manning Marable, *W.E.B. Du Bois: Black Radical Democrat* (Boston: Twayne Publishers, 1986), p. 102.
[41] Louis, *Great Britain and Germany's Lost Colonies*, p. 7.

adopted without unanimous consent, despite the fact that unanimity was not required to pass motions at the conference.[42] Thus, the Peace Conference and the Covenant of the League embodied and reproduced the racial/Eurocentric hierarchy of the nineteenth century, while foreshadowing and articulating the belief in self-determination that would dominate the diplomacy of the mid-twentieth century.

Negotiations over the Mandate system were some of the most intense of the Paris Peace Conference.[43] Consistent with the ambivalent views of the day, the Mandate system was a compromise between the three main ideas on the table about what to do with former colonies: annexation, international control and administration, or self-determination. The system that ultimately grew out of Smuts' and Wilson's draft covenants, and articulated in Article 22 of the Covenant of the League of Nations, was a combination of continued colonialism, its regulation, and a foreshadowing promise of decolonization. The compromise thus acknowledged the widespread belief that annexation was not appropriate but also embodied the view that the inhabitants of these former colonies were not yet suited for independence. Specifically, Article 22 said that to those "colonies and territories . . . inhabited by peoples not yet able to stand by themselves under the strenuous conditions of the modern world . . . should be applied the principle that the well-being and development of such peoples form a sacred trust of civilization. . . ."[44] The idea was "tutelage" in a paternalistic sense. Further, Article 22 states that the "character of the Mandate must differ according to the stage of development of the people, the geographical situation of the territory, its economic conditions and other similar circumstances."[45]

Reflecting perceived differences in "development" and levels of "civilization," Article 22 created three classes of Mandate. In the language of the Covenant, and according to the mandatory agreements, the former lands of the Turkish empire became Class A mandates, having reached a "stage of development" where they, with some assistance, would soon be "able to stand alone." The Class B mandates, were "at such a stage,

---

[42] See Lauren, *Power and Prejudice*, pp. 82–103.

[43] On the negotiations over the Mandate system and Article 22 at the conference see Wright, *Mandates Under the League*, pp. 24–43. It is important to recall that not all the captured or disputed territory went into the Mandate system. Areas in Europe were allocated either to one power or another, or in the case of the Saar region of Germany, placed under an International Commission of five members chaired by its British member and including one native of the Saar Basin.

[44] Covenant of the League of Nations, Article 22, paragraph no. 1.

[45] Covenant of the League of Nations, Article 22, paragraph no. 3.

that the Mandatory must be responsible for the administration of the territory under conditions which will guarantee freedom of conscience and religion, subject only to the maintenance of public order and morals, the prohibition of abuses such as the slave trade, the arms traffic, the liquor traffic . . . " The Class C Mandate territories were those which, "owing to the sparseness of their population, or their small size, or their remoteness from the centre of civilisation . . . can be best administered under the laws of the Mandatory as integral portions of its territory, subject to the safeguards above mentioned in the interests of the indigenous population." As Wm. Roger Louis says, the Class C mandates were "regarded, in the phrase current at the time, as 'colonies in all but name.' "[46] Rather than deal with all the issues at Paris, the former colonies that were to be in these categories were defined at a later date by the Allied Supreme Council (Britain, France, Italy, Japan and the US), and individual agreements were written for each mandate in 1919 and 1920 and confirmed over the next two years.[47] The allocation of territory to mandatory powers was, though decided by a committee, actually based on which power took over the territory from Turkey or Germany during the war.[48] France and Britain had mandates in Togo and Cameroons by an agreement in 1919. There was never an official mandate agreement between Britain and the League on Iraq, only a treaty. The Palestine and Transjordan mandates were split, early on, as were later the mandates for Syria and Lebanon.[49]

Other parts of the Covenant made space for colonial reform. Article 23 charged members of the League to "undertake to secure just treatment of the native inhabitants of the territories under their control." Article 1

[46] Wm. Roger Louis, "The Era of the Mandates System and the Non-European World," in Hedley Bull and Adam Watson, eds., *The Expansion of International Society* (Oxford: Oxford University Press, 1984), pp. 201–213: 204.
[47] See Hall, *Mandates, Dependencies and Trusteeships*, pp. 130–161. Mandatory agreements were not between the inhabitants of the territories and the mandatory power, but rather between the League and the mandatory government. Significantly, and completely in line with the paternalistic belief of the day, it was rare that the inhabitants of any territory were consulted about their status after the war. For exceptions, see Cassese, *Self-determination of Peoples*. The Anti-Slavery and Aborigines Protection Society drew up a draft proposed mandate agreement and submitted it to the Permanent Mandates Commission in July 1919. Rather more comprehensive than most mandatory agreements that actually came into force over the next few years, they made their draft "Memorandum on Colonial Mandates" public in the October 1919 issue of the *Anti-Slavery Reporter and Aborigines' Friend*, pp. 63–68.
[48] Of course, not all captured territory became mandates, only former colonies.
[49] League of Nations, *The Mandates System: Origin, Principles, Application* (Geneva: League of Nations, 1945).

Table 6.1 *League of Nations Mandates*

Class	Territory	Administrative power
A	Iraq	Great Britain
	Palestine and Transjordan	Great Britain
	Syria and Lebanon	France
B	Togoland	France
	Togoland	Great Britain
	Cameroons	France
	Cameroons	Great Britain
	Tanganyika	Great Britain
	Ruanda Urundi	Belgium
C	South West Africa	South Africa
	New Guinea	Australia
	Nauru	Great Britain/Australia
	Samoa	New Zealand
	Pacific Islands: Marshall, Carolines and Marianas	Japan

Source: League of Nations, *The Mandates system: Origin, Principles, Application* (Geneva: League of Nations).

noted that "any fully self-governing State, Dominion, or Colony . . . may become a Member of the League," if it was voted in by the League Assembly and the prospective member agreed to comply with the obligations and regulations required of members. Further, the 1885 General Act of Berlin and the 1890 Brussels Act were revised after the Peace Conference in a separate agreement, the Convention on the Revision of the General Act of February 26, 1885, and of the General Act and Declaration of Brussels of July 2, 1890. Significantly, the Convention retained the emphasis of both prior agreements on commercial openness in Africa but also, in Article 11 committed signatories to "continue to watch over the preservation of the native populations and to supervise the improvement of the conditions of their moral and material well-being."[50] Thus, after World War I, principles and beliefs that were essential elements of a decolonization regime – self-determination, nationalism, human rights, and an international interest in the affairs of colonial administration – were codified in this major international treaty and used to structure international relations.

[50] Convention quoted in Hall, *Mandates, Dependencies and Trusteeship*, pp. 323–328: 326.

Obviously, however, the League of Nations Mandate system, and the mention of just treatment elsewhere in the Covenant, were a far cry from advocating or implementing decolonization.[51] As M.E. Chamberlain notes, "The Mandatory power was required only to provide good and humane government, to refrain from exploitation, and to suppress evils such as the remnants of the slave trade."[52] Rather, the Mandate system was first primarily a method of monitoring the treatment of the subjects of mandate territories by means of annual reports by the mandatory power, as required by the Covenant, to the Permanent Mandates Commission. And, as Quincy Wright argued, "Probably none of the mandatory governments has been enthusiastic for the system. They prefer mandates to nothing but doubtless would prefer colonies to mandates."[53]

Yet, despite the narrow intentions of its authors (and perhaps in part due to strong criticism of the Mandate system from the left, as not actually much different than colonialism), the Mandate system grew to be more than its framers – or the mandatory powers – intended, ultimately striking a wedge in the colonial system.[54] The first edge of the wedge is found in the content of specific mandate agreements, where modest, but still significant, protections for natives were built into the language of the mandatory agreements.[55] For example, in the Mandate over East Africa, Britain agreed that land transfers "shall take into consideration native laws and customs."[56]

Further, League mandates were the site of increasing scrutiny of colonial labor practices. Besides the enforcement of the anti-slavery regime, forced labor was to be discouraged in League mandate territories.[57] Forced labor was prohibited, for example, in South West Africa "except

---

[51] Critics, such as Stalin, believed the Mandate system was simply imperialism.

[52] M.E. Chamberlain, *Decolonization: The Fall of the European Empires* (Oxford: Basil Blackwell, 1985), pp. 7–8; Dorothy V. Jones, "The League of Nations Experiment in International Protection," *Ethics & International Affairs* 8 (1994), 77–95.

[53] Wright, *Mandates Under the League*, p. 97.

[54] Analysis and mild criticism from the US left came, for instance, from Rayford Logan, "The Operation of the Mandate System in Africa," *The Journal of Negro History* 13 (October 1928), 423–477. Some drafters of the League Covenant took a cynical view. See Lansing, *The Peace Negotiations*, pp. 155–160. Miller, *The Drafting of the Covenant, I*, p. 47.

[55] It must be borne in mind that so-called treaties of protection between natives and colonizers had made some of these promises before. The key differences were international oversight and accountability.

[56] Text of the British Mandate for East Africa, in Hall, *Mandates, Dependencies and Trusteeship*, p. 304.

[57] According to their agreements as Mandatory powers, Mandatories were not to arm and use the indigenous populations for military and police, except for domestic purposes.

for essential public works and services, and then only for adequate remuneration."[58] Similarly, using almost the same language, the text for the British Mandate for East Africa, says the mandatory power "shall prohibit all forms of forced or compulsory labour, except for essential public works and services, and then only in return for adequate remuneration."[59] As mandatory in East Africa, Britain agreed that it, "shall protect the natives from abuse and measures of fraud and force by the careful supervision of labour contracts and the recruiting of labour."[60]

The Permanent Mandates Commission

Beyond the language of mandatory agreements, the greatest power of the Mandate system to change colonial practice lay in an underrated institution, the Permanent Mandates Commission (PMC) of the League. The PMC's official role was oversight. But, from the perspective of ethical argument, the PMC was a venue for arguments about colonial practice within the mandates and colonies more generally. As such, it (inadvertently) promoted the deconstruction of colonialism (denormalizing and delegitimizing elements of colonial practice) and the construction of a new paradigm. The PMC, in publicizing the conditions in the mandates, also reframed colonial practice. Working in conjunction with the rest of the League of Nations system and the mandatory administrations, the PMC also articulated criteria for good colonial administration and created new forms of knowledge and practice about colonialism in the general public and among colonial administrators, and was thus the engine for institutionalizing the new normative beliefs about colonial governance. The ultimately revolutionary impact of the PMC was inadvertent because many PMC members were former colonial administrators who were ardent advocates of colonialism. Further, the PMC had little or no direct say in the administration of mandates. Because it could not directly intervene – even its questions and recommendations on matters of governance had to be conveyed through the League Council – the PMC exercised indirect influence.

Understanding how ethical argument, reframing, and the institutionalization of new normative beliefs occurred and worked – especially

[58] Text of the Mandate for German South West Africa in T.D. Gill, *South West Africa and the Sacred Trust, 1919–1972* (The Hague: T.M.C. Asser Instituut, 1984), pp. 104–105: 105.
[59] Text of the British Mandate for East Africa, in Hall, *Mandates, Dependencies and Trusteeship*, pp. 303–306: 304.
[60] Ibid.

how transparency, accountability, and the idea of progress for "natives" was promoted by the process – requires an understanding of the entire apparatus of the Mandate system, where three bodies, the League Council, the League Assembly, and the Permanent Mandates Commission had roles in supervising mandatory administration. According to the League Covenant, the mandatory power was to submit annual reports to the Council; the mandatory and the Council would agree, for each mandate, on the authority of the mandatory power; and a permanent commission would "receive and examine annual reports of the Mandatories and advise the Council on all matters relating to the observance of the mandates."[61] Since the instructions for the PMC were not explicit in every detail, the League Assembly, the Council, and the Commission devised the rules and procedures of mandate supervision and the composition of the permanent commission.[62] Table 6.2 outlines the main steps in the process of mandatory supervision by the League.

Established by the Council of the League in November 1920, the PMC sat in Geneva and usually met twice a year. After some debate over the constitution of the PMC, the Assembly decided that the majority of the ten-member commission would consist of "non-Mandatory Powers." PMC members were to be experts sitting in a private capacity, and were to recuse themselves if they were citizens of a country whose mandate was being discussed.[63] Further, a representative of the International Labor Organization usually attended Commission sessions. The PMC was linked to the secretary general of the League by a secretary who directed a small staff, known as the Mandates section or secretariat. PMC and secretariat membership had remarkable continuity over the nearly two decades it met. For example, there were only three secretaries from 1921 to 1939 and only two Commission chairmen. Most commissioners served several years, but many served much longer, for example, Marquis Théodoli of Italy served from 1921 to December 1937, and

---

[61] Article 22, paragraphs 7–9.

[62] The membership, organization, and procedures were adopted by the Council on 1 December 1920 and the Rules of Procedure were devised by the Commission at their first session in 1921. Some rules were later clarified or revised with amendments at sessions of the Commission. See League of Nations, *The Mandates System*, p. 35. Further, according to the Mandatory agreements, the Permanent Court of International Justice, established by the League, could hear disputes as well.

[63] There were originally nine commission members. The first secretary was made an extra-ordinary member in 1924 and a tenth member was added in 1926. Commissioners came from Italy, Portugal, Spain, Germany, Norway, and Sweden and from the Mandatory powers of Belgium, Great Britain, the Netherlands, and Japan.

Table 6.2 *Process of League Mandate supervision*

===

1. The mandatory administration submitted an annual report to the Council of the League, answering questions posed to it by the Permanent Mandates Commission.
2. The Mandate Secretariat received and studied the annual reports, and distributed the reports to the PMC members. The Secretariat staff also prepared and distributed questions and background information on the annual reports to members of the PMC, and drafted reports on the petitions to the PMC.
3. Members of the PMC examined the reports, petitions, and any supplementary material sent to it by the Secretariat.
4. The PMC met twice annually to discuss the annual reports and to question the accredited representatives of the Mandatory power on the content of their reports and conditions in the Mandate. Each commission member had an area of expertise, though all, including the secretary and the representative from the ILO, could participate in the questioning and discussion.
5. The Mandate secretariat staff prepared the minutes of the PMC and helped the PMC write its report to the Council. Reports could contain questions, observations and, rarely, recommendations. The Secretariat staff also kept a file of the Mandatory power's replies to the Permanent Mandate Commission's questions and observations.
6. The Council passed on the PMC report and their own comments to the League Assembly and/or the Sixth (Political) Committee of the League Assembly. The Assembly, made up primarily of non-colonial powers, discussed the reports and sometimes made recommendations to the League Council.
7. The League Council, which included mandatory powers, communicated questions and recommendations of the PMC and the Assembly to the League. The Council also had the power to appoint PMC members, settle disputes, and decide when a mandate was ready for independence.
8. Minutes of the PMC, the PMC report, and the discussion and any resolutions of the Council and the Assembly were published.

===

Frederick Lugard, of Britain served from July 1923 to July 1936.[64] Two of the shorter terms were the British Commissioners W. Ormsby-Gore and Lord Hankey who resigned the PMC to become members of the British Cabinet.

At least some PMC members were conscious of their role as framers of public impressions about mandatory government and used the PMC's authority to publicize conditions in the mandate territories. The minutes, which include the (sometimes verbatim) records of interactions between commission members and representatives of the mandatory powers,

---

[64] The PMC held thirty-seven sessions, the first in February 1921, and the last in December 1939.

were printed annually in English and French, and made available to the general public, usually within two months of the session.[65] In 1929, the PMC acknowledged publishing its minutes so that it could "secure the assistance of public opinion in the moral control incumbent upon the Commission."[66] As Lord Hailey, British member of the Commission from 1936 to 1939 wrote in 1938, "only those who have had experience in the internal working of an official administration, in circumstances where there is no organization of public opinion, can appreciate the strength of the influence which can be exerted by publicity of the nature of that involved in the proceedings of the Commission and Council."[67]

As important as publicity was in reframing colonial practice, the more subtle but powerful innovation of the Mandate system was its institutionalization of international oversight of colonial reform practices, which changed colonialism in a way that made decolonization more likely.[68] Normative beliefs about accountability and just treatment of the "natives" were institutionalized when the PMC articulated the terms of oversight, specified indicators of just treatment, devised measures of progress, and reviewed the annual reports of the mandatory powers to the Permanent Mandates Commission. Institutionalization made the new normative beliefs concrete and simultaneously helped to defamiliarize, denormalize, and delegitimize old-style colonialism.

The most important technique for indirectly governing the colonies and institutionalizing new normative beliefs was the process of annual reports by the mandatory powers. Each year the same questions were asked, and each year mandatory administrations submitted reports and testified before the PMC.[69] It is not surprising that reports by mandatory administrators on the conditions within mandates, and their own actions, tended to put mandatory administration in the best possible light. The oral questioning of mandatory power representatives by the

---

[65] The minutes of the Permanent Mandates Commission (PMC) total over 8,000 pages according to one estimate. League of Nations, *The Mandates System*, p. 49.

[66] PMC, *Minutes of the Fifteenth Session, 1929*, p. 15.

[67] Hailey, quoted in Hall, *Mandates, Dependencies, and Trusteeship*, p. 212. Hall believed that the PMC was not as successful as the Congo reform movement in using publicity and pointed out: "In an autocratic system, where free publicity is not possible, no Mandate or trusteeship system could operate." Ibid.

[68] Of course the Berlin West Africa Conference and its General Act changed colonialism too, but in a way (by specifying "effective occupation") that primarily reinforced the institution.

[69] The reports of the mandatory powers to the PMC were not generally printed in the *Official Journal* of the League of Nations or in the minutes of the Permanent Mandates Commission. The League printed one set in 1925, but decided that it was too costly to keep up the practice.

PMC was an important innovation of the Commission that helped commissioners clarify conditions in the mandates and hold administrators accountable.

But the Commission limited its oversight in two other respects: the PMC decided that it would not send missions of inquiry to mandate territories, nor could inhabitants of the territories directly petition the PMC. Inhabitants had to go through the mandatory government to make their petitions, although third parties could send petitions directly to the chair of the Commission. The right of petition was usually used by Europeans in the mandate territories, and the mandatory power usually sent its own comments about the petitions along with the petitions it chose to transmit. The PMC argued that to hear petitions directly or to send missions to mandate territories could undermine confidence and authority in the administering powers and would also put the Commission in the position of being a judicial body, whereas its official role was one of advising the Council of the League.[70]

Perhaps the best illustration of how PMC members saw, in practical terms, "the principle that the well-being and development of such peoples form a sacred trust of civilization," and how the new normative beliefs about colonialism were articulated and institutionalized by the PMC is the evolution of its questionnaires on mandates.[71] In 1921, its first year of operation, the PMC drew up a list of about sixty questions that it wanted mandatory powers to answer in their reports with regard to B and C class mandates. The PMC questionnaire was intended to elicit information about compliance with international normative beliefs as stated in the Covenant. Because the focus and language of the questions was negotiated among members of the Commission, their content is worth noting as an articulation of the least common denominator of beliefs about colonial administration. The questions covered slavery, labor, arms traffic, trade and manufacture of alcohol and drugs, freedom of conscience, economic equality, education, public health, systems of land tenure, public finances, demographic statistics, and moral, social, and material well being. The Commission also asked for copies of all legislative and administrative decisions with regard to each territory.

---

[70] See League of Nations, *The Mandates System*, pp. 38–46; Wright, *Mandates Under the League*, pp. 169–184; Hall, *Mandates, Dependencies, and Trusteeships*, pp. 198–207. The League Council did, on occasion, usually to resolve border issues, send special commissions to mandated territories. See League of Nations, *The Mandates System*, p. 45.
[71] From Article 22, paragraph 1 of the Covenant.

Despite prohibitions on exploitation and the fact that the administering powers were legally obliged to promote the well being of inhabitants, the forced labor that was widespread in non-mandate colonies was also practiced in the League mandate territories, especially in Africa. On labor, the Commission asked whether and how free and forced labor were regulated and "protected." Specifically, with regard to Class B mandates the questionnaire asked, "1. What are the measures intended to ensure the prohibition of forced labour for purposes other than essential public works and services and what are the effective results of these measures? 2. For what public works and services is forced native labour required? How is this regulated? 3. Are there any other forms of forced labour, such as labour in lieu of taxation, maintenance of highways, etc. If in the affirmative, how are these regulated?"[72]

At its ninth session, the PMC expanded the questionnaire to about 275 questions, adding more questions about the status of native inhabitants, labor, and public health. The enlarged scope of inquiry indicates how the least common denominator of colonial reformism moved toward more autonomy and self-determination for the "natives" under mandatory administration. One entirely new set of questions focused on "native participation" in their own government: "12. Do natives take part in the general administration and, if so, to what extent? Are any posts in the public service open to natives? Have councils of native notables been created? 13. Are there any native communities organized under native rulers and recognized by the Government? What degree of autonomy do they possess and what are their relations with the Administration? Do village councils exist?" With regard to "Judicial Organization," another new set of questions asked: "30. How are the courts and tribunals of the various instances [civil and criminal] constituted? 31. Do they recognize native customary law, and if so, in what cases and under what conditions? 32. Are natives entitled to officiate in the courts and tribunals: for example as assessors or members of the jury?"

Other new questions were oriented toward protecting native rights and welfare, and the section of questions on labor issues was expanded and renamed from simply "Labour" to "Conditions and Regulation of Labour."[73] The content of these questions shows a widening scope of

[72] "Questionnaire Intended to Facilitate the Preparation of the Annual Reports from the Mandatory Powers." Reprinted in Hall, *Mandates, Dependencies and Trusteeship*, pp. 319–322: 319–320.
[73] Minutes of the Permanent Mandates Commission, "B and C Mandates, List of Questions Which the Permanent Mandates Commission Desires Should Be Dealt With in the Annual

critical attention from abolishing slavery to extending "native" worker's rights.

55. Are there any laws and regulations regarding labour, particularly concerning:

Labour contracts and penalties to which employers and employed are liable in the case of their breach?
Rates of wages and methods of payments?
Hours of work?
Disciplinary powers possessed by employers?
Housing and sanitary conditions in the camps or villages of workers?
Medical inspection before and on completion of employment; medical assistance to workers?
Compensation in the event of accident, disease or incapacity arising out of, and in the course of, employment?
Insurance against sickness, old age or unemployment?

. . .

61. Does the existing law provide for compulsory labour for essential public works and services?

What authority is competent to decide what are public works and services the essential nature of which justifies recourse to compulsory labour?
What payment is made to the workers?
May such compulsory labour be commuted for a money payment?
Are all such classes of the population liable to such labour?
For what period can this labour be exacted?

. . .

69. Are there any trade unions in the territory? If so, have these unions put forward any protests or demands?

Some governments objected to the more comprehensive PMC questionnaire. South Africa, Britain, and Japan opposed the new questionnaire in part on the grounds that it was too long.[74] Other mandatory powers did not object as much, but at its eleventh session, the Commission decided that mandatory powers were free to decide whether or not to use the longer questionnaire. Nevertheless, according to observers,

Reports of the Mandatory Powers," Distributed to the Council, the Members of the League and the Delegates at the Assembly, Geneva, June 25th, 1926, *Publications of the League of Nations*, VI.A. Mandates, 1926, 7 pages.
[74] Wright, *Mandates Under the League*, p. 162. Hall, *Mandates, Dependencies, and Trusteeship*, p. 206.

mandatory government reports "tended to become fuller and clearer as the years go by."[75]

> The more complete the annual reports became, and the longer and more closely the Commission and the accredited representatives worked together, the more committed the governments were to carrying out the principles of the mandates. The more complete the background statistics given by the mandatory powers and the longer the period of years over which the information stretched, the more they were committed to telling the truth and nothing but the truth. It became part of the wisdom of the Geneva experience that a government which gave statistics committed its future. For once it had begun to give ordered data, nothing was more likely to come quickly to light than a serious inaccuracy. To the trained eye of an international body – and its secretariat – . . . a serious inaccuracy, or even the variant fact, stood out as red lights on the page and invited immediate question and comment.[76]

Thus the PMC reframed colonial practice by questioning and publicizing conditions in the mandates. New normative beliefs about progress were institutionalized as the meaning of "well-being and development" were articulated and given more precise qualitative and quantitative measure. The content of the questions tended to articulate specific milestones and signs for making practical the belief that more, not less, autonomy should be given to the people who inhabited the mandates, especially the "native" inhabitants, and thus change in a positive direction was implied, indeed demanded. Because the mandatory administration's reports were annual, and they were expected to show evidence of improvement in the economic, political, and social conditions of natives, the mandatory had an incentive to improve those conditions. The fact that international surveillance was indirect, via self-reports by mandatory administrations, meant that to a certain degree, the standards and expectations of the mandates system was internalized by mandatory powers. The legitimate mission of colonialism became development, rather than exploitation. Exploitation was delegitimized and greater native rights and autonomy institutionalized. The role of the PMC as a

[75] James C. Hale, "The Creation and Application of the Mandate System: A Study in International Colonial Supervision," *Transactions of the Grotius Society*, vol. XXV (London: Grotius Society, 1940), p. 218. "The mandatory Powers, in fact, have continually sought to render their annual reports more comprehensive, and to include in them all relevant information concerning points of special interest to the members of the Commission." League of Nations, *The Mandates System*, p. 37.
[76] Hall, *Mandates, Dependencies, and Trusteeship*, p. 188.

venue for ethical arguments is illustrated by following the discussion of PMC supervision of South Africa's administration of their mandate.

South West Africa as a mandate

While there were certainly many arguments about South West Africa within the Permanent Mandates Commission, it is one of the hardest cases in which to demonstrate that status as a League of Nations Mandate and supervision by the PMC made a difference. South West Africa was the last League Mandate territory to become independent – indeed, it was one of the last of any of the world's colonies to become independent when South Africa finally left in 1990. Further, South West Africa's independence came after decades of guerrilla war. What difference did South West Africa's status as a mandate make in the lives of South West Africans? Were the "natives" protected from the rapes, lynching, concentration camps, and massacres that characterized German colonial rule? Was South Africa at all deterred from formal annexation by the fact of supervision by the PMC and the League?

South West Africa was occupied by South African forces fighting with the Allies early in World War I and ruled under martial law from mid 1915 until 31 December 1920. When the war ended, thousands of Germans living in South West Africa were repatriated to Germany, but thousands remained, and were joined by more than 10,000 new South African occupiers.[77] General Jan Smuts of South Africa thought German colonies in Africa too "barbaric" for inclusion in the Mandate system and he wanted to annex South West Africa. The South African government certainly had the military might to do so. Nevertheless, President Wilson's vision of the Mandate system prevailed in Paris and South West Africa became a mandate in 1921.

South West Africa was the only territory specifically named in Article 22 of the League of Nations Covenant.

> There are territories such as South West Africa and certain of the Pacific Islands, which, owing to the sparseness of their population, or their small size, or their remoteness from the centres of civilisation, or their geographical contiguity to the territory of the Mandatory, and other circumstances, can be best administered under the laws of the

---

[77] The majority of the population, over 208,000 people, were "native and coloured," and about 19,000 were European according to the 1921 South African census. League of Nations, *The Mandate System*, p. 115.

Mandatory as integral portions of its territory, subject to the safeguards above mentioned in the interests of the indigenous population."[78]

In its mandate agreement, signed on 17 December 1920, and in promises to the natives, South African officials pledged to administer the territory better than the Germans. Specifically, Article 2 of the agreement stated that "the mandate shall promote to the utmost the material and moral well-being and the social progress of the inhabitants of the territory . . . " South Africa was also given "full power of administration and legislation over the territory subject to the present Mandate as an integral portion of the Union of South Africa."[79] Given this language, it is no wonder that Smuts told the Union of South Africa Parliament in 1925 that mandate status was close enough to annexation: "It gives the Union such complete sovereignty, not only administrative, but legislative, that we need not ask for anything more."[80]

Although the South Africans regularly contrasted their administration with what they portrayed as the more brutal rule of the Germans, South African administration of South West Africa was brutal from the start and ostensibly little different than old-fashioned colonialism.[81] Already practicing what it called "segregation" at home, South Africa moved to institute the same arrangement in South West Africa by, for example, confining African "natives" to "native reserves" and taking the best land for whites, as it had done in South Africa in 1913.[82] Well over 90 percent of South West Africa's native population was thus restricted to less than 10 percent of the land. South West Africans were also required to pay relatively high taxes, which both subsidized mandatory administration and forced Africans to work in wage labor on white farms.

In 1923 the PMC questioned the purpose of the native reserve system. In reply, the South African representative said native reserves were "entirely in the interest of the natives." The reasoning was that, "natives, if allowed to live with the white people, eventually parted with their land and became vagrants and a source of danger. The only way

[78] League of Nations Covenant, Article 22, paragraph 7.
[79] The complete text of the mandate is found in John Dugard, ed., *The South West Africa/ Namibia Dispute: Documents and Scholarly Writings on the Controversy Between South Africa and the United Nations* (Berkeley: University of California Press, 1973), pp. 72–74.
[80] I. Goldblatt, *History of South West Africa from the beginning of the Nineteenth Century* (Cape Town: Juta & Company Limited, 1971), p. 210.
[81] See David Soggot, *Namibia: The Violent Heritage* (London: Rex Collings, 1986).
[82] The Germans had also used a native reserve system in South West Africa.

to preserve the native was to bring him gradually under the influence of civilisation, as was done in South Africa."[83] This nineteenth-century language did not fare well in the PMC. The chairman of the commission asked simply, "whether the system could be reconciled with the spirit of the mandates and the civilising mission with which the Mandatory was entrusted."[84] The South African representative then backpedaled and attempted to conceal the nature of the system by describing it in vague terms, saying that the "natives originally had their own land which they lost as a consequence of rebellion."[85] South African evasiveness, and the doggedness of the PMC, is apparent in the same session during questioning of the South African representative about labor recruitment practices in South West Africa. The questioner, Mr. Grimshaw, was the ILO expert who sat with the PMC.

> Mr. GRIMSHAW asked whether vagrants were liable to imprisonment and compulsory employment.
>
> Major HERBST said that punishment for vagrancy might take the form of compulsory employment at a private farm, or at public works, in return for pay . . .
>
> Mr. GRIMSHAW pointed out that on page 21 of the report, the number of Ovambos recruited for work was a little over 1,000 "apart from those going of their own accord". Did the recruited natives go under compulsion?
>
> Major HERBST said that some pressure was exercised by the native chiefs. There was a European officer in Ovamboland, who was in-formed of the requirements of the mines. He made these requirements known to the chiefs, who themselves persuaded the natives to recruit. . .
>
> Mr. GRIMSHAW asked whether men were directly compelled to work.
>
> Major HERBST said there was no compulsion if they could show means of subsistence.[86]

As this exchange demonstrates, members of the PMC sought to ascertain the conditions for natives working in the mandate, while South African representatives tried to put the best face on these conditions and to justify their policies in light of dominant beliefs. If normative beliefs and legitimacy did not matter, neither side would have bothered with such a discussion.

[83] PMC, *Minutes of the Third Session, 1923*, p. 103.
[84] Ibid., p. 104.   [85] Ibid., p. 104.   [86] Ibid., p. 108.

The role of argument is also illustrated in an incident known as the Bondelswarts affair. Not surprisingly, African resistance to South African mandatory rule was evident from the beginning and South Africa often used force to crush that resistance.[87] In 1917, the South African administration imposed a tax on dogs and the tax was increased in 1921. The Bondelswarts, located in the southern part of the mandate, apparently refused to pay the tax and also resisted handing over five men, including Abraham Morris, for whom arrest warrants had been issued in April. Morris had re-entered South West Africa illegally from South Africa, and he was apparently armed. This dispute capped a long period of Bondelswart ill-feeling about taxes, wages, and other mandatory administration policies.[88] Accounts of what happened next vary. Most agree that in May 1922 the Bondelswarts prepared to fight, or at least defend themselves, and the mandatory administration moved to crush what they called a rebellion of 500 to 600 people, of which 200 were said to be armed (although only about 40 weapons were captured after the Bondelswarts were crushed). The mandate administrator, Gysbert Hofmeyr, then raised a force of about 400 men, armed with rifles and four machine guns, and called in aircraft to bomb the Bondelswarts. This resulted in what some called a massacre: 100 rebels died, including Morris and a small number of Bondelswart women and children. Another 468 of the Bondelswart men were wounded and/or taken prisoner.[89]

The Bondelswarts incident was widely reported in South Africa, where the press and members of parliament called for an investigation. One opposition member of the South African parliament, Arthur Barlow, said that "black men" in the League of Nations would seize upon the incident and "our name was going to stink in the nostrils of the countries of the world."[90] But, despite widespread criticism, the prime minister of South Africa, General Jan Smuts, stood up for the actions of Hofmeyr, who submitted a report of the event to the government shortly

[87] See Petet Katjavivi, *A History of Resistance in Namibia* (Trenton, NJ: Africa World Press, 1988); Colin Leys and John S. Saul, *et al.*, *Namibia's Liberation Struggle: The Two Edged Sword* (London: James Currey, 1995); Isaak I. Dore, *The International Mandate System and Namibia* (Boulder: Westview Press, 1985).
[88] John H. Wellington, *South West Africa and its Human Issues* (Oxford: Oxford University Press, 1967), pp. 285–286.
[89] See A.M. Davey, *The Bondelzwarts Affair: A Study of the Repercussions* (Pretoria: University of South Africa, 1961), pp. 5–8. Also see Goldblatt, *History of South West Africa from the beginning of the Nineteenth Century* and Wellington, *South West Africa and its Human Issues*. PMC, *Minutes of the Third Session, 1923* (Geneva: League of Nations, 1923).
[90] Quoted in Davey, *The Bondelzwarts Affair*, p. 10.

afterwards. Later, under pressure from the South African parliament, Smuts agreed to an investigation by the Native Affairs Commission of South Africa.

Reaction abroad was also critical. In Britain, the secretary of state for colonial affairs, Winston Churchill, was questioned about the incident in the House of Commons. Of more concern to South Africa, news of the incident also reached the League of Nations Assembly where the PMC, and the Haitian representative to the League Assembly, Mr. Bellegarde, called for an investigation. Shortly after the Bondelswarts affair, South Africa was due to answer questions on its annual report to the PMC. But, South Africa did not send a representative to the PMC in 1922 to answer questions on its very brief report. The minutes of the meeting say simply that the PMC regretted the absence of a representative of South Africa, that it "drew attention to the term 'Protectorate' bestowed upon the mandatory territory in some of the official communications of the mandatory Power", and that the PMC would like information about the rebellion and its "repression."[91] Later that year, in diplomatic language, the League Assembly unanimously passed a resolution, "moved by feelings of great anxiety for the welfare and relief of the survivor," expressing its desire to see the full report on the action that South Africa had promised to produce.[92]

In 1923, South Africa supplied the PMC with the required annual report and two special reports on the Bondelswarts incident prepared by the administrator of South West Africa and the panel appointed by Smuts. On 23 July 1923, the Anti-Slavery and Aborigines' Protection Society wrote to the secretary general of the League to point out serious omissions in the two reports and to note that even according to the South Africans themselves, the fighting appeared to have been started by the Mandatory government and that the Bondelswarts were defending themselves. Further, the Society urged the PMC to hear "someone on behalf of the Hottentots" rather than only to hear from Major Herbst, "who took part in the attack."[93] Over the course of several days, PMC members closely questioned the South African representatives on

---

[91] PMC, *Minutes of the Second Session, 1922*, p. 10. The first opportunity for the PMC to comment on South Africa's policies came in 1922 but the South African government did not send anyone to represent the mandatory government at the PMC. South Africa was the only Mandatory administration which failed to send a representative to the PMC that year. In fact, nearly every mandatory government sent a high-ranking representative each year.

[92] League of Nations, Assembly Resolution Number 5, Geneva, 20 September 1922.

[93] Letter printed as Annex 8, PMC, *Minutes of the Third Session, 1923*, pp. 287–288.

events, focusing their inquiry on the deep roots of the trouble, the immediate causes of the uprising, South African conduct in repressing it, and the conditions of the Bondelswarts people following suppression of the rebellion.[94] After a relatively brief discussion of how the fighting arose and was conducted, PMC questioning concentrated on the political and economic causes of the dispute. PMC members asked why the Bondelswarts could not have some form of self-government. The South African representatives said that the Bondelswarts, though they wanted their own chief to be recognized, could not revert to a "primitive" system since the "tribes had been broken up by the previous government due to the constant wars in which they had engaged."[95] The minutes note that the PMC found South African arguments shifting and contradictory:

> The Chairman did not quite understand the conditions prevailing. At one moment it seemed that the natives had reached some degree of civilisation; at other times they seemed to be wholly barbarous. They found on the one hand that there was a tax on dogs, and on the other that there was no Customs ... The Commission was informed that cattle owners must pay a fine if their cattle were not vaccinated or branded, a regulation that seemed to show that the organisation of the country was fairly complete. They [the PMC] were now dealing with a question of credit and of advances, which was difficult to understand if the people in question were in a primitive stage.[96]

The PMC concluded that the uprising itself could have been prevented by better administration and that its "repression appears to have been carried out with excessive severity, and, had it been preceded by a demonstration of the overwhelming force at the command of the military authority, an immediate and perhaps bloodless surrender might have been anticipated."[97]

Upon learning of the PMC's forthcoming conclusions, the South African representative, Major Herbst, requested a second hearing, where he said: "I intended to let the case rest where we finished the other day ... I had not then considered that it was possible that we might get an adverse verdict on this matter from the Commission ... " Saying that

---

[94] In a departure from the usual style, where remarks of Commission members and mandatory representatives were summarized in the third person, the exchange between the South African representatives and the Commission members were apparently recorded and published verbatim. PMC, *Minutes of the Third Session, 1923*, 31 July, 1 August, and 7 August respectively, pp. 113–125; 126–136; 183–187.
[95] Ibid., p. 128.   [96] Ibid., p. 130.   [97] Ibid., p. 136.

the administrator, Hofmeyr, had done what nine out of ten administrators would have done in similar circumstances, Herbst tried to reframe the incident by arguing that the PMC should see the issue as one not of pre-existing native grievances and a just rebellion harshly crushed, but as the breach of law by the Bondelswarts. He continued:

> What would be the effect on an Administrator of such a censure coming from a body like the Permanent Mandates Commission? Could he possibly, with any self-respect, continue in occupation of the post? . . . Unless action against the Government is suppressed as speedily as possible, we cannot foresee the consequences . . . We still have natives there who are only impressed by show of force; that is all they recognise as appertaining to a government . . . I would ask the Commission to seriously consider the effect of an adverse criticism in South Africa. We are going to have an immediate outcry.[98]

Despite Herbst's plea, the PMC report submitted to the Council of the League and forwarded to the League Assembly, and the separate statement by PMC Chairman Alberto Théodoli, were critical of the South African conduct before, during, and especially after the rebellion. The Commission's report was more diplomatic than the chairman's statement, yet even it was critical of specific practices of the mandatory administration, including the dog tax and the administration's decree requiring natives to purchase branding irons for their cattle ("The whites actually received their branding-irons, but those which were bought by natives were kept by the Administration"). The report was particularly critical of the vagrancy law.

> The Vagrancy Law of 1920 as interpreted by the Administration made any native wandering abroad liable to arrest if he could not prove legal ownership of at least 10 head of cattle or 50 head of small stock.

> The magistrate was authorised, in lieu of the punishment prescribed, to adjudge the accused to a term of service on public works or to employment under any municipality or private person other than the complainant, for a term not exceeding that for which imprisonment might be imposed, at such wages as the magistrate deemed fair. This power of imposing forced labour for the benefit of private individuals in lieu of the sentence of the Court is a practice which cannot be approved.[99]

[98] Ibid., pp. 183–184, 186, 187.
[99] PMC, "Report on the Bondelswarts Rebellion," in PMC, *Minutes of the Third Session, 1923*, pp. 290–296: 293.

PMC Chairman Théodoli of Italy was more blunt in his assessment. He argued that the principles which govern mandates and colonies are different: "As far as the mandated territories are concerned, the Covenant of the League of Nations . . . has profoundly and substantially altered colonial law and colonial administration." Quoting the Covenant, Théodoli argued that the actions of governments ought to be in line with the purpose of the Mandate system, namely, "the well-being and development of less-advanced peoples." He said: "First in importance come the interests of the natives, second the interests of the whites." He argued that although the PMC did not have all the information it needed, "my fundamental impression is that the administration of the territory of South-West Africa, before, during, and after the incident, seems above all to have been concerned with maintaining its own authority in defence of the interests of the minority consisting of the white population." Chairman Théodoli concludes:

> The Administration ought, on the contrary, in my opinion from the beginning to have carried on a policy and adopted an administrative practice calculated to lessen the racial prejudice, which in those territories has always been the fundamental cause of the hostility which has invariably existed between the native population and the whites.
>
> I think, therefore, that the Administration has pursued a policy of force rather than of persuasion, and further, that this policy has always been conceived and applied in the interest of the colonists rather than in the interest of the natives.
>
> I admit that circumstances in the past, special conditions on the spot, and the particular characteristics of the population may make the task of the mandatory Power a very difficult one. My conscience, however, will not allow me to admit that these difficulties justify a departure from the principles of the mandate . . .[100]

On 23 August 1923, the South African representative to the League, E.H. Walton, replied to the PMC report and the chairman's statement, taking strong exception to the criticism in both.[101] As a result of the Commission's work, the Council of the League passed a resolution that, in diplomatic language, censored South Africa for its behavior in the affair and expressed its hope that, in the future, South Africa would

[100] "Statement made by the Chairman, Marquis Alberto Théodoli," in PMC, *Minutes of the Third Session, 1923,* p. 296.
[101] E.H. Walton, "Comments of the Accredited Representative of the Union of South Africa on the Commission's Report on the Bondelswarts Rebellion." Annexed to PMC, *Minutes of the Third Session, 1923.*

report improvement in the condition of the Bondelswarts. This might seem like very little. Still, the South African government protested the resolution.[102]

Though South West Africans continued to resist South African government the administration was much more moderate in response to protests, such as the conflict in Rehobeth in 1925 that could, like the Bondelswarts incident, have led to a massacre.[103] The PMC continued to watch the South African administration carefully and to note when it did not seem to be working in the spirit of the Mandate system. For example, in 1925, when the South African parliament enacted legislation that granted the territory's white population a measure of representative government, the PMC noted that this did not take the natives into account. In 1926 and 1927, the PMC, the Council of the League and the League Assembly all protested a phrase in the treaty between South Africa and Portugal, which settled the boundary between Angola and South West Africa, because the language of the treaty referred to South Africa's sovereignty over South West Africa. In 1933, when the South African Parliament proposed granting representation to the mandate's white population in the Union Parliament, the PMC, departing from its usual diplomatic language, criticized South Africa's administration in 1934. The PMC argued that turning South West Africa, in effect into the fifth province of South Africa was, "to undermine the principles of the mandate."[104] The South African government then stalled and eventually backed off under cover of a new South West Africa Commission which said that although such an arrangement would not violate the mandate, in any case it was not necessary to take such a step at that time. After the opinion of the South African commission on this point was communicated to the PMC in South Africa's annual report, the PMC then agreed to reserve judgment on the situation.[105]

[102] Wright, *Mandates Under the League*, p. 210.
[103] On the 1925 campaign of resistance by the Rehoboth community, a petition by the Rehoboth to the PMC, and South Africa's negotiated resolution of the dispute, see Wright, *Mandates Under the League*, pp. 210–211; Goldblatt, *History of South West Africa*, pp. 223–225. In 1922, members of the South West African Universal Negro Improvement Association and African Communities League (founded in Luderitz in 1921) went to Geneva to petition the League for black rule in South West Africa. Tony Emmett, "Popular Resistance in Namibia, 1920–5," in Brian Wood, ed., *Namibia, 1884–1984: Readings on Namibia's History and Society* (Lusaka: United Nations Institute for Namibia, 1988), pp. 224–258: 237.
[104] PMC, *Minutes of the Twenty-Seventh Session, 1934*, p. 63.
[105] PMC, *Minutes of the Thirty-First Session, 1937*, p. 192. Goldblatt, *History of South West Africa*, p. 235. Solomon Slonim, *South West Africa and the United Nations: An International Mandate in Dispute* (Baltimore: The Johns Hopkins University Press, 1973), p. 55.

South Africa had to regularly justify its behavior and publicly answer to the normative standards articulated by the PMC. The regularity and intensity of outside oversight by the PMC and the League held South West Africa under international scrutiny and made it accountable in ways that would not otherwise have been the case. Thus, while South West Africans were still treated badly, status as a mandate under the League probably prevented South Africa from annexing the territory and perhaps deterred the South African government from perpetrating even more terrible abuses on the African population.

Effects and effectiveness of the Mandate system

The impact of the Mandate system may be assessed on three levels. First, did conditions improve inside mandates? Second, did the Mandate system have a concrete impact on colonialism as a set of practices in non-mandate territories? Were the beliefs, arguments, and practices articulated and developed with regard to League mandates generalized beyond the mandate territories and put into effect in other, non-mandate, colonies? Of course, if conditions simultaneously improved in mandates and colonies, then we cannot establish a causal relationship from mandates to other colonies unless it was the same set of beliefs that led to the Mandate system which also affected the general conception of colonialism and led to changes in all colonies. Third, did the Mandate system (inadvertently) affect how colonialism was understood, and thus reframe the colonial system?

The answer to the first question, is a qualified yes. International supervision of the mandatory powers by the PMC and the League did affect the conduct of the mandatory powers in individual mandate territories. As envisaged by the language of the covenant, some class A mandate territories achieved independence, specifically Iraq in 1932, and Transjordan and Lebanon in 1944 and 1946.[106] However, this

---

[106] Iraqis rebelled in 1920 against British rule, costing the British 400 lives to squash the uprising. There were disagreements over controlling Iraq's newly discovered oil resources and the British established a monarchy in Iraq where there had been none before. The same year that Iraq became a League mandate territory, the Kurds of northern Iraq were promised autonomy in the Treaty of Sevres and the opportunity, at a later date, to apply to the League for status as a sovereign state. The exact boundaries of Iraq in the Kurdish region were disputed with Turkey, the former colonizers, until the League sided with Iraq in 1925 (with the provisos that Turkey would get 10 percent of Iraqi oil revenues from the Kurdish area and that the rights of the Kurdish population would be respected). Even after formal independence from Britain in 1932, foreign affairs were still controlled by Whitehall.

"independence" was not always complete. In the case of Iraq, for example, Britain retained control of foreign policy and defense until after World War II. But nominal independence was hardly the outcome for the majority of League mandate territories.

However, if most mandates did not become independent, did the Mandate system protect the inhabitants of mandate territories from the abuses that were typical of colonialism? One key point of control in the complex colonial system was government regulation of labor, and this is implicitly recognized by the attention the PMC gave to labor in its questionnaires and oversight. Did labor conditions improve for the subjects of mandates? In one important respect – at least in Africa – condition for labor was essentially the same regardless of colonial status: colonial and mandatory governments alike continued to change the system of labor from subsistence to wage labor, and forced labor was a feature of both systems. Indeed, as labor historians have shown, the coerced proletarianization of native labor, whether through forced labor or taxation, is the great legacy of colonialism all over the world.

On the other hand, there were certainly important differences between colonial and mandatory labor practices. For example, the recruitment and periods of forced labor in mandates was regularly scrutinized by the PMC. The period of forced labor required in the Belgian mandate territory of Ruanda declined in the late 1920s and early 1930s from 29 to 13 days per year while forced labor requirements remained high in Belgium's other African territory, the Congo, where it reached 120 days in World War II. Indeed, compulsory labor grew in some non-mandate territories: forced labor went from 7 to 12 days per year in French West and East Africa during the interwar period and in the Portuguese colonies in Africa forced labor was officially six months per year for men 14–60 years old. Head taxes in the Portuguese colonies could further increase the amount of labor required, since the tax was payable with three months of labor per year.[107]

The greater length of forced labor in the Belgian Congo colony versus forced labor in a Belgian mandate raises the question of whether there was any transfer of attitudes from mandate to colony. Were innovations in mandate policy or the notion of sacred trust extended to non-mandate colonies? At least in Britain, the bureaucratic distinction between colonies and mandates was not firm. The General Division

[107] C. Coquery-Vidrovitch, "The Colonial Economy of the Former French, Belgian and Portuguese Zones, 1914–35," in Boahen, ed., *Africa Under Colonial Domination*, pp. 351–381: 360, 363, 367.

of Britain's Colonial Office had the responsibility of dealing with the League mandates. British Secretary of State for the Colonies Ormsby-Gore, who had previously served on the Permanent Mandates Commission, told the Foreign Policy Committee of the Cabinet in 1937, that although Article 22 formally applied only to mandates, the principles "were, in practice, identical with the principles by which His Majesty's Government was guided in its general administration of the Colonies."[108] Some transfer of principles and practice was also inevitable in cases such as British mandate territories and colonies in East Africa, which were economically and politically integrated.[109] And, as will be discussed in Chapter 7, the Mandate system influenced the treatment of colonies in the later United Nations Trusteeship System and the Declaration on Non-Self-Governing Territories.

But, most concretely, the Mandate system appears to have influenced labor practices in all colonies. After 1927, four members of the PMC sat on the newly created Native Labor Committee of the International Labor Organization. The Native Labor Committee focused on forced labor and long-term labor contracts in all colonies and dependencies, not just in mandates. As Duncan Hall argues, the conventions on labor that came out of the Native Labor Committee's work "aimed at extending to dependencies in general safeguards first given international recognition in the provisions of the League mandates."[110] In 1930 the ILO Conference adopted the "Forced Labour Convention" with 93 votes in favor and 63 abstentions (including France, Belgium, and Portugal); "no delegations could bring themselves to a principled defense of forced labor."[111] The Convention's goal was the suppression of forced labor "in all its forms within the shortest possible period."[112]

Did the Mandate system affect how colonialism itself was understood and framed? The Mandate system was supervised by men and women like Lord Frederick Lugard of Britain, who, prior to his service on the Permanent Mandates Commission, was a colonial officer and the governor

---

[108] D. J. Morgan, *The Official History of Colonial Development, Vol. 1: The Origins of British Aid Policy, 1924–1945* (London: Macmillan Press, 1980), p. 17.

[109] Hall, *Mandates, Dependencies, and Trusteeship*, pp. 232–233.

[110] Ibid., p. 250.

[111] Frederick Cooper, *Decolonization and African Society: The Labor Question in French and British Africa* (Cambridge: Cambridge University Press, 1996), p. 29.

[112] The Forced Labor Convention said that forced labor could not be used for private purposes, but only for public works for at most sixty days per year, with wages and limited hours. The League of Nations Slavery Convention of 1926 also mentioned forced labor in the context of preventing forced labor "from developing into conditions analogous to slavery."

of Nigeria, for Britain. Lugard's notion of the Mandate system was aggressive humanitarianism, rather than reform. "British methods," he said, "have not in all cases produced ideal results, but I am profoundly convinced that there can be no question but that British rule has promoted the happiness and welfare of the primitive races."[113] Lugard believed in British colonialism: "We hold these countries because it is the genius of our race to colonize, to trade, and to govern. The task in which England is engaged in the tropics – alike in Africa and the East – has become part of her tradition, and she has ever given of her best in the cause of liberty and civilization."[114] Could he and the other true believers in colonialism who served on the PMC have intended that the Mandate system would change the way colonialism was understood and ultimately undermine the institution? Probably not. Nevertheless, that was the unintended consequence.

Britain's reforms in its largest colony, India, are an example of the effects of the Mandate system on non-mandate colonies. Indians, of course, had long fought for autonomy, and reforms had begun well before the Mandate system was put in place, for example, with the mutiny of Indian soldiers in the Bengal Army in 1857 and the formation of the nationalist Indian National Congress in 1885. British reforms allowed greater Indian participation in "responsible" government with the Indian Councils Acts of 1892 and 1909, but they were not enough for most activist Indians. Mahatma Gandhi, who gradually developed his ideas of non-violent resistance, *satyagraha*, during his decades of activism on behalf of Indians in South Africa, returned to India in 1915 and took up his moral campaign there. The 1917 Montague Declaration called for the "gradual development of self governing institutions," but two years later the British government in India passed the Rowlett Acts which continued the political restrictions that Britain had imposed during World War I.

Indians peacefully protested these restrictions but the British cracked down on the protesters. The most famous incident occurred when, in Amritsar on 13 April 1919, British General Dyer ordered his troops to fire, without warning, on several thousand people who were peacefully disobeying a ban on public meetings. Ultimately, the soldiers killed 379 people and wounded more than 1,000 other protesters. An official British inquiry into the massacre and subsequent floggings during martial law,

[113] Lord Lugard, *The Dual Mandate in British Tropical Africa* (New York: Frank Cass (1922) 1965), p. 618.
[114] Ibid., p. 619.

found against Dyer.[115] Thus, while similar crackdowns had been unremarkable, the reframing of the colonial mission, in part exemplified and in part generated by the League of Nations Mandate System, meant that the Dyer's action was understood differently than before.

In part as a reaction to charges of hypocrisy, Britain again reformed its India policy with the 1919 Government of India Act that enunciated a principle of "dyarchy," where "some spheres, such as education and health, were 'transferred' to Indian control at the provincial level, while others such as public order were 'reserved' and remained under British control."[116] In 1924, the Royal Commission on Indianization set goals for increasing the numbers of Indians in the civil service and police force. From 1927 to 1930, the Simon (Parliamentary) Commission developed a plan to introduce representative government to India, though there were no Indian representatives on the Simon Commission. The non-violent movement in India, protesting the lack of a direct voice in constitutional reform, grew to have thousands of adherents in the 1930s and staged many non-violent protests to British rule, attracting world-wide attention. The 1935 Government of India Act gave an Indian federal government nominal domestic authority but retained British control over foreign and military affairs.[117] Thus, Britain reformed the governance of its largest colony in parallel with the reforms it undertook in its mandates.

Conclusion

There are several conclusions to draw from this discussion of the Mandate system. First, public pressure, deployed in the form of ethical argument, led to the innovation of mandates. Second, ethical arguments, which took place in the forum of the Permanent Mandates Commission, were part of the process of institutionalizing reformist beliefs. Third, this institutionalization within the Mandate System was generalized to colonies through various mechanisms – colonial administration, imitation, and international law.

This last point is controversial, but contemporary observers thought that mainstream beliefs about colonialism shifted because of the Mandate system and in fact consciously sought to extend mandate

---

[115] See Chamberlain, *Decolonization*, on this incident, p.16.

[116] Ibid., pp. 6, 16.

[117] The first provincial elections in 1937 resulted in Congress Party victories in six of eleven provinces and Gandhi's party could therefore claim significant political support.

principles to all colonies. For example, in a report to the Grotius Society, James C. Hale claimed that the Mandate system was better than colonialism for inhabitants of mandates. Under the Mandate system, Hale argued, "the natives' rights are more fully protected, white settlers are prevented from exploiting the natural resources of the territory to their sole advantage, and all States members of the League of Nations are given an equal voice in this supervision, with a view to maintaining the trust undertaken by the League on behalf of civilisation."[118]

Notably, one of Hale's early reports on the Mandate system was subtitled, "A Study in International Colonial Supervision." Claiming that it was "better than the old colonial system," Hale argued that, "The Mandatory is merely carrying out a trust, the avowed aim of which is to help the inhabitants of the territory to stand by themselves, and not to govern them for its sole advantage."[119] Hale's report the following year was titled, "The Reform and Extension of the Mandates System: A Legal Solution to the Colonial Problem." Hale said: "despite the diversity of colonial aims in the nineteenth century, it is clear that since the institution of the Mandate System, the governing principle behind all colonial administration is that of trusteeship."[120] Hale believed that colonialism was already quite changed because of the Mandate system.

> In other words, several of the colonial Powers of the present day, departing from the principle of the exploitation of colonies for economic purposes, tend towards the principle that they are administering the territories with a view to furthering the interests of the natives and raising their standard of civilisation, so that they may one day take their place in the community of nations. The guardianship is to be seen in the increase in educational and health services, in the granting of greater powers to native authorities, and to the encouragement of native hierarchies.[121]

The table on which arguments about colonialism occurred was thus forever changed because of the League Mandate system. The idea of a Mandate system, and the eventual end of colonialism through such a system, was no longer simply the opinion of the colonial reformers in social movement organizations like the Anti-Slavery and Aborigines

[118] Hale, "The Creation and Application of the Mandate System," pp. 185–284: 204.
[119] Ibid., p. 282.
[120] James C. Hale, "The Reform and Extension of the Mandates System: A Legal Solution to the Colonial Problem," *Transactions of the Grotius Society*, vol. XXVI (London: Grotius Society, 1941), pp. 153–210: 155.
[121] Ibid., p. 155.

Protection Society. Rather, there was now a "colonial problem" which could be solved by extending the Mandate system. Or as Quincy Wright suggested in 1930:

> The question of extending the system to other areas in the administrative sense is of less importance than the extension of its principles. The system has already resulted in wider recognition of the principle of trusteeship, that dependencies should be administered in the interests of their inhabitants; in the principle of tutelage, that the cultivation of the capacity for self-government is such an interest; of the principle of international mandate, that states are responsible to the international community for the exercise of power over backward peoples even if that responsibility is not fully organized.[122]

In sum, at the end of World War I, the political rule, military occupation, and economic domination which characterized colonialism in previous centuries was still in place, and with the successful crushing of anti-colonial revolts that occurred during the war, the colonizers were generally quite secure militarily in their colonies. Yet, in one of the great reversals of international politics, the leaders of the same powers that practiced colonialism on a scale never before seen in the world, would construct, with the League of Nations Mandate system, an institutional mechanism that would gradually deconstruct colonialism. This was an outcome the architects of the Mandate system never intended, nor apparently even foresaw, yet it was a consequence of their ethical and practical arguments. Colonialism was thus denormalized, delegitimized, and an alternative reformist conception was put on the table and gradually institutionalized. As Edward Grigg told members of the British House of Commons in 1935, "The attack on our position in Africa is not, in my opinion, coming from Africans or from anybody outside ourselves. It is coming from within our own ranks...If that kind of propaganda goes on it will undermine the peace of the Colonial Empire, not because of its effects in Africa, but because of its great effect upon ourselves."[123]

[122] Wright, *Mandates Under the League*, p. 588. A later observer wrote: "The mandated territories became colonial showcases because of the amount of publicity given to them. The impact of specific colonial policies extended beyond the boundaries of the particular mandate. The care taken with the pronouncements of 'native policy' in the mandated territory of Tanganyika, for example, had repercussions in Kenya and Uganda." Wm. Roger Louis, *Imperialism at Bay: The United States and the Decolonization of the British Empire, 1941–1945* (New York: Oxford University Press, 1978), p. 93.
[123] Edward Grigg, quoted in R.D. Pearce, *The Turning Point in Africa: British Colonial Policy 1938–48* (London: Frank Cass, 1982), p. 12.

As opinion shifted from supporting empire to questioning colonialism, it was no longer possible for colonizers to simply massacre those who disagreed with colonial government. Indeed, when unrest led to deaths in colonies, it was increasingly shocking. Mandate became a new standard of conduct against which all colonial administration was measured. When colonial administrations failed to show progress of the sort expected in mandates, as was made evident in reports on labor unrest, poverty, and malnutrition in the British colonies in the West Indies and Africa during the 1930s, colonial powers were understood to be failing a sacred trust.[124] The questioning occasioned by these reports led to commissions to study various colonial "problems," gradual reforms, and the inauguration of "development" assistance to the colonies. This shift is captured in the writings of a staunch advocate of colonialism for economic gain, the prominent French colonial official, Albert Sarraut. In his 1931 book, *Grandeur et servitudes coloniales*, he wrote: "The natives are people like ourselves. They must be treated as such, which means securing for them the basic guarantees of such individual and personal rights as we claim for ourselves. This is a categorical demand of association policy: it has moral and practical consequences." Exemplifying the mix of motives and beliefs which characterized the period (pragmatic and moral reformism), Sarraut continued:

> Secondly, the colonized races must be protected from the diseases which strike and decimate them and which reduce the yield of this mighty workforce. This is the task of medical aid. They should be protected against acts of violence and fraud which may threaten their person, work or possessions. From this arises, with the concern for general security in the country, the effort towards a guarantee for personal security through the work of a non-partisan, regular judiciary ... The native worker must be protected appropriately by means of humane work regulations. The moral and spiritual value of this mass of human beings must be raised. This means the development of education....

> Finally, our protégés must be rendered capable of taking part to a legitimate and appropriate extent in the administration of their own countries. It must therefore be made possible for them to hold public office, and the setting-up of representative bodies must enable them to express their wishes. In a word, they should be associates, and not

[124] See Pearce, *The Turning Point in Africa*, pp. 17–18; Cooper, *Decolonization and African Society*, pp. 57–109; Morgan, *The Official History of Colonial Development*, vol. I.

serfs, of the power that has taken the fate of their fatherland into its hands.[125]

The idea of colonialism had thus moved from mere exploitation to development with an eye toward greater self-determination. The view of colonial subjects had changed from less than human to peoples with rights, although in the view of many, they still needed paternalistic guidance. These transformations in belief in turn created greater openings for anti-colonial independence movements to argue and organize politically for self-government which they were able to exploit in the coming decades.

[125] Quoted in Hans Ansprenger, *The Dissolution of Colonial Empires* (New York: Routledge, 1981), pp. 79–80.

7 Self-determination

Empires fall; but imperialism is ever resurrected.[1]

The British did not relinquish their Empire by accident. They ceased to believe in it.[2]

Both the Colonial Office and the Colonial Governments have been caught in the ever-present struggle of our nation to resolve the dilemma of being autocratic abroad and democratic at home.[3]

Many histories and analyses of decolonization stress the post-World War II era, which seems sensible since this is the period when most decolonization occurred – in seventy territories between 1945 and 1979, many of these by 1960 – and when anti-colonial normative beliefs were fully articulated.[4] Yet although European colonialism in Africa and Asia looked strong in 1945, the foundations for the change in argument, belief, and culture were laid well before that period. Between 1750 and the

[1] Ronald Robinson and John Gallagher with Alice Denny, *Africa and the Victorians: The Official Mind of Imperialism* (London: Macmillan, 1961), p. v.
[2] A.J.P. Taylor quoted in correspondence to Wm. Roger Louis, *Imperialism at Bay: The United States and the Decolonization of the British Empire, 1941–1945* (New York: Oxford University Press, 1978), p. xiii.
[3] F.D. Corfield, chief native commissioner, in *Report on Native Affairs for Kenya: Historical Survey of the Origins and Growth of Mau Mau* (London: Her Majesty's Stationery Office, 1960), p. 28. Quoted in Roxanne Lynn Doty, *Imperial Encounters: The Politics of Representation in North–South Relations* (Minneapolis: University of Minnesota, 1996), p. 106.
[4] For example, Robert H. Jackson, "The Weight of Ideas in Decolonization: Normative Change in International Relations," in Judith Goldstein and Robert Keohane, eds., *Ideas and Foreign Policy: Beliefs, Institutions, and Political Change* (Ithaca: Cornell University Press, 1993), pp. 111–138; John Darwin, *Britain and Decolonization: The Retreat from Empire in the Post-War World* (New York: St. Martin's Press, 1988); Henry S. Wilson, *African Decolonization* (New York: Edward Arnold, 1994). Exceptions to post-1945 era focus are Franz Ansprenger, *The Dissolution of Colonial Empires* (New York: Routledge, 1989) and Antonio Cassese, *Self-determination of Peoples: A Legal Reappraisal* (Cambridge: Cambridge University Press, 1995).

1930s, arguments made by reformers against the fundamental constitutive practices of colonialism – slavery and forced labor – challenged and ultimately led to changes in important aspects of the institution, so that it was no longer possible to view colonialism itself as legitimate.[5] These changes in colonial practices were significant enough to say that the colonialism which ended in the mid-twentieth century was not quite the same institution that had reached its zenith in the eighteenth and nineteenth centuries.

Post-World War II decolonization may be considered the implementation and extension of already articulated normative beliefs and arguments. Thus, at this point, much of my explanatory purchase rests on path dependent processes and institutionalization. Yet one cannot ignore the events of World War II and the arguments and events of the post-1945 period, if only because colonialism was still in place at the end of the war. Nearly 600 million people lived in colonies, mandates, or protectorates in 1945: Britain had over 60 overseas colonies, mandates, or protectorates including over 450 million people; France had over 30 colonies, mandates, or protectorates, controlling over 65 million people; the Dutch had 3 colonies with 53 million people.[6]

Several processes contributed to making the post-1945 period the era of decolonization and, with the exception of continuing attention on South West Africa/Namibia, they are the focus in this chapter. I emphasize the relationship between ethical argument, normative belief, colonial practice, and political opportunity. Again, my approach is intended to highlight the process of argument and the role, in particular, of ethical arguments in the growth of anti-colonial sentiments, the decline of racist beliefs, decreasing public support for maintaining colonialism, and the institutionalization of the normative belief in self-determination. Though some may find the description too thick, it is surely too thin since the force of my argument about ethical arguments, and the role of argument more generally, rests on the content of arguments and the institutionalization of beliefs in the activities of the United Nations and the practices of colonial governments. Four trends are highlighted: stronger

[5] This did not pose a fundamental legitimation crisis for the colonial regimes themselves so much as create a policy legitimation crisis. To solve the crisis, colonialism had to be at least reformed if not ended.

[6] Spain had five colonies including Spanish Morocco with over 1 million people; the Portuguese Empire included eight colonies with about 11 million people; Belgium had two African colonies with about 14 million people. See Muriel E. Chamberlain, *The Longman Companion to European Decolonization in the Twentieth Century* (London: Longman, 1998).

292

anti-colonial resistance; the delegitimation of racist beliefs; ethical arguments leading to declining public support for colonialism within the metropole; and the continuing institutionalization of normative beliefs in, for example, the United Nations Trusteeship System.

First, anti-colonial movements grew in both the West and the colonies themselves after 1945. Anti-colonial activists used ethical arguments, political organizing and military force. This is sometimes described as a sudden political awakening, though in most cases, anti-colonial political organizations had deep roots in previous movements that had greater or lesser degrees of success under colonialism. In the post-1945 period, anti-colonial activists achieved greater success in organizing colonial populations, they increased coordination across colonies, and in some cases their associated guerrilla movements acquired better military equipment. Most anti-colonial movements simply wanted the exit of colonial administrations, and self-government along the lines of a nationalist political program that took state sovereignty as a given. Few successful movements had in mind anything more radical. In addition, there was greater international solidarity, especially among descendants of African slaves in the Americas, Pan-Africanists, who identified with colonial people and pressed for the modification and ultimately the end of colonialism.

Second, during the interwar and post-war period, racist beliefs that underpinned colonialism were undermined as "scientific" racism and social Darwinism were challenged within the scholarly community and wider liberal culture. This coincided with the increased emphasis on political and human rights during and after the war. In other words, the political and cultural basis for anti-colonial arguments shifted from regarding "natives" as inferior or non-human, to at least potentially politically equal. Third, public support within colonial powers for maintaining colonialism declined as a consequence of the previous generation's successful ethical argumentation regarding colonialism.

Fourth, though the Mandate system died with the League of Nations, the institutional momentum and mechanisms of the system were carried forward and enlarged by the United Nations with, for instance, the formation of the United Nations Trusteeship System and UN oversight of "non-self-governing" territories. In addition, the UN began in the late 1940s to monitor and in some cases conduct plebiscites in UN Trust Territories and colonies, ensuring that inhabitants were at least consulted about their fates. By the 1960s, the UN was a force for decolonization and the normative belief in decolonization was backed by sanctions against those states, especially Portugal and South Africa, which continued a practice viewed increasingly as an anachronism: unmodified colonialism. Continuing to focus on South West Africa as an indicator and illustration of the role of particular legal arguments, and because South West Africa's situation became important in changing the attitudes and practices of the UN, I discuss early international efforts to change the status of South West Africa.

World War II and colonial arguments: changing opportunity

Even during World War II, it was not clear that colonialism would soon end. The war heightened the actual and perceived importance of colonies to the metropole, especially for France and Britain. Speaking in San Francisco after the war, Great Britain's Lord Cranborne "maintained that liberty could not have been preserved in the Second World War without" colonial empire.[7] As they had during World War I, both France and Britain relied on the raw materials and food produced in the colonies, conscripting workers to boost production. Further, hundreds of thousands of Africans served in the British and French armies, many serving outside Africa. For example, by June 1940, almost 10 percent of the French army in France was African.[8] More than 370,000 Africans served in the British armed forces and tens of thousands more worked as forced labor on farms and in factories.[9] Indians also served for Britain in Europe, Africa, and Asia. Even non-combatant Belgium increased the use of forced labor, requiring 120 days compulsory labor in Congo, its African colony, and in Ruanda-Urundi, its mandate territory.[10]

War also catalyzed both positive and negative changes for the colonies. Poor wage and labor conditions during the war provoked

[7] Harold K. Jacobson, "The United Nations and Colonialism: A Tentative Appraisal," *International Organization* 16 (Winter 1962), 37–56. Reprinted in Leland M. Goodrich and David A. Kay, eds., *International Organization: Politics and Process* (Madison: University of Wisconsin Press, 1973), pp. 287–306: 306; Harold Macmillan on the "War Effort and Colonial Policy," a speech to the House of Commons, reprinted in A.N. Porter and A.J. Stockwell, eds., *British Imperial Policy, 1938–64, Volume 1, 1938–51* (London: Macmillan Press, 1987), pp. 109–124.
[8] John D. Hargreaves, *Decolonization in Africa* (London: Longman, 1988), p. 49.
[9] See Immanuel Geiss, *Pan-Africanism: A History of Pan-Africanism in America, Europe and Africa* (New York: Africana, 1974), p. 365. Frederick Cooper, *Decolonization and African Society: The Labor Question in French and British Africa* (Cambridge: Cambridge University Press, 1996), p. 125.
[10] Michael Crowder, "Africa Under British and Belgian Domination, 1935–45," in Ali Mazrui, ed., *Africa Since 1935* (Berkeley: University of California, 1993), pp. 76–101: 94.

strikes and desertion although in some cases, wages were raised, and work conditions improved to encourage greater worker compliance and productivity.[11] As it had during World War I, labor organizing in the colonies became an increasingly effective form of political activism, as labor saw it had greater leverage. Anti-colonial activism during the war occasioned alarm for the colonizers, as when the British viceroy in India, Lord Linlithgow, wrote to Winston Churchill on 31 August 1942: "I am engaged here in meeting by far the most serious rebellion since 1857, the gravity and extent of which we have so far concealed from the world for reasons of military security."[12] While greater political freedom was allowed in India during the war, in other cases the autonomy won between the wars was taken away during World War II. For example, the former British mandate Iraq, given independence in 1932, was occupied by Britain from June 1941 to the end of World War II because the Iraqi government refused to break off ties with the Axis powers.

The British White Paper "Statement of Policy on Colonial Development and Welfare" of February 1940, which became the basis for the subsequent Colonial Development and Welfare Act of July 1940, outlined a policy of providing assistance to the colonies so that they could improve their welfare. As Malcolm MacDonald, then minister of health but formerly of the Colonial Office, noted, the previous Colonial Development Act of 1929 was enacted "in order to stimulate that development mostly to bring additional work to idle hands in this country." The 1940 Act, he argued, "breaks new ground. It established the duty of taxpayers . . . to contribute directly and for its own sake towards the development in the widest sense of the word of colonial peoples for whose good government the taxpayers of this country are ultimately responsible."[13] This was a significant financial commitment: the Act provided for £55 million over ten years. The goals of colonialism had become rather like the goals of the Mandate system, at least rhetorically, although the colonial system itself was not fundamentally questioned at this time by the British Cabinet or most members of Parliament.[14]

[11] Cooper, *Decolonization and African Society*, pp. 110–166.
[12] Quoted in Louis, *Imperialism at Bay*, p. 8.
[13] Speech in the House of Commons by Malcolm MacDonald on the Colonial Development and Welfare Bill, 21 May 1940, *Hansard Parliamentary Debates* (1939–1940), vol. 361, cols. 41–48, 50–51, in Porter and Stockwell, eds., *British Imperial Policy*, pp. 94–100: 97.
[14] "Statement of Policy on Colonial Development and Welfare," discussed in D.J. Morgan, *The Official History of Colonial Development, Vol. 1: The Origins of British Aid Policy, 1924–1945* (London: Macmillan, 1980).

On the other hand, during World War II the Allies' public rhetoric was filled with calls for self-determination, and colonialism became a significant partisan political issue in Britain during the war. For example, the Soviet Union championed a right to self-determination, consistent with V.I. Lenin and Joseph Stalin's arguments in favor of it, and pushed the most radical of any government's positions on decolonization.[15] The British Labour Party announced in February 1940 its view that:

> For colonial peoples, Labour demands that everywhere they should move forward, as speedily as possible, towards self-government. In the administration of colonies not yet ready for self-government the interests of the native population should be paramount, and should be safeguarded through an extension and strengthening of the Mandate System. There must be equal opportunity of access for all peaceful peoples to raw materials and markets in these colonial territories.[16]

The Atlantic Charter signed by Winston Churchill and Franklin Roosevelt in August 1941 stated, in part, that they "desire to see no territorial changes that do not accord with the freely expressed wishes of the peoples concerned," and that they "respect the right of all people to choose the form of government under which they will live; and they wish to see sovereign rights and self-government restored to those who have been forcibly deprived of them."[17] African independence activists then used the Atlantic Charter to frame arguments for self-determination and independence. For example, a prominent Nigerian activist, Nnamdi Azikiwe, published "The Charter and British West Africa," and a member of the legislative council in Ghana, G.E. Moore, argued in 1943 that if there was "the right of all peoples to choose the form of government under which they live it was a right to which the Africans share."[18]

The parts of the Atlantic Charter that dealt with self-determination sparked immediate debate. Not surprisingly, the Labour Party claimed the Charter applied to the colonies, as well as to Europe (meta-argument), while members of the Foreign and Colonial Offices often

---

[15] Cassese, *Self-determination of Peoples*, pp. 14–19.

[16] Labour quoted in James C. Hale, "The Reform and Extension of the Mandates System: A Legal Solution to the Colonial Problem," *Transactions of the Grotius Society*, vol. XXVI (London: Grotius Society, 1941), pp. 153–210: 161.

[17] Atlantic Charter, reprinted in Porter and Stockwell, eds., *British Imperial Policy*, pp. 101–102.

[18] Quoted in Jean Suret-Canale and A. Adu Boahen, "West Africa 1945–1960," in Ali Mazrui, ed., *Africa Since 1935* (Berkeley: University of California, 1993), pp. 161–191: 161.

disagreed about how to deal with the implications of the Atlantic Charter.[19] Although President Roosevelt argued that the Atlantic Charter's emphasis on self-determination was universally applicable, in September 1941 Tory Prime Minister Churchill told the House of Commons that the Atlantic Charter was intended to apply only to the states under Nazi control and was "quite a separate problem from the progressive evolution of self-governing institutions in regions whose peoples owe allegiance to the British crown."[20] On 27 October 1942, Roosevelt said the Charter applied "to all humanity."[21] On 10 November 1942, Churchill said, "I have not become the King's First Minister in order to preside over the liquidation of the British Empire."[22] Churchill was not alone in the British government in publicly resisting the extension of the Atlantic Charter to colonies. Home Secretary Herbert Morrison, in remarks published in the *Manchester Guardian* in January 1943, said: "It would be ignorant, dangerous nonsense to talk about grants of full self-government to many of the dependent territories for some time to come. In those instances it would be like giving a child of ten a latch key, a bank account, and a shot-gun."[23] In private, the secretary of state for the colonies wrote to the deputy prime minister:

> The truth, I suppose, is that we do not think the Atlantic Charter at present applicable in its entirety to Colonial territories. There is, for instance, the principle of self-determination, which finds a prominent place in the Charter. Can it possibly be said that the African Colonies are fit for the application of this principle? Or the West Indies? Or the Pacific Islands? ... The Atlantic Charter was originally intended, as I understand it, to be concerned primarily with the European countries at present overrun by Hitler. They are adult nations, capable of deciding their own fate. No doubt, the time may come when even the most backward of our Colonies [will] also become adult nations. But at present they are children and must be treated as such. Ought we not to say so, so as to avoid further misunderstanding?[24]

---

[19] On some of the memos between British colonial officials regarding the application of the Atlantic Charter to colonies, see D.J. Morgan, *The Official History of Colonial Development, Vol. 5: Guidance Towards Self-Government in British Colonies, 1941–1971* (London: Macmillan, 1980), pp. 1–5.

[20] Churchill's remarks reprinted in Porter and Stockwell, eds., *British Imperial Policy*, pp. 103–105: 105. Also see Heather A. Wilson, *International Law and the Use of Force by National Liberation Movements* (Oxford: Clarendon Press, 1988), p. 58.

[21] Quoted in Morgan, *The Official History of Colonial Development*, vol. I, p. xxvii.

[22] Quoted in ibid.   [23] Quoted in Louis, *Imperialism at Bay*, p. 14.

[24] Secretary of State for the Colonies, Cranborne, to Deputy Prime Minister Atlee, 14 January 1943, in Porter and Stockwell, eds., *British Imperial Policy*, p. 142.

But it was difficult to prevent the Atlantic Charter from being app-lied to Britain's colonies because important elements of the colonial institution were already denormalized and delegitimized. Like the US, New Zealand's and Australia's political leadership were in favor of ex-tending the Mandate system in some way; only South Africa and France supported the British position. Despite Churchill's reluctance, the US and Britain did discuss colonial policy at ministerial and head of state levels. To clarify the issue, the US and Britain drafted a Joint Declaration on colonial policy in 1943, promising that "Parent" or "Trustee" states would "guide and develop the social, economic and political institutions of the Colonial peoples until they are able without danger to themselves and others to discharge the responsibilities of government."[25]

The fact that the legitimacy of colonialism was in increasingly deep trouble in Britain is also illustrated by British government discussions during 1944 about whether to renew and extend the 1940 Colonial De-velopment and Welfare Act. The argument against extending the act turned in part on the expense of colonial welfare during the war. The contribution of the colonies to the war effort was noted with apprecia-tion but finances were still tight. While the private exchanges within the government over the Act focus on the amount of money involved, they also mention the concern of legitimizing British colonial government. For example, Colonial Secretary Oliver Stanley wrote to Chancellor of the Exchequer John Anderson: "I make no pretence, however, that this is going to be a profitable transaction on a purely financial calculation. The overriding reason why I feel that these proposals are essential is the necessity to justify our position as a Colonial Power."[26] In explain-ing how he could not whole-heartedly support the request to boost the colonial development budget – because of the expense involved – but could support a smaller increase, Anderson told Stanley, "I recognise the desirability of making some substantial gesture to justify ourselves before world opinion as a great Colonial power and also to assure the Colonies themselves of our intentions."[27] In other words, while the is-sue was ostensibly the amount of the grants to colonies, the pressure to make substantial grants was evidence of the problem of justifying colonial government. This was also well illustrated when Stanley, in a

[25] Quoted in Morgan, *The Official History of Colonial Development*, vol. V, p. 8.
[26] Secretary of State for the Colonies to Chancellor of the Exchequer, 21 September 1944 in Porter and Stockwell, eds., *British Imperial Policy*, pp. 202–205: 204.
[27] Chancellor of the Exchequer to Secretary of State for the Colonies, in Porter and Stockwell, eds., *British Imperial Policy*, pp. 206–207: 206.

secret memorandum to the War Cabinet arguing for a larger commitment than that recommended by the chancellor of the exchequer, made ethical, identity, and practical appeals in favor of increasing expenditures on colonial welfare.

> 9. I am not pretending that the assistance to the Colonies which I propose will not impose some burden upon this country. I do, however, feel that the Colonial Empire means so much to us that we should be prepared to assume some burden for its future. If we are unable or unwilling to do so, are we justified in retaining, or shall we be able to retain, a Colonial Empire? The burden, however, is infinitesimal compared to the gigantic sums in which we are and shall be dealing. Nor is the apparent burden wholly real. If these sums are wisely spent, and the plans devoted to increasing the real productive power of the Colonies, there will in the long run accrue considerable benefit to us, either in the form of increased exports to us of commodities which otherwise we should have to obtain from hard currency countries, or in the form of increased exports from the Colonies, as part of the sterling area to the hard currency countries outside.
>
> 10. But I am not basing my argument on material gains to ourselves, important as I think these may be. My feeling is that in the years to come, without the Commonwealth and Empire, this country will play a small role in world affairs, and that here we have an opportunity which may never recur, at a cost which is not extravagant, of setting the Colonial Empire on lines of development which will keep it in close and loyal contact with us. To say now in 1945 that with these great stakes at issue we shall not be able to afford £15 million in 1949, or £20 million in 1953, is a confession of our national impotence in the future.[28]

Stanley argued, "Finally, it is the moment at which to kill the enemy propaganda lie that the policy announced in 1940 was forced on us by our critical situation and that we never meant to implement it. Nothing would better confirm our faith in our sincerity than that at the height of our success we should confirm and amplify this policy which was first announced in the depth of our disaster."[29] Ultimately the Act was renewed and the amount increased to £120 million over the period of 1945–1956.[30] Thus, by the end of the war, colonialism was delegitimized to the extent that a reformist agenda was dominant in the Anglo-American world.

---

[28] Stanley Memorandum of 15 November 1944 quoted in ibid., pp. 208–211: 210–211.
[29] Louis, *Imperialism at Bay*, p. 102.   [30] Also see ibid., pp. 101–102.

Similarly, the French were reluctantly moved to take colonial reform seriously, although during the war it was not clear they would do so. General Charles de Gaulle and other French exiles explicitly declared their desire to win back and keep all their colonies. De Gaulle told Roosevelt, "I know that you are preparing to aid France materially, and that aid will be valuable to her. But it is in the political realm that she must recover her vigor, her self-reliance, and consequently, her role. How can she do this ... if she loses her African and Asian territories ... if the settlement of the war imposes on her the psychology of the vanquished?"[31]

But, during the war, colonial reform reluctantly became French policy. De Gaulle promised in 1941 to give independence to France's League of Nations mandates in the Middle East, Syria, and Lebanon. At the 1944 French Africa Conference in Brazzaville, attended by colonial administrators and De Gaulle, Commissioner of the Colonies René Pleven said, "In Colonial France, there are no peoples to free, no racial discrimination to abolish. There are populations who feel French and who wish to take a larger part in French life ... They should be led toward political personality and franchise step by step, not wishing to know any other independence than that of France."[32] At the meeting's close the French resolved that, "The aims of the civilizing labours of France in the Colonies exclude all possibilities of development outside of the French imperial system: the eventual formation even in the distant future of self-government in the colonies must be dismissed."[33] They further stated, "It is also desired that the colonial peoples should experience this liberty and that their sense of responsibility should be developed little by little so that they may find themselves associated in the management of public affairs in their countries."[34] Although the aim of the Brazzaville meeting was to discuss issues such as agriculture, economics, medicine, and administration, and although participants explicitly rejected independence as a goal, the meeting ended up discussing "participation" by Africans in their own government.

[31] Quoted in James W. Silver, 'Framing a Balance Sheet for French Decolonization: Raymond Aron, Raymond Cartier and the Debate over the African Empire' (Cambridge, MA: Harvard University Honors Thesis), p. 47.
[32] Quoted in Dorothy Shipley White, *Black Africa and De Gaulle: From the French Empire to Independence* (University Park: The Pennsylvania State University Press, 1979), p. 121.
[33] Quoted in Timothy Weiskel, "Independence and the *Longue Durée*: The Ivory Coast 'Miracle' Reconsidered," in Prosser Gifford and Wm. Roger Louis, eds., *Decolonization and African Independence: The Transfer of Power, 1960–1980* (New Haven: Yale University Press, 1988), pp. 347–380: 357.
[34] Quoted in White, *Black Africa and De Gaulle*, p. 124.

French colonial policy in the immediate post-war period reflected public ambivalence. Colonial reforms such as allowing trade unions in 1944, abolishing forced labor in 1946, instituting local assemblies, and granting representation of territories in the French National Assembly, all had the effect of granting greater rights and representation for Africans.[35] Also in 1946, the Lamine Guéye law made all colonial "subjects" into citizens. On the other hand, French police cracked down on demonstrations for independence in Algeria in 1945, killing thousands in the region around Sétif, and in 1946 France began an eight-year war to hold on to Indochina. So much had changed in terms of the laws, if not yet the use of force, that Minister of Overseas France, Marius Moutet, said in 1946 that, "The brutal colonial fact, the fact of conquest, the imposition of one nation on other nations, the maintenance of sovereignty that rests only on force, is impossible today. The historic period of colonization is passed."[36] Perhaps what Moutet meant was that the use of brute force against inferior subjects was no longer unquestioned and unfettered; France still frequently used force, but greater political and economic freedom was also part of the colonial policy.

Pan-Africanism and anti-colonial solidarity

Pan-Africanism, the solidarity of people of African descent, was both a cultural idea and a political program with roots in the mid and late nineteenth-century writings of Ethiopianists and West African scholars such as John Africanus Horton, James Johnson, and Edward Blyden.[37]

---

[35] See Louis, *Imperialism at Bay*, pp. 44–47; Suret-Canale and Boahen, "West Africa 1945–1960," pp. 173–174; Majhemount Diop, in collaboration with David Birmingham, Ivan Hrbek, Alfredo Margrido, and Djibril Tamsir Niane, "Tropical and Equatorial Africa under French, Portuguese and Spanish Domination, 1935–45," in Ali Mazrui, ed., *Africa Since 1935* (Berkeley: University of California, 1993), pp. 58–75: 72–74; Elikai M'Bokolo, "French Colonial Policy in Equatorial Africa in the 1940s and 1950s," in Gifford and Louis, eds., *The Transfer of Power in Africa*, pp. 173–210; and Rudolf von Albertini, *Decolonization: The Administration of Future Colonies, 1919–1960* (Garden City, NY: Doubleday & Company, 1971), pp. 364–371.

French colonies were grouped into two federations, French Equatorial Africa or AEF, consisting of what was known as Middle Congo, Chad, Ubangu-Chari (Central African Republic), and Gabon. French West Africa or AOF consisted of Senegal, French Sudan (Mali), French Guinea, Upper Volta (Burkina Faso), Côte d'Ivoire, Dahomey (Benin), Niger, and Mauritania.

[36] Quoted in White, *De Gaulle and Black Africa*, p. 148.

[37] Ethiopianism was primarily concerned with developing an African Christianity, but it also refuted racist beliefs. The later Negritude, black consciousness, and black pride movements, which stressed a cultural as well as political and economic analysis of the situation of African people, often had a Pan-African component. See P. Olisanwuche Esedebe,

The Pan-Africanists' main tools were discursive: education and argument. One of their most common rhetorical techniques was to expose hypocrisy and call for consistency between the words and principles of democratic nations and their overseas practices. Their other tool was political organizing.

From primarily being based among West African, Afro-British, and African-American intellectuals, during the period between the two world wars, a world-wide Pan-African movement grew to include more Africans. Pan-Africans also developed a less paternalistic program for African liberation, and came to have a more sharply focused articulation of their analysis of colonial economics. The Second Pan-African conference, which held sessions in London, Brussels, and Paris in 1921, endorsed a declaration stressing racism as a problem and proposed "self-government for backward groups." Going farther than they had in 1919, conference participants argued that the "habit of democracy must be made to encircle the earth. Despite the attempts to prove that its practice is the secret and divine gift of a few, no habit is more natural or widespread among primitive people, or more easily capable of development among masses. Local self-government with a minimum of help and oversight can be established tomorrow in Asia, in Africa, America, and the isles of the sea."[38] A delegation from the conference then traveled to the Permanent Mandates Commission to present a petition which politely suggested that, as "the spirit of the world moves towards self-government," mandated areas, "being peopled as they are by black folk, have a right to ask that men of Negro descent, properly fitted in character and training, be appointed a member of the Mandates Commission as soon as a vacancy occurs."[39] The delegation also asked the League to "take a firm stand on the absolute equality of races."[40] This was certainly ethical argument: it denormalized and delegitimized both racism and colonialism and offered an alternative which met normative goals already articulated and widely held. The form of the argument was logical inference and side-ways reasoning; after rejecting racism, analogy suggested that there was no limit to democratic principles and therefore no limit to their practice.

Pan-Africanism: The Idea and Movement, 1776–1963 (Washington, DC: Howard University Press, 1982); A. Adu Boahen, *African Perspectives on Colonialism* (Baltimore: Johns Hopkins University Press, 1987).

[38] Quoted in George Padmore, *Pan-Africanism or Communism* (Garden City, NY: Anchor Books, 1971), pp. 108–109.

[39] Quoted in ibid., p. 112.   [40] Quoted in ibid., p. 112.

Pan-Africanists organized two other congresses before World War II. In 1923, the Third Pan-African Congress held sessions in London and Lisbon with wider participation than previous meetings. Again, most of the demands were modest, requesting that Africans have a "voice in their own governments . . . access to land and its resources . . . trial by juries of their peers under established procedures of law . . . development of Africa for the benefit of Africans, and not merely for the profit of Europeans." The most radical statement was the demand for the "organization of commerce and industry so as to make the main objects of capital and labour the welfare of the many rather than the enriching of the few."[41] The 1927 Pan-African Congress held in New York involved over 200 delegates from eleven countries.

During the interwar period and World War II, many in the African-American elite were increasingly active in denouncing colonialism and imperialism. Before and during World War II, even the moderate US National Association for the Advancement of Colored People (NAACP) was sharply anti-colonial and had strong links and overlapping membership with other more radical anti-colonial organizations. NAACP Secretary Walter White wrote to US President Roosevelt in September 1944 to urge that, "the U.S. government will not be a party to the perpetuation of colonial exploitation and to appoint qualified Negroes to serve at U.S. government conferences determining war or post war policies."[42] According to historian Penny Von Eschen, the African-American press kept up a strong critique of the Europeans' conduct of the war: "There was fierce criticism of the Allies' coercive use of unarmed Africans for transport and labor battalions. This practice caused such high casualties, the *Defender* [April 1942] charged, that it was 'a contradiction of the very principles of liberty and humanity for which we claim to be fighting.'"[43] But the critique of colonialism was deeper, as the State Department reported in 1944: "Leading Negro journals like *The Crisis*, official organ of the National Association for the Advancement of Colored People, the

[41] Quoted in ibid., p. 118.
[42] Quoted in Penny M. Von Eschen, *Race Against Empire: Black Americans and Anticolonialism, 1937–1957* (Ithaca: Cornell University Press, 1997), p. 74. Also see Hollis R. Lynch, *Black American Radicals and Liberation of Africa: The Council on African Affairs, 1937–1955* (Ithaca: Africana Studies and Research Center, Cornell University, 1978); Hollis R. Lynch, "Pan-African Responses in the United States to British Colonial Rule in Africa in the 1940s," in Prosser Gifford and Wm. Roger Louis, eds., *The Transfer of Power in Africa: Decolonization 1940–1960* (New Haven: Yale University Press, 1982), pp. 57–86; Suret-Canale and Boahen, "West Africa 1945–1960," pp. 165–166.
[43] Von Eschen, *Race Against Empire*, p. 33.

relatively conservative *New York Amsterdam News* and the militant left-wing organ, the *People's Voice* conduct a perpetual and bitter campaign against 'white imperialism.' "[44]

One of the most important anti-colonial groups in the US, the Council on African Affairs, publicized conditions in colonies and supported liberation movements. Begun in 1937 as the International Committee on African Affairs to educate Americans about Africa, the Committee was reorganized into the Council on African Affairs (CAA) in 1942, with a more explicit Pan-African analysis and liberation agenda. Much of its work on behalf of Africa was dedicated to public education and outreach. The CAA organized rallies featuring some of its famous supporters, including the African-American intellectual W.E.B. Du Bois and the enormously popular entertainer Paul Robeson. For example, the CAA organized a Colonial Conference in New York, at a branch of a public library on 135th St., on 6 April 1945, which included Kwame Nkrumah and the African-American intellectuals Rayford Logan and Du Bois, along with West Indians and Africans. Conference participants called for an international Colonial Commission to "oversee and facilitate the transition of peoples from colonial status to such autonomy as colonial peoples themselves may desire."[45]

Many other groups questioned colonialism. In June 1945 an All Colonial People's Conference met to call for independence. The Pan-African Conference met in Manchester, England in October 1945 with the goal of "complete and absolute independence," and the decolonization strategy discussed included mass organization through trade unions and political parties.[46] The meeting included sessions on colonialism in the West Indies, Asia, and Africa, and participants came from Antigua, Barbados, Bermuda, Jamaica, Gambia, Uganda, Tanganyika, Nigeria, Sierra Leone, and other colonies. It included, as usual, W.E.B. Du Bois, but also three future African heads of state, Kwame Nkrumah of Gold Coast (later Ghana), Jomo Kenyatta of Kenya, and Hastings Banda of Malawi.

In the United States in the immediate post-war period, the CAA and NAACP continued to promote anti-colonial activism through public

[44] State Department report quoted in ibid., p. 42.   [45] Quoted in ibid., p. 77.
[46] In addition, the All Colonial People's Conference included the Pan-African Federation, the Federation of Indian Associations in Britain, the West African Students' Union, the Ceylon Students' Association and Burma Association. Paul Gordon Lauren, *Power and Prejudice: The Politics and Diplomacy of Racial Discrimination* (Boulder: Westview Press, 1996), p. 173. See Geiss, *Pan-Africanism*, pp. 401, 408.

education and by directly lobbying government officials. The CAA published the monthly journal *New Africa*, which included news and analysis of conditions in Africa.[47] In April 1944 members of the CAA's executive board met the officials of the newly organized Africa Division of the State Department, and in March 1945, Max Yergan and Alpheus Hunton of the CAA met with Assistant Secretary of State Archibald MacLeish. When the San Francisco Conference on the United Nations opened on 25 April 1945, the NAACP had the status of consultant to the US delegation.[48] The CAA also sent its program for Africa in the peace settlement, "Text and Analysis of the Colonial Provisions of the United Nations Charter," to the Secretary of State and US representative to the UN and published a pamphlet, "The San Francisco Conference and the Colonial Issue," which they sent to all the delegates at the UN conference.[49]

In addition to lobbying the US government and the UN, the CAA attempted to focus US public opinion against colonialism with large public rallies. A CAA rally at Madison Square Garden in 1946, intended to "organize 'anti-imperialist and democratic forces' to influence American foreign policy," attracted 19,000 people.[50] The day before the rally, the *New York Herald Tribune* printed a letter to the editor that "sketched the problems of land and labor in West Africa, Kenya, and South Africa and spelled out the inadequacies of American policy on Africa and the attempts by the South African government to annex South-West Africa."[51] The rally itself was widely covered in the *New York Herald Tribune* and the *New York Times*. The CAA rally in New York for "Africa and Colonial Freedom through a Strong UN" in April 1947 critiqued South African policies. Another CAA rally at New York's Madison Square Garden in September 1947 attracted 15,000 people to hear Lena Horne, Paul Robeson, and former Vice President Henry Wallace.[52]

Despite initial unity and the large public response, the anti-colonial movement among black Americans fractured after the anti-communist

---

[47] At its peak in 1946, circulation for *New Africa* was more than 3,000. "But, *New Africa*'s influence was considerably larger than its circulation suggests, as it was subscribed to by church, labor, educational, and political organizations, and was also read by U.S. government officials. It also circulated in Europe, particularly among British leftist and government circles, and in Africa among nationalist and labor groups. Indeed by 1950 there was a government ban on it in three African countries – Kenya, South Africa, and the Belgian Congo." Lynch, "Pan-African Responses," p. 60.
[48] Von Eschen, *Race Against Empire*, p. 81.
[49] Ibid., p. 83; Lynch, "Pan-African Responses," pp. 61–62.
[50] Von Eschen, *Race Against Empire*, p. 103.
[51] Ibid., pp. 103–104.   [52] Ibid., pp. 92–93.

Truman Doctrine was announced in Congress in March 1947. NAACP leader, Walter White, supported both the Truman Doctrine and the Marshall Plan, while Paul Robeson and others, including the Progressive Citizens of America (PCA), opposed the Truman Doctrine and Cold War polarization. The leadership of the CAA split in 1948 between those who supported Truman and those, such as Du Bois and Robeson, who backed Henry Wallace as a candidate for president in 1948. In 1950 the US government revoked Paul Robeson's passport because, they said, he was "extremely active in behalf of the independence for the colonial peoples of Africa."[53]

But while anti-colonial activism among African Americans was dampened by the Cold War, it grew in the rest of the world. The 1955 Bandung Conference, held in Indonesia, was hailed as the "first international conference of colored peoples in the history of mankind" by Indonesia's president Sukarno, who spoke of being united against colonialism and racism.[54] African and Asian delegates from twenty-nine countries, including colonies and newly independent nations, criticized Western racism as the foundation of colonialism. As Carlos Romulo, president of the Philippines, said, "To bolster his rule, to justify his own power to himself, Western white man assumed that his superiority lay in his very bones, in the color of his skin. This made the lowliest drunk superior, in colonial society, to the highest product of culture and scholarship and industry among the subject people."[55]

Colonial culture and the decline of scientific racism

Twentieth-century Pan-Africanists and other anti-colonial activists recognized the centrality of racist beliefs and the Europeans' sense of racial superiority as a foundation of colonialism and challenged the West on this account. Although Social Darwinism, or the belief in the natural

[53] US State Department quoted in ibid., p. 124. In 1947, the Attorney General included the CAA on its list of subversive organizations and in 1952 the US Attorney General's Subversive Activities Control Board labeled the CAA as "substantially directed and controlled by the Communist Party, USA." Ibid., pp. 115 and 134. Von Eschen writes that, "The pervasive psychologizing of racism marginalized intellectuals such as Du Bois and Hunton, who located racism in the history of slavery and colonialism." Ibid., p. 158. Though the CAA denied an association with the Communist Party in 1955 it disbanded. The American Committee on Africa (ACOA) was founded in 1953 and TransAfrica continued solidarity and anti-colonial work.
[54] Lauren, *Power and Prejudice*, p. 224.   [55] Romulo quoted in ibid., p. 225.

superiority of those who dominate others, was prevalent in scientific and popular culture of the West during the late nineteenth century, Africans had consistently rejected European arguments about African inferiority, publishing refutations of European racism and championing African values over European culture.[56] Yet scientific racism and other racist beliefs were still widespread during the early twentieth century.

The impetus for Western scientists to reevaluate scientific racism and social Darwinism came from both the scientific community and the popular reaction to Nazism.[57] One early challenge by the famous American anthropologist Franz Boas, who published *The Mind of Primitive Man* in 1911, questioned the idea of a difference between the primitive and the civilized in intelligence. Doubt about the science of race continued to grow in part because of the difficulty in proving distinct racial types. The anthropomorphic physical anthropology of human measurement was failing to meet the scientists' own criteria for good science. There was simply too much variation within so-called racial groups to maintain rigid typologies based on measurements, and moreover, there was no single agreed-upon measurement scheme.[58]

But more important, perhaps, was the growing desire in the 1930s among European and American scientists to refute the Nazis' views about race. Adolf Hitler's, *Mein Kampf* (1925), and the racial ideas of the Nazi movement, received greater attention after Hitler's election to chancellor in 1933. In the US, Franz Boas organized anthropologists and other social scientists to refute racist science. In England, Julian Huxley and Alfred Haddon in 1935 published *We Europeans, a Survey of 'Racial' Problems With A Chapter on Europe Overseas*, questioning racial science. The scholarly journals *Nature* and *Science* published articles, letters, and editorials about racial science. Scientists also convened conferences on race and Nazi science.[59] In December 1938, 1,284 scientists in the US, including three Nobel laureates, published a Scientist's Manifesto critical of "pseudo-scientific racialism."[60]

[56] Boahen, *African Perspectives on Colonialism*, pp. 20–22.
[57] Turn of the century American intellectual critics of social Darwinism, for instance Boas and William James, were also often critical of imperialism. See Richard Hofstadter, *Social Darwinism in American Thought*, revd edn (New York: George Braziller, 1955), pp. 192–200.
[58] Nancy Stepan, *The Idea of Race in Science: Great Britain, 1800–1960* (London: Macmillan, 1982), pp. 162–169.
[59] See ibid., and Elazar Barkan, *The Retreat of Scientific Racism: Changing Concepts of Race in Britain and the United States Between the World Wars* (Cambridge: Cambridge University Press, 1992), pp. 279–346.
[60] Barkan, *The Retreat of Scientific Racism*, p. 337.

World War II itself brought race to the forefront. The Western powers and the Japanese fought a war filled with racial stereotypes and racist appeals to national solidarity, while the Nazis carried out their extermination policy based on racial ideas.[61] As British Labour politician Clement Atlee told his party in August 1941, "Our enemies, the Nazis, set up a monstrous and ridiculous racial doctrine. They declare themselves to be a master-race to which the rest of us are inferior, and if they assert that claim in respect to Europeans you may be quite assured they are going to apply it to everyone else – Asiatics, Africans, and everyone."[62] At the same time, racism faced serious challenge in the US when the military became increasingly integrated along racial lines and the war prompted the elimination of some racial barriers in the private sector.[63] During the war, the famous scholar Ashley Montague (a former Boas student) published *Man's Most Dangerous Myth: The Fallacy of Race*. Intent on using a scientific argument for larger political goals, Montague wrote:

> In our time, the problem of *race* has assumed an alarmingly exaggerated importance. Alarming, because racial dogmas have been made the basis for an inhumanly brutal political philosophy which has already resulted in the death or social disenfranchisement of millions of innocent individuals; exaggerated because when the nature of contemporary "race" theory is scientifically analyzed and understood it ceases to be of any significance for social or any other kind of action . . . It is highly desirable, therefore, that the facts about "race" as science has come to know them should be widely disseminated and clearly understood.[64]

Intellectuals continued their assault on scientific racism after the war. The anthropologist Claude Lévi-Strauss published *Race et Histoire* in 1952 challenging crude cultural evolutionism and hierarchies of societies.[65] Similarly, the United Nations Educational, Scientific and Cultural Organization (UNESCO) convened meetings and published statements on race concluding that the capacities of all races were similar.

[61] See John Dower, *War Without Mercy: Race and Power in the Pacific War* (New York: Pantheon, 1986).
[62] Quoted in Louis, *Imperialism at Bay*, p. 125.
[63] See Lauren, *Power and Prejudice*, pp. 108–144.
[64] Ashley Montague, *Man's Most Dangerous Myth: The Fallacy of Race* (New York: Columbia University Press, 1942), p. ix, quoted in Pat Shipman, *The Evolution of Racism: Human Difference and the Use and Abuse of Science* (New York: Simon and Schuster, 1994), p. 161.
[65] Paul Clay Sorum, *Intellectuals and Decolonization in France* (Chapel Hill: University of North Carolina Press, 1977), pp. 224–232.

UNESCO's July 1950 statement said, in part, "Biological differences between ethnic groups should be disregarded from the standpoint of social acceptance and social action . . . According to present knowledge, there is no proof that the groups of mankind differ in their innate mental characteristics, whether in respect to intelligence or temperament. The scientific evidence indicates that the range of mental capacities in all other ethnic groups is much the same."[66] The UNESCO position and other such statements were widely debated among intellectuals, but, by the 1950s, most scientific racism had been refuted by official bodies such as UNESCO, and it was no longer possible to make crudely racist statements without challenge.[67] Thus, although, revulsion toward Nazi views shaped the content of the critique of scientific racism, views about the "darker" races were also challenged and revised. The argument moved forward by analogy: if anti-Semitism was wrong, other forms of racism were wrong. Colonialism could no longer be normal or legitimate once scientific racism was dethroned.

UN trusteeship and institutionalization of anti-colonialism

Though it would not formally disband until May 1946, the League of Nations essentially died during World War II. And although not officially on the table at the Dumbarton Oaks Conference of 1944 which set the outlines of the United Nations, the idea of a trusteeship system to replace the League Mandate system had been discussed by Allied governments during the war and among members of the public.[68] Further, draft plans developed in the US State Department, starting in August 1942, envisaged a system of international supervision encompassing all dependent territories, not just mandates. A March 1943 draft proposal written under the direction of Secretary of State Cordell Hull foresaw establishing "at the earliest possible moments" dates when these areas would achieve the "status of full independence within a system of

---

[66] The statement was drafted by Montague and rewritten after debates in scientific and anthropology journals as well as in the popular press. Quoted in Shipman, *The Evolution of Racism*, p. 163.

[67] See Barkan, *The Retreat of Scientific Racism*, p. 341 and Shipman, *The Evolution of Racism*, pp. 156–170.

[68] A sample of the debate is a special issue of *African Affairs* 43 (October 1944) and subsequent issues of the same journal. The *Round Table* also published a discussion in December 1944. See James N. Murray, *The United Nations Trusteeship System* (Urbana: The University of Illinois Press, 1957) and Louis, *Imperialism at Bay*, pp. 448–460.

general security."[69] During the Allies' Yalta meeting in February 1945, the US pushed for what it called a trusteeship formula for all colonies, even while Churchill rejected the notion outright and said he did not want it discussed at the San Francisco Conference to establish the United Nations in May and June 1945. Churchill said:

> I absolutely disagree. I will not have one scrap of British territory flung into that area. After we have done our best to fight this war and have done no crime to anyone I will have no suggestion that the British Empire is to be put into the dock and examined by everybody to see whether it is up to their standard. No one will induce me as long as I am Prime Minister to let any representative of Great Britain go to a conference where we will be placed in the dock and asked to justify our right to live in a world we have tried to save.[70]

Britain clearly hoped to retain its empire, though Churchill also obviously knew he would have to muster arguments in favor of it. As Lord Cranborne, speaking at the San Francisco Conference, said: "Do not let us rule out independence as the ultimate destiny of some of these territories. It is not ruled out ... But to have it as a universal goal of colonial policy would, we believe, be unrealistic and prejudicial to peace and security. Nor am I sure it is in the minds or desires of the vast majority of colonial peoples themselves." Cranborne continued, "What do these people want? They want liberty. Let us give them liberty. They want justice. Let us give them justice ... Let us help them climb up the rungs of the ladder of self-government. That is the purpose ... so that ultimately dependent or independent they may play their full part in a peaceful, prosperous and independent world."[71]

The arguments in San Francisco among and within delegations over trusteeship and the fate of all the colonies, as at the Paris Peace Conference after World War I, was finally resolved by compromise, this time among the so-called Big Five powers – the US, Britain, France, the Soviet Union, and China – with input from non-governmental organizations and from other states.[72] Churchill ultimately backed down, agreeing to the trusteeship system, Chapter XII of the UN Charter, once he was assured participation was voluntary. Thus, the British were pushed by a change in international political capabilities (as a result of a shift in the

---

[69] Quoted in Murray, *The United Nations Trusteeship System*, p. 25.
[70] Quoted in Louis, *Imperialism at Bay*, p. 458.   [71] Quoted in ibid., p. 547.
[72] Much of the work was done in Committee II/4. See Murray, *The United Nations Trusteeship System*, pp. 31–45.

balance of international belief) to do, if not an about face, a right angle turn. Why? By 1945, ethical arguments had succeeded in denormalizing earlier, more violent forms of colonial rule, delegitimizing the purposes of the system, and putting an alternative system of trusteeship on the table that would be the model for all "dependencies," as they were called. Further, new normative beliefs were institutionalized as the balance of belief and capability shifted; Britain was no longer able to dictate the normative terms of the international order.

Still, the UN Charter ultimately did not go as far as many, notably Egypt, India, Iraq, and the Soviet Union, would have liked in terms of protecting and expanding the rights of "dependent" peoples. Part of the difficulty was in specifying the meaning of self-determination. As the Venezuelan delegate to the meeting said, "If it means self-government, the right of a country to provide its own government, yes, we would certainly like it to be included; but if it were to be interpreted, on the other hand, as connoting a withdrawal, the *right of withdrawal or secession*, then we would regard that as tantamount to *international anarchy* and we should not desire that it should be included in the text of the Charter."[73] But the trusteeship system went further than the League Mandate system. Specifically, after first stating that the purposes of the UN were to maintain international peace and security, Article 1 (2) stated that a purpose was to "develop friendly relations among nations based on respect for the principle of equal rights and self-determination of peoples, and to take other appropriate measures to strengthen universal peace." As Antonio Cassese argues, the article "had a snowball effect, for it lent moral and political force to the aspirations of colonial countries, strongly backed up by socialist States. Thus, Article 1(2) was eventually perceived and relied upon as a legal entitlement to decolonization. More importantly, the United Nations served as an international forum promoting and channeling the gradual crystallization of legal rules governing this amorphous subject."[74]

The broad language of the opening Chapter of the UN Charter was specified in Chapters XII and XIII, respectively establishing a Trusteeship System and Trusteeship Council. Although there was no explicit discussion of a date to end trusteeship status in the Charter, eventual independence was implied by the language of Article 76 (b) of Chapter XII, which stated that the objectives of trusteeship included: "to promote the political, economic, social and educational advancement of the

---

[73] Quoted in Cassese, *Self-determination of Peoples*, pp. 39–40.   [74] Ibid., p. 65.

inhabitants of the trust territories, and their progressive development toward self-government or independence as may be appropriate to the particular circumstances of each territory and its peoples and the freely expressed wishes of the people concerned . . ." Human rights and racial equality were also explicitly linked to the trust territory system in Article 76 (c and d) where other purposes of trusteeship were outlined: "to encourage respect for human rights and for fundamental freedoms for all without distinction as to race, sex, language, or religion . . . to ensure equal treatment in social, economic, and commercial matters . . . [and] in the administration of justice . . ."

The trusteeship system was small since most of the A class mandates were already independent by 1945. In January 1946 all the Mandatory powers of B and C class territories, except South Africa, declared their intention to draw up trusteeship agreements for their territories. Still, the portion of people living in trusteeship, out of the total number living in old fashioned colonies, was small. "Counting the dependencies of Portugal and Spain, there were more than eight times as many non-self-governing territories outside the trusteeship system, and they contained over ten times as many people."[75] As with League of Nations mandates, each UN trust territory was set up with an individual agreement between the trust power and the UN. The following table describes the United Nations trust territories and their dates of eventual independence.

The UN trusteeship system continued and expanded the mandate concept, illustrating how the table on which arguments were made had been altered by the institutionalization of the Mandate system. For example, the Trusteeship Council, like the Permanent Mandates Commission, was to hear reports from trustee powers about their administration of trust territories in response to a questionnaire based on the one used by the League of Nations Permanent Mandates Commission. However, the Trusteeship questionnaire was more detailed than the League questionnaire and indicates institutionalization of beliefs in trusteeship and self-determination. Specifically, the questionnaire contained the following sections: political advancement in terms of general administration and judicial organization, economic advancement, social advancement including human rights, labor conditions and regulations, public health, penal administration, and education. Further, the reports should answer questions regarding the implementation of UN

[75] Jacobson, "The United Nations and Colonialism," p. 295.

Table 7.1 *United Nations Trust Territories*

Trust	Administering power	Previous status	Date of independence
British Cameroons	Great Britain	League Mandate	1961 Northern part incorporated into Nigeria. Southern part incorporated into Cameroon
French Cameroons	France	League Mandate	1960 (Cameroon)
New Guinea	Australia	League Mandate	1975
Ruanda-Urundi	Belgium	League Mandate	1962 Became two states: Rwanda and Burundi
Nauru	Australia	League Mandate	1968
Pacific Islands (Carolines, Marshall, and Marianas Islands)	US	League Mandate (under Japan)	Palau independent in 1994; Marshall Islands independent in 1991; Marianas and Federated States of Micronesia (including Carolines) became US self-governing territories in 1975 and 1979 respectively.
Somaliland	Italy	Italian Colony	1960 (Somalia)
Tanganyika	Great Britain	League Mandate	1961 (Tanzania)
British Togoland	Great Britain	League Mandate	1957 Incorporated into Ghana by plebiscite
French Togoland	France	League Mandate	1960 (Togo)
Western Samoa	New Zealand	League Mandate	1962

General Assembly and Trusteeship Council resolutions with regard to the trusteeship territory.[76] The emphasis was clearly on "advancement" in these areas, with the expectation that UN supervision would aid in this

---

[76] Murray, *The United Nations Trusteeship System*, pp. 131–139.

process. Further, the UN Trusteeship Council was given greater authority than the League Permanent Mandates Commission in two important respects. The Council was empowered to make "periodic visits" to the trust territories, which it did on occasion.[77] And the Trusteeship Council could hear petitions by the inhabitants of trust territories without having those petitions first screened and forwarded by the administering authority.[78]

The trusteeship system became the model for decolonization of non-trust colonies, or in UN parlance, the "non-self-governing" areas discussed in Chapter XI of the UN Charter, the "Declaration Regarding Non-Self-Governing Territories." The language of Chapter XI shows how deeply beliefs in self-determination had penetrated: "Members of the United Nations which have or assume responsibilities for the administration of territories whose people have not yet attained a full measure of self-government recognize the principle that the interests of the inhabitants of these territories are paramount, and accept as a sacred trust the obligation to promote to the utmost, within the system of international peace and security established by the present Charter, the well-being of the inhabitants of these territories..." The administering powers, according to Article 73, should "ensure due respect for the culture of the people concerned...develop self-government, to take account of the political aspirations of the peoples...to promote constructive measures of development," and report on the "economic, social and educational conditions" in these territories. And as with the trusteeship system, administering governments were required to submit annual reports, extending the system of accountability to all colonies.[79] To monitor implementation of the goals for non-self-governing territories, the General Assembly later established the "Committee on Information from Non-Self-Governing Territories." The template of mandate and

[77] Article 87 of the Charter. At first the British resisted the idea of inspections, fearing their political impact. Louis, *Imperialism at Bay*, pp. 95–96.
[78] Rules of Procedure for the Trusteeship Council, approved 23 April 1947, reprinted in H. Duncan Hall, *Mandates, Dependencies and Trusteeships* (Washington: Carnegie Endowment for International Peace, 1948), pp. 371–385. Other differences in procedure and substance are discussed in Hall, *Mandates, Dependencies and Trusteeships*, pp. 277–281.
[79] Further, the 1948 Universal Declaration of Human Rights extended political rights to "all human beings [who] are born free and equal in dignity and rights." Illustrating how self-determination was the starting point of debate in the post-war world, the relevant portions of the Declaration state that "Everyone has the right to recognition everywhere as a person before the law ... Everyone has the right to take part in the government of his country, directly or through freely chosen representatives ... The will of the people shall be the basis of the authority of government."

trusteeship was applied by analogy to all colonies through the Committee on Information:

> The substantive recommendations of the Trusteeship Council and the Committee on Information have been strikingly similar ... Both bodies have advocated the same things: increased educational facilities for the indigenous inhabitants; enlarged social welfare programs with emphasis on community development; more extensive and comprehensive economic programs which would aim at diversification; and greater opportunity for inhabitants to participate in decision-making.[80]

Thus, normative beliefs in self-government and self-determination first expressed and institutionalized in the League Mandate system were extended to other colonies and institutionalized into standard operating procedures characteristic of the PMC. But the extent of UN activism was still the subject of argument within the world body. Some members favored an activist policy on the part of the UN in promoting self-determination and decolonization. As the Indian delegate to the Fourth Committee of the UN said in late 1946:

> the final object, which was the autonomy of those territories, should be clearly stated, and ... the right of the natives to election and participation in the administration should be affirmed in detail. In particular it should be explicitly stated that no racial discrimination, and no monopoly should be admitted in theory or in fact. Freedom of speech, freedom of the press, freedom of assembly, and freedom to present petitions would have to be guaranteed. No authority should be given to establish a base without the approval of the United Nations ... Finally, it was desirable that as with the Americans in the Philippines, a date limit for the transitional regime should be fixed.[81]

But the UN Charter did not promote immediate decolonization in non-trust territories and there was also disagreement with the Trusteeship Council based on differing visions of the purposes of the system. Thus, as Heather Wilson shows, some of the first post-war challenges to colonialism went unsupported by the United Nations despite appeals by nationalist groups seeking self-government and independence. For example, in both "1950 and 1951 the question of [French] Morocco

---

[80] Jacobson, "The United Nations and Colonialism," p. 296.
[81] *Official Record of the Second Part of the First Session of the General Assembly, Plenary Meetings* (October–December 1946), *Fourth Committee, Trusteeship, Part I* (November–December 1946), p. 70, quoted in Murray, *The United Nations Trusteeship System*, pp. 54–55.

appeared on the agenda of the General Assembly but no debate took place," despite appeals by members of the Arab League for discussion of Morocco's status.[82] The French resisted discussion of Morocco in the UN, claiming that it was a domestic matter. In 1953 the UN General Assembly adopted a weak resolution urging continued negotiations between Moroccans and the French, but in 1953 the UN failed to adopt a draft resolution that recognized "the right of the people of Morocco to complete self-determination."[83] Similarly, the United Nations took a soft line on French human rights behavior in Tunisia in the early 1950s. On the other hand, by 1960, although in previous years such resolutions had been defeated, the UN was ready to recognize the Algerians' right to self-determination.[84] The unsuccessful French war to hold on to Algeria ultimately cost more than 500,000 lives over seven years.

The increasingly active role of the UN in decolonization efforts during the 1950s and 1960s, was due perhaps primarily to the greater portion of former colonies in the UN, but also to the institutionalization of anti-colonial normative beliefs.[85] As Harold Jacobson suggests, the "most salient motive force underlying the UN's recommendations seems to have been a feeling that all racial discrimination should cease and that the indigenous inhabitants of dependent territories are entitled to a position of full equality."[86] It was inconsistent and thus incoherent to keep colonies if colonialism was no longer acceptable among civilized peoples, once the humanity and at least theoretical equality of those in colonies was granted. In other words, the UN's activism was a consequence of both normative beliefs and ethical arguments as well as a change in political capabilities. Though some former colonies, e.g. the US sometimes voted in support of colonialism, the majority of votes in the General Assembly could not be counted in favor of colonialism.

The scope of self-determination gradually expanded through ethical argument. UN delegates continually debated the meaning of self-determination, with some favoring an anti-colonial interpretation of external

[82] Wilson, *International Law and the Use of Force*, p. 63.
[83] Draft Resolution A/2526, 22 October 1953, quoted in ibid., p. 64.
[84] Ibid., pp. 65–66.
[85] This shift in membership was most dramatic in terms of new African states: in 1946 African states comprised less than 10 percent of membership and in 1991 African states were 33 percent of UN members.
[86] Jacobson, "The United Nations and Colonialism," p. 296.

self-determination, and others promoting internal self-determination or democracy as paramount. Third World and socialist states generally favored defining the concept as external self-determination, while Western countries generally pushed for a conception that stressed internal self-government, arguing that an emphasis on sovereignty would encourage separatism and weaken the international order. Only Chile proposed, in 1952, to include a right to control natural resources.[87]

Culminating decades of ethical argument, in 1960 the UN General Assembly passed Resolution 1514, the "Declaration on the Granting of Independence to Colonial Countries and Peoples," which said all dependent people had a "right to complete independence."[88] Drafted and pushed by the African and Asian members of the UN that had recently won their independence, the language closely resembled that used at the 1955 Bandung Conference. The resolution condemned colonialism as "alien subjugation, domination, and exploitation," and said that colonialism "constitutes a denial of fundamental human rights." Moreover, the resolution declared that "armed action or repressive measures of all kinds directed against dependent peoples shall cease in order to enable them to exercise peacefully and freely their right to complete independence . . . " The Declaration further instructed all states to observe the provisions of the UN Charter, the UN Declaration of Human Rights (1948) and "the present Declaration on the basis of equality, non-interference in the internal affairs of all States, and respect for the sovereign rights of all peoples and their territorial integrity." Also notable was the fact that *not even the states that still held colonies dared to vote against the measure.* Rather, the colonial powers formed the majority of the nine abstentions. South Africa, Australia, Belgium, France, Spain, Portugal, Great Britain, the United States, and the Dominican Republic abstained, while eighty-nine states voted in favor of Resolution 1514, and none voted against.

The UN further institutionalized and articulated beliefs in equality and self-determination in 1961 when the General Assembly established the Special Committee on Colonialism to implement the 1960 Declaration.[89] The Special Committee immediately took an activist role

---

[87] See Cassese, *Self-determination of Peoples*, pp. 44–52.

[88] Resolution 1514 (XV). Thomas Franke argues that the declaration is contradictory because it does not consistently use the principle of self-determination. *The Power of Legitimacy Among Nations* (Oxford: Oxford University Press, 1990), pp. 163–165.

[89] The UNGA also created other committees, namely the Special Committee on South West Africa and the Special Committee on Portuguese Territories, both established in 1961. In

in the decolonization process, leading the General Assembly and Security Council to take stronger positions. From the beginning of its work, the Special Committee gave priority to Africa under the logic that "it was in Africa that the largest number of people were still living under colonialism and that it was here that the largest colonial territories still existed."[90] For example, the Special Committee spent fifteen of its first twenty-six meetings on the problem of white minority rule in Rhodesia.[91] The Committee heard petitions from Africans who were organizing for political and economic rights and urged that the government release all political prisoners. Prior to the British colony's 1965 Unilateral Declaration of Independence (UDI), the Special Committee urged Britain to take a stronger line on Rhodesia's racial policies and requested that all member states refrain from sending arms and ammunition to Southern Rhodesia. Only after the UDI did the UN General Assembly and Security Council, along with Great Britain, gradually impose mandatory sanctions on Rhodesian imports and exports. Those sanctions remained in force until an agreement for majority rule was reached in 1979.[92]

Although by the mid-1960s decolonization was a fact for many former colonies, the UN continued to argue about colonialism. In December 1966 the UN General Assembly adopted the "International Covenant on Civil and Political Rights," which stated in part that "all peoples have the right to self-determination." Further, the Covenant said that all parties to it, "including those having responsibility for the administration of Non-Self-Governing and Trust Territories, shall promote the realization of the right to self-determination, and shall respect that right in conformity with the provisions of the Charter of the United Nations."[93]

1962 the General Assembly dissolved these committees and the much older Committee on Information, transferring their function to the Special Committee on the Situation with regard to the Implementation on the Granting of Independence to Colonial Countries and Peoples, commonly known as the Special Committee or the Committee of Twenty-Four.

[90] UN, *The United Nations and Decolonization: Summary of the Work of the Special Committee of Twenty-Four* (New York: United Nations, 1965), p. 9.

[91] David A. Kay, "The Politics of Decolonization: The New Nations and the United Nations Political Process," *International Organization* 21 (Autumn 1967), 786–811 reprinted in Goodrich and Kay, *International Organization*, pp. 307–332: 317.

[92] A chronology of UN efforts and sanctions is found in Gary Clyde Hufbauer, Jeffrey Schott, and Kimberly Ann Elliot, *Economic Sanctions Reconsidered: History and Current Policy*, 2nd edn (Washington, DC: Institute for International Economics, 1990), Case 65–3, pp. 285–293.

[93] The Covenant on Civil and Political Rights also says: "All peoples may, for their own ends, freely dispose of their natural wealth and resources without prejudice to any obligations arising out of an international economic cooperation, based upon the principle

In October 1970 UN General Assembly Resolution 2621 (XXV) resolved that colonialism was a "crime" that violated the principles of international law and the UN Charter. It also proposed a "Programme of Action for the Full Implementation of the Declaration on the Granting of Independence to Colonial Countries and Peoples," that consisted of assisting freedom fighters with material aid, attacking financial interests that aided colonialism, and publishing the negative aspects of colonialism as well as UN activities in support of decolonization. Notably, this resolution passed 85:5:15. The Programme was followed by numerous resolutions recognizing and supporting the struggles of people under colonial or alien rule, including those persons under Portuguese, Rhodesian, South African, Indonesian (East Timor) and Moroccan (Western Sahara) domination. Further, individual governments gave financial and in some cases military support to anti-colonial organizations. On the other hand, when twenty-six of fifty members of the Organization of African Unity recognized the independence movement in Western Sahara in 1982, it caused a year-long schism within the organization. By the early 1970s the governments of the Soviet Union, Denmark, and Canada all supported Popular Movement for the Liberation of Angola (MPLA).[94]

The United Nations' firmest actions in support of decolonization were perhaps its sanctions against Portugal, Rhodesia, and South Africa.[95] For example, the United Nations implemented a voluntary arms embargo against South Africa in 1963 to hasten Namibian independence and increase the pressure to reform apartheid, and made the embargo mandatory in 1977. During the 1970s and 1980s, the UN also assisted Namibian efforts for independence from South Africa. In 1984 and 1986 the UN arms embargo against South Africa was tightened to include spare parts and ammunition. Similarly, the UN imposed economic sanctions against Portugal and Rhodesia, lifting those only after majority rule was certain to be instituted in Mozambique, Angola, and Zimbabwe.[96]

of mutual benefit, and international law. In no case may a people be deprived of its own means of subsistence."
[94] Kenneth Maxwell, "Portugal and Africa: The Last Empire," in Prosser Gifford and Wm. Roger Louis, eds., *The Transfer of Power in Africa: Decolonization 1940–1960* (New Haven: Yale University Press, 1982), pp. 337–385: 347–348.
[95] In 1990 the United Nations began the International Decade for the Eradication of Colonialism. Robert Aldrich and John Connell, *The Last Colonies* (Cambridge: Cambridge University Press, 1998), p. 159.
[96] The UN was not the only international organization that promoted decolonization: the Organization of African Unity (OAU), founded in 1963, proclaimed the elimination

Anti-colonial movements and negotiated decolonization

Decolonization after World War II generally followed one of three routes: peaceful negotiated transfers of power; internationally mediated and supervised independence processes, such as plebiscites and UN Trusteeship; or anti-colonial military rebellions. Although strong anti-colonial movements in the colonies pressed for reform and independence, war was the exception; negotiated transfer or plebiscite was the rule.

There were several guerrilla wars for independence in the post-war period, often involving more than one nationalist political movement struggling for the liberation of a single colony. France was the most active in trying to maintain its colonies by force against determined guerrilla resistance in Tunisia, Algeria, Vietnam, and Morocco. In Algeria, the French faced the Front de Libération National (FNL) between 1954 and 1962 before De Gaulle negotiated an agreement for French withdrawal. Both the Vietnamese and the Algerians were met with brutal force in response to their rebellions against the French. Nevertheless, France lost decisively at Dien Bien Phu in 1954, and despite great military success in the late 1950s, negotiated its way out of Algeria in 1962.[97] Multiple independence movements fought against the Portuguese in Angola (1961–1974), Mozambique (1963–1974), and Guinea-Buissau (1963–1974), finally gaining their independence when the Portuguese government fell to a military coup in 1975 and the new government negotiated a withdrawal.[98] Similarly, Portugal's colony in East Timor was promised independence after the coup, but was invaded by Indonesia in 1975, which occupied the territory until 1999. When Spain left its colony Rio de Oro (Spanish Sahara) in 1976, the land was occupied by its neighbors Mauritania and Morocco. The occupants of Western Sahara, as it

---

of colonialism as one of its main purposes. The OAU also proclaimed its determination "to safeguard and consolidate the hard-won independence as well as the sovereignty and territorial integrity of our States, and to resist *neo-colonialism* in all its forms." Charter of the Organization of African Unity, adopted on 25 May 1962, emphasis added. The OAU was more forthcoming than the UN with material and political support for decolonization efforts in Africa. The OAU took a stand against Portugal earlier than the UN when it instituted an economic and diplomatic boycott against Portugal's colonial policies in 1963; the UN General Assembly called for an arms embargo and economic sanctions against Portugal in late 1965. In other cases, particularly when the UN needed guidance on which, of sometimes several, independence movements to recognize in an African state, it looked to the organizations recognized by the OAU.

[97] See Anthony Clayton, *The Wars of French Decolonization* (London: Longman, 1994).

[98] See Norrie MacQueen, *The Decolonization of Portuguese Africa: Metropolitan Revolution and the Dissolution of Empire* (London: Longman, 1997).

became known, then began a long, complex, guerrilla, and legal struggle by the people – under the Front for the Liberation of Saguia el Hamra and Rio de Oro, or the Polisario Front – for independence from their neighbors.

Colonial rebellion was not confined to indigenous peoples; European colonists also fought to retain their political domination. For example, Portuguese and Dutch settlers attempted small rebellions against the metropole, and French *colons* rebelled in Algeria in 1957 and 1960. The most successful rebellion was the Unilateral Declaration of Independence (UDI) from Britain by the European colonial settlers of Southern Rhodesia in 1965. They succeeded in maintaining power until 1980 when a negotiated solution ended their war with the Zimbabwean liberation armies.

Despite these armed revolts, decolonization was more often the consequence of a negotiated transition, where independence leaders, working with labor and political organizations, struggled for peaceful and legal transfers of power following elections. British colonies, for example, often gained independence through staged legal transfers. The white-settler dominated British dominions of Australia, Canada, New Zealand, and South Africa had already achieved a *de facto* independence which was recognized at the Imperial Conference of 1926. In Asia, after the British regained Burma from Japanese control, elections led to Burmese independence in 1948.

Some nationalist leaders had long histories of working with or in colonial administrations in order to negotiate a transition to self-rule and political independence. For example, the first French Constituent Assemblies elected in October 1945 and June 1946 included sixty-three members from overseas colonies. Some of these members had many years of experience in colonial administration, including men who would become future leaders of their independent states, such as Félix Houphouët-Boigny (Ivory Coast) and Léopold Sedar Senghor (Senegal). Kwame Nkrumah, the noted Pan-African activist who became the first leader of Ghana, Africa's first colony to achieve independence after World War II, was part of a long tradition of African activism and participation in the British colonial government of the Gold Coast going back to when two Africans sat on the Legislative Council in 1888. Nkrumah served as leader of government business after elections in 1951, while subsequent elections gave increasing autonomy to Ghana, which finally became independent in 1957. In the West Indies, Norman Manley and his cousin Alexander Bustamante, who led two relatively evenly matched political parties, negotiated greater autonomy and ultimately independence for Jamaica over the course of many years.[99]

The independence in 1947 of India, Britain's largest imperial holding, was one of the first post-World War II cases of a largely peaceful transfer of power. Decolonization was a protracted process which Indians had been struggling to achieve for decades and some devolution of power had already occurred before World War II. Unsatisfied with the pace and content of reforms, however, Indians continued to push for complete independence, in a largely non-violent effort, but the British managed to postpone independence until after World War II, partly by jailing most leaders of the popular Indian Congress Party during the war. Still, there was a shift in public opinion in Britain toward Indian aspirations for independence, which was reflected in the change of stance taken by political parties toward decolonization. For example, Britain's Labour government of 1945–1951 "was more sympathetic than the Conservatives to colonial aspirations, identifying them to some extent with the struggles of the British working classes for their own form of self-determination."[100]

In India and elsewhere, it was explicit British policy to make sure that the transition from colonial rule to greater self-government and eventual independence was gradual. As Secretary of State for the Colonies A. Creech Jones said in 1948, "The central purpose of British Colonial Policy is simple. It is to guide the Colonial territories to responsible government within the Commonwealth in conditions that ensure to the people concerned both a fair standard of living and freedom from oppression from any quarter."[101] In part, gradualism was intended to preserve as much control over the process as possible. But the Colonial Office also believed that it would take time to train natives in the mechanics of self-rule. To that end, the British gradually increased the number of native civil servants in government administrative posts in many of its colonies and very gradually gave up some of the functions of local government to colonial inhabitants. In addition, British policymakers believed that implementing a Commonwealth among Britain's former colonies could preserve the connection of the empire. As Frederick Cooper argues, "In the end, officials' belief in the universal

[99] See Victor Stafford Reid, *The Horses of the Morning* (Kingston, Jamaica: Caribbean Authors Publishing Co., 1985).
[100] M.E. Chamberlain, *Decolonization: The Fall of the European Empires* (Oxford: Basil Blackwell, 1985), p. 76.
[101] Morgan, *The Official History of Colonial Development*, vol. V, p. 20.

value of European social knowledge did not serve to preserve empire, but instead to convince French and British officials that they could give it up, believing that they had molded some Africans to the norms of modernity and that they could bequeath to that elite the task of super-intending those who had not made the transition."[102]

French decolonization was, like the British process, a slow evolution toward greater recognition of the rights of colonial subjects, as well as the harsh wrenching of freedom through violent means that occurred in Algeria and Vietnam. But violence was the exception. French policy had long been one of assimilation and as a consequence, some formal recognition of the colonial subjects was already part of French policy. For instance, the West African Blaise Diagne had been a member of the French parliament for Senegal during and after World War I and was given a large role in the colonial administration of Africa after the war. In the late 1920s, French Indochina was granted a representative body, dominated by the French but including a large number of elected Indochinese. As Arthur Girault, an interwar theorist of French colonial-ism, wrote in 1927, "The policy of assimilation is the safety valve which prevents the rupture: To the man whom we prevent from being prime minister in his own country because his country is a colony, we must offer in exchange the possibility of being prime minister of France. The people we forbid local patriotism must be inspired with love for the common fatherland, the cult of the Empire."[103]

During World War II nationalist elites grew more explicit in demand-ing changes that would lead from colonialism to self-government in French Equatorial Africa and French West Africa. While at the 1944 French Africa Conference in Brazzaville, African elites had pressed for an "Empire citizenship" for Africans that would give them equal civil and political rights with the metropolitan French, by the late 1940s and early 1950s Africans were making more radical demands. An uprising against France in Madagascar was brutally crushed in 1947. On the other hand, after the war the French allowed and organized elections for mu-nicipal and colonial representation, and set up the political structures to accommodate this new level of governance by Africans. In addition, in 1955 the French began to give preference to Africans over Europeans to fill vacant posts in colonial administration. "Any position that can be filled correctly by an African must be entrusted to him rather than to

[102] Cooper, *Decolonization and African Society*, p. 20.
[103] Quoted in Albertini, *Decolonization*, pp. 290–291.

a European ... Between equally qualified candidates, the African must always receive preference."[104]

In 1956, the French legislature passed the *Loi Cadre*, or framework law, that created territorial assemblies, and eventually led to a vote in September 1958 in France's black African colonies over the kind of relationship they wanted with France. The choice was independence or a relationship of "community" where members would enjoy both greater autonomy and economic advantages. Most French colonies in West Africa voted for community, except for Guinea, which voted for immediate independence. Yet in relatively short order, Mali, the Ivory Coast, Niger, Dahomy (now Benin), and Upper Volta (now Burkina Faso) peacefully negotiated their independence in 1960. Other French African territories, including Togo, Madagascar, the Republic of the Congo, and Gabon achieved independence in 1960 following roughly the same path.

Finally, in some cases, the UN facilitated plebiscites in non-self-governing territories. Plebiscites by international organizations were not a new feature of world politics. In 1935, for instance, the Council of the League of Nations had solved a dispute over whether Germany or France should govern the Saar region with an internationally observed plebiscite.[105] The United Nations made greater use of plebiscites to help decide the future of territories and the shape of governments. For example, the areas of British and French administration in Togoland conducted plebiscites under UN supervision with inhabitants of British Togoland deciding in 1956 to join Ghana rather than remain a trust territory, while the Chamber of Deputies of French Togoland voted in 1958 for independence. Most recently, the United Nations Mission in East Timor (UNAMET) held a referendum on East Timor's status in August

---

[104] French policy quoted in M'Bokolo, "French Colonial Policy in Equatorial Africa," p. 206.

[105] At the end of World War I, France demanded the Saar region as compensation for war losses. France did not get the Saar, and the area was placed under the government of an international commission from 1919 to 1935. Germany demanded the return of the Saar in 1933. A Plebiscite Commission oversaw the voting in 1935. Most residents voted for reunion with Germany, with the second largest number casting their ballots for continued trusteeship. See Yves Beigbeder, *International Monitoring of Plebiscites, Referenda and National Elections: Self-determination and Transition to Democracy* (Boston: Martinus Nijhoff Publishers, 1994), pp. 84–86. Plebiscites were also used by the French in 1790, 1791, and 1793 to decide the fate of Alsace, Avignon, and Belgium and the Palatinate. Of course other territories were created or annexed without plebiscite after World War I: Poland and Czechoslovakia were created; portions of Europe formerly belonging to Germany and Austria were given to Italy and Poland; and the mandate territories formerly belonging to Germany and Turkey were all allocated without a vote on the part of the inhabitants. See Cassese, *Self-determination of Peoples*, pp. 12, 24–25.

1999 where over 98 percent of those registered to vote cast ballots, and of those an overwhelming majority, over 78 percent, rejected continued government by Indonesia. When violence threatened the result, and the lives of the people of East Timor, UN member states led by Australia intervened and the UN ultimately set up a "transitional administration" to assist the recovery and self-determination of East Timor. Table 7.2 lists some UN supervised referenda. The resort to internationally supervised plebiscite is perhaps the best example of the institutionalization of the principle of self-determination.[106]

Changing power: declining public support in the core

Colonial reform movements, from the Congo Reform Association to the Aborigines Protection Societies, were of course long active in the metropolitan countries. After World War II however, anti-colonial sentiment grew in the colonial powers and new organizations, for example the international League Against Imperialism, pressed for decolonization.[107] By the middle of the twentieth century, colonial powers were increasingly constrained by domestic politics as the colonial consensus cracked. Ultimately, as Gann and Duignan suggest, the majority of the intelligentsia in France and Britain "experienced a revulsion against imperial ideals."[108] Why was this?

In part, the brutality of anti-colonial conflicts often led to declining domestic support for colonial policy within the metropole, as happened at the turn of the century with Britain's prosecution of the Boer War. Ethical arguments bolstered by reports of colonial brutality changed the domestic balance of power within states and made colonial empire difficult to maintain. For example, British suppression of Malayan communists (1948–1957) became unpopular in Britain.

In France, left and mainstream French public intellectuals, such as Albert Camus, Jean Paul Sartre, and Raymond Aron, questioned the morality and utility of colonies.[109] Initially supportive of French colonial policy after World War II, the press also mounted criticism of colonial policy and French conduct in their wars in Tunisia, Vietnam, and Algeria. In 1956, journalist Raymond Cartier published articles in the journal *Paris Match*, questioning the economic wisdom of maintaining colonies.

[106] See Aldrich and Connell, *The Last Colonies*.   [107] Davidson, *Let Freedom Come*, p. 190.
[108] Gann and Duignan, *Burden of Empire*, p. 73.
[109] Silver, *Framing a Balance Sheet*; Sorum, *Intellectuals and Decolonization*.

Table 7.2 *International plebiscites and referenda*

Location and Date	Supervisor/ Authority	Issue and outcome
British Togoland 1956	UN UNGA Res. 944(X)	Population voted in favor of union with the Gold Coast rather than continued Trusteeship
French Togoland 1958	UN UNGA Res. 1182 (XII)	Elections for a Chamber of Deputies in April 1958 followed by Chamber of Deputies vote for independence
British Northern Cameroon 1959	UN UNGA Res 1350 (XIII)	Population voted to postpone a decision on whether to join Nigeria
British Northern and Southern Cameroon 1961	UN	Northern Cameroon decided to join Nigeria and Southern Cameroon decided to join the Republic of Cameroun. Results were endorsed by a UN GA res.
Rwanda 1961	UN UNGA Res 1580 (XV)	Population voted against a monarchy system
Western Samoa 1961	UN UNGA Res 1569 (XV)	Population endorsed the constitution drafted by the Constitutional Convention in 1960 and decided to become independent
Malaysia 1963	UN	Future of the Sabah and Sarawak decided before establishing the Federation of Malaysia
Cook Islands 1965	UN UNGA Res 2005 (XIX)	General elections; became a self-governing territory. Residents are New Zealand citizens.
Aden 1967	UN	Election supervision mission failed
Equatorial Guinea 1968	UN	August referendum on independence; September, general elections
West Irian 1969	UN	Self-determination
Bahrain 1970	UN	Determine wishes of people
Papua New Guinea 1972	UN UNGA Res 2156 (XXXVIII)	Trusteeship Council sent observers to the elections for the House of Assembly
Niue Island 1974	UN	New Zealand invited the UN to send authorities to the referendum on self-determination where the population voted in favor of self-government in Free Association with New Zealand; the UN endorsed the results. Islanders are New Zealand citizens

Table 7.2 *(cont.)*

Location and Date	Supervisor/ Authority	Issue and outcome
Ellice Island 1974	UN	UK requested a UN mission to observe a referendum on the separation of Ellice Island from the Gilbert Islands; the population voted in favor of separation and became Tuvalu
Mariana Islands 1974	UN Trusteeship Council	UN Trusteeship Council observed a plebiscite in the Mariana Islands portion of the Pacific Islands Trust Territory
Comoro Islands 1974 and 1976	UN	In 1974, the majority of the population of Anjouan, Grand Comore, and Moheli voted for independence while Mayotte voted in 1947 and 1976 to remain part of France
French Somaliland 1977	UN	Election observed
Trust Territory of the Pacific Islands 1978	UN	Referendum; several districts of the Territory voted to form a Federation under the Constitution of the Federated States of Micronesia (FSM); in 1982 FSM signed a compact of Free Association with the US which came into force in 1986
Palau, Trust Territory of the Pacific Islands 1979, 1983, 1986, 1987, 1990	UN	Plebiscites on the Island's status; finally determined that the island's trusteeship status would have a Compact of "Free Association with the US"; Became independent in 1994
Namibia 1989	UN	Elections for democratic government
East Timor 1999	UN	Referendum on East Timor's relationship with Indonesia; East Timorese voted to end their relationship with Indonesia
Western Sahara ?	UN	Morocco has agreed in principle but has stalled implementation of a vote

Sources: Aldrich and Connell, *The Last Colonies*; Beigbeder, *International Monitoring*; Cassese, *Self-determination of Peoples*; UN Document A/46/609, 19 November 1991, "Human Rights Questions."

Other French intellectuals, by emphasizing torture and the denial of due process in the colonies, stressed the hypocrisy and ironies of French colonial rule. As Pierre-Henri Simon argued in his *Contre la torture* (1957), France, by using torture in the colonies "is less menaced by the action of its enemies than by the ruin of its principle."[110] Another anticolonialist, Jean-Marie Domenach, argued in the journal *Esprit* in 1957: "The right to independence is a consequence of the right of peoples to self-determination, of which France made itself the historical promoter. To oppose it would be to oppose our very tradition, our reason to be heard in the world."[111] Domenach also said of the war in Algeria: "French youth has been placed in this untenable situation of resisting a people struggling for its dignity."[112] The French state knew it was vulnerable to these arguments and tried to conceal the evidence for them; from 1955 to 1962, of the 269 times when issues of newspapers or magazines were seized by the government, some "40 percent of the cases concerned publications revealing torture, executions or bad conditions in prisons or internment camps."[113] Critics of French policy then argued that colonialism was increasing the danger of *domestic* fascism.

French support for using the war in Indochina to reestablish order fell from 37 percent in January 1947 to 7 percent in February 1954, while those favoring negotiations with the Vietminh grew from 15 percent to 42 percent of those polled in the same period. Further, by February, 18 percent favored abandoning Indochina altogether and recalling the troops.[114] The French war against Algerian nationalists (1954–1962), eventually engaging about 500,000 troops, grew to be extremely unpopular in France. By the late 1950s, enough reports of torture and brutality had made it back to France, despite heavy government censorship, to prompt a debate about the conduct of the war. French opinion in favor of decolonization, as opposed to those favoring the use of military force to crush the Algerian rebellion, grew from 39 percent in early 1956 to 56 percent in early 1958.[115]

Perhaps the most extreme domestic political reaction to continued colonialism occurred in Portugal. The Portuguese fought anti-colonial rebellions at great cost in Guinea-Bissau, Mozambique, and Angola, and

---

[110] Quoted in Sorum, *Intellectuals and Decolonization*, p. 125.
[111] Quoted in ibid., p. 71.   [112] Quoted in ibid., p. 148.
[113] Jacques van Doorn and Willem J. Hendrix, *The Process of Decolonization: The Military Experience in Comparative Perspective* (Rotterdam: Comparative Asian Studies Program, 1987), p. 36.
[114] *Sondages* polling data reported in Sorum, *Intellectuals and Decolonization*, p. 10.
[115] Van Doorn and Hendrix, *Process of Decolonization*, pp. 7, 26, 36.

faced opposition to their rule in their other, smaller colonies as well. On average, Portugal stationed 105,000 troops in its African colonies from 1961 to 1973, a high proportion of them Portuguese rather than African, and nearly 9,000 died in the wars.[116] After initially backing repression of the guerrilla movements, elite consensus on colonial policy gradually fractured. Some wanted more substantial reform while others thought the minor colonial reforms of the Caetano government, allowing some legislative and judicial control in the African colonies, were too much. A top general in the Portuguese military, Antonió de Spinola, wrote *Portugal and the Future*, which was critical of the policies. Eventually, top level disagreements in the government about the strategy in Africa – whether to continue the status quo of war or to gradually allow a transition to independence – plus the grievances of junior officers, left room for a military coup in April 1974 by junior officers of the Armed Forces Movement (MFA), who opposed continued empire. As MFA saw it, "Those who benefited from the war were the same financial groups that exploited the people in the metropolis and, comfortably installed in Lisbon or Oporto or abroad, by means of venal government obliged the Portuguese people to fight in Africa in defense of their immense profits."[117] In July 1974, the new regime passed Law 7/74, which "recognized the right to self-determination, with all of its consequences, including the acceptance of the independence of the overseas territories."[118] In 1975, Portugal withdrew from its African colonies.

Ethical argument was not, however, always successful at altering public opinion. In contrast to the British, French, and Portuguese experiences, the population of the Netherlands supported military occupation of Indonesia. The Dutch campaign against West New Guinea nationalists for more than a decade (1950–1962) was popularly supported in the metropole. "Even in 1961, shortly before the actual transition to rule by Indonesia, 56% [of Dutch opinion polled] thought that Papua's 'coming of age'" was necessary before independence.[119]

South West Africa and failed arguments

South West Africa's transition from colony to independence as Namibia was complex. It involved negotiations, guerrilla war, Cold War tension

[116] MacQueen, *The Decolonization of Portuguese Africa*, p. 37.
[117] Quoted in Maxwell, "Portugal and Africa: The Last Empire," p. 359.
[118] Law quoted in MacQueen, *The Decolonization of Portuguese Africa*, p. 88.
[119] Van Doorn and Hendrix, *Process of Decolonization*, p. 8.

and cooperation, and action by the UN General Assembly, the Security Council, and the International Court of Justice (ICJ). In many ways this case is both typical and unusual and extreme. In this discussion, I review the arguments South Africa made to the world community in their attempt to keep South West Africa, the arguments made by advocates of Namibian independence, and the logic of International Court of Justice decisions. South African claims may seem absurd now, but, at the time, they were persuasive with some, and this is more understandable if we recall the cultural context, especially in the time between the creation of the UN and the mid-1960s, when South Africa's arguments about South West Africa were finally rejected in the world body. The case illustrates the use of ethical arguments by the colonial power, the international observers who sought to modify South Africa's rule, and anti-colonial activists and guerrillas, notably the South West Africa People's Organization (SWAPO). South African arguments were only ultimately rejected when scientific racism was rejected and Namibians themselves were able to press their case against occupation. However, ethical arguments failed to change the status of South West Africa through most of this period, but nor was South Africa able to persuade the rest of the world that their occupation was just.

South Africans persistently argued that South West Africa's status as a mandate should end and the territory should be incorporated into South Africa. South African Prime Minister Jan Smuts argued in South Africa's House of Assembly on 20 March 1945 that "If the League of Nations lapses, then the mandatory system also lapses . . . The mandate will have to be abolished, and the territory can be incorporated as a province of the Union . . ."[120] At the San Francisco conference of the United Nations, South Africa claimed that it had treated the inhabitants of South-West Africa well and "faithfully performed its obligations under the mandate." Because of South West Africa's "ethnological" similarity with South Africa, and its economic dependence, "There is no prospect of the Territory ever existing as a separate State, and the ultimate objective of the mandatory principle is therefore impossible of achievement."[121] Using results of a "consultation" of native tribal leaders (where independence was not an option), the South African representative to the UN also claimed that the people of South West Africa

---

[120] Quoted in John Dugard, ed., *The South West Africa/Namibia Dispute: Documents and Scholarly Writing on the Controversy Between South Africa and the United Nations* (Berkeley: University of California Press, 1973), p. 98.
[121] Dugard, ed., *South West Africa/Namibia Dispute*, pp. 89–90: 90.

"freely and unequivocably" wanted to become part of South Africa.[122] South African diplomats then claimed that the mandate should be dissolved and that South West Africa should be incorporated into the Union of South Africa.[123]

Pan-Africanists, anti-colonial activists, and of course South West Africans immediately challenged South Africa's version of international law and history. In early 1946, A. B. Xuma, president of South Africa's African National Congress, sent a cable from Johannesburg to the UN saying, "We have long experience of South Africa's policies, and would not like hundreds of thousands more innocent victims to be brought under South Africa's race and colour dominated policies."[124] Xuma urged the UN to "save their black brothers living in the mandated territory of Southwest Africa from annexation by the Jan Smuts' government of the Union of South Africa."[125] In April 1946, the Namibians living in exile in neighboring Botswana sent a memo to the UN protesting South Africa's efforts to annex South West Africa, and the white South African, Reverend Michael Scott of the Anglican Church, carried a petition from South West Africans to the United Nations in 1947.[126] In October 1946, the Council on African Affairs petitioned the UN Human Rights Commission for an investigation of South Africa's request to annex South West Africa, and Alpheus Hunton circulated the CAA's pamphlet "Seeing is Believing – The Truth About South Africa." The CAA also worked with the Indian government, the ANC, the Indian National Congress, and the Joint Passive Resistance Council of South Africa to protest the treatment of Indians in South Africa in 1946 and 1947. In 1946, when the interim Indian government filed charges with the UNGA that Indians living in South Africa were discriminated against, the CAA organized letters to Truman, the State Department and the US delegate to the UN "urging 'full support to the Indian government's petition to the United

---

[122] Quoted in ibid., p. 109. James Barber and John Barratt, *South Africa's Foreign Policy: The Search for Status and Security 1945–1988* (Cambridge: Cambridge University Press, 1990), pp. 23, 357–358.

[123] On South African arguments at the last session of the League of Nations in 1946 see Solomon Slonim, *South West Africa and the United Nations: An International Mandate in Dispute* (Baltimore: Johns Hopkins University Press, 1973), pp. 68–72.

[124] Quoted in Peter Katjavivi, "The Development of Anti-Colonial Forces in Namibia," in Brian Wood, ed., *Namibia, 1884–1984: Readings on Namibia's History and Society* (Lusaka: United Nations Institute for Namibia, 1988), pp. 557–584: 564.

[125] Quoted in Von Eschen, *Race Against Empire*, p. 88 .

[126] Peter H. Katjavivi, *A History of Resistance in Namibia* (London: James Currey, 1988), pp. 37–39.

Nations ...'"[127] CAA arguments were successful in affecting at least the African-American community's understanding: South Africa's post World War II efforts to annex South West Africa were "universally condemned in African American press."[128]

Responding to criticism, the South African delegation presented the UN with a long memo in October 1946. South Africa made four arguments: granting that the principle of mandates and trusteeship was ultimately self-government, South Africa claimed that "the backwardness of the vast majority of the population" in South West Africa made such a goal impossible; it would be very expensive for the mandate to develop; uncertainty about the future led to difficulty in promoting racial peace and development; and finally, they repeated their claim that the people of South West Africa had already said in a "consultation" of their views that they wanted incorporation into South Africa.[129]

Debate in the General Assembly over South West Africa was sharp. For example, the so-called consultation of the South West Africans through their tribal authorities was derided – since no actual votes by the people were taken – and contrasted with actual voting by whites in the Territory. In December 1946 the UNGA passed a resolution saying that South Africa should place South West Africa under trusteeship.[130] The South Africa representative to the UN refused, but nevertheless promised to continue submitting reports to the United Nations on its administration and said it would "administer the Territory in the spirit of the existing Mandate."[131] South Africa continued to press the UN to "accede" to the incorporation of South West Africa into South Africa, again arguing that the native and European inhabitants had been consulted and that it would provide for the welfare of both populations.

Because opinion was not uniform within South Africa itself, the government had to argue its case there as well and reassure doubters that South Africa's external arguments would succeed. In the South African

---

[127] Von Eschen, *Race Against Empire*, p. 86. Also see Lynch, "Pan-African Responses in the United States to British Colonial Rule in Africa in the 1940s," p. 67.
[128] Von Eschen, *Race Against Empire*, p. 88.
[129] Summarized in Slonim, *South West Africa*, p. 79.
[130] UNGA Resolution 65 (1), 14 December 1946. Besides recommending that South West Africa be placed in the trusteeship system the resolution clearly articulates the view that the people of South West Africa are undeveloped politically. "*Considering* that the African inhabitants of South West Africa have not yet secured political autonomy or reached a stage of political development enabling them to express a considered opinion which the Assembly could recognize on such an important question as incorporation of their territory ...." Ibid.
[131] Quoted in Dugard, ed., *South West Africa/Namibia Dispute*, p. 112.

House of Assembly during March 1947, members and Prime Minister Smuts, clearly mindful of the role of argument, spoke of South Africa's "case" in the world. Member of the South African Parliament Eric Louw said, "South Africa's case is good. The grounds on which we base our case are sound. They are sound juridically. They are sound factually, and I say let us not hesitate. I believe that in this matter we have hesitated too long. Already there has been some talk of sanctions . . . May I suggest that we must not allow ourselves to be scared by talk of sanctions, nor to be deflected from our course by any such suggestions."[132] In reply, Smuts said that he also thought South Africa had a good case but should still refrain from using "language which looks like a challenge which may appear provocative and which may put the bristles up of stronger nations than ourselves and make our case more difficult. It is not wisdom to use language that looks like a challenge."[133]

Prime Minister Smuts attempted to reframe the situation by suggesting that South West Africa was no longer a mandate and had not become a trust territory. Smuts argued that with the termination of the Mandate system, the reports by South Africa to the UN fell under Chapter XI, on non-self-governing territories: "I should rather associate our position with that of colonial territories, which do not fall under trusteeship, but under the colonial system."[134] Seeking to impose this frame on the UN, South Africa then submitted a report on South West Africa to the UN, stating that it assumed the report would not be examined by the Trusteeship Council. After considering the issue of where to examine the report, the UNGA nevertheless sent it to the Trusteeship Council.

---

[132] Quoted in ibid., p. 124.   [133] Smuts quoted in ibid., p. 124.

[134] Quoted in ibid., p. 116. On the question of submitting reports to the UN versus the League of Nations, Eric Louw, said in March 1947: "I can speak from personal experience, having on two occasions had the honour of submitting the South-West Africa report to the League of Nations Mandates Commission. And Mr. Speaker, let me say this, that the Mandates Commission of those days was a body of sympathetic affable gentlemen. And yet, on each occasion I was examined and cross-examined for two full days by the Commission. I was cross-examined very closely on the Union's administration of South-West Africa. But I suggest that when these reports . . . go to the UNO, it is going to be a very different story. The examination of the Union by the UNO Trusteeship Committee will be very different from what it was in the days of the old League of Nations, because the old League, with possibly half a dozen exceptions, was a white organisation, an organisation of predominantly European powers . . . But the UNO is a horse of a very different colour, because the UNO is predominantly coloured; it consists of predominantly coloured and Asiatic nations and of off-colour nations. A considerable number of South and Central American nations are predominantly of mixed blood. And the position is going to be very different when our representative – I pity the poor man – turns up to submit his report on South-West Africa, to the UNO as at present constituted." Quoted in Dugard, ed., *South West Africa/Namibia Dispute*, pp. 118–119.

When the document was considered in 1947, the Trusteeship Council noted that it was incomplete and requested replies by South Africa to fifty questions, including requests for information on the participation of non-Europeans in the government of South West Africa. When South Africa's delegates replied to the Trusteeship Council's questions in 1948, they reiterated their position that South West Africa was not a trust and that its replies should not be taken to imply that South Africa would be accountable to the UN. The Trusteeship Council rejected the South African frame, and adopted a negative report on South Africa's administration of South West Africa, in particular emphasizing the imbalance between resources available to European and native populations.[135]

In 1949, South Africa declared that the mandate was over. In an implicit recognition of the role of ethical argument, South Africa said it would no longer submit reports to the UN since this created a situation where the Trusteeship Council became a "forum for unjustified criticism and censure of the Union Government's administration, not only in South West Africa but in the Union [of South Africa] as well."[136] South Africa, however, continued to make implicit ethical arguments, for instance when South Africa informed the UN of the South West Africa Affairs Act 23 of 1949, under which six white representatives of South West Africa would sit in the South African House of Assembly, and four would sit in the Senate. In a nod to the principle of political representation, one of the white delegates to the Senate would have "thorough acquaintance, by reason of his official experience or otherwise, with the reasonable wants and wishes of the coloured races of the Territory."[137]

Despite South African recalcitrance, the UN kept trying to get South West Africa into the trusteeship system. India introduced a resolution, passed in the Fourth Committee of the UN by a vote of twenty-seven to twenty in October 1947, urging South Africa to place South West Africa under international trusteeship. The US, UK, and all other colonial powers voted against the resolution. In 1949, the UN Fourth Committee again heard testimony from Reverend Michael Scott on behalf of South West African natives. Also in 1949, the UNGA adopted a resolution to

---

[135] See Slonim, *South West Africa*, pp. 91–95.
[136] South Africa's letter to the UN on 11 July 1949 quoted in Slonim, *South West Africa and the United Nations*, p. 100. A longer excerpt is in Dugard, ed., *South West Africa/Namibia Dispute*, pp. 119–120.
[137] Quoted in Dugard, ed., *South West Africa/Namibia Dispute*, p. 120.

take the question of South West Africa to the International Court of Justice. After hearing arguments from South Africa, Egypt, India, the US and Poland, the ICJ gave the first of several rulings on South West Africa in its 1950 advisory opinion. In sum, the opinion said that South Africa was not obliged to put South West Africa under the Trusteeship system, but neither could the South African government legally ignore South West Africa's status as a mandate: South Africa was obliged to promote the "material and moral well-being and social progress of the inhabitants." The Court also affirmed the UN's right to supervise the mandate, essentially substituting the UN for the League.[138] Following the ICJ ruling, in 1951 the UN set up an Ad Hoc Committee to implement the advisory opinion and hopefully to negotiate a trusteeship agreement with South Africa. South Africa argued, however, that the ICJ opinion was invalid and that they had no obligation to negotiate a trusteeship agreement for South West Africa with the UN. When South Africa refused to cooperate, the Fourth Committee heard testimony from South West Africans and again from Reverend Scott about conditions in South West Africa.

Since there had been no progress in getting South Africa to put South West Africa under trusteeship, the UN began to treat South West Africa as a trust territory in all but name. In 1953 the UNGA voted to replace its Ad Hoc Committee with a new Committee on South West Africa that would, among other things, examine South Africa's administration of South West Africa "within the scope of the Questionnaire adopted by the Permanent Mandates Commission of the League of Nations in 1926."[139] In 1954, the Committee on South West Africa invited South Africa to submit a report on the territory covering the years for which the UN had no report. When South Africa refused, the Committee examined relevant information and wrote its own report which concluded that "after thirty-five years of administration under the Mandates System, the Native inhabitants are still not participating in the political development of the Territory, that their participation in the economic development is restricted to that of labourers and that the social and educational services for their benefit are far from satisfactory."[140] South Africa refused to supply reports the following years, and the 1955 and 1956 reports of the Committee on South West Africa were again quite critical,

[138] Advisory Opinion is summarized and discussed in Slonim, *South West Africa*, pp. 110–122. Most of the text of the opinion is excerpted in Dugard, ed., *South West Africa/Namibia Dispute*, pp. 131–143.
[139] Slonim, *South West Africa*, p. 141.   [140] Quoted in ibid., p. 144.

if anything, growing increasingly harsh as South Africa began to extend the apartheid system more completely to South West Africa.[141] The UN then established a Good Offices Committee which tried, again unsuccessfully, to bring South West Africa into the Trusteeship system.

The UNGA continued to invite South Africa to put South West Africa under trusteeship until 1959 and South Africa repeatedly declined to do so. Given these failures, in November 1960, Ethiopia and Liberia, as former members of the League of Nations, asked the ICJ for a binding judgment that Namibia remained a Mandate territory and that South Africa's governance of Namibia (in exporting apartheid to the territory) was contrary to its obligations as a mandatory power.[142] South Africa argued that the ICJ lacked jurisdiction. The UNGA passed a resolution supporting the Ethiopian and Liberian effort, and in the following years continued to pass resolutions stating that South Africa had failed to carry out its responsibilities as a mandate.[143]

While the ICJ case was pending, the independence movement in South West Africa achieved greater external recognition and support.[144] The South West African People's Organization (SWAPO) and the South West Africa National Union (SWANU), had grown out of the early anti-German resistance efforts and years of political organizing under South African rule. Denied access to South West Africa, the UN's Special Committee for South West Africa went to Accra, Dar es Salaam, and Cairo in 1961 to hear petitions from SWAPO and SWANU representatives urging that South Africa's mandate be terminated and that self-government based on "one man, one vote" be set up.[145] The Committee report concluded that South Africa was unfit to govern South West Africa, that it should be removed from the territory, and called for the independence of South West Africa.[146] In 1963 the UNGA adopted a resolution which defined any further attempt by South Africa to annex South West Africa as an act of "aggression" which threatened international peace and security.[147]

[141] Slonim, *South West Africa*, pp. 155, 167. South Africa's extension of apartheid to South West Africa ironically opened South Africa itself to greater criticism of its racial policies as the area of domestic jurisdiction (Article 2) of the UN Charter, was blurred by the South Africans themselves.
[142] For the text of submissions to the ICJ, see Slonim, *South West Africa*, pp. 375–378.
[143] UNGA Resolutions 1565 (XV), 1596 (XV), 1702 (XVI), and 2674 (XX).
[144] On this early period see Tony Emmett, "Popular Resistance in Namibia, 1920–5," in Wood, ed., *Namibia, 1884–1984*, pp. 224–225.
[145] Dugard, ed., *South West Africa/Namibia Dispute*, pp. 223–225.
[146] Ibid., pp. 225–226.   [147] UNGA Resolution 1899 (XVIII), 13 November 1963.

When the ICJ ruling finally came in July 1966, the Court found that Ethiopia and Liberia did not have any legal rights or interests in the territory. The South African government proclaimed victory and attacked guerrilla camps in the Ovamboland region of South West Africa, while SWAPO and SWANU interpreted the ruling as a sign that they should intensify their effort for independence, including armed struggle.[148] South African repression of Namibian independence efforts intensified in response, and the independence movement guerrillas were labeled terrorists. In spite of the ICJ opinion, by 1966 the vast majority of UNGA members had come to believe that if an administering power had failed to live up to either the "sacred trust" obligation of the League Mandate system, or of the UN Charter obligations to promote the "well-being" of the inhabitants of trust territories, then the trusteeship had been vitiated by the administering power. This view was clearly articulated in a 1966 UNGA resolution, which passed by a vote of 114 to 2 (with 3 abstentions), terminating South Africa's right to administer South West Africa and stating that South West Africa was therefore a direct responsibility of the UN.

> [C]onvinced that the administration of the Mandated Territory by South Africa has been conducted in a manner contrary to the Mandate, the Charter of the United Nations and the Universal Declaration of Human Rights ... *Declares* that South Africa has failed to fulfill its obligations in respect to administration of the Mandated Territory and to ensure the moral and material well-being and security of the indigenous inhabitants of South West Africa ...[149]

The following year, the UNGA passed a resolution creating the UN Council for South West Africa and set June 1968 as the target date for South West African independence.[150] South Africa tried to deflect international scrutiny by adopting some of the language of self-determination, albeit without the substance. In 1968 South Africa moved to create six areas in South West Africa as "self-governing nations" by passing the Development of Self-Government for Native Nations in South West Africa Act. The 1968 Act explicitly uses the language of self-determination in its preamble: "Whereas it is desirable that the native nations in the territory of South-West Africa should in the realization

---

[148] See Dugard, ed., *South West Africa/Namibia Dispute*, p. 377.
[149] Resolution 2145 (XXI), 27 October 1966. The negative votes were South Africa and Portugal; the abstentions were France, the UK, and Malawi.
[150] Resolution 2248 (S-V), 19 May 1967.

of their right of self-determination develop in an orderly manner to self-governing nations and independence."[151]

Meanwhile, South Africa kept defending its role in South West Africa at the UN, for example, sending the UN a letter in September 1969 outlining its position and arguing that the UN did not have the authority to revoke its mandate. But the General Assembly and Security Council rejected the Self-Government Act.[152] The Security Council called upon "all states to refrain from all dealings with the Government of South Africa purporting to act on behalf of the territory of Namibia" and further requested all states to "increase their moral and material assistance to the people of Namibia in their struggle against foreign occupation."[153] In response, the South African Department of Foreign Affairs published a 115 page analysis of the legal status of South West Africa. This pattern of UN resolution and South Africa reply continued over the next several years. The South African government continually rejected the UN position and consistently argued until the 1970s that South West Africa ought to be part of South Africa.

The UN General Assembly and Security Council nevertheless found South Africa's arguments without merit and in 1970 asked the International Court of Justice to rule on the consequences of South Africa's presence in Namibia. The Finnish delegate to the Security Council hoped that a correct ruling by the ICJ would "help ... to mobilize public opinion."[154] In 1971, after reviewing the legal arguments, South Africa's policies, the relevant UN resolutions, and the Court's previous decisions, the ICJ found that South Africa's occupation, being illegal, had to end. The principle of self-determination applied to Namibia. Further, "Member States of the United Nations are ... under obligation to recognize the illegality and invalidity of South Africa's continued presence in Namibia [and] to refrain from lending any support or any form of assistance to South Africa with reference to its occupation in Namibia."[155] The ruling cleared the way for substantial UN support for the inhabitants of South West Africa and SWAPO.

Not surprisingly, South African Prime Minster B.J. Vorster rejected the ICJ opinion, claiming that the court was packed against South Africa and

---

[151] On the 1968 Act, see Dugard, ed., *South West Africa/Namibia Dispute*, pp. 431–435: 433.
[152] See Slonim, *South West Africa*, p. 328. See UNGA Resolution 2403 (XXIII), 16 December 1968 and UNSC Resolution 264 (1969).
[153] UNSC Resolution 269 (1969).
[154] Quoted in Slonim, *South West Africa*, p. 330. A long excerpt of the opinion is in Dugard, ed., *South West Africa/Namibia Dispute*, pp. 453–481.
[155] Quoted in Slonim, *South West Africa*, p. 337.

that the ICJ ruling was "the result of political maneuvering instead of objective jurisprudence."[156] Further, Vorster said, "It is our duty to administer South West Africa so as to promote the well-being and progress of its inhabitants."[157] Thus, over the course of several years, South Africa's arguments for occupying Namibia were found unpersuasive, and the UN and ICJ moved to push South Africa out by mobilizing public opinion against South Africa's occupation.

International opposition to South Africa's behavior in the region and inside South Africa itself grew in the 1970s and 1980s. As is well known, there was also vocal opposition to South Africa's domestic government among African states. In 1969, several independent African states issued a statement outlining their opposition to minority rule in Southern Africa. The Lusaka Manifesto of April 1969, signed by Burundi, Central African Republic, Chad, Congo, Ethiopia, Kenya, Rwanda, Somalia, Sudan, Tanzania, Uganda, and Zambia, proclaimed that signatory states "do not accept that any individual or group has any right to govern any other group of sane adults, without their consent, and we affirm that only the people of a society, acting together as equals, can determine what is, for them, a good society and a good social, economic, or political organization."[158] The Manifesto also urged that South Africa, because of its "denial of human equality," be excluded from United Nations agencies and the UN itself and that South Africa should be "ostracized from the world community . . . isolated from world trade patterns and left to be self-sufficient if it can."[159]

Why was South Africa so interested in South West Africa that it would risk such international reaction? Although this is discussed at greater length in chapter 8, simply put, South West Africa was valuable economically because of its vast natural resource wealth in the form of diamonds, uranium, zinc, and other minerals. Further, as long as South Africa held South West Africa's mineral wealth, this was another potential lever of influencing Western government policies toward South Africa itself. Finally, South West Africa was part of a "cordon sanitaire" for white minority rule in South Africa which was, according to the South African government, under assault from communism and "terrorism."

---

[156] Quoted in ibid., p. 344.
[157] Quoted in Dugard, ed., *South West Africa/Namibia Dispute*, p. 491.
[158] "Lusaka Manifesto," April 1969, reprinted in Colin Legum and John Drysdale, eds., *Africa Contemporary Record* (New York: Africana Publishing Company, 1971), vol. II, 1969–1970, pp. C41–C45: C41–C42.
[159] Ibid., p. C44.

If South West Africa was so important, why did South Africa refrain from annexing South West Africa outright? And why did the South African government keep trying to convince the ICJ and the UN of the legitimacy of South African position? Part of the answer has to do with the political culture of Afrikaners and English speaking South Africans. Many white South Africans truly believed in the rule of law and that they could persuade others that they were right. This belief in law and public persuasion is evident even in their internal use of law to enact apartheid and to round up and try political dissidents in the famous "treason" trials of the 1950s and 1960s. Second, as Smuts said, the South Africans felt they had no reason to alarm the outside community since they had many of the benefits of annexation without proclaiming it. A proclamation would only have heightened the distance between South Africa and the United Nations, which increasingly threw its political, and financial, support behind SWAPO and the anti-apartheid movement.

Remaining colonies, free associations, and late decolonization

Throughout, I have argued that colonialism has ended as a distinct practice of international politics. In the sense that it is no longer acceptable for states to take territory against the wishes of the inhabitants and to govern the people there without political representation, colonialism is over. In another sense, however, colonialism continues for several million people who live in lands variously described by the governing authorities as crown colonies, dependencies, overseas territories, or autonomous communities. Most of these places are islands, many of them beautiful tourist destinations, with small populations.

In many cases, "administering" states made reports to the United Nations justifying their treatment of the inhabitants of these territories and often "voluntarily" conducted referenda to show that the people chose their status, or at least approved of it after the fact. Referenda or plebiscites were held during the 1980s and 1990s in several of these territories, some conducted under international supervision. For example, the US-held territories of the Marshall Islands, Palau, the Virgin Islands, and Puerto Rico conducted plebiscites in the 1980s and 1990s to determine their status. When the last UN Territory, Palau, became independent in 1994, the UN Trusteeship Council suspended its operations. Curaçao, Bermuda, Christmas Island, and New Caledonia, held respectively by the Netherlands, Britain, Australia, and France, also conducted referenda in the 1980s and 1990s.[160] In some cases, such as in Puerto Rico, the population voted to keep their status as self-governing dependencies. In other cases, such as East Timor and Tibet where the colonizers, Indonesia and China respectively, resisted any change, long, hard-fought movements for independence or at least greater autonomy developed and achieved international recognition. In the case of Western Sahara, after a long war for independence by the Polisario Front, Morocco agreed in principle to a UN referendum, though it has managed to stall its implementation through the 1990s.

What is important about these situations from the perspective of my argument about ethical arguments and normative belief is the widespread presumption that the people in these territories should have some say about who governs them and how. In other words, the starting point or topoi of discussion and arguments about status is now self-determination; old-fashioned colonialism is illegitimate even in these remaining colonies. Thus, decolonization and self-determination are the standards by which present political relations are judged. Even in cases where colonies remain, most of the governments have gone to great pains to show that their government is legitimate and desired by the inhabitants.

In cases where legitimacy is in question because the land was recently taken by force and there are strong independence and autonomy movements, such as East Timor and Tibet, Indonesia and China respectively have come under tremendous international criticism by human rights groups, governments, and international organizations. The success of their ethical arguments, if not in every instance their political movements, is illustrated by the fact that leaders of both East Timor and Tibet's independence movements have been recognized internationally by the press and with Nobel Peace Prizes. In neither case, however, were Western governments willing to expend significant political capital to help bring self-determination to these lands.

The belated political success of East Timorese independence versus the failure of Tibetans to achieve independence is thus a consequence of at least five factors. First, the political and cultural relationship between China and Tibet is extremely complex and cannot be easily framed. Rather, much of the discourse is still at the meta-argument phase where some characterize Tibet as a sovereign state invaded by a colonizer, while others suggest the relation is a more complex religious, cultural, and

---

[160] See Aldrich and Connell, *The Last Colonies*.

political interrelationship.[161] Second, the Tibetans have not conducted a large-scale guerrilla conflict that has provoked brutal Chinese repression, and hence, the sympathies of the world have not been engaged by the emotional outrage that now accompanies brutal repression. East Timorese were massacred in large numbers after 1975 by Indonesian armed forces and reports of these massacres, and continued violent repression, were used to great effect by those who argued against the occupation. When militias destroyed much of East Timor's infrastructure and terrorized its population following the East Timorese vote for independence in 1999, international observers were outraged. Third, the invasion of Tibet in 1950 occurred before decolonization norms were fully articulated and institutionalized, while Tibet's *de facto* and *de jure* status as an independent nation was ostensibly less clear in the international law of the time. By contrast, East Timor had been colonized by a Western power, and, when Portugal left, there was an opportunity for independence. Fourth, China has no powerful domestic opposition to colonialism to constrain their government or support decolonization. The transition to relative democracy in Indonesia in 1998 created an opening for domestic and international public opinion on East Timor, and hence an opening for ethical argument. When the East Timorese population voted overwhelmingly in 1999 for independence, in a UN supervised vote, Indonesian rule could no longer be considered legitimate by any current standard. Fifth, China's potentially enormous military and economic power has deterred Western governments from showing serious and sustained interest in confronting China on human rights issues. Western governments are unlikely to act until an ethically based transnational movement mobilizes support for Tibetans on a scale to rival or exceed the global anti-apartheid movement of the 1980s. If the status of Tibet can be reframed through ethical (and practical) argument, change will become more likely.

[161] See Tsering Shakya, *The Dragon in the Land of Snows: A History of Modern Tibet Since 1947* (New York: Columbia University Press, 1999); Melvyn C. Goldstein, *The Snow Lion and the Dragon: China, Tibet, and the Dalai Lama* (Berkeley: University of California Press, 1997).

8 Alternative explanations, counterfactuals, and causation

> I am very busy here going through the Indies archives and calculating the profit which Spain made then and makes now out of her colonies.[1]

> I know enough tribes in Africa. They all have the same mentality insofar as they yield only to force. It was and remains my policy to apply this force by unmitigated terrorism and even cruelty. I shall destroy the rebellious tribes by shedding rivers of blood and money.[2]

> One of the problems in writing about decolonization is that we know the end of the story. Whether self-government is seen as the outcome of a process of preparation carried out by a colonial state or as a triumph wrested from the colonizers by national movements, the story lends itself to be read backwards and to privilege the process of ending colonial rule over anything else that was happening in those years.[3]

The content of argument, belief, and culture enables, shapes, and limits, providing a discursive structure to world politics that is as real as the military forces of states or the balance of power among them. Previous chapters highlight the use of ethical arguments by agents to bolster or undermine colonial practices and institutions, but scientific, identity, and practical arguments were also part of colonial and anti-colonial discourses. Yet, as acknowledged, there are powerful alternative explanations for the rise of colonial empire, the demise of slavery, and the end of colonialism that stress economic and balance-of-power forces rather than discursive forces. Although it is impossible to completely separate

---

[1] King Leopold quoted in Adam Hochschild, *King Leopold's Ghost: A Story of Greed, Terror and Heroism in Colonial Africa* (Boston: Houghton Mifflin Company, 1998), p. 37.
[2] Lothor von Trotha quoted in Horst Drechsler, *"Let Us Die Fighting:" The Struggle of the Herero and Nama against German Imperialism (1884–1915)* (London: Zed Press, 1980), p. 154.
[3] Frederick Cooper, *Decolonization and African Society: The Labor Question in French and British Africa* (Cambridge: Cambridge University Press, 1996), p. 6.

the "material" from the "ideational" – since humans make arguments about the nature of the economic and military world and how to best act in it, and persuasive arguments may lead to behavioral changes which meet up against constraints in the material world, or change that material world – it might be useful to try to do so now in order to see the limits of a causal explanation that rests on argument and how the two realms overlap.

This chapter examines the most powerful alternative explanations – those that rest on "material" factors – for the end of colonialism, concludes the discussion of Namibia, and suggests some counterfactuals in order to highlight just which conditions were crucial for decolonization to occur and to recall the role of contingency. I conclude by summarizing my, now qualified, causal arguments.

Alternative explanations for post-World War II decolonization

Why the sudden shift toward decolonization as the international norm after World War II? Though it would be a legitimate inquiry, the focus here is not on why one imperial power or another was forced to relinquish, or voluntarily gave up, its colonial holdings, but rather on why colonialism ceased to be a dominant practice and became, instead, one that was viewed as wrong.[4] Still, in explaining the end of colonialism as an accepted practice, as an accepted relationship among states (at least from the perspective of the colonizer), one cannot entirely ignore the specifics of these endings, for there may be some underlying economic or political reasons why all these colonialisms ended that explains the demise of colonialism and the rise of decolonization as the behavioral norm. Such are the realist and Marxist arguments, which stress power-political and economic causes for colonialism's demise.

There are several versions of economic and power-political explanations for post-1945 decolonization – growing effectiveness of national liberation movements; increased expense versus declining profits; and the exhaustion of the colonizer – and these factors are often linked, even occasionally to ethical explanations. R.F. Betts argues, for example, "In large measure, colonial rule ultimately collapsed in Africa because of the declining ability – a combined financial, military and moral

---

[4] In understanding particular decolonizations, one must delve deeply into the history of the metropole, its political, military, and cultural relationship to the colony in question, and the strength of the liberation movements in the colony.

condition – of Europeans to continue it in the face of African nation-alist pressure."[5]

Liberation movements

One version of the power politics explanation stresses how indigenous efforts for national liberation became more effective, tipping the bal-ance of military and political power away from the colonizer. According to this account, peaceful and legal movements of intelligentsia and/or guerrilla wars for self-determination were fueled by the insults of colo-nialism and growing nationalist sentiments within the colonies. This view emphasizes indigenous efforts for "national liberation" rather than the mobilization of reformers within imperial states, or arguments made by the colonized.

This view relies on demonstrating that there were increasingly strong nationalist anti-colonial movements. And there is no doubt that these efforts became better organized and more effective. For example, during the twentieth century, the legal movements for change and non-violent organization, such as the Indian National Congress in India, and the Convention Peoples Party in Ghana, sought liberation through political reform and at the ballot box. Armed resistance to colonial powers – e.g. in the United States in 1776, in Haiti in 1804, culminating in the guerrilla wars of the twentieth century in Algeria, Rhodesia, Vietnam, and Namibia – also became harder to defeat. Moreover, independence movements could develop and draw upon nationalist sentiments and pan-national support from their neighbors.[6]

Scholars of decolonization movements give several (primarily idea driven) explanations for growing nationalism in the early twentieth century, ranging from increased literacy and the transfer of European nationalist ideals, as natives with Western education returned to the colonies, to what Hedley Bull describes as "the psychological or spiritual awakening of Asian, African, Caribbean and Pacific peoples . . ."[7] This

---

[5] R.F. Betts, "Methods and Institutions of European Domination," in A. Adu Boahen, ed., *Africa Under Colonial Domination, UNESCO General History of Africa*, vol. VII (Paris: UNESCO, 1985), pp. 313–331: 330.

[6] On the other hand there were native "collaborators" who benefited from slavery, forced labor, and other economic institutions of colonialism who facilitated and supported colo-nial practices.

[7] Hedley Bull, "The Revolt Against the West," in Hedley Bull and Adam Watson, eds., *The Expansion of International Society* (Oxford: Oxford University Press, 1984), pp. 217–228: 224. In his famous winds of change speech to the South African Parliament in 1960, Harold Macmillan said, "We have seen the awakening of national consciousness in peoples who

awakening began, Bull argues, "among small groups of the Western-educated, later affecting masses of peoples that led them to perceive the old order no longer as a fact of nature, but as something that could be changed, to recognize that by mobilizing themselves to this end they could indeed change it, to abandon a passive for a politically active role in world politics."[8] Similarly, Margery Perham claims with regard to Africa, that:

> Most of the tribes quickly accepted European rule as part of an irresistible order, one which brought many benefits, above all, peace, and exciting novelties, railways and roads, lamps, bicycles, ploughs . . . For the ruling classes it brought new strength and security of status and new forms of wealth and power . . . It was not until a small minority, through their attainment of the higher levels of Western education, and above all through travel came to understand something of the world at large and of their own place in it that the spell of acceptance began to be broken. Excited by the wine of these ideas, and smarting, perhaps, from some experience of the colour bar in Europe, and especially in Britain the young African would return after some years to his country to preach the idea that only by self-government could Africans escape from personal humiliation and win equality of status in a world of which they were at last becoming aware.[9]

Explanations focusing on indigenous efforts also stress the growing military effectiveness of resistance movements as they were able to supply themselves with arms and ammunition.[10] What made colonialism

---

have for centuries lived in dependence upon some other power . . . In different places it takes different forms but it is happening everywhere. The wind of change is blowing through this continent and, whether we like it or not, the growth of national consciousness is a political fact. We must all accept it as a fact, and our national policies must take account of it." Harold Macmillan, "The Wind of Change," in A.N Porter and A.J. Stockwell, eds., *British Imperial Policy, 1938–64, Volume 2: 1951–1964* (London: Macmillan Press, 1987), pp. 522–531: 524–525.

[8] Bull, "The Revolt Against the West," p. 224. As D.K. Fieldhouse argues: "On the one hand it caused resentment by what it destroyed; on the other hand it encouraged its subjects to think as Europeans, and in so doing narrowed the gap between ruler and ruled. Once a sufficient minority of them had acquired European skills and adopted European assumptions about, for example freedom and equality, alien rule would seem as intolerable an anomaly as that of one European state by another . . . In these ways and for these reasons modern colonialism contained the seeds of its own destruction and decolonization was the inevitable outcome." D.K. Fieldhouse, *Colonialism 1870–1945: An Introduction* (New York: St. Martin's, 1981), p. 24.

[9] Quoted in A. Adu Boahen, *African Perspectives on Colonialism* (Baltimore: Johns Hopkins, 1987), p. 62.

[10] For a summary of European military-technical advantages, including paternalistic references to indigenous peoples, see Michael Howard, "The Military Factor in European Expansion," in Bull and Watson, eds., *The Expansion of International Society*, pp. 33–42.

possible on such a large scale as existed at the beginning of the twentieth century was overwhelming military force on the part of the colonizers. Fieldhouse is typical when he argues that though resistance to colonialism was "widespread at the start and was never entirely eliminated . . . it could everywhere be suppressed or contained because the imperialist possessed far superior military resources and better political organization and there were no external powers to support resistance movements as there were after 1945."[11] According to the balance-of-forces argument, after World War II the colonizers had long lines of communication, often several colonies to "defend" at once, but few of the advantages traditionally associated with defending one's own territory, even as the colonized were gaining military might. As Michael Doyle argues, "Independence became possible . . . when the balance shifted to the opponents of continued rule and the metropole was not in a position to apply overwhelming force."[12] Thus, although European military might continued to grow, and was at its peak just as decolonization began, the argument is that the ratio of military force between colonizer and colonized shifted; effective resistance became possible in situations where military resistance and revolt had previously been ineffective.

Economics of empire

Other explanations for decolonization emphasize the *growing expense of empire*. The imperial elite's understanding of the costs and benefits of empire changed because empire was *in fact* less profitable than in the past. This explanation also presumes that one of, or the only, cause of colonialism was the economic and strategic utility of colonies; when this utility declined, if it did, rational colonizers let their colonies go. As Michael Howard argues, "On the part of the imperial powers, empires – at least, formal empires – were seen to bring neither political power nor economic advantage commensurate with the effort involved in maintaining them."[13] European elites realized that neocolonialism (informal domination of colonial economies and politics) was less costly than direct military occupation and formal political control.[14] As M. E. Chamberlain argues:

[11] Fieldhouse, *Colonialism*, p. 25.
[12] Michael W. Doyle, *Empires* (Ithaca: Cornell University Press, 1986), p. 369.
[13] Howard, "The Military Factor in European Expansion," p. 41.
[14] In 1930, US State Department official Benjamin Gerig argued in *The Open Door and the Mandates System: A Study of Economic Equality before and since the Establishment of the Mandates System* that international mandates were preferable because they were open doors. "The Mandates System is undoubtedly the most effective instrument yet devised

By the 1950s it had become clear that empire could be expensive in both monetary terms and, if you chose to defend it militarily, as the French and Portuguese were to do, in terms of human resources and of political stability at home as well. Was it worth it? Almost certainly not, if you could leave behind a sufficiently stable political structure to provide a satisfactory trading partner; that after all ... was what the Europeans had been seeking in the nineteenth century; they had only moved to formal political control when they could not find it. The growing nationalist movements seemed likely to provide such a political structure.[15]

Quincy Wright also stresses an economic calculus:

Presently humanitarianism was strengthened by a new appreciation of economic expediency. In the exploitation of thinly populated temperate regions extermination of the natives was little loss to the imperial power and perhaps a gain. Immigrants could fill the gap, supplying better labor than the natives and also relieving population pressure in the home territory. But with thickly settled acquisitions like India or tropical acquisitions like Central Africa it began to be seen that the native was an important economic asset. Without his labor the territory could not produce. Thus the ablest administrators like Sir Frederick Lugard in Nigeria began to study the native and cater not only to his material but to his psychological welfare with highly gratifying economic results.[16]

For some, an "efficiency" rationale was probably a persuasive reason for colonizers to engage, at a minimum, in pragmatic reforms or even to drop their opposition to decolonization. A parallel argument advanced by both Marxist and non-Marxist theorists of international political economy suggests that imperialism was increasingly expensive at the same time that changes in modes of production made colonialism less profitable. In other words, when the costs of maintaining empire rose, colonialism was no longer seen as profitable compared with the benefits of trade among already industrialized states.

to make the Open Door effective. The mandates principle is irreconcilable with that of national economic imperialism." Quoted in Wm. Roger Louis, *Imperialism at Bay: The United States and the Decolonization of the British Empire, 1941–1945* (New York: Oxford University Press, 1978), p. 91.

[15] M. E. Chamberlain, *Decolonization: The Fall of the European Empires* (New York: Basil Blackwell, 1985), p. 76.

[16] Quincy Wright, *Mandates Under the League of Nations* (Chicago: University of Chicago Press, 1930), pp. 9–10.

Exhaustion and overreach

Exhaustion arguments have a long pedigree and are often related to an "over-extension" or imperial "over-reach" thesis. As Edward Gibbon argues in *The Decline and Fall of the Roman Empire*, "the decline of Rome was the natural and inevitable effect of immoderate greatness. Prosperity ripened the principle of decay; the causes of destruction multiplied with the extent of conquest; and as soon as time, or accident, had removed artificial supports, the stupendous fabric yielded to the pressure of its own weight."[17] The exhaustion explanation for decolonization is that the colonial powers' ability to maintain empire declined due to the drain of the two world wars and the Great Depression, while armed resistance in the colonies grew. One interwar observer, M.J. Bonn, wrote, "The success of these decolonization movements was not so much due to their own innate strength as to the war-tiredness of the great empires. After four years' fighting on far-flung fronts, the glamour of adventure had gone. Even the most reckless spirits had drunk their fill and long for peace, cleanliness, quiet and rest."[18] Similarly, Gann and Duignan argue, that after World War I, "Britain and France stood at the zenith of their imperial might, but at the very moment of success, real power was slipping from their grasp. They were exhausted."[19]

Moreover, if colonial powers were fatigued and overstretched at the end of World War I, by the end of World War II the great powers were in deep trouble financially; Britain, for instance, had overseas debts of £3,355 million. Increasingly financially strapped and "exhausted," great powers could not bear the expense of policing the empires. J.D. Hargreaves argues, in addition, that one of the first causes of a stirring for African independence was the Great Depression, which led to a decline in commodity prices for sectors of the African agricultural

---

[17] Quoted in Anthony Pagden, *Lords of All the World: Ideologies of Empire in Spain, Britain and France, c. 1500–1800* (New Haven: Yale University Press, 1995), p. 162.

[18] M. J. Bonn, *The Crumbling of Empire: The Disintegration of the World Economy* (London: Allen and Unwin, 1938), p. 152.

[19] L.H. Gann and Peter Duignan, *Burden of Empire: An Appraisal of Western Colonialism in Africa South of the Sahara* (New York: Praeger, 1967), p. 72. On overreach, also see Paul Kennedy, *The Rise and Fall of the Great Powers* (New York: Random House, 1988) and Jack Snyder, *Myths of Empire: Domestic Politics and International Ambition* (Ithaca: Cornell University Press, 1991). One could also argue that the Cold War and the desire of the European powers to mobilize to defend against the threat of Soviet expansion caused the colonial powers to reorient their priorities from defense of empire to European defense. However, this does not take into account uses of empire in the past as a part of the European balancing system.

economy, displaced rural Africans, and decreased the metropolitan power's ability to pay for empire.[20]

A reply to the alternative explanations

While these alternative explanations for post-1945 decolonization – increasingly effective liberation movements, greater expense of empire, and the exhaustion and/or overextension of the great colonial powers – are important in individual cases, they are insufficient as an account of the end of colonialism as a legitimate practice. When linked together – stronger liberation movements increased the expense of maintaining empire just as profits were declining and the great powers were weakened by wars with each other – the alternative accounts are more plausible, but still not entirely convincing.

On the argument that growing nationalism and anti-colonialism, which became increasingly effective, brought decolonization, I have shown throughout that resistance to colonialism by the colonized – from the conquest of the Aztecs to the invasion of East Timor – was constant. No one in the colonies suddenly awoke to their oppression and began to fight it; anti-colonial movements resisted the colonizers politically and militarily from the outset. The question is: why were liberation movements increasingly effective after 1945? Anti-colonial movements certainly became better coordinated politically and were also supported by labor movements within the metropole and other sympathetic international actors. Thus, mobilization by liberation movements was crucial in determining the precise timing and manner of decolonization in particular cases. But anti-colonial movements were not necessarily better armed in relation to the colonizer. Rather, what became increasingly evident was the declining willingness of colonizers to fight for colonies in the same brutal ways they had in the past.

Do economic factors account for post-1945 decolonization? Answers depend on economics at several levels and for several kinds of actors. Colonies were extremely important during and after the world wars for those European states which had colonial holdings: colonies supplied raw materials, cheap labor, and hundreds of thousands of soldiers.[21]

[20] J. D. Hargreaves, *Decolonization in Africa* (London: Longman, 1988), pp. 32–34.
[21] Recall that not only did France and Britain use conscripts from the colonies to maintain colonial rule, but conscripts were used both during and after the World Wars to supplement the European militaries in Europe, for instance occupying the Rhineland for France after World War I. Clemenceau, in 1919 decided to make conscription mandatory in French West Africa in order to make up for French manpower shortages due to the carnage of World

Colonies also partially financed, through taxation, the post-war recon-struction of colonial European states. Thus, as one observer notes, "The great irony of decolonization in Africa is that it came almost imme-diately after the post-1945 period wher the metropolitan powers had regarded their colonies as an essential economic foundation for their own recovery and future development."[22]

Still, the benefits of colonies could have been less than the costs of maintaining them. However, arguments stressing the costs of empire often fail to take fully into account the fact that inhabitants of colonies were generally taxed for the privilege of being colonies (taxation with-out representation) and in some cases, taxes apparently paid for the occupation, as during British rule of India during the late nineteenth century. Further, tariffs on imports to colonies also offset the costs of military occupation.[23] Even later, when "development" came onto the agenda, profits likely outweighed the expense of colonial rule in most cases. "A rough calculation suggests that between 1945 and 1951 Britain extracted some £140 million from her colonies, putting in only about £40 million under the Colonial Development and Welfare acts."[24] But in 1952, with falling commodity prices, the colonies were not such an asset.

This brings us to the core question: was colonialism profitable? In terms of the average settler, metropolitan citizen, investor, or native colonial subject there is no one-size-fits-all answer to the question of colonialism and profit: the economics of colonialism were profitable for some and not for others, depending on the period. For Portugal, which was in a difficult economic situation in the post-World War II era, its African colonies provided valuable revenue. Portuguese Angola was rich in iron, diamonds, and oil. And as Kenneth Maxwell notes of Portugal, "the large surplus from the African territories would be painful to lose." Portuguese revenue from its African colonies was sub-stantial, not only subsidizing occupation, but bolstering the Portuguese government even in the last years of Portuguese colonialism.

> In 1973 such earnings represented as much as 5 percent of the gross national product, about $540 million. All the cotton of Mozambique

War I. Myron Echenberg, *Colonial Conscripts: The* Tirailleurs Sénégalais *in French West Africa 1857–1960* (London: James Currey, 1991), pp. 42–46. Also see Gann and Duignan, *Burden of Empire*, p. 213.
[22] David Fieldhouse, "Arrested Development in Anglophone Black Africa?" in Prosser Gifford and Wm. Roger Louis, eds., *Decolonization and African Independence: The Transfer of Power, 1960–1980* (New Haven: Yale University Press, 1988), pp. 135–158: 139.
[23] See Doyle, *Empires*, pp. 236, 251, 253.
[24] Fieldhouse, "Arrested Development?" p. 140.

was exported to Portugal and 99.7 percent of its sugar, both at well below world prices. At the same time, the wages of the Mozambique miners working in South Africa were converted into gold shipments to Lisbon – in effect a hidden subsidy to the Portuguese war effort, since the bullion was valued at the official rate of $42.20 an ounce instead of the world market price of close to $200 an ounce in 1974. During the three years before the coup, the official value of this gold amounted to at least $180 million.[25]

Still, profitability was not uniformly distributed. For example, in their study of the economics of the British colonial empire, Lance Davis and Robert Huttenback argue, "The British as a whole certainly did not benefit economically from the Empire. On the other hand, individual investors did. In the Empire itself, the level of benefits depended upon whom one asked and how one calculated. For the colonies of white settlement the answer is unambiguous: They paid for little and received a great deal. In the dependent Empire the white settlers, such as there were, almost certainly gained as well."[26] On the other hand, Davis and Huttenback argue, "As far as the indigenous population was concerned, while they received a market basket of government commodities at truly wholesale prices, there is no evidence to suggest that, had they been given a free choice, they would have bought the particular commodities offered, even at the bargain-basement rates."[27]

Most damaging to the economic argument is that the world's largest colonial power, Great Britain, was uncertain about the economic and strategic benefits of its colonial holdings in the crucial period after World War II. British government documents show that officials simply did not know if colonial empire paid, or if so, how much. In a 1957 memo to the Colonial Policy Committee, which he copied to the colonial secretary, Prime Minister Harold Macmillan requested an account of the colonial balance sheet. Macmillan wrote, "I should also like to see something like a profit and loss account for each of our Colonial possessions, so that we may be better able to gauge whether, from the financial and economic point of view, we are likely to gain or lose by its departure. This would need, of course, to be weighed against the political and strategic considerations involved in each case." What the prime minister says

[25] Kenneth Maxwell, "Portugal and Africa: The Last Empire," in Prosser Gifford and Wm. Roger Louis, eds., *The Transfer of Power in Africa: Decolonization 1940–1960* (New Haven: Yale University Press, 1982), pp. 337–385: 358.
[26] Lance E. Davis and Robert A. Huttenback, *Mammon and the Pursuit of Empire: The Economics of British Imperialism* (Cambridge: Cambridge University Press, 1988), p. 267.
[27] Davis and Huttenback, *Mammon and the Pursuit of Empire*, p. 267.

352

next suggests that he was attempting to make a rational decision about Britain's colonial policy. "And it might perhaps be better to attempt an estimate of the balance of advantage, taking all these considerations into account, of losing or keeping each particular territory. There are presumably places where it is of vital interest to us that we should maintain our influence, and others where there is no United Kingdom interest in resisting constitutional change even if it seems likely to lead eventually to secession from the Commonwealth."[28] On the other hand, it is also clear from the statement that colonies may have been kept despite their profitability or strategic importance.

Macmillan's request for a balance sheet was a bit late and the answer he received was ambiguous. Three studies were done, and in the last, "the conclusion was drawn that the economic considerations were fairly evenly matched. Consequently it was felt that the economic interests of the United Kingdom were unlikely in themselves to be decisive in determining whether or not a territory should become independent. Nor was it believed that strategic considerations should be uppermost, as the maintenance of bases against the will of the local Government and people would seriously limit their usefulness."[29] Nor was there a clear consensus during the 1950s on the profitability of the colonies among England's educated public; rather, it was a topic of heated debate among politicians and intellectuals.

To decide whether material constraints forced colonizers to decolonize, or declining profits decreased their willingness to pay the costs of occupation, would require a complex balance sheet. Then scholars would have to decide whether gains by individual merchants, capitalists, or states were offset by the losses of metropolitan taxpayers, and just what the significance of these numerical figures was in terms of politics and capacity to act. Moreover, one would have to know whether these calculations were done by the imperial offices for the cabinets of colonial powers. At least in one case, Britain, the calculations were done very late, well after decolonization had begun.

[28] Macmillan also wrote: "It would be good if Ministers could know more clearly which territories are likely to become ripe for independence over the next few years – or, even if they are not ready for it, will demand it so insistently that their claims cannot be denied – and at what date that stage is likely to be reached in each case." Personal Minute from the Prime Minister to the Lord President of the Council, 28 January 1957, reprinted in Porter and Stockwell, eds., *British Imperial Policy, 1938–64*, vol. II, p. 451.
[29] D.J. Morgan, *The Official History of Colonial Development, Vol. 5: Guidance Towards Self-Government in British Colonies, 1941–1971* (London: Macmillan, 1980), p. 102.

Explanations that stress declining profitability also fail to explain why – if imperial powers recognized or began to believe that empire was no longer profitable – colonizers often stayed on, and in some cases fought extremely costly wars to maintain imperial control. If economic explanations for colonialism and for decolonization are to make sense, one must conclude that leaders of colonial powers were slow learners or that other interests and beliefs kept states interested in colonies.[30] Alternatively, one may conclude that empire was actually profitable for certain classes and those classes pushed the rest of the state, through coalition logrolling, to take and maintain colonies. When the coalitions fell through, their colonial policies were abandoned. And if empire became less profitable, this was in part due to the efforts of reformers: the mission became humanitarian development, and such development in the form of schools, clinics, and infrastructure did not come cheap.

What about the argument that formal imperialism (direct occupation and control) became more expensive than informal imperialism (the informal control of neocolonialism)? The problems with this account are several. First, wasn't it always the case that it is cheaper over the long run to trade than raid or coerce? If this is so, why would any rational government have colonies? Second, if formal colonialism was necessary to turn colonial subjects into wage laborers, to create the infrastructure of roads, railways, and ports, and to build the economic assets of plantations and mines, could not colonizers have left most colonies much earlier? Why maintain, for instance, Jamaica or Ghana, decades after each had infrastructure, markets, and wage labor economies?

What about the exhaustion/overextension thesis? These arguments take several forms: the colonizer was outnumbered, colonizers faced greater logistic or financial problems, or the colonizers' militaries were relatively weak. The exhaustion/overextension argument is the one best supported by evidence. For example, by fighting three guerrilla wars at once, Portugal, never an economic powerhouse, was apparently overextended in Africa during the 1960s and 1970s. "By 1974, over a million Portuguese had seen service overseas. One of every four adult males was in the armed forces."[31] Similarly, colonizers were overextended

---

[30] Despite his own emphasis on the economics of French colonialism, Raymond Aron argued: "The leaders of France have always thought of the national destiny in political terms rather than economic terms." He believed that France had "aspired to glory rather than profit, preferred crusades to commerce." Quoted in Silver, *Framing a Balance Sheet*, p. 37.

[31] Maxwell, "Portugal and Africa," p. 339. Also see R.J. Hammond, *Portugal and Africa, 1815–1910: A Study in Uneconomic Imperialism* (Stanford: Stanford University Press, 1966).

in the first wave of Latin American decolonization from Spain in the early nineteenth century. Whereas Haiti achieved independence from France via a slave revolt in the late 1700s, several Spanish colonies in South America achieved independence as a consequence of the over-throw and occupation of Spain by Napoleonic France in 1808. While some colonial settlers remained loyal to Spain, most notably in Cuba, others used the opportunity to rebel, sparking civil wars in Mexico and Venezuela and revolts elsewhere in Spain's American empire. When Spain restored its monarchy and recovered from French occupation, it sent troops in 1812 to restore its empire in the Americas. Yet Simón Bolívar, Miguel Hidalgo, José de San Martín, and other rebels man-aged to free large swaths of the empire, notably Ecuador, Venezuela, Columbia, and Chile and Spain was forced to retreat from New World colonialism.[32]

Yet all the exhaustion arguments, when applied to the decolonization of the mid-twentieth century, face the problem that there was nothing new about population ratios or distance. Specifically, the colonizer was almost always outnumbered and facing long lines of communication. At the beginning of the twentieth century, for example, about 12 percent of the British Empire's population was British or European; in 1914 French Africa was controlled by a "handful of some 4,200 white Frenchmen, dispersed over a territory fourteen times the size of the metropole and inhabited by between 15 and 16 million" Africans.[33]

If always historically outnumbered, did colonizers, after World War II, face greater logistical difficulty maintaining long lines of communica-tion to the colonies? On the contrary, improvements in transportation and communication in the post-war era actually decreased logistical problems. If the thesis is that colonizers could not pay, they also probably found it difficult to pay for repression after World War I, yet they con-tinued to do so for decades following the war. Why did not colonial empires fall apart after World War I? Were there cumulative effects of

[32] See Jorge I. Dominguez, *Insurrection or Loyalty: The Breakdown of the Spanish American Empire* (Cambridge, MA: Harvard University Press, 1980). Portuguese loss of control over Brazil was more gradual, though it was also sparked by Napoleonic advances in Europe. In any case, settler revolts did not dramatically change the social and economic structure of Latin American states; the hierarchy of Spanish descendent settlers over mestizos, Indians and slaves remained essentially in place.
[33] Dennis Judd, *Empire: The British Imperial Experience from 1765 to the Present* (New York: Basic Books, 1996), p. 3; Henri Brunschwig, "The Decolonization of French Black Africa," in Prosser Gifford and Wm. Roger Louis, eds., *The Transfer of Power in Africa: Decolonization 1940–1960* (New Haven: Yale University Press, 1982), pp. 211–224: 216.

both world wars and the subsequent Cold War on human, material, and financial resources, gradually decreasing the ability of the colonizers to hold onto their colonies? Colonial empires for the most part remained intact until ten and fifteen years after World War II. Or did these world wars make the colonies appear, as the British said, even more valuable to the colonizer?

If the exhaustion is said to be military, the evidence is only partly supportive. Britain and France were much stronger militarily at mid-century *vis-à-vis* their colonies than they were before and they could have likely kept their colonies if they had chosen to do so. After defeating Hitler, both countries were secure at home and could have put their military forces to work repressing the anti-colonial militaries. In some cases, notably Vietnam and Algeria, France did so. Only marginal powers – defeated Spain, weak Portugal, and apartheid South Africa under sanctions – found colonialism a great military and economic burden and were forced to retreat.

Thus, various economic or power-political explanations for decolonization may seem plausible at first glance, but this set of arguments is less persuasive when one considers four additional points. First, if the great colonial powers had chosen to use their military might to defeat rebellious colonies in the mid-twentieth century, they would likely have won, the efficiency of guerrilla tactics and the advantages of fighting from one's own territory notwithstanding.[34] To be successful, the colonial powers would simply have had to resort to the time-tested techniques of Germany's von Trotha – extermination. Notably, von Trotha went to the effort of killing more than half the native population of Namibia before it had been established that the colony would be profitable. Only an ethical argument explanation can suggest why extermination was no longer on the table.

Second, evidence for economic explanations of colonialism and decolonization is ambiguous and may be indeterminate. Economic arguments assume that, at the end of European colonialism in the twentieth century, colonies were less profitable and therefore less important to the metropolitan powers. Again, the argument is that imperial expansion resulted from the capitalist desire to find new markets, cheap labor, and inexpensive raw materials, and so on. But if one examines the economic history of European contact with non-European regions, colonies

[34] The exception is Portugal which was not a great economic power by the 1960s and did not have the great military resources of France or Britain.

356

were not always associated with significant profitability, and on the other hand, in some instances, trade occurred on terms extremely favorable to Europeans, yet colonies were not always established. As Peter Liberman shows, even the conquest and economic exploitation of industrialized states can be profitable, if less than efficient.[35] Thus, decolonization was not economically determined: decolonizing powers could have held onto the formal political control of their colonies for economic reasons. Still, as emphasized below, economic (practical) *arguments* were certainly important in helping to sustain or dissolve support for colonialism.

Third, the seeds of the decolonization regime articulated in the League of Nations Mandate system began to germinate in the late nineteenth and early twentieth centuries. This was precisely when colonies were considered necessary by the colonial powers for economic and strategic reasons, and when colonies were, on the whole, considered to be quite profitable. Few disputed the economic and strategic benefits of colonialism until mid-century, when the system was already in deep normative trouble.

Finally, economic and military conditions for the end of particular colonial empires (a high-cost, low-benefit ratio, military defeat, and overextension and exhaustion) have obtained in the past when colonies were lost in war or were temporarily too costly to maintain, but colonial empire as an institution was never outlawed or the subject of sanctions before the mid-twentieth century. Colonies had been abandoned, lost, or exchanged throughout history. What was different about the decolonization of the mid-twentieth century was its systematic-ness, and the fact that it would be very difficult today, and in the foreseeable future, to practice colonialism. Though colonizers might have desired the wealth that came with holding colonies, the public and influential elites in the metropole were gradually persuaded that colonialism itself was an abhorrent practice, and they were no longer willing to tolerate and pay for it as they had in the past. As Fieldhouse argues, "at least in the West European democracies, governments were vulnerable to criticism of brutality by liberals and humanitarians such as the British Anti-Slavery Society."[36]

[35] Peter Liberman, *Does Conquest Pay? The Exploitation of Occupied Industrial Societies* (Princeton: Princeton University Press, 1996). For qualifications, see Stephen G. Brooks, "The Globalization of Production and the Changing Benefits of Conquest," *Journal of Conflict Resolution* 43 (October 1999), 646–670.
[36] Fieldhouse, *Colonialism*.

Practical arguments

Ethical arguments about colonialism were deployed alongside scientific and identity arguments about the practice. In addition, practical arguments about the profitability and strategic value of colonialism were deployed by proponents of colonialism, reform, and decolonization and indeed were as ubiquitous as ethical arguments about the practice.

Advocates of empire often argued that colonies were profitable. Even Adam Smith, a critic of colonies on the grounds that they were protectionist and inhibited free trade, wrote in the *Wealth of Nations*, "To propose that Great Britain should voluntarily give up all authority over her colonies . . . would be to propose such a measure as never was, and never will be adopted, by any nation in the world."[37] As noted earlier, the nineteenth-century French advocate of empire, Prime Minister Jules Ferry, argued, "Colonies are for rich countries one of the most lucrative methods of investing capital . . . I say that France, which is glutted with capital and which has exported considerable quantities, has an interest in looking at this side of the question."[38] After World War I, the advocates of French colonialism frequently touted the economic and strategic virtues of colonies. "Yesterday, France needed colonial contingents for the war. Tomorrow it will need them in order to refashion its military instrument. Henceforth its security will be a tributary of its colonies."[39] Albert Sarraut, France's colonial minister from 1920 to 1924, wrote several studies of French colonialism in which he argued that colonies offered the opportunity for great economic gain. His *La Mise en Valeur des Colonies* published in 1922–1923 urged greater investment in the colonies in order to boost France's own economy: "to supply, without any delay, to the needs of our national life the increased amount of primary products that it demands, this is the aim."[40] In the 1930s, the German Office for Colonial Policy, whose job in part consisted of convincing the German people of the virtues of colonies, often used economic arguments. The 1939 speaker's guide for the office included this talking point: "Colonies are needed because of Germany's lack of space. They are to provide raw materials and markets . . . Aside from their material

[37] Adam Smith, *Wealth of Nations* (London: 1966), vol. II, pp. 112–113.
[38] Quoted in A. Adu Boahen, *African Perspectives on Colonialism* (Baltimore: Johns Hopkins University Press, 1987), p. 31.
[39] Albert Sarraut quoted in Rudolf von Albertini, *Decolonization: The Administration and future of the Colonies, 1919–1960* (Garden City, NY: Doubleday & Company Inc., 1971), p. 268.
[40] Quoted in ibid., p. 270.

value, colonies must be sought by the Reich in order to provide German youth with a testing ground for character."[41] Similarly, Britain's Lord Lugard, in *The Dual Mandate*, argued that war proved the value of the colonies against the arguments of the "Little Englanders."[42]

The argument that colonies were economically important was also deployed by advocates of colonial rule after World War II. For example, after the discovery of oil in the Sahara, France's Resident Minister Robert Locoste said in April 1957, "These discoveries which are, it appears, of world importance, must confirm our country in her African vocation and justify all the more the effort of the metropole to reintroduce calm into Algeria, which is the key to the Sahara."[43] Similarly, British Conservatives in power during World War II tended to argue that the colonies were crucial economically and therefore essential for Britain's world position.

Conversely, critics of colonialism also frequently used economic arguments. Some claimed that colonialism, because it typically involved protectionism, was inherently less profitable than free trade. Indeed, protectionism was characteristic of European colonialism. For example, for two centuries during the height of mercantilism, from the 1650s to the 1850s, British tariff regulations required that all colonial trade must be carried on ships owned and registered in Britain and that all goods imported to the colonies must either be the product of Britain or transshipped through Britain, with duties paid there. British colonies were forbidden to manufacture or export most goods, with only limited manufacturing allowed. Proponents of free trade objected to this system, arguing that competition would be more profitable. Others argued that the value of British trade with its colonies was small and generally diminishing. And others argued that only a few benefit from imperialism: "Although the new Imperialism has been bad business for the nation, it has been good business for certain classes and certain trades within the nation. The vast expenditure

---

[41] Wolf W. Schmokel, *Dream of Empire: German Colonialism, 1919–1945* (New Haven: Yale University Press, 1964), pp. 34–35.
[42] Lord Lugard, *The Dual Mandate in British Tropical Africa* (London: Frank Cass, (1922) 1965), p. 609.
[43] Quoted in James W. Silver, 'Framing a Balance Sheet for French Decolonization: Raymond Aron, Raymond Cartier and the Debate over the African Empire' (Cambridge, MA: Harvard University Honors Thesis), pp. 12–13. Further, this view seems to have been widely shared. When the journal of the French Institute of Public Opinion, *Sondages*, published the answer to the question, "Do you think France will be able to exploit the Saharan petroleum reserves if Algeria becomes Independent," in September 1957, 18 percent answered yes, and 53 percent said no. Silver, *Framing a Balance Sheet*, p. 13.

on armaments, the costly wars, the grave risks and embarrassments of foreign policy, the stoppage of political and social reforms within Great Britain, though fraught with great injury to the nation, have served well the present business interests of certain industries and professions."[44]

Individual colonies were also singled out for criticism on the grounds that they were unprofitable. In 1865, British colonial reformer Charles Adderly claimed that Britain's possessions in West Africa, costing a million pounds a year, were a waste, and the parliamentary Committee on West African Affairs, in agreement with Adderly, said: "All further extension of territory or assumption of government, or new treaties offering protection to native tribes, would be inexpedient . . ."[45] After World War I, one British observer wrote, "The glorious days when the native could be squeezed for the benefit of the Crown, as well as for the planters' and merchants' profits, are gone forever. From the budgetary point of view, colonies cost more than they bring in. Tributes have gone out of fashion and subsidies are the rule."[46]

In the 1930s the scholar Grover Clark set about computing what he called *The Balance Sheets of Imperialism: Facts and Figures on Colonies.* "Three main claims have been made as to the value of colonies: that they provided important outlets for population; that the possession of them gave important opportunities for profitable trade which otherwise would not be available; that control over the sources of raw materials in colonies added to a nation's security in time of war and gave it important advantages in times of peace."[47] Clark concluded that colonies

---

[44] J.A. Hobson, *Imperialism: A Study* (New York: James Pott & Co., 1902), pp. 51–52. Hobson did not think, however, that the economic motive was the chief cause of imperialism. Rather, he emphasized the causal role of "the non-economic factors of patriotism, adventure, military enterprise, political ambition, and philanthropy" and argued that "the motor power of Imperialism is not chiefly financial: finance is rather the governor of the imperial engine, directing the energy and determining its work: it does not constitute the fuel of the engine, nor does it directly generate the power. Finance manipulates the patriotic forces which politicians, soldiers, philanthropists, and traders generate." Ibid., p. 66.
[45] Quoted Davis and Huttenback, *Mammon and the Pursuit of Empire*, p. 9.
[46] Bonn, *The Crumbling of Empire*, p. 333.
[47] Grover Clark, *The Balance Sheets of Imperialism: Facts and Figures on Colonies* (New York: Columbia University Press, 1936), p. v. He comments on the moral dimensions of colonialism when he says of early colonial activity: "What they were after was trade, or loot, or both – and in many cases they were none too scrupulous about the methods they used to get what they wanted." Ibid., p.6. Clark describes an "anemic little clerk," the British colonist, Cecil Rhodes, as a "quite unscrupulous but vastly interesting and able empire builder . . ." Grover Clark, *A Place in the Sun* (New York: The Macmillan Company, 1936), p. 33.

might have been profitable before 1800 but were certainly not so after 1880, and "each of these claims is essentially fallacious."

> For the eight decades preceding the new drive for colonies which started in the 1880s, the governments as such spent considerably more on expansion than they received directly from it. These losses ultimately fell on the taxpayers. But private interests were making good profits on trade with the overseas territories, and the governmental expenditures were much less than they came to be later. Perhaps the private profits roughly equaled the governments' losses. In any case, between 1800 and 1880, the balance for the people as a whole in the colony-holding countries was not large on either the debit or the credit side of the ledger.
>
> Since 1880, however, the cash costs to the countries which have used force to get or keep control of colonies unquestionably have been very substantially more than any possible cash profits derived from the trade with the territories controlled.[48]

Focusing on the period from 1878 to 1934, Clark provides extensive empirical support for his claims that colonialism does not provide profit, resources, or benefits from migration but actually sows instability and war as countries compete for these prizes. Clark ends his book with a call to keep political control of the colonies – since independence would probably lead, especially in Africa and the Pacific, to "chaos" – but to open colonies to trade in order to "insure real equality of economic opportunity in the colonies for the nationals of all countries."[49]

Britain's Labour party, after World War II, held that colonialism mainly benefited capitalists. As John Strachey, a post-war Secretary of State for War argued, "Exactly contrary to the popular prejudice, a nation is likely to-day [*sic*] to be strong or weak in inverse ratio to imperial possessions."[50] In France, Raymond Aron stressed economic reasons for French withdrawal from Algeria in *La Tragédie algerienne* and *L'Algérie et la Républic*, published in 1957 and 1958. Despite the ostensible importance of colonies to the French economy, Aron argued, the war in Algeria was a diversion of resources from France while the withdrawal of young men from the French economy to fight the war tightened the labor market, and led to

[48] Clark, *Balance Sheets of Imperialism*, p. 3.
[49] Ibid., p. 18. Clark approved of the Mandate system but thought it did not do enough to protect and promote free trade.
[50] Quoted in Louis, *Imperialism at Bay*, p. 34.

growing inflationary pressure. He said France could simply buy the oil it needed and did not have to physically control the Saharan oil supplies. "It is the currency of payment, not sovereignty on the drilling sites or on the pipelines that is essential."[51] Similarly, Raymond Cartier published many articles in *Paris-Match* in the late 1950s questioning the economic wisdom of colonies.

> In Black Africa, France pays. It assumes for the metropolitan budget the salaries of the governors, administrators, magistrates, police. It takes on the costs of meteorology, the geographic service, the radio stations . . . of principal airports. It completely covers the military expenses which have risen up to 50 billion [Francs per year] for all the overseas territories. It covers currency shortages, the budget deficits, subsidizes in growing proportions the majority of colonial projects.[52]

Thus, practical arguments were a feature of colonial and anti-colonial discourse. Strategic, balance-of-power arguments were also common. During the Cold War, for example, some argued that decolonization posed an increased risk of political instability for the colonizer.

But beginning in the late nineteenth century colonialism was less and less considered a legitimate means to the ends of profit and security. As noted in chapter 7, beliefs about what it was good and right to do in terms of economic exploitation were already divided at the middle part of the twentieth century. A 1946 opinion poll asked, "Should we administer our colonies above all for the profit of France, or above all for the profit of the indigenous populations?" Asking the question illustrates that the economic motive for colonialism was already denormalized. French opinion was roughly evenly divided, with 31 percent saying for the profit of France, 28 percent for the profit of the natives, and 25 percent for the profit of both.[53]

Non-economic arguments in favor of colonialism – religious and civilizing missions based on the presumed inferiority of non-Europeans – were also delegitimized at the same time that the ideas of self-determination and sovereignty were more widely believed and applied. This is why colonizers did not continue to use the same methods of imprisonment, mutilation, and massacre that they had in the past employed with great success to control and intimidate. Thus, colonialism ended not because it was less profitable or because the

---

[51] Quoted in Silver, *Framing a Balance Sheet*, p. 14.   [52] Quoted in ibid., p. 32.
[53] Paul Clay Sorum, *Intellectuals and Decolonization in France* (Chapel Hill: University of North Carolina Press, 1977), p. 16.

material balance between colonizer and colonized changed. Colonialism was no longer legitimate for economic, military, or civilizing reasons.

Alternative explanations for South Africa's exit from Namibia

What accounts for South Africa's withdrawal from Namibia in 1990? SWAPO began its armed struggle in 1966 and South Africa began a war against Angola in 1975 that featured several large-scale assaults.[54] At the peak of its regional military engagement, the South African Defence Force (SADF) occupied one-third of Angolan territory as it fought SWAPO and conducted a campaign of military destabilization over the entire Southern African region. A negotiated settlement to South Africa's war in Angola, brokered in 1988 by the United States and the Soviet Union, included South African withdrawal from Namibia. This case thus exemplifies the complex relationships among economic, strategic, and normative factors and indicates the limits of an ethical argument explanation. South West Africa/Namibia was both extremely profitable and costly to maintain. South African foreign policy meant that it was increasingly overextended in the region, while international sanctions weakened the South African military. South Africa's wars against Angola and SWAPO eventually ground to a stalemate, and though South Africa had nuclear, chemical, and biological weapons, it did not escalate their use.

Economics of occupation

Was it reasonable, in purely economic terms, for South Africa to hold on to South West Africa/Namibia after the UN revoked South Africa's mandate in 1966? Though economic statistics regarding Namibia were generally withheld – after 1966, South Africa included the figures for Namibian mining in statistics for South African mining – the occupation does appear to have been profitable. First, Namibia provided an outlet for South African goods, making it valuable to South Africa's private sector when economic sanctions against South Africa were anticipated

---

[54] See in Colin Leys and John S. Saul, *et al.*, *Namibia's Liberation Struggle: The Two Edged Sword* (London: James Currey, 1995); Peter H. Katjavivi, *A History of Resistance in Namibia* (London: James Currey, 1988); Dennis Herbstein and John Evenson, *The Devils Are Among Us: The War for Namibia* (London: Zed Books, 1989).

and then imposed. Second, South Africa exploited Namibia's significant mineral resources, the most profitable of which were diamonds and uranium. Specifically, Namibian diamond production accounted for 22 percent of the South African De Beers corporation's after-tax profits in 1978. Third, labor was cheap in Namibia due to the suppression of black wages, increasing the profit margin of Namibia's most lucrative sector, the mining industry.

Was occupation of Namibia overly expensive? Because figures detailing the full costs of the occupation were never published by South Africa, it is difficult to know whether costs outweighed profits and how the cost–benefit ratio changed over time. For example, the South West Africa administration's spending on police and defense for 1987–1988 were, respectively, R136 million and R191.9 million.[55] But the share of the total South African defense budget spent on Namibia is unknown – and not likely ever to be known. South Africa also subsidized expenditures for the South West African Territorial Force and the administration of the territory of Namibia. The occupation of Namibia cost R1.7 million per day in the mid 1980s while the "cost of killing a single SWAPO insurgent has risen to R600,000."[56] In 1988, the war in Namibia cost South Africa $1 million (R2.15 million) per day, not including the subsidy to the Namibian government which Pretoria put at $400 million a year (R860 million).[57] The total cost of the twenty-three-year war against SWAPO was some R8 billion ($3 billion).[58] Fortunately for South Africa, the SWA/Namibian mining industry subsidized their occupation of Namibia through taxation. For example, from 1 April 1987 to 31 March 1988, R255 million of the R600 million in Namibian government revenue that came from taxes and duties came from the mining industry. Much of that money, R130 million, came from diamond production.[59] Lead, zinc, silver, copper, and tin mined in Namibia were all taxed at 40 percent; diamonds were taxed at 60 percent; and taxation for uranium was a sliding scale, rising to as much as 70 percent. Profits remained substantial, however, because of low wages.

---

[55] *Africa South of the Sahara 1991* (London: Europa Publications Limited, 1990), p. 749.
[56] Christopher Coker, *South Africa's Security Dilemmas* (New York: Preager, 1987), p. 45.
[57] *Africa Research Bulletin, Political Series* 25 (15 December 1988), 9062.
[58] Susan Brown, "Diplomacy by Other Means: SWAPO's Liberation War," in Leys and Saul, *Namibia's Liberation Struggle*, pp. 19–39: 37.
[59] *Africa South of the Sahara 1991*, p. 749.

Was South Africa exhausted or over-extended?

Three elements of potential exhaustion and overextension must be considered: the South African military's loss of life during the decades of occupation and war; the resource drain of occupation at a time when South Africa faced international sanctions; and South Africa's self-encirclement as the region responded to its destabilization policies.

While it should not be difficult to determine, it is hard to know whether the South African military was increasingly drained by the occupation of SWA/Namibia and the Angolan war. The South African government appeared to systematically under-report the deaths resulting from combat, malaria, and other causes. An SADF archivist interviewed shortly after the conflicts ended claims that no overall tally of casualties in Namibia and Angola were ever made because they were "too few to count." He continued, "no one believes me when I say that, but it's true. There were just too few to count."[60] Indeed, the official SADF figures were confusing. Thus, the South African public never had complete figures, even after the war ended, although unofficial figures for combat related deaths totaled 715 for all South African forces, including police, SADF, and SWATF.[61]

Whatever the real number of deaths and injuries due to combat, disease, and accidents, white casualties were obviously a concern for South African decisionmakers, and the SADF took several measures to decrease casualties and to convince the public that the numbers were low. To decrease their dependency on white South African troops, and to keep white South Africans, especially those in the part-time services, away from the brunt of the fighting in Namibia, South Africa increasingly relied on black Namibians and on "non-white" soldiers from South Africa. The "Namibianization" of the occupation forces in South West Africa began in the early 1970s. In the mid-1970s, South Africa organized bantustan (black "homeland") based units linked to the ethnic homelands in Namibia, and in 1980 South Africa formally established the South West African Territorial Force (SWATF), an indigenous army designed to take over the brunt of the repression inside Namibia. South Africa introduced compulsory service for all Namibians in 1981. The SWATF was rapidly mobilized to a force of 20,000–24,000, and grew to 35,000 in early 1989, with duties in both Namibia and Angola.[62] As

---

[60] Interview with the author, Pretoria, 27 May 1991.
[61] Brown, "Diplomacy by Other Means," p. 37.
[62] "Free at Last?," *Washington Notes On Africa* (Spring 1989), p. 2.

one white South African noted, "deaths of black troops, who now carry the brunt of the fighting, are hardly ever reported – since 1976 it has been official SADF policy not to reveal their names or provide statistics."[63] By 1986, South Africa claimed that SWATF provided 51 percent of all South African commanded soldiers in Namibia and the SADF noted that the expansion of SWATF "resulted in a gradual decline in the call-up of Citizen Force members for service in the SWA operational area."[64]

SWAPO and South Africa made conflicting claims regarding casualties, but both sides agree that South African losses grew.[65] In early 1977, the South African Defence Ministry reported 33 "security force" casualties in Namibia since April 1975.[66] In 1982 the SADF said 77 troops were killed in action in Namibia, 149 died of other causes, and 259 deaths were "accidents."[67] The SADF claimed that 30 members of the security forces in Namibia were killed in 1985 and that 32 were killed the following year.[68] In late 1985, the South African government said 560 South African lives had been lost in Namibia since the late 1970s.[69] SWAPO figures suggest a much higher rate of casualties. In 1984 SWAPO's People's Liberation Army of Namibia (PLAN) claimed to have killed 71 SADF and SWATF troops in May, June, and July alone.[70] In the month of August 1988 alone, PLAN reported that they killed 113 "enemy soldiers," wounded many others, and captured or destroyed South African military vehicles in twenty separate military actions.[71]

---

[63] Gavin Cawthra, *Brutal Force: The Apartheid War Machine* (London: International Defence & Aid Fund for Southern Africa, 1986), p. 178.

[64] Republic of South Africa (RSA), *White Paper on Defence and Armaments Supply 1986*, p. 18. Mark Phillips, "The Nuts and Bolts of Military Power: The Structure of the SADF," in Jacklyn Cock and Laurie Nathan, eds., *Society at War: The Militarization of South Africa* (New York: St. Martin's Press, 1989), pp. 16–27: 26; Cawthra, *Brutal Force*, pp. 199–204.

[65] Over 10,000 Namibian people were killed (1 percent of the population), and over 100,000 fled the country to neighboring states, mostly, approximately 72,000, to Angola. Tony Weaver, "The South African Defence Force in Namibia," in Cock and Nathan, eds., *Society at War*, pp. 90–102: 90.

[66] RSA, *White Paper on Defence 1977*, p. 7.

[67] Note that for 1982, SWAPO figures for total deaths are less than SADF figures, assuming that SADF figures for deaths by accidents and other causes are actually combat deaths. PLAN claimed that over 2,000 enemy soldiers were wounded and 466 killed. "The SADF also claimed to have killed a thousand PLAN combatants – though only 157 were accounted for by reports of specific actions." Reported in "Namibia – a Nation Under Siege," *Resister*, no. 27 (August–September 1983), 12–13: 12.

[68] Reported by the End Conscription Campaign, "Militarization Facts and Figures," p. 3.

[69] Coker, *South Africa's Security Dilemmas*, p. 29, citing *The Times* (London) report of 18 September 1985, is imprecise about the dates that these figures cover, but the context suggests that these were SADF deaths since 1978.

[70] Cawthra, *Brutal Force*, p. 179.

[71] "News from the Battlefield," *The Combatant* (August 1988), 19–21.

The SADF did admit many casualties due to accidents in operational areas, including occupied southern Angola; between January 1979 and June 1983 accidents claimed the lives of 647 servicemen and injured over 3,000. As Christopher Coker notes: "Only 107 were reported killed in action. These figures seem highly suspect. Either the South African army is unusually accident prone or else casualties in the field have been deliberately disguised as accident statistics."[72] Interviews with white South Africans after South Africa's withdrawal from Namibia and Angola indicate that some soldiers injured in battle were instructed to lie about the cause of their injuries: a common excuse for the loss of limbs was for individuals to say that they had been in an auto accident in South Africa.[73]

Was SWAPO increasingly effective? SWAPO claims about SADF and SWATF casualties may have been exaggerated to bolster morale or because of incomplete information on the fate of South African wounded. Nevertheless, it appears that in several engagements during the 1980s in both Angola and Namibia, South Africa lost more troops than ever before even though the SWATF and the 32 Battalion (primarily composed of mercenaries), took over more of the direct fighting with SWAPO's military arm, PLAN.

South African casualties probably grew for three reasons. First, South Africa faced increasingly active and effective military opposition from SWAPO. Second, the very repressiveness and horror of South Africa's occupation of Namibia seemed to increase SWAPO's determination.[74] Third, the policy of recruiting black Namibians into SWATF and the SWA police met with increasing resistance: for example, in January 1981, 5,000 Namibian refugees arrived in Angola to avoid conscription.[75] Namibian resistance to conscription meant that more SADF troops were brought into operational areas from South Africa.

Was South Africa overextended? After 1974, South Africa conducted a regional destabilization strategy which gradually prompted the state to mobilize large numbers of its white citizens and also increased the pressure for international sanctions against South Africa. When the Portuguese government fell in a military coup in April 1974, the new Portuguese government immediately began negotiations with the liberation movements in Angola and Mozambique, leading to independence

---

[72] Coker, *South Africa's Security Dilemmas*, p. 44.
[73] Interviews by the author in Johannesburg, May 1991.
[74] Coker, *South Africa's Security Dilemmas*, p. 42.   [75] Cawthra, *Brutal Force*, p. 202.

for both in 1975. While South African Prime Minister Vorster said publicly that South Africa had nothing to fear from a black government in Mozambique, officials also said that South Africa had lost its "cordon sanitaire," was under "total onslaught," and ought to respond with a "total strategy."[76]

Under the total strategy, South Africa began a program of regional destabilization and war, which eventually led to self-encirclement and contributed to South Africa's economic stress. No direct *military* threat was perceived: "[T]he military threat to the R.S.A. finds its only actual physical expression in the existence of armed elements of banned political organizations accommodated in neighboring states. They attempt to infiltrate the R.S.A. for the purposes of terrorism, sabotage and subversion with a view to overthrowing the existing order."[77] South Africa would use all available means – "military, psychological, economic, political, sociological, technological, diplomatic, ideological, cultural etc." – to eliminate the threat posed by communism, the ANC, and its supporters.[78]

South Africa tried diplomacy and economic embrace to influence the new regimes in Angola and Mozambique.[79] Also in 1974, South Africa suggested the creation of a greater Ovambo Bantustan (African homeland) straddling the Angola–South West Africa border which could have reduced South Africa's problems with what they believed to be the most militant element of SWAPO, the northern Namibian Ovambo people, and isolated the largest component of SWAPO military strength. It would also have decreased Angolan territory.[80] Diplomacy failed.

---

[76] Colin Legum, "Southern Africa: The Secret Diplomacy of Detente," in Colin Legum, ed., *Africa Contemporary Record, 1974–1975* (New York: Africana Publishing Company, 1975), vol. VII, pp. A3–A15: A7.

[77] RSA, *White Paper on Defence and Armament Production, 1975*, p. 7. The total strategy concept is drawn from André Beaufre, a French strategist. André Beaufre, *An Introduction to Strategy* (New York: Preager, 1965). As one observer notes: "when one looks at the total strategy in depth and in relation to Beaufre's writings, it appears to have very little authenticity of its own. Total strategy . . . is essentially Beaufre writ large in the particular counter-revolutionary context of contemporary South Africa." Philip H. Frankel, *Pretoria's Praetorians: Civil–Military Relations in South Africa* (Cambridge: Cambridge University Press, 1984), pp. 29–70: 46. Also see Steven Metz, "Pretoria's 'Total Strategy' and Low-Intensity Warfare in Southern Africa," *Comparative Strategy* 6 (1987), pp. 437–469.

[78] RSA, *White Paper on Defence 1977*, p. 4. The White Paper also says that it is important to "achieve understanding by governments and citizens of other countries of the RSA's internal policies and the western humanistic tradition upon which they are based." p. 9.

[79] *Africa Contemporary Record, 1970–1971*, vol. III, pp. A11–A17; Legum, "Southern Africa: The Secret Diplomacy of Detente," p. A9.

[80] Robert S. Jaster, *The Defence of White Power: South African Foreign Policy Under Pressure*, (London: Macmillan, 1988), p. 69.

For Angola and Namibia, the total strategy meant almost continuous use of military force. South Africa also sponsored the Mozambican National Resistance (MNR or Renamo) against Mozambique, even after signing an agreement to halt support for the MNR in 1984. Against Botswana, Lesotho, Swaziland, and Zimbabwe, South Africa mixed relatively lost-cost military actions, including air and ground raids against suspected "terrorists," with economic incentives and economic coercion.

The total strategy – because it involved total military and economic mobilization – put tremendous stress on the South African military, economy, and society both directly, as the government mobilized, and indirectly, as the international community sanctioned South Africa for its regional aggression and apartheid. White males were drawn out of the economy for military service, the industrial sector was pushed to develop weapons, and public support for the occupation gradually waned. Ironically, South African foreign policy thus helped to undermine the apartheid system it was designed to save.[81]

Between 1975 and 1990, South Africa more than doubled its full-time military forces by increasing conscription rates.[82] In 1977, the national service period for white conscripts was increased from one to two years in order to respond to the decision to wage war in Angola and meet the determined resistance of the Namibians. By the early 1980s, one of every ten white South African males was in the armed services at any one time.[83]

Full-time forces were supplemented by part-time "Citizen" forces and "commandos" who were regularly called to do up to three months of "border-camp" service in the "operational areas" of Namibia and Angola.[84] The entire white male population of apartheid South Africa was subject to military service from ages 16 to 65.

[81] Neta C. Crawford, *The Domestic Sources and Consequences of Aggressive Foreign Policies: The Folly of South Africa's "Total Strategy,"* Working Paper, no. 41 (Centre for Southern African Studies, University of the Western Cape, South Africa, 1995).
[82] South Africa's "full time" (permanent force) military in 1965 was 26,500, with 13,500 in the Citizen Force and 51,500 in the Commandos. In 1970 "full time" military was 43,800, with 26,550 in the Citizen Force and 58,000 in the Commandos. IISS, *The Military Balance,* for 1965–1966 and 1970–1971.
[83] M. Brzoska, "South Africa: Evading the Embargo," in Michael Brzoska and Thomas Ohlson, *Arms Production in the Third World,* eds. (London: Taylor & Francis, 1986), pp. 193–214: 194.
[84] The "average number of camps per member [of the Citizen Force], over a period of three years, was 2.09 (authorized number 3)" while the "average number of days of service over a period of three years was 87 (authorized number is 120 days in two years)." RSA, *White Paper on Defence and Armaments Supply 1986,* p. 5.

All white males must register for military service at 16, while still in school. They are then liable for service in the full-time force. Those who do not make a career in the permanent force are required either before or after tertiary education to render two years of national service ... After this they are placed in the part-time citizen force for twelve years, during which time, they must serve up to 720 days in annual 30-, 60- or 90-day "camps". Then they are placed in the active citizen force reserve for five years and may be required to serve 12 days a year in a local commando unit until the age of 55. Finally, they are placed on the national reserve until they are age 65.[85]

In June 1979, SADF 8,000 reservists were deployed to Namibia to track down SWAPO forces.[86] By 1988 there were 175,000 in the Citizen Force and 150,000 in the Active Citizen Force Reserve. Between 1980 and 1990, there were also 90,000 to 140,000 commandos serving part time.[87] Mobilization of all SADF full- and part-time forces in the mid-1980s would perhaps have totaled between 500,000 and 1 million men, and "would rapidly bring the economy to its knees."[88] Finally, to reduce dependency on white soldiers, South Africa gradually integrated its military during the 1970s, and by 1986, almost one quarter of full-time SADF forces (24 percent) were either black (12 percent), coloured (11 percent), or Indian (1 percent).[89] Other militaries in the region mobilized to keep pace with the South African threat.[90]

South Africa's regional aggression and its occupation of Namibia provoked an international response. The UN Security Council adopted a voluntary arms embargo against South Africa in August 1963, calling upon all states to "cease forthwith the sale and shipment of arms, ammunition of all types and military vehicles to South Africa."[91] In response, South Africa developed an indigenous military production base, and in 1968, South Africa established foundations for the Armaments Development and Production Corporation of South Africa (Armscor), several companies closely affiliated and coordinated by the state to ensure that the weapons needed by the SADF were produced

[85] Phillips, "The Nuts and Bolts of Military Power," p. 18.
[86] Jaster, *The Defence of White Power*, p. 93.
[87] IISS, *The Military Balance* (London: Brassey's) for the years 1980–1990.
[88] Phillips, "The Nuts and Bolts of Military Power," p. 19.
[89] RSA, *White Paper on Defence and Armament Supply 1986*, p. 17.
[90] Of course the governments of Angola and Mozambique were fighting South African supported guerrilla forces, which also caused them to increase their military forces.
[91] UN Security Council (SC) Resolution 181, 7 August 1963. See Neta C. Crawford, "How Arms Embargoes Work," in Neta C. Crawford and Audie Klotz, eds., *How Sanctions Work: Lessons From South Africa* (New York: St. Martin's, 1999), pp. 45–74.

Table 8.1 *Numbers in the armed forces of Angola, Mozambique, South Africa, and Zimbabwe, 1975–1990*

	Angola	Mozambique	South Africa[a]	Rhodesia/Zimbabwe[b]
1975	30,000	20,000	50,000	15,000
1976	35,000	21,000	59,000	17,000
1977	47,000	26,000	67,000	17,000
1978	47,000	25,000	78,000	24,000
1979	47,000	30,000	70,000	38,000
1980	47,000	30,000	70,000	94,000
1981	53,000	30,000	78,000	74,000
1982	54,000	30,000	78,000	50,000
1983	54,000	32,000	77,000	46,000
1984	60,000	34,000	97,000	46,000
1985	66,000	35,000	95,000	46,000
1986	70,000	65,000	90,000	45,000
1987	74,000	65,000	102,000	45,000
1988	107,000	65,000	100,000	45,000
1989	100,000E	71,000	103,000	49,500
1990	100,000E	72,000	77,400	56,400

E: estimated.
[a] Full-time military.
[b] Zimbabwe became a majority rule government in early 1980. The figures noted prior to 1979 are for the armed forces of the white controlled government.
Sources: Figures for 1975–1977 are taken from the US Arms Control and Disarmament Agency, *World Military Expenditures and Arms Transfers, 1987*; for 1978–1988 from *World Military Expenditures and Arms Transfers 1989*, (Washington, DC: US Government Printing Office, 1987, 1990; for 1989–1990 from International Institute for Strategic Studies, *The Military Balance 1989–1990*, and *1990–1991* (London: Brassey's, 1990).

by South African industries or procured abroad. In the mid-1970s, in anticipation of a mandatory UN arms embargo, South Africa increased its procurement schedule and domestic production, saying, "The RSA must, as far as practicable, be self-sufficient in the provision of arms and ensure their continued production."[92]

In 1977, the UN Security Council condemned South Africa for its "acts of repression" and "attacks" on its neighbors, arguing that "the military build-up by South Africa and its persistent acts of aggression against the neighboring States seriously disturb the security of those states." It also declared that the "acquisition by South Africa of arms and

[92] RSA, *White Paper on Defence 1977*, p. 9.

related *matériel* constitutes a threat to the maintenance of international peace and security."[93] The Security Council imposed a mandatory arms embargo on South Africa, prohibiting exports of weapons, ammunition, military vehicles and equipment, paramilitary and police equipment, and spare parts, while also prohibiting states from granting licensing arrangements to manufacture military equipment in South Africa. When the SADF moved into South African townships, and increased regional military aggression, the UN Security Council passed a resolution in December 1984 requesting that all states refrain from importing South African produced arms, ammunition, and military vehicles.

If South Africa wanted to remain at war in Namibia and Angola, with the UN arms embargo in place, it had to increase its domestic arms production. "Before 1963, South Africa spent 70 percent of its military budget on arms procurement overseas, most of it from the UK. But by 1984, almost 100 percent was spent within South Africa for local arms production."[94] By 1990, South Africa had 975 private contractors engaged by Armscor.[95] Arms procurement and military industry became an enormous drain on the South African economy during the 1970s and 1980s: "The absorption of scarce resources (capital, labour and foreign exchange) and the crowding out of non-military public and private investment and of non-military R&D not only exacerbated many of the existing structural problems in the apartheid economy . . . but also contributed to the underdevelopment, declining productivity and poor international competitiveness of the civilian economy."[96] Table 8.2 shows the growth in official expenditures for acquisitions by Armscor.[97]

While the embargo, and arms production to counter it, strained the South African economy, South Africa's tightly linked military and foreign policies toward Angola and Namibia led to military overextension. In 1975 South Africa articulated increasing alarm over the actual and potential military collaboration between SWAPO guerrillas and the

---

[93] UN SC Resolution 418, 4 November 1977.
[94] Signe Landgren, *Embargo Disimplemented: South Africa's Military Industry* (London: Oxford University Press, 1989), p. 9. Also see William Cobbett, "Apartheid's Army and the Arms Embargo," in Cock and Nathan, eds., *Society at War*, pp. 232–243.
[95] RSA, *Briefing on the Organization and Functions of the South African Defence Force and the Armaments Corporation of South Africa, Limited 1990*, p. 66.
[96] Peter Batchelor and Susan Willett, *Disarmament and Defence Industrial Adjustment in South Africa* (Oxford: Oxford University Press, 1998), p. 48.
[97] It is unlikely that the clandestine purchase of armaments is included in official South African government figures.

Table 8.2 *South Africa's expenditures*
for arms acquisition

Year ending	Millions of Rand[a]
1967	23
1969	52
1971	68
1973	102
1975	296
1977	689
1979	921
1980	1,178
1981	1,235
1982	1,450
1983	1,591
1984	1,571
1985	1,865
1986	2,463
1987	2,300
1988	2,743
1989	4,845

[a] Not in constant Rand.
Source: RSA, *Briefing on the Organization
and Functions of the South African Defence
Force and the Armaments Corporation of South
Africa, Limited 1990*, p. 66.

Angolan independence movements. South Africa saw Angola, dominated by the Marxist MPLA, as a haven for the ANC and SWAPO and
as a launching pad for Soviet aggression. Fighting among three major independence movements in Angola – the MPLA, UNITA and the
FNLA – also threatened South African economic interests in Angola,
particularly the Calueque dam on the Cunene River.

SADF invaded Angola in July and August 1975, saying, "South Africa
responded to a call from the workers in the Calueque–Ruacana scheme
to protect them . . . This military intervention was then extended in order to deflect the effects of the Angolan civil war from the northern
border of South-West Africa and inhibit SWAPO efforts to capitalize
on the unstable situation in the southern region of Angola."[98] The initial invasion was small, involving about 500 SADF troops taking up

[98] RSA, *White Paper on Defence 1977*, p. 6.

positions near the hydroelectric installations along the Cunene River, and disarming UNITA, FNLA, and MPLA troops.[99] By late August, South Africa occupied a strip of territory 50 km (*c.* 31 miles) deep along the border. In September and October of 1975, the SADF escalated and moved up the Angolan coast while Zairean and FNLA troops attempted to crush the MPLA from the north. In response, Cuba sent just under 500 military instructors in October to assist the MPLA, and in November sent 650 troops to help the MPLA turn back the invaders. Thus, despite coming within 100 miles of the capital, South Africa was forced to retreat. "The SADF columns had outrun their supply lines while the MPLA forces were rapidly reinforcing themselves with heavy arms."[100]

Western support, particularly covert assistance from the US Central Intelligence Agency, was not enough to ensure a quick SADF or UNITA victory in Angola. By December, SADF forces were suffering what they considered significant losses. SADF retreated in early 1976, but the invasion became the prototype for the basic pattern of South African behavior toward Angola over the next ten years: frequent small-scale sabotage, periodic large-scale military incursions, the occupation of southern Angola, and military support of UNITA.[101] It is unlikely that UNITA could have survived without South African government support in the form of weapons, vehicles, and fuel: "From a demoralized band of 3,000 men who fled into the bush [in 1976], UNITA's leader Jonas Savimbi claims to have built a force of 30,000 who are active in every province up to the tenth parallel."[102] In addition, former FNLA guerrillas were trained by South Africa and organized into the "32 Battalion" which later became a permanent 4,000 member element of the SADF.[103]

---

[99] Christopher Coker, "South Africa: A New Military Role in Southern Africa 1969–1982," in Robert Jaster, ed., *Southern Africa: Regional Security Problems and Prospects* (New York: St. Martin's Press, 1985), pp. 142–150: 143.

[100] Cawthra, *Brutal Force*, p. 147.

[101] The relationship from the mid-1970s to the late 1980s between South Africa and UNITA was quite close. UNITA, an indigenous organization, grew to depend quite heavily on South African weapons, training and logistical support. In some cases, as documented by Phyllis Johnson and David Martin, *Apartheid Terrorism: The Destabilization Report*, The Commonwealth Secretariat (Bloomington: Indiana University Press, 1989), SADF forces performed covert sabotage missions in Angola but left evidence to suggest that it was UNITA's work.

[102] Coker, "South Africa: A New Military Role in Southern Africa 1969–1982," p. 145.

[103] Robert S. Jaster, "The 1988 Peace Accords and the Future of South-Western Africa," *Adelphi Papers*, no. 253 (Autumn 1990), pp. 10–11; Coker, *South Africa's Security Dilemmas*, p. 39.

South Africa intensified its military effort in Angola, attempting to defeat the Angolan government and crush SWAPO, but the "bush war," as they called it, suffered from both the UN arms embargo and the Cuban military presence. In June 1980 and August 1981, SADF launched large-scale military incursions into Angola and occupied Cunene Province.[104] Cuban military assistance to Angola increased so that by late 1983, when South Africa launched another effort, "Operation Askari," Cuban aid was able to make a difference in the battle for Cuvelai, Angola. The SADF lost at least ten aircraft, including four sophisticated Mirage fighter aircraft. This was a significant blow given the inability to replace any Mirage lost from their already small inventory because of the arms embargo.[105] Moreover, the embargo led to a spare parts shortage: of the fewer than 70 sophisticated French Mirage aircraft in the South African arsenal, in the late 1980s, more than half of the aircraft were grounded due to the lack of spare parts.[106]

After invading Angola again in 1983, South Africa, under the Lusaka Accords of February 1984, agreed to withdraw from Angola's Cunene province by the end of March. But South Africa never completely withdrew. In July 1984, South Africa admitted that it had halted withdrawal on the rationale that SWAPO, which had not been part of the agreement, was still operating in the region.

Escalation and stalemate

Between 1985 and 1988, there were numerous military clashes between the Angolan military and UNITA anti-government guerrillas and the SADF. Moreover, the scale of South African operations in support of UNITA, including sabotage, increased.[107] In 1985, the United States Congress repealed the Clark Amendment banning US aid to UNITA, and in 1986 US military support resumed. Since South Africa had been funding UNITA, this amounted to a subsidy of South African foreign policy:

---

[104] Coker, "South Africa: A New Military Role in Southern Africa 1969–1982," p. 144. Coker, p. 143, argues: "Although these operations have been described as raids the term is somewhat misleading. Most recently they have amounted to full-scale invasions involving armoured cars, fighter bombers and large detachments of troops."
[105] In 1980 there were six Canberra B and six Buccaneer bombers with 32 Mirage F1AZ fighters in the arsenal; by 1987 there was one less Canberra, six Buccaneer, and 15 Mirage F1AZ. IISS, *Military Balance* for 1980–1981 and 1987–1988.
[106] Coker, *South Africa's Security Dilemmas*, pp. 33–34.
[107] Angola blamed over 3,000 acts of sabotage from 1976 to June 1987 on the economically vital Buengela Railway on SADF and UNITA. See Johnson and Martin, *Apartheid Terrorism*, pp. 129, 130 and Cawthra, *Brutal Force*, p. 159.

US aid to UNITA was $15 million in 1986, and again in 1987.[108] Despite external assistance, neither South Africa nor UNITA was able to defeat Angola's People's Armed Forces for the Liberation of Angola (FAPLA).

The turning points were two battles: for UNITA occupied Mavinga in 1985, and the siege of Cuito Cuanavale from 1987 to 1988. When Angola lost a bid to oust UNITA from Mavinga in the fall of 1985, due to the intervention of South African forces, the Angolans purchased sophisticated aircraft and radar from the Soviet Union and in May 1986 Angola received the new equipment. South Africa remained in southern Angola, and the US sent sophisticated anti-aircraft equipment to UNITA.[109]

In August 1987, FAPLA began a counter-offensive against UNITA forces in Mavinga, and SADF forces sought to take Cuito Cuanavale because it was the site of an important Angolan airfield. The battle for Cuito lasted months, but the Angolans held. The SADF sent in 3,000 men and perhaps 2,000 SWATF troops to support the estimated 10,000 well-trained UNITA forces already in Mavinga.[110] SADF encircled the Angolan military, and FAPLA retreated to their base in Cuito Cuanavale about 200 miles from the border from October to December 1987. "South Africa continued to incur (as well as inflict) substantial losses during this period . . . From September to November, South Africa listed thirty-five SADF members killed in combat: a record for any like period in the war." Another twenty-six died from cerebral malaria.[111] In November 1987, South Africa's head of state, P.W. Botha, visited a base in southern Angola to boost the morale of SADF forces. In December South Africa rejected a UN resolution for South Africa to withdraw from Angola and the siege continued.

In March 1988, Cuba sent 15,000 fresh troops. But instead of staying in rear positions as was characteristic of past deployments, the Cubans

---

[108] In 1988, US assistance to UNITA rose to $30–45 million; in 1989, aid was $50–60 million; in 1990, aid was $65–80 million. "U.S. Still Fuels War in Angola," *Washington Notes on Africa*, Spring 1990, pp. 10–11; "US Aid to Unita . . . The Beginning of the End?" *Washington Notes on Africa*, Winter 1990, pp. 4–6.

[109] On US and Soviet assistance, to UNITA and the MPLA respectively, see Gerald Bender, "The Eagle and the Bear in Angola," *The Annals of the American Academy of Political and Social Science* 489 (January 1987), 123–132; Michael McFaul, "Rethinking the 'Reagan Doctrine' in Angola," *International Security* 14 (Winter 1989/90), 99–135.

[110] South Africa "never had more than 9 000 troops inside Angola, although most sources claim the number was closer to 3 000." Thomas Ohlson, "The Cuito Cuanavale Syndrome: Revealing SADF Vulnerabilities," *South African Review* 5 (Braamfontein: Raven Press, 1989), pp. 181–190: 185.

[111] Jaster, "The 1988 Peace Accords," p. 18.

participated in the counter-attack which ultimately turned the battle in Angola's favor. Angola's "anti-aircraft defences made the loss of irreplaceable aircraft costly for the South Africa air force, and armoured cars were stopped with anti-tank missiles."[112] SADF troops were driven to defensive positions around the Calueque dam in Southern Angola. On 27 June, a SADF commander led an assault on Cuban troops and killed 150 men. The Cubans retaliated with an air assault on the Calueque position, killing twelve SADF members. Moreover, SWATF forces mutinied and 360, mostly black soldiers, were imprisoned because they refused to fight. A senior SADF military commander said of the 1988 confrontation and Cuban build-up: "This was more than we could handle. Had the Cubans attacked [Namibia] they would have overrun the place. We could not have stopped them."[113] SADF claimed that only fifty-two whites died in the entire operation.

The war inside Namibia also grew in intensity and scale, but the ratio of the opposing military forces appears to have been rather lopsided. Portraying its military actions in Southern Africa as peacekeeping, anti-terrorism, and training, South Africa justified attacks against Namibian refugee camps during 1978 and 1979 as against SWAPO supporters and members. A May 1978 SADF attack on Kassinga refugee camp in southern Angola left over 600 Namibians dead, and nearly half of those killed were children.[114] In March 1979, South Africa attacked SWAPO camps in Zambia, and Angola reported numerous small-scale incursions by South Africa in 1979.[115] In 1979, the SADF said, "The protection of South-West Africa and her peoples against terrorism remains a priority task which has been one of the most important activities of the SA Army in the past year... The operational task in SWA also affords an important opportunity for members of the SA Army to acquire practical experience in that type of warfare which, in fact, serves as a very important rounding off of the SA Army's training

---

[112] Johnson and Martin, *Apartheid Terrorism*, p. 147.

[113] Quoted in Jaster, "The 1988 Peace Accords," p. 23. This assessment appears to be a slight exaggeration. First, the Cubans clearly stated that they were not interested in crossing the border between Angola and Namibia and they never did so. Second, while the disposition of South African forces in the March 1988 battle is not clear, it seems that if Cuban and Angolan forces had crossed the border, there were sufficient troops and equipment to at least have produced a stalemate at the border. But such a battle would have cost even more white South African lives.

[114] Cawthra, *Brutal Force*, 149; Johnson and Martin, *Apartheid Terrorism*, p. 140. The Angolan government reported that 700 men, women, and children were killed at Kassinga. UN, *Namibia Bulletin*, no. 3 (September 1978), p. 11.

[115] UN, *Namibia Bulletin*, no. 3 (October 1979), pp. 13–16.

program."[116] One British mercenary, Trevor Edwards, deserted after serving for nine months in the SADF 32 Battalion:

> Our main job is to take an area and clear it. We sweep through it and we kill everything in front of us, cattle, goats, people, everything. We are out to stop SWAPO and so we stop them getting into the villages for food and water. But half the time the locals don't know what's going on. We're just fucking them up and it gets out of hand. Some of the guys get a bit carried away. And SWAPO still get by us and cross the cut-line between Angola and Namibia. It's not as if we are stopping them.[117]

SWAPO's military presence in the region was small, with fewer than 2,000 guerrillas in 1980, but grew to between 6,000 and 8,000 troops during the mid 1980s.[118] Estimates of South African forces committed to Namibia vary but the number seemed to sharply increase in the late 1970s and 1980s. In 1977, there were an estimated 53,200 SADF in Namibia; in May 1979 SWAPO testified in the UN that there were about 75,000 SADF troops and personnel in Namibia.[119] In 1982 Defence Minister D.F. Malan admitted that there had been a "fiftyfold" increase in the number of South African troops in Namibia and South Africa since 1975.[120] By 1986, the UN estimated that South Africa's total occupation was "more than 100,000 troops in Namibia, comprising mercenaries, additional reinforcements that are frequently airlifted into the Territory, as well as locally recruited elements and an increasingly armed white settler community."[121]

Throughout the 1980s, SWAPO claimed modest military successes, which South Africa persistently denied. SADF also denied UN reports that it was engaged in violent repression inside Namibia, although a South African Air Force song, to the tune of "Ghost Riders in the Sky," captures the feeling and SADF strategy: "The Billy Boys were loading up, One dark and windy night, Six bombs each, Mark 82s, It was a fearsome

---

[116] RSA, *White Paper on Defence and Armaments Supply 1979*, p. 18. Abbreviations are in the original.
[117] Quoted in Nick Davies, *The Guardian* (London), 29 January 1981. Reprinted in UN, *Namibia Bulletin*, no. 1 (1981), pp. 29–32: 29.
[118] Coker, *South Africa's Security Dilemmas*, p. 30.
[119] UN, *Namibia Bulletin*, no. 2, (July 1977), pp. 18–19; UN, *Namibia Bulletin*, no. 2, (July 1979) p. 20.
[120] UN, *The Military Situation in and Relating to Namibia* (New York: United Nations, 1983), p. 5. This is an odd number.
[121] UN, *The Military Situation in and Relating to Namibia* (New York: United Nations, 1987), p. 2.

sight, To strike at dawn, that was their task, Against the Swapo swine, To Kill the commies in a group, Before they cross the line . . . The bombs were right on line, The Swaps were taken by surprise, Death came so quick and fast, No more would they terrorize, They'd met their end at last . . .″[122]

The UN reported evidence of terrible brutality committed in Namibia by SADF, SWATF, and the 2,000 to 3,000 mercenaries from Western nations fighting for South Africa. A former member of the SADF, Bill Anderson, told the United Nations in 1976 of SADF activities in Namibia.

> His unit had been involved mostly in sweeping areas of suspected guerrillas and in guarding the northern Namibian border. Orders had been given to capture every male over the age of puberty and to kill those who ran away. His batallion [*sic*] had captured between 200 and 300 men. The prisoners were kept blindfolded, with their hands tied tightly behind their backs. They were frequently assaulted, punched, burnt with cigarettes or had sand stuffed into their mouths by men of all ranks, even in the presence of senior officers. The interrogations themselves were conducted in special tents and were accompanied by various forms of torture, include [*sic*] water torture and electric shock.[123]

Could South Africa have won the war in Angola and kept Namibia if it had used all its military might? South Africa lost its conventional military edge because the UN arms embargo made it difficult to replace equipment. For example, losses of twenty-two aircraft in battle and another twelve due to accident or error between 1974 and 1989 were large given the small size of its total inventory.[124] On the other hand, despite the UN embargo, South Africa successfully pursued the development of nuclear weapons during the 1970s and 1980s to offset its numerical disadvantage in Africa.[125] Because South Africa was unwilling to use its six nuclear weapons, its declining conventional military capabilities were thus significant. Ultimately, the arms embargo meant that South Africa was far enough behind in military technology to help turn the balance in Angola's favor when, in the late 1980s, Soviet weapons

---

[122] Excerpt of "The Billy Boys' Song," words by Rick Culpan. Dick Lord, *Vlamgat: The Story of the Mirage F1 in the South African Air Force* (Weltevreden Park, South Africa: Covos-Day Books, 2000), pp. 269–270: 269.

[123] UN, *Namibia Bulletin*, no. 1, (April 1977), pp. 9–10.

[124] Lord, *Vlamgat*, pp. 267–268.

[125] David Fig, "Sanctions and the Nuclear Industry," in Crawford and Klotz, eds., *How Sanctions Work*, pp. 75–102.

and thousands of Cuban military forces were pumped into Angola at the request of the Angolan government. Thus, the combination of South Africa's relative military isolation and the increased quality of Angolan arms led to a shift in the balance of forces.

But South Africa did not use all its military capabilities. For example, why did South Africa forgo using its nuclear weapons? Were the constraints strategic – there were few or no military targets worth the expenditure of an expensive nuclear weapon – or normative/political, specifically, the fear of international approbation, increased isolation, and sanctions?

Negotiating Namibian independence

In the 1960s and early 1970s South Africa discussed Namibia with UN representatives. In April 1977, Britain, France, West Germany, and the United States formed a "Contact Group" to negotiate with South Africa over Namibia. Under intensified pressure, South Africa accepted UN Security Council Resolution 435 of 29 September 1978 which called for the "withdrawal of South Africa's illegal administration from Namibia and the transfer of power to the people of Namibia with the assistance of the United Nations. . . " Resolution 435 also established a United Nations Transition Assistance Group (UNTAG) to supervise independence elections. The Contact Group initiative foundered when South Africa added more conditions to its withdrawal. Still seeking international legitimacy for the occupation, South Africa also reformed its government of South West Africa by agreeing to elections for a Constituent Assembly. South Africa sponsored the Democratic Turnhalle Alliance (DTA) and SWAPO boycotted the December 1978 elections. The international community called the unsupervised elections illegal, and not surprisingly, the DTA won. Thus, as one scholar noted, "South Africa managed to give the appearance of co-operating with the Contact Group and moving the negotiations forward, while in fact avoiding firm commitments and blocking progress."[126]

In 1981, the Reagan administration proclaimed a new US policy toward South Africa, "constructive engagement." The Reagan administration opposed sanctions against South Africa, and Contact Group efforts dissolved into trilateral negotiations, as the chief State Department officer on Africa, Chester Crocker, began talks with Angola and

---

[126] Jaster, "The 1988 Peace Accords," p. 12. Also see Jaster, *The Defence of White Power*, pp. 106–108.

South Africa. In 1984 South Africa signed separate agreements to cease military operations against Angola and Mozambique but soon abrogated both. The Reagan administration began openly supporting UNITA, eventually convincing the Congress to repeal the Clark Amendment in 1985, and proposed a "linkage" strategy: South Africa would agree to withdraw from Namibia if and when Cuban troops aiding Angola withdrew. The Angolan government briefly withdrew from US mediated negotiations in early 1986 but returned to the bargaining table in mid July 1987. The Soviets joined the diplomatic effort, and in May 1988 Cuba entered the negotiations. In late July 1988 the parties agreed in principle that South Africa would leave Namibia and that Cuba would withdraw its troops. From the point when Cuba joined the negotiations and agreed to linkage, much of the bargaining was over the pace of Cuban withdrawal from Angola and the timing of Namibian independence.[127] There were no SWAPO representatives at the negotiations. In December 1988, the Brazzaville Protocol agreement to end the war between Angola and South Africa was formally signed.

Implementation of the agreement was not flawless, nor did peace immediately follow in Angola and Namibia. Indeed, one of the largest battles in the war in Namibia occurred in early April 1989: SWAPO troops returning to Namibia were attacked by the SADF and more than 200 SWAPO fighters died. Demobilization nevertheless continued and elections were held under UN supervision. SWAPO won a majority and Namibia became independent on 21 March 1990 under a SWAPO government.[128] One member of a South African psychological action (propaganda) team deployed in Namibia, said "I don't understand how SWAPO won" the independence elections in 1990 – "no one we met in the villages said they supported SWAPO."[129] However, the Namibian government publicly expressed concern that plots uncovered to overthrow the SWAPO government in 1990 were orchestrated by South Africa.[130] Indeed, in 1991 Nico Basson, a white South African

[127] See Gerald J. Bender, "Peacemaking in Southern Africa: the Luanda-Pretoria tug-of-war," *Third World Quarterly* 11 (January 1989), 15–30; and Gillian Gunn, "A Guide to the Intricacies of the Angola-Namibia Negotiations,"*CSIS Africa Notes*, no. 90 (8 September 1988).
[128] The transition was also not without bitterness: "In some predominantly white suburbs around Windhoek [Namibia's capital], residents are flying the swastika," according to Mark Verbaan, "Namibia: Opening a New Chapter,"*Africa Report* 35 (May–June 1990), 25–28: 26.
[129] Interview with the author, 27 May 1991, Pretoria, South Africa.
[130] *Africa Research Bulletin, Political Series,* 27 (August 1990), 9804.

who worked for the South African-backed Democratic Turnhalle Alliance, described SADF efforts to influence the 1989 election, infiltrate SWAPO, and sabotage the UN forces supervising the transition process in 1989.[131]

Ethical argument

At many points in the history of South West Africa/Namibia, it has seemed as if brute force rather than ethical argument was decisive. Yet ethical argument played a role throughout, shaping the material and normative constraints felt by South Africa. First, sanctions by Western governments – whose interest in South Africa's mineral wealth would have argued against embargos – were imposed primarily as a consequence of ethical arguments made by the international anti-apartheid movement. These sanctions placed military and economic constraints on South Africa and hastened South Africa's overextension. The oil and arms embargoes were particularly harmful, exacerbating the military constraints South Africa faced in Angola and Namibia.[132] Again, sanctions were put in place as a consequence of normative beliefs held by anti-apartheid activists who made successful ethical arguments and would have been unlikely, even unthinkable, fifty or one hundred years earlier when dominant normative beliefs favored colonialism.[133] Second, South Africa faced increasingly effective resistance inside Namibia, in part because SWAPO was able to use ethical arguments to mobilize the international community in support of their struggle for independence. The UN's recognition of SWAPO as the "sole and authentic" representatives of the Namibian people "meant that South Africa never felt sufficiently confident to ban SWAPO's legal political presence" in Namibia.[134] And without financial and material support from the UN and others, SWAPO would have found it much more difficult to fight the apartheid regime.

Third, although most of the political ferment in South Africa during the 1970s and 1980s concerned apartheid, there were ethical arguments inside South Africa about policy toward Namibia and South Africa's

---

[131] Christopher S. Wren, "South African Describes Army Namibia Plot," *The New York Times*, 1 July 1991, p. A7.
[132] Neta C. Crawford, "Trump Card or Theatre: An Introduction to Two Sanctions Debates," pp. 3–24; "How Arms Embargoes Work," pp. 45–74; and "Oil Sanctions Against Apartheid," pp. 103–126, in Crawford and Klotz, eds., *How Sanctions Work*.
[133] Audie Klotz, *Norms in International Relations: The Struggle Against Apartheid* (Ithaca: Cornell University Press, 1995).
[134] Leys and Saul, *Namibia's Liberation Struggle*, p. 14.

other neighbors. Ultimately, opinion about South African foreign policy inside white South Africa became divided in the 1980s even as the government attempted to silence dissenters and discredit their arguments.[135] White South African males began to resist conscription in larger and more vocal numbers, although some just quietly refused to appear for their national service or yearly Citizen Force camps, and some left the country, ostensibly to pursue higher education. The End Conscription Campaign (ECC) formed in South Africa in 1983 mobilized white males of draft age in South Africa and was supported by human rights, religious, women's, and student groups. As resistance to conscription grew, ECC activists were detained and police raided the homes and offices of ECC members. The army formed a unit to track down draft resisters in 1987, and in 1988 the government banned the ECC.[136] In August 1988, just two weeks before the banning, the ECC organized a public announcement by 143 white males of their refusal to serve in the SADF. The ECC engaged in political education campaigns about South African foreign policy: immediately after formation in 1983 the ECC embarked on a "No War in Namibia" campaign.[137] In addition, the Committee on South African War Resistance, formed in 1978, published a four part series focusing on South Africa's occupation of Namibia in its journal *Resister*.[138] In September 1989, 771 conscripts publicly refused to serve in the SADF.[139] The Deputy Minister of Defence accused the ECC members of being weak: "lacking in the moral fibre to defend the country against Russia and its surrogates."[140]

---

[135] During the 1980s, activists from all racial groups were subjected to government banning, detention, harassment, and assassination. For example, in 1985 the Congress of South African Students was banned. In 1988 alone, 528 students, scholars, and teachers were detained, while about 570 trade unionists, workers, and community political organizers were detained. From 1976 through the first six months of 1988 18,675 people were detained under security legislation and an estimated additional 40,996 were detained under state of emergency regulations from 21 July 1985 to December 1988. David Webster and Maggie Friedman, "Repression and the State of Emergency: June 1987 – March 1989," *South African Review 5*, (Braamfontein, SA: Raven Press, 1989), pp. 16–41.
[136] Laurie Nathan, "Marching to a Different Beat," in Cock and Nathan, eds., *Society at War*, pp. 308–323.
[137] The best account of the ECC through 1988 is Nathan, "Marching to a Different Beat." The white anti-conscription movement is chronicled in the periodical, *Resister: Journal of the Committee on South African War Resistance*, published in Britain until 1991. Also see *Out of Step: War Resistance in South Africa* (London: Catholic Institute of International Relations, 1989).
[138] The series began in *Resister*, no. 27 (August–September 1983).
[139] "We Say No to the SADF: National and International Registers Launched," *Resister*, no. 64 (First Quarter 1990), 6–7: 7.
[140] Quoted in Nathan, "Marching to a Different Beat," p. 317.

Between 1975 and 1978, on average some 1,750 conscripts failed to report for national service induction. In 1985, 7,589 conscripts failed to report, 50 percent of the number to be inducted. The government said later that most of these no-shows were accounted for, but stopped announcing induction figures for subsequent call-ups. The 1986 Defence White Paper flatly stated that "the objections of churches to national service will result in the Defence Force being reduced to inefficiency."[141] In a government brochure describing national service commitments for white males, the role of the anti-conscription movement was minimized. The brochure states that the "reduction of the initial national service period announced by the State President on 7 December 1989, was the final result of an investigation which was launched on our own initiative earlier in the year and not in any way due to pressure from informal pressure groups."[142] Thus, the ethical arguments of the war resisters – who did not have to make arguments which could have led to government harassment, abuse, and arrest – contributed to the weakening of South Africa's military capabilities. In addition, there appeared to be increased desertion among SADF troops serving in Namibia. In 1981, of the 577 held in SADF detention centers, "519 were serving sentences for refusing to serve in the field or for going absent without leave."[143] Moreover, SADF conscripts were known to be deliberately vandalizing military equipment in operational areas.[144]

Finally, the anti-war movement in South Africa had some success in changing white opinion. White support for South Africa's policy of attacking "terrorist/guerrilla bases in neighboring states" declined. In 1982, 81.1 percent of white South Africans agreed with this policy. In May 1988, a poll showed 63 percent of whites supporting attacks and by January 1990, 58.7 percent thought South Africa should attack such bases. The intensity of white support also declined, with 60 percent of those who "definitely agree" with the policy in 1982 and 1984 declining to 23.9 percent definitely agreeing in 1990.[145]

Thus, my analysis of the South West Africa case throughout the book has shown the limits of an ethical argument explanation. Yet it also demonstrates that what some call material factors – namely the

---

[141] RSA, *White Paper on Defence and Armaments Supply 1986*, p. 7.
[142] RSA, SADF brochure, "National Service," p. 12.
[143] Coker, *South Africa's Security Dilemmas*, p. 44.   [144] Ibid., p. 45.
[145] André Du Pisani, "What Do We Think? A Survey of White Opinion on Foreign Policy Issues, No. 5" (Johannesburg: The South African Institute for International Affairs, May 1990), p. 10.

economic benefits of occupation, the costs of sanctions, more effective resistance in Namibia and Angola, and South Africa's declining military capability – were affected by ethical argument. As bad as the German and South African rule of South West Africa was, if there had been no ethical argument, the situation would likely have been much worse for the inhabitants of the region.

Counterfactuals

The strength and limits of an explanation are often tested by comparing the actual turn of events to counterfactuals.[146] If key conditions had been different could colonialism have survived the twentieth century as a legitimate institution? I briefly discuss three counterfactuals.

First, if Germany had won World War I, how would the world be different with respect to colonialism? There would certainly have been no League of Nations since the League idea came out of the Anglo-American community that won the war. Without the victory of the Western allies, there would also likely have been no German or Turkish territories to dispose of in some way or another. Further, without a League and captured territory, there would have been no Mandate system, no International Labor Organization, and no dominant powers with populations interested in championing self-determination and institutionalizing those beliefs.

The fact that Germany lost World War I, and had its colonies stripped from its possession, contributed not only to the Mandate system, but to Germany's post-war grievances. A German colonial lobby formed after World War I to protest the peace settlement persistently called for recolonization and both private and government resources were devoted to persuading Germans of the values of colonies. They argued that they needed "living space" and that their former African colonies, the League mandates, had been stolen from them and should be returned.[147]

During the mid-1930s, the Nazi government raised what became known as the "Colonial Question." Germany argued that Britain had exaggerated or lied about their ill-treatment of South West Africans

---

[146] I thank Jon Mercer for reminding me of the importance of explicitly discussing counterfactuals. A useful introduction is Philip E. Tetlock and Aaron Belkin, eds., *Counterfactual Thought Experiments in World Politics: Logical, Methodological, and Psychological Perspectives* (Princeton: Princeton University Press, 1996).

[147] See Wolfe W. Schmokel, *Dream of Empire: German Colonialism, 1919–1945* (New Haven: Yale University Press, 1964).

and others and used official government publications to counter the "colonial guilt lie." When the Nazis and Italians raised the Colonial Question to British diplomats in the 1930s, there was a serious discussion of the issues in Britain, although the British ultimately, for several reasons, decided against returning the colonies to their former colonial masters. Some argued that return would break up British lines of communication on the African continent. The British public was also against returning the colonies. Further, ethical arguments supposing that a change in the language spoken in the mandated territory would harm education efforts implied the Africans right to self-determination. According to the Labour Party, this "might well put back the clock of advancement for the indigenous population for a generation, and that population has a moral right to veto them which the Labour Party should uphold."[148] In the House of Commons Debate on the question on 7 December 1938, the Secretary of State for the Colonies, Malcolm MacDonald, "assured the House that both the wishes of the inhabitants of the territories and of the House itself would have to be considered before any decision was taken."[149]

What if Germany, Italy, and Japan had won World War II? The German Reich was explicitly bent on re-establishing German colonial territory, and Germany's "place in the sun," and there is good evidence to believe the German government would have undertaken new colonization if it had been successful in the war. Further, in 1939, the German government undertook planning for a colonial empire that included, among other things, a reliance on forced labor.[150] Germany, Italy, and Japan also took territory and established colonies during the war. If the Axis powers had won, the League of Nations, already essentially ended at the outset of World War II, would likely not have had a successor in the form of the United Nations. There would have been no United Nations Trusteeship System and no Declaration on Non-Self-Governing Territories. Further, if the Nazis had won, Nazi Germany's racist beliefs would probably not have been so thoroughly discounted in the West.

Both of these counterfactual scenarios highlight the key conditions of democratic normative beliefs and culture. Specifically, the outlines of

---

[148] Labour Party, *The Demand for Colonial Territories and Equality of Economic Opportunity* (memorandum, March 1937), p. 48 quoted in D.J. Morgan, *The Official History of Colonial Development, Vol. 1: The Origins of British Aid Policy, 1924–1945* (London: Macmillan, 1980), p. 21.

[149] Morgan, *The Official History of Colonial Development*, vol. I, p. 21.

[150] Schmokel, *Dream of Empire: German Colonialism, 1919–1945*, pp. 137–184.

the colonial policies and practices of Germany, Italy, and Japan were little different from those of Britain or France. The differences were in their domestic political orders. The defeat of Germany and its allies by more democratic states who were willing and able to impose their democratic norms on the conquered ensured the triumph of political liberalism, specifically the greater articulation and extension of democratic normative beliefs and practices in both the core democracies of the West and in those powers' relations to their colonies. The necessity to articulate the principles at stake in the two wars solidified and heightened the commitment to democracy and self-determination in the victorious states. The contradictions and hypocrisy of colonialism by self-proclaimed democracies were also highlighted and heightened by the wars. The cluster of principles and normative beliefs that fed into the evolving practice and emergent norm of decolonization – principles of equality, self-determination, nationalism, democracy, human rights, non-intervention, and anti-racism – gained broader persuasive power as they were increasingly applied in the heart of the colonial powers, the "mother" countries, and as these arguments were generalized beyond the privileged members of colonial society.

Would the colonizers have remained had colonial resistance movements been less effective? Most anti-colonial resistance movements were never great military threats to colonial powers. But they did raise the ethical stakes by posing the problem of how the colonial power would respond. And the political effectiveness of anti-colonial movements was significant. They articulated ethical dilemmas, publicized colonial government atrocities, and humanized the colonized in the eyes of the colonizer. Moreover, to the extent that anti-colonial movements were able to force concessions such as unionization, political representation, and judicial reform, they were an integral part of the decolonization process. Less effective anti-colonial movements would thus likely have meant a longer life for colonialism.

How ethical arguments undermined colonialism

Practitioners of colonialism made arguments in favor of the practice based on religious/philosophical, practical, scientific, and identity beliefs. The core of these arguments contained a sharp distinction between Europeans and outsiders and the belief in Western European religious, economic, cultural, biological, and scientific superiority. Yet there were always Europeans, and of course Native Americans, Africans, and Asians, who questioned the beliefs and practices of colonialism, and in particular its most harsh elements, slavery and forced labor. Indeed, the main arguments about colonialism between 1492 and 1900 concerned the ethics of its two primary constitutive practices, slavery and forced labor, rather than any serious questioning of colonialism itself.

The ethical explanation for decolonization stresses two consequences of ethical argument. First, ethical arguments fostered growing disbelief in the normality, legitimacy, and necessity for slavery and colonialism, ultimately nurturing what became a widespread normative distaste for colonial empire among the political elites and mass public of colonial powers. Slavery and colonialism depend logically on a belief in human inequality while arguments about the rights of humans are cumulative and expanding by the nature of their content. Specifically, there was no *logical* limit to applying human rights and self-determination arguments once people began to believe, at least in principle, in human equality.

What is the "logical" connection between the end of slavery and forced labor, and decolonization? The cluster of principles and normative beliefs that fed into the evolving practice and emergent behavioral norm of decolonization are: equality, self-determination, nationalism, democracy, human rights, non-intervention, and anti-racism. What these normative beliefs have in common is respect for the other and non-violent relations – that is their core value. These values were extended (often imperfectly and sometimes hypocritically) from sovereigns to individual humans in the core with increased democratization for white males, to the idea of universal human freedom (the abolition of slavery) to other historically weak groups (women and minorities) and states (decolonization and non-intervention).

Early advocates of colonial reform and later proponents of decolonization called on colonizers to act in ways that were consistent with their (evolving) identities, including their newly discovered empathy with the other, colonial subjects. Ultimately, persuasive ethical arguments caused a shift in opinion on the issue of the legitimacy of colonialism among non-colonial powers, and then reformers and anti-imperialists inside the colonial powers. Later, the non-colonial states pressured reluctant colonial powers into granting their colonies independence. Ethical arguments about reforming colonialism harnessed the emotions of embarrassment and shame on the part of colonizers. And ethical arguments (as well as practical and identity arguments) were used by the colonized to mobilize their peers to resist it.[151]

Second, persuasive ethical arguments changed the economic and political context for colonialism: by making slavery illegitimate, persuasive ethical arguments increased the costs of colonialism and decreased its profits; and by making aspects of colonial rule illegitimate, persuasive ethical arguments decreased the willingness of domestic populations in the metropole to support colonialism. Specifically, because of persuasive ethical arguments, two important constituent practices of colonialism, slavery and forced labor, became increasingly suspect (they were defamiliarized and delegitimized) as colonial powers democratized. Normative beliefs and ethical arguments helped anti-slavery movements outlaw slavery and regulate forced labor. As the colonizer had to pay for labor, some of the costs of colonialism increased and the greater expense was used as evidence that colonialism was no longer in the economic interests of great powers. The belief systems and practices surrounding and supporting colonialism as the dominant practice among great powers were thus modified by the changing view of the normality of its constitutive and related practices.

Further, persuasive ethical arguments shifted colonial actors' conceptions of their interests and altered the capabilities of the colonizers as the growing normative revulsion for empire and its constitutive practices was accompanied by domestic resistance to the burdens of empire.[152] The domestic populations of colonial powers increasingly resisted the taxes and conscription required to maintain colonial holdings. The source for this domestic revulsion and resistance among the publics of the colonizers was the sense that empire was not right – and certainly not worth the torture, repression, and vast sums of money required to maintain it. Domestic resistance to empire was not new – what was perhaps new in the twentieth century was the role of international media and thus the extent to which the publics of colonizers were aware of the techniques their governments used to sustain empire. What was also new was the unwillingness of colonial publics to use violence, especially genocide and torture, to maintain empire. And it was no longer glorious for colonizers to die for empire because of these new identity

---

[151] Hendrik Spruyt, "The End of Empire and the Extension of the Westphalian System: The Normative Basis of the Modern State Order," *International Studies Review* 2 (Summer 2000), 65–92.
[152] This discussion should not be taken to mean that public sentiments in favor of, or against, colonialism were the same among all European colonizers.

and normative beliefs. Thus, the ability of colonial powers to impose colonialism declined as the balance of belief shifted from supporters of colonialism to supporters of reform and decolonization. There was no longer an international consensus on the virtues of maintaining colonial rule.

It also became harder to mobilize domestic populations for colonial occupation at the same time as resistance inside the colonies increased, altering the capabilities of actors in the colonial–anti-colonial equation. It was no longer possible, as the great powers had done in the late nineteenth century with their embargo on shipping arms to Africa, to deny support to anti-colonial movements. Mainstream liberals and socialists were willing, and frequently eager, to supply anti-colonial movements with money, and sometimes weapons. The greater legitimacy and international support for anti-colonial independence movements led to stronger guerrilla movements and legal challenges to colonial rule as outsiders sent aid to independence forces.

How and why did new normative beliefs come to be applied to colonial subjects? There were two catalysts for the shift toward recognizing a principle and then a right to self-determination in the colonies: the end of slavery and the articulation, by colonial subjects, of their rights. Both of these catalysts fostered a long-term movement toward the humanization of the other, in this case, those who were different from those with military power: "the growing acknowledgment by states and societies that all individuals, regardless of their citizenship, race, religion, or other defining characteristics, are entitled to basic protections of life, property, and contract."[153]

Perhaps as important as the end of slavery was the fact that Western educated members of the colonial empires were able to press their case themselves, in increasing numbers after World Wars I and II, using the language and the legal justificatory modes of the colonizers. This is not the same as the argument that European nationalism spread to the colonies and infected indigenous peoples with national aspirations. Nor is it to say that anti-colonial ethical arguments "originated in

[153] Ethan Nadelmann, "Global Prohibition Regimes: The Evolution of Norms in International Society," *International Organization* 44 (Autumn 1990), 479–526: 483. Moreover, as the historian Michael Adas has argued, the very brutality of World War I contributed to the sense that the so-called civilized nations were not so civilized. Michael Adas, *Machines as the Measure of Men: Science, Technology, and Ideologies of Western Dominance* (Ithaca: Cornell University Press, 1989), ch. 6.

the West."[154] Rather, the publics and political elites of the great powers found it increasingly difficult to argue that the "subject" races were incapable of self-government – "not yet able to stand by themselves" – when clearly intelligent and articulate members of those peoples fought with Europeans during the world wars and then came to Europe to present their own case, in the language of the colonizers and from within the logic of their dominant belief systems of Christianity, democracy, and free markets. Thus, the identities of both the colonizer and the colonized were reconstructed through anti-colonial arguments made by the colonized and the colonizer became more receptive to decolonization arguments.

Emotions, specifically, empathy and identification, were also important in the decolonization process but their causal role is deeply intertwined with the role of arguments.[155] As long as the colonizer could hate and disdain the colonized, it was easier to maintain beliefs in European superiority and the right, indeed obligation, to replace the political, social, and economic systems of the colonized with those of the colonizer. The belief in European superiority also interfered with the colonizer's ability to appreciate and empathize with the victims of slavery, forced labor, mutilation, and torture. Decolonization became possible only in an era when the beliefs about colonial "subjects" were reassessed. The ethical arguments that challenged colonial beliefs about the colonized would likely not have been as persuasive had not the colonizer begun to *feel* differently about the colonized; the colonizer would likely not have felt differently about the colonized had they maintained their belief in European superiority.

The process of institutionalizing normative beliefs in international treaties and the procedures of international organization was also extremely important. Once certain normative beliefs were put into practice and institutionalized, for instance by translating the belief into colonial law or by making a practice subject to the international oversight of the Permanent Mandates Commission, the colonial world was changed.

[154] Robert H. Jackson, "The Weight of Ideas in Decolonization: Normative Change in International Relations," in Judith Goldstein and Robert Keohane, eds., *Ideas and Foreign Policy: Beliefs, Institutions, and Political Change* (Ithaca: Cornell University Press, 1993), pp. 111–138: 112, 119, 134.
[155] I am not the first to point out the importance of emotions in this context. Ethan Nadelmann argues that "norms emerge and are promoted because they reflect not only the economic and security interests of dominant members of international society but also their moral interests and emotional dispositions."Nadelmann, "Global Prohibition Regimes," p. 524.

Thus, ending slavery changed the economic and political context of colonialism; the articulation and implementation of good labor practices in the colonies after World War I enabled labor to appeal unfair practices, and it lowered barriers to labor organizing; and the articulation and implementation of the normative belief in sacred trust and development eventually led to a greater role for colonial subjects in their own government, creating sites where native critics of colonial policy could make their arguments heard and affect other colonial practices. This was a sort of ethical boot-strapping: successful ethical arguments led to institutionalization of new normative beliefs, and when the standard operating procedures of colonialism changed, the social movement mobilization for decolonization became easier.

This is not to say, as Robert Jackson does, that there is "an irreversibility about these political norms."[156] Nor is it to argue, as Jackson does, that the "normative ideas of self-determination not only preempted colonialism but also precluded its reform into international trusteeship, say, or associate statehood."[157] He suggests that as "an indication of the preemptive character of anti-colonial ideas, colonial institutions and policies are not only untenable but even unthinkable."[158]

Rather, as the humanitarian intervention debate of the early and mid-1990s shows, ethical arguments can support a variety of institutions and practices including the reinstitution of colonialism or the Mandate System. For example, advocates of humanitarian intervention have argued that humanitarian interventions to "save" the "failed states" of the world are in the self-interests (in terms of economic gains and global stability) of the great powers.[159] Similarly, historian Paul Johnson's proposed solution to the problems of corrupt government and economic disaster is international trusteeship managed by the "civilized" countries: "The Security Council could commit a territory where authority has irretrievably broken down to one or more trustees . . . empowered not merely to impose order by force but to assume political functions." He suggests that the mandate of the trustees would "usually be of limited duration – 5, 10, 20 years . . . and their ultimate object would be to take constitutional measures to insure a return to effective self-government with all deliberate speed." But "the mandate may

---

[156] Jackson, "The Weight of Ideas," p. 137; also see pp. 113, 138.
[157] Ibid., p. 115.   [158] Ibid., p. 138.
[159] Gerald B. Helman and Steven R. Ratner, "Saving Failed States," *Foreign Policy* 89 (Winter 1992–1993), 3–20.

last 50 years, or 100."[160] He argues: "The only satisfaction will be the unspoken gratitude of millions of misgoverned or ungoverned people who will find in this altruistic revival of colonialism the only way out of their present intractable miseries."[161] Johnson attempts to make his argument persuasive in a context where colonialism is thoroughly delegitemized by painting a picture of past colonialism as a benevolent institution, reluctantly initiated by colonizers (who thought they were doing good), and maintained for the purpose of obtaining trade and spreading civilization and stability. "They [the Europeans] could not trade without stability, and to get stability they had to impose it. So they built little forts, which became bigger and eventually turned into the nucleus of colonies. European colonialism in its origins was to some extent a reluctant and involuntary process."[162] But Johnson's argument is less persuasive now than it might have been during the 1960s.

What has changed over the last one thousand years is the growth of the belief in human equality. Yet, decolonization did not become the behavioral norm simply because of the end of slavery or the presence of Indians, Asians, and Africans in the midst of the imperial powers. Rather, it was the arguments that were framed, extended, or sparked by these events, and the contradictions these arguments exposed (between the rhetoric of self-determination that was so widely proclaimed during the world wars and the actual conditions of the people in the colonies) that led to a growing recognition and influence of ideas about the equality of the "other" that formed the core of the decolonization regime.[163] Social movements denormalized and delegitimized both slavery and colonialism. The publicity efforts of the social movements, as well as press coverage, were crucial in this process. Reformers both inside the colonies and in the metropole exposed and publicized the colonial condition, especially the facts that imprisonment, censorship and torture were important elements of maintaining colonialism and suppressing indigenous movements.[164] They were able to reframe these practices – from

---

[160] Paul Johnson, "Colonialism's Back – And Not a Moment Too Soon," *New York Times Magazine* 18 April 1993, pp. 22, 43–44: 44.

[161] Ibid., p. 44.   [162] Ibid., p. 43.

[163] As M.J. Bonn said: "The democracies of the West had become genuine democracies; they realized the incongruity of vast empires ruled by democracy. Imperialism, as a missionary creed, did not appeal to the masses any longer." Bonn, *The Crumbling of Empire*, p. 153.

[164] On transnational social movements see Margaret E. Keck and Kathryn Sikkink, *Activists Beyond Borders: Advocacy Networks in Transnational Politics* (Ithaca: Cornell University Press, 1998).

being understood as necessary and ultimately benevolent – and represent them as horrific, counterproductive, and alien to the values and identity of Europeans.

Anti-colonial arguments had been made for centuries before the twentieth–century process of decolonization began; what made those arguments persuasive to more people were changes in the culture of the metropole. Military repression and crude exploitation were increasingly distasteful to colonizers because, and to the extent that, the culture of those societies had become more democratic. But, this is only part of the causal story; without a shift in the interests and capabilities within the colonial powers (partially driven by these shifting normative beliefs) formal colonialism would probably not have given way to decolonization. This is why it is so important to understand how normative beliefs and ethical arguments can become institutionalized and change the economic and political context.

Was it primarily the delegitimation of colonialism that led to decolonization or did ethical arguments contribute to changing assessments within the colonial powers of the values they assigned to empire, and hence to changing the very interests of the imperial powers? Or did ethical arguments and normative beliefs play little independent role, with most of the impetus for decolonization borne by the changing interests and capabilities of the colonizers? As Nadelmann has argued, "It is difficult and often impossible to determine whether those who conform to a particular norm do so because they believe the norm is just and should be followed, or because adherence to the norm coincides with their other principle interests, or because they fear the consequences that flow from defying the norm, or simply because conforming to the norm has become a matter of habit or custom."[165]

The ethical argument explanation for the end of colonialism passes the tests I proposed in chapter 2 for demonstrating the causal importance of normative belief and ethical argument. First, there is the temporal test. Normative beliefs should be raised and ethical arguments should be given and found persuasive *before* practices are changed. Years, if not several decades, of ethical argument preceded changing colonial practices. Indeed one of the findings of this book is just how long it takes to alter deeply embedded, widespread, taken for granted social practices. Second, after an ethical argument succeeds, that is, convinces a sufficient number of people so that a once taken for granted practice is no

[165] Nadelmann, "Global Prohibition Regimes," p. 480.

longer a given, one would expect a (not necessarily universal) congruence between the normative beliefs that underpinned the ethical arguments and the behavior. In other words, if slavery and forced labor are
found to be wrong, they should no longer be widely practiced. Indeed,
although it took decades, both slavery and colonialism were largely
eliminated. Where they do continue to exist, these practices are either
not tolerated, as in the case of slavery and unmodified colonialism, or
the institution has been modified, as with colonialism, so that it does not
have the same features as the older institution. Even where colonies remain, they have political institutions which involve significant political
participation for the colonized and some form of self-government.

The third "test" is whether normative beliefs that underpin arguments for changing a practice are used in arguments about correct behavior, and those who use them are not ignored or mocked.
This occurred in the case of colonialism with the normative belief
in self-determination initially expressed by Woodrow Wilson, W.E.B.
Du Bois, and other leaders of this generation. International leaders
of the next generation, for example, Prime Minister Churchill (a former colonial minister), who balked at the application of the Atlantic
Charter to British colonies, felt bound not only to use the words of
self-determination, but to help institutionalize the process of decolonization by consenting to elements of the UN Charter that applied to
"non-self-governing territories." By the early 1960s, even the colonial
powers were unwilling to vote against anti-colonial resolutions at the
United Nations and the prime minister of Britain was compelled to make
a speech about the independence "wind of change" blowing through
Africa.

Fourth, we can believe that normative beliefs and ethical arguments
have some causal force if, when their prescriptions for behavior are not
adhered to, those who flout them attempt to justify their (non-normal)
behavior on ethical or practical grounds. South Africa for decades tried
to do this at both the United Nations and the International Court of
Justice. That South Africa felt compelled to make its arguments about
South West Africa on ethical grounds showed the dominance of particular normative beliefs and the importance of the process of argument.

A fifth "test," that normative beliefs should be linked with other normative beliefs, and become part of the arguments used to advance
these other beliefs – a test for coherence – was certainly satisfied.
Anti-slavery, human rights, and self-determination beliefs were discussed together, with each normative belief's reasoning being used to

legitimize the other normative beliefs. This cluster of beliefs became a rich, deeply intertwined, discourse of both argument and law. The cluster of normative beliefs associated with decolonization were linked in arguments and increasingly applied to UN resolutions and actions that supported human rights in colonial and newly independent states. If normative beliefs were unimportant, and ethical arguments unpersuasive, then no one would bother using them as the foundation for other normative beliefs or ethical arguments.

Sixth, if ethical arguments and normative beliefs have power, we should expect the use of international sanctions, by the majority of the international community, to change the behavior of those who violate the normative prescriptions, or to punish those who support such norm violators. Sanctions were used against violators of the anti-colonial normative prescription. For example, an arms embargo and other sanctions were put in place by states and international organizations against South Africa because of its occupation of Namibia. In addition, as UN and OAU sanctions against Portugal and South Africa demonstrated, sanctions were not only discussed and approved, they were applied.[166] Still, there were no significant international sanctions against China for its occupation of Tibet, at least by 2001.

Finally, since we would never expect "rational" actors to behave contrary to their "interests," ethical arguments may be viewed as causally important whether, and to the extent that, actors with incentives to violate normative prescriptions act counter to their "interests" and follow the new normative prescriptions, or re-frame their interests in light of coming to hold new normative beliefs. For this last test to be valid three conditions should hold: states (or the influential elites that shape government policies) should "know" their interests (or at least believe they do); actors should not have been compelled by other (non-normative) circumstances, such as a change in their ability to pursue their interests because of, for example, sanctions; and actors must not have found some other way of achieving the same ends, while not technically violating the normative prescriptions that followed from ethical arguments.[167]

---

[166] Sanctions were not universally applied by members of the international community. See Landgren, *Embargo Disimplemented*; George W. Shephard, ed., *Effective Economic Sanctions* (New York: Preager, 1991); and Crawford and Klotz, eds., *How Sanctions Work*.
[167] Of course if actors change their behavior due to sanctions imposed by others acting from normative convictions, then an ethical explanation *is* appropriate. Similarly, if actors change their means for achieving the same ends, they may have done so as to appear in compliance with normative beliefs.

The "rational interest" test is, of course, problematic because actors' understanding of their interests change as their normative beliefs change. As implied above, we might better ask about the degree to which actors' understanding of their interests change as a consequence of normative beliefs. This simple "interest" test of the effectiveness of normative arguments – do actors act counter to their interests? – ought not to be seen as putting a firm barrier or making a dichotomy between the normative and the self-interested behavior of actors. Nevertheless, for the sake of clarity, I will consider the interest versus normative belief argument in its pure form here.

Colonial powers frequently acted against their "interests" and often could not demonstrate their economic interests were being met in any given colonial enterprise. Further, those interests were as much ethical, cultural, and religious as they were economic. Still, if one takes a narrow interpretation of interests as economic or strategic, there is some evidence that normative beliefs and ethical arguments on occasion trumped material interests. Certainly, the greatest colonial power in the nineteenth and twentieth centuries, acted against its perceived "interests" by outlawing the slave trade and peacefully withdrawing from several of its colonies. British elites openly and privately discussed their fears that ending slavery or decolonizing might hurt them economically. Yet they did both anyway.

I have throughout emphasized the mechanisms of argument and change. Yet we must also ask more generally why some arguments are persuasive, and others not. In the context of decolonization, I have shown how advocates of change (and somewhat unwittingly, the pragmatic reformers) overcame the extrinsic and intrinsic constraints on successful argument. But change did not go as far as it could have gone. Specifically, some argue that neocolonialism – the informal penetration and control of weaker states by the great powers and multinational corporations based in the former colonial powers – is such an effective means of extraction that the colonizers simply shifted from one method of exploitation to another. In other words, the colonizers gave up on formal empire without much resistance because they found a more efficient and less distasteful (to their publics) method of domination. However, if neocolonialism was recognized by the political and business leaders of colonial states to be efficient, why didn't all great and small powers immediately move to set up neocolonial relations and withdraw from colonies the moment they had established the means for informal control? Raising or framing the condition of neocolonial relations shows both the penetration of normative beliefs about self-determination and the discursive and institutional limits of those beliefs as they developed historically. In other words, to ask why decolonization was limited in most ways to the granting of political control is to articulate the extent to which the belief in self-determination, understood as a political and physical right, has penetrated our understanding of relations between peoples. Decolonization was limited primarily to the political realm because the emphasis of the decolonization process, as it developed out of the anti-slavery and colonial reform movement and the League of Nations Mandate system, was on decolonizing bodies and granting political representation. As Antonio Cassese argues, "the term 'alien domination' or 'subjugation' does not contemplate economic exploitation. Rather 'alien subjugation, domination, and exploitation' cover situations in which one Power *dominates* the people of *a foreign territory* by recourse to *force*."[168]

Neocolonialism has not escaped critique. It is just that the challenge is relatively weak – at the first stages of a meta-argument framing economic relations between former colonies and colonizers as exploitation, and then denormalizing and delegitimizing unequal relations. Free market capitalism is still the dominant belief system, or as Antonio Gramsci would say, it is hegemonic. In fact, capitalist beliefs and culture have obviously grown stronger with the end of Soviet style communism and the weakening of European and non-aligned movement experiments in socialism. Before economic relations between former colonizers and their former colonies can significantly change, both the ethical and practical arguments of those who argue against neocolonialism will have to become more persuasive. Persuasive ethical arguments that change complex social systems must first reframe the dominant practice. Reformers' arguments must denormalize and delegitimize the dominant practice. Activists must also propose an alternative and work to change the balance of political power that supports the dominant practice. But ultimately their success depends on gradually institutionalizing new normative beliefs. This is hard work, it may take decades or even centuries, and the ripple effects of argument and change may go in directions unanticipated by reformers.

[168] Antonio Cassese, *Self-determination of Peoples: A Legal Reappraisal* (Cambridge: Cambridge University Press, 1995), p. 99.

9 Poiesis and praxis: toward ethical world politics

> Violence is for the morally infallible. If you are convinced that you alone
> have truth, there is little recourse but to threaten, intimidate, bribe or
> coerce those who disagree with you if they do not come around to your
> view – or ultimately if these methods are unavailing, to use force. That,
> more or less, is what we see on the international scene today.[1]

While the last decade of the twentieth century was characterized by
the reconfiguration of world politics with the end of the Cold War, it was
also marked by arguments about humanitarian interventions (e.g. Haiti,
Somalia, Kosovo) and the failure to intervene (Rwanda). In some cases,
most dramatically in Rwanda where a genocide occurred before the eyes
of the world in 1994, the failure to undertake humanitarian intervention
prompted, for some, remorse and a desire to act more quickly. Remorse
was heightened when General Romeo Delaire of Canada, who commanded the UN force in Kigali prior to the 1994 genocide in Rwanda,
said that a force of 5,000 trained soldiers could have prevented much
of the killing. On the other hand, some fear that easing the legal and
political path to humanitarian interventions will lead to more interventions undertaken for self-interested or strategic reasons. The legitimacy
and conduct of humanitarian intervention – the threat or use of military
force to protect or promote human rights – is thus likely to remain one of
the central problems of world politics. At issue is the future of millions
of people who, if not rescued by the international community, or some
benevolent power, may be left to suffer or die at the hands of brutal dic-
tators or genocidal aggressors. Or perhaps the subjects of humanitarian

---

[1] Robert Holmes, *On War and Morality* (Princeton: Princeton University Press, 1989),
p. 288.

intervention will be "rescued" but still suffer under the inept, if benevolent and paternalistic, guiding hand of their saviors who set up short or medium-term governments to save "failed states." Humanitarian interventions may slide down the slippery slope to humanitarian occupations and state building.[2] It is thus crucial to ask how the recourse to humanitarian intervention will be decided and how such interventions will be conducted.

Although the change from analysis to prescription and from colonialism and decolonization to issues of humanitarian intervention may seem abrupt, I take up these questions for several reasons. First, debates about humanitarian intervention are in many ways a continuation of arguments about colonialism and decolonization. When scholars, policymakers, and citizens propose intervening to save failed states or to halt humanitarian disasters, they may do so because they fear the instability that can result from such crises. But interveners also often articulate a moral or religious obligation to act to protect others.[3] The impulses and arguments in favor of humanitarian intervention are thus not dissimilar to colonial arguments: advocates of humanitarian intervention pose justifications that recall the civilizing mission of colonialism, while the subjects of these interventions also often articulate uneasiness with their conduct, likening them to recolonization. As President Robert Mugabe of Zimbabwe said at the Millennium Summit: "If the new millennium, like the last, remains an age of hegemonic empires and conquerors doing the same old things in new technological ways, remains the age of the master race, the master economy and the master state, then I am afraid we in developing countries will have to stand up as a matter of principle and say, 'Not again.' "[4]

Second, decolonization and humanitarian interventions are historically linked through the mandate and trusteeship systems and specifically through United Nations activism in the transition from South West Africa to Namibia. Namibia is perhaps the prototype case of the international community taking an activist role in preventing human rights abuse, sending troops to protect human rights, and using its capacity to build states.

---

[2] Ernst B. Haas, "Beware the Slippery Slope: Notes toward the Definition of Justifiable Intervention," in Laura Reed and Carl Kaysen, eds., *Emerging Norms of Justified Intervention* (Cambridge: American Academy of Arts and Sciences, 1983), pp. 63–87.

[3] See Cecelia Lynch, "Acting on Belief: Christian Perspectives on Suffering and Violence," *Ethics & International Affairs* 14 (2000), 83–97.

[4] Quoted in Barbara Crossette, "U.N. Meeting Ends With Declaration of Common Values," *The New York Times*, 9 September 2000, A1.

The UN's role in South West Africa evolved over the course of four decades from witnessing, documenting, and publicizing South African abuse, to assisting Namibia's independence movement, to determining the structure and process of the transition from South African occupation and rule toward independence. In 1967 the UN essentially set up a shadow government of Namibia when the UNGA passed a resolution creating the UN Council for South West Africa, and the UN began to give significant resources to SWAPO. In 1978, the UN Security Council passed Resolution 435 which set up a transition assistance group to assist with new elections when they should occur. In 1982, the UN drew up a Settlement Plan which contained the principles for a Constituent Assembly in Namibia and for a Constitution. The UN also developed an informal checklist for the impartial governance of Namibia during what would be a period of transition from the illegal government of South Africa to the legal government of Namibia. In 1989 the UN Transition Assistance Group (UNTAG) was finally created and put in place to supervise elections and a transition to democracy for Namibia. Concrete planning for decolonization and state-building thus occurred over the course of about seven years. The plans included a code of conduct for the elections, agreed to by all parties, and plans for the demobilization, disarmament, and reintegration of about 30,000 former combatants, restructuring of the police force, and democratization. UN assistance for elections for decolonization was not new; what was new was the complexity of the mission – the UN Special Representative and UNTAG were engaged in the detailed logistics of the demilitarization of South West Africa at the same time that it set up a shadow government, provided humanitarian assistance, and supervised elections. Before the UN forces arrived in 1989 there was a terrible clash between South African forces and SWAPO. Demilitarization and a more or less peaceful democratic transition were guaranteed by the UNTAG military presence which numbered about 8,000 in total, from 110 countries, functioning as civilian police monitors, election supervisors, and military personnel in UNTAG in 1989. UNTAG was considered a success and a model: SWAPO wanted help, the world provided it, and elections were declared free and fair with the new government taking over peacefully in 1990.

Third, the possibility and practice of humanitarian interventions raises the question of how to reconcile clashing normative beliefs. Specifically, the development of Western theories of sovereignty, as well as the long history of colonialism and the struggle for decolonization, generated a deserved respect for the legal and political concepts of self-determination and non-intervention. On the other hand, the development of human rights norms – which helped to create the conditions for decolonization – elevates the status of the individual in world politics and challenges the inviolability of sovereignty as a legal protection for states which violate human rights. Some even argue that states vitiate their sovereignty when they violate the social contract by allowing or engaging in human rights abuses. Humanitarian intervention thus pits powerful normative beliefs and international legal conventions against each other: state sovereignty and the rule of law may be violated to protect or promote individual rights.

Fourth, the discussion in the preceding chapters about the uses of ethical argument, emotion, and strategic political action to abolish slavery, curb forced labor, and end colonialism illustrates how nascent beliefs may become dominant and how an informal international polity may coalesce to govern specific issue areas and change dominant practices. Arguments and beliefs make the world as much or more than economic factors or a drive for power. I showed that normative beliefs shaped colonial practice and ethical arguments were used to uphold colonialism. I also showed how colonial reformers and anti-colonial activists deployed ethical (as well as practical and scientific) arguments to undermine the practices and ultimately the legitimacy of colonialism; new normative beliefs were institutionalized in international organizations and colonies, further undermining colonial practice. When the majority of states, expressing and acting on the political will of those who sought to end slavery and colonialism, changed their practices and developed new laws, they both purposely and inadvertently reformed world politics. It is possible to do so again with regard to the related problem of humanitarian intervention.

This chapter develops a framework for a poiesis and praxis of ethical argument using discourse ethics and thus marks a sea change in the tone and substantive focus of the book from analysis to suggestions for practical action. Poiesis is the Greek word for the process of making something, and praxis is the utilization of theoretical knowledge in a practical activity. I propose a discourse ethical approach to the problem of humanitarian intervention. Specifically, I suggest that interested actors consciously conduct an ethical argument on the questions of when the resort to humanitarian intervention is just, and how such interventions shall be conducted, using techniques based on discourse ethics. The aim is to develop a convention on humanitarian intervention.

But before proceeding to a discussion of how humanitarian intervention may be usefully addressed through discourse ethics, I establish a role for both ethics and ethical argument in world politics. I then turn to the question of why ethical arguments, which might clash with self-interests narrowly defined, are sometimes appealing. I then review discourse ethics, suggesting how it might be used to address the problem of humanitarian intervention.

Potential for ethical praxis

There are at least three conflicting arguments widely heard about the potential of international ethics.[5] Realists argue that there are no ethics in international life – morality is a fig-leaf for interests. "Human rights have purely instrumental value in the political culture; they provide a useful tool for propaganda, nothing more."[6] The ethics of international life is the ethics of the dominant powers; the strong do as they will, the weak as they must, and "morality is the product of power."[7] The preceding chapters on the role of normative beliefs and ethical arguments were intended to persuade you that such a view is, at the least, questionable.

A second view, held by liberals, asserts that morality is already woven into the fabric of international politics. A more ethical world order is possible, if only we practice our politics in line with universally valid norms. There are such things as universal human rights which ought to be protected and extended.[8] Indeed, the 1948 Universal Declaration of Human Rights unselfconsciously rests on naturalist foundations: "All human beings are born free and equal in dignity and rights . . . Everyone has the right to life, liberty, and security of person."[9] As Ken Booth argues, "just because many Western ideas were spread by commerce and the Gatling

[5] This section is a substantially revised version of Neta C. Crawford, "Postmodern Ethical Conditions and a Critical Response," *Ethics & International Affairs* 12 (1998), 121–140.
[6] Noam Chomsky, "'Humanitarian Intervention,'" *Boston Review* 18 (December–January 1993–1994), 3–6: 5.
[7] Edward Hallett Carr, *The Twenty Years' Crisis, 1919–1939: An Introduction to the Study of International Relations* (New York: Harper & Row: 1964), p. 81.
[8] See for example, Charles R. Beitz, *Political Theory and International Relations* (Princeton: Princeton University Press, 1979); John Vincent, *Human Rights and International Relations* (Cambridge: Cambridge University Press, 1986); John Rawls, *The Law of Peoples* (Cambridge, MA: Harvard University Press, 1999).
[9] Universal Declaration of Human Rights, Articles 1 and 3.

gun, it does not follow that every idea originating in the West, or backed by Western opinion, should therefore simply be labeled 'imperialist' and rejected. There are some ethnocentric ideas – and individual human rights is one of them – for which we should not apologize."[10] The problem, from this perspective, is getting others to recognize rights and to put justice above the narrowly defined interests of states.

Poststructural and critical theorists argue that whether or not we think that there are ethics in international life, or that there ought to be, there are no firm grounds for any particular ethical belief; ethics is contextual. Critical theorists question the foundations of belief – even the possibility of providing ahistorical, timeless, and decontextualized foundations – and disagree with both liberals and realists, arguing that although people and states do act on the basis of moral convictions and normative beliefs, there is nothing objective or timeless about those beliefs.[11] Jürgen Habermas argues that Enlightenment faith in reason has been profoundly shaken by its own logic.

> After a century that, more than any other, has taught us the horror of existing unreason, the last remains of an essentialist trust in reason have been destroyed. Yet modernity, now aware of its contingencies, depends all the more on a procedural reason, that is a reason that puts itself on trial. The critique of reason is its own work: this double meaning...is due to the radically anti-Platonist insight that there is neither a higher nor a deeper reality to which we could appeal...[12]

As Habermas notes, "Under the ethnomethodologist's microscope even the most ordinary features of everyday life become something strange."[13] Since there are no universally valid foundations for normative beliefs, it is not clear why one culture's answers to problems

---

[10] Ken Booth, "Human Wrongs and International Relations," *International Affairs* 71 (January 1995), 103–126: 113.
[11] While there are *significant* differences among them, feminist, postmodern, poststructural, and critical theoretical perspectives share a critical attitude toward positivism, naturalism, and universalism, asserting that our understandings of the social and natural world are social constructions. Following from Nietzsche, Horkeimer, and Foucault, these theorists are "post" and "critical" in the sense of questioning the promise of the Enlightenment. For introductions, see Drucilla Cornell, *The Philosophy of the Limit* (New York: Routledge, 1992); David Couzens Hoy and Thomas McCarthy, *Critical Theory* (Oxford: Blackwell, 1994); Jim George, *Discourses of Global Politics: A Critical (Re)Introduction to International Relations* (Boulder: Lynn Reinner, 1994).
[12] Jürgen Habermas, *Between Facts and Norms: Contributions to a Discourse Theory of Law and Democracy* (Cambridge, MA: MIT Press, 1996), p. xli.
[13] Jürgen Habermas, "Reconstruction and Interpretation in the Social Sciences," in *Moral Consciousness and Communicative Action* (Cambridge, MA: MIT Press, 1990), pp. 21–42: 42.

of international ethics should be privileged. Post-structuralists suggest that we come to hold particular beliefs both through the operations of power (a view not dissimilar from E.H. Carr's analysis) or through the process of building a social consensus. In other words, we argue about our beliefs, provide evidence, and occasionally change our minds.

None of these views is dominant, and thus, the status of ethics in contemporary world politics is ambiguous and paradoxical. As realists charge, world politics is frequently characterized by the nasty and the brutish to the point where some suggest that the phrase "international ethics" is an oxymoron. Conversely, as liberals suppose, international law has become characterized by substantive propositions about how we ought to act. Specifically, the principles of respect for self-determination, non-intervention, and the rule of law were codified in international law starting in the late 1800s.[14] The content of international law has thus enabled its process, fostering the conditions for non-coercive relations among states and respect for individual humans. As Steven Lukes argues, "The principle that human rights must be defended has become one of the commonplaces of our age" even as human rights are "violated virtually everywhere."[15] We notice and are disturbed by those violations.

But, as critical theorists suggest, many scholars and activists are increasingly uncertain about how to ground liberal propositions. The shoring up of the legal-normative foundations for the sovereign state system occurred just as states came under increasingly obvious assault in the practical realm of day-to-day inter-state interactions (via, for example, the globalization of financial flows, powerful multinational corporations, the internationalization of information, the media, and cultural expression, and transnational social movements) and as state sovereignty was thoroughly denaturalized by critical and constructivist approaches to international relations theory.[16] The end of colonialism put Western cultural arrogance on notice. "We are troubled not solely

[14] Dorothy V. Jones, "The Declaratory Tradition in Modern International Law," in Terry Nardin and David R. Mapel, eds., *Traditions of International Ethics* (Cambridge: Cambridge University Press, 1992); Dorothy V. Jones, *Code of Peace: Ethics and Security in the World of Warlord States* (Chicago: University of Chicago Press, 1989).
[15] Steven Lukes, "Five Fables About Human Rights," in Stephen Shute and Susan Hurley, eds., *On Human Rights: The Oxford Amnesty Lectures 1993* (New York: Basic Books, 1993), pp. 19–40: 20.
[16] Jens Bartelson, *A Genealogy of Sovereignty* (Cambridge: Cambridge University Press, 1995); Cynthia Weber, *Simulating Sovereignty: Intervention, the State and Symbolic Exchange* (Cambridge: Cambridge University Press, 1995); Thomas J. Biersteker and Cynthia Weber, eds., *State Sovereignty as Social Construct* (Cambridge: Cambridge University Press, 1996).

by injustice, but also by theoretical scruples about the universality of any given view of justice and human rights as a basis for intervention. The relationship between the theory and practice of human rights is problematic."[17] Foundations are under assault even as human rights foundationalism serves to undermine the sovereignty of states in principle and in practice. This is similar to what Antonio Cassese has noted about the effects of believing in self-determination: "The ascendancy of international norms governing human rights has forced the traditionally rigid, pure-statist regime to recognise individuals as legal subjects . . . "[18]

Advocates thus find it necessary to defend the notion of universal human rights – so self-evidently proclaimed after World War II – against relativism and critical theory.[19] Perhaps in the past it was possible to unselfconsciously argue the primacy of sovereign states and that might makes right, possible to assert that our creator endowed us with certain rights, but, due to the self-consciousness of the postmodern perspective, we no longer uncritically accept such assertions. Yet even critical theorists take an ethical stance when they deny the legitimacy of "systems of exclusion."[20]

The appeal of human rights and ethical arguments

Realist, liberal, and critical perspectives sit uneasily side by side in world politics. Some scholars attempt to reconcile this cacophony through an appeal to intuition. For instance, as Richard Rorty notes, "human rights foundationalism is *outmoded*."[21] Why then is the human rights realm so resilient against critique? Rorty, building on the work of Eduardo Rabossi, argues that we are now a "human rights culture" and suggests that we can accept this cultural fact without trying to ground it in something natural. Rorty says "the most philosophy can hope to do is to summarize our culturally influenced intuitions about the right thing to do in various situations . . . We see the formulation of such

---

[17] Stephen Shute and Susan Hurley, "Introduction," in Shute and Hurley, eds., *On Human Rights*, pp. 2–18: 3.
[18] Antonio Cassese, *Self-determination of Peoples: A Legal Reappraisal* (Cambridge: Cambridge University Press, 1995), p. 165.
[19] Michael J. Perry, "Are Human Rights Universal? The Relativist Challenge and Related Matters," *Human Rights Quarterly* 19 (August 1997), 461–509; Thomas M. Frank, "Are Human Rights Universal?" *Foreign Affairs* 80 (January–February 2001), 191–204.
[20] Andrew Linklater, *The Transformation of Political Community: Ethical Foundations of the Post-Westphalian Era* (Cambridge: Polity Press, 1998), p. 10.
[21] Richard Rorty, "Human Rights, Rationality, and Sentimentality," in Shute and Hurley, eds., *On Human Rights*, pp. 111–134: 116.

summarizing generalizations as increasing the predictability, and thus the power and efficiency, of our institutions, thereby heightening the sense of shared moral identity which brings us together in a moral community."[22] Habermas also appeals to intuition as a ground for normative belief – "moral philosophy concerns itself with clarifying the everyday intuitions into which we are socialized."[23] Situating human rights and morality in historical context and arguing that human rights discourse is generalization that summarizes our intuitions – is both a relief and profoundly unsatisfactory. It is a relief to stop searching for foundations and recognize that they are historically based.

But to replace foundations, e.g., Judeo-Christian commandments and the Kantian categorical imperative to treat others as ends and not means, and the recourse to universal reason with "intuition" does not solve the problem of what to do. What if our "intuitions" are quite harmful to some individuals or classes of people? What if "intuitions" conflict? Moreover, using the word "intuition" glosses over the complexity of ethical reasoning, its situatedness in the experiences of individuals and cultures (whether that culture is of epistemic communities, formal organizations, bounded political communities such as nations and states, civilizations, or global), and the relationship of ethical reasoning to ethical argument. For example, liberal "intuitions" about humanitarian intervention can be traced. Specifically, decolonization laid the groundwork for current arguments about humanitarian intervention by extending the idea of respect for sovereignty from the Western core to the global level, while it also limits sovereignty by elevating the status of human rights. The discourse about humanitarian intervention takes the shape it does, and is deeply problematic, because it occurs in the context of a decolonization regime that stresses sovereignty and self-determination.

It is useful then to adopt only part of the argument about intuition. We can recognize that the contemporary era is characterized by belief in human rights. And we can, in order to act, stop searching for firm grounds for human rights other than that most of us believe in them. But we should probably not look to intuition as a pseudo-ground for

---

[22] Ibid., p. 117.
[23] Jürgen Habermas, "Discourse Ethics: Notes on a Program of Philosophical Justification," *Moral Consciousness and Communicative Action*, 43–115: 48. "Moral intuitions ... instruct us on how best to behave in situations where it is in our power to counteract the extreme vulnerability of others by being thoughtful and considerate." Jürgen Habermas, "Morality and Ethical Life: Does Hegel's Critique of Kant Apply to Discourse Ethics," *Moral Consciousness and Communicative Action*, pp. 195–215: 199.

human rights, or any other normative beliefs, even as we recognize that this is exactly what we are, in part, doing. It is still worthwhile to try to articulate good reasons for human rights and other normative beliefs. This means recognizing that functional utility arguments (e.g., "community works better when there are egalitarian ethical standards," and "there is less social unrest if we treat all well") and reciprocity ("do unto others as you would have them do unto you") are two good reasons for human rights, and for ethical action more generally, but that they are not the only grounds.

The preceding analysis of colonial arguments and the explanation of the role of argument in decolonization illustrate that the grounds of particular normative beliefs are historically contingent, specific to cultures, and that we hold certain normative beliefs because we learned they are good, or we later came to be persuaded of their goodness. If we struggled to articulate the grounds of our intuitions, we might well be able to say what it is we have learned and why we think those things are convincing. In the future, if we are open to persuasion, we may well believe that something else is good. Intuition is thus another word for socialization, empathy, and conviction.

While one can stress the process of ethical argument, we must still account for the persuasive appeal of particular ethical arguments and normative beliefs. Why would individuals find normative beliefs about equality and human rights appealing – so much so that they are sometimes willing to forgo the advantages of exploitation and even sometimes bear the costs of working for change? What makes ethical arguments persuasive? There are at least three possible reasons why human rights beliefs are appealing (beyond the view that we are obliged to believe in human rights) which are not mutually exclusive: coherence, self-interest, and practical-emotional.

The coherence view suggests that egalitarian normative beliefs are attractive because they are part of a larger belief system that individuals and groups hold. To hold human rights beliefs is to be consistent with the web of other philosophical/religious, identity, normative, and practical beliefs that individuals have become convinced are good. There is nothing particularly unique about human rights beliefs in this view; they are merely consistent with other beliefs and rules.

A self-interest explanation suggests that human rights beliefs are appealing because individuals conceive of themselves, regardless of their actual position, as potential objects of discrimination and unequal treatment. Thus, humans support equal rights, even if they would benefit from inequality, because they recognize that "but for the grace of god" (or luck), they too could be in an inferior position. The sense of contingency is initiated and bolstered by egalitarian beliefs – there is no divine right or biological superiority – that counterbalance the greed, arrogance, and solipsism that are left once inferiority of the other can no longer be used to justify and legitimize inequality. Principles of justice and fairness that all could live with follow.[24]

The practical-emotional view says that individuals find normative beliefs about equality and human rights appealing because humans live in community and, in fact, usually crave positive contact with others.[25] Our sociability is both practical and emotional: alone we cannot fend for ourselves emotionally or physically, nor can we continue our species and achieve many of our goals. The most efficient and emotionally satisfying way to run community may be consensually, or at least democratically; efficient because non-democratic forms require coercion (or brain-washing), and socially satisfying because humans, for the most part, appear to prefer social harmony over prolonged acrimony. Repression might be desirable for self-interest reasons (it may bring the oppressor wealth and power) but it is undesirable for emotional reasons, which explains why oppressors go to such great lengths to deny, even to themselves, that they are oppressors. Thus, democratic norms may be appealing over the long run because they satisfy community/social interests in harmonious relations. Humans may prefer to feel they are taking others into account just as they wish others to take their views into account. It may simply feel better.[26] Carried to a conclusion one might argue that humans are inherently other regarding.

As I argued above, much of what led to the end of slavery and the delegitimization of colonialism was ethical argument. Another element was the empathy elicited by the victims and critics of these practices. The subjects of slavery, colonialism, and apartheid participated in their own humanization in the eyes of the oppressor and those who actively and passively supported oppressors. Slave narratives, novels, plays, media accounts of atrocities, all brought the reality and the humanity of the oppressed "other" into sharper emotional focus. One could not hear

[24] See John Rawls, *A Theory of Justice* (Cambridge, MA: Harvard University Press, 1971); Beitz, *Political Theory and International Relations*.

[25] This is not a communitarian argument, though communitarians might find it compatible with elements of their views.

[26] On other aspects of emotion in world politics, see Neta C. Crawford, "The Passion of World Politics: Propositions on Emotion and Emotional Relationships," *International Security* 24 (Spring 2000), 116–156.

and be persuaded by ethical arguments that took the other into account as deserving of good treatment and agency if the image of the other was extremely negative. I am inclined to this third view but think all three – coherentist, self-interest, and practical-emotional – may account for the ever-widening appeal of human rights and democratic norms.

Decisions about how to act in international politics are permeated through and through with normative assumptions, assertions, and ethical arguments, but the place of ethics in international politics is ambivalent and paradoxical, while the appeal of ethical arguments is not clear. Charismatic and religious authority are no longer invested with the same legitimacy they once were, brute force no longer makes right, yet we cannot always agree on the substance of normative beliefs in order to act. "Under modern conditions of life none of the various rival traditions can claim prima facie general validity any longer. Even in answering questions of direct practical relevance, convincing reasons can no longer appeal to the authority of unquestioned traditions."[27] It is hard to know which grounds, if any, are correct, and then how to make decisions. If there are no firm *a priori* logical grounds for international ethics, or we cannot agree on the substance of ethics in world politics, how can actors legitimately decide what to do when faced with ethical dilemmas?

Discourse ethics: deciding how to decide

The way to proceed in a pluralist world where ethical beliefs clash, even beliefs about the existence and foundation of ethics, is to agree on legitimate procedures for decisionmaking. "The turn to discourse, which includes but is not limited to communicative ethics, is in part a move from a substantive to a procedural conception of moral and political theory. Rather than providing values grounded in an account of human nature or reason, discourse based approaches offer a set of procedures that, if followed, would yield principles legitimating social practices and institutions."[28] Procedure does not guarantee a consensual outcome, but it does make violent conflict over the outcome less likely.

---

[27] Jürgen Habermas, "Morality, Society and Ethics: An Interview with Torben Hviid Nielsen," in Jürgen Habermas, *Justification and Application: Remarks on Discourse Ethics* (Cambridge, MA: MIT Press, 1993), pp. 147–176: 151.
[28] J. Donald Moon, "Practical Discourse and Communicative Ethics," in Stephen K. White, ed., *The Cambridge Companion to Habermas* (Cambridge: Cambridge University Press, 1995), pp. 143–164: 143.

Perhaps the most fully articulated views of discourse ethics are found in the scholarship of Habermas, building on the work of Karl-Otto Apel, and in the arguments of Iris Marion Young, writing from a feminist perspective.[29] I use Habermas' understanding of discourse ethics as a starting point, criticize it, and modify it for use as a praxis of world politics.

The starting point for discourse ethics is the belief that for decisions and normative beliefs to be followed, they must be justified – they must be seen to be normatively good, they must be done for good reason, and all those affected by a decision must consent on some level. For Habermas, only "those norms deserve to be valid that could meet with the approval of those potentially affected insofar as the latter participate in rational discourses."[30] The approval develops through a process of dialogue.

> Only when [a] decision emerges from argumentation, only when it comes about in accordance with pragmatic rules of discourse, do we consider the resulting norm justified. One has to make sure everyone concerned has had a chance to freely give his consent. Argumentation is designed to prevent some from simply suggesting or prescribing to others what is good for them . . . [T]he rules of discourse themselves have a normative quality, for they neutralize imbalances of power and provide for equal opportunities to realize one's interests.[31]

Normative validity and legitimate decisions are arrived at through communicative action where participants seek consensus.

Habermasian discourse ethics occurs in an "ideal speech" situation where interlocutors hope to come to an uncoerced understanding: only the force of the better argument convinces. Communicative action presumes that actors attribute the same meaning to particular expressions, that what they say is comprehensible/understandable to the hearer, that their propositions are true, and that their propositions are right in the

[29] Karl-Otto Apel, "Is the Ethics of the Ideal Communication Community a Utopia? On the Relationship Between Ethics, Utopia, and the Critique of Utopia," in Seyla Benhabib and Fred Dallmayr, *The Communicative Ethics Controversy* (Cambridge, MA: MIT, 1995), pp. 23–59; Habermas, "Discourse Ethics"; Iris Marion Young, *Justice and the Politics of Difference* (Princeton: Princeton University Press, 1990). Also see Christian Reus-Smit, "The Constitutional Structure of International Society and the Nature of Fundamental Institutions," *International Organization* 51 (Autumn 1997), 555–589.
[30] Habermas, *Between Facts and Norms*, p. 127. Habermas argues that law works either through coercion and fear of sanction, or because people want to obey when they believe the law is right.
[31] Habermas, "Discourse Ethics," p. 71.

sense of being based on norms (normative beliefs) that can be redeemed, that is, shown to be valid. Further, one assumes that participants are sincere, and that they are ready to take on the obligations that result from reaching consensus.[32] Discourse ethics also entails the "universal exchange of roles" in which participants come to understand each other through a dialogue where interlocutors *listen* to each other.[33]

But, before all this can occur, certain preconditions should obtain. First, the argument must be minimally logical (coherent). Second, assuming some relief from pressure to act, the procedure must allow actors to test validity claims and question any assertion, while interlocutors must give reasons for disputing a proposition. Third, the structure of the situation must "rule out all external or internal coercion other than the force of the better argument and thereby neutralize all motives other than the cooperative search for truth."[34] Every *competent* subject must be allowed to participate, to bring any assertion into the discourse, and to express their attitudes, desires, and needs.[35]

Habermasian discourse ethics also entails five basic categories of rights within legal communities. First, each person is "owed a right to the greatest possible measure of *equal* liberties that are mutually compatible." Second, rights are guaranteed to those who are members of a particular community, with the community determining membership. Third, individuals are guaranteed equal treatment; those who feel their rights have been infringed upon must be able to make a claim against the community. Fourth, citizens must have basic rights to participate in processes of opinion and will formation. Fifth, these civil rights "imply" that there are "basic rights to the provision of living conditions that are socially, technologically, and ecologically safeguarded, insofar as the current circumstances make this necessary if citizens are to have equal opportunities to utilize [their] civil rights."[36]

Of course, Habermas recognizes that not all action is communicative. With strategic action, actors seek to "*influence* the behavior of another by means of the threat of sanctions or the prospect of gratification in order to *cause* the interaction to continue as the first actor desires."[37] Speech is not always ideal because "real human beings are driven by other motives in addition to the one permitted motive of the search for truth."[38] The problem of democratic politics becomes one of expanding

---

[32] Habermas, *Between Facts and Norms*, pp. 4–5, 19.
[33] Habermas, "Discourse Ethics," p. 65.   [34] Ibid., p. 89.   [35] Ibid., p. 89.
[36] Habermas, *Between Facts and Norms*, pp. 122–125.
[37] Habermas, "Discourse Ethics," p. 58.   [38] Ibid., p. 92.

the scope of communicative action and prescribing limits for strategic action.

Critique of pure discourse ethics

It is common to dismiss discourse ethics as utopian. Recognizing that world politics is already characterized by argument, on the other hand, creates room to consider the possibilities of discourse ethics. Taking discourse ethics seriously, however, entails recognizing that the process has both practical and discursive limits, some of which may be overcome.

First, logistics must be taken into account. "Discourses take place in particular social contexts and are subject to the limitations of time and space . . . Topics and contributions have to be organized. The opening, adjournment, and resumption of discussions must be arranged."[39] Someone, or all participants, must set agendas, organize discussion, and end arguments; and we know that the process of agenda setting itself has substantive consequences. Thus, Habermas notes:

> Because of all of these factors, institutional measures are needed to sufficiently neutralize empirical limitations and avoidable internal and external interference so that the idealized conditions always already predisposed by participants in argumentation can at least be adequately approximated . . . [A]ttempts at institutionalization are subject in turn to normative conceptions and their goal, which spring *spontaneously* from our intuitive grasp of what argumentation is. This assertion can be verified empirically by studying the authorizations, exemptions, and procedural rules that have been used to institutionalize theoretical discourse in science or practical discourse in parliamentary activity.[40]

Second, discourse ethics may be inefficient and slow, and better suited to developing normative consensus over a long period of time, rather than for making quick decisions in contexts that require immediate action. But political issues often seem quite urgent and many actors are involved. How can we slow the effects of war, poverty, or social unrest while we deliberate? Part of the solution may lie in organizing discourse so that large numbers of actors work in caucuses and several caucuses work at once. To speed future deliberation, scholars of international ethics might also make it their job to revisit the past and constantly reevaluate how humans acted in particular ethical dilemmas. Lessons

[39] Ibid., p. 92.   [40] Ibid., p. 92.

of the past cannot be applied like a cookie cutter, but the habits of con-textually based reasoning will aid deliberation. Pre-discourse, or what scholars of mediation call pre-negotiation, is vital in instances where actors who don't share the same understanding of events and the good, must develop a shared vocabulary.

Urgency is less an issue for ethical world politics than one might think because almost all have already agreed that certain situations deserve immediate action: specifically, genocide and wars of aggression. What remains in those cases is to agree that the events being observed are actu-ally genocide or aggression, and certainly this process of interpretation can be painfully slow as those who do not want to act, or simply dis-agree, contest the interpretation. In categories of urgent cases, majority rule may have to suffice as a guide to action.

Third, Habermas presupposes that all actors confer the same meaning on linguistic expressions. "The world . . . is constituted only for an inter-pretation community whose members engage, before the background of an intersubjectively shared lifeworld, in processes of reaching under-standing with one another about things in the world."[41] Habermas also suggests that "The condition for the truth of statements is the potential agreement of everyone else."[42] This assumption, problematic even in contexts where the background consensus is wide and deep, is even more difficult to sustain in the context of discourses among commu-nities that hold different belief systems. Discourse ethics among those who do not share a lifeworld thus requires pre-discourse, where the meaning of terms and the background for beliefs is agreed upon, and so actors agree on truth (or at least the terms of the debate and the scope of disagreement).

Fourth, Habermas emphasizes that practical discourse and commu-nicative action rest on our shared background assumptions – the life-world – and on the authority of "archaic" institutions that we take for granted. "The lifeworld forms both the horizon for speech situa-tions and the source of interpretations, while it in turn reproduces itself only through ongoing communicative interactions."[43] If Habermas is right about the dependence of practical arguments on a background consensus, when interlocutors' lifeworlds are narrow, we can expect

[41] Habermas, *Between Facts and Norms*, p. 14.
[42] Jürgen Habermas, *Vorstudien und Ergazugen zur Theorie des Kommunkativen Handelns* (Frankfurt: Surkamp, 1984), p. 107 quoted in William Outwaite, *Habermas: A Critical Introduction* (Stanford: Stanford University Press, 1994), p. 41.
[43] Habermas, *Between Facts and Norms*, p. 22.

414

little creativity from actors searching for solutions. Are lifeworlds rich enough for us to critique dominant practices and find creative solutions to them? If one believes in essential identities, our points of view will be narrow and our interests narrowly conceived. But as feminist theories of identity and difference suggest, "all subjects" are "mutually and multiply constituted."[44] Further, it is possible for humans to empathize and take other roles to understand different points of view.

This is quite unlike Beitz' arguments, based on Rawls, that international justice based on principles that all actors would derive in an original position (under a veil of ignorance) would require interlocutors to step outside identities.[45] Participants in an argument, even if they did not know their social position, could not climb out of their cultural lifeworld context without abandoning their linguistic communicative competence. Habermasian "practical discourses depend on content brought to them from outside. It would be utterly pointless to engage in practical discourse without a horizon provided by the lifeworld of a specific social group and without real conflicts in a concrete situation in which the actors consider it incumbent upon them to reach a consensual means of regulating some controversial social matter."[46]

Fifth, while Habermas wants all those potentially affected by a norm to have a chance to speak, his formulation of discourse ethics nevertheless restricts participation in deliberation. On the one hand, Habermas says that humans have a basic right to living conditions that make it possible for them to use their civil rights. This is a significant condition that has radical implications for democratic participation. But, Habermas does not take into account other restrictions on who can speak. Specifically, discourse takes place within communities, and those communities determine group membership. People who are displaced, or for some reason defined as outside a community, at least in Habermas' formulation, have no right to participate. International politics must find ways to accommodate the speech of the millions who are internally and internationally displaced.

Further, Habermas argues, "[e]very subject with the *competence* to speak and act is allowed to take part in a discourse."[47] Competence

---

[44] Jane Flax, "Displacing Woman: Toward an Ethics of Multiplicity," in Bat-Ami Bar On and Ann Ferguson, eds., *Daring to Be Good: Essays in Feminist Ethico-Politics* (New York: Routledge, 1998), pp. 143–155: 145.
[45] Rawls, *A Theory of Justice*; Beitz, *Political Theory and International Relations*; Rawls, *The Law of Peoples with "The Idea of Public Reason Revisited."*
[46] Habermas, "Discourse Ethics," p. 103.   [47] Ibid., p. 89, emphasis added.

includes *communicative* competence that is – beyond agreement about the language itself – the ability to produce grammatically correct sentences. Competence also includes the ability to reason in the ways that are *recognized* as reason. So, Young argues, "Habermas retains vestiges of a dichotomy between reason and affectivity. He rather firmly separates discourse about feelings from discourse about norms."[48] Those who are radically different in their beliefs, understanding of causality, and even in their view about the utility of language versus other forms of expression to persuade, may not be able to effectively argue with others. The different will not necessarily be denied access to arguments; rather, they will not be understood, and they may even be dismissed out of hand.[49] "A dominating or hegemonic discourse provides a 'regime of truth,' a means of assessing not only whether statements are true or false but also whether they have any meaning at all or are mere nonsense."[50] Moreover, others will not always be able to speak with persuasive force. Specifically, the very young and those understood to be mentally ill are not generally considered competent, although experience tells us that they can often participate in discourse. Further, on the occasions when individuals are in too much physical or emotional pain to think or speak, they cannot effectively participate.

Thus, it would perhaps be better to think of communicative capability or capacity rather than competence, turning competence criteria from a restriction into an exhortation to enhance the capacities of both speakers *and* hearers. The capacity of interlocutors to listen and understand each other, vital in situations where interlocutors are equally powerful, is even more important when a weaker party needs a more powerful party's assistance (e.g. intervention and foreign aid). Along these lines, Richard Rorty argues that our desire to promote human rights changes because our feelings about the other change: "most of the work of changing moral intuitions is being done by manipulating our feelings rather than increasing our knowledge."[51] Rorty suggests that "the emergence of the human rights culture seems to owe nothing to increased moral knowledge and everything to hearing sad and sentimental stories."[52]

---

[48] Young, *Justice and the Politics of Difference*, p. 118.
[49] Thomas Kuhn, *The Structure of Scientific Revolutions* (Chicago: University of Chicago Press, 1962); Michel Foucault, *The Archaeology of Knowledge and the Discourse on Language* (New York: Pantheon, 1972).
[50] James F. Keeley, "Toward a Foucauldian Analysis of International Regimes," *International Organization* 44, 1 (Winter 1990), pp. 83–105: 91.
[51] Rorty, "Human Rights," p. 118.   [52] Ibid., pp. 118–119.

Dialogue encourages the telling of these stories in their complexity, and helps ensure that assistance is welcome.

Sixth, discourse ethics must take political power into account.[53] Power is ubiquitous in politics, whether we define it as the ability to use physical force to coerce others, the ability to command instant authority, the power of shared beliefs, or the capacity to set agendas. Indeed, as I have emphasized, recognizing power is crucial to understanding the process of political argument as it really occurs. Political argument does not occur on a level playing field, and when change occurs due to political argument, it is because the balance of belief, and the authority associated with it, has shifted.

A discourse ethical approach has to avoid the pitfall of taking discourse out of its political context. In other words, discourse ethics that stresses dialogue between two others can be depoliticizing if "hearing sad and sentimental stories" yields a person-to-person or case-by-case response to problems when what is required are institutional changes designed to level the playing field. However, in discourse ethical situations, power differences are less important if all actors' assertions are open to tests of their validity. As soon as I am able to question the basis of your arguments, the power differential has been at least partially bridged. Discourse ethics practiced as part of "ethic of care," as discussed below, may prevent the process from losing sight of larger political, economic, and social contexts, and mistaking personal responsibility for institutional responsibility. In addition, as long as some are unable to be heard – because of lack of access to media and relevant institutional fora where opinions are shaped and policies set, then the conditions for discourse ethical politics have not been met.

Seventh, discourse ethics seems, at least on the surface, to be too rational. Indeed, the process depends on actors being able to listen to each other and to dispassionately withstand probing and testing of their validity claims. How can those who have little or no trust in others ever hope to engage in discourse ethical dialogue? Indeed, if empathy and other emotions play a crucial role in determining our ability to understand others, and our willingness to help them, then those of us who wish to increase the scope for argument must work to increase empathy. Rorty suggests this is done through sentimental education that "sufficiently acquaints people of different kinds with one another so

[53] Habermas, *Between Facts and Norms*, pp. 132–168.

they are less tempted to think of those different from themselves as only quasi-human."[54] Rorty also regards the provision of basic needs as crucial. "Security and sympathy go together . . . The tougher things are, the more you have to be afraid of, the more dangerous your situation, the less you can afford the time or effort to think about what things might be like for people with whom you do not immediately identify. Sentimental education only works on people who can relax enough to listen."[55] Though there is little reason to infer this from Rorty's own words, his argument should not be used to say that the poor are unfit to engage in dialogue or that they cannot feel empathy for others. Rather, Habermas' and Rorty's arguments should be read as an obligation to increase the capacity of all to engage in dialogue. Aspects of globaliza-tion that increase contact among cultures, that allow us to comprehend the beliefs, poetry, and agency of others, increase the background of empathetic understanding.[56] However, if discourse ethics is to work in situations where actors have a history of violent conflict and ethnocen-tric disregard for the other, much more emotional work must be done to increase the capacity of interlocutors to listen to each other. The prob-lems of competence/capacity, power, and standards of rationality and reason, require institutional guarantees of access for all speakers.

Finally, Habermas (at some points) seems to suppose that the goal of discourse ethics is the agreement of *all* on the *best* solution. There is also the possibility that in searching for single best solutions, interlocu-tors will become mired and pass up sub-optimal solutions that could avoid stalemate. As Beitz argues, "actual agreement of everyone con-cerned is too stringent a requirement to place on the justification of moral principles."[57] It is impossible to eliminate all difference of opin-ion and understanding, though this is not necessarily bad. Habermas argues that because there will be areas where all affected cannot agree, we will tend to agree to norms that are least constricting, and that tol-erant diversity will result. "The more abstract the agreements become, the more diverse the disagreements with which we can non-violently live."[58] This outcome would ideally encourage respect for difference but it is not clear where boundaries begin and end.

---

[54] Rorty, "Human Rights," pp. 122–123.   [55] Ibid., p. 128.

[56] Of course other aspects of globalization do just the opposite, as difference, and even some cultures, are overwhelmed and sometimes obliterated by the march of mainly Western ideas, commodities, and practices.

[57] Beitz, *Political Theory and International Relations*, p. 19.

[58] Jürgen Habermas, *Postmetaphysical Thinking* (Cambridge, MA: MIT Press, 1992), p. 140.

Because the standard, almost rote, critique of discourse ethics is that it is too utopian for domestic contexts, much less for world politics, most of these issues are not discussed by scholars of world politics, or even by political theorists. Yet, as suggested above, many criticisms of discourse ethics can be answered. Can discourse ethics be applied to world politics?

Discourse ethics and world politics

The analysis of colonialism and decolonization shows that though ethical argument is ubiquitous and consequential, world politics does not follow discourse ethics. But some have suggested that it can and should. Jürgen Haacke argues that "discourse theory targets precisely those questions [with] which students of international politics are perennially confronted: how do we and how can we address interpersonal, intergroup, intersocietal, or interstate conflicts that inevitably arise given the plethora of competing views, values, identities, interests, and needs espoused by humanity."[59] Similarly, Thomas Risse argues that true reasoning, or the logic of arguing in a Habermasian sense, is already evident in world politics.[60] Andrew Linklater proposes to use discourse ethics and an ethics of care to create social relations that are more universalistic, sensitive to cultural difference, and less unequal.[61]

Despite these assertions, it appears on the surface that discourse ethics is particularly ill-suited for international politics. Characteristics that might allow for discourse ethics in domestic politics do not appear to be in place in world politics. Authority in domestic politics is found in both legitimate procedures and in established institutions that derive their authority through either their acceptance as part of the lifeworld or through their connection to other taken-for-granted institutions. Habermas assumes that there is a background consensus for domestic politics – the lifeworld and archaic institutions undergirding communicative action and discourse ethics – but international politics is surely characterized by different lifeworlds and few archaic institutions. International ethics in the current era occurs in a context of anarchy – nominal sovereign equality among states and the absence of an enforcer – and

[59] Jürgen Haacke, "Theory and Praxis in International Relations: Habermas, Self-Reflection, Rational Argumentation," *Millennium* 25 (Summer 1996), 255–289: 261.
[60] Thomas Risse, "'Let's Argue!' Communicative Action in World Politics," *International Organization* 54 (Winter 2000), 1–39.
[61] Linklater, *The Transformation of Political Community*.

real inequality and hierarchy. Moreover, force is omnipresent in international politics. "Like all argumentation, practical discourses resemble islands threatened with inundation in a sea of practice where the pattern of consensual conflict resolution is by no means the dominant one. The means of reaching agreement are repeatedly thrust aside by the instruments of force."[62] And, finally, some see the possibilities for peaceful coexistence and discourse slipping further away in the post-Cold War world where the "great divisions among humankind and the dominating source of conflict will be cultural."[63] How could discourse ethics work in the context of anarchy; "clashing" civilizations that regard each other's lifeworlds as irrational; a dearth of accepted, legitimate, and effective institutions; unequal power and ability among states to participate in speech and to act; and the constant possibility of recourse to force?

Yet world politics is closer to the conditions for discourse ethics than it appears at first glance. As Beitz argues, "the international realm is coming more and more to resemble domestic society in many of the features usually thought relevant to the justification of (domestic) political principles."[64] World politics already depends as much on the process and content of arguments as on coercion and relations of military power. But there are differences between argument as a mode of persuasion, either of the other or of third parties, and the much less common form of discourse ethical argument as a search for understanding, consensus, or as a form of social or public reasoning. How could actors in world politics begin to apply discourse ethical processes?

The content of international law has increasingly provided for the possibility and even occasionally the reality of non-coercive relations among states. Respect for individual human rights has grown. So has respect for sovereign states. In fact, sovereign equality as a normative belief, and the decreasing legitimacy of the use of force, already enables states and some non-state actors to engage in argument and potentially in discourse ethics. The primary condition of ideal speech, freedom from coercion, is thus partially present in the dominant ideology of world politics. And, in the twentieth century, individuals and states established

[62] Habermas, "Discourse Ethics," p. 106.
[63] Samuel Huntington, "The Clash of Civilizations?" *Foreign Affairs* 72 (Summer 1993), pp. 22–49: 22.
[64] Beitz, *Political Theory and International Relations*, p. 8.

international institutions that serve as venues for argument for states and peoples.[65] These venues, such as the UN General Assembly, though they certainly embody global inequalities of wealth and military power, are at least formally equal and organized to facilitate speech among the representatives of all states. Ironically, sovereignty may also cover the violation of rights if governments characterized by widespread and systemic human rights abuses at home sit on international commissions and at the United Nations, and make use of the democratic procedures of those bodies. Because sovereignty is valued and non-democratic states are allowed to participate in international deliberations, democracy at the international level may not be mirrored at the domestic level.

International institutions thus only potentially provide a framework for the procedural guarantees necessary to overcome the obstacles discussed above in implementing discourse ethics. Therefore, it is vitally important for the process of discourse ethics that states not be the only interlocutors. Non-governmental organizations, social movement organizations, and cultural exchanges are already also venues for discourse. Further, epistemic communities create and maintain regimes of truth and, to a certain degree, follow discourse ethics.

Discourse ethics is possible in world politics among representatives of states and civil society. There are, even under anarchy, incentives to be honest and fair. To be taken seriously in their future interactions – have their statements and commitments be seen as credible – interlocutors have an incentive to be sincere, truthful, and willing to follow through (*pacta sunt servanda*) with the actions required by the consensus achieved through their discourse.

Moreover, the diversity of perspectives in world politics is a strength, rather than an obstacle, in the process of deliberation. Though humans share elements of a common history, they do not share an understanding of that history; nor do all humans agree on a set of values and goals for the present and future. A dearth of perspectives (lifeworlds) is not an immediate concern at this historical moment. Because, in most matters, states and people acting in world politics cannot rely on the illusion of preexisting consensus, the need for *procedural* versus substantive (rule based) morality among states and people is more blatantly obvious in

---

[65] Of course argument among the representatives of states occurred prior to the twentieth century.

world politics than in domestic politics. It is precisely because we cannot rest on preexisting agreement that democracy in the form of discourse ethics is vital. And because we cannot assume that we know what others mean by their statements in world politics, and that their values and interests are the same, we must be particularly attentive to their speech and also be willing to make our arguments transparent.

Meanwhile, other international institutions such as global news media, globally available culture, and more frequent and genuine interactions among people, help to produce the empathy that facilitates role taking and also the background of shared experiences and assumptions on which discourse can rest, at least for a moment. (This is not unproblematic: the BBC's and CNN's views still come primarily from the West.) Because sovereign equality is presumed (though not actual) and the overt hegemonic imposition of norms is illegitimate, there is more room for the operations of discourse ethics than ever before in world politics.

Finally, consensus does not always have to be achieved, nor should it necessarily be the goal. As the history of world politics and international law indicates, there are ways for states to act together without consensus, and without using sanctions. There are also ways to allow variations in behavior. This is done by striving to develop principles rather than immediately moving to develop law and institutionalizing procedures. As Cassese argues, international principles serve an important function. "When States cannot agree on definite and specific standards of behaviour because of their principled, opposing attitudes, but need, however, some sort of basic guideline for their conduct, their actions and discussions eventually lead to the formulation of principles."[66] International legal principles, such as self-determination, according to Cassese, have both a "high degree of generality and abstraction" and they reflect the dominant culture. Cassese argues:

> In this respect principles are a typical expression of the present world community, whereas in the old community – relatively homogenous and less conflictual – specific and precise rules prevailed. Principles, being general, loose and multifaceted, lend themselves to various and even contradictory applications, and in addition are susceptible to being manipulated and used for conflicting purposes. On the other hand,

[66] "Principles do not differ from treaty or customary rules simply in that they are more general and less precise . . . Rather, principles differ from legal rules in that they are the expression and result of conflicting views of States on matters of crucial importance." Cassese, *Self-determination of Peoples*, p. 128.

principles have great normative potential and dynamic force: among other things, one can deduce from them specific rules, to the extent that these rules are not at variance with State practice.[67]

Hard cases

Two questions must be addressed: who can participate in discourse ethics and how should actors proceed if they cannot come to agreement? Discourse ethics requires democratic practices among interlocutors and implies that collectivities, in order to be legitimate in discourse ethical practice, are themselves democratic. What if potential participants are not democratic in their internal structure and process? Non-democracies can and do participate in institutions which at least formally ascribe to discourse ethical principles. But ought they be allowed to do so? Are interventions into the internal life of states in instances where the right to life is not at issue ever justifiable?

Ethical issues, which arise in specific historical contexts and have unique features, cannot be (and are not usually) decided in the abstract. We cannot know for certain how to act in a situation without considering its particulars, and we are always confronted by new situations. However, it seems foolish and impractical to throw everything into the category of "to be decided" and renegotiated. One suspects that some things ought to be taken for granted – such as the protection of the right to participate in decisions – if all actors want to guarantee their ability to speak regardless of their particular individual status and if we would like to respond to urgent problems within a time period that allows for decisions to have some possibility of being relevant. Thus, there are guides to action on even the hard cases.

In the first hard case, what if actors cannot come to agreement? What if, after an attempt at discourse, actors cannot agree even on general principles? What if one side refuses to engage in dialogue and uses force to get their way? In some cases, it may be fine to decide not to act. But inaction may have dire consequences for those who cannot control others but are still affected by their actions. In these situations, we may have to act somehow if inaction would threaten our well-being or our existence. What can be done? The first answer is simply to try harder. Agreement may not seem possible unless interlocutors reason backward to what they can agree on and then forward to the particulars of the

---

[67] Ibid., pp. 128–129.

problem. Only then may it be possible for them to agree on something. In some cases they may have to go even further, to the realm of possible futures where imagination is another realm of experience. The hard cases then demand a form of dialogue, and, in particular, a form of listening that is not possible until participants in arguments have learned to listen empathetically.[68] The presumption must be against the use of force.

Taking democracy seriously also means that we must learn to accept, at least for the moment, outcomes we don't like if the practice does not affect us directly. This does not mean that everything is allowed and ought to be praised. "Culture can be torture and 'authenticity' the means of maintaining oppressive power structures."[69] Ethical argument is at work when novelists, human rights organizations, and politicians publicize female circumcision, call it genital mutilation, and elicit our help in stopping the practice. We must also accept that others will find it impossible to accept outcomes they don't like and will continue to argue with their opponents. It is not ethical to sanction those one disagrees with, as a first resort. If interlocutors cannot come to a normative consensus, it may be more fruitful to shift to other kinds of argument, such as practical or scientific arguments. In the case of female circumcision/genital mutilation, a scientific argument against the practice would stress potential and likely medical consequences of such a procedure, while practical arguments would emphasize the opportunity costs of using public health moneys to treat people for the complications of an elective surgical procedure.

If actors do not behave according to discourse ethical principles, then it may be just to engage in strategic action and sanctions. Taking discourse ethics seriously – that is, only those norms deserve to be valid that meet or could meet with the approval of all affected in their capacity as participants in a practical discourse – thus has implications for the legitimacy of interlocutors. Non-democratic states are not legitimate interlocutors. That is, if the laws of a state are not derived democratically because participants are systematically denied the opportunity to participate in discourse, these states are not fit for communicative action with other communities.

Does this mean that non-democratic states should be left out of international deliberations? In theory, yes. In practice, non-democratic states

---

[68] See Flax, "Displacing Woman"; David Campbell, *Politics Without Principle: Sovereignty, Ethics, and the Narrative of the Gulf War* (Boulder: Lynn Rienner, 1993).
[69] Booth, "Human Wrongs," p. 115.

should be the subject of strategic action – sanctions, bargaining, threats, and incentives – rather than communicative action. As Beitz argues, "unjust institutions do not enjoy the same prima facie protection against external interference as do just institutions, and in fact, other things equal, interference with unjust institutions might be justified when it has a high probability of promoting domestic social justice."[70] Yet this does not mean total isolation or embargo is always appropriate. Non-democracies may be allowed to participate in institutions that follow discourse ethical procedures with certain conditions attached to their participation. Democratic states that seek to sanction other states ought to be able to justify and convince their own populations, and those of other democratic states, that sanctions are appropriate. Further, in line with the obligation to provide living conditions for people to practice their civil rights, sanctions must include humanitarian exemptions and direct aid to those persons who are most vulnerable. Discourse should simultaneously proceed with those parts of the community that are democratic and therefore legitimate.

Humanitarian intervention and discourse ethics

International law, including the UN Charter, building on the tradition of respect for sovereignty articulated in the Treaty of Westphalia, prohibits the use of force by states, except in self-defense. Humanitarian intervention seems to be prohibited as well.[71] Yet interventions that are at least nominally motivated for humanitarian purposes are conducted and may well seem imperative in some situations. Is it ever appropriate to intervene with military force to promote or protect human rights values? Is it legitimate for international society to impose normative beliefs *inside* a community, for instance to promote human rights or forms of economic life?

In the context of a decolonization regime, the only instances that seem to warrant interventions into the domestic affairs of others are those where a state or group within the state is depriving its citizens of the right to life, and their ability to speak. The UN and other bodies have provided assistance or even conducted plebiscites, referenda, and elections so that people could form independent states and begin the process of self-determination. On the other hand, while there is great sympathy

---

[70] Beitz, *Political Theory and International Relations*, p. 121.
[71] Simon Chesterman, *Just War or Just Peace? Humanitarian Intervention and International Law* (Oxford: Oxford University Press, 2001).

for the idea of preventing or halting grave human rights abuses, especially genocide, there is similarly skepticism about the possibility of disinterested humanitarian interventions. As Hans Morgenthau said, "it is futile to search for an abstract principle which would allow us to distinguish in a concrete case between legitimate and illegitimate intervention."[72] He argues that, "All nations will continue to be guided in their decisions to intervene and their choice of means of intervention by what they regard as their respective national interests."[73]

If communities, like individuals, have rights to the greatest possible extent as long as their actions do not harm others, then intervention is warranted only when one community's actions infringe upon the rights of other communities to determine their lives. It follows that states that use force against other states and people ought to be stopped: aggression justifies intervention. Should it matter if the aggression occurs within state boundaries? International law is ambivalent on this point, as is international practice. The genocide in Rwanda in 1994 occurred without humanitarian intervention to halt it, and intervention to halt Serbian aggression in Bosnia (a region of Yugoslavia) was very slow in coming. Humanitarian intervention in Somalia by the US and UN in 1993 occurred but then went sour, with the interveners becoming combatants. And intervention by West African troops in Sierra Leone in January 1999 to halt a civil war was characterized by terrible brutality on the part of the intervening forces.

"Humanitarian" intervention thus poses a complex set of problems. What is the difference between humanitarian assistance and intervention. When is *humanitarian* intervention warranted? How can humanitarian interventions be implemented so that they at least do no harm and hopefully do some good? What are the limits of humanitarian intervention? In addressing these questions actors face difficult conceptual tasks as well as tensions and contradictions between intentions and consequences. And this is not to mention the political dilemmas of securing the will to intervene and mounting adequate force.

The main theories of world politics leave us ill-prepared to address issues of humanitarian intervention. Realists, stressing self-interested actors seeking power, argue that truly humanitarian interventions are impossible: so-called humanitarian interventions must be a cover or justification for state interests. States should only intervene when vital

---

[72] Hans Morgenthau, "To Intervene or Not to Intervene," *Foreign Affairs* 45 (April 1967), 425–436: 430.
[73] Ibid., p. 430.

interests are at stake, in which case the resort to "humanitarian inter-vention" is likely to be rare. Liberals who believe that humans have other attributes besides self-interest – namely empathy, benevolence, and a respect for human rights – grant the possibility of humanitar-ian interventions, but have difficulty theorizing the who, what, where, when, why, and how of humanitarian interventions. Liberals want to do good, and they try, but they are troubled by the difficulty of doing so, in part because the historical context of colonialism and decoloniza-tion makes any intervention suspect. Constructivists, emphasizing the historical and social construction of institutions and practices, can tell us that the practice and problems of humanitarian intervention are not new, but the meaning of humanitarian intervention is not necessarily constant. Constructivists and poststructuralists can help us contextu-alize the present understanding of humanitarian intervention, and can show us how we got to where we are in terms of law and institutions. But constructivists have little to say about what to do.

If theories of world politics are unsatisfactory, can theories of moral-ity and ethics help us decide the questions of when to act and how to conduct humanitarian intervention? Utilitarian ethical approaches offer one possibility: we could simply decide that humanitarian interventions ought to be undertaken when the benefits of action outweigh the costs and risks of inaction. But how do we know the benefits of action, and what if costs and risks are very high? How are we to value the inde-pendence of a people, their right to live without fear of massacre, and against the cost of lives sent to preserve their rights? And what of the opportunity costs of action? Which things should we forgo at home so that others can live? How shall we measure the costs of inaction? Would we feel right letting others suffer if the material costs of action outweigh the benefits?

If utilitarianism is deficient, perhaps a deontological approach that starts with universal normative beliefs could offer guidance. However, there is insufficient agreement within and among states about interna-tional ethics beyond the bare minimum principles of non-intervention except in cases of genocide and aggression. Yet even in the case that would most clearly seem to warrant humanitarian intervention – genocide – the duty of a particular response is not entirely clear. The 1948 Genocide Convention, which defines the crime of genocide, states that perpetrators of genocide "shall be punished" after the fact. But the Convention does not articulate a clear method to prevent or halt genocide. Rather, Article 8 of the Genocide Convention says:

427

"Any Contracting Party may call upon the competent organs of the United Nations to take *such action under the Charter of the United Nations as they consider appropriate* for the prevention and suppression of acts of genocide . . . "[74] Further, it appears that there were very few, if any, instances of humanitarian intervention to prevent genocide either before or after the Genocide Convention came into force. It is difficult to recall a single clear international effort to prevent or halt genocide in the last century where some other motive for intervention was not also at work. If genocide is an undisputed instance justifying humanitarian interventions, why are interventions to halt it so rare?

Nor is there a consensus, beyond the problem of genocide, within the activist community about the other sorts of crises that are the legitimate triggers for humanitarian intervention. Does inept government, civil war, or famine warrant humanitarian intervention? International law would seem to prohibit such interventions. Further, even if they were allowed, what if the intervened upon don't want such help? Moreover, some principles conflict.

More troubling, there are fundamental ontological and ethical problems that destabilize the discussion of humanitarian intervention. As attractive as they are, deontological approaches beg the question of why we should find particular rules persuasive enough to be bound by them, and not some other rule. What is the good? How shall we seek to do good? How do we decide in cases where we disagree? Who is the relevant "we" who decides and acts? What is any one person's obligation to another?[75]

Humanitarian intervention is thus a real conundrum for theorists. Moreover, the practice of humanitarian intervention – and it will not stop even as diplomats and scholars try to sort out the problems – is extremely complex, involving many different actors with sometimes conflicting views of the aims and best methods for conducting humanitarian interventions. The subjects of humanitarian intervention are rarely asked what they would like, and sometimes when they are able to be heard, because in fact they have been speaking all along, we do not listen. Finally, humanitarian interventions sometimes make situations worse, while interventions that fail to take into account the wishes of

---

[74] Convention on the Prevention and Punishment of the Crime of Genocide. Approved and proposed for signature and ratification or accession by General Assembly resolution 260 A (III) of 9 December 1948, entry into force 12 January 1951, Article 8.
[75] Stanley Hoffman, *Duties Beyond Borders* (Syracuse, NY: Syracuse University Press, 1981).

the intervened upon, which do not even allow that they have agency, are of questionable legitimacy and likely also to face serious practical problems.

This last feature of the practice of humanitarian intervention, the failure to treat the intervened upon as if they were active agents, links colonialism and present-day humanitarianism. Often the impetus for humanitarian interventions was and is increased empathy for the other. When we think of the other as more like us, it is not acceptable that we should let them be subject to the ills we could prevent, such as genocide, starvation, and bad government. But, from the perspective of the intervened upon, there is also a strong element of arrogant paternalism (not dissimilar to the paternalism that supported colonialism) in the drive to promote liberal markets, human rights, and democracy through foreign aid, trade policy, economic sanctions, and military interventions.

Feminist scholars have developed ideas about an ethic of care that might help us sort out exactly when and how to intervene to help others in a way that is welcome and not idiosyncratic.[76] Joan Tronto, taking an anti-naturalist, anti-essentialist perspective, argues that care is both a practice and a disposition aimed at "maintaining, continuing, or repairing the world."[77] She says, "What is definitive about care . . . seems to be a perspective of taking the other's needs as the starting point for what must be done."[78] Tronto emphasizes that "perceptions of needs can be wrong. Even if the perception of the need is correct, how the care-givers choose to meet the need can cause new problems."[79] An ethic of care, she argues, requires us to be attentive, responsible, competent, and responsive in care giving. Addressing the criticism that this is a private morality which leaves in place political and structural obstacles to care, Tronto argues that conceiving of morality and politics from the perspective of an ethic of care has revolutionary implications for social relations in that we will see how care, primarily done by the weak, is currently organized to suit the powerful. If the challenge is to heighten regard for others over self-interest narrowly defined, and to broaden the conception of community to include others who seem quite different, then an ethic of care is well suited to solving moral problems.

[76] Nel Noddings, *Caring: A Feminine Approach to Ethics and Moral Education* (Berkeley: University of California Press, 1984); Sarah Ruddick, *Maternal Thinking: Towards a Politics of Peace* (Boston: Beacon Press, 1989).
[77] Joan C. Tronto, *Moral Boundaries: A Political Argument for an Ethic of Care* (New York: Routledge, 1993), p. 104.
[78] Ibid., p. 105.   [79] Ibid., pp. 107–108.

An ethic of care could be useful then in promoting an attitude that arrests the potential paternalism in the discourse and practice of humanitarian intervention. Specifically, those who would be intervened upon by great powers must be part of any discourse about potential humanitarian intervention. As Michael Shapiro argues, an "ethics of encounter" must necessarily recognize that we cannot know the other and must not attempt to fix their identities with our narratives. We must be open to their understanding of themselves.[80]

As important as this dialogue might be, as Fiona Robinson suggests, the ethics of care demands that we ask not only should we intervene in this or that crisis. Rather, "moral attention needs to be paid to developing an understanding of the moral relations which exist, and the moral decisions that are constantly being taken, both before and after the question of humanitarian intervention actually arises; this in turn demands a critical analysis of the social relations which exist within societies, and between societies in the global context."[81] In other words, humanitarian crises do not generally arise, full blown and out of nowhere. Rather, the everyday foreign policies of states and the individual actions of citizens may promote conditions that lead to the violation of human rights or help prevent them. States which violate human rights, like all states in the international system, have allies or at least regular economic interactions with other states. Human rights violators need guns, fuel, training in the techniques of torture, and so on. They also need or would like, external recognition of their legitimacy as a government. This is exactly what the great powers often provided to governments such as Indonesia, Chad, South Africa, the Sudan, and Cambodia during the Cold War. As one African observer of the Senegalese human rights case against the former dictator of Chad, Hissene Habré, remarked: "Hissene Habré was received and honored in Paris as a head of state and ally. France never regarded him as a dictator. This case is much more complex than the role of Habré. There is the role of France that supported him. There is the role of the United States that supported him. If we are to judge Hissene Habré, we have to also judge those who supported him."[82] Following that logic backwards along the causal chain, if we are to prevent

[80] See Michael J. Shapiro, "The Ethics of Encounter: Unreading, Unmapping the Imperium," in David Campbell and Michael J. Shapiro, eds., *Moral Boundaries: Rethinking Ethics and World Politics* (Minneapolis: University of Minnesota, 1999), pp. 57–91.
[81] Fiona Robinson, *Globalizing Care: Ethics, Feminist Theory, and International Relations* (Boulder: Westview Press, 1999), p. 146.
[82] Babacar Sine, quoted in Norimitsu Onishi, "African Dictator Faces Trial Where He Once Took Refuge," *The New York Times*, 1 March 2000, pp. A1 and A3: A3.

abuses, we must prevent the active and passive support of those abuses. Holding an attitude of care entails holding a long view of how our actions and inactions affect the life possibilities of others. Citizens may put pressure on their governments to withdraw support from those countries which engage in torture, expulsions, and murders. This is a step short of comprehensive and formal international sanctions that may obviate the need for later humanitarian interventions.

A convention on humanitarian intervention

It is precisely because we cannot agree on substance – even in the case of genocide, where the Genocide Convention of 1948 prohibits genocide and says states ought to act to prevent it, but provides no clear guidance on how to halt or prevent genocidal acts – that I propose a procedural method for moving forward which borrows from and modifies discourse ethics. Bearing in mind the problems and promise of discourse ethics and an ethics of care, I propose that interested actors from all over the globe begin a discourse ethical dialogue with the object of developing a convention on humanitarian intervention. There have been attempts at developing guidelines for humanitarian intervention before and others have proposed working to develop a consensus.[83] My call differs from those efforts in stressing a discourse ethical procedure.

The procedural aim must be to conduct a discourse with all potential actors who will then develop an approach to deciding questions of humanitarian intervention. The substantive aim would be to establish general procedures for avoiding humanitarian crises and, when necessary, conducting humanitarian interventions. As it is now, there are some general and specific guidelines on the conduct of humanitarian interventions developed by UN agencies, non-governmental organizations, and some governments, but there is no global framework, in part because the legality of humanitarian intervention is questionable.

Without getting deeply into the substance – which must be decided through a global discourse – any convention probably has to answer at least the following questions. What are the causes of humanitarian crises? How can humanitarian crises be prevented? What is a "humanitarian" intervention versus a political intervention? What kinds of humanitarian crises demand an international response? What are the limits of

---

[83] See Richard Caplan, "Humanitarian Intervention: Which Way Forward?" *Ethics & International Affairs* 14 (2000), 23–38: 31–34.

humanitarian intervention, for example, can state building properly be considered humanitarian intervention? Who can legitimately call for humanitarian interventions? Who shall be consulted when the need arises to intervene? Who, specifically which organizations, are authorized to undertake humanitarian interventions? What shall be the nature of legitimate humanitarian intervention practice; is deadly force acceptable and in what instances? When elements of humanitarian interventions go awry, how shall those responsible be identified and treated?

The authors of the convention will not be able to devise 'one size fits all' answers to these questions. They must devise a set of principles that is flexible enough to suit the kinds of instances the international community agrees ought to be the objects of humanitarian intervention. While each case will be unique, there are two generic scenarios that the authors of a convention should consider addressing: preventing genocide; halting ongoing genocide.

The irony of using discourse ethics to develop a protocol for the use of force to protect others' rights, is obvious. But this irony heightens the necessity of such an approach. Without a conversation open to all and where all presuppositions and arguments are open to challenge, humanitarian intervention may become a practice that resembles colonial interventions. In other words, humanitarian intervention violates discourse ethical principles and this is precisely why a discourse ethical practice must be used to decide when force can or must be used. Without a wider and sustained conversation, truly humanitarian interventions, already rare and deeply contradictory in theory and practice, may become more rare, while interventions under the rubric of "humanitarian intervention" may proliferate, despite the fact that such interventions are about something else, such as promoting a political or economic form of life preferred by the powerful. Thus it is crucial that a convention on humanitarian intervention should not be drawn up only by representatives of likely interveners. All peoples should participate in the discourse, including non-state actors. Indeed, those who are subjects of humanitarian intervention are already speaking. The issue is whether they are heard. Such an open dialogue will be emotional and political; the scars of colonialism have not healed, while the failures of recent humanitarian interventions have perhaps only deepened those wounds.

A convention would take years to accomplish, and no doubt more than one humanitarian crisis will arise before a convention is achieved. What could a long, probably simultaneously emotional and legalistic, discourse do to help in cases of urgent humanitarian crises?

A world-wide discourse on humanitarian intervention could have several important benefits, many of which would occur before a convention is articulated.

Dialogue could help actors see the consequences of their actions, in the long chain of events, which help create humanitarian crises (such as great powers sending arms to authoritarian regimes to promote the "interests" of the great power), and help actors avoid, prevent, or halt those actions. Avoiding the crises that lead to humanitarian interventions – by being attentive to the ways that external actors are setting the groundwork for crises or failing to act to discourage early abuse – would clearly be better than intervening after the fact.

The process of reaching agreement on the language of a covenant would help articulate and shape the international normative beliefs that must be clarified before crises can even be identified. Discourse leading to a convention on humanitarian intervention could help actors develop the context to understand complex crises and develop better causal models for dealing with them. The discourse might also help actors decide which features of crises frame it as humanitarian, and allow them to respond more quickly than the years it took to help Bosnian Muslims. Finally, the process of dialogue could contribute to creating the respect for difference necessary to making world politics more ethical. Greater legitimacy might be attached to interventions if the entire international community were part of the discourse that leads to a convention on humanitarian intervention. In sum, this approach melds principle with process, emotion with reason.

Devising a convention on humanitarian intervention is clearly an enormous challenge. To add to the complexity, a convention on humanitarian intervention must provide for its own revision. Still, we already have a head start on the content of such a convention. Discourse ethics and the critical perspective of an ethics of care/encounter imply a very narrow scope of just interventions. Murder justifies intervention and sanctions. Political repression only justifies sanctions against states – if those who are repressed call for them – not intervention.

Because comprehensive economic sanctions may have enormous consequences – both intended and unintended, we must also consider comprehensive international sanctions as a form of intervention. Inept government, or the urge to save failed states, does not justify comprehensive sanctions by states. Sanctions and intervention to change economic organization or political arrangements that we simply disagree with (such as no-growth economies or anarchist political organization)

thus ought not to be permitted. Sanctions that cost lives to promote political and economic systems are not acceptable; political and economic
forms of life that cost life justify sanctions and intervention. Persuasion
ought to be the rule. On the other hand, if individuals and groups do not
wish to participate or interact with regimes that they find abhorrent, no
laws should force that interaction. Conversely, those who would avoid
contact should allow others to interact. Each side may seek to persuade
the other to change their policy.

Realizing ethical world politics

In those instances when we must interact with others and we find ourselves in conflict over ends or means, if we do not at first see an obvious
way to act in matters that concern all of us, we can use discourse ethical
principles to find that way. Yet, in many ways, world politics is very far
from conditions of communicative action, discourse ethics, and an ethics
of care. My arguments about the importance of the table on which arguments rest and are understood, specifically the ways the background of
culture and preexisting belief constrain and enable the persuasiveness of
arguments, show why normative change is often slow, incremental, and
path-dependent. Yet the history of colonial reform and decolonization
suggests that ethical arguments are already an important part of the
process of world politics. Decolonization is a necessary precondition
for discourse ethics in world politics, but it is certainly not sufficient.
Movement toward ethical world political relations would be helped by
an ethical discourse on humanitarian intervention, the next frontier of
ethical world politics. And, despite many problems, there are signs that
world politics is moving in the direction of realizing discourse ethics
and an ethic of care. Anarchy – the absence of hierarchy – in the context of international organizations, transnational contact, local activism,
and traditions of international law that constrain the use of force, provides opportunities to deliberate. World government is *not* necessary
for discourse ethics to work. Anarchy and the clash of civilizations are
a virtue, not an obstacle to the development of ethical world politics.
Because no one can presume understanding, it is obvious that we must
work toward it.

But some conditions of world politics do have to change to allow
greater scope for discourse ethics and ethical world politics. Most importantly, taking discursive democracy seriously as the foundation of
ethics in world politics means that human needs rise to the top of the

agenda – they are not solely a matter of benevolence but crucial to legitimacy. A procedural commitment to ethics implies that the world community has obligations to promote the capacity of its members to participate in deliberation on issues that affect them. Both discourse ethics and the ethics of care underscore the importance, indeed our obligation, to better the material conditions of the least well-off, and to increase the sensitivity of the already well-off so that all are able to participate in the construction of their communities and able to empathize enough with the other to know when and how they are to act in a caring way. The ways that the actions of the well-off directly and indirectly hurt the poor and weak must be clarified and corrected. It is not enough to say that the poor or the different have the right to speak, we must remove the economic and institutional obstacles to their participation.

As we lower the material and institutional barriers to discourse ethical dialogue, we must also lower the barriers of arrogance, hostility, and fear. To be in an ethical relation with another is to be in an emotional and other-regarding relationship: the other deserves and has our tolerant respect and sympathy. We need to start in an ethical relation in order to have discourse ethics, and discourse ethics allows us to maintain and deepen the ethical relation.

Discourse ethics is certainly difficult and not easily achieved within households, much less within states or across boundaries of culture and political systems. Yet taking argument analysis, discourse ethics, and the skepticism of critical perspectives seriously expands the possibilities for ethical world politics. Little of the discourse ethical dialogue that I advocate will be easy and much of it will be extremely difficult, especially when it comes to questioning cherished assumptions, changing comfortable ways of being in the world, and making real changes in relations of power. Consistent with the postmodern literary theorists' analytical emphasis on discourse as a social construction that materially reproduces the world's norms, hierarchies, and values, argument analysis and discourse ethics emphasize how our arguments can, with difficulty and persistence, change the world.

Appendix. African decolonization

Current country name	Colonizer at independence	Date	Method of decolonization
Algeria	France	1962	Guerrilla war and negotiated independence.
Angola	Portugal	1975	Guerrilla war and negotiated Portuguese withdrawal followed by long civil war and South African intervention.
Benin	France	1960	Self-governing territory in 1958. Negotiated transition→ granted independence.
Botswana	Britain	1966	Negotiated transition→ granted independence.
Burkina Faso	France	1960	Self-governing territory in 1958. Negotiated transition→ granted independence.
Burundi	Belgium Trust	1962	UN supervised referendum in 1961 decided against monarchy; separated from Rwanda in 1962.
Cameroon	France and Britain Trust	1960 1961	Former French Trust Territory Cameroun united in 1961 with British Trust Territory after UN supervised plebiscite in 1961.
Canary Islands	Spain		Became an "autonomous community" of Spain with two legislatures under 1978 constitution.
Cape Verde	Portugal	1975	Negotiated transition.

(cont.)

Continued

Current country name	Colonizer at independence	Date	Method of decolonization
Central African Republic	France	1960	Self-governing territory in 1958. Negotiated transition→ granted independence.
Chad	France	1960	Self-governing Territory in 1958. Negotiated transition→ granted independence.
Comoros	France	1975	Voted to remain French in 1958; Plebiscites in 1974; three main islands voted for independence and declared it unilaterally. In 1976, one island voted to remain French.
Congo	Belgium	1960	Negotiated transition→ granted independence.
Djibouti	France	1977	In a May 1977 referendum, inhabitants overwhelmingly voted to become independent, leading to independence in June.
Egypt	Britain	1922	Protectorate terminated in 1922 and Egypt was declared sovereign; Britain only gradually withdrew. Out in 1956.
Equatorial Guinea	Spain	1968	UN-supervised referendum on independence in 1968, followed by UN-supervised general elections.
Eritrea	Italy/ Britain/ Ethiopia	1993	Occupied by Italy 1885–1941; British occupation/Trusteeship, 1941–1952; Guerrilla war against Ethiopia and referendum in 1993.
Ethiopia	Italy	1941	Italian Occupation 1936–1941 opposed by the League of Nations.
Gabon	France	1960	1958 Referendum granted self-government.
Gambia	Britain	1965	Negotiated and granted independence.
Ghana	Britain	1957	Negotiated and granted independence. British Togoland voted for union with the Gold Coast in 1956 (UNGA Res. 944 (X))

(cont.)

Current country name	Colonizer at independence	Date	Method of decolonization
Guinea	France	1958	Negotiated transition→ granted independence.
Guinea-Bissau	Portugal	1974	Guerrilla Movement
Ivory Coast	France	1960	1958 Referendum granted self-government.
Kenya	Britain	1963	Negotiated transition→ granted independence.
Lesotho	Britain	1966	Negotiated transition→ granted independence.
Liberia	private	1847	Settled by US born African-Americans.[a]
Libya	Italy	1951	British and French admin. 1943–1951, then negotiated transition→ granted independence.
Madagascar	France	1960	Major rebellion in 1947; 1958 referendum granted self-government.
Malawi	Britain	1964	Negotiated transition→ granted independence.
Mali	France	1960	Negotiated transition→ granted independence.
Mauritania	France	1960	1958 Referendum granted self-government.
Morocco	France	1956	Guerrilla war and negotiated independence.
Mozambique	Portugal	1975	Guerrilla war and negotiated Portuguese withdrawal followed by long civil war.
Namibia	South Africa Mandate	1990	Guerrilla war and negotiated South African withdrawal. UN supervised elections in 1989.
Niger	France	1960	1958 Referendum granted self-government.
Nigeria	Britain	1960	British territory of Northern Cameroon decided to join Nigeria in 1961 UN supervised plebiscite.
Rwanda	Belgium Trust	1962	UN supervised referendum in 1961 decided against monarchy; separated from Burundi in 1962.
Sao Tomé and Principe	Portugal	1975	Granted independence.

(cont.)

Continued

Current country name	Colonizer at independence	Date	Method of decolonization
Senegal	France	1960	1958 Referendum granted self-government.
Sierra Leone	Britain	1961	Negotiated transition→ granted independence.
Somalia	Italy, Britain Trust	1960	Negotiated transition→ granted independence.
South Africa	Britain	1910	Granted white settlers self-government, followed by long struggle for majority rule which succeeded in 1994.
Sudan	Britain	1956	Negotiated transition→ granted independence.
Swaziland	Britain	1968	Negotiated transition→ granted independence.
Tanzania	Britain Trust	1961	Negotiated transition→ granted independence.
Togo	France Trust	1960	UN supervised elections in 1958 UNGA Res 1182 (XII).
Tunisia	France	1956	Guerrilla war and negotiated independence
Uganda	Britain	1962	Negotiated transition→ granted independence.
Walvis Bay	South Africa	1994	Negotiated transition to Namibia.
Western Sahara	Spain/ Morocco		Africa's last colony. Morocco and Mauritania invaded in December 1975; Mauritania withdrew in 1979; Polisario declared Saharan Arab Democratic Republic; ceasefire in 1991. UN referendum and settlement is stalled.
Zambia	Britain	1964	Negotiated transition→ granted independence.
Zimbabwe (Rhodesia)	Britain	1965	Unilateral Declaration of Independence by white settlers, followed by guerrilla war for majority rule which succeeded in 1980.

[a] The African-American settlers of Liberia, despite their own and their ancestors' histories of slavery, and notwithstanding the strong influence of the US Constitution on their own constitutional arrangements, did not establish a political system that treated natives and African-Americans equally. Thus, the ideas of self-determination and equality were not always applied even by those who had benefited from the abolition of slavery.

Select bibliography

Adas, Michael, *Machines as the Measure of Men: Science, Technology, and Ideologies of Western Dominance* (Ithaca: Cornell University Press, 1989).

Adler, Emanuel, "Seizing the Middle Ground: Constructivism in World Politics," *European Journal of International Relations* 3 (September 1997), 319–364.

Africa South of the Sahara 1991 (London: Europa Publications Limited, 1990).

Albertini, Rudolf von, *Decolonization: The Administration and Future of the Colonies, 1919–1960* (Garden City, NY: Doubleday & Company, 1971).

Aldrich, Robert and Connell, John, *The Last Colonies* (Cambridge: Cambridge University Press, 1998).

Alker, Hayward R., *Rediscoveries and Reformulations: Humanistic Methodologies for International Studies* (Cambridge: Cambridge University Press, 1996).

Alker, Hayward R., "The Dialectical Logic of Thucydides Melian Dialogue," *American Political Science Review* 82 (September 1988), 805–820.

Andrews William L., and Gates, Henry Louis (eds.), *Slave Narratives* (New York: Library of America, 2000).

Ansprenger, Hans, *The Dissolution of Colonial Empires* (New York: Routledge, 1981).

Anstey, Roger, *The Atlantic Slave Trade and British Abolition 1760–1810* (London: Macmillan, 1975).

Anti-Slavery Reporter and Aborigines' Friend (London: Published under the sanction of the Anti-Slavery & Aborigines Protection Society, 1909–1980).

Apel, Karl-Otto, "Is the Ethics of the Ideal Communication Community a Utopia? On the Relationship Between Ethics, Utopia, and the Critique of Utopia," in Seyla Benhabib and Fred Dallmayr (eds.), *The Communicative Ethics Controversy* (Cambridge: Massachusetts Institute of Technology: 1995), pp. 23–59.

Aristotle, *Politics*, translated H. Rackham (Cambridge, MA: Harvard University Press, 1990).

The Art of Rhetoric, translated with an introduction by H.C. Lawson-Tancred (New York: Penguin Books, 1991).

The Nichomachean Ethics, translated with an Introduction by David Ross (Oxford: Oxford University Press, 1980).

Audi, Robert, *Practical Reasoning* (New York: Routledge, 1989).

Axelrod, Robert, "An Evolutionary Approach to Norms," *American Political Science Review* 80 (December 1986), 1095–1111.

Bannister, Robert, *Social Darwinism: Science and Myth in Anglo-American Social Thought* (Philadelphia: Temple University Press, 1979).

Banton, Michael, *Racial Theories*, 2nd edn (Cambridge: Cambridge University Press, 1998).

Barkan, Elazar, *The Retreat of Scientific Racism: Changing Concepts of Race in Britain and the United States Between the World Wars* (Cambridge: Cambridge University Press, 1992).

Barry, Brian M., *Political Argument: A Reissue with a New Introduction* (London: Routledge, 1990).

Batchelor, Peter and Willett, Susan, *Disarmament and Defence Industrial Adjustment in South Africa* (Oxford: Oxford University Press, 1998).

Beer, George Louis, *African Questions at the Paris Peace Conference* (New York: Macmillan, 1923).

Beigbeder, Yves, *International Monitoring of Plebiscites, Referenda and National Elections: Self-determination and Transition to Democracy* (Boston: Martinus Nijhoff Publishers, 1994).

Beitz, Charles R., *Political Theory and International Relations* (Princeton: Princeton University Press, 1979).

Bell, David E., Raiffa, Howard, and Tversky, Amos (eds.), *Decision Making: Descriptive, Normative, and Prescriptive Interactions* (Cambridge: Cambridge University Press, 1988).

Bender, Gerald J., "Peacemaking in Southern Africa: The Luanda-Pretoria Tug-of-war," *Third World Quarterly* 11 (January 1989), 15–30.

Bender, Gerald, "The Eagle and the Bear in Angola," *The Annals of the American Academy of Political and Social Science*, 489 (January 1987), 123–132.

Bender, Thomas (ed.), *The Anti-Slavery Debate: Capitalism and Abolitionism as a Problem in Historical Interpretation* (Berkeley: University of California Press, 1992).

Berlin, Ira, *Many Thousands Gone: The First Two Centuries of Slavery in North America* (Cambridge, MA: Harvard University Press, 1998).

Betts, R.F., "Methods and Institutions of European Domination," in Boahen, ed., *Africa Under Colonial Domination*, 313–331.

Bley, Helmut, *Namibia Under German Rule* (Hamburg: LIT Verlag, 1996).

Boahen, A. Adu, *African Perspectives on Colonialism* (Baltimore: Johns Hopkins University Press, 1987).

Boahen, A. Adu (ed.), *Africa Under Colonial Domination, UNESCO General History of Africa*, VII (Paris: UNESCO, 1985).

Bolt, Christine, *The Anti-Slavery Movement and Reconstruction: A Study in Anglo-American Co-operation, 1833–77* (Oxford: Oxford University Press, 1969).

Select bibliography

Bonn, M.J., *The Crumbling of Empire: The Disintegration of the World Economy* (London: Allen and Unwin, 1938).

Booth, Ken, "Human Wrongs and International Relations," *International Affairs* 71 (January 1995), 103–126.

Bridgman, Jon M., *The Revolt of the Hereros* (Berkeley: University of California Press, 1981).

Brown, Susan, "Diplomacy by Other Means: SWAPO's Liberation War," in Leys and Saul *et al.*, *Namibia's Liberation Struggle*, 19–39.

Brzoska, M., "South Africa: Evading the Embargo," in Michael Brzoska and Thomas Ohlson (eds.), *Arms Production in the Third World* (London: Taylor & Francis, 1986), 193–214.

Bull, Hedley, "The Revolt Against the West," in Bull and Watson (eds.), *The Expansion of International Society*, 217–228.

Bull, Hedley and Watson, Adam (eds.), *The Expansion of International Society* (Oxford: Oxford University Press, 1984).

Campbell, David, *Politics Without Principle: Sovereignty, Ethics, and the Narrative of the Gulf War* (Boulder: Lynn Rienner, 1993).

Carr, Edward Hallett, *The Twenty Years' Crisis, 1919–1939: An Introduction to the Study of International Relations* (New York: Harper & Row, 1964).

Cassese, Antonio, *Self-determination of Peoples: A Legal Reappraisal* (Cambridge: Cambridge University Press, 1995).

Cawthra, Gavin, *Brutal Force: The Apartheid War Machine* (London: International Defence & Aid Fund for Southern Africa, 1986).

Chamberlain, M.E., *Decolonization: The Fall of the European Empires* (Oxford: Basil Blackwell, 1985).

The Longman Companion to European Decolonization in the Twentieth Century (London: Longman, 1998).

Chesterman, Simon, *Just War or Just Peace? Humanitarian Intervention and International Law* (Oxford: Oxford University Press, 2001).

Chilton, Paul, *Security Metaphors: Cold War Discourse from Containment to Common House* (New York: Peter Lang, 1996).

Chomsky, Noam, " 'Humanitarian Intervention,' " *Boston Review* 18 (December–January 1993–1994), 3–6.

Clayton, Anthony, *The Wars of French Decolonization* (London: Longman, 1994).

Cobbett, William, "Apartheid's Army and the Arms Embargo," in Cock and Nathan (eds.), *Society at War*, pp. 232–243.

Cock, Jacklyn and Nathan, Laurie (eds.), *Society at War: The Militarization of South Africa* (New York: St. Martin's Press, 1989).

Cohen, Joshua, "The Arc of the Moral Universe," *Philosophy & Public Affairs* 26 (Spring 1997), 91–134.

Coker, Christopher, *South Africa's Security Dilemmas* (New York: Preager, 1987).

"South Africa: A New Military Role in Southern Africa 1969–1982," in Robert Jaster (ed.), *Southern Africa: Regional Security Problems and Prospects* (New York: St. Martin's Press, 1985), 142–150.

442

Commission on International Justice and Goodwill, *The System of Forced Labor in Africa* (New York: Federal Council of the Churches of Christ in America, 1926).

Conklin, Alice, *A Mission to Civilize: The Republican Idea of Empire in France and West Africa, 1895–1930* (Stanford: Stanford University Press, 1997).

Coombes, Annie, *Reinventing Africa: Museums, Material Culture and Popular Imagination* (New Haven: Yale University Press, 1994).

Cooper, Frederick, *Decolonization and African Society: The Labor Question in French and British Africa* (Cambridge: Cambridge University Press, 1996).

Corwin, Arthur F., *Spain and the Abolition of Slavery in Cuba, 1817–1886* (Austin: University of Texas Press, 1967).

Craton, Michael, "Emancipation from Below? The Role of British West Indies Slaves in the Emancipation Movement, 1816–34," in Jack Hayward (ed.), *Out of Slavery: Abolition and After* (London: Frank Cass, 1985).

Craven, Paul and Hay, Douglas, "The Criminalization of 'Free' Labour: Master and Servant in Comparative Perspective," in Lovejoy and Rogers (eds.), *Unfree Labour*, 71–101.

Crawford, Neta C., "Decolonization as an International Norm: The Evolution of Practices, Arguments, and Beliefs," in Laura Reed and Carl Kaysen (eds.), *Emerging Norms of Justified Intervention* (Cambridge: American Academy of Arts and Sciences, 1983), 37–61.

The Domestic Sources and Consequences of Aggressive Foreign Policies: The Folly of South Africa's "Total Strategy," Working Paper, no. 41 (Centre for Southern African Studies, University of the Western Cape, South Africa, 1995).

"Postmodern Ethical Conditions and a Critical Response," *Ethics & International Affairs* 12 (1998), 121–140.

"How Arms Embargoes Work," in Crawford and Klotz (eds.), *How Sanctions Work*, pp. 45–74.

"Oil Sanctions Against Apartheid," in Crawford and Klotz (eds.), *How Sanctions Work*, 103–126.

"Trump Card or Theatre: An Introduction to Two Sanctions Debates," in Crawford and Klotz (eds.), *How Sanctions Work*, 3–24.

"The Passion of World Politics: Propositions on Emotion and Emotional Relationships," *International Security* 24 (Spring 2000), 116–156.

Crawford, Neta C., and Klotz, Audie (eds.), *How Sanctions Work: Lessons From South Africa* (New York: St. Martin's, 1999).

Crowe, S.E., *The Berlin West Africa Conference, 1884–1885* (London: Longmans, Green and Co., 1942).

Curtin, Philip D., *The Atlantic Slave Trade: A Census* (Madison, WI: University of Wisconsin Press, 1969).

Darwin, John, *Britain and Decolonization: The Retreat from Empire in the Post-War World* (New York: St. Martin's Press, 1988).

Davey, A.M., *The Bondelzwarts Affair: A Study of the Repercussions* (Pretoria: University of South Africa, 1961).

Davidson, Basil, *Let Freedom Come: Africa in Modern History* (Boston: Little, Brown and Company, 1978).

Davis, David Brion, *The Problem of Slavery in Western Culture* (Ithaca: Cornell University Press, 1966).

Slavery and Human Progress (Oxford: Oxford University Press, 1984).

Davis, Lance E. and Huttenback, Robert A., *Mammon and the Pursuit of Empire: The Economics of British Imperialism* (Cambridge: Cambridge University Press, 1988).

Der Derian, James, *On Diplomacy: A Genealogy of Estrangement* (New York: Basil Blackwell, 1987).

Dore, Isaak I., *The International Mandate System and Namibia* (Boulder: Westview Press, 1985).

Doty, Roxanne Lynn, *Imperial Encounters: The Politics of Representation in North-South Relations* (Minneapolis: University of Minnesota Press, 1996).

Doyle, Michael W., *Empires* (Ithaca: Cornell University Press, 1986).

Drechsler, Horst, *"Let Us Die Fighting": The Struggle of the Herero and Nama against German Imperialism (1884–1915)*, (London: Zed Press, 1980).

Drescher, Seymour, *Capitalism and Antislavery: British Mobilization in Comparative Perspective* (Oxford: Oxford University Press, 1987).

Du Bois, W.E. Burghardt, *The Suppression of the African Slave Trade to the United States of America, 1638–1870* (New York: Longmans, Green, and Co., 1896).

The World and Africa: An Inquiry into the Part Which Africa Has Played in World History (New York: International Publishers, 1965).

Duffy, Gavan, Federking, Brian K., and Tucker, Seth A., "Language Games: Dialogical Analysis of INF Negotiations," *International Studies Quarterly* 42 (June 1998), 271–294.

Dugard, John (ed.), *The South West Africa/ Namibia Dispute: Documents and Scholarly Writings on the Controversy Between South Africa and the United Nations* (Berkeley: University of California Press, 1973).

Echenberg, Myron, *Colonial Conscripts: The* Tirailleurs Sénégalais *in French West Africa 1857–1960* (London: James Currey, 1991).

Eden, Lynn, *Whole World on Fire: The Making of Organizational Knowledge about U.S. Nuclear Weapons Effects* (Ithaca: Cornell University Press, forthcoming).

Elbourne, Elizabeth, "Freedom at Issue: Vagrancy Legislation and the Meaning of Freedom in Britain and the Cape Colony, 1799–1842," in Lovejoy and Rogers (eds.), *Unfree Labour*, 114–150.

Eltis, David, *Economic Growth and the Ending of the Transatlantic Slave Trade* (Oxford: Oxford University Press, 1987).

Emmett, Tony, "Popular Resistance in Namibia, 1920–5," in Brian Wood (ed.), *Namibia, 1884–1984*, 224–258.

Esedebe, Olisanwuche, *Pan-Africanism: The Idea and Movement, 1776–1963* (Washington, DC: Howard University Press, 1982).

Evangelista, Matthew, *Unarmed Forces: The Transnational Movement to End the Cold War* (Ithaca: Cornell University Press, 1999).

Extracts from the Evidence Taken Before Committees of the Two Houses of Parliament Relative to the Slave Trade, with Illustrations from Collateral Sources of Information (London: Davidson, 1851) reprinted (New York: Negro Universities Press (1851) 1969).

Farrell, Thomas B., *Norms of Rhetorical Culture* (New Haven: Yale University Press, 1993).

Fieldhouse, D.K., *Colonialism 1870–1945: An Introduction* (New York: St. Martin's, 1981).

Fieldhouse, David, "Arrested Development in Anglophone Black Africa?" in Gifford and Louis (eds.), *Decolonization and African Independence*, 135–158.

Finnemore, Martha, "Constructing Norms of Humanitarian Intervention," in Katzenstein (ed.), *Culture of National Security* (1996), 153–185.

"Norms, Culture, and World Politics: Insights from Sociology's Institutionalism," *International Organization* 50 (Spring 1996), 325–347.

Finnemore, Martha and Sikkink, Kathryn, "International Norm Dynamics and Political Change," *International Organization* 52 (Autumn 1998), 887–917.

Flax, Jane, "Displacing Woman: Toward an Ethics of Multiplicity," in Bat-Ami Bar On and Ann Ferguson (eds.), *Daring to Be Good: Essays in Feminist Ethico-Politics* (New York: Routledge, 1998), 143–155.

Florini, Ann, "The Evolution of International Norms," *International Studies Quarterly* 40 (September 1996), 363–389.

Foner, Philip S. and Winchester, Richard C. (eds.), *The Anti-Imperialist Reader: A Documentary History of Anti-Imperialism in the United States. Volume I, From the Mexican War to the Election of 1900* (New York: Holmes & Meier, 1984).

Foucault, Michel, *The Archaeology of Knowledge and the Discourse on Language* (New York: Pantheon, 1972).

Discipline and Punish: The Birth of the Prison (New York: Vintage Books, 1979).

"The Subject and Power," in Herbert L. Dreyfus and Paul Rabinow (eds.), *Michel Foucault: Beyond Structuralism and Hermeneutics*, 2nd edn (Chicago: University of Chicago Press, 1984), 208–226.

Frankel, Philip H., *Pretoria's Praetorians: Civil-military Relations in South Africa* (Cambridge: Cambridge University Press, 1984).

Gann, L.H. and Duignan, Peter, *Burden of Empire: An Appraisal of Western Colonialism in Africa South of the Sahara* (New York: Praeger, 1967).

Gavin, R.J. and Betley, J.A., *The Scramble for Africa: Documents on the Berlin West Africa Conference and Related Subjects 1884/1885* (Ibadan, Nigeria: Ibadan University Press, 1973).

Geiss, Immanuel, *The Pan-African Movement: A History of Pan-Africanism in America, Europe and Africa* (New York: Africana Publishing, 1974).

Gelpi, Christopher, "Crime and Punishment: The Role of Norms in Crisis Bargaining," *American Political Science Review* 91 (June 1997), 339–360.

Gemery, Henry A. and Hogendorn, Jan S. (eds.), *The Uncommon Market: Essays in the Economic History of the Atlantic Slave Trade* (New York: Academic Press, 1979).

Geortz, Gary, *Contexts of International Politics* (Cambridge: Cambridge University Press, 1994).

Geortz, Gary and Diehl, Paul F., "Toward a Theory of International Norms: Some Conceptual and Measurement Issues," *Journal of Conflict Resolution* 36 (December 1992), 634–666.

Gifford, Prosser and Louis, Wm. Roger (eds.), *The Transfer of Power in Africa: Decolonization 1940–1960* (New Haven: Yale University Press, 1982).

Decolonization and African Independence: The Transfer of Power, 1960–1980 (New Haven: Yale University Press, 1988).

Gill, T.D., *South West Africa and the Sacred Trust, 1919–1972* (The Hague: T.M.C. Asser Instituut, 1984).

Goffman, Erving, *Frame Analysis* (New York: Harper, 1974).

Goldblatt, I., *History of South West Africa from the Beginning of the Nineteenth Century* (Cape Town: Jutta & Company Limited, 1971).

Goldstein, Melvyn C., *The Snow Lion and the Dragon: China, Tibet, and the Dalai Lama* (Berkeley: University of California Press, 1997).

Green, William A., *British Slave Emancipation: The Sugar Colonies and the Great Experiment, 1830–1865* (Oxford: Clarendon Press, 1976),

Greenblatt, Stephen, *Marvelous Possessions: The Wonder of the New World* (Chicago: University of Chicago Press, 1991).

Gunn, Gillian, "A Guide to the Intricacies of the Angola-Namibia Negotiations," *CSIS Africa Notes*, no. 90 (8 September 1988).

Haacke, Jürgen, "Theory and Praxis in International Relations: Habermas, Self-Reflection, Rational Argumentation," *Millennium* 25 (Summer 1996), 255–289.

Haas, Ernst B., "Beware the Slippery Slope: Notes toward the Definition of Justifiable Intervention," in Laura Reed and Carl Kaysen (eds.), *Emerging Norms of Justified Intervention* (Cambridge: American Academy of Arts and Sciences, 1983), 63–87.

Habermas, Jürgen, *Theory of Communicative Action, Volume One: Reason and the Rationalization of Society*, translated Thomas McCarthy (Boston: Beacon Press, 1984).

Moral Consciousness and Communicative Action (Cambridge: MIT Press, 1990).

Postmetaphysical Thinking (Cambridge: MIT Press, 1992).

Justification and Application: Remarks on Discourse Ethics (Cambridge: MIT Press, 1993).

Between Facts and Norms: Contributions to a Discourse Theory of Law and Democracy (Cambridge: MIT Press, 1996).

Hale, James C., "The Creation and Application of the Mandate System: A Study in International Colonial Supervision," *Transactions of the Grotius Society*, vol. XXV (London: Grotius Society, 1940).

"The Reform and Extension of the Mandates System: A Legal Solution to the Colonial Problem," *Transactions of the Grotius Society*, vol. XXVI (London: Grotius Society, 1941), 153–210.

Hall, H. Duncan, *Mandates, Dependencies and Trusteeship* (Washington: Carnegie Endowment for International Peace, 1948).

Hanke, Lewis, *All Mankind is One: A Study of the Disputation Between Bartolomé de Las Casas and Juan Ginés de Sepulveda in 1550 on the Intellectual and Religious Capacity of the American Indians* (DeKalb, IL: Northern Illinois University Press, 1974).

Hargreaves, J.D., *Decolonization in Africa* (London: Longman, 1988).

Helman, Gerald B. and Ratner, Steven R., "Saving Failed States," *Foreign Policy* 89 (Winter 1992–1993), 3–20.

Henderson, W.O., *The German Colonial Empire, 1884–1919* (London: Frank Cass, 1993).

Herbstein, Dennis and Evenson, John, *The Devils are Among Us: The War for Namibia* (London: Zed Books, 1989).

Hermann, Charles F., Kegley Jr., Charles W., and Rosenau, James N. (eds.), *New Directions in the Study of Foreign Policy* (London: HarperCollins Academic, 1987).

Hobson, J.A., *Imperialism: A Study* (New York: James Pott & Co., 1902).

Hochschild, Adam, *King Leopold's Ghost: A Story of Greed, Terror and Heroism in Colonial Africa* (Boston: Houghton Mifflin Company, 1998).

Hoffman, Stanley, *Duties Beyond Borders* (Syracuse, NY: Syracuse University Press, 1981).

Hofstadter, Richard, *Social Darwinism in American Thought*, revised edn (New York: George Braziller, 1955).

Homer-Dixon, Thomas F. and Karapin, Roger S., "Graphical Argument Analysis: A New Approach to Understanding Arguments Applied to a Debate about the Window of Vulnerability," *International Studies Quarterly* 33 (September 1989), 389–410.

Isaacman, Alan F., *The Tradition of Resistance in Mozambique: Anti-Colonial Activity in the Zambesi Valley, 1850–1921* (London: Heinemann, 1976).

Isaacs, Tracy, "Cultural Context and Moral Responsibility," *Ethics* 107 (July 1997), 684–760.

Jackson, Robert H., "The Weight of Ideas in Decolonization: Normative Change in International Relations," in Judith Goldstein and Robert Keohane (eds.), *Ideas and Foreign Policy: Beliefs, Institutions, and Political Change* (Ithaca: Cornell University Press, 1993), 111–138.

Janis, Irving, *Groupthink: Psychological Studies of Policy Decisions and Fiascoes* (Boston: Houghton Mifflin, 1982).

Jaster, Robert S., *The Defence of White Power: South African Foreign Policy Under Pressure* (London: Macmillan, 1988).

"The 1988 Peace Accords and the Future of South-western Africa," *Adelphi Papers*, no. 253 (Autumn 1990).

Jennings, Lawrence C., *French Reaction to British Slave Emancipation* (Baton Rouge: Louisiana State University Press, 1988).

Jervis, Robert, *Perception and Misperception in International Politics* (Princeton: Princeton University Press, 1976).

System Effects: Complexity in Social and Political Life (Princeton: Princeton University Press, 1997).

Johnson, Paul, "Colonialism's Back – And Not a Moment Too Soon," *New York Times Magazine*, 18 April 1993, pp. 22, 43–44.

Jones, Dorothy V., *License for Empire: Colonialism by Treaty in Early America* (Chicago: University of Chicago Press, 1982).

Code of Peace: Ethics and Security in the World of Warlord States (Chicago: University of Chicago Press, 1989).

"The Declaratory Tradition in Modern International Law," in Terry Nardin and David R. Mapel (eds.), *Traditions of International Ethics* (Cambridge: Cambridge University Press, 1992).

"The League of Nations Experiment in International Protection," *Ethics and International Affairs* 8 (1994), 77–95.

Jones, Greta, *Social Darwinism and English Thought: The Interaction Between Biological and Social Theory* (Atlantic Highlands, NJ: Humanities Press, 1980).

Jonsen, Albert R. and Toulmin, Stephen, *The Abuse of Casuistry: A History of Moral Reasoning* (Berkeley: University of California Press, 1988).

Katjavivi, Peter, *A History of Resistance in Namibia* (Trenton, NJ: Africa World Press, 1988).

"The Development of Anti-Colonial Forces in Namibia," in Wood (ed.) *Namibia, 1884–1984*, 557–584.

Katzenstein, Peter J. (ed.), *The Culture of National Security: Norms and Identity in World Politics* (New York: Columbia University Press, 1996).

Kaufmann, Chaim D. and Pape, Robert A., "Explaining Costly International Moral Action: Britain's Sixty-year Campaign Against the Atlantic Slave Trade," *International Organization* 53 (Autumn 1999), 631–668.

Keck, Margaret E. and Sikkink, Kathryn, *Activists Beyond Borders: Advocacy Networks in International Politics* (Ithaca: Cornell University Press, 1998).

Keeley, James F., "Toward a Foucauldian Analysis of International Regimes," *International Organization* 44, 1 (Winter 1990), 83–105.

Kennedy, Paul, *The Rise and Fall of the Great Powers* (New York: Random House, 1988).

Keohane, Robert O., "The Demand for International Regimes," in Stephen D. Krasner (ed.), *International Regimes* (Ithaca: Cornell University Press, 1983), 141–171.

Khong, Yuen Foong, *Analogies at War: Korea, Munich, Dien Bien Phu, and the Vietnam Decisions of 1965* (Princeton: Princeton University Press, 1992).

Kier, Elizabeth, *Imagining War: French and British Military Doctrine Between the Wars* (Princeton: Princeton University Press, 1997).

Klein, Martin A., "Slavery, the International Labour Market and the Emancipation of Slaves in the Nineteenth Century," in Lovejoy and Rogers (eds.), *Unfree Labour in the Development of the Atlantic World*, 197–229.

Kloosterboer, W., *Involuntary Labour Since the Abolition of Slavery: A Survey of Compulsory Labour Throughout the World* (Leiden: E.J. Brill, 1960).

Klotz, Audie, *Norms in International Relations: The Struggle Against Apartheid* (Ithaca, NY: Cornell University Press, 1995).

Knopf, Jeffrey W., *Domestic Society and International Cooperation: The Impact of Protest on U.S. Arms Control Policy* (Cambridge: Cambridge University Press, 1998).

Koskenniemi, Martti, *From Apology to Utopia: The Structure of International Legal Argument* (Helsinki: Finnish Lawyers' Publishing Company: 1989).

Kratochwil, Friedrich, *Rules Norms and Decisions: On the Conditions of Practical and Legal Reasoning in International Relations and Domestic Affairs* (Cambridge: Cambridge University Press, 1989).

Kuhn, Thomas, *The Structure of Scientific Revolutions* (Chicago: University of Chicago Press, 1955).

Laffey, Mark and Weldes, Jutta, "Beyond Belief: Ideas and Symbolic Technologies in the Study of International Relations," *European Journal of International Relations* 3 (1997), 193–237.

Landgren, Signe, *Embargo Disimplemented: South Africa's Military Industry* (London: Oxford University Press, 1989).

Langley, J. Ayo, *Ideologies of Liberation in Black Africa, 1856–1970: Documents on Modern Africa Political Thought from Colonial Times to the Present* (London: Rex Collings, 1979).

Las Casas, Bartolomé de, *In Defense of the Indians Against the Persecutors and Slanders of the Peoples of the New World Discovered Across the Seas*, translated and edited by Poole, Stafford (DeKalb, IL: Northern Illinois University Press, 1974).

Lasswell, Harold, *World Politics and Personal Insecurity* (New York: The Free Press, (1935) 1965).

Lauren, Paul Gordon, *Power and Prejudice: The Politics and Diplomacy of Racial Discrimination* (Boulder: Westview Press, 1996).

League of Nations, *The Mandates System: Origin, Principles, Application* (Geneva: League of Nations, 1945).

League of Nations Permanent Mandates Commission, *Minutes* (Geneva), various years including 1922, 1923, 1926, 1934, 1937.

LeVeen, E. Phillip, *The British Slave Trade Suppression Policies, 1821–1865* (New York: Arno Press, 1977).

Levy, Jack S., "Learning and Foreign Policy: Sweeping a Conceptual Minefield," *International Organization* 48 (Spring 1994), 279–312.

Lewy, Guenter, "The Case for Humanitarian Intervention," *Orbis* 37 (Fall 1993), 621–632.

Leys, Colin and Saul, John S., contributions by Brown, Susan, Steenkamp, Philip, Maseko, Sipho S., Tapscott, Chris, and Dobell, Lauren, *Namibia's Liberation Struggle: the Two Edged Sword* (London: James Currey, 1995).

Linklater, Andrew, *The Transformation of Political Community: Ethical Foundations of the Post-Westphalian Era* (Cambridge: Polity Press, 1998).

Litfin, Karen, *Ozone Discourses: Science and Politics in Global Environmental Cooperation* (New York: Columbia University Press, 1994).

Lloyd, Christopher, *The Navy and The Slave Trade: The Suppression of the African Slave Trade in the Nineteenth Century* (London: Frank Cass, (1949) 1968).

Logan, Rayford, "The Operation of the Mandate System in Africa," *The Journal of Negro History* 13 (October 1928), 423–477.

Lord, Dick, *Vlamgat: The Story of the Mirage F1 in the South African Air Force* (Weltevreden Park, South Africa: Covos-Day Books, 2000).

Louis, Wm. Roger, *Great Britain and Germany's Lost Colonies, 1914–1919* (Oxford: Clarendon Press, 1967).

Imperialism at Bay: The United States and the Decolonization of the British Empire, 1941–1945 (New York: Oxford University Press, 1978).

"Morel and the Congo Reform Association 1904–1913" in Louis and Stengers (eds.), *E.D. Morel's History of the Congo Reform Movement*, 171–220.

"The Era of the Mandates System and the Non-European World," in Bull and Watson (eds.), *The Expansion of International Society*, 201–213.

Louis Wm. Roger, and Stengers, Jean (eds.), *E.D. Morel's History of the Congo Reform Movement* (London: Oxford University Press, 1968).

Lovejoy, Paul E. and Rogers, Nicholas (eds.), *Unfree Labour in the Development of the Atlantic World* (Portland, OR: Frank Cass, 1994).

Luard, Evan, *War in International Society* (New Haven: Yale University Press, 1986).

Lugard, Frederick, *The Dual Mandate in British Tropical Africa* (New York: Frank Cass (1922) 1965).

Lukes, Steven, "Five Fables About Human Rights," in Shute, and Hurley (eds.), *On Human Rights*, 19–40.

Lumsdaine, David Halloran, *Moral Vision in International Politics: The Foreign Aid Regime, 1949–1989* (Princeton: Princeton University Press, 1993).

Lynch, Cecelia, "Acting on Belief: Christian Perspectives on Suffering and Violence," *Ethics & International Affairs* 14 (2000), 83–97.

Lynch, Hollis R., *Black American Radicals and Liberation of Africa: The Council on African Affairs, 1937–1955* (Ithaca: Africana Studies and Research Center, Cornell University, 1978).

"Pan-African Responses in the United States to British Colonial Rule in Africa in the 1940s," in Gifford and Louis (eds.), *The Transfer of Power in Africa: Decolonization 1940–1960*, 57–86.

Mandelbaum, Michael, "The Reluctance to Intervene," *Foreign Policy*, 95 (Summer 1994), 3–18.

Maxwell, Kenneth, "Portugal and Africa: The Last Empire," in Gifford and Louis (eds.), *The Transfer of Power in Africa: Decolonization 1940–1960*, 337–385.

Mazrui, Ali A. (ed.), *UNESCO General History of Africa VIII: Africa Since 1935* (Oxford: James Curry, 1999).

McAdam, Doug, McCarthy, John D., Zald, Mayer N. (eds.), *Comparative Perspectives on Social Movements: Political Opportunity, Mobilizing Structures, and Cultural Framings* (Cambridge: Cambridge University Press, 1996).

McFaul, Michael, "Rethinking the 'Reagan Doctrine' in Angola," *International Security* 14 (Winter 1989/90), 99–135.

Mefford, Dwain, "Analogical Reasoning and the Definition of the Situation: Back to Snyder for Concepts and Forward to Artificial Intelligence for Method," in Hermann, Kegley, and Rosenau (eds.), *New Directions in the Study of Foreign Policy*, 221–244.

Merrim, Stephanie, "The Counter-Discourse of Las Casas," in Williams and Lewis (eds.), *Early Images of the Americas*, 149–162.

Metz, Steven, "Pretoria's 'Total Strategy' and Low-Intensity Warfare in Southern Africa," *Comparative Strategy* 6 (1987), 437–469.

Midgley, Claire, "Slave Sugar Boycotts, Female Activism and the Domestic Base of British Anti-Slavery Culture," *Slavery and Abolition* 13 (December 1996), 137–162.

Miers, Suzanne, *Britain and the Ending of the Slave Trade* (New York: Longman Group, 1975).

Miers, Suzanne and Roberts, Richard (eds.), *The End of Slavery in Africa* (Madison: University of Wisconsin Press, 1988).

Miller, David Hunter, *The Drafting of the Covenant* (New York: G.P. Putnam's Sons, 1928), 2 vols.

Miller, William Lee, *Arguing About Slavery: The Great Battle in the United States Congress* (New York: Alfred A. Knopf, 1996).

Moon, J. Donald, "Practical Discourse and Communicative Ethics," in Stephen K. White (ed.), *The Cambridge Companion to Habermas* (Cambridge: Cambridge University Press, 1995), 143–164.

Morel, E.D., *Africa and the Peace of Europe* (London: National Labour Press, 1917).

Morgan, D.J., *The Official History of Colonial Development, Vol. 1: The Origins of British Aid Policy, 1924–1945* (London: Macmillan Press, 1980).

The Official History of Colonial Development, Vol. 5: Guidance Towards Self-Government in British Colonies, 1941–1971 (London: Macmillan, 1980).

Morgenthau, Hans J., *Politics Among Nations: The Struggle for Power and Peace*, 6th edition, revised by Kenneth W. Thompson (New York: Knopf, 1985).

Morris, Thomas D., *Southern Slavery and the Law, 1619–1860* (Chapell Hill: University of North Carolina Press, 1996).

Mueller, John, "Changing Attitudes Towards War: The Impact of the First World War," *British Journal of Political Science* 21 (January 1991), 1–28.

Murray, James N., *The United Nations Trusteeship System* (Urbana: The University of Illinois Press, 1957).

Nadelmann, Ethan, "Global Prohibition Regimes: The Evolution of Norms in International Society," *International Organization* 44 (Autumn 1990), 479–526.

Nardin, Terry and Mapel, David R. (eds.), *Traditions of International Ethics* (Cambridge: Cambridge University Press, 1992).

Oldfield, J.R., *Popular Politics and British Anti-Slavery: The Mobilization of Public Opinion Against the Slave Trade, 1787–1807* (Manchester: Manchester University Press, 1995).

Onuf, Nicholas Greenwood, *World of Our Making: Rules and Rule in Social Theory and International Relations* (Columbia: University of South Carolina Press, 1989).

Padmore, George, *Pan-Africanism or Communism* (Garden City, NY: Anchor Books, 1971).

Pagden, Anthony, *European Encounters with the New World: From Renaissance to Romanticism* (New Haven: Yale, 1993).

 Lords of All the World: Ideologies of Empire in Spain, Britain and France, c. 1500–1800 (New Haven: Yale University Press, 1995).

Patterson, Orlando, *Slavery and Social Death: A Comparative Study* (Cambridge: Harvard University Press, 1982).

Payne, Rodger, "Persuasion, Frames, and Norm Construction," unpublished manuscript (University of Louisville, 2000).

Pearce, R.D., *The Turning Point in Africa: British Colonial Policy 1938–48* (London: Frank Cass, 1982).

Persell, Stuart Michael, *The French Colonial Lobby, 1889–1938* (Stanford, CA: Hoover Institution Press, 1983).

Phillips, Mark, "The Nuts and Bolts of Military Power: The Structure of the SADF," in Cock and Nathan (eds.), *Society at War*, 16–27.

Porter, A.N. and Stockwell, A.J. (eds.), *British Imperial Policy, 1938–64, Volume 1, 1938–51* (London: Macmillan Press, 1987).

 British Imperial Policy, 1938–64, Volume 2: 1951–1964 (London: Macmillan Press, 1987).

Powell, Walter, "Expanding the Scope of Institutional Analysis," in Powell, Walter and DiMaggio, Paul (eds.), *The New Institutionalism in Organizational Analysis* (Chicago: University of Chicago, Press, 1991), 183–202.

Rapoport, Anatol, *Fights, Games, and Debates* (Ann Arbor: University of Michigan, 1960).

Rawls, John, *The Law of Peoples* (Cambridge, MA: Harvard University Press, 1999).

Ray, James Lee, "The Abolition of Slavery and the End of International War" *International Organization* 43 (Summer 1989), 405–439.

Raymond, Gregory A., "Problems and Prospects in the Study of International Norms," *Mershon International Studies Review* 41 (November 1997), 205–245.

Reiter, Dan, *Crucible of Beliefs: Learning, Alliances, and World Wars* (Ithaca: Cornell University Press, 1996).

Republic of South Africa (RSA), *White Papers on Defence*, various years.

Resister (journal of the End Conscription Campaign), various years.

Reus-Smit, Christian, "The Constitutional Structure of International Society and the Nature of Fundamental Institutions," *International Organization* 51 (Autumn 1997), 555–589.

452

Risse, Thomas, "'Let's Argue!' Communicative Action in World Politics, *International Organization* 54 (Winter 2000), 1–39.

Risse, Thomas, Ropp, Stephen C., and Sikkink, Kathryn (eds.), *The Power of Human Rights: International Norms and Domestic Change* (Cambridge: Cambridge University Press, 1999).

Rivera, Luis N., *A Violent Evangelism: The Political and Religious Conquest of the Americas* (Louisville, KY: Westminster/John Knox Press, 1992).

Robinson, Fiona, *Globalizing Care: Ethics, Feminist Theory, and International Relations* (Boulder: Westview Press, 1999).

Robinson, Ronald and Gallagher, John, with Denny, Alice, *Africa and the Victorians: The Official Mind of Imperialism* (London: Macmillan, 1961).

Rogers, Nicholas, "Vagrancy, Impressment and the Regulation of Labour in Eighteenth-Century Britain," in Lovejoy and Rogers (eds.), *Unfree Labour*, 102–113.

Rorty, Richard, "Human Rights, Rationality, and Sentimentality," in Shute and Hurley (eds.), *On Human Rights*, 111–134.

Sahlins, Marshall, *Culture and Practical Reason* (Chicago: University of Chicago, 1976).

Sampson, Martin W., "Cultural Influences on Foreign Policy," in Hermann, Kegley, and Rosenau (eds.), *New Directions*, 384–405.

Sawyer, Roger, *Slavery in the Twentieth Century* (Routledge & Kegan Paul: London, 1986).

Schmokel, Wolfe W., *Dream of Empire: German Colonialism, 1919–1945* (New Haven: Yale University Press, 1964).

Seed, Patricia, "Taking Possession and Reading Texts: Establishing the Authority of Overseas Empires," in Williams and Lewis (eds.), *Early Images of the Americas*, 111–147.

Shakya, Tsering, *The Dragon in the Land of Snows: A History of Modern Tibet Since 1947* (New York: Columbia University Press, 1999).

Shannon, Vaughn P., "Norms are What States Make of Them: The Political Psychology of Norm Violation," *International Studies Quarterly*, 44 (June 2000), 293–316.

Shapiro, Michael J., "Representing World Politics: The Sports/War Intertext," in Der Derian, James and Shapiro, Michael J. (eds.), *International/Intertextual Relations: Postmodern Readings of World Politics* (Lexington: Lexington Books, 1989).

"The Ethics of Encounter: Unreading, Unmapping the Imperium," in Campbell, David and Shapiro, Michael J. (eds.), *Moral Boundaries: Rethinking Ethics and World Politics* (Minneapolis: University of Minnesota, 1999), 57–91.

Shephard, George W. (ed.), *Effective Economic Sanctions* (New York: Preager, 1991).

Sherman, William L., *Forced Native Labor in Sixteenth-Century Central America* (Lincoln: University of Nebraska Press, 1979).

Shipman, Pat, *The Evolution of Racism: Human Differences and the Use and Abuse of Science* (New York: Simon and Schuster, 1994).

Shute, Stephen and Hurley, Susan (eds.), *On Human Rights: The Oxford Amnesty Lectures 1993* (New York: Basic Books, 1993).

Sikkink, Kathryn, "The Power of Principled Ideas: Human Rights Policies in the United States and Western Europe," in Goldstein and Keohane (eds.), *Ideas and Foreign Policy*, 139–170.

Silver, James W., *Framing a Balance Sheet for French Decolonization: Raymond Aron, Raymond Cartier and the Debate over the African Empire* (Cambridge, MA: Harvard University Honors Thesis).

Slonim, Solomon, *South West Africa and the United Nations: An International Mandate in Dispute* (Baltimore: Johns Hopkins University Press, 1973).

Slovic, Paul, Fischhoff, Baruch, and Lichtenstein, Sara, "Response Mode, Framing, and Information-Processing Effects in Risk Assessment," in Bell, Raiffa, and Tversky (eds.), *Decision Making*, 152–166.

Smith, Adam, *An Inquiry into the Nature and Causes of the Wealth of Nations* (New York: Modern Library, 1994).

Smith, Helmut Walser, "The Talk of Genocide, the Rhetoric of Miscegenation: Notes on Debates in the German Reichstag Concerning South West Africa, 1904–14," in Friedrichsmeyer, Sara, Lennox, Sara, and Zantop, Susanne (eds.), *The Imperialist Imagination: German Colonialism and its Legacy* (Ann Arbor: The University of Michigan Press, 1998), 107–123.

Snow, Alpheus Henry, *The Question of Aborigines in the Law and Practice of Nations* (New York: G.P. Putnam's Sons, 1921).

Snyder, Jack, *Myths of Empire: Domestic Politics and International Ambition* (Ithaca: Cornell University Press, 1991).

Sorum, Paul Clay, *Intellectuals and Decolonization in France* (Chapel Hill: University of North Carolina Press, 1977).

Spruyt, Hendrik, "The End of Empire and the Extension of the Westphalian System: The Normative Basis of the Modern "State Order," *International Studies Review* 2 (Summer 2000), 65–92.

Stepan, Nancy, *The Idea of Race in Science: Great Britain 1800–1860* (London: Macmillan, 1982).

Substance of the Debates on a Resolution for Abolishing the Slave Trade which was moved in the House of Commons 10th June 1806 and in the House of Lords 24th June 1806 (London: Dawsons of Pall Mall, 1968).

Sylvan, Donald A. and Voss, James F. (eds.), *Problem Representation in Foreign Policy Decision Making* (Cambridge: Cambridge University Press, 1998), 187–212.

Temperley, Howard, *British Antislavery, 1833–1870* (London: Longman, 1972).

Temperley, H.W.V. (ed.), *A History of the Peace Conference of Paris* (London: H. Frowde, and Hodder & Stoughton, 1920–1924), 6 vols.

The Combatant (journal of the People's Liberation Army of Namibia (PLAN)). Various years.

Thomas, Hugh, *The Slave Trade: The Story of the Atlantic Slave Trade, 1440–1870* (New York: Simon and Schuster, 1997).

Thompson, Janice E., "Norms in International Relations: A Conceptual Analysis," *International Journal of Group Tensions* 23 (1993), 67–83.

Toulmin, Stephen, *The Uses of Argument* (Cambridge: Cambridge University Press, 1958).

Toulmin, Stephen, Rieke, Richard, and Janik, Allan, *An Introduction to Reasoning* (New York: Macmillan, 1979).

Traboulay, David, *Columbus and Las Casas: The Conquest and Christianization of America, 1492–1566* (New York: University Press of America, 1994).

Tronto, Joan C., *Moral Boundaries: A Political Argument for an Ethic of Care* (New York: Routledge, 1993).

Turley, David, *The Culture of English Antislavery, 1780–1860* (London: Routledge, 1991).

Tushnet, Mark V., *The American Law of Slavery, 1810–1860: Considerations of Humanity and Interest* (Princeton: Princeton University Press, 1981).

Tversky, Amos, and Kahneman, Daniel, "Rational Choice and the Framing of Decisions," Bell, Raiffa, and Tversky (eds.), *Decision Making*, 167–192.

Union of South Africa, *Report on the Natives of South-West Africa and their Treatment by Germany* (London: His Majesty's Stationery Office, 1918).

United Nations, *Namibia Bulletin* (New York: United Nations). Various years.
   The United Nations and Decolonization: Summary of the Work of the Special Committee of Twenty-Four (New York: United Nations, 1965).
   The Military Situation in and Relating to Namibia (New York: UN, 1983).

Upthegrove, Campbell L., *Empire by Mandate: A History of the Relations of Great Britain with the Permanent Mandates Commission of the League of Nations* (New York: Bookman Associates, 1954).

van Eemeren, Frans H., Grootendorst, Rob, Jackson, Sally and Jacobs, Scott, *Reconstructing Argumentative Discourse* (Tuscaloosa: University of Alabama Press, 1993).

Vandervort, Bruce, *Wars of Imperial Conquest in Africa, 1830–1914* (Bloomington, IN: Indiana University Press, 1998).

Vertzberger, Yaacov Y.I., *The World in Their Minds: Information Processing, Cognition, and Perception in Foreign Policy* (Stanford: Stanford University Press, 1990).

Vincent, John, *Human Rights and International Relations* (Cambridge: Cambridge University Press, 1986).

Vincent, R.J., *Nonintervention and International Order* (Princeton: Princeton University Press, 1974).

Voeltz, Richard A., *German Colonialism and the South West Africa Company, 1884–1914* (Athens, OH: Ohio University Center for International Studies, 1988).

Von Eschen, Penny M., *Race Against Empire: Black Americans and Anticolonialism, 1937–1957* (Ithaca: Cornell University Press, 1997).

von Wright, Georg Henrik, "Norms, Truth and Logic," in Georg Henrik von Wright, *Practical Reason* (Ithaca: Cornell University Press, 1983), 130–209.

Walvin, James, *An African's Life: The Life and Times of Olaudah Equiano, 1745–1797* (London: Cassell, 1998).

"Freedom and Slavery and the Shaping of Victorian Britain," in Lovejoy and Rogers (eds.), *Unfree Labour in the Development of the Atlantic World*, 246–259.

Walzer, Michael, *Just and Unjust Wars: A Moral Argument with Historical Illustrations*, 2nd edn (New York: Basic Books, 1992).

Wapner, Paul, "Politics Beyond the State: Environmental Activism and World Civic Politics," *World Politics* 47 (April 1995), 311–340.

Watson, Alan, *Slave Law in the Americas* (Athens, GA: University of Georgia Press, 1989).

Weaver, Tony, "The South African Defence Force in Namibia," in Cock and Nathan (eds.), *Society at War*, 90–102.

Weisband, Edward, "Discursive Multilateralism: Global Benchmarks, Shame, and Learning in the ILO Labour Standards Monitoring Regime," *International Studies Quarterly* 44 (December 2000), 643–666.

Welch, David, *Justice and the Genesis of War* (Cambridge: Cambridge University Press, 1993).

Wellington, John H., *South West Africa and its Human Issues* (Oxford: Oxford University Press, 1967).

Wendt, Alexander, *Social Theory of International Politics* (Cambridge: Cambridge University Press, 1999).

White, Dorothy Shipley, *Black Africa and De Gaulle: From the French Empire to Independence* (University Park: The Pennsylvania State University Press, 1979).

Williams, Eric, *Capitalism and Slavery* (Chapel Hill, NC: University of North Carolina, 1944).

Williams, Jerry M. and Lewis, Robert E. (eds.), *Early Images of the Americas: Transfer and Invention* (Tucson: The University of Arizona Press, 1993).

Wilson, Heather A., *International Law and the Use of Force by National Liberation Movements* (Oxford: Clarendon Press, 1988).

Wilson, Henry S., *African Decolonization* (New York: Edward Arnold, 1994).

Wood, Brian (ed.), *Namibia, 1884–1984: Readings on Namibia's History and Society* (Lusaka: United Nations Institute for Namibia, 1988).

Wright, Quincy, *Mandates Under the League of Nations* (Chicago: University of Chicago Press, 1930).

Young, Iris Marion, *Justice and the Politics of Difference* (Princeton: Princeton University Press, 1990).

456

Index

CAMBRIDGE STUDIES IN INTERNATIONAL RELATIONS